LIVING ISSUES IN PHILOSOPHY

FOURTH EDITION

LIVING ISSUES IN PHILOSOPHY

FOURTH EDITION

LIVING ISSUES
IN PHILOSOPHY

An Introductory Textbook

HAROLD H. TITUS

Denison University

FOURTH EDITION

AMERICAN BOOK COMPANY

NEW YORK

7 9 EP 10 8

PREFACE

The favorable reception given the first three editions of *Living Issues in Philosophy* and the growing list of adoptions have encouraged the publisher and the author to bring out a Fourth Edition. The new edition, it is hoped, has been strengthened in a number of ways.

The author believes more firmly than ever that philosophy should come out of its "ivory tower," simplify its technical language wherever possible without loss of meaning, and deal with the living issues facing men today. Philosophy, as well as giving attention to some special areas, needs to set forth a unifying view of life that embraces the different areas of human experience. A first course in philosophy needs to deal with vital questions of human interest in science, religion, art, morality, education, and social policy. This text is an attempt to meet that need.

As in the first three editions, the author has kept four requirements constantly in mind. The first is that an introductory text be clear and readable. Insofar as possible, the material is presented in language that is nontechnical and clear. New terms and the building of a vocabulary are necessary, of course, as one moves into a new field. Where special or technical terms are essential to make the meaning exact, these terms are defined or explained, in the text itself and in the glossary, so that they will be clear to the beginning student. If we do not make a conundrum of it, philosophy can be one of the most thrilling and intellectually stimulating subjects in the college curriculum.

The second requisite is that the book deal with issues closely related to life. Philosophy can help students see the basic issues of human existence and discern the values of life. A first course, therefore, should not place its emphasis on negative criticism, nor should it treat exclusively—or even chiefly—the history of thought. Philosophy should not be merely a narrow specialty or only methodology. A first course should give students some appreciation of the importance of philosophy for their own lives and start them on the way to building a philosophy of their own. When it does so, many students will be eager to go on to the more specialized courses, such as ethics, logic, the history of philosophy, and social philosophy.

The third requisite is that the text recognize the problem of organization for classroom use. In this text the chapters are neither excessively long nor unduly short. The division of the book into five parts makes it easy for the instructor to omit an entire part, as well as certain chapters, or to add topics if he wishes to do so. The order of presentation of topics also may be changed if a teacher wishes to begin with, say, values, or with social issues, before he discusses the problem of knowledge or methods of inquiry. Questions and projects and an annotated reading list are provided at the end of each chapter.

A fourth requisite that the author has recognized is that the text be comprehensive—that it open up the field of philosophy rather than deal exclusively with some special interest of the author. A genuine attempt has been made to be fair to the various systems of thought or points of view. While some of the author's convictions are presented, the text leaves leeway for the thinking and convictions of the teachers and students who use it.

For more than two thousand years, philosophy has helped build the intellectual, moral, and religious foundations of civilization. During the last fifty or sixty years, along with the growth of specialization in the sciences, philosophy has sometimes become a narrow specialty concerned almost exclusively with the problems of logic and language or with reporting the views of the philosophers of the past. Where this has happened, philosophy has abandoned its task of integrating the piecemeal knowledge of the day and the quest for some comprehensive view of life and the world. From various sources, however, there is evident a renewed conviction that one important function of philosophy is an integration of or orientation to the various phases of human experience, that philosophy should be made available and intelligible to as many students and other members of the community as possible, and that it should play a more vital role in shaping world affairs. Men have to make decisions and to act, and philosophy should help them work out a scale of values and a philosophy of life by which they may live.

Special thanks are due to a number of persons. Suggestions have come from those who have used the first three editions: some in letters to the author, some in conversations at professional meetings, and some as comments made to representatives of the publisher. Not all the suggestions could be adopted, of course, but all have been appreciated and considered. Unfortunately, it is not feasible to name all of the persons who have made valuable suggestions. My wife has helped me at innumerable points. My colleagues in the Department of Philosophy at Denison have been helpful: Maylon H. Hepp has read the entire manuscript and made valuable suggestions; Francis C. Bayley has read the chapters dealing with scientific method; and Robert A. Macoskey has read the chapter dealing with the philosophy of education. The chemist Conrad E. Ronneberg has read the chapter entitled "The Physical Sciences and Philosophical Problems." James A. Pait, Chairman of the Division of Humanities at Miami-Dade Junior College, Miami, Florida, has made a number of useful suggestions. Thanks are due to the administration of Denison University for the time and space in which to do the work, to the library staff for their continued assistance, to Helen Dunfield, Diane Carlson, and Loris Brakeman for excellent work in typing the manuscript, and to the publishers who have granted permission to quote from their publications.

HAROLD H. TITUS
Granville, Ohio

CONTENTS

PART TWO

MAN AND HIS PLACE IN THE WORLD

PART THREE
THE TYPES OF PHILOSOPHY

PART FOUR
THE REALM OF VALUES

LIVING ISSUES IN PHILOSOPHY

FOURTH EDITION

LIVING ISSUES IN PHILOSOPHY

FOURTH EDITION

ONE

PHILOSOPHY AND THE CONTEMPORARY SCENE

Today we are moving into a new and fascinating age in which we look at the world and human affairs from a viewpoint different from that of former generations. John Glenn may not have been the first man to orbit the earth and to view it from outer space, but he *was* the first of the astronauts to do it while millions around the earth looked on and listened with breathless suspense and with a realization that we are entering a new era. In this new era many older ways of looking at things are obsolete. Even "modern man" is obsolete. A few years ago an airplane passenger, using a telescopic lens, took a picture of a building when he was over Athens, Greece. He had a previous picture, taken on the ground, of the same building. When he showed the two pictures to a number of his friends, none of them recognized the pictures as of the same building. The building was the Parthenon, of which until recently no human being had ever seen an aerial view. Modern man must face new perspectives in nearly all areas of life, not only in the physical world but also in social relations and especially in the world of thought.

Our attention recently has been captured by events which have led to what we sometimes describe as the atomic age or the age of outer space. But the hydrogen bomb and astronaut's orbit are only the more dramatic and highly publicized new phenomena in our world. In this century, especially in the last few decades, we have seen great advances in knowledge—in general science, technology, agriculture, medicine, the social sciences, and education. Men and women live longer, travel faster, have more comforts and labor-saving devices, and produce more goods in fewer man-hours than ever before. The extension of the "age of automation" undoubtedly will eliminate much more drudgery and further increase production and reduce working hours. Controlling new sources of energy from the atom—and possibly from the sun, the tides, and the winds—is likely to change our lives beyond even our wildest imaginings. Harnessing the atom and conquering the air will enable men to lift their sights from mastery of the land and seas of the earth to conquest of the moon, planets, and outer space. With the turn of a switch men today can see events taking place thousands of miles away, and they can bring into their living rooms the accumulated wisdom and knowledge of the race.

Along with these advances, we are witnessing in our world a great struggle for the minds and loyalties of men. Military power, great wealth, and placing men on the moon or on other planets will not solely determine the outcome of this battle of ideas. Modern civilization is in danger because many of our inherited values concerning the nature and rights of man, the structure of human society, and the meaning of the human venture have increasingly become confused and then separated from our everyday lives and decisions. In the decades ahead can we win the battle for civilization? Will we acquire the understanding, the insight, and the courage that a great age demands? Can the crucial battle of ideas or the struggle for the minds and the loyalties of men be won?

CONFLICTING TRENDS IN A REVOLUTIONARY AGE

We are living through what many people call a "world revolution." Changes are occurring which reach to the very foundations of human life and society. There has recently been a "shortening of the time-span between notable changes" in society.[1] In the past men could expect to live under relatively fixed conditions; the time-span of significant changes was considerably longer than that of a human life. Now great changes are taking place within a fraction of the life-span of single individuals, and this situation creates unprecedented problems in both human living conditions and human thinking. We are living in a period which resembles the late stages of the Graeco-Roman civilization, the Renaissance, the Reformation, and the Industrial Revolution, when basic shifts took place in the thinking, values, and practices of men. But in our age the changes are world-wide, and they are happening at a greatly accelerated rate.

Yet in spite of our amazing advances, many thoughtful people are disturbed and anxious. They are concerned over a situation in which our physical power, scientific knowledge, and wealth stand in sharp contrast with the failure of governments and individuals to come to grips with the pressing intellectual and moral problems of life. Knowledge seems divorced from values; it is possible to have great power without insight. With few exceptions, the many books on the philosophy of history and civilization that have appeared during the last few decades agree that, though our civilization is making progress in science and technology, in other areas, including the ethical and nonmaterial, there is widespread confusion and possibly disintegration. While these writers differ as to what they feel can and should be

1 Alfred North Whitehead, *Adventures of Ideas* (New York: New American Library of World Literature, 1953), p. 99. (Mentor ed.) See also Ch. VI, pp. 110–126.

done, most of them believe that revival is possible and that dangerous trends can be discovered and controlled if men have vision, courage, and determination.

Many older ethical standards, as well as interpretations of life and the universe, have been weakened or destroyed, and many people find it difficult to establish new and stable foundations for living. In speaking about the "personal fragmentation" that leads to insecurity, one writer says, "There is in the climate of the modern world a sense of impending disaster, a rootlessness of the person, a pervasive tenseness which points to certainties dissolved and emotional centers displaced."[2] After speaking about the uneasiness which exists today and saying that "we are not living up to our moral capacity in the world," the editor of *The Saturday Review* goes on: "We have been living half a life. We have been developing our appetites—but we have been starving our purposes. We have been concerned with bigger salaries, bigger television screens, bigger cars—and now with bigger missiles—instead of with the big ideas on which our lives and freedoms depend."[3]

The concern in our time is not only about what is happening to many individuals, but about the very future of our type of civilization and perhaps of civilization itself. James P. Warburg says, "The decline of the West is undeniable, but in the writer's opinion it is by no means irreversible. The renaissance of Western civilization must begin within Western society. The key element in Western society is Individual Man." Again he says, "Our civilization has for centuries practiced neither the Jewish teaching of justice under moral law nor the Greek teaching of rational thought and behavior, and least of all the Christian teaching of love, compassion, and human brotherhood."[4] Lewis Mumford speaks about "the invisible breakdown in our civilization," the "erosion of values, the dissipation of humane purposes, the denial of any distinction between good or bad, right or wrong, the reversion to sub-human levels of conduct."[5] A psychologist, after consulting other psychologists, psychiatrists, and social scientists in many countries of the world in an attempt to discover the reasons for the tension and anxiety gripping the world, says: "The melancholy truth about the course of world history is that we are well along the road to disintegration." He concludes that there has been a "deterioration of personal, political, and social morals."[6]

---

2 Albert William Levi, *Philosophy and the Modern World* (Bloomington: Indiana U. Press, 1959), p. 5.
3 Norman Cousins, "Is America Living Half a Life?" *The Saturday Review*, 40 (November 16, 1957): 26.
4 *The West in Crisis* (Garden City: Doubleday, 1959), pp. 16–17, 26.
5 *The Conduct of Life* (New York: Harcourt, Brace & World, 1951), p. 148.
6 George W. Kisker (ed.), *World Tension—The Psychopathology of International Relations* (Englewood Cliffs: Prentice-Hall, 1951), pp. 296–297.

The events of recent decades have made it clear that something has indeed gone tragically wrong with human affairs. Man has gained great new powers in science and technology, but too frequently these powers have been used for destructive purposes. Man has rapidly extended the range and quantity of his knowledge, but he has advanced little if at all toward happiness and well-being. He has devised numerous plans and organizations for gaining greater security and comfort, yet he suffers from intellectual and emotional insecurity because he is uncertain about the meaning of life, the nature of the world in which he lives, and the kind of life he wants to live with his fellows.

World War II was a war of ideas, as well as of men, materials, and con-flicting national interests. It was in large part a conflict between two irrecon-cilable philosophies competing for the allegiance of men. The difference between life in the democratic and in the fascist countries was not so much a difference in technology, or in science, or even in general education; it was a difference in ideas, ideals, and loyalties. The "cold war" that has existed since the end of World War II is a similar conflict between philosophies of life. Communism challenges our traditional beliefs and intensifies the struggle for the minds and hearts of men. If in this conflict our civilization has appeared weak at times, it is not because large numbers of leaders in the "free" societies have been communists or have wished to be "soft" toward communism. The real reason appears to be a lack of a strong sense of direction.

After calling attention to the lack of a sense of national purpose, to the overwhelming drive for personal comfort, amusement, and new gadgets, to industrial stoppages due to a lack of social discipline, to an educational system which all too frequently sacrifices quality to quantity, and to other conditions which tend to weaken our society, George F. Kennan, one of our outstanding diplomats who has served under both political parties, said, "If you ask me—as an historian—whether such a country has, over the long run, good chances of competing with a purposeful, serious and disciplined society such as that of the Soviet Union, I must say that the answer is 'no.' "[7]

All the men quoted above speak of the need for a revitalization of our society. They feel that our trouble is mainly intellectual and moral confusion leading to cultural instability. For some, however, "the prospect of the coming quarter-century is exhilarating," since we are likely to see and to participate in "centuries of development telescoped into a brief span."[8] One student of philosophy comes to the defense of modern man. While admitting that "it is frightening when intelligence is applied in a moral void," and acknowledging that something very fundamental has gone wrong and that "an extraordinary number of men and women . . . are asking whether

[7] Quoted by Steve Allen in *The Saturday Review*, 43 (August 20, 1960): 14.
[8] David Sarnoff, *The Fabulous Future: America in 1980* (New York: Dutton, 1956), p. 14.

our civilization has not been on the wrong path for a long time," he thinks that the "doom-filled prophecies are unwarranted."9

Civilization is basically a set of ideas and ideals by which man lives. These ideas and ideals are embodied in rules of living and in institutions. They give life its unity and meaning. When they are lost sight of or fail to motivate, the civilization either changes or tends to decline. Medieval civilization was inspired primarily by a belief in salvation and a supernatural order. During the late Middle Ages this belief apparently ceased to be, of itself, sufficient motivation for a living society, and we can conjecture that if other beliefs had not emerged, Western civilization would have died.

Changes in ways of doing things and in history usually begin with people who are convinced of the worth of some ideal or who are captured by some vision of a different way of life. Following the Middle Ages, many people began to conceive of a way of life motivated to a much larger extent by a belief that life on this earth is worthwhile in itself. In the broadest sense, this belief made possible the Renaissance, the Reformation, and our modern world, with its factories, mass production, money and banks, rapid transportation and, more recently, atomic power and exploration of outer space. All these things are calculated to make this world better and to give man more control over it. But unless we develop some fairly consistent view of the nature of man, the nature of the total order within which man lives, and some reasonable scale of values based on an order beyond mere human desires, such things are not likely to provide an enduring basis for our world.

With man's rapidly increasing knowledge and power over the physical and intellectual world, his potentialities for good as well as for evil are greater than ever before. We may come to live in a better world than man has ever known. What our world becomes depends in large part on whether we have the intelligence, the sense of responsibility, the courage, and the determination to reconstruct a set of values in which we can believe. Philosophy, in conjunction with other disciplines, plays a central role in personal integration and social reconstruction and stability.

WHAT IS PHILOSOPHY?

In a general sense, a person's philosophy is the sum of his fundamental beliefs and convictions. In this sense everyone has a philosophy, even though he does not realize it. All people have some ideas concerning physical objects, man, the meaning of life, nature, death, God, right and wrong, and beauty and ugliness. Of course, these ideas are acquired in a variety of ways. Especially during the early years of our lives, we are continuously engaged, with

9 Charles Frankel, *The Case for Modern Man* (New York: Harper, 1956), pp. 2, 196.

varying degrees of consciousness, in acquiring views and attitudes from our family, from companions, and from various other individuals and groups. These attitudes may come to us through custom and tradition as expressed by behavior in home, school, and church. They may be influenced by the movies, radio, television, and books. They may be the result of some thinking on our part; or they may be largely the result of convention and emotional bias. This broad, popular, or man-in-the-street view of philosophy is not adequate for our purposes. It does not describe the work and task of the philosopher. We need to define philosophy more specifically, since the broad view does not distinguish philosophy from many vague, confused, and superficial beliefs.

The word *philosophy* is derived from the Greek words *philos* ("loving") and *sophia* ("wisdom") and means "the love of knowledge and wisdom." But philosophy can be approached or defined from a number of different points of view. Here we present five that are supplementary rather than contradictory, although some philosophers may wish to exclude one or more of them. Each approach must be kept in mind for a clear understanding of the many meanings of *philosophy* and what particular philosophers may say about the nature and function of philosophy.

1. *Philosophy is a personal attitude toward life and the universe.* When a person goes through some crisis or unusual experience, often we inquire, "How does he take it?" or "How does it affect him?" Sometimes the answer is, "He takes it philosophically." This means that he sees the problem in its broad perspective or as a part of a larger scheme of things; hence he faces the situation calmly and reflectively, with poise and composure.

The mature philosophical attitude is the searching and critical attitude; it is also the open-minded, tolerant attitude expressed in the willingness to look at all sides of an issue. It includes a readiness to accept life and the world as they are, and to try to see life in all its relationships. This does not mean enslavement to the present or to what exists now, however, because philosophy is willing to look beyond the actualities to the possibilities.

To philosophize is not merely to read and to know philosophy; it is also to think and to feel philosophically. Philosophy begins in wonder, doubt, and curiosity. It grows out of our developing awareness of the problems of human existence. Consequently, philosophy is in part the speculative attitude that does not shrink from facing the difficult and unsolved problems of life.

2. *Philosophy is a method of reflective thinking and reasoned inquiry.* This method is not the exclusive property of philosophy, as will readily be seen; it is the method of all careful and accurate thinking. Philosophy, however, is more inclusive or synoptic than are the various sciences. Philosophical method is reflective and critical. It involves the attempt to think through

one's problems and to face all the facts involved. The accumulation of more knowledge does not by itself lead to understanding, since it does not necessarily teach the mind to make a critical evaluation of facts or enable a person to live his life according to consistent principles.

There are varieties of philosophical methods, as will be seen when the problems of knowledge are studied in greater detail. Philosophers differ in the extent to which they emphasize and accept or reject authority, reason, sense experience, and intuition. These topics will be considered in Part One, Methods of Inquiry.

3. *Philosophy is an attempt to gain a view of the whole.* Philosophy seeks to combine the conclusions of the various sciences and long human experience into some kind of consistent world view. The philosopher wishes to see life, not with the specialized slant of the scientist or the businessman or the artist, but with the over-all view of someone cognizant of life as a totality. In speaking of "speculative philosophy," which he distinguishes from "critical philosophy," C. D. Broad says, "Its object is to take over the results of the various sciences, to add to them the results of the religious and ethical experiences of mankind, and then to reflect upon the whole. The hope is that, by this means, we may be able to reach some general conclusions as to the nature of the universe, and as to our position and prospects in it."[10]

Since the direction of learning during the past century has been toward analysis, specialization, and the fragmentation of knowledge, it is well to keep in mind that many of the great philosophers have refused to confine their attention to some one or even a few aspects of experience. Plato, Aristotle, Aquinas, Hegel, Bergson, Dewey, and Whitehead, to mention only a few, have sought to gain a comprehensive vision of things.

While there are difficulties and dangers in setting forth any world view, there are also dangers in confining one's attention to fragments of human experience. "The dangers of the sort of narrow specialization which either refuses to look beyond its own little province or treats as nonsensical attempts to go beyond it far outweigh the risks of attempting a world view."[11]

4. *Philosophy is the logical analysis of language and the clarification of the meaning of words and concepts.* Certainly this is one function of philosophy. In fact, nearly all philosophers have used methods of analysis and have sought to clarify the meaning of terms and the use of language. There are some philosophers, indeed, who see this as the main task of philosophy, and a few who claim this is the only legitimate function of philosophy. Such persons consider philosophy a specialized field serving the sciences and aiding in the clarification of language rather than a broad field reflecting upon all of life's

10 *Scientific Thought* (New York: Harcourt, Brace, 1923), p. 20.
11 Lewis E. Hahn, "Philosophy as Comprehensive Vision," *Philosophy and Phenomenological Research*, 22 (September, 1961): 16–25.

experiences. This outlook is recent and has gained considerable support during the last half century. It would limit what we call *knowledge* to statements about *observable facts* and their interrelations—that is, to the business of the various sciences. All linguistic analysts, however, do not define *knowledge* so narrowly. While they do reject and try to "clean up" many nonscientific assertions, many of them think that we can have knowledge of ethical principles and the like, though this knowledge is also experientially derived. Those who take the narrower view neglect, when they do not deny, all generalized world views and life views, as well as traditional moral philosophy and theology. From this more narrow point of view the aim of philosophy is to expose confusion and nonsense and to clarify the meaning and use of terms in science and everyday affairs.

The discussions centering around "philosophical analysis" as the function and method of philosophy are involved and technical. The groups supporting this general position have not been unified, as we shall see in Chapter 16. We do need to emphasize here that there are no philosophical schools which do not rely on analysis in some form. We are using the terms *philosophical analysis* and *linguistic analysis* to describe those philosophers who see this as the sole or at least the major task of philosophy.

5. *Philosophy is a group of problems as well as theories about the solution of these problems.* There are certain perennial problems which interest mankind and for which philosophers have always sought answers. Philosophy presses its inquiry into the deeper problems of human existence beyond what eye hath seen or ear heard. Some questions raised in the past have been answered in a manner satisfactory to most men. For example, the existence of innate or inborn ideas has been denied since the time of John Locke in the seventeenth century. Many questions, however, have been answered only tentatively, and many problems remain unsolved.

What are philosophical questions? The question "Did John Doe make a false statement on his income tax return?" is merely a question of fact. But the questions "What is truth?" and "What is the distinction between right and wrong?" have philosophical importance.

Most of us stop at times—sometimes because of startling events, often out of sheer curiosity—and think seriously about fundamental life issues: What is life and why am I here? What is the place of life in this great universe? Is the universe friendly or unfriendly? Do things operate by chance or through sheer mechanism, or is there some plan or purpose or intelligence at the heart of things? Is my life controlled by outside forces or do I have a determining or even a partial degree of control? Why do men struggle and strive for their rights, for justice, for better things in the future? What do concepts like "right" and "justice" mean, and what are the marks of a good society?

Often men and women have been asked to sacrifice their lives, if need be, for certain values and ideals. What are the genuine values of life and how can they be attained? Is there really a fundamental distinction between right and wrong, or is it just a matter of one's own opinions? What is beauty? Should religion still count in a person's life? Is it intellectually respectable to believe in God? Is there any possibility of a "life after death"? Is there any way we can get an answer to these and many related questions? Where does knowledge come from, and can we have any assurances that anything is true?

These questions are all philosophical. The attempt to seek answers or solutions to them has given rise to theories and systems of thought, such as *idealism, realism, pragmatism, logical empiricism, humanism,* and *materialism.* Philosophy also means the various theories or systems of thought developed by the great philosophers—men like Socrates, Plato, Aristotle, Augustine, Aquinas, Descartes, Spinoza, Locke, Berkeley, Kant, Royce, James, and others. Without these men and their thoughts, philosophy would not have the rich content it has today. Even though we may be unconscious of the fact, we are constantly influenced by ideas that have come down to us in the traditions of society.

So far we have been talking about philosophy in general. However, philosophy also deals with the systematic body of principles and assumptions underlying a particular field of experience. For example, there are philosophies of science, education, art, music, history, law, mathematics, and religion. Any subject pursued far enough reveals within itself philosophical problems.

THE RELEVANCE OF PHILOSOPHY TO EVERYDAY LIVING

Occasionally we hear it said that it does not matter what a person believes so long as he does the right thing. Some people, in other words, have a tendency to value action or deeds over beliefs and convictions. But ideas are the foundation of action, and a person is not likely to make any determined effort to act unless he believes something. Communism as we know it would probably not have come into being if Marx had not laid its foundations in his philosophy; once men accepted his ideas, it was almost inevitable that these ideas should be expressed in action. There is a deep tendency in us all to become whatever we think ourselves to be; as a result, ideas have a decisive power in human history. One writer says:

> This capacity to believe is the most significant and fundamental human faculty, and the most important thing about a man is what he believes in the depth of his being. This is the thing that makes him what he is; the thing that organizes him and feeds him; the thing that keeps him going in the face of untoward circumstances; the thing that gives him resistance and drive. Let neutrality, confusion, indifference or skepticism enter this inner place, and the very springs

of life will cease to flow. Men will quit, lose heart, yield, give up, become bitter
or cynical, become sunk in bleakness or emptiness, commit suicide, turn to
criminality, or retreat into a realm of phantasy.[12]

Let us summarize briefly some of the things that philosophy can do for us,
showing why it is that a person needs a philosophy.

1. *Each person must make decisions and act.* If we are to decide wisely and act
consistently, we need to discover values and the meaning of things. Life
forces us to make choices and to act on the basis of some scale of values.
We have to decide questions of truth and falsity, of beauty and ugliness, and
of right and wrong. The search for standards and goals is an important part
of the task of philosophy. Philosophy is interested in the qualitative aspect of
things. It refuses to disregard any authentic aspect of human experience and
seeks to formulate standards and goals in the most reasonable way.

After asking the question, "What is the use of philosophy?" Jacques
Maritain says that it reminds men "of the supreme utility of those things
which do not deal with means, but with ends. For men do not live only by
bread, vitamins, and technological discoveries. They live by values and
realities which are above time and are worth knowing for their own sake."[13]

2. *Our conduct is our own, and we are really free only when we rely upon inner
controls or self-chosen ends.* If a man acts as he does merely because of custom or
tradition or the law, he is not genuinely free. When asked what good his
philosophy did him, Aristotle remarked that it enabled him to do willingly
what other men did merely because of fear of the law. That man is free who
is the author of the principles and the laws by which he lives. In an ideal
society, each person would agree with every law or, if he did not like the law,
would criticize it and agitate for a change. He would do this on the basis of
facts and principles which were consistent.

3. *Philosophy is one of the best means to foster the habit of reflection.* Philosophy
can help us to enlarge the areas of our awareness—to become more alive,
more discerning, more critical, and more intelligent. In many specialized
fields of knowledge there is a definite and specific body of facts, and students
are given problems so that they will gain practice in arriving at the right
answers quickly and easily. In philosophy, however, there are different points
of view to be considered, and there are unsolved problems which are important for life. Consequently, the student's sense of wonder, his curiosity,
and his speculative interest are kept alive.

4. *We live in an age of uncertainty and change, when many of the older beliefs
and ways of doing things are inadequate.* Under such conditions we need a scale
of values and a sense of direction. Just as we feel physical discomfort when we

---

12 From Hugh Stevenson Tigner, *No Sign Shall Be Given* (New York: Macmillan, 1942),
p. 109. By permission of The Macmillan Company, publishers.
13 *On the Use of Philosophy* (Princeton: Princeton U. Press, 1961), pp. 6–7.

are in the midst of material disorder and moral discomfort when we are confronted with cruelty and injustice, so there is intellectual discomfort in the presence of fragmentary and confused views of the world. Without some unity of outlook and response, there may result, as Irwin Edman has pointed out,[14] a divided self, which in turn may lead to psychological tensions or nervous collapse. One way we can gain unity in a world in turmoil is to achieve an inner integration, to know what to approve and what to disapprove, and to gain a sense of the meaning of human existence.

THE FUNCTION OF PHILOSOPHY IN LIBERAL ARTS EDUCATION

What part does philosophy play in a liberal arts education? Let us ask, first, what *is* a liberal arts education? There is considerable agreement that it has some if not all of the following aims: (1) It should train men to think critically and constructively. (2) It should give some insight into moral, aesthetic, and religious values, and help men to discriminate among values. (3) It should train men for constructive citizenship in a free and growing society—that is, it should make men free and enable them to use their freedom wisely. (4) While liberal arts education, as such, is not aimed directly at the acquisition of special or technical skills, it should provide the intellectual background helpful to success in business and professional areas.

What is the function of philosophy in such an educational program? At one time "philosophy" included all the special sciences.[15] During and after the Renaissance, mathematics and physics separated from philosophy; later the other sciences followed. Psychology has been a separate science only in recent decades; in some institutions it is still linked to philosophy. Today there are so many sciences and such a maze of specialties within some of these sciences that many persons tend to forget the matrix, or the whole, of which these sciences are only a part.

In 1943 a Commission on the Function of Philosophy in Liberal Education was appointed by the officers of the American Philosophical Association. This commission undertook an extensive study of the role philosophy might play in modern education and the postwar world, publishing its report in 1945 in a book called *Philosophy in American Education*.[16] Writing in this

---

[14] "Philosophy," in *On Going to College: A Symposium* (New York: Oxford U. Press, 1938), pp. 196–198.

[15] The influence of that earlier situation is still with us. For example, one may earn a degree of Doctor of Philosophy (Ph.D.) in fields such as physics, chemistry, biology, and psychology, as well as in the field of philosophy itself. The Ph.D. degree is the highest that can be earned in any field of study.

[16] Published by Harper. The members of the commission were Brand Blanshard, Curt J. Ducasse, Charles W. Hendel, Arthur E. Murphy, and Max C. Otto. The study was aided by a grant from the Rockefeller Foundation to the American Philosophical Association.

report on "The Climate of Opinion," Brand Blanshard says that "the major demands on philosophy" are for "integration," for "community of mind," for a "reinterpretation of democracy," and for a "philosophy of life." Of the demand for integration, he says, "one of the great historic tasks of philosophy has been the putting together of the results of human inquiry, religious, historical, scientific, into a consistent view of the world." Philosophy should not be just another specialty, as it is occasionally represented.

The great issues of our time are philosophical problems. They have to do with questions of right, justice, freedom, man, society, and nature. Tomorrow's inventions will not make them obsolete. Philosophical problems are not only central but timeless. "No civilization can survive," says Robert Ulich, "without a deeper and uniting definition of truths and values. . . . Only the mediocre person is satisfied with a mass of incoherent and isolated knowledge."[17] Facts alone are not enough. The mature person wants to understand himself, the society in which he lives, and his relation to the universe. Philosophy provides the means for the student to systematize, assimilate, and evaluate the huge mass of knowledge. Philosophical reflection or discussion is one of the best ways to achieve perspective.

Of the function of philosophy in a liberal education program, one teacher of philosophy said:

> Philosophy has traditionally been a foundation stone for the liberal arts education of a college student, in the humanistic area. It should be admitted that Philosophy, as the "Love of Wisdom," cannot, in the ordinary sense, be taught. It is not a skill like typewriting, nor a science like physics. It is closer to the arts, in that the teacher of philosophy can only hope to evoke from the student a deep and enduring desire to pursue, lovingly and religiously, the wisdom that will give his whole life a more profound meaning in relation to himself and to others.
>
> Nevertheless, the academic aspect of philosophy can reasonably expect to instruct the student in the history of *ideas* and *ideals* of great philosophers, so that the wisdom of others may be utilized by the student in finding his own wisdom of life. We may also expect to provide the student with some skill in logical or discursive thinking, as an intellectual tool for seeking wisdom.
>
> Since, in philosophy, we may philosophize about anything, we find that our course work may be devoted to such subjects as philosophy of religion, philosophy of morality (ethics), philosophy of the arts (aesthetics) and of literature, philosophy of the sciences, philosophy of law, philosophy of history, etc. In all such areas, we desire to provide the student with some basic insight into liberal arts subjects and to satisfy his need to relate that insight to an intellectually balanced and emotionally mature way of life.

[17] *History of Educational Thought* (New York: American Book, 1945), p. 341. See also Ulich's *The Human Career* (New York: Harper, 1955); and *Philosophy of Education* (New York: American Book, 1961).

Underlying all traditional philosophy is metaphysics—the inquiry into the nature of ultimate reality, and into the nature of knowledge, meaning, and truth. Analysis of these fundamental questions, which pervade all of the great philosophical systems, and all of our courses, serves to make the student sensitive to the often naive character of his own views on these all-important problems. His intellectual perspectives are broadened and liberalized, so that he may become consciously and sympathetically aware of honestly differing opinions on these subjects. In the type of world in which we are living, where metaphysical differences make a difference (e.g. the dialectical materialism of communism versus a Christian conception of God and man), it is essential that our students become clearly cognizant of the grounds for these differences. To live adequately in our world, is to live with a compassionate understanding of our ideological differences. The study of Philosophy may hope to engender such understanding.[18]

PHILOSOPHY AND RELATED FIELDS

There are many approaches to an understanding of the world in which we live. Human aspirations, interest, and activity have expressed themselves in four basic fields—philosophy, science, art, and religion. Since each of these fields is considered later in this study, we shall merely distinguish among them at this time.

Philosophy, as we have seen, is an attempt to understand the world, its meaning, and its values. Its field is broad and inclusive. It attempts to answer questions about the kind of universe in which we live and what the ends of life may reasonably be. Philosophy, while using the facts and descriptive material presented by specialized fields of study, goes beyond description to inquire into the nature, the values, and the possibilities of things. Its goals are *understanding* and *wisdom*.

Philosophy and science have much in common. Both grow out of the reflective, inquiring attitude and are prompted by an impartial love of truth. The sciences, however, deal with special or restricted fields. Their purpose is to describe the world so that it may be interpreted in exact or mathematical terms, and then to control it mechanically, where possible. Science has as its goals *description, prediction, experimentation,* and *control.* Chapters 5 to 8 consider the scientific methods and interpretations of the universe given us by the natural sciences, and the relation between philosophy and science.

The insight of the artist enriches our lives through his creating of beauty and heightening of the aesthetic aspects of experience. An important part of man's life has to do with enjoyment of music, drama, poetry, painting, sculpture, and architecture. The field of aesthetics and the philosophy of art deal with the problems of the nature of beauty and the arts. To live a full life, man needs to cultivate his sensitivity to this area of human experience. The

[18] C. W. Berenda, "The Liberal Arts Function of Philosophy," *The Journal of Philosophy,* 54 (January 3, 1957): 19–20.

goals of art are not *knowledge* and *understanding*, as in philosophy, nor *description* and *control*, as in science, but *creativity, perfection, form, beauty, communication*, and *expression*, and above all the *aesthetic response*.

A philosophy is not a religion, but any mature religion will have or will imply some philosophical background or some set of beliefs about life and the universe. Religion, it has been said, begins at the point where philosophy moves into personal commitment and action. A religion is more than a mere belief or an understanding of something; it implies the reaction of a man's whole being to that on which he feels dependent. It is life lived in the conviction that "what is highest in spirit is deepest in nature."

Religion implies devotion and an object of worship. In religion, worship rather than knowledge is central. The person wishes to secure harmony or adjustment between himself and his world. Yet conviction should be related to reality, and philosophy can help men build their religious convictions on foundations that are intellectually mature. Philosophy may support one's religious beliefs, provided such beliefs are not dependent on prescientific, outworn, narrow, and dogmatic conceptions. The main concerns of religion are *harmony, adjustment, commitment, worship, peace, righteousness, salvation*, and *God*.

Philosophy is thus a comprehensive approach to life and the world, one closely related to all the main areas of human experience. It seeks to unify the results of the sciences and the insights of moral philosophy, aesthetics, and religion. Philosophers from ancient to modern times have sought for a unified vision of life and its meaning and have attempted to give a "reasoned conception of the universe and of man's place in it."

QUESTIONS AND PROJECTS

NOTE: The *Review Questions*, number *1* in this and the following chapters, are questions on the content of the chapter and are not meant as examination questions, although some of them could be used as such. To think on a subject, a student must be familiar with terminology and some basic facts and ideas. These questions are intended to say to the reader, "As you read this chapter these are some of the things to which you need to pay special attention." With this in mind the author has not hesitated at times to list a number of terms and ideas in one question.

1. Review Questions

(1) What justification is there for saying that our age is facing unprecedented problems? Are these problems any different, except in degree and intensity, from the problems of past ages?

(2) Why are many thoughtful people disturbed and anxious? Is the phrase *world revolution* a reasonable one? Why or why not?

(3) Which contemporary conditions or trends do you think encouraging, and which discouraging?

(4) Consider the statements in the chapter regarding the times in which we live. All of these statements were made by thoughtful students of our society and world affairs. Give your reactions to these quotations, indicating the extent to which you agree or disagree with them.

(5) What is meant by the statement that "civilization is basically a set of ideas and ideals"?

(6) Why does each person need a philosophy? Can we really choose whether or not we are to have a philosophy of life? What is the issue here?

(7) In this chapter we have presented five approaches to philosophy or points of view from which it may be defined. Make clear these different points of view, and indicate whether or not you think they are of equal importance.

(8) How may philosophical questions be distinguished from those which have little or no philosophical importance?

(9) How may one defend the statement that "philosophy is relevant to everyday living," or that beliefs and convictions are important for a person and for a society?

(10) What are the crucial elements in a liberal arts education?

(11) Discuss the functions and tasks of philosophy in a liberal arts education.

(12) Distinguish between philosophy and science, art, and religion.

2. Organize some of your present beliefs and convictions regarding life and the world and write out a statement of not more than 2000 words. A copy of this statement should be kept and compared with a similar statement written after you have completed the course.

3. Has your secondary school and college education developed in you any set of convictions or values regarding your personal life, social relationships, and the world in general? Should education be concerned with such questions or only with descriptive knowledge in specialized areas? Discuss.

4. Outline the field of philosophy, exhibiting in chart or graphic form its main divisions (such as axiology, epistemology, and metaphysics) and the subdivisions within these fields. The following will help you: J. Donald Butler, *Four Philosophies and Their Practice in Education and Religion* (New York: Harper, 1951), pp. 41–47; Milton D. Hunnex, *Philosophies and Philosophers* (San Francisco: Chandler, 1961); George T. W. Patrick, *Introduction to Philosophy* (rev. ed.; Boston: Houghton Mifflin, 1935), Ch. VI, "Philosophical Themes"; Daniel S. Robinson, *An Anthology of Recent Philosophy* (New York: Thomas Y. Crowell, 1929), Ch. IV.

5. Think about the following statements for a few minutes after you have read them; then indicate the extent and areas of your agreement or disagreement.

(1) "There is no more direct way of elevating our life than by elevating our ideas."—Ernest Dimnet

(2) "Make it thy business to know thyself, which is the most difficult lesson in the world."—Cervantes

(3) "Money buys everything except love, personality, freedom, immorality, silence, and peace."—Carl Sandburg

6. The philosophical journals are an important storehouse of current thinking in the field. Familiarize yourself with as many of them as you can. The following is a partial list: (1) *Ethics;* (2) *Hibbert Journal;* (3) *Humanist;* (4) *Journal of Philosophy;* (5) *Journal of the History of Ideas;* (6) *Mind;* (7) *New Scholasticism;* (8) *Pacific Philosophy Forum;* (9) *Personalist;* (10) *Philosophical Review;* (11) *Philosophical Studies;* (12) *Philosophy;* (13) *Philosophy and Phenomenological Research;* (14) *Philosophy East and West;* (15) *Philosophy of Science;* (16) *Proceedings of the Aristotelian Society;* (17) *Review of Metaphysics.*

SUGGESTED READINGS

BALDWIN, ROBERT C., AND MCPEEK, JAMES A. S. *An Introduction to Philosophy Through Literature.* New York: Ronald, 1950.
Philosophy is introduced by selections from the "literature of ideas." The selections are organized around philosophical themes.

DOWNS, ROBERT B. *Molders of the Modern Mind: 111 Books That Shaped Western Civilization.* New York: Barnes & Noble, 1961.
Brief descriptions of books that have influenced the course of Western society. Useful as a checklist for future reading.

DURANT, WILL. *The Pleasures of Philosophy.* New York: Simon and Schuster, 1953. (Paperback.)
The author discusses the main problems of philosophy in an attempt to set forth a consistent philosophy of life for the interested beginner.

EWING, A. C. *The Fundamental Questions of Philosophy.* New York: Macmillan, 1952.
A book written to give readers an idea of "what philosophy is and of the great topics with which it deals." See Chapter 1, "What Philosophy Is and Why It Is Worth Studying," pp. 2–25.

GRANT, GEORGE P. *Philosophy in the Mass Age.* New York: Hill & Wang, 1960.
A small book which, contending that American civilization is morally confused, stresses the need to recognize natural law that is rational and God-given.

JOAD, C. E. M. *Guide to Philosophy.* New York: Random House, 1936. (Dover, paperback, 1956.)
A good comprehensive survey of philosophy.

KAPLAN, ABRAHAM. *The New World of Philosophy.* New York: Random House, 1961.
An introduction on the nature of philosophy is followed by nine lectures dealing with various Occidental and Oriental philosophies.

LEVI, ALBERT WILLIAM. *Philosophy and the Modern World.* Bloomington: Indiana U. Press, 1959.
A stimulating and informative interpretation of twentieth-century intellectual history in which Part One deals with the problems and Part Two with sixteen of the leaders from Bergson to Wittgenstein and Whitehead.

LODGE, RUPERT C. *Applying Philosophy*. Boston: Beacon, 1951.
Philosophy presented as "reflective living." The implications and limitations of applying philosophy to everyday life. Clear and readable.

LONG, MARCUS. *The Spirit of Philosophy*. New York: Norton, 1953.
A book for the beginner, which deals with topics such as the meaning of philosophy, space and time, causality, teleology, and God.

MELZER, JOHN HENRY. *Philosophy in the Classroom: A Report*. Lincoln: U. of Nebraska Press, 1954.
The report of a study of how philosophy is being taught. Teachers who answered a questionnaire tell how they conduct their courses.

MOORE, GEORGE EDWARD. *Some Main Problems of Philosophy*. New York: Macmillan, 1953. (Collier Books, paperback, 1962.)
Twenty lectures on a variety of topics by an outstanding English philosopher—for the more mature student.

ORTEGA Y GASSET, JOSÉ. *What is Philosophy?* New York: Norton, 1960.
A series of lectures written over a period of years and dealing with the nature of philosophy and its importance in the present world.

WINN, RALPH B. *Philosophy at Work: A Constructive Approach*. New York: Pageant, 1960.
In Part One the author shows how philosophy deals with the problems of today. Part Two is a collection of readings on many topics.

SELECTED READINGS IN PHILOSOPHY

BRONSTEIN, DANIEL J., *et al.* (eds.). *Basic Problems of Philosophy*. 2nd ed.; New York: Prentice-Hall, 1955.

DAVIDSON, ROBERT F. (ed.). *The Search for Meaning in Life*. New York: Holt, Rinehart and Winston, 1962.

MANDELBAUM, MAURICE, *et al.* (eds.). *Philosophic Problems: An Introductory Book of Readings*. New York: Macmillan, 1957.

RADER, MELVIN (ed.). *The Enduring Questions: Main Problems in Philosophy*. New York: Holt, 1956.

RANDALL, JOHN H., *et al.* (eds.). *Readings in Philosophy*. 2nd ed.; New York: Barnes & Noble, 1950.

SINGER, MARCUS G., AND AMMERMAN, ROBERT T. (eds.). *Introductory Readings in Philosophy*. New York: Scribner's, 1962.

PART ONE

METHODS OF INQUIRY

❧ TWO ❧

THE SOURCES OF
KNOWLEDGE

In this and the next two chapters we face one of the most important as well as one of the most difficult questions in the field of philosophy:[1] What is the nature of human knowledge? What is the human mind capable of knowing? Do we have any genuine knowledge upon which we can depend, or must we be satisfied with mere opinions and guesses? Are we limited to the bare facts of experience, or are we able to go beyond what the senses reveal?

The technical term for the theory of knowledge is *epistemology*, which comes from the Greek word *episteme,* meaning "knowledge." There are three central questions or problems in this field: (1) What are the *sources* of knowledge? Where does genuine knowledge come from, or how do we know? This is the question of origins. (2) What is the *nature* of knowledge? Is there a real world outside the mind, and if so, can we know it? This is the question of appearance versus reality. (3) Is our knowledge *valid?* How do we distinguish truth from error? This is the question of the tests of truth, of verification. These questions are considered in this and the next two chapters.

Many beliefs once thought to be genuine knowledge have turned out to be false. Men once firmly believed that the earth was flat, that disease demons could be driven out by loud noises, and that in dreams our souls actually visited spots distant in time and space. These beliefs, once so securely held, have now been almost universally discarded. May the same thing be true of much of our present-day knowledge?

TRADITION AND COMMON SENSE

Philosophy is a comparatively recent development in man's long struggle to understand the conditions of living. Even in the West today, only a small

[1] Logically, this question of the nature of knowledge should be considered prior to a discussion of most other questions. However, some readers and teachers may wish to take up these questions later or just before they consider The Types of Philosophy, Part Three.

percentage of the population has any real insight into the fundamental problems of human existence with which philosophers are concerned. The vast majority subscribe to opinions or beliefs based largely on tradition and custom. Let us consider briefly this less specialized fund of opinions before we examine the main sources of knowledge.

We are born into social groups which have definite ways of acting, feeling, and thinking. We become conscious of ourselves and of a world around us. We get acquainted with other persons and with things through an ever-widening range of experience. Our emerging consciousness includes the sensations of touch, sight, sound, taste, and smell. As objects (or relations, qualities, and so on) and sounds are brought together through association or deliberate conditioning, we form words and learn the names of things. Words are grouped into sentences as we acquire a language. The events of our consciousness are distinctly private, since no one else can be aware of our sensations. We assume, however, that the experiences of others are similar to our own.

As we grow and have further experiences, we acquire habits, feelings, thoughts, beliefs, and memories that appear to be fairly reliable. These ways of acting and thinking, engaged in without serious doubt or questioning by the members of a group, are the customs and traditions that tend to hold the individual in line. Men tend to look to group opinion to provide clues to the opinions they should hold. Ways of acting and thinking are passed on from generation to generation by tradition, imitation, and instruction. These common ways of looking at things are often referred to as *common sense*. *Common sense* is thus a broad term for the fund of opinion each member of the group is expected to have.

This acquired wisdom may include practical maxims and proverbs, opinions about the practices that people are expected to follow, and the unarticulated beliefs held by members of the group. That children ought to obey their parents, that animal organisms have a definite life span, that objects heavier than air fall to the ground, and that things exist independently of us and our knowledge of them—all these may be included among the countless convictions growing out of human experience.

Among the *characteristics of common-sense opinion,* the following four are worthy of note: First, common-sense opinion tends to be habitual and imitative—that is, to be inherited largely from the past. It rests on custom and tradition. What is custom and tradition for the group tends to become habit and belief for the individual. These common-sense beliefs are sometimes stated as proverbs or maxims coming down from the past. For example, "Spare the rod, and spoil the child." Common-sense belief places limits on the whims and the caprices of the individual, and emphasizes the tested and approved ways of the group. For this reason *common sense* is often considered to be synonymous with *good sense,* and a man of common sense is considered a man of sound judgment.

Second, common-sense opinion is often vague and ambiguous. It is superficially grounded and may vary from individual to individual, from group to group, or from area to area. It is a mixture of fact and prejudice, of wisdom and emotional bias. It includes notions and opinions that have been formed without careful reflection and criticism: for example, "The good die young." Furthermore, common-sense opinion is inclusive of all areas of life in the sense that it is unspecialized belief. At times this may be an element of strength and balance. It enables men to appeal to common sense as opposed to the one-sided and extreme claims of some specialists, who may see the world and life from a very narrow point of view. Common-sense belief, however, may lead people astray as well as lead them in the right direction. In a complex and rapidly changing world, it is frequently inadequate to meet or to cope with new and unfamiliar situations.

Third, common-sense opinion is in considerable part untested belief. It is not, as some are prone to believe, a mere statement of "facts" based on first-hand sensations or other experiences. For example, "Red-headed people are quick-tempered." Like people who are not red-headed, some are quick-tempered and some are not. Positive cases seem to confirm the opinion; negative cases are seldom used to refute the belief. While those who hold these notions may think they are self-evident, they are actually based on assumptions that are often unexamined and that need to be checked and criticized. While some notions of common sense can be verified, the history of science and of philosophy makes it clear that the "first look" is not always correct, and that things are not always what they appear to be.

Fourth, common-sense opinions are seldom accompanied by explanations of why things are as they are alleged to be. Explanations are missing or, if they are present, are usually so general that they overlook exceptions and limiting conditions. For example, if water is said to freeze at low temperatures, why is this; and why is it that flowing water and salt water do not freeze under the same conditions as still and fresh water? In distinguishing science from common sense, Ernest Nagel says, "It is the desire for explanations which are at once systematic and controllable by factual evidence that generates science; and it is the organization and classification of knowledge on the basis of explanatory principles that is the distinctive goal of the sciences."[2]

We never leave common-sense belief wholly behind us, regardless of how far our education may carry us or how specialized our knowledge may become. And it may be fortunate that we never completely abandon common-sense belief, since it may serve as a check against the "blind spots"

[2] *The Structure of Science* (New York: Harcourt, Brace & World, 1961), p. 4.

some people develop through intensive specialization. But common-sense belief, if it is to serve this useful purpose, needs constant and careful re-examination.

OBSTACLES TO CLEAR THINKING

Just as there are speech defects that may prevent a person from speaking plainly, so there are thought impediments that may prevent a man from thinking clearly. Emotion, personal interests, or outside pressures may lead our thinking astray. These obstacles to clear thinking may cause our science and our philosophy to be biased, and they are especially likely to influence and to distort our fund of common-sense opinions.

Francis Bacon (1561–1626) has given us a classic statement of the errors of thinking in his famous "Idols of the Mind."[3] These are, first, the Idols of the Tribe. Men are prone to recognize evidence and incidents favorable to their own side or group (tribe or nation). Second, there are the Idols of the Cave. We tend to see ourselves as the center of the world and to stress our own limited outlook. Third, the Idols of the Market Place cause us to be influenced by the words and names with which we are familiar in everyday discourse. We are led astray by emotionally toned words—for example, in our society such words as *communist* or *radical*. Finally, the Idols of the Theater arise from our attachment to parties, creeds, and cults. These fads, fashions, and schools of thought are like stage plays in the sense that they lead us into imaginary worlds; ultimately, the Idols of the Theater lead us to biased conclusions.

Handicaps to clear thinking may be stated in other than the classic terms above. Some that we would recognize are prejudice, susceptibility to propaganda, authoritarianism.

Prejudice always inhibits clear thinking. The human mind frequently finds it difficult to suspend judgment until all the evidence is in.[4] Even after the evidence has been gathered, our prejudices make it difficult to draw accurate conclusions. A prejudice is a prejudgment, a mental bias, which leads us to ignore or to minimize some of the evidence and to overestimate other parts of it. Prejudices usually rest on emotional grounds and tend to be in line with our comfort, pride, and self-interest. When confronted with our prejudices, we are likely to try to rationalize them—that is, we try to find "reasons" or arguments for continuing to believe what we wish to believe.

Another obstacle to clear thinking is our susceptibility to propaganda. Even when we want to face facts and think clearly, our thinking may go

---

[3] *Bacon Selections,* ed. Matthew Thompson McClure (New York: Scribner's, 1928), pp. 288–290. (Modern Student's Library.)

[4] There are situations, as William James and others have made clear, in which it is undesirable or impossible to suspend judgment. In cases where immediate action is demanded, we have to act on the basis of the evidence we have at the time.

astray because our information is tainted or manipulated by its sources. The propagandists of special-interest groups use radio, television, the press, and motion pictures in an attempt to control our thinking. Propagandists attempt, first, to arouse in us a strong emotion or desire, and then, through suggestion, to present a line of action that appears to be a satisfactory way of expressing the emotion or satisfying the desire. There is, however, no necessary—that is, logical—connection between the emotion to be aroused, such as a man's love for his wife, and the proposed line of action, which may be buying anything from flowers to a grand piano.

The uncritical or blind appeal to authority is an unphilosophical and unscientific method of gaining knowledge. This is true whether the authority is custom, tradition, the family, the church, the state, or the mass media of communication. This uncritical acceptance of authority is called *authoritarianism*.

Authoritarianism means something different from the mere acceptance of the views of a particular authority on certain occasions. It is the belief that knowledge is guaranteed or validated by the authority. When a person accepts authority uncritically, he ceases his independent efforts to find out what is true or false. Regardless of its form, testimony that is accepted on blind faith, and without regard to the extent to which it does or does not harmonize with experience and reason, is a dangerous thing.

The weaknesses and dangers of authoritarianism are numerous. First, as a dominant attitude, which uses no tests for knowledge except authority, it tends to block progress and to be a substitute for thinking and further investigation. We live in a rapidly changing social order, in which the beliefs and practices of one age may be quite inadequate in a later period. Second, when authorities disagree or conflict, as they frequently do, we are left in confusion unless we have other sources to which to turn. Third, we are likely to be led astray by the prestige of our authority and fail to realize when he speaks outside the range of his competence. A person who is competent in one field is quite likely to be believed when he speaks on some other subject about which he may have no special knowledge. Fourth, we may be led astray by the fact that a belief has been persistent and widespread. Such widespread acceptance may add to its prestige and appeal and make it difficult for us to discover ancient errors. It is well to remember that many of these beliefs may be wrong; indeed, many have been disproved.

As a classic illustration of authoritarianism we may cite the scholastic thinkers of the Middle Ages, who dared not deviate from the teachings of the Church and the writings of Aristotle. Modern counterparts exist; the communist "party line" is perhaps the example which comes to mind most quickly, but the reader might well make his own list.

Many people welcome authority because they have little confidence in themselves or are intellectually lazy: to accept the word of someone else is to take the easy way of gaining comfort and assurance. People in general tend to be imitative, credulous, and suggestible. To hear or to read is to believe, and so they accept the idea, "get on the band wagon," "toe the party line." To follow the crowd and fall in line with public opinion is the refuge, too, of confused and weary minds. Such conformist tendencies in human beings create fertile soil for modern high-pressure advertising and propaganda.

The pressure of public opinion, prejudice, propaganda, and blind acceptance of authority are not the only obstacles to thinking. We are all creatures of impulse and habit. While habits are very useful in taking care of the routine details of life, they do not help and sometimes they hinder us when we are faced with new and unfamiliar situations.

There is also a wide range of fallacies in thinking or violations of the principles of logic and consistency. These are sometimes divided into three groups. The semantical fallacies have to do with the careless or improper use of words. Words may shift in meaning as we proceed with our discussion. For example, if the term *law* in a discussion of natural law is changed surreptitiously to refer to a legislative enactment or to moral law in the sense of a rule of conduct, we have a shift in meaning. The formal fallacies cause us to draw invalid conclusions from our premises. We may make an assertion about all the members of a group when the premises permit us to speak only of some. The empirical fallacies arise from our hasty generalizations. Because one event came after another, we may wrongly insist that there is a direct causal relationship.

To avoid hasty generalizations we need to know the types of premises from which we can draw valid conclusions, and also the conditions under which we may reasonably generalize from a knowledge of particular instances. Deduction and induction are both processes of reasoning that we need to understand if we are to avoid serious fallacies in our thinking. They are terms used to describe methods by which we move from evidence to conclusions based on the evidence. Deduction is that process by which we draw a conclusion from one or more premises. If our inference is correct and the conclusion does follow, we say that the deduction is valid. For example: if we say, "All men are mortal" and "Socrates is a man," we may conclude that "Socrates is mortal." Here the premises are all the evidence that is relevant to the soundness of the conclusion. Induction, on the other hand, is empirical, in that it deals with matters of fact. It attempts to draw conclusions concerning all the members of a class after examining only some of them or concerning an unexamined member of a class. The aim is to make statements or propositions that are true. For example, after examining some crows, or even a large number, may we conclude that all crows are black? May we conclude that the next crow we see will be black? The types of deduction and induction are too numerous to mention here, but the reader unacquainted with these methods of reasoning and the forms they may take, as well as the many fallacies that may lead thinking astray, is advised to consult any good book on logic.[5]

THE POSSIBLE SOURCES OF KNOWLEDGE

In his well-known *Essay Concerning Human Understanding*, John Locke points out how this problem of the sources of knowledge is the first and fundamental question to be settled.

> Were it fit to trouble thee with the history of this Essay, I should tell thee, that five or six friends meeting at my chamber, and discoursing on a subject very remote from this, found themselves quickly at a stand, by the difficulties that arose on every side. After we had a while puzzled ourselves, without coming any nearer a resolution of those doubts which perplexed us, it came into my thoughts, that we took a wrong course; and that before we set ourselves upon inquiries of that nature, it was necessary to examine our own abilities, and see what objects our understandings were, or were not, fitted to deal with. This I proposed to the company, who all readily assented; and thereupon it was agreed, that this should be our first inquiry.[6]

Immanuel Kant also placed this issue first among the central questions of life. Since the time of Locke and of Kant, the problem of knowledge has occupied a prominent place in philosophical discussions.

Where did we get the beliefs we now hold? Is there some one source of knowledge, or are there many sources of knowledge? If there are many sources, are some more important than others? There are usually four sources of knowledge recognized in modern discussions, and we shall consider these sources here.

TESTIMONY AS A SOURCE: THE APPEAL TO AUTHORITY

How do we know that Socrates and Julius Caesar ever lived? Are they perhaps fictitious characters, like many others about whom we read in ancient mythology and in modern novels? We know that Socrates and Julius Caesar lived because of the testimony of their contemporaries and of the historians. In fact, the most common way of gaining knowledge about the past is to rely on the testimony of others—that is, upon authority. Much of the knowledge we use in everyday living has also been gained in that way. It is the way in which most of us have gained what knowledge we have of the thoughts of other men and the facts in the special fields of the various sciences. We have gained this knowledge neither by intuition, nor by thinking it out for ourselves, nor by personal experience.

---

[5] For example, see Maylon H. Hepp, *Thinking Things Through* (New York: Scribner's, 1956), Ch. 31, for a summary of the common pitfalls in thinking.
[6] From *Locke Selections*, ed. Sterling P. Lamprecht (New York: Scribner's, 1928), pp. 84–85.

Authority as a source of knowledge has its values as well as its dangers. Testimony or authority that is open to free and honest inquiry as to its validity is a legitimate source of knowledge. We need to accept such testimony in areas which we cannot investigate adequately for ourselves. We should make reasonably certain, however, that those we accept as authorities are people of integrity who have had more opportunity than we to gain the information desired. We need to know that these people have used the best methods available at the time. We must leave the solution of some questions to experts in whose knowledge and skill we have reasonable confidence. The testimony of others may be valuable in bringing us a summary of the conclusions to which they have been led by their experience. Such testimony may suggest to us where and how to look for evidence and so direct our attention to what might otherwise be overlooked. In discussing "the grounds of belief" Max Black says, "Among the most useful tests of qualification applied to alleged authorities are *recognition by other authorities* (especially as evidenced by such official signs of respectability as titles, diplomas, and degrees), *agreement with other authorities,* and *special competence* ('being in a position to know')."[7]

Testimony or authority, it must be kept clearly in mind, is a secondary source, not a primary one. When we ask, "From what source did our authority gain his knowledge?" we should not be satisfied with merely additional authorities. We want to know whether he gained his information by experience, or reason, or some other way, and whether we can examine the steps by which the conclusions were reached.

We need to keep in mind both the values and the dangers of the appeal to authority. Authority as a source of knowledge is dangerous only when we surrender our independent judgment and make no effort to discover what is true or false. In the previous section we considered some of the main dangers of the blind acceptance of tradition and authority.

THE SENSES AS A SOURCE: THE APPEAL TO SENSE PERCEPTION

How do we know that water will freeze or that it will revive the drooping plant? We may say that we know by means of our sensory organs from our own past experience.

What we see, hear, touch, smell, and taste—that is, our concrete experience—constitutes the realm of knowledge, according to the empiricists. Empiricism stresses man's power of perception, or observation, or what the senses receive from the environment. Knowledge is obtained by forming ideas in accordance with observed facts. Stated briefly, empiricism maintains that we know what we have found out from our senses.

Empiricism may take a number of forms. As a narrow sensationalism (that

[7] *Critical Thinking* (New York: Prentice-Hall, 1952), p. 256.

is, referring to the senses), it asserts that knowledge is essentially sensation and that there is no other knowledge. In the eighteenth century, John Locke regarded the mind as analogous to a piece of wax: as wax shows the form of what is pressed against it, so the mind registers impressions as they come from the world outside. More recent empiricism has abandoned this theory of knowledge. Pragmatism, as a form of "radical empiricism," views the mind as active in selecting and molding its experiences in accordance with the interests and purposes of the organism. It emphasizes the changing world of experience. Pragmatism is considered separately as a type of philosophy in Part Three.

Modern science, which is especially interested in particular facts and relations, is empirical. Scientists are interested in controlled observations and experiments, not in mere general sense perceptions and experiences, and they strive to keep irrelevant factors from disturbing the examination of some special problem or event. Items can be changed or manipulated, and the effects can be recorded. Furthermore, if the conditions are controlled, the experiment can be repeated by other observers; thus more accurate and objective information can be obtained. Special instruments can be used to aid observation, help eliminate errors, and measure results. The conclusions, however, are always tentative and are set forth in the form of hypotheses, theories, or possibly laws, which, after further observation and research, may need to be modified or changed. The process of building up the great body of scientific knowledge is a slow one, involving the labor of countless thousands in many parts of the world. This knowledge enables us to exercise considerable control over our world, and it is of constant service in our daily lives.

While we depend on empirical knowledge for our acquaintance with the particular facts and relations of our everyday world, we do need to exercise caution and to realize that we can be led astray even in the area of sense data. Prejudices and emotions may distort our view so that we select our "facts" to support our expectations. We tend to see what we expect to see or are trained to see. Our knowledge is infected with a personal and subjective coloration. The ease with which some philosophers and scientists have cast doubt upon just what it is that is outside or beyond us should keep us humble. To what extent the world as we know it is appearance or reality is considered in the next chapter.

THINKING AS A SOURCE: THE APPEAL TO REASON

How do we know that two contradictory statements cannot be true at the same time? How do we know that if two things each equal a third thing, they are equal to each other? We say that such things are self-evident or that they appeal to our reason.

The thinkers who stress reasoning or thought as the central factor in knowledge are known as *rationalists*. Rationalism is the view that we know what we have thought out, that the mind has the ability to discover truth by itself, or that knowledge is obtained by comparing ideas with ideas. The rationalist, in emphasizing man's power of thought and what the mind contributes to knowledge, is likely to assert that the senses, by themselves, cannot give us coherent and universally valid judgments. The highest kind of knowledge consists in universally valid judgments that are consistent with one another. The sensations and experiences which we gain through the senses—sight, sound, touch, taste, and smell—are just the raw material of knowledge. These sensations must be organized by the mind into a meaningful system before they become knowledge. For the rationalist, knowledge is found in concepts, principles, and laws, not just in raw sensations.

In its less extreme form, rationalism makes the claim that man has the power to know, with certainty, various truths about the universe which the senses alone cannot give us. For example, if A is greater than B and B is greater than C, then A is greater than C. We know that this is true quite independently of any actual instances. We know that it applies generally to boxes, to cities, or to men, even when we have not experienced it or tried it out. Other "necessary truths"—truths which do not depend on observation for either their discovery or their verification—are: five plus five equals ten; the three interior angles of a triangle are equal to two right angles.

In its more extreme form, rationalism may make the claim that men are capable of arriving at irrefutable knowledge independently of sense experience. From this point of view, the rationalist claims to be able to provide us with genuine knowledge, truths (laws) about the world and not merely laws of thought. Furthermore, the thoroughgoing rationalist is likely to interpret these laws, discovered by thought, as basic principles of nature in general.

The question as to whether or not there is any a priori knowledge, or knowledge that does not spring from experience, is exceedingly controversial. The examples most frequently used are the formal disciplines of logic and mathematics, where the principles used appear to have a high degree of certainty and universality. Logic and mathematics are products, not of the senses, but of reason; yet they give us reliable knowledge. For example, consider the statements: "If equals are added to equals, the sums are equal." "A thing cannot both exist and not exist at the same time." We can see by *thinking* about them that these principles and relations must be true, although we have not tested them out in all possible situations. Concrete experience does not increase or diminish our assurance of them. To think clearly, men are obliged to accept the validity of certain laws of thought. These would include: the Principle of Identity, "If p is true, then p is true" (All A is A);

the Principle of Noncontradiction, "Not both p is true and p is false" (Not both A and not A); and the Principle of Excluded Middle, "p is either true or false" (Either A or not A).[8] The mind, it is said, has certain ready-made principles or certain innate ways of operating. The empiricist (the person who emphasizes sense perception or experience) will regard these principles as the laws of thinking—directives without which meaningful discourse cannot occur—and not genuine knowledge.

We admit that we do possess some knowledge not directly derived from sense experience. We must be careful, however, not to extend the claims for the power of reason too far, as some of the more extreme rationalists do. One criticism of the rationalist's position is that it is probable that some sense experience is necessary to draw out or to make clear these general principles. We need, it is pointed out, to deal with particular things before we get a sense of numbers, and to experience lines, angles, and triangles before we can build geometrical systems. This criticism, however, misses the point because it confuses psychological and temporal priority with the real question, which is logical priority. The issue, for example, is not whether we have sense experience before we can know certain mathematical truth, but whether the justification of such truth consists in an appeal to sense experience. The rationalist will insist that the question is one of logical priority and what is required for verification. Another criticism is that it appears to be clear that such a priori knowledge as we have in fields like logic and mathematics is purely formal or abstract, and that it does not inform us of what actually exists in the world. Such knowledge deals not with the existing external world, but with our world of relations and meanings. All this knowledge is of the "if . . . then . . . ." variety. To say that "five plus five equals ten" is not to say that any particular thing exists; it is to say that if you have five items (of anything) and five other items, then you have ten items. So far as the external world is concerned, we learn about its rich variety by means of the senses and not by means of any a priori knowledge.

The danger of the extreme forms of rationalism is that men may substitute their deductive reasoning for empirical observation. In so doing they may come to accept some system that has logical consistency but little relevance to the world in which we live. The medieval schoolmen, as well as Descartes, Spinoza, Kant, and other thinkers past and present, have set forth systems of thought that have a high degree of logical consistency. Quite obviously they cannot all be true. The medieval schoolmen, assuming that perfect motions were circular and that planetary motions were perfect, reasoned that planetary motions must be circular motions; yet this conclusion is false, as observation has proved.

---

[8] John Hospers, *An Introduction to Philosophical Analysis* (Englewood Cliffs: Prentice-Hall, 1953), p. 123.

INSIGHT AS A SOURCE: THE APPEAL TO INTUITION

How do we know, as we occasionally seem to know when we meet some-one for the first time, that here is a person who can be trusted? Some people do feel that they know such things. Similarly some people fall in love almost at first sight. Do we have some sense or intuition that sometimes gives us immediate insight into situations?

A possible source of knowledge is intuition, or the direct apprehension of knowledge that is not the result of conscious reasoning or of immediate sense perception. In the literature dealing with intuition, one comes across such expressions as "immediate feeling of certainty," "imagination touched with conviction," a "total response" to some "total situation," and a "direct insight into truth." We may note the following positions men hold regarding intuition.

1. There is an element of intuition present in all knowledge. George Santayana uses *intuition* to mean our awareness of the immediate data of consciousness. W. E. Hocking speaks of self-knowledge as the "best case for intuition." Knowledge of oneself appears to be present as an element in all knowledge of other objects.[9] When I hear a whistle, in addition to hearing it I am aware of my hearing and aware of myself as the one who does the hearing. Intuition is present in the knowledge of oneself and one's own life, and in the axioms of mathematics. It is present in our understanding of the connection between the propositions that constitute the various steps of an argument. Reasoning itself depends on some connection that we grasp or fail to grasp.[10] An intuitive element is the foundation of our recognition of the beautiful, of the moral standards that men accept, and of religious values.

2. Intuition is merely the result of the accumulation of one's past experience and thinking. Valid intuitions are shortcuts to the knowledge that the senses and reflective thinking would reveal. They are the outcome of subconscious induction or deduction. Those who have had considerable experience in thinking and working in a field are more likely than others to have good intuitions in that area. "The following are among the most frequently accepted uses of the term 'intuition' in contemporary scientific literature: quick perception, imagination, abbreviated reason, and sound judgment."[11] Scientific insight comes to those who have labored persistently over scientific problems; poetic inspirations come to those who are practiced in writing poetry; musical inspirations come to those who know and practice music; philosophical and religious intuitions come to those who devote time and attention to these fields.

3. Intuition is a higher kind of knowledge, different in nature from that

9 *Types of Philosophy* (3rd ed.; New York: Scribner's, 1959), p. 123.
10 Alfred C. Ewing, *Reason and Intuition* (New York: Oxford U. Press, 1942).
11 Mario Bunge, *Intuition and Science* (Englewood Cliffs: Prentice-Hall, 1962), p. 68. (Spectrum Book.)

disclosed by the senses or by the intellect. The outstanding representative of this point of view is Henri Bergson (1859–1941), the French philosopher. For Bergson intuition and intelligence are pointed in opposite directions. Intelligence, or intellect, is the tool science uses to deal with matter. It deals with things and with quantitative relations. It solidifies whatever it touches and is incapable of dealing with the nature of life or with duration. Intuition, which is instinct become self-conscious, can lead us to the very inwardness of life. If intuition can extend itself, it will give us the clue to vital operations. We discover the *élan vital,* the vital impulse of the world, by intuition, which is inward and immediate, rather than by intellect, which is external and which describes the living in static terms. The student should note the metaphorical language in this and the following position, and attempt to explain just what is being asserted here.

4. Intuition, according to the mystics, may enable us to gain a vision of reality, to receive the inspirations of an immanent God, or to experience a unity with God. Followers of all the great religions have declared that their leaders gained a unique insight into religious and moral truths. The teachings of Zoroaster, Gautama Buddha, the Hebrew prophets, Christ, Saint Paul, Saint Augustine, Mohammed, Bernard of Clairvaux, Meister Eckhart, and a host of others bear testimony to the strength of these convictions.

Wherever there is feeling, there is an awareness of some object or situation. Fear, anger, and jealousy arise because of our awareness of some unpleasant situation. Love, sympathy, and laughter involve knowledge. Feeling appears to contain essential elements of truth needed to meet various life situations and bring about our adjustment to them. Animals have a "feeling knowledge" in connection with food-getting, nest-building, and migration which gives a true sense of situations and which sustains the life of the organism. W. E. Hocking, in pointing out such facts, suggests the possibility of this feeling sense becoming in man a "valuable organ of knowledge." The intuitionists believe that a "total response to the total situation" may supplement the particular senses and the efforts of the intellect. The student of this problem will need to watch two series of experiments. The first, by Kuo, Rowan, and others, deals with possible causative factors in the behavior of rats and the migration of birds.[12] The second is the experiments in human extrasensory perception carried on at Duke University[13] and elsewhere, particularly in England.

Intuition may function more adequately in connection with elemental, or basic, life interests as distinct from those judgments that are complex, or composite. William Pepperell Montague says:

[12] See Leland W. Crafts, *et al., Recent Experiments in Psychology* (2nd ed.; New York: McGraw-Hill, 1950), Chs. I, II.

[13] See Joseph B. Rhine, *New Frontiers of the Mind* (New York: Rinehart, 1937); *The Reach of the Mind* (New York: Sloane, 1947); *New World of the Mind* (New York: Sloane, 1953).

We might take as an example of an elemental interest romantic love and the judgment of faith on which it is based. It would surely be a vain and preposterous undertaking to discover one's true sweetheart by accepting the authority of others, by using deductive reasoning and calculation, by cold-blooded empirical analysis of her perceivable qualities, or by considering the extent to which she might be a practical utility. All of these nonmystical methods would doubtless be appropriate in the selection of a business partner, a housekeeper, or even in making a marriage of convenience. But no one either could or would fall in love for any other reason than that the beloved appealed in a direct and unanalyzable manner to his heart or his feelings. In other words, the lover as such is and must always remain a mystic. And even in forming the belief on which one bases his choice of a friend, intuition is almost as indispensable as in choosing a sweetheart. True friendship is certainly not based upon either calculation or utility, but upon the direct appeal to our sympathies and affections. The same might be said of objects of art, the primary enjoyment of which is not based upon considerations that are rationally analyzable.[14]

The weakness or danger of intuition is that it does not seem to be a safe method of obtaining knowledge when used alone. It goes astray very easily and may lead to absurd claims unless it is controlled or checked by reason and the senses. "No intuition or experience is so secure that it can elude rational criticism."[15] It must turn to the percepts of the sense organs and the concepts of reason when it attempts to communicate and explain itself or to defend itself against false interpretations or attacks. Intuition seems to presuppose and to be affected by our previous experience and thought. An intuited "truth," supported by evidence, may be acceptable where intuition alone or reason alone would be insufficient.

Whether we think of intuition as present to some extent in all awareness and knowledge, as the accumulation of our experiences, as immediate insight into the totality of some situation, or as supersensuous revelation, there appears to be an element of intuition in knowledge. Intuition, however, must abandon any claim to certainty or infallibility. Intuition, intellect, and sense experience must be utilized together in our quest for knowledge.

THE OCCIDENT AND THE ORIENT: CONTRASTING ATTITUDES

Men in the West have tended to emphasize the objective world of the senses, and this emphasis has led to modern science and technology, in which the West excels. It is a way of thinking inherited mainly from the Greeks. It has produced a philosophy of nature that supports and branches out into

---

14 From William Pepperell Montague, *The Ways of Knowing*, ed. J. H. Muirhead (London: Allen and Unwin, 1925), p. 226. By permission of The Macmillan Company, publishers.
15 Bunge, *Intuition and Science*, p. 25.

the various sciences. The resulting knowledge is departmentalized, specialized, and detached, and it tends to be empirical and descriptive. When knowledge goes beyond this immediate world of the senses, it becomes theoretical and is expressed in various verbal or mathematical symbols. Knowledge must be such that it may be either stated in empirical descriptive terms or communicated according to the rules of logic and scientific verification.

The Eastern, or Oriental, thinker is more concerned with the inner and personal nature of the self and with a reality "beyond" this present empirical world. For many Eastern philosophers, the world of the senses is ephemeral and illusory. The Eastern philosopher is concerned with the "inner" nature of things and is not content to accept the "outer" view of things. He wants not merely to see but *to be* the "real." He is more likely to stress "knowledge by acquaintance," and he is more ready to accept as trustworthy the experience and testimony of ancestors, history, and intuition. Philosophy is a way of life, an experiment in living. The nature of things is to be discovered not so much by logical inference from the piecemeal facts of this world as by acquaintance through one's personal experience. To gain this acquaintance or insight, the mind must be cleared of the obstacles of selfish desires and disturbing emotions. Discipline and self-control are essential. This discipline is intellectual and moral, as well as emotional and physical.[16]

For Hindu philosophers there are at least three sources of knowledge. Swami Nikhilananda says:

> According to Hindu philosophers a conclusion regarding a spiritual truth depends for its validity on three factors: the scriptures, reason, and personal experience. . . . Neither the Vedas [the ancient sacred literature of the Hindus], however, nor reasoning, nor experience can independently create genuine conviction. By depending solely upon the scriptures one becomes dogmatic. Reason, by itself, cannot give certainty, and often it is found that reasoning conceals the rationalizing of man's desire; he proves what he wants to prove. Personal experience by itself can also be deceptive in that it may project one's own favourite ideas. But when all three factors jointly lead to the same conclusion, one may be reasonably assured of having reached the truth. . . .[17]

Buddhists in their search for truth and enlightenment have relied on reason, experience, and intuition. Gautama rejected the authority of the ancient Vedic (Hindu) scriptures and tradition, as well as all claim to a special revelation of truth. He based his philosophy on reason and the everyday experience of men. He counseled his followers not to accept anything merely

---

16 See Swami Nikhilananda, "Concentration and Meditation as Methods in Indian Philosophy," in *Essays in East-West Philosophy*, Charles A. Moore (ed.) (Honolulu: U. of Hawaii Press, 1951), pp. 89–102; William S. Haas, *The Destiny of the Mind, East and West* (New York: Macmillan, 1956), Ch. XI, "The Yoga Technique," pp. 214–235.

17 *Hinduism: Its Meaning for the Liberation of the Spirit* (New York: Harper, 1958), p. 4.

because it is tradition or has the support of some revered sage, priest, or teacher. They were advised to accept only what agrees with their own experience when it has been subjected to investigation and the test of reason, and when it contributes to the welfare of themselves and others. An immediate or intuitive grasp of reality, however, is valued more than analytical speculation. While one should have regard for the experience and testimony of others, authorities disagree; thus a man needs to base his beliefs on his own experience as interpreted by reason.

THE SOURCES AS COMPLEMENTARY

The various sources of knowledge, in the view of the author, are complementary and not antagonistic in attempts to discover truth. The senses, reason, and intuition, as well as the secondary sources of the testimony of others, are genuine sources of knowledge. Each has value and something to contribute, and each may be superior to the others in certain areas.

A number of men, writing from various points of view, have stressed the complementary nature of these sources of knowledge. In *The Ways of Knowing*, Montague discusses the "federation of the methods." He sees them as complementary methods for the discovery of knowledge: "neither can be substituted for the other; neither can contradict the other." He says that the empiricists "acquire the food of science," while the rationalists "digest and assimilate it."[18]

In discussing empiricism and rationalism, J. A. Leighton says:

> The sound position may be called *rational empiricism* or *empirical rationalism*. In contrast with *a priori* rationalism, it stresses the dependence of all our knowledge on experience. In contrast with sensationalistic empiricism, it insists on the purposive activity of the mind in knowing and holds that the success of this activity implies a vital intercourse between the mind and reality. Such a point of view makes an organic synthesis of the valid claims of both rationalism and empiricism. From this standpoint we explicitly hold that the materials of knowledge come to us in experience, but the materials thus given are organized by the activity of reason into the texture of our science.[19]

In various writings John Dewey has pointed out that a new conception of experience and of the relation between sense perception and reason is needed to conform to the newer developments in biology and psychology.[20] Wherever there is life there is activity or behavior. There is a continuous interaction between the organism and the environment; each tends to mold

[18] *Ways of Knowing*, pp. 126, 130.
[19] *The Field of Philosophy* (rev. and enl. ed.; New York: D. Appleton-Century, 1930), p. 555.
[20] See especially *Reconstruction in Philosophy* (enl. ed.; Boston: Beacon, 1948). (Beacon Paperback, 1957, Ch. IV.)

or to modify the other. The higher the form of life, the greater the control exercised over the environment. An organism with interests explores and interacts constantly with its environment, and knowledge is gained in the process. Knowledge is experience that is organized by the self or mind. This is sometimes called the *genetic approach* to knowledge.

Knowledge thus is not something that comes in neat packages which can be easily traced to separate sources. It is rather the result of growth in which a living organism with interests and drives is in constant contact and interaction with a changing environment. Out of this relationship awareness arises. An organism becomes aware of various specific things, relations, events, and persons; acquaintance, language, meaning, and thinking emerge.

QUESTIONS AND PROJECTS

1. Review Questions

(1) Explain in your own words the central questions or problems of epistemology, or the theory of knowledge.

(2) Describe some of the steps by which we acquire our earliest beliefs and ways of acting, feeling, and thinking, and indicate how these are related to the customs and traditions of our social groups.

(3) What is common sense? Indicate its main characteristics, its advantages, and its disadvantages or dangers.

(4) Set forth the main "obstacles to clear thinking" as described by Francis Bacon and more recent thinkers. Why is it often very difficult to rid ourselves and others of these obstacles?

(5) Describe *authoritarianism*, indicating (a) why some people easily welcome authority, (b) when the appeal to authority is justified and when not, and (c) the main weaknesses or dangers of authoritarianism in the advance of knowledge.

(6) Discuss *empiricism*, indicating the forms it may take, its strong points, and the dangers of radical empiricism.

(7) Are all people who think *rationalists?* State the position known as rationalism, and indicate the forms it may take. In what fields does reason appear to be predominant? What is meant by a priori knowledge and by the "laws of thought"?

(8) Explain the different ways in which the term *intuition* is used and defined. Are there areas in which you think intuition may be a valid source of knowledge? Indicate the values and dangers of using intuition as a source of knowledge.

(9) Discuss briefly the differences between the Orient and the Occident regarding views as to the sources of knowledge.

(10) Give your reaction to the claim that "the sources of knowledge are complementary" and that we need a "federation of the methods." Is the "genetic approach" to knowledge as set forth by John Dewey a way of overcoming the older conflict between empiricism and rationalism?

2. The twentieth century exhibits a conflict, inherited in part from the eighteenth and nineteenth centuries, between rationality and irrationality. Our age has been called "the retreat from reason." In your judgment what people, groups, institutions, and social philosophies ("isms" or ideologies) are lined up on the two sides? What part do the authoritarian attitude, emotion, tradition, intuition, the appeal to empirical evidence, reason, and the like play in this problem?

3. How far or to what extent can we accept authority: (1) in the physical sciences; (2) for the facts of history, including causal explanations; (3) as a source of moral standards; (4) in politics, social philosophy, and religion?

4. Are some of the natural sciences more empirical and some more rational? Some students of the sciences speak of sciences like botany as more simply descriptive and less highly developed than sciences like physics, which involve a high degree of mathematical insight, logical analysis, and the formulation of abstract principles.

5. Are there any inborn or innate ideas? Until the late seventeenth century many men thought there were. In his *Essay Concerning Human Understanding* John Locke made such a strong case against innate ideas that few men since then have been able to accept the notion. What are Locke's arguments? His essay or any good history of philosophy will enable you to restate his position.

6. We sometimes hear it said that "on the whole, women are more intuitive and men more rational" in their general reactions. Can you find any evidence to support such a statement?

7. In *The Crisis of Our Age* (New York: Dutton, 1957), P. A. Sorokin says that we live in a sensate culture—that is, one that stresses empirical knowledge and sensory enjoyment. Such a culture is materialistic, hedonistic, and utilitarian. Sorokin thinks that our extreme empiricism is one important cause of the crisis in which modern society finds itself. Read especially his chapter on "The Crisis in the System of Truth," and report on whether you agree or disagree with him.

8. Some conservative religious people use the term *rational* in a derogatory sense and imply that reason is a danger in the realm of religion. What explains this fear of reason? Is reason an obstacle to religious belief, or may it be used in defense of religion?

9. Should faith and revelation be included as possible sources of knowledge? Faith may be a prerequisite for discovery and achievement in all areas of action, including science. Revelation and discovery may be different aspects of one dynamic process. (In a later chapter we consider questions of religious knowledge.)

SUGGESTED READINGS

BOAS, GEORGE. *The Limits of Reason.* New York: Harper, 1961.
   While stressing the importance of reason, the author maintains that life is more than reason, and that traditions, emotions, and myths are also necessary.

BUNGE, MARIO. *Intuition and Science.* Englewood Cliffs: Prentice-Hall, 1962.
A critical evaluation of intuitions and intuitionism in the fields of "philosophy, mathematics, and factual science."

CASSIRER, ERNST. *The Problem of Knowledge: Philosophy, Science, and History since Hegel.* Trans. by William H. Woglom and Charles W. Hendel. New Haven: Yale U. Press, 1950. (Preface by Charles W. Hendel.)
The final volume in a series that deals with the relation of knowledge to the sciences and philosophy in recent times.

DESCARTES, RENÉ. *Selections.* Ed. by Ralph M. Eaton. New York: Scribner's, 1927. (Modern Student's Library.)
See the Introduction by Ralph M. Eaton, pp. v–xl; selections from Descartes' On Method, pp. 1–37; and selections from "The Rules for the Direction of the Mind," pp. 38–83.

EWING, ALFRED C. *Reason and Intuition.* New York: Oxford U. Press, 1942.
A clear presentation of the view that reason and intuition are closely related and that both are necessary.

JOAD, C. E. M. *Guide to Philosophy.* New York: Random House, 1936. (Dover, paperback, 1956.)
See Chapter IV, "Rationalism and Empiricism," pp. 107–125. Questions concerning a priori knowledge, sense experience, and intuition also are discussed. Readable.

LOCKE, JOHN. *An Essay Concerning Human Understanding.* Abridged and ed. by Raymond Wilburn. New York: Dutton, 1947. (Everyman's Library.)
A classic essay in the field of knowledge that attempts to show, through an examination of the facts of experience, how our ideas originate. Locke disposes of innate ideas and attempts to show that all ideas originate in experience.

LONERGAN, BERNARD J. F. *Insight: A Study of Human Understanding.* New York: Longmans, Green, 1958.
A Jesuit scholar examines the act of organizing knowledge to see if the insights of mathematicians, scientists, and men of common sense can be brought within a single perspective.

MASLOW, PAUL. *Intuition Versus Intellect.* Valley Stream: Life Science, 1957.
A discussion of the two aspects of man's life and approaches to the world: the one, man's genetic memory and intuitive impulses; the other, his increasing intelligence and knowledge.

MONTAGUE, WILLIAM PEPPERELL. *The Ways of Knowing.* New York: Macmillan, 1925.
A comprehensive and critical examination of the theories and problems of knowing. For a discussion of the sources of knowledge, see Part I, which considers six ways of attaining knowledge.

PASCH, ALAN. *Experience and the Analytic: A Reconsideration of Empiricism.* Chicago: U. of Chicago Press, 1958.
A critical study of the various interpretations of experience and a suggestion as to the direction empiricism must take if knowledge is to be both rational and empirical.

RUSSELL, BERTRAND. *Human Knowledge: Its Scope and Limits.* New York: Simon and Schuster, 1948.

The author presents his theory of knowledge in an attempt to show the relation between individual experience and the general body of scientific knowledge. Fairly difficult.

TAYLOR, STANLEY. *Conceptions of Institutions and the Theory of Knowledge.* New York: Bookman, 1956.
A study in the sociology of knowledge, dealing with individualism, sociological positivism, and historical relativism. Knowledge is viewed as a product of group life in an institutional and cultural context.

THE NATURE OF
KNOWLEDGE

Is there a real, objective world outside the mind, or is the world, in part at least, a mental construct? The problem of appearance versus reality, or of subjectivism versus objectivism, is the second question we are to consider in epistemology. This issue of the nature of knowledge is fundamental, since the answer we give will have a bearing on many other questions we are to discuss.

THE COMMON-SENSE VIEW

The common-sense view of the world, held quite generally by "the man in the street," is known as *naïve realism*. According to this view, the distinctions between thoughts and things (physical objects), past and present, present and absent, knower and object known, are comparatively fixed and are common to all spectators. People see stars, rocks, trees, houses, tables, and other things. These things exist in their own right quite independently of our perceiving or thinking about them. We may become aware of them; when we do so, we perceive them just as they are in and of themselves. Consciousness, like a flashlight or a searchlight, lights up or illuminates the events and objects of our experience. Our senses are thought of as something like windows, which enable us to perceive the world and to know it as it is. Things seem to be nonmental, or neutral, and common to all observers who examine or come to know them. Furthermore, the things, processes, and relations that we experience are continuous—they go on all the time, whether or not we happen to experience them.

As part of this common-sense view of the world, some people distinguish between substances and their qualities. The external world consists of substances like rocks, wood, and water. These possess qualities. For example, a thing may be hard, smooth, brittle, and black or soft, rough, pliable, and red. The person with some knowledge of chemistry and physics speaks of solids, chemical compounds, molecules, atoms, electrons, and protons. He probably thinks of these things as being external to, and independent of, all observers. He also thinks that he knows the difference between the real and the imaginary, and knows what is genuine knowledge as distinct from mere opinion.

DIFFICULTIES WITH THE COMMON-SENSE VIEW

When philosophers and others reflect on the nature of knowledge and on the world which we are attempting to understand, they find that it is much more complicated and baffling than most people realize. They attempt neither to confuse the public nor to belittle our popular assumptions, but to understand the world more adequately. Let us look at some of the problems that arise in sense perception, using some of the simpler examples that occur frequently in the literature on the subject.

The Sense of Sight   As we look at objects, they appear to have some color. Where or what is color? If I put on blue-colored glasses, the world looks blue. If I put on red glasses, the world looks red. If we get an overdose of santonin or put it in our eyes, everything looks yellow. Color appears to be either wholly or in part affected by the condition of our visual organs. In the cases mentioned, nothing has been done to the "outer" world. A man with "normal" vision may see an object and call it red, while a color-blind person sees it as grayish. But if two people with supposedly normal eyes look at the same object and call it red, have we any assurance that they both see the same shade of red? Even if they do see exactly the same thing, does that mean anything more than that they both have the same type and quality of visual apparatus?

If our eyes were constructed more like microscopes, would we live in the world that we now inhabit? On the other hand, if they were gauged more like telescopes, we would live in a still different world, would we not? Some animals, we are told, can see by ultraviolet light, which gives man no color sensation. Light from some of the stars I saw last evening took thousands of years to come to the earth. What I see is not the star but a little bit of light. It is possible that the star disappeared years ago.

There is a coin on my desk. People say it is circular, but from most points of view it looks elliptical. There are only two points from which it appears circular: that directly over it and that directly under it. Many observers could have many different "coin-like" sense data. Apparently the sense data and the coin (whatever it is) are not identical.

When I say that I "see" a book on my desk, what I see ordinarily is a part of the cover or jacket and one end or one side of the book. The book is in part perceived, but it is in part a mental construct. This is characteristic of most of the objects we are said to experience. When I apply pressure to my eyeball at precisely the right place, I see double; for example, I can see two pencils on my desk, not just one. If all of us had grown up with a bone pressing at that point, would we all see two things where we now see just one?

The Sense of Sound In hearing we are presented with problems similar to those in vision. If I am standing by the railway tracks and a whistling locomotive rushes past me, the pitch of the whistle changes very definitely as the engine approaches me, is opposite me, and recedes. The engineer or the fireman will insist that the pitch was the same throughout. Here are two different sense data apparently from one object.

At a track meet the starting pistol must sound before any of the runners leave the starting line. If you are at the far end of some tracks, you can see the runners start before you hear the pistol report—that is, the order of your sense data reverses what other observers insist are the "facts" of the situation. As we shall see in the case of dreams and hallucinations, we may have a vivid impression of voices or other sounds when there are no corresponding external factors.

The Sense of Touch As the philosopher George Berkeley pointed out years ago, water may feel warm to one hand and cool to the other if, when we plunge both hands into the same water, one of our hands is cool and the other is warm.

If I stand near the fire, I experience the sensation of heat. In common practice we speak of the heat as a quality of the fire. But is it? As I move nearer the fire or into it, I experience the sensation of pain from the greater degree of heat. Yet the pain is my pain and not in the fire. Is the heat, also, a sensation of mine rather than a property of the fire? Raise the temperature of our bodies only a few degrees and the world will feel and look different. C. E. M. Joad, who points out some of these facts,[1] suggests that there is no particular reason that the sensations possessed by a "Nordic" adult with a body temperature of 98.4° should be privileged to be considered "real."

If parts of our nervous system are appropriately stimulated, we can get various sensations of touch. There is much testimony that a man may lose a limb and still experience a sense of touch, or of twitching, or of pain in the missing limb, as if it were still there.

The Senses of Smell and Taste The sense organs of smell and of taste are especially fickle, as many people can testify. They are sometimes influenced by what we have just been eating or smelling, and a head cold may greatly diminish their range and consistency. Here again our experiences seem to be affected by the nature and the condition of the sense organs, as well as by what may be "out there."

Memory, Dreams, and Hallucinations We can remember past objects,

[1] *Guide to Philosophy* (New York: Random House, 1936), p. 30.

people, and events. Sometimes our memory is very clear and vivid. We can imagine all sorts of things with equal vividness. In dreams and hallucinations we seem to see, hear, touch, smell, and taste that which has no present position in the spatiotemporal order, as we and others may judge the situation at a later time. There is a dualism here that leads men to ask whether or not in ordinary perceptions we may be creating our sense data wholly or in part. What is appearance, and what is reality? What do we mean by the "real" world?

SENSATIONS AND SENSE DATA

Before proceeding further let us distinguish between two terms which we shall have occasion to use, that is, between a *sensation* and a *sense datum*. A *sensation* is a state of consciousness, an awareness, or a mental event. While it may be associated with one or more of the senses it may be a thought, memory, or emotion of some sort. A *sense datum,* on the other hand, is something of which we are immediately aware and directly experience, such as a color, sound, or the like. It is occasionally said that "we *sense* sense data," whereas "we *have* sensations." It is conceivable that two or more of us might sense the same sense-datum. A sensation is private, personal, and peculiarly our own.

SUBJECTIVISM

Subjectivism, or what is more technically called *epistemological idealism,* is the view that objects and the qualities which we perceive through our senses do not exist independently of a consciousness of them. Reality consists of consciousness and its states, though not necessarily *my* consciousness and *my* states of mind.

The reader is urged to ask himself the following questions and to take time to reflect on their meaning and possible answers. (If you are not willing to take each step yourself, can you see how another person might with some justification take the step?) Montague sets forth seven stages of subjectivism.[2] The stages are partly historical and partly logical in their development. Our questions follow these stages in a general way.

Where are the things in dreams located—in the world outside us or in our subjective or inner personal experiences? Just what is the nature of dreams? Some of these experiences seem clear and genuine. They may be so vivid that we can relate the details a long time afterward. They may stir us to a high pitch of emotional excitement. They may be pleasant or terrifying. Primitive man was so impressed by these experiences that he thought his self had wandered off and had these experiences. In addition to dreams, we all

2 *The Ways of Knowing* (New York: Macmillan, 1925), pp. 265–290.

have illusions at times and perhaps occasionally hallucinations. Drugs or fever may induce hallucinations. In illusions we mistake the identity of some person or object and give what we call a false interpretation; the hallucination is something we have created, in the sense that it has no external basis or counterpart. We put the objects of these experiences in the mind or within ourselves and not in the outer world. That is, we call them subjective. If you are willing to accept the subjectivity of such experiences as dreams, hallucinations, illusions, you have taken the first step toward subjectivism.

What is the nature of my images or sense data? The image in the dream, we say, was subjective or uniquely mine. As we have seen earlier in the chapter, we can have many images of one object, such as a mountain. Evidently there is a distinction between what is "out there" and my sense data. These sense data seem to vary from time to time and to be peculiarly mine. If two things can vary independently, they are not identical. As between the various sense data of the mountain and what we call the real mountain, what is mere appearance and what is "out there" in the "real" world? If you accept the subjectivity of these images, and sense data in general, then you have taken step number two.

What is the nature of qualities such as color, sound, taste, smell, and tactual qualities? Here we are talking not just about the images we get of them, but of the qualities themselves, which are called "secondary qualities." John Locke (1632–1704), who believed in the reality of material substance, spiritual or thinking substance, and ideas, separated the qualities of material substance into two rather distinct groups. There were the primary qualities, such as form, extension, solidity, motion, number, and so on, which belong to the external world. Then there were the secondary qualities, such as color, sound, taste, odor, and so on, which do not belong to bodies in the external world. Colors and sounds are merely the effect of light and sound waves of certain lengths on human sensory organs. Philosophers like Locke, and various modern scientists as well, have attributed only quantitative relations to the outer world, and have attributed the nonquantitative qualities to conscious states. These secondary qualities vary from person to person, and may vary within the experience of one person as he views his world under different circumstances. These qualities are said to be in the mind, in states of consciousness, or to be subjective. The way we experience secondary qualities depends on the nature of our sensory equipment. Can you accept the subjectivity of these secondary qualities? If so, you have taken step number three.

If you can accept or at least understand the subjectivity of secondary qualities, are you now ready to take another step and accept the subjectivity of the primary qualities, which include extension, figure, motion, mass, size, and shape? Experience indicates that the primary qualities, like the secondary qualities, seem to vary or change and to be affected by the condition of the sensory organs. Historically this position is most ably defended by the philosopher George Berkeley (1685–1753). His famous expression is, "To be is to be perceived." Berkeley accepted Locke's arguments for the subjectivity of the secondary qualities, and then went on to show that the same arguments can be applied to the primary qualities. If all the qualities, both secondary *and* primary, are mental constructs, the concept of material substance as the place where primary qualities reside is no longer needed. There are only spiritual substances and ideas, or conscious beings and their sensations and ideas. If both the primary and the secondary qualities are in the mind, what is left to the object itself? All that the term *matter* can mean is a certain group of qualities, impressions, or ideas. Berkeley called his position *immaterialism*.

If this fourth step is taken, we have arrived at the stage of subjectivism proper, or the belief that there is no reality outside of experience. When we take this step, we pass from epistemological dualism to epistemological monism, since there is now a single realm consisting of conscious beings and their ideas. How, then, does one account for the distinctions that men have made between primary and secondary qualities? The primary qualities seem to be fixed and measurable. That is why they have been called physical qualities or states, to distinguish them from the qualities productive of variable and unmeasurable, purely private experiences, which we call mental or psychical.

Berkeley says that these common or measurable experiences, the primary qualities of our world, are caused by something beyond ourselves, and are different from the secondary qualities, which arise out of our own mental activity. The agency is still, however, a conscious being or a conscious will infinitely wise and more powerful than we are. The order of nature arises, according to Berkeley, from the ideas in the mind of God. While we shall return to this issue in the chapter on idealism, the reader should study Berkeley's *Principles of Human Knowledge* to get the full force of his arguments and the clever way in which he attempts to refute objections.

Are you able to go a step further, a fifth step, and interpret space and time and the order and laws of nature as forms of the mind? Man cannot think except in spatial and temporal terms. Does this mean that these are mind-dependent, functions of a universal mind, or essentially subjective? The work of Berkeley did not reach to the laws or relations that unite the various experiences of men, but Immanuel Kant (1724–1804) gave attention to this problem. The mind, he said, imposes its own forms of organization or synthesis upon the unorganized sensations it receives from an unknown source. The mind functions through the three faculties of sensibility, understanding, and reason. The first set of forms consists of space and time. The second set is called the "categories," the higher classes or divisions within which things are organized. These include such forms of relationship as quality, quantity, cause, effect, unity, and plurality. The third set is the "ideas." When, as scientists, we marvel over the mathematical relations and harmonies of the world, we are merely projecting onto the outer world the relations and the harmonies of our own minds.

Kant's arguments are difficult and complicated and cannot be presented here in detail. A brief statement regarding his arguments for the subjectivity of space and time is in order. A person can imagine the nonexistence of any particular object in space and time—say the building we occupy—but he cannot imagine the nonexistence of space and time themselves. Try to think of a limit to space. What is beyond your limit? Is there "a time when time was not"? That time and space adhere or stick to the mind is a proof of their subjectivity. They exist, therefore, in Kant's view, logically and existentially, prior to the bodies that occupy them. Space and time exist *within* consciousness. Our thinking about the properties of space and time appears to possess a certainty and a necessity that are not present when we think about the various objects of our world. This can be explained most adequately by the assumption that they are forms of the mind itself. If space and time were objective, we would have to think of them as either finite or infinite; yet we are unable to do so. If we think of them as finite, we can easily pass in thought beyond their limit. To think of them as infinite seems, according to Kant, to imply their completion. To call infinite a completed or actually existent series would be self-contradictory; it would imply the completion of that which, according to his definition, was incomplete.

The argument from selective relativity, as Montague points out, can be used here as well as in the earlier stages of the development of our position of subjectivity. The object in time and space and the various time and space relationships that we experience are determined, in this point of view, primarily by the nature and condition of the conscious self, and only secondarily by whatever (unknown and unknowable) may exist beyond the experiences of conscious selves.

The five steps we have listed will seem to some to take us to the limit of subjectivity. Two additional steps, however, are possible. A sixth step has been taken by a few philosophers. Are you able to conceive of one single cosmic self or absolute mind that is the ground of all existence and of all the forms and relations of human experience? The deeper selves in each of us are said to constitute or to be aspects of one universal self, just as one drop of water is part of the totality of water and partakes of its nature. If we take this sixth step, the many selves in each of us become parts of one all-inclusive self. At this point we have a monism, one reality. This position has been accepted by some post-Kantian philosophers in the West and by some Oriental thinkers. The outstanding representative in the Occident is Hegel (1770–1831), whom we consider briefly in the chapter on idealism.

Have you ever wondered whether you alone exist and the world were your idea? A final possible stage in the line of thought we have been developing is *solipsism*. Solipsism is the view that the individual self alone exists, or the view of "the subjectivity of the absolute subject." This position has not been held by any school of philosophers nor by any outstanding thinker. The term *solipsism* comes from the Latin *solus,* meaning "alone," and *ipse,* meaning "self." It is the *reductio ad absurdum* of subjectivism.

The problem before us in this section on subjectivism is what Ralph Barton Perry called the *egocentric predicament.* No matter what we do or how hard we try, we cannot get outside or beyond our own experience. All our knowledge of objects is of the subject-object variety. What the object would be apart from this relationship, there is no way of knowing. When you think of any object, you must think of it as having various sensorially perceived qualities. The object is red or smooth or sour. We have already seen that mental factors and the condition of the sense organs enter into the perception of objects. Possibly there are no independent objects; the world may be a mental construct. To say that you can think of objects and can experience them as existing independently does not alter the situation, since you are still dealing with your perceptions or sense data.

OBJECTIVISM

Objectivists, or *epistemological realists,* reject the view of Berkeley that to exist is to be a mind or an idea in some mind. They insist that there is an independent reality apart from minds. In the early part of the chapter we considered naïve realism, which maintains that we perceive the physical object itself. In the chapter on realism we shall find that the new realists hold a position rather close to this. During the eighteenth century the "copy theory" or "representative realism" of John Locke was widely accepted. For him, primary qualities were in the outer world, and the secondary qualities were in the mind. The mind knows the copies or images of the external things. The critical realists of the twentieth century would claim that what we perceive are sense data, not objects. Realism, its types, and its general philosophical implications are considered in a later chapter. Here we are interested in understanding the epistemological claims of objectivism.

Before considering the case for objectivism, let us ask: *Where* are the sense data (*sensa*)? Where are these elements of our experience that we think are immediately in consciousness? This is one of the most baffling issues in philosophy. Let us state some possibilities, without elaborating the answers.

First, the qualities that produce sensa may be out in the physical world, where they seem to be. If they are in the outer world, then they may exist independently of their being sensed, or they may be created in the outer world by the knower at the time of perception. These views seem difficult to hold in the light of the facts presented earlier in the chapter, but a few realists have held the belief that sense-qualities exist independently of perception, or in the physical objects about us. Second, the sensa may exist within the person who is the knower or perceiver. In that case they may be the result of stimulation of the nervous system, or they may be explained as mental events that imply a dualism of mind and matter. Third, what produces sensa may not be located anywhere in particular. We cannot locate them exclusively in the outer world or within the person. Excitations or signals in the form of a wave pattern produce, it is said, a pattern of "brain events," which correspond to the events from which the excitations come. The sensa then would be imaginative projections that arise as a result of organic events stimulated by, say, light waves.

Let us turn next to some of the simpler arguments in the case for objectivism. Some of these arguments are negative in that they attempt to show the weakness of the subjectivist's position; others are positive.

1. Objectivists accuse the subjective idealists of the fallacy of *non sequitur,* or of drawing a false conclusion from a true proposition.

> The true proposition is, "It is impossible to discover anything that is not known," since it becomes known by the mere process of being discovered. From this proposition it follows that it is impossible to discover with certainty what characteristics things possess when they are not known. The idealist then proceeds falsely to conclude, "Things have no characteristics when they are not known; therefore, the characteristic of being known is that which constitutes their existence: therefore, things only exist when they are known."[3]

The only valid conclusion is that "all known things are known," and this is merely a tautology. The fact that we cannot tell for certain what characteristics things possess when they are not known does not mean that all things are known or that being known is a prerequisite to existence. The fact that we cannot know a thing unless it has been experienced does not mean that there cannot be unexperienced things.

2. The subjectivists are accused of a misuse of the word *idea* when they use it both for "the concept held by the knower" and for "the object known." This double use of the word really "begs the question" and assumes without proof that there is no real difference between the mind and that toward which the mind's experience is directed. Bertrand Russell says:

[3] Joad, *Guide to Philosophy*, pp. 65–66.

There is a confusion engendered by the use of the word "idea." We think of an idea as essentially something *in* somebody's mind, and thus when we are told that a tree consists entirely of ideas, it is natural to suppose that, if so, the tree must be entirely in minds. But the notion of being "in" the mind is ambiguous. We speak of bearing a person in mind, not meaning that the person is in our minds, but that a thought of him is in our minds. When a man says that some business he had to arrange went clean out of his mind, he does not mean to imply that the business itself was ever in his mind, but only that a thought of the business was formerly in his mind, but afterwards ceased to be in his mind. And so when Berkeley says that the tree must be in our minds if we can know it, all that he really has a right to say is that a thought of the tree must be in our minds. To argue that the tree itself must be in our minds is like arguing that a person whom we bear in mind is himself in our minds.[4]

The object of an act of thought should be clearly distinguished from the act of thought itself.

3. Belief in the existence of a world quite independent of our experience and knowledge of it conforms to the assumptions of everyday life and is implied in all our special sciences. Such an assumption, while it cannot be proved with finality, explains the events and the peculiarities of our lives better than any alternative approach. In all our conscious acts we are aware of something outside of or beyond ourselves. We are not only aware, but at times we are aware that we are aware. A common characteristic both of our sense perceptions and of our moments of reflection is that we are aware of something other than ourselves. This something, most men believe, is unaffected by our consciousness of it.

The fact that the evidence from the different sense organs converges and builds up a unified picture of our world furnishes us with additional evidence. Elements of time and space fit into the series of events and appear to be genuine aspects of a world outside us. Astronomers, geologists, historians, and others report the details of a long process of development, which seems to be explained most adequately as an environing nature that we are gradually learning to describe.

Within our human experience there appears to be a clear distinction between those experiences that we ourselves create, such as our imaginings, thoughts, and dreams, and the sense perceptions that are forced upon us by an external world. If objectivism is to some degree true, this distinction is easily understood. If it is false, then the distinction is rather baffling. Our sense perceptions are ordinarily vivid, steady, and consistent, whereas these other images are less distinct, unsteady, and often confused. This leads us to the next point.

4 *The Problems of Philosophy* (London: Oxford U. Press, 1912), pp. 62–63. (*Home University Library*, No. 35.)

4. Causal interactions are going on both within and beyond the realm of our experiences. Our perceptions or experiences must also have a cause. Events that break into our field of consciousness are often quite unrelated to our previous train of thought. Furthermore, these events seem to obey laws which are quite independent of our minds, so that we are unable to get rid of them even by great effort.

A fire is burning briskly in our fireplace. We leave it, then return an hour or two later to find that it has burned low. These and other events lead man to believe that causal sequences continue to operate in the same way whether or not they are being perceived by anyone. Both Berkeley and Kant recognized this problem and attempted to meet it. Berkeley said that God was the cause of the order of the external world. Kant posited a thing-in-itself that was unknown and unknowable. The realist would say that to accept the world of our experience at its face value is to hold the most reasonable position.

A NOTE ON INTERMEDIATE POSITIONS

Between subjectivism and objectivism, according to some writers, are positions known as *phenomenalism* and *epistemological dualism*. The position of the phenomenalist, of which Kant is a representative, is that we can only know phenomena; we cannot know ultimate reality. The external world, *as we perceive it,* is not necessarily the same as or even similar to the external world that stimulates our sense organs. In attempting to answer the question, "What can we know?" Kant divided the world into three parts: an inner world of subjective states (images, sensations, and the like), which is not the realm of knowledge; the world of ultimate reality (noumenon, or thing-in-itself), which is unknown and unknowable by sense perception; and the world of nature or of experience, the phenomenal realm, which is the realm of human knowledge. The mind is active and forms into a system of knowledge all the materials brought in by the senses. Whether you call this position "phenomenalistic realism" or "Kantian idealism" or just "phenomenalism" will depend upon what aspects of this approach you choose to emphasize.

Epistemological dualism recognizes two separate areas that are involved in the knowledge process. There are, first, the sense data, or those elements that are immediately present in our consciousness. There is, second, the external order of nature that is inferred from the sense data. Epistemological dualism may take many different forms, since both of these areas may be physical or mental, or one may be mental and the other physical. It has been called the "copy theory" and the "representative theory." My image of the mountain is not the mountain itself but a copy or a representative of it. In the position called critical realism we have one example of this point of view.

CONCLUSIONS

The answer to the problem of the nature of knowledge will depend, at least in part, on the type of philosophy (as considered later) a person is inclined to accept. In a problem that is so complex, it is especially easy to take some part of the knowledge situation and attempt to make that part appear to be the whole. Both the more extreme forms of subjectivism and the more extreme forms of objectivism are equally guilty of this error. Undoubtedly there are important subjective elements in our knowledge. We experience things from a particular frame of reference and by a particular set of sense organs, which might be quite different from what they are. Our perceptions are relative to the self. When I see a tree or a man, there is a specific neural or organic process that is the condition of that experience. As the conditions of our organism vary, the objects of our experience change. The world of things is in some sense relative to the conscious self that experiences those things. On the other hand, there is a "given" from outside us. That there are objects which have an existence quite independent of our experiences appears to be certain. It seems to be the most tenable assumption that enables us not only to explain and to reconcile the numerous experiences we have but also to relate these experiences to those of our fellow men.

While we cannot prove for certain the existence of an external world, it appears that such facts as the sequence of events in our world, the discovery of objects which are unexpected and which "break in" upon our consciousness, and the assumptions of everyday living and of scientific progress are explained more adequately by the hypothesis of the existence of an external world than by any of the more extreme forms of subjectivism. Later, the discussion of the various types of philosophy will indicate additional approaches to this problem.

QUESTIONS AND PROJECTS

1. Review Questions

(1) Explain what is meant by the problem of the nature of knowledge. Why is it one of the more difficult problems in philosophy?

(2) State in your own words the common-sense view of the nature of knowledge? Why is it called the "common-sense" view?

(3) What difficulties arise when the common-sense view of the nature of knowledge is subjected to careful examination? Illustrate the difficulties in the areas of the senses of sight, sound, and touch.

(4) In this chapter you may have found some terms with which you were not familiar. Be ready to explain the meaning and philosophical significance of such terms

and phrases as: *subjectivism,* or *epistemological idealism; objectivism,* or *epistemological realism; phenomenalism; epistemological dualism;* and *egocentric predicament.*
The Glossary, as well as the discussion in this chapter, may help clarify the meanings.

(5) In the section on subjectivism you were asked a series of questions which moved further and further toward complete subjectivism. How many of these steps were you able to take, and why did you stop at some stage? Be prepared to write a short essay on "The Problem of Subjectivism."

(6) What special problems do we face in explaining space and time?

(7) What is the case for objectivism? Do the facts that this position is closer than subjectivism to the common-sense view and is implied in the various sciences carry much weight with you?

(8) State as clearly as you can your own position regarding the nature of knowledge. Evaluate the concluding statements of the chapter.

2. Think about the ways in which our sense data and images may vary apart from actual changes in the objects of our experience. See if you can supply examples other than those given in the chapter. Do objects appear to be independent of our perception of them?

3. Some animals can "see in the dark"; others are color-blind. Is it true that "every animal species inhabits a homemade universe" and that this world of sense perception is only a small part of the world as a whole? If we possessed other or different types of sense organs or if the range and power of our senses were keener or duller than they are now would the world vary accordingly?

4. Do our training or education and our past experiences affect our perception? Is it true that we see largely what we are trained to see or expect to see? Consider the following experiment: By the use of a stereopticon, different pictures are shown to the right eye and left eye of the same person simultaneously. When people from the United States and Mexico are shown, by this means, a baseball player and a bullfighter, the former tend to see the baseball player and the latter the bullfighter.[5] Can you give some other examples in which training and experience tend to influence perception?

5. Are you able to accept the assertion that "What a man is determines what he can know"? Certain basic elements in our experience appear to be incommunicable. We find it impossible to describe light and color to a person who has always been totally blind. Some people do not experience what others do in the presence of music and the beauties of nature. An experience may be private and subjective in that we cannot communicate it to those who have not yet experienced it, though it may not be private in the sense that in principle it is open to all.

6. Even though a person may accept objectivism and a realistic approach to epistemology, does it appear that there are some subjective elements in all our knowledge? For example, Ralph Barton Perry has spoken about the egocentric predicament, and John Dewey has said that he was never able to get beyond or outside of his own experience. Note also that there are many differing interpretations of history and many psychologies and philosophies set forth by very able thinkers. Discuss.

5 Hadley Cantril, "Perception and Interpersonal Relations," *American Journal of Psychiatry,* 114 (August, 1957): 119–126.

7. Discuss the statement: "I know that physical objects exist and are real because I see and feel them."

8. The problem of appearance versus reality, or subjectivism versus objectivism, is an old issue in philosophy. If we never penetrate beyond sense data so that we can compare sense data with what is beyond sense data, how can we make such distinctions? Think about this question and indicate some of the conclusions to which you are led.

SUGGESTED READINGS

BLANSHARD, BRAND. *The Nature of Thought.* 2 vols.; New York: Macmillan, 1940.
An outstanding idealist carefully examines human thought and knowledge. The first volume is concerned with sense perception and ideas, the second volume with creative thinking and the nature and tests of truth.

FARBER, MARVIN. *Naturalism and Subjectivism.* Springfield: Charles C Thomas, 1959.
The author discusses the place and the limits of subjectivism and the conflict between naturalism and subjectivism.

FRIEDRICK, L. W. (ed.). *The Nature of Physical Knowledge.* Bloomington: Indiana U. Press, 1960.
A study based on a symposium at Marquette University in which the contributors consider whether there is only one or more than one form of knowledge.

HARRIS, ERROL E. *Nature, Mind, and Modern Science.* New York: Macmillan, 1954.
A historical discussion of the problem of knowledge that attempts to gain perspective on contemporary views. The author, an idealist, is especially critical of logical empiricism and of any philosophy that would reject the immanence of mind in nature.

HILL, THOMAS ENGLISH. *Contemporary Theories of Knowledge.* New York: Ronald, 1961.
A presentation of idealist, realist, mediating, pragmatist, and analytic theories of knowledge as set forth by major representatives of the various views.

JOAD, C. E. M. *Guide to Philosophy.* New York: Random House, 1936. (Dover, paperback, 1956.)
See Chapters 1–3, pp. 23–106 for a statement of the problem of knowledge and the answers of subjective idealism and of realism.

LEWIS, CLARENCE IRVING. *An Analysis of Knowledge and Valuation.* LaSalle: Open Court, 1946.
This comprehensive work relates the problem of knowledge to the realm of values. The author contends that judgments of value are empirical judgments and are true or false, depending upon the evidence.

MARTIN, WILLIAM OLIVER. *The Order and Integration of Knowledge.* Ann Arbor: U. of Michigan Press, 1957.

A careful examination of the different types and fields of knowledge. The author, a realist, insists that being and knowing are related, but not identical.

MONTAGUE, WILLIAM PEPPERELL. *The Ways of Knowing*. New York: Macmillan, 1925.

A comprehensive examination of the problems of knowledge. For the problem of the nature of knowledge, see Part III, where there are chapters dealing with objectivism, epistemological dualism, subjectivism, and so on.

O'NEILL, REGINALD F. *Theories of Knowledge*. Englewood Cliffs: Prentice-Hall, 1960.

A realist theory of knowledge is presented in Part One, followed by an evaluation of other theories.

POLANYI, MICHAEL. *Personal Knowledge: Towards a Post-Critical Philosophy*. Chicago: U. of Chicago Press, 1958.

The author says that in every act of knowing, including that involving scientific knowledge, there is a personal element and the fusion of the personal and the objective. For a simple presentation of the author's point of view, see The Study of Man.

SINCLAIR, WILLIAM ANGUS. *The Conditions of Knowing*. New York: Harcourt, Brace, 1951.

The author sets forth a theory of knowledge that emphasizes the attitudes of individuals. In Part III questions of appearance and reality are discussed.

Selections from the following classics will be found in the Philosophy Series of the Modern Student's Library (New York: Scribner's): Plato's *Theaetetus;* Descartes' *On the Nature of the Human Mind;* Locke's *An Essay on the Human Understanding;* Berkeley's *Principles of Human Knowledge* and *Three Dialogues Between Hylas and Philonus;* Hume's *An Inquiry Concerning Human Understanding.*

FOUR

THE VALIDITY OF
KNOWLEDGE

Many beliefs once thought to be true have later been discovered to be false. What makes some beliefs true and others false? Can we ever be sure that we have discovered the truth? Is the human mind capable of discovering or finding any genuine knowledge? When or under what conditions may we have reasonable assurance that we are dealing with facts rather than mere opinions? Centuries ago, when Jesus stood trial before him, Pilate asked, "What is truth?" Before this, Socrates, Plato, and other Greek philosophers had thought about the question. Men are still seeking the answer.

Throughout time, opinions and beliefs have changed—not only the common everyday beliefs but also the beliefs of science and philosophy. Scientific theories that were once accepted as true have been replaced by other theories. Are these beliefs more than guesses or opinions based on the "climate of opinion" of the day? Things by themselves are neither true nor false; they just are or are not. Our judgment about things and our propositions are true or false. Truth has to do with the assertions or the claims that we make about things. Among the philosophers of the past and of the present there has been and is a great diversity of belief.

THREE TESTS OF TRUTH

In attempting to determine what beliefs are true, philosophers have relied, in the main, on three tests of truth. Men believed many things and acted on the basis of those beliefs before it occurred to them to ask: Why are some beliefs true and others false? Today few informed people would accept custom or tradition as a sufficient justification for declaring something to be true. While customs and traditions often are valuable, they may also lead one astray. They sometimes contain conflicts, and they do not provide for change and progress. The appeal to "universal agreement" is equally insecure, since some beliefs that have been widespread and firmly believed over long periods (for example, that the earth was flat) have later been found to be false. Other thinkers, in the past, have appealed to instinct. The instinct theory, however, has been under attack, and many things formerly explained as "instincts" are now explained more adequately as the results of "conditioning." Still other people have appealed to the strong feeling that a thing is true; yet feelings may be determined by our moods, health, or training.

We shall find that there is no complete agreement regarding the tests of truth. Each answer will call forth some severe criticisms from people with opposing points of view. The reader will do well to ask: Is only one of these tests sound, or does each test contribute some insight? Do the tests need to be combined in some way? The three theories of the test of truth that we shall consider are the correspondence theory, the coherence or consistency theory, and the pragmatic theory.

THE CORRESPONDENCE THEORY: THE TEST OF AGREEMENT WITH "FACT"

The test of truth called the correspondence theory is the one most widely accepted by the realists. According to this theory, truth is "fidelity to objective reality." Truth is the agreement between the statement of fact and the actual fact, or between the judgment and the situation the judgment claims to describe. Truth has to do with the assertions or the claims that we make about things.

If I state that the United States is bounded on the north by Canada, my statement is true, according to this approach, not because it happens to agree with other statements previously made or because it happens to work, but because it corresponds to the actual geographical situation. This, it is said, is what the word *truth* means in everyday usage. It is also the characteristic view of the scientific man, who checks his ideas with his data or findings and is glad to submit his conclusions to similar objective tests by others.

According to the correspondence theory, the presence or absence of belief has no direct bearing on the issue of truth or falsity, since truth and falsity depend on the conditions that have been affirmed or denied. If a judgment corresponds with the facts, it is true; if not, it is false. If I say, "There is an automobile parked in our driveway," my statement can be verified by empirical investigation.

The critics of the correspondence theory, however, do not think that the question of the verification of statements can be as clear and self-evident as the supporters of the correspondence theory affirm. The first critical question is usually this: "How can we compare our ideas with reality?" We know only our own experiences. How can we get outside our experiences so that we can compare our ideas with reality as it actually is? The correspondence theory, they say, assumes that we know not only our judgments but also the actual circumstances apart from our experiences.

The theory of correspondence seems to assume that our sense data are clear and accurate, that they disclose the nature of the world just as it is. Idealists and pragmatists seriously question this assumption, and point out that in perception the mind tends to enter into and modify our views of the world. If our powers of perception were diminished or increased or if we possessed fewer or more sense organs, the world might appear quite different. Since we cannot know an object or an event apart from our sense data, it is foolish to talk about whether or not our judgments correspond with the thing as it is in itself.

Finally, we have knowledge of meanings (definitions), relations, and values, as in mathematics, logic, and ethics. Some of the ideas that we want to verify have no objects outside the area of human thought with which we can make comparisons and check for correspondence. In these areas, at least, the correspondence theory of truth does not seem to apply. Yet the knowledge in these fields possesses a high degree of certainty. Supporters of the correspondence theory would reply to this latter criticism by pointing out that in mathematics and logic no truth claims *about the world* are made and therefore they do not have to be verified except for consistency, since they are of the "if . . . then" variety of statements.

THE COHERENCE THEORY: THE TEST OF CONSISTENCY

The coherence, or consistency, theory is the test of truth quite generally accepted by idealists, although its acceptance is not confined to that school of thought. Since we cannot directly compare our ideas and judgments with the world as it is, the coherence theory places its trust in the consistency or harmony of all our judgments. A judgment is true if it is consistent with other judgments that are accepted as true. True judgments are those logically coherent with other relevant judgments.

Under ordinary circumstances, we often judge a statement to be true or false on the ground that it is or is not in harmony with what we have already decided is true. On this basis we reject many ideas as absurd and denounce some experiences as illusions or false perceptions. They do not "fit in" with what has happened in the past or with what, from our past experience, we may reasonably expect to happen. This does not mean, however, that we reject new ideas or new truths without careful examination. Occasionally new facts or ideas will force themselves upon us and impress us so strongly with their truth that we need to revise many of our previous conceptions, if not a whole system of thought. The Copernican world view and the biological theory of evolution are examples of new ideas that led to outstanding changes. We accepted them because they gave us a larger degree of coherence and consistency—they explained some things previously unexplained.

The simplest form of the coherence theory demands an inner or formal consistency in the particular system under consideration, quite apart from any interpretation of the universe as a whole. For example, in mathematics, assuming certain definitions and axioms, men can build up the system of geometry implied by the definitions and axioms consistent with them. This system is then accepted as true. The principle of consistency or logical implication underlies our systems of mathematics and formal logic and, to a considerable extent, any science or organized body of knowledge. Conformity to certain formal laws of thought—like the law of noncontradiction, which it seems altogether impossible to deny—is the very basis of such systems of truth, according to this approach.

The idealists tend to enlarge the principle of coherence, or consistency, to include an "all-inclusive and self-consistent whole of reality." Plato, as well as modern philosophers like Hegel, Bradley, and Royce, enlarged the principle of coherence to include the universe, so that every true judgment and every partial truth system is continuous with the whole of reality and derives its meaning from that whole. "This leads us to the idealistic principle of consistency according to which truth is a reciprocally consistent *system of propositions, each of which gets its truth from the whole system.*" The idealists add: "it is the consistency of our human beliefs with that whole which makes them true when they are true. Thus purely formal consistency is abandoned and coherence with reality is made the essence of truth. It is this aspect which justifies calling this a metaphysical form of the coherence theory."[1]

Adherents of the coherence theory claim that any adequate theory of truth, besides satisfying other requirements, must be able to explain "the relativity of truth," or how a belief can be held to be true at one time and false at a later time. The coherence theory meets this requirement. Insofar as every judgment is merely partial when separated from the whole, it is to some extent one-sided and possesses only a degree of truth. From this viewpoint, truth grows, and it would never be complete or final until it encompassed all of reality.

While inconsistency and incoherence are disturbing and lead men to seek unity, the critics of the coherence theory point out that we can construct false as well as true coherent systems. The theory, they say, does not distinguish between consistent truth and consistent error. To say that "a judgment is true if it is consistent with other judgments that are accepted as true" could lead to a dangerous circularity in which we have a number of false statements each one of which claims to be true because it is consistent with the others. The critics point to numerous past systems which, though logically consistent, were apparently quite false. Correspondence to fact is a

[1] Daniel S. Robinson, *An Introduction to Living Philosophy* (New York: Thomas Y. Crowell, 1932), pp. 104–105.

condition even the most self-consistent system must meet. If, however, our view of coherence embraces *inclusiveness, simplicity,* and systematic *orderliness* as well as consistency, these criticisms have less point.

Critics of the coherence theory say also that it is rationalistic and intellectualistic and deals mainly with the logical relations among propositions. Because of this, it fails to furnish an adequate test for the judgments of everyday experience. If the test of coherence is used, then it needs to be stated more with reference to factual consistency, that is, the agreement between a judgment and a definite environmental situation. This, of course, is really a correspondence, and not a coherence test. Other critics of these tests of truth suggest a different approach—the test of utility.

THE PRAGMATIC THEORY: THE TEST OF UTILITY

Pragmatism as a philosophy is considered in a later chapter. Here we give merely a brief statement of the pragmatic conception of truth and of the tests of truth.

Truth cannot be correspondence with reality, since we know only our experiences. On the other hand, the coherence theory is formal and rationalistic. Pragmatism claims that we can know nothing about "substances," "essences," and "ultimate realities." It opposes all authoritarianism, intellectualism, and rationalism. The pragmatists are thoroughgoing empiricists in their interpretation of the flux of experience. For the pragmatists the test of truth is utility, workability, or satisfactory consequences. There is no such thing as static or absolute truth. Truth is redefined to mean something that happens to a judgment or an idea. Truth is made in the process of human adjustment. According to William James, *"True ideas are those that we can assimilate, validate, corroborate, and verify. False ideas are those that we can not."*[2] John Dewey says:

> That which guides us truly is true—demonstrated capacity for such guidance is precisely what is meant by truth. . . . When the claim or pretension or plan is acted upon, it guides us truly or falsely; it leads us to our end or away from it. Its active, dynamic function is the all-important thing about it, and in the quality of activity induced by it lies all its truth and falsity. The hypothesis that works is the true one; and *truth* is an abstract noun applied to the collection of cases, actual, foreseen and desired, that receive confirmation in their works and consequences.[3]

This redefinition of the nature of truth leads naturally to a repudiation of

[2] "Pragmatism's Conception of Truth," in *Essays in Pragmatism,* Alburey Castell (ed.) (New York: Hafner, 1955), p. 160.
[3] *Reconstruction in Philosophy* (New York: Holt, 1920), pp. 156–157. (Enl. ed., Beacon, 1948. Beacon Paperback, 1957.)

the older tests of truth and to the defense of new ones. An idea or a theory or a hypothesis is true if it works out in practice, if it leads to satisfactory results. The phrase "satisfactory results" may be highly ambiguous. The supporters of this test of truth, however, have tended to stress one or more of three approaches, as follows: (1) That is true which satisfies the desire or purposes of men. True beliefs must satisfy not just some whims but our whole natures, and satisfy them over a period of time. An important question here is whether a belief that satisfies us thereby demonstrates its truth or merely its comfort-value. (2) That is true which can be demonstrated experimentally. This test, it is claimed, is in harmony with the spirit and practice of modern science. Whether in the laboratory or in daily life, when a question of truth and falsity arises we should "try it and see." (3) That is true which aids in the biological struggle for existence. The instrumentalism of John Dewey, discussed in a later chapter, stresses the biological function of ideas and doctrines.

The test of workability, or utility, has keen critics as well as able supporters. Critics have called it a "dangerous doctrine," since it seems to justify many satisfying beliefs that ought not to be held unless they conform to the facts. Many beliefs that comfort and fortify people are plainly untrue. In our everyday life we had better not believe that the price of common stock we hold is going up because it gives us comfort to think so when in reality it is not, or that some business venture in which we are interested is going to prosper just because it is an inspiring belief. We are more likely to use this test, the critics say, in the areas where we can more safely live in happy illusion and where we are not likely to be checked by more stringent tests.

To define truth in this way and to accept satisfactory consequences as a test of truth is to imply, at least, that there can be one truth for you and another for me. Such relativism tends to blind our judgment and make us less able to judge evidence impartially and objectively. We ought to learn to view things as they are and to control our hopes, wishes, cravings, and prejudices.

Innumerable theories—in religion, economic life, science, and other fields—have "worked" for considerable lengths of time. Untrue ideas often lead to what many people call "satisfactory results." On the other hand, some judgments cannot be pragmatically verified. While beliefs that are true tend to work in the long run, it is not necessarily the case that beliefs which work are therefore true.

EVALUATION OF THE TESTS OF TRUTH

Before we attempt to evaluate the three main "tests of truth" that have survived the philosophical discussions of recent centuries, let us question the underlying assumption that there *is* such a thing as truth and that we can hope to discover it. How can we meet the skeptic when he claims that there is no such thing as valid knowledge or expresses an attitude of uncertainty and doubt?

Skepticism is an expression of doubt or disbelief, which in its stricter meaning is a denial of the possibility of knowledge, and in its broader meaning is an attitude of suspending judgment until critical analysis is complete or all available evidence is at hand. Skepticism arose in ancient Greece, and it is connected with certain Sophists like Gorgias (c. 483–376 B.C.), and with Pyrrho (c. 360–270 B.C.) in the later Graeco-Roman period. In more recent times David Hume (1711–1776) is one of the best-known skeptics.

Skepticism, in its narrow sense, is the position that knowledge is impossible and that the quest for truth is in vain. Gorgias asserted that nothing exists; and that if it did, we couldn't know it; and that even if a man did come to know anything, he could not impart this knowledge to his fellows. Anatole France said that "it is plain that we can know nothing, that all things combine to deceive us, and that nature is only making a cruel sport of our ignorance and helplessness. . . ."[4]

A thoroughgoing skepticism would lead to an attitude so noncommittal as to make any intelligent and consistent action almost impossible; as such, it is not a satisfactory ideal for personal life or society. Very few outstanding thinkers have denied the possibility of knowledge. Skepticism is self-refuting, since the denial of all knowledge is a claim that refutes itself. If nothing can be known, then how does the skeptic know that his position is a valid one? If he affirms his own position as the truth, he is attempting to distinguish between the true and the false. He must have some idea of what the truth is to appeal to the principles of valid reasoning in arguing against the possibility of truth.

In its broader meaning skepticism may be merely the attitude of questioning any assumption or conclusion until it can be subjected to rigorous examination. The skeptics in this sense tend to stress the possibilities for error inherent in the various ways of attempting to gain knowledge. They point out that all knowledge is human, that our human faculties are frail and limited, and that the senses and reason seem to be equally unreliable. They remind us that even the so-called experts in all areas have greatly diverse opinions.

A certain amount of skepticism has tended to precede and stimulate philosophical reflection. It is a reminder of the need for caution and the dangers of dogmatism. It says to us: "Don't be too sure." "Don't be dogmatic." "You may be wrong." "Be tolerant and open-minded." This type of skepticism, represented by the questioning attitude of Socrates, has much in its favor, since it helps free men from superstition, prejudice, and error and clears the way for intellectual progress.

---

[4] *The Garden of Epicurus*, trans. Alfred Allinson (2nd ed.; London: John Lane, Bodley Head, 1920), p. 72.

A position closely related to skepticism and sometimes confused with it in meaning is *agnosticism,* which comes from the Greek term for "unknown" or "without knowledge." The term is associated with the names of Thomas Huxley and Herbert Spencer in the nineteenth century. The agnostic's position is a profession of ignorance rather than a positive denial of any valid knowledge. Agnosticism implies man's ignorance of the real nature of such "ultimates" as matter, mind, and God.

Let us turn now to the more positive side of our evaluation of the tests of truth. Each of the separate tests of truth appears to have value under certain circumstances.[5] The test of correspondence is widely used in everyday experience, as well as in the various sciences. There are many occasions on which we seem to be able to check our "ideas" with the "facts," and to receive confirmation after other investigators have checked our results. Frequently, however, in complicated areas of human experience and thought, the correspondence theory does not seem to apply. In such cases we may have to appeal to coherence, or consistency. At still other times we may properly defend the theory behind a concept like democracy by showing that it has actually worked well and has produced satisfactory results in human experience.

Because the theories supplement rather than directly contradict each other, they can be combined in a definition of truth: Truth is the faithful adherence of our judgments and ideas to the facts of experience or to the world as it is; but since we cannot always compare our judgments with the actual situations, we test them by their consistency with other judgments that we believe are valid and true, or we test them by their usefulness and practical consequences.

SPHERES OF INTELLECTUAL DISCOURSE

There are different levels of existence as we pass from the inorganic, the realm of nonliving things, to the organic, the realm of plants and animals, to the realm of human beings, with self-consciousness and a wide range of new powers. (These human characteristics are to be considered in later chapters.) These levels of existence may require different means to be understood. The ways of knowing may be many, and may depend in part on the level of existence being considered.

At least four levels or spheres of intellectual discourse have been identified and defended. The question of whether there are only one or two or more conceptions of rationality is controversial—a few philosophers and scientists wish us to confine our attention to one or two of these levels. Most of the

---

5 For a discussion of these tests of truth by a philosopher who believes that we cannot do with only one criterion of truth, see A. C. Ewing, *The Fundamental Questions of Philosophy* (New York: Macmillan, 1952), Ch. 3.

influential thinkers of the past and the present, however, have recognized four spheres of intellectual discourse that move toward understanding and the attainment of truth.

First, there is formal logic. This type of thinking was first given systematic expression by Aristotle in ancient Greece, but it has undergone refinement and elaboration by logicians, especially during the last century. In pure logic and pure mathematics, as distinct from the applied branches of these disciplines, it finds its clearest expression. This form of rationality is concerned with internal coherence and universal validity. If A is greater than B and B is greater than C, then A is greater than C. Two plus two equals four. These statements are true regardless of what the letters A, B, and C represent or to what the words *two* and *four* apply.

These laws of thought are of crucial importance, since they determine clear thinking in all realms of human experience. Yet logic as a formal discipline has nothing to do with the world of experience in which we live and act. It places emphasis on concepts and universals rather than on the world of individuals and existence. "Logic . . . has nothing to do with history. In the world of logic nothing happens; things do not come into being and pass away; nothing grows; there is no hope, no disappointment, no courage, no cowardice, no love, no hate."[6] The principles of logic, however, need to be known and applied to all human thinking.

Second, there is the level of empirical inquiry, or factual rationality. Here men add the perceptual or the sensory to formal logic, and we enter the area of the various sciences. Our knowledge of the particular events that take place in space and time requires the union of logic and the changing world of experience and existence. Science is the elaboration, refinement, and checking of our perceptual knowledge. It brings in instruments and experimentation to aid the search for truth. It is thus more reliable than our untested, everyday or common-sense opinions, even though its conclusions give us only a greater or lesser degree of probability, rather than absolute certainty.

The issue of probability versus certainty, or of fallibilism versus non-fallibilism, has given rise to much philosophical controversy. There are some people who will question the statement that empirical inquiry can give us only probable knowledge. They will claim that some empirical statements that assert only one thing, such as, this swan is white, or this is my finger, can be accepted as certain when we come to the point where no further tests or checks seem possible and there is no real point in further doubt. In these situations, they say, we can say not merely that I *feel* certain but that it *is* certain. The fallibilist will reply, however, that no empirical proposition is

6 George Boas, *The Limits of Reason* (New York: Harper, 1961), p. 42.

ever really certain since there are an infinite number of sense-data for any object and all the evidence is never in or at hand.[7]

Some people will claim that the factual knowledge given by the objective methods of the sciences is the only real knowledge obtainable. The doctrine that stops at this point and rules out all of man's normative, religious, and philosophical experiences and insights of a more general nature as providing no further knowledge of the human venture is sometimes called "scientism." It is a philosophy that scientists, as well as others, may or may not accept; it is not science, nor is it a requirement of science. To limit knowledge so drastically in the interest of an objective method would appear to ignore wide ranges of human experience. The following chapters give consideration to this problem and to the nature of science in general.

The third level of rationality is the normative, or evaluative. Here we judge things to be better or worse, right or wrong, good or evil, beautiful or ugly, holy or profane, and the like. As we enter this realm of investigation we do not leave either logical or factual rationality behind. We do, however, become more inclusive in our outlook. To ignore this area of experience would do violence to man's distinctively human traits and reduce him to the level of mere animality. Many of man's beliefs and actions would be meaningless if he took the position that value judgments have no objective validity and that no such judgment is any better or worse than any other.

The fact that there are differences of opinion and that certain questions cannot be definitely decided does not imply that any judgment is as good as any other. Furthermore, a value judgment is not invalidated because some or even many men neither accept nor follow it. Every society professes some standards of conduct and judges some things desirable or undesirable, admirable, or contemptible. Indignation about and resentment toward injury and injustice are almost universally present in human affairs. So long as men have common needs and face common problems, their choices and judgments will agree insofar as they recognize certain facts and think clearly and consistently. Man's critical faculties need to be brought to bear on his value judgments, whether these are concerned with moral standards, aesthetic insights, or religious experiences.

In contending that these value experiences may bring us genuine knowledge, Theodore M. Greene, says:

> It means, first, the recognition that man is capable of having experiences of a distinctive character which we are justified in labeling "moral" and "aesthetic."
> It means, second, the acceptance of these experiences as at least possible confron-

[7] For a brief discussion of these opposing views, see John Hospers, *An Introduction to Philosophical Analysis* (Englewood Cliffs: Prentice-Hall; 1953), pp. 160–164, 421–425.

tations or encounters with something which we call "goodness" and "beauty"—qualities which have a recognizable character of their own. The beauty and goodness thus encountered are, like other ultimates in human experience, ineffable. . . . The good and the beautiful are encounterable, explorable, knowable, communicable, but not translatable.

Third, what we encounter in our moral and aesthetic experiences, if we take them seriously, is found to be, in its own way, as coercive and orderly as are the distinctive characteristics of the perceptual world of nature. The more we find and explore goodness and beauty, the more convinced we become that they have a distinctive character of their own which we must accept, and which therefore "obligates" us to respond to them in an appropriate manner. They obligate us, however, not by enforcing our response (like a causal law, which we cannot evade or break), but by putting us under a distinctive type of moral or aesthetic obligation which we can ignore or repudiate if we choose to do so, though only by doing violence to our own moral and aesthetic nature.[8]

Fourth, there is the level of synoptic or comprehensive rationality. This is the most inclusive level of thinking, since it utilizes and moves beyond the knowledge of the previous levels. It is found where men seek integration and achieve some comprehensive vision of things. This stage of rationality is reached as men set forth life views and world views and critically evaluate the evidence and arguments for the stand they have accepted. Alfred North Whitehead says that such speculative philosophy is "the endeavor to frame a coherent, logical, necessary system of general ideas in terms of which every element of our experience can be interpreted."[9] George P. Adams speaks of "man's sense of the claims made upon his life and thought by that which transcends the phenomenal and empirical order of nature's events." He calls this man's "metaphysical sense."[10] Philosophy thus seeks to "envisage the nature of things in the widest possible perspective." In this area, too, are found those religious convictions that go beyond the merely traditional and authoritarian.

In the search for what is real and for some over-all unity and consistency, the thoughts of men, whether philosophical or religious, have tended to group themselves into one of a few systems of thought. We can, with Stephen C. Pepper, call such general views "world hypotheses." Out of his experience and thinking, a man hypothesizes that the world is of a certain nature. He makes selections and decisions as if this were the case. When he finds that continued reflection and living, on the basis of these presuppositions and commitments, furnish him additional evidence, he thinks he has

[8] *Moral, Aesthetic, and Religious Insight* (New Brunswick: Rutgers U. Press, 1957), pp. 125–126.
[9] *Adventures of Ideas* (New York: New American Library of World Literature, 1953), p. 285. (Mentor ed.)
[10] *Man and Metaphysics* (New York: Columbia U. Press, 1948), p. V.

good reasons for its continued acceptance. That these beliefs *may* be partially or even wholly mistaken must be admitted. But this is true of all our beliefs about the world. In any case, we cannot expect the degree of agreement that is found in the sciences, which investigate the strictly objective aspects of reality. We need to subject our philosophical and religious views to the recognized tests of truth. They should be open to criticism, to remolding, and to replacement by more adequate views whenever the evidence warrants such revision.

> If rationality is defined most narrowly, in purely logical terms, even factual judgments must be condemned as irrational. If only factual rationality is added, moral and aesthetic judgments must be declared irrational. If rationality is defined to exclude all religious faith, no such faith, however enlightened, can satisfy such a criterion. But why *need* rationality be narrowly defined? Why condemn a priori whole areas and dimensions of human experience which are of such crucial significance for man? Is it not far more reasonable to assume that Reality is endlessly complex, that man can encounter different facets of Reality in different types of experiences, and that all these experiences, if they are orderly, coercive, and sharable in their respective ways, should be presumed, *in principle,* to be capable of providing him with precious and unique clues to this or that aspect of the Real?[11]

In addition to the distinction among the four types or stages of discourse, we need to make a distinction between two different kinds of knowledge. If the distinction is valid, then possibly the way we come to know some facts may differ from the way we come to know others. There is, first, *knowledge by description,* or knowledge *about* a thing. This is the matter-of-fact knowledge, which we gain of the objects and events around us and which has its most accurate expression in the natural sciences. There is, second, *knowledge by acquaintance,* which is intimate appreciation, such as friends have of one another. For example, there is a difference between a scientific description of love, whether from a chemical or a psychological point of view, and the actual experience of being in love. Similarly, there is a difference between the description of a symphony and the deep emotional and aesthetic responses a performance of the symphony evokes.

While people can acquire much accurate knowledge from scientific descriptions of living organisms, there is a quality about life that can be known only by acquaintance. What a man knows of the "inner nature" of life depends primarily on the "depth and the range of his own personal experience," his "imaginative sympathy" with the experiences of others, and the "extent to which he has reflected on the material so presented."[12] Further-

---

[11] Greene, *Moral, Aesthetic, and Religious Insight,* pp. 140–141.
[12] Burnett H. Streeter, *Reality* (New York: Macmillan, 1926), p. 36.

more, some of the basic elements in human experience appear to be difficult if not impossible to communicate. Another person cannot be given the knowledge; he must experience it himself. Even such simple sensations as light and color cannot be clearly and vividly described to one who has known nothing but darkness.

The testimony of various Oriental students of the problem of knowledge lends weight to the view that we need to recognize more than one way of knowing and more than one test of truth. For example, in speaking about Indian culture, with its metaphysical leanings, rationalistic spirit, and mysticism, Radhakrishnan says:

> Creative life is possible only for those who are capable of concentration and integrity, who have the courage to be lonely in their minds. It is in moments of solitariness that we glimpse visions of truth and beauty, bring them down to earth, clothe them with emotions, carve them into words, cast them into movements or frame them into philosophies. If our minds are to become vehicles of spirit, solitude and meditation are essential. All growth is from within outwards. Spirit is freedom. True wealth is in being, not in having. A free mind is not a herd mind.

> Early in India's history a definite direction has been given to man's mind. To be, to hold the soul in its serenity is the end of man. There is in us the principle of subjectivity which is free from the pressure of external influences. Ordinarily we are automata; our words and deeds, our moods and emotions, our thoughts and ideas are produced by external forces. But man must learn to act from a different basis. He must become a different being. He must not be satisfied with what he is. He must be born again or renewed in his consciousness. He whose life is cumbered with distractions and luxuries is not necessarily on a higher level than he who pursues the inward way, grows from within, develops new qualities and powers that he does not now possess. Man cannot be satisfied with earthly possessions, not even with knowledge which instructs, informs, and even entertains. He has another destiny, the realisation of the spirit in him.[13]

Knowledge, then, according to this point of view, is of two quite different kinds. The first kind deals with the phenomenal world. The knowledge sensorially derived or reasoned from the data of sense perception is limited and does not disclose the real nature of things. This includes the scientific knowledge so highly prized in the West. The other type of knowledge, which brings understanding, requires rigorous detachment, self-control, and concentration. This knowledge, which leads to direct and immediate insight, is achieved by the whole personality. Through the former kind of knowledge a person overcomes physical limitations, such as disease and poverty. Through the latter type of knowledge a person is said, especially by

13 S. Radhakrishnan, *East and West* (New York: Harper, 1956), p. 21.

many Eastern thinkers, to attain insight, enlightenment, and perhaps immortality.

If there are various levels of existence as we pass from the inorganic, to the organic, to the realm of self-consciousness, then these levels may require different means to be understood. The ways of knowledge may be many rather than one.

CONCLUSIONS

1. Knowledge is acquired through continuous growth and constant quest. Man's experience is never complete, and his knowledge grows with his experience. Growth is one of the fundamental facts of existence. Man needs to strive constantly to be informed, to cultivate mental flexibility, and to face the realities of the world in which he lives.

2. No one can claim rightly to have final knowledge of the world. We must avoid both irresponsibility and fanaticism. The way of knowledge is neither a dogmatism that takes present knowledge as certain and final, nor a skepticism that believes that knowledge is impossible. All mental processes are subject to human limitations, to the interplay of personal interest and desire, and to the social, economic, and religious outlook of the time. These factors enter into seemingly objective scientific discussions, as well as into philosophical and religious doctrines.

3. Truth is not a man-made principle or convention, to be taken up or cast aside at will. Our knowledge discloses a world that is to some extent strongly present and objective. Our vision may at times be warped and distorted, but ours is not a phantom world. There is a "given" of some sort to which we must adjust ourselves.

Our growing body of knowledge has been built up by the efforts of countless thousands of persons throughout the ages. It is ours by inheritance, we must add to it and pass it on to others. As new facts and insights are discovered, this knowledge is remolded or restated in more satisfactory or more illuminating terms.

4. We accept a philosophical theory as tentatively verified or true if it has been formed after a careful and impartial examination of all the relevant data, including the testimony of history and of present experience, and if it is in harmony with the well-established principles of science and philosophy. Life is a continuous process of forming, testing, and remolding our knowledge of the universe and our basic convictions regarding life. We need to live confidently and courageously by what we know today, but to be ready to change these convictions as new evidence appears.

QUESTIONS AND PROJECTS

1. Review Questions

(1) Elaborate on some of the main questions connected with the problem of the validity of knowledge. Is there any knowledge that is final or infallible?

(2) Define and then evaluate critically: (a) the correspondence theory, (b) the coherence theory, and (c) the pragmatic theory of truth. Indicate the strengths and weaknesses of each of the tests.

(3) Distinguish between skepticism and agnosticism, and indicate the degrees or types of skepticism. What are the dangers of these negative attitudes toward knowledge, and what values can we nevertheless derive from them?

(4) How would you define truth? You need not follow or accept the definition given in this chapter, but be ready to defend your position.

(5) What are the four spheres of intellectual discourse? Since the last two are more likely to be questioned, be ready to discuss them fully. Do the positions of Theodore M. Greene and Sir S. Radhakrishnan appear acceptable or unacceptable? Discuss.

(6) Indicate why you accept or reject the distinction between "knowledge by description" and "knowledge by acquaintance."

(7) State the general conclusions that may be drawn from a study of the validity of knowledge. You may wish to use some of the tentative conclusions given at the end of the chapter, but feel free to depart from them and to formulate your own answer.

(8) When may a philosophical theory reasonably be accepted as tentatively verified or true?

2. How would you answer the student who asked, "How do we know that the intelligent life is really the best?"

3. State as clearly as you can the distinctions among reason, rationalism, and rationalization. Why do people frequently confuse these terms?

4. Why do we need to be tolerant of different views and avoid dogmatism in setting forth our own convictions?

5. Give examples of the problems that may arise when an expert in a particular field tries to speak in another field.

6. Give your reaction to the following statement: "Any truth is many sided, even simple truths. But the complex truth of today needs approach by many different methods and many different types of mind before we can arrive at even an approximation of the truth." (Attributed to Lord Stamp of England, who was killed in an air raid on London during World War II.)

7. In court witnesses are asked to swear "to tell the truth, the whole truth, and nothing but the truth." What assumptions underlie this oath? Are you able to accept these assumptions?

8. Some people have claimed that those who demand evidence for and logical proof of a belief have grave doubts about the truth of that belief or have actually ceased to

believe. Do people look for evidence only when they are uncertain or unable to defend the belief in the face of criticism?

SUGGESTED READINGS

AYER, ALFRED JULES. *The Problem of Knowledge*. New York: St. Martin's, 1956.
Deals with such questions as philosophy and knowledge, skepticism and certainty, perception, memory, and our knowledge of ourselves and others, from the point of view of logical positivism.

BOAS, GEORGE. *The Inquiring Mind*. LaSalle: Open Court, 1959.
A philosopher discusses the techniques of thinking, the basic metaphors, and the principles of explanation that philosophers have used. Difficult for beginners.

BOULDING, KENNETH E. *The Image*. Ann Arbor: U. of Michigan Press, 1956.
An organic theory of knowledge discussed in the light of the images, private and public, that govern our behavior.

BRIGHTMAN, EDGAR SHEFFIELD. *An Introduction to Philosophy*. rev. ed.; New York: Holt, 1951.
See Chapter II, "What Methods Do Philosophers Use?" pp. 25–43; and Chapter III, "How Can We Distinguish Truth from Error?" pp. 44–74. Written by an outstanding personalist.

DEWEY, JOHN. *The Quest for Certainty*. New York: Putnam's, 1929.
A discussion of the relation between thought and action. Truth is obtained, according to the author, by the experimental methods of science.

———. *Reconstruction in Philosophy*. enl. ed.; Boston: Beacon, 1948. (Beacon paperback, 1957.)
The author points out the defects of traditional philosophy and calls for a type of creative thinking that emphasizes satisfactory results in human affairs.

FERRÉ, NELS F. S. *Faith and Reason*. New York: Harper, 1946.
An examination of faith and reason in their relation to science, philosophy, religion, and the quest for truth.

GREENE, THEODORE MEYER. *Moral, Aesthetic, and Religious Insight*. New Brunswick: Rutgers U. Press, 1957.
A small book that presents the author's neo-Kantian approach to knowledge and the various types of rationality.

HIGHET, GILBERT. *Man's Unconquerable Mind*. New York: Columbia U. Press, 1960. (Paperback.)
A small, readable book.

MCKEON, RICHARD. *Thought, Action, and Passion*. Chicago: U. of Chicago Press, 1954.
Four essays, including one on "Truth and the History of Ideas," that deal with such problems as the relation between knowledge and action.

RUSSELL, BERTRAND. *Human Knowledge: Its Scope and Limits.* New York: Simon and Schuster, 1948.
    A book written not primarily for philosophers but for "that much larger public which is interested in philosophical questions." Among the topics treated are science, language, perception, knowledge, and probability. See also Russell's Inquiry into Meaning and Truth *and* Logic and Knowledge.

STARK, WERNER. *The Sociology of Knowledge: An Essay in Aid of a Deeper Understanding of Ideas.* London: Routledge and Kegan Paul, 1958.
    The author posits that the sociology of knowledge can throw light on the origins of truth and help us eliminate error.

VIAND, GASTON. *Intelligence, Its Evolution and Forms.* New York: Harper, 1960.
    A small book that treats intelligence in its evolutionary perspective—animals to beings that think conceptually.

WILSON, JOHN. *Language and the Pursuit of Truth.* New York: Cambridge U. Press, 1956.
    Deals with the meaning of words and statements, their logical classification, and methods of verification. The author holds that the discovery of truth depends on an understanding of language.

❧ FIVE ☙

PHILOSOPHY AND SCIENTIFIC METHODS OF INQUIRY

Some scientists have said that there has been more scientific progress in the last century and a half than in all previous history. Certainly the pace of science has been greatly accelerated, so much so that our age is frequently called the age of science and technology. The development of science is predominantly the work of Western civilization in its modern period. Other civilizations have made important contributions to human progress, of course, but mainly in nonscientific fields. The early Greeks made many advances in philosophy, art, and government. When they turned their attention to science, they showed interest chiefly in pure science or in theory. During this period philosophy and science were practically the same, and little or no distinction was made between them. The ancient Hebrews are known for their insights in religion and morality. The Romans were administrators, lawgivers, and practical builders. Theology was one of the main interests of the medieval period. Since the Renaissance, however, and especially during the last century, the climate of opinion in the West has favored science and its practical applications.

PHILOSOPHY AND THE DEVELOPMENT OF SCIENCE

Science has been called "trained and organized common sense." Its distinctive characteristic is its critical and accurate observation and description of things and events. The term *science* comes from the Latin *scire,* "to know." Today the word *science* is used in a narrower sense to designate a quantitative and objective knowledge of nature. Such knowledge for its own sake, without consideration for any practical application, is often called basic, or pure, science. When scientific knowledge is put to practical use, it is called applied science. The development of science is one of the greatest achievements of the human mind. Without some knowledge of the growth of science, it is difficult to understand modern history.[1]

Early civilization, with primitive agriculture and industrial arts, appears to have originated in or near the valleys of great rivers, such as the Nile, the Euphrates, and the Yellow. The land was fertile and water was available for men and herds. More than two thousand years before the Christian era began, the Babylonians and Egyptians possessed a considerable body of knowledge. They used fixed units of measurement, such as standards of length, weight, and volume, a multiplication table, tables of squares and cubes, and a decimal system based on man's ten fingers. In Egypt the periodic rise of the waters of the Nile, resulting in lost boundary marks, led to a system of land-surveying that stimulated the growth of geometry. Instruments such as set squares, levels, beam balances, and plumb lines, as well as a considerable amount of mathematical knowledge, were needed to build the pyramids. Weaving and spinning were practiced, and wheeled chariots were in use.

For both the Egyptians and the Babylonians, the world was thought to resemble a box, of which the earth was the floor. There was a rudimentary astronomy based on man's observations of the regularities of the "heavenly bodies." The days of the week were named after the sun, the moon, and the five known planets, and the months and the years were determined from the movement of the moon and the apparent movement of the sun. By the sixth century B.C., eclipses could be predicted, and there was a calendar containing 365 days. In India and China, too, progress was being made. Paper and the compass were invented in China. The system of numerals we use today came from India by way of Arabia.

With the Greeks, human consciousness and interest in man and nature expanded rapidly. The Greeks wanted to know for the sake of knowing, and the scientific as well as the philosophical spirit was born. The contribution of the Greeks was so great that many of the scientific and philosophical terms which we use today originated with them. Thales, the first Ionian nature-philosopher, who lived in the Greek colonial city of Miletus in Asia Minor, is reported to have visited Egypt and to have become acquainted with the system of land-surveying in use there. Later he advanced geometry and set forth his views about the watery nature of the world. Other pre-Socratic thinkers were instrumental in advancing man's interest and knowledge in areas that were to become important for the development of science and

[1] See one of the many good histories of science, such as Sir William Cecil Dampier's *History of Science and Its Relations with Philosophy and Religion* (4th ed.; New York: Cambridge U. Press, 1949); and L. W. H. Hull, *History and Philosophy of Science: An Introduction* (New York: Longmans, Green, 1959). See also "Some Recent Books on the History of Science" by I. Bernard Cohen, in *Roots of Scientific Thought,* Selections from *Journal of the History of Ideas,* Philip P. Wiener and Aaron Noland (eds.) (New York: Basic Books, 1957), pp. 627–656.

philosophy. Socrates was interested primarily in morals and the good life and had little interest in questions about the nonhuman world.

Plato (c. 427–347 B.C.) has had a great influence on the development of philosophy. He was concerned with concepts, universals, or Ideas, rather than with material things. Influenced by Pythagoras, he had great reverence for mathematics, but was not interested in the application of mathematics in studying the world. Knowledge for Plato consisted of acquaintance with the supersensory world of Ideas, which alone had reality. The senses did not yield genuine knowledge. Because of this outlook some historians of science say that he retarded the development of empirical science.

Aristotle (384–322 B.C.), in contrast with Plato, was more of a realist interested in this world and in things. He systematized and extended the knowledge of his day. Indeed, until the Renaissance no one was his scientific equal. He studied some five hundred species of animals, and his system of classification profoundly affected thinking in the biological sciences. He made many mistakes, of course. He located intelligence in the heart and considered the brain a cooling system! He rejected the atomic theory of Democritus, and he thought that the earth was a sphere at rest, rejecting Pythagoras' theory of the sun as the center of the universe. Yet, without experimental equipment, he made many remarkable contributions to scientific thought as well as outstanding contributions in the field of philosophy. Perhaps the greatest of his achievements was the ordering of thought itself; it was Aristotle who created formal or syllogistic logic, a logic that remained largely unchanged until the modern age.

Additional fields to which the Greeks made contributions include the atomic theory of matter (Leucippus and Democritus), medicine (Hippocrates), deductive geometry (Euclid), astronomy (Ptolemy and Aristarchus), and mechanics (Archimedes). Through Pythagoras and the philosopher-scientists whom he influenced, some Greeks came to believe that in numbers and mathematics they had found the key to the nature of the universe.

The Romans were a practical people who excelled as administrators and builders. They had little interest in pure science or knowledge for its own sake. Their amphitheaters, aqueducts, forums, and roads reflected their concern with engineering and the practical or useful arts.

For a thousand years, during the Middle Ages, Europe made only slight advances in science. During the earlier part of the Middle Ages, the influence of Plato's philosophy was strong and Aristotle was known mainly for his logic. During the later part, the period of cultural flowering, Aristotle's philosophy was accepted as the great authority. The men of that period looked to deductive reasoning (syllogistic logic) and revelation as their sources of knowledge. They thought they knew the meaning and the purpose of their own lives and of the universe. The main contribution of the scholastic philosophers and theologians to science was their idea of nature as a rational, orderly whole. This concept is basic to modern science.

During the Renaissance Aristotle's authority was replaced by a new method and a new view of the universe. The scientific changes are often spoken of as the Copernican Revolution. An illustrious group of scientists, including Copernicus (1473–1543), Galileo (1564–1642), and Newton (1642–1727), established scientific observation and experimentation on a firm foundation. Copernicus pointed out that the sun is the center of our solar system and that the earth is one of the planets. Galileo accepted the atomic theory and gave mechanics an experimental and mathematical basis. Newton's astronomy and mechanics synthesized the newer developments.

The accompanying philosophical changes are sometimes referred to as the Cartesian Revolution, since René Descartes (1596–1650), a French philosopher, gave philosophical expression to the new mechanical views of the universe. Men's minds were turned from purposes and perfections to a conception of universal law operating in the mechanical world of nature. The newer views suggested to some men a mechanistic or materialistic view of things. The period from the Renaissance to the end of the eighteenth century saw the physical sciences effectively organized, with a firm mathematical basis. During the eighteenth century there were also many practical inventions, the most important of which was the steam engine.

The nineteenth century witnessed the rapid growth of science and industry. John Dalton (1766–1844) and others advanced the atomic theory, which has had a profound effect on physics and chemistry. There was significant growth in the studies of electricity and heat. In the main, however, this was a time of consolidation in the physical sciences. The great work of the nineteenth century was in the application of scientific methods to the study of living organisms. While the idea of evolution had been known to some Greek philosophers, it was not widely accepted before Charles Darwin (1809–1882) published *The Origin of Species* in 1859. The concept of evolution has had widespread influence on modern throught.

The twentieth century has brought unparalleled advances in many fields of science and the breakup of many interpretations that had been taken for granted during the two or three previous centuries. The sciences of the nineteenth century, for example, took matter, space, and time as basic and fixed entities. Matter was thought to be composed of simple and indivisible atoms existing in a definite space and time. Concepts of relativity, the quantum theory, and the electronic theory of matter have profoundly altered the older views. The outstanding names are too numerous to mention, but the list would include J. J. Thomson, Lord Rutherford, Einstein, Bohr, and Planck. Science is now closely tied to the systems of higher mathematics and is much more conscious than formerly of its limitations and the vast areas yet to be explored. Recently scientific inquiry has been directed to psychological and social studies. Some of these modern views of the universe and life are considered in later chapters.

SCIENCE AND SCIENTIFIC METHODS

Since the terms *science* and *scientific method* are both used in a number of different ways, an examination of some of these different usages will help us understand the nature of the processes and the terms involved.

THREE POSSIBLE MEANINGS OF THE TERM *Science*

The word *science* is used, first, to denote the many sciences. These include physics, chemistry, astronomy, geology, biology, and psychology. Mathematics and logic are sometimes referred to as formal or abstract sciences, and disciplines like botany and mineralogy are often called descriptive or empirical sciences. There are, then, a great many sciences, and their fields overlap.

Second, the term *science* may be used for a body of systematic knowledge including the hypotheses, theories, and laws that have been built up by the work of numerous scientists through the years. This knowledge is mainly theoretical, in contrast with the practical skills and the arts. Conant appears to have this use of the term in mind when he defines science as "an interconnected series of concepts and conceptual schemes that have developed as a result of experimentation and observation and are fruitful of further experimentation and observations."[2]

Third, for a considerable number of people the term *science* is used to designate a method of obtaining knowledge that is objective and verifiable. In this sense the term is practically synonymous with *scientific method*.

A VARIETY OF SCIENTIFIC METHODS

There is no universal agreement, even among scientists, as to what is meant by *scientific method*. Science has evolved from common sense, and the transition from one to the other is gradual and continuous. A careful examination of the sciences, such as physics, astronomy, and psychology, fails to reveal any single method in use. Sciences like astronomy proceed by means of observation and mathematical calculations from these observations. Other sciences, like physics and chemistry, emphasize controlled experimentation. In still other sciences trial and error, statistics, and sampling are used. We need, then, to speak about scientific methods rather than *the* scientific method.[3] The method used depends on the nature of the material or on the problem to be studied.

---

[2] James Bryant Conant, *Science and Common Sense* (New Haven: Yale U. Press, 1951), p. 25.
[3] *Ibid.,* pp. 45, 50.

Observation   Some sciences, such as astronomy and botany, have been built up by careful and methodical observation. Observation is a matter of sense perception: we see, hear, touch, feel, or smell something. On the basis of our observations we draw conclusions regarding relations, causal sequences, and the meaning of the situation.

The *method of agreement,* one of the inductive methods, is sometimes called the *observational* method of agreement. The principle involved is that "the sole invariable circumstance accompanying a phenomenon is causally connected with the phenomenon." For example, some years ago eight well-known leaders in the United States lumber industry became ill and died. Even though they lived in widely separated areas of the country, the fact that they all died within a short period of time led to the belief that there might be a common cause. On examination of the circumstances of the deaths and the events leading up to them, it was noted not only that all the men had died of amoebic dysentery but also that all of them had attended a conference of lumber dealers in the same city a few weeks before. All of them had stayed at the same hotel and had used water that was later found to be contaminated with dysentery germs from the backing-up of the sewage system. In the light of all the circumstances, the contaminated water at the hotel was identified as the cause of the untimely deaths, or "the sole invariable circumstance." There were, of course, a number of common conditions besides the use of the contaminated water. In such circumstances one needs to make a judgment of relevance based on general knowledge and past experience. In this case the water supply was first assumed to be the cause; further investigation disclosed that this water was contaminated and was actually the cause of the disease.

Accurate observation is crucial to scientific investigation. The following conditions are exceedingly important.

1. *Normal or sound sense organs.* While all the senses aid in observation, keen sight and hearing are especially important.

2. *Intellectual maturity.* This includes not only the ability to think but familiarity with the appropriate intellectual instruments, such as terms and concepts, and the ability to use symbols.

3. *Physical instruments.* Telescopes, microscopes, and devices for measurement of time, space, weight, and the like are necessary to obtain accurate results. The history of some sciences is in considerable part the story of the improvement of certain instruments. For example, the development of astronomy is closely related to and dependent on the improvement of the telescope. Progress in biology is similarly related to the improvement of the microscope.

4. *The appropriate position, place, or condition for observation.* The point of view of the observer is receiving more and more attention, as we shall see.

We need to be concerned about the proper conditions for observation—to give attention to factors like time, place, motion, temperature, light, atmospheric conditions, and noise. Faulty observation resulting from some distorting factor can easily lead us to mistaken conclusions.

5. *A knowledge of the field.* Other things being equal, the person who knows the field, its history, and its relationship to other fields of study and experience will have an advantage.

Trial and Error   The method of trial and error, sometimes called trial and success, or trial and chance, is quite universal and well known and does not need lengthy discussion. Trial and error is used by animals as they try to solve their problems. It is a technique studied as well as used by the psychologist as he works with animals and men. We see the method in operation as the rat tries to get out of a maze or around some obstacle in his path. We see it used as the chimpanzee tries various means to secure food that is out of reach. A man will often use this method to find out how some gadget works. The method is thus used automatically by animals, more deliberately by the handyman trying to open a lock for which the key has been lost, and most deliberately by scientists as they try different hypotheses and by philosophers as they test ideas and systems of thought for coherence and factual and logical consistency. The "happy solution" that gives satisfaction is likely to become part of our body of accepted beliefs.

While the trial-and-error method may be called "learning by doing" rather than "learning by thinking," in all but its simplest forms it does involve reflection. Reflective thinking has been called "trial and error by ideas." In reflective thinking, the fumbling is done in the imagination. We may carry out in our imagination a number of proposals or hypotheses and conclude that some may work and others will not. Trial and error in the ideological and imaginative stage saves time, energy, and often life itself.

Experimentation   Active experimentation is the principal method of discovering and verifying causes. Experimentation involves manipulation and control. While observation and trial and error have been widely used, they have their limitations. Great advances in scientific research were made possible when techniques of control were discovered and put to use. In an experiment the observer controls the conditions relating to the subject of his study. He then manipulates these conditions, changing one factor at a time so that he may record the results. The *method of difference,* sometimes called the *experimental* method of difference, is widely used in science. The rule for this method is to vary only one factor or condition at a time, keeping all other factors unchanged or constant. The investigator "makes a difference to see whether it will make a difference" in the result.

A simple illustration of the method of difference is the coin and feather experiment in physics. Why does a feather fall to the ground more slowly than a coin? An experiment is designed to see whether the cause is the resistance of the air. A coin and a feather are dropped at the same time in the chamber of an air pump in which air is present. The coin drops quickly and the feather is retarded. With the other factors kept constant, the air is pumped from the chamber. The coin and the feather are dropped again. This time they reach the bottom of the receiver at the same time. This indicates that the air pressure slows the fall of the feather.

Another method, *concomitant variation,* which deals with the relationship between two phenomena that vary as a result of some common causal connection, may be either observational or experimental. This method may show that two phenomena increase or decrease together, or that one increases as the other decreases. The method of concomitant variation is used in the experiment with the bell jar, which shows that air is a necessary medium for the transmission of sound waves. When the bell is struck with air in the bell jar, sound is heard. As the air is pumped out, the sound diminishes, until the air and the sound disappear at the same time.

Statistical Methods   The term *statistics* refers to the science of the collection, analysis, and classification of numerical data as a basis for induction. Statistical methods arose in early times to help rulers and states gather information about population, births, deaths, wealth, taxes, and the like. These methods have been greatly refined, and today statistical methods are used in everyday affairs, in business and financial activities, and in many of the sciences. Counting, measurement, averages, means, medians—all enable us to make our information exact and to find the order in a mass of detail. Statistics help us see processes that we could not otherwise observe, to explain causes and effects, to describe types of phenomena, and to make comparisons through the use of tables, charts, and graphs. Statistics also enable us to predict some future events with a high degree of accuracy.

The Method of Sampling   Sampling is the method in which we take the nature of certain members of a class as an indication of the nature of the whole membership. When is a single instance likely to be an accurate representative of the whole and when is it not likely to be? When the material to be examined is known to be homogeneous throughout, a single sample will give accurate results. A random natural sample will suffice, since there are no varying conditions whose distribution must be considered. Such samples are often valuable for comparison with material of this type at some different time or place.

As the heterogeneity of the material increases, the number of samples taken must increase. If we know that the sand on a seashore is uniform, then a single sample may be sufficient. If we suspect that the sand is not uniform throughout, then we will take samples at many different places. These can be mixed, and we can "sample the sample."

When differences among items must be taken into account, as in public polls, the investigator must be careful to see that his sample is representative. He may consider questions of age, sex, occupation, economic status, education, and sometimes religion, politics, and other factors that may influence the results. In this case the sample constructed needs to be a cross section of the population or the group to be studied. The bacterial content of water in a pond may vary in different regions of the pond and be affected by inlet or outlet, running or stagnant areas, surface or depth, vegetation and wind direction. In this situation a sample from each area may need to be examined.

A METHOD OF REFLECTIVE THINKING

The methods we have been considering are not separate and distinct; they are interrelated and supplement one another. In fact, it is not possible to use one of them apart from the others. In a general way, we may say that *scientific method* is a collective term designating and denoting the numerous processes and steps by which the various sciences are built up. More specifically, it is a method for acquiring knowledge. Ordinarily this method consists of six steps.[4]

1. *There is an awareness of a problem.* Thinking ordinarily begins when there is some definite obstacle, or difficulty, or possibly when we are merely curious about something. It is crucial to state the problem clearly and correctly. Without a clear definition of the problem, we do not know what facts to collect.

2. *The available and relevant data are collected.* For a simple problem this material may be readily available; for more complicated problems it may take months or years of careful investigation to collect. What the "facts" are will sometimes be known only after careful research.

3. *The data are organized*—that is, they are enumerated, analyzed, and classified. There is an attempt to note comparisons and contrasts, and to put the data in some meaningful order. Enumeration, analysis, and classification are basic to scientific method.

4. *Hypotheses are formulated.* Various tentative solutions may occur to the scientist in the process of analysis and classification. These suggestions or educated guesses are likely to arise as the investigator examines the problem or the subject matter with which he is dealing. He is likely to select first for testing the one that appears to be most probable on the basis of the evidence he has collected to date. There are no limits to the number of hypotheses that may be set forth. While there are no rigid rules for its formulation, a hypothesis should be reasonable, should give rise to deductions that can be tested, and should be a guide to further research.

[4] In *How We Think* (New York: Heath, 1933), John Dewey set forth five steps in reflection. These have been restated many times by various writers. The five steps are included in the six set forth here.

5. *Deductions are drawn from the hypotheses.* In our inferences at this point, the principles of formal logic will come to our aid. Mathematics may also help us disclose the type of order and relationship to be found in the subject matter. In reasoning out the consequences of the various tentative solutions, we reason hypothetically—that is, we say, "If A and B are true, then C must be true." This leads to the next step.

6. *Verification is the final stage.* Having determined, by deductive analysis, what else will be true if our hypothesis is true, we then attempt to see whether this other fact or condition is, as a matter of fact, true. If it turns out to be true, our hypothesis is confirmed or tentatively verified. This process of verification may be carried on by means of observation, by experimentation, or by checking the consistency of the hypothesis with related facts that are believed to be true. If a hypothesis is eliminated as false, we select another hypothesis and proceed as before. Verification will be only approximate or give us a degree of probability. In some cases this may be so high a degree as to approach certainty, but we must hold our conclusions tentatively and be ready to change them when new evidence indicates the need for further investigation.

These six steps may be followed in any area where reflective thinking is carried on. If scientific method is understood in these general terms, it may be applied to any and every area of human experience. Those who claim that scientific method is limited are usually thinking of the more restricted meaning of the term, in which the material is objective and the results must be stated in mathematical or quantitative terms. For example, some men working in the natural sciences object to the use of the terms *science* and *scientific method* when applied to the social studies.

SCIENTIFIC POSTULATES

All proof must begin with certain assumptions. This is true in science, philosophy, or religion. Some ideas or facts must be accepted as *postulates*— that is, must be taken for granted. These include the fundamental laws of thought or logic, such as the principles of identity ("all A is A"), noncontradiction ("not both A and not A"), and excluded middle ("either A or not A"); these are commonly spoken of as self-evident. Ordinarily we also accept the evidence of immediate experience. Men working in the sciences usually proceed on the basis of some or all of the following basic assumptions, postulates, axioms, or conditions.

1. The principle of *causality* is the belief that every event has a cause and that, in identical situations, the same cause always produces the same effect.

2. The principle of *predictive uniformity* states that a group of events will

show the same degree of interconnection or relationship in the future as they showed in the past or do show in the present.

3. The principle of *objectivity* requires the investigator to be impartial with regard to the data before him. The facts must be such that they can be experienced in exactly the same way by all normal people. The aim is to eliminate all subjective and personal elements insofar as possible and to concentrate on the object being studied.

4. The principle of *empiricism* lets the investigator assume that his sense impressions are reliable and that he may test truth by an appeal to the "experienced facts." Knowing is the result of observation, experience, and experiment, as opposed to authority, intuition, or reason alone.

5. The principle of *parsimony* suggests that, other things being equal, a person takes the simplest explanation as the most valid one. This principle is a check on unnecessary intricacy. It cautions against complicated explanations. It is sometimes called "Occam's razor," since William of Occam, a fourteenth-century English philosopher, said that "entities should not be multiplied beyond necessity."

6. The principle of *isolation,* or *segregation,* requires that the phenomenon under investigation be segregated so that it can be studied by itself.

7. The principle of *control* emphasizes controls as essential, at least for experimentation. Otherwise, many factors may vary at the same time, and the experiment could not be repeated in the same way. If the conditions change while the experiment is being conducted, the results may be invalid.

8. The principle of *exact measurement* requires results to be such that they can be stated in quantitative or mathematical terms. This is the goal at least of the physical sciences.

A scientist, E. G. Conklin, raises the question of whether there can be such a thing as a "purely objective science." He reminds us that there can be "no observation without an observer, no experiment without an experimenter, no classification without a classifier."[5] In the physical or inorganic sciences the postulates and conditions set forth above can be met fairly adequately. We can isolate and control and measure with a high degree of success. We need to keep in mind, however, Heisenberg's principle of uncertainty or indeterminacy and the realization that the principles of science are undergoing significant revision.[6] Electrons change position in an unpredictable manner. The very act of observation is said to affect the way subatomic particles act. When we come to a study of living creatures, especially man and his society, new and difficult conditions are also encountered. Life on its

[5] *Man, Real and Ideal* (New York: Scribner's, 1943), p. 5.
[6] Werner Heisenberg, *Physics and Philosophy: The Revolution in Modern Science* (New York: Harper, 1958).

higher levels cannot be isolated and controlled without altering the nature of that which is to be studied. Separate a person from society and you change the nature of his being.

SOME CONCLUSIONS AND IMPLICATIONS

1. Neither the scientist nor the philosopher has any secrets or methods of obtaining knowledge that are not open to people in general. Science differs from ordinary common sense in that it is more critical, more penetrating, and more controlled and exact in its observations and analyses. We all use observation, but the scientist is trained to observe more carefully in his particular field. We all use the trial-and-error method and we all experiment at times, but the scientist is more rigorous. He takes special care to guard against errors. He is trained in the proper use of accurate instruments. He usually knows the history of the field. He is acquainted with the progress and the mistakes that have already been made; thus he is able to avoid many blind alleys and mistakes of the past.

2. There is no *science* in general, except as the term is used collectively to denote the various natural sciences or the body of facts that they have accumulated. No investigator is a scientist in general; he is a specialist in one field, or at most in a few fields. There are a great many sciences whose fields overlap. These sciences are to be distinguished not so much by separate areas or by separate subject matter as by the units, classes, categories, and concepts under which we think of that subject matter.

3. Scientific method can be divided into two parts: the logical methods and the technical or technological methods. The logical methods are those of reasoning or drawing inferences. The logical processes are the same in all the sciences, in philosophy, and in all clear and accurate thinking. They include such principles of reasoning as the method of agreement, the method of difference, and the method of concomitant variation. (The reader interested in further discussion should consult books on logic and scientific method, where he will find the inductive and deductive methods of reasoning explained and illustrated in great detail.)

The technical methods are those of manipulating the phenomena under investigation. This is what many people think of as "science." These methods are many and varied. Here we include the constantly growing mass of apparatus and equipment that aids in observation and experimentation. These instruments are the things that immediately come to our attention as we enter a scientific laboratory. They extend our powers of observation and control. Without a knowledge of the field and the methods of reasoning, however, they are of little use.

4. The scientific methods we have been considering are the most valuable

methods we have found for the discovery of objective knowledge. They are the result of the thinking and work of thousands of men through many centuries. These methods have been worked out in an effort to avoid the obstacles and biases that impede the search for truth. They are still being refined and adapted to the different types of material under study. Some people believe that we will eventually develop methods to take care of everything with which we have to deal, including the qualitative as well as the quantitative aspects of things.

QUESTIONS AND PROJECTS

1. Review Questions

(1) On pages 21–24 the characteristics of common-sense opinion were given. State these in your own words; then indicate how scientific methods and science differ from common sense.

(2) List some of the major steps and key men involved in the development of science.

(3) State three possible meanings or uses of the term *science*.

(4) Justify the statement that there are "a variety of scientific methods" rather than one method only. Give examples.

(5) Discuss briefly the methods, problems, and possible disadvantages involved in observation, experimentation, and statistical procedure and sampling.

(6) State the six steps in reflective thinking; these steps should be thought out and not memorized. Do you think it satisfactory to describe scientific methods in these general terms?

(7) List the main assumptions or postulates underlying scientific method or methods as used in the natural sciences. Be ready to discuss and challenge or defend these postulates.

(8) State the general conclusions that may be drawn from a study of scientific methods. Do not confine yourself to the few conclusions set forth at the end of this chapter.

2. Have you had occasion in your daily activities to use the various scientific methods outlined on pp. 77–82? What do you do, for example, when your automobile refuses to start and you attempt to locate the trouble yourself instead of calling a service man? Do you recognize any or all of the six steps of reflective thinking in such a situation?

3. Look up and clarify in your own mind the different uses of the term *law*. For example, differentiate a scientific law, a statutory law, and a moral law.

4. What kinds of questions does science ask and attempt to answer? In giving your own views, comment on the following quotation: "The kinds of questions which science is designed to answer are questions which arise when we are considering the means of doing something, and not the kinds of questions which arise when we are considering what is worth doing. Science, in the last analysis, is knowledge of how to use the means at our disposal to achieve our purposes. It is not knowledge of what purposes are good. . . . [Scientific knowledge is] instrumental knowledge."[7]

5. The motives or incentives behind scientific advances may be of two kinds: intellectual curiosity or pure science, and technological or practical interests associated with such things as the building of bridges, factories, bombs, and rapid travel and communication. Babylonian, Egyptian, Roman, and much modern science is practical in emphasis. In Greek and Renaissance science, intellectual curiosity is dominant. Speaking of "the jealousy of modern governments for scientific secrets," L. W. H. Hull says, "Science is publicly valued as an aid to wealth and power. . . . Its place, besides religion, philosophy and the arts, among the elements of gracious civilization, is forgotten."[8] Discuss modern science as the product of these contrasting motives. What is the emphasis today, and do you consider the present situation desirable?

6. Morris R. Cohen says that "scientists themselves are not always possessed of clear and sound ideas" concerning the nature of scientific method.[9] Men in scientific research tend to follow "techniques that are established habits or routines in their field." When forced to generalize about the methods used, they are likely to repeat the conventional answers. Comment on this.

7. Read the following quotations, discuss their implications, and indicate why you agree or disagree with them.

(1) "[A]ll scientific descriptions of facts are highly selective, . . . they always depend upon theories. . . . Similarly, a scientific description will depend, largely, upon our point of view, our interests, which are as a rule connected with the theory or hypothesis we wish to test; although it will also depend upon the facts described."[10] —K. R. Popper.

(2) Warren Weaver says, "Science is what scientists do . . . and scientists are human." Scientists, he points out, differ from people in general only in their "schooling in scientific method, their knowledge of the vast successes which science has had, their proud partnership in the profession that has measured the star, split the atom, and probed the cell. This inheritance is, I am bound to tell you, magnificent but dangerous."[11]

8. What is the status of the principle of the uniformity of nature? Do we just accept it on faith or is there evidence for it? Can it be proved?

7 John Macmurray, *The Boundaries of Science* (London: Faber and Faber, 1939), p. 104.
8 *History and Philosophy of Science*, p. 324.
9 *Studies in Philosophy and Science* (New York: Holt, 1949), p. 48.
10 *The Open Society and Its Enemies* (London: Routledge, 1945), II, p. 247.
11 "Science and the Citizen," *Bulletin of the Atomic Scientists*, XIII (December, 1957): 365; *Science*, 126 (December 13, 1957): 1228.

SUGGESTED READINGS

BACON, FRANCIS. *Selections.* Ed. by M. T. McClure. New York: Scribner's, 1928. (Modern Student's Library.)
Selections from Bacon's more important works that indicate his method and outlook. See especially Advancement of Learning *and* Novum Organum.

BROWN, G. BURNISTON. *Science: Its Method and Its Philosophy.* New York: Norton 1950.
An attempt to answer the following questions: What is scientific method? How has it arisen? What is a scientific outlook?

BUTTERFIELD, HERBERT (ed.). *The History of Science.* Glencoe: Free Press, 1958.
Fifteen British scientists, philosophers, and historians discuss the leaders in science, their achievements, and the landmarks in the scientific revolution of Western civilization.

CAMPBELL, NORMAN R. *What is Science?* New York: Dover, 1952.
A readable book dealing with the nature, methods, laws, and applications of science.

CONANT, JAMES BRYANT. *Modern Science and Modern Man.* New York: Doubleday, 1953. (Anchor Book.)
A discussion of the changing scientific scene and the role science plays in the life of man. See also the author's other works, including Science and Common Sense *and* On Understanding Science.

DAMPIER, SIR WILLIAM CECIL. *A History of Science and Its Relations with Philosophy and Religion.* 4th ed. rev. and enl.; New York: Cambridge U. Press, 1949.
An account of the development of science, from ancient times to the present, that gives attention to the religious and philosophical implications of the scientific outlook. See A Shorter History of Science *by the same author for an abbreviated account.*

FRANK, PHILIPP G. (ed.). *The Validation of Scientific Knowledge.* Boston: Beacon, 1956.
Contains papers read at a special conference, arranged by the Institute for the Unity of Science, on the "Validation of Scientific Theories."

HEPP, MAYLON H. *Thinking Things Through.* New York: Scribner's, 1956.
An introduction to logic and scientific method. Part III deals with problems of factual inquiry in everyday life and the sciences.

HULL, L. W. H. *History and Philosophy of Science: An Introduction.* New York: Longmans, Green, 1959.
The author discusses scientific method and ideas from a historical and philosophical perspective. The last chapter deals with twentieth-century trends.

KANTON, J. R. *The Logic of Modern Science.* Bloomington: Principia, 1953.
A study of science based on interbehavioral psychology that attempts "to free the logic of science from the historical epistemologies, ontologies," and "spiritistic entities."

LACKMAN, SHELDON J. *The Foundations of Science.* Detroit: Hamilton, 1956.
A monograph, prepared for the junior-college level, that considers the objectives, assumptions, operating conceptions, and methodology of science.

LERNER, DANIEL (ed.). *Parts and Wholes*. Glencoe: Free Press, 1962. (The Hayden Colloquium on Scientific Method and Concept.)
Eight scholars from various fields discuss the limited nature of human knowledge and the fact that empirical knowledge is concerned with parts and not with wholes.

MADDEN, EDWARD H. (ed.). *Theories of Scientific Method: The Renaissance through the Nineteenth Century*. Seattle: U. of Washington Press, 1960.
Thirteen studies that give the theories of scientific method held by certain men of the period under consideration. See also Edward H. Madden (ed.), The Structure of Scientific Thought.

Mid-Century Convocation on the Social Implications of Scientific Progress. Ed. and ann. by John Bly Burchard. New York: Technology Press M. I. T. and Wiley, 1950. (Massachusetts Institute of Technology, 1949.)
Forty scholars and men of affairs discuss the relation of science to society and exchange views regarding the problems raised by science for the twentieth century.

NAGEL, ERNEST. *The Structure of Science: Problems in the Logic of Scientific Explanation*. New York: Harcourt, Brace & World, 1961.
Essays discussing the methods, laws, patterns of explanation, and theories of science. Some essays deal with special fields such as physics, biology, the social sciences, and historical inquiry.

NEWMAN, JAMES R. (ed.). *What Is Science?* New York: Simon and Schuster, 1955.
Twelve scientists and philosophers explain the methods used in their respective fields and the ways in which the search for knowledge proceeds.

WERKMEISTER, W. H. *A Philosophy of Science*. New York: Harper, 1940.
A comprehensive text in the philosophy of science. See especially Chapter I, "The Dawn of Modern Science," and Chapter II, "The Method of Science."

❧ SIX ❧

SCIENCE AND PHILOSOPHY

In this chapter we shall consider the relationship between science and philosophy. There are at least two reasons for doing so. In the first place, many people now claim that science is the *only* way of obtaining knowledge, that it is the "sole authentic mode of revelation," and that to know is to be able to state things in quantitative terms. The question "Can science save us?" is answered in the affirmative by some.[1] There are scientists and a considerable number of young people who have specialized in one field or area of science who have come to believe that no other mental activity is worth much consideration. Scientific method, they say, has no limitation.

In the second place, there are, in contrast, numerous attacks on science, or on what is sometimes called "scientism."[2] Phrases like "the superstition of science" are occasionally seen, not just in books and articles written by philosophers, religious leaders, and others, but in those written by scientists themselves. There is much to be gained by facing such criticisms frankly. They are more frequently directed against the attitudes and philosophy of some scientists than against science itself.

THE VALUE AND ACHIEVEMENTS OF SCIENCE

The great achievements of the sciences and the value of scientific method are almost universally recognized. The fact that practically all sciences have made breathtaking advances in recent years is well known to all educated people. We have considered some of them briefly in the preceding chapters. Theoretical advances dealing with matter, space, time, evolution, and the

[1] George A. Lundberg, *Can Science Save Us?* (New York: Longmans, Green, 1947).

[2] See Fulton J. Sheen, *Philosophies At War* (New York: Scribner's, 1943), pp. 50 ff.; Hugh Stevenson Tigner, *Our Prodigal Son Culture* (New York: Harper, 1940), Ch. IX; and Anthony Standen, *Science Is a Sacred Cow* (New York: Dutton, 1950). (Dutton Everyman Paperback, 1958.)

like have given us a new outlook on the world. The practical application of scientific knowledge to technology and mechanization touches our lives daily at innumerable points. We are beginning to believe that there is no area of life about which scientific methods cannot produce some information.

The sciences have enabled us to reduce the barriers of space and time by rapid methods of communication, travel, and transportation. The human voice can now travel distances that would have been considered unbridgeable a few decades ago. Science is responsible for the development of the modern age of power, for new sources of food supply and the expansion of agricultural production, and for progress in medicine and disease-control. We have been released from many of the age-old fears and hazards to life and happiness. We have gained control over many of our traditional enemies. Cold, heat, darkness, and storms do not hold the terrors they once did. Our understanding of the processes of our own bodies, as well as of the world in which we live, has been greatly increased.

With the help of certain sciences we can be forewarned of events; we can make predictions in many areas of life. We can observe trends that otherwise would escape us. The application of the methods of the sciences to the problems of social relations and human behavior gives us new hope that we shall be able one day to deal more adequately with some of the baffling problems of our modern civilization.

In addition to these practical advantages and achievements, science helps satisfy our disinterested curiosity in the quest for truth. At times it provides the contemplative imagination with new vistas of insight, such as some new theory of evolution or space-time relativity. It may also disclose objects of great aesthetic charm, such as the order and regularity of the planets as they circle the sun. Mathematicians have sometimes used aesthetic terms to express their elation after the solution of some difficult problem.

On the whole, scientists have done their work so thoroughly and so accurately that today there is a strong presumption in favor of any idea that is set forth in the name of science. We have almost come to believe that "science" can explain everything and do nearly anything.

But the very fact that scientific methods are so valuable and have so much prestige is likely to blind us to certain errors into which both the scientist and the general public are inclined to fall. Men in all walks of life easily develop "blind spots." This is particularly true of the specialist. Even an exceptionally careful investigator, after completing his research, will sometimes make claims not warranted by the facts he has discovered. Let us consider some of the things that will help us avoid misunderstanding in this area.

LIMITATIONS OF SCIENTIFIC METHODS

In our discussion in this section we are thinking of *science* and *scientific methods* in the more restricted sense—as the terms are used by most scientists in the natural sciences, where the methods are strictly empirical and objective and the purpose is to interpret the world quantitatively and mathematically. We are assuming that scientists are free to investigate anything with which their methods are capable of dealing. The purpose of this section is not to urge that the sciences be kept out of any particular areas of human experience; rather, it is to indicate the limitations inherent in scientific methods.

If one reads widely in the literature of the sciences, many questions arise in his mind. For example, why are there "the seven psychologies," each claiming to be the valid approach and to represent the truth? What are the dominant factors in human behavior and social progress? Are they geographical, hereditary, psychological, cultural, religious, or economic, to mention just a few of the possible answers? The conflicting evidence and claims are very bewildering.

There are principles that will help to point up some of the limitations of science. Keep these suggestions in mind when considering science and scientific methods.

1. *In scientific research, you can find only that which your methods and your instruments are capable of finding.* You can discover only that which is discoverable with the technique you use. This seems so obvious that one wonders why it is so frequently overlooked. If you use an objective method, you find only what can be stated objectively. If you proceed on the basis of the postulates of physics and chemistry, you find only what can be stated in physical or chemical terms. If you get in touch with your friend by telephone, you hear his voice; you get what the instrument transmits, and nothing more. If you investigate an object with a pair of scales, you get its weight. There may be other interesting things about it, but you are entitled to claim as scientifically valid knowledge only what your instrument and method are capable of giving you.

Sir Arthur S. Eddington's illustration of the elephant is well known.[3] If a student reads "an elephant slides down a grassy hillside" in a problem in physics, he knows that he need not pay much attention to the form of the expression. When he finds that the elephant weighs two tons, the idea of elephant disappears and a mass of two tons takes its place. When the slope of the hill is found to be sixty degrees, the picture of a hill vanishes and in its place the student thinks of an angle of sixty degrees. The idea of the turf is replaced by a coefficient of friction, and so on for the other data of the

---

[3] *The Nature of the Physical World* (New York: Macmillan, 1937), pp. 251 ff.

problem. Thus what we might call the "poetry" fades out of the picture, and we are left with pointer-readings and numbers. And if only pointer-readings or their equivalents enter into our scientific calculations, that is all we can expect to find in our solution.[4] Eddington emphasizes the fact that the subject matter of science consists of pointer-readings and similar indications, and that when we state the properties of a body in physical quantities, we are indicating the response of various measuring instruments to the body, and nothing more.

In *Modern Science and Materialism*[5] Hugh Elliot argues that since there is no place for "spirit" or "purpose" in astronomy or physics, nothing of that nature exists. He says, "No sign of purpose can be detected in any part of the vast universe disclosed by our most powerful telescopes." He concludes that there is nothing but "the physical laws of matter." But should a person expect to find purpose by looking through a telescope?

2. *Scientific classification gives valuable information, but no single classification includes everything in the subject being classified.* Classification is one of the fundamental bases of scientific knowledge. We do not know what a thing is until we can classify it or put it into a meaningful context. If a thing cannot be analyzed and classified, it eludes science.

The kind of classification, however, depends on our purpose in making it. Things may be classified in many different ways. Buildings may be classified according to location, type, or valuation. Sick people may be classified according to their ailments, the doctors attending them, their ages, races, economic statuses, and so on. It is especially obvious in the case of sick people that classification is a means of dealing with things by the simple device of disregarding their differences. For example, several people with many different characteristics may all be classed as typhoid fever patients. Scientific classification frequently includes details of the differences by the use of subdivisions or subclasses. However, the fact remains that the original classification was based on some one common characteristic. Therefore we are justified in asserting that simple classification treats a group of people or a group of things that have certain qualities in common as if they possessed only those qualities. The scientist is entirely justified in doing this, if he does not forget what he has done.

3. *The whole may have qualities absent in the parts.* If we analyze an object, its elements or simple units are not more real than the object or event with

4 A friend with a literary flare who read this illustration suggested how much the scientist who recognizes nothing but "facts" misses. He writes: "Gone is the exotic thrill of just thinking about a massive beast swinging his trunk and tail and conducting himself like a lad at play, of a pleasant breeze swaying the tall grass on a rising slope, and the delightfully zany joke which stirs something within us."

5 New York: Longmans, Green, 1919. See also Roy Wood Sellars, *et al.* (eds.), *Philosophy for the Future: The Quest of Modern Materialism* (New York: Macmillan, 1949).

which we began. Scientific method is concerned with breaking objects down into their constituent elements. Some people are inclined to believe that these simple units have a reality not possessed by the complex object. This may be called the fallacy of reduction. Scientific analyses and explanations do not alter the gross facts of experience. The explanations of science add something to our knowledge; they give us new facts or point out things that we would have overlooked otherwise, but they do not take anything away from the actual world. To explain is not to explain away. To explain the colors of the sunset as electromagnetic vibrations is not to explain away the sunset, but merely to interpret it, to add to our knowledge of the nature of light and colors.[6]

Science advances by a method of analysis. But there are qualities in total situations that are not discovered by an analysis of any one part of the whole or even of all the parts examined separately. Water is composed of hydrogen and oxygen, which are gases with all the qualities and properties of gases. These gases will not quench thirst, or revive drooping plants, or freeze at zero degrees centigrade—all of which things water will do. Moreover, water is a liquid with the characteristics of liquids.

If we analyze a living organism, we do not find life in any one of the parts. Yet there is life in the total organism; the whole has a quality not found in any of its parts.

When we analyze things into simple units, it is a mistake to believe that these units are more "real" than the whole of which they were parts, or of the same kind of reality as the whole. The real nature of things is found as much in wholes and in qualities as in the elements or parts. The world which any science gives us may be a real world, but it is not the whole world nor the only world. No one can interpret adequately any situation without considering it as a whole, as well as knowing its parts and the relations of those parts.

4. *There may be many interpretations of a thing, a person, or an event, each of which is true as far as it goes.* Each interpretation may be illuminating from one point of view. The farmer who sees the boys stealing his apples gets greatly excited. The psychologist describes the state of the man by saying that a stimulus has called forth an emotional response. The physiologist explains it as accelerated heart action and increased oxidation. The physicist may explain it by reference to the increased velocity of the molecules in the blood. A bystander may simply remark that the old boy is angry.[7] Each is explaining the event properly from his own viewpoint.

[6] In this and in the succeeding point the author has been influenced by the excellent discussion on "The Function of Exploration in Physics," Ch. VI of *An Introduction to Reflective Thinking* by Columbia Associates in Philosophy (Boston: Houghton Mifflin, 1923).

[7] *Ibid.*, p. 145.

The uncritical attempt to explain or describe everything in one language or with reference to one principle or type of interpretation is one of the more frequent misuses of the scientific methods. It may be called the fallacy of oversimplification or hasty monism. It occurs whenever all things are thought to be exhaustively treated by inclusion in some one category. Examples of hasty monism would include the monistic explanations of history or of human conduct. Some explain history solely on the basis of climatic changes, others solely on the basis of economic forces, and still others on the basis of biological factors, to mention just a few of the possible interpretations. Human conduct has been explained entirely by glandular conditions, by psychological urges, by environmental pressures. While all these factors are important, we may well be suspicious of attempts to explain complex events with reference to a single set of concepts.

There are multiple points of view and multiple approaches to understanding our world. Truth appears to be of many kinds, and there is more than one window on reality. As one scientist expressed it: "It requires a long-necked observer to see the whole firmament out of one window."

5. *When we consider anything that is in a process of development, we find the later stages as real as the earlier stages, and probably more informative as to the nature of the process.* A prevalent mistake is that of regarding what is earlier in development as more real than what follows. The genetic method, which traces things back to their beginnings, is very useful if it does not cause us to neglect the more advanced stages. Of course, the whole process must be taken into account. We cannot explain later stages adequately or fully by the earlier stages. If we could see the earth as it was many millions of years ago, we would be impressed by the fact that no life was present. Later we might see life but no evidence of man. Of the first view, we would say that only mechanical forces were present. It would be observed still later that living organisms were present. Eventually the process produced man, with self-consciousness and a degree of intelligence.

Aristotle once asked how one should study an oak tree. Where shall one start? Shall he start with the acorn or the young sapling, with the tree in its maturity or in its period of decay? Clearly all the processes belong to the concept "oak tree," and a mere description of its parts or a cross section of it at any one period does not describe the unity of the organism. For Aristotle, reality was a process of development from potentiality to actuality. The later stages of an evolutionary process indicate most clearly the nature of the force or forces that have been present throughout the process.

6. *The sciences are dependent upon man's sense organs and upon his general intellectual equipment.* We may increase the range of man's senses with instruments like the telescope, microscope, and computer, but we cannot provide him with new ones nor change the nature of the organs man has. When we observe, it is always with some "interest." There is a tendency to see what

we are trained to see or expect to see. After we receive the image or the sensation, we have to move on to inference or generalization. This involves the logical operation of the human mind. Observation and theories develop hand in hand. Different observations lead to different theories, and different theories lead us to make different observations. Science depends on the human sense organs and the processes of human reason. The "standpoint of the observer" is increasingly coming to be recognized in all fields. Since science is often said to be based on observation and experimentation, it is well to emphasize again that scientific knowledge depends also on assumptions and postulates, and that these in turn rest essentially on faith.

Many sciences, perhaps all of them, ought to employ objective, quantitative, and mechanical methods because of the greater simplicity and accuracy of these methods. When they are used, however, it must be remembered that the sciences are not telling the whole story. Scientific methods are among man's most useful intellectual tools, but, like the others, they can be misused. Abuses arise not only when these techniques get into the hands of evil men, but also when a good man comes to believe that the aspect of nature he is studying is the only aspect.

THE RELATION OF PHILOSOPHY TO SCIENCE

It is not easy to present a simple, clear-cut statement of the relation between philosophy and science, indicating the agreements and differences. There are different definitions and conceptions of science and different interpretations of the nature and task of philosophy. Scientists do not agree among themselves about the nature and limitations of the sciences. Philosophers also do not agree regarding the methods and tasks of philosophy. For example, in a very broad sense, science may be interpreted as any classified and systematized body of facts in some particular area. From this point of view— more frequently found among writers in continental Europe than in the United States and Britain—even subjects like ethics and theology may be called sciences. Most people working in the sciences, however, define *science* as a method of objective investigation with the purpose of describing and interpreting in exact and quantitative terms. The term thus means knowledge that has been gained through observation, experimentation, classification, and analysis. Science aims to eliminate the personal or human element insofar as possible. The purpose of science is to obtain knowledge of the facts, laws, and processes of nature.

The author of one of the outstanding histories of science has this to say:

> Men of science, most of whom used naively to assume that they were dealing with ultimate reality, are coming to see more clearly the true nature of their

work. The methods of science are primarily analytic, and lead, as far as may be, to the explanation of phenomena in mathematical form and in terms of physical concepts. But the fundamental concepts of physical science, it is now understood, are abstractions, framed by our minds so as to bring order and simplicity into an apparent chaos of phenomena. The approach to reality through science, therefore, gives only aspects of reality, pictures drawn on simplified lines, but not reality itself. Nevertheless, even philosophers are coming to see that, in a metaphysical study of reality, the methods and results of science are the best available evidence, and that a new realism, if possible at all, must be built up by their means.[8]

In "The Physical Scientist at His Work," Kirtley F. Mather says:

One of the first considerations that I would recommend to the embryo physical scientist is the recognition of the limitations of science, hand in hand with his obviously justified respect for the power of science. The man of science is not the whole man. The well-rounded individual is an artist and a philosopher as well as a scientist. Human life, as distinct from other animal life, involves the recognition of aesthetic and ethical values that transcend the immediate requirements for mere existence. Almost every day, in the life of every scientific worker, a point is reached where the man of science must bow out and the philosopher must take over.

On the field of battle where ethical and moral values are appealing for recognition, appraisal, and loyalty, the physical sciences are forever neutral. To be sure, science provides the only means for the realization of values, but it does not create them, and in the final, ultimate analysis it does not discriminate among them. The release of atomic energy from nuclear fission by chain reaction has no moral significance, in and of itself. It is what men do with this new and spectacularly dynamic form of energy that is either good or bad.[9]

Philosophers, we have said, differ among themselves as to the meaning and task of philosophy. In a narrow sense, philosophy is a science dealing with logical method or with the logical analysis of language and meanings. Philosophy may be considered the "science of sciences," with its main task the critical analysis of the assumptions and concepts of the sciences and possibly the systematization or organization of knowledge. In a broader sense, philosophy attempts to integrate man's knowledge from the various areas of human experience and to set forth a comprehensive view of the universe and of life and its meaning. This interpretation of philosophy neither excludes the function of critical analysis mentioned above nor limits philosophy to any one subject matter. We are using the term *philosophy* in this more inclusive sense.

[8] Sir William Cecil Dampier, *A History of Science and Its Relations with Philosophy and Religion* (4th ed. rev. and enl.; New York: Cambridge U. Press, 1949), pp. vii-viii.
[9] In *motive* (December, 1951): 19.

AREAS OF AGREEMENT BETWEEN PHILOSOPHY AND SCIENCE

There are various points on which philosophy and science agree. During the last few centuries philosophy has developed in close association with science. Many of the outstanding philosophers have made important contributions in the sciences. For example, Leibniz shared in the discovery of the differential calculus. The contributions of Alfred North Whitehead and Bertrand Russell to mathematical theory are well known. Both philosophy and science use the methods of reflective thinking in their attempt to face the facts of the world and of life. Both exhibit a critical, open-minded attitude and an impartial concern for the truth. They are interested in organized and systematized knowledge.

Science supplies philosophy with a large amount of factual and descriptive material essential in the building of a philosophy. Indeed, the philosophy of any period tends to reflect the scientific outlook of that period.[10] Science exerts a check upon philosophy by helping to eliminate such ideas as are incompatible with scientific knowledge.

Philosophy takes the piecemeal knowledge of the various sciences and organizes it into a more complete and integrated world view. In this connection the very progress of the sciences makes philosophy necessary, since the discovery of new facts and relationships forces men to revise their notions and interpretations not only in the sciences but in most other fields. For instance, the acceptance of the concept of evolution forced men to revise their thinking in nearly all other areas. Further contributions of philosophy to science are the criticism by philosophy of the assumptions and postulates of the sciences and the critical analysis of many of the terms used.

AREAS OF DIFFERENCE BETWEEN PHILOSOPHY AND SCIENCE

The contrasts between philosophy and science generally represent tendencies or points of emphasis, not absolute distinctions. Whereas particular sciences deal with restricted or limited fields, philosophy attempts to deal with the whole of experience. Philosophy is thus inclusive rather than exclusive; it attempts to include in its body of knowledge what is common to all fields and to human experience in general. Philosophy thus attempts to gain a more comprehensive view of things. Whereas science is more analytic and descriptive in its approach, philosophy is more synthetic or synoptic, dealing with the properties and qualities of nature and life as a whole. Science attempts to analyze the whole into its constituent elements or the organism into organs; philosophy attempts to combine things in interpretative syntheses and to discover the significance of things. Whereas science tends to eliminate the personal factor and to ignore values in its drive for objectivity, philosophy is interested in personality, in values, and in all

10 We will examine current scientific views of life and the universe in the next two chapters.

realms of experience. Science is interested in the nature of things as they are; philosophy is interested not only in the real aspects but also in the possibilities of things and in their worth and meaning. To observe nature and to control processes is the aim of science; to criticize, evaluate, and coordinate ends is part of the task of philosophy.

Both science and philosophy are interested in explanations and meanings. In science, however, the emphasis is more on a description of the laws of phenomena and on causal relationships. Philosophy is interested in "why" as well as "how," in questions of purpose, and in the relation between particular facts and the larger scheme of things. Science employs observation, experimentation, and a classification of the data of sense experience. Philosophy, because of the nature of its problems, seeks to relate the findings of the sciences to the claims of religion, ethics, and the arts.

While there are many areas in which the scientist gives us much knowledge, there are other areas into which, as a scientist, he does not venture. Such areas as religious commitment, devotion, and worship, the values, ends, and purposes of life, beauty in the arts and literature, a life view and a world view that integrate man's knowledge and insights—all these are areas with which the scientist, as scientist, is not concerned.

In a discussion of "fact, motive, and intention," John Macmurray says:

> The reconciliation of intentions, the harmonization of wills, and not merely of motives, is the basic condition of any satisfactory social order. Its possibility within limits is demonstrated by the fact of human community and by the peculiar skill which certain people show in mediating between persons whose wills are at enmity and bringing about a reconciliation. There is surely involved in this a kind of knowledge of the intentionality of human action which provides a basis for a form of systematic reflection which could extend and deepen the possibility which it reveals. At least we may reach one negative conclusion which seems to be indubitable, and which events in our own generation are forcing increasingly upon our notice. If there can be no knowledge of matters of intention, if scientific knowledge is the only form of knowledge which is possible to us, then all human life must be the sport of a blind chance. For scientific knowledge, being instrumental knowledge, has the effect of increasing almost without limit our power to realize our intentions. But whether it is employed for good or bad purposes, for construction or for destruction, to increase happiness or to increase misery, depends upon the character of the intentions which it serves.[11]

The extreme rationalist, who stresses reason as the important or central factor in knowledge, will make a more complete separation between science and philosophy than we have made. He may wish to confine the term *science*

---

11 *The Boundaries of Science* (London: Faber and Faber, 1939), pp. 258–259.

to the description of the data of sense perception. On the other hand, he believes that philosophy, through reason, is capable of discovering irrefutable knowledge apart from sense experience.

Let us emphasize again that the differences between pure science and philosophy are in considerable part differences of degree and emphasis. In all serious thinking, the processes of analysis and synthesis are combined. Many scientists are also philosophers. Philosophers are trained in the scientific methods and often pursue special interests in some of the sciences. Both philosophers and scientists gain perspective as they come to understand and to appreciate each others' discipline.

NEW PROBLEMS FACING THE SCIENTIST

The scientist has problems the philosopher does not have, at least not to the same extent. This is because recent developments in the sciences are changing society at a rapid rate and have great implications for good or evil in the future. Science, especially applied science or technology, has become a key factor in the power struggle between special-interest groups on the national scene and between nations or power blocs in the international arena. Scientists are becoming deeply involved in military affairs, foreign policy, social planning, communication, and economic competition, as well as in fields like engineering and medicine.

Until recent decades most scientists worked in university or small private laboratories, alone or in small groups, on projects involving relatively small financial outlays, and with little attention from the public. These conditions have changed or are changing for large numbers of scientists. Probably a million people were involved in the various projects that led to nuclear fission and the first bombs. Political and industrial groups that have a big stake in the results are now furnishing the financial support for a large part of the scientific research under way. These groups frequently want to control or profit by the results of the research. "As the power of scientific research to change the world increases, so concomitantly will the influence of scientists over their research decrease."[12]

A generation ago the scientist worked on problems in which he was especially interested. His aim was the discovery of truth and he usually shared his findings with his fellow scientists around the world. Now he works on projects for which money is available, and sometimes he does not know the exact nature or purpose of the work in which he is engaged. This has a tendency to undermine his sense of moral responsibility. As he becomes the center of attention and as his work results in public controversy, a sense of uneasiness may result. Most scientists are dedicated to the discovery of truth

---

[12] Philip Siekevitz, "A New Ethics for Science," *The Nation,* 186 (March 15, 1958): 223.

and the promotion of human welfare. They are rightly disturbed when their work comes under criticism and they are charged with lack of concern for their fellowmen or called "destroyers of life."

Scientific advance has important implications for philosophy, religion, and society in general. New problems in the realm of human values are arising that we cannot discuss in this chapter.[13] In the future is science to be free or under pressure and in chains? To do his best work, the scientist must have a large measure of freedom, congenial conditions under which to work, a sense of the importance of his task, and a dedication to truth and human development.

QUESTIONS AND PROJECTS

1. Review Questions

(1) What are two rather sharply contrasting attitudes toward science?

(2) Why is it important to clarify our thinking about the relation between science and philosophy?

(3) Show how the outstanding achievements of science and their relation to the advancement of human welfare may at times blind us to some of the dangers of specialization.

(4) State some principles or generalizations that need to be kept clearly in mind if we are to eliminate some of the errors of science and extreme claims which are occasionally made in its name. You may wish to criticize some of these statements or to suggest others that might well be included in the list.

(5) Defend or attack Eddington's statement that the subject matter of science consists mainly of pointer-readings.

(6) Point out the things we especially need to keep in mind about scientific classification, the relation between parts and the whole, varying interpretations of events, and things that are in process of development.

(7) Show how science cannot avoid the problems of epistemology, and how special problems may arise in connection with scientific observation and the condition of our sense organs.

(8) What is the relationship between science and philosophy, and where do they agree and diverge?

(9) Indicate some of the contributions of science to philosophy and of philosophy to the sciences.

(10) What new and disturbing problems are facing many scientists as they carry on their work in the contemporary world?

13 For special problems in the relation of science to government see C. P. Snow, *Science and Government* (Cambridge: Harvard U. Press, 1961); and *Perspectives on Government and Science,* ed. Norman Wengert, *The Annals of the American Academy of Political and Social Science,* 327 (Philadelphia: January, 1960).

2. Luther Burbank was given some squash seeds, bean seeds, and kernels of corn that had been found in an Arizona cliff dwelling. There were two ways of examining them. One way was to analyze them; another was to plant them and see what they would become. Discuss possible ways of studying these seeds and the implications of the different methods.

3. What are the differences among the scientific, the practical, and the philosophical moods? A scientist, J. Arthur Thomson, in *Introduction to Science* (New York: Holt, 1911), Ch. 1, discusses the scientific mood and contrasts it with the practical mood and the emotional mood. A philosopher, E. S. Brightman, in *Introduction to Philosophy* (New York: Holt, 1925), Ch. 1, discusses the philosophical spirit or mood. These statements, though written some years ago, are still highly meaningful. Contrast and discuss these different moods, and indicate whether or not there are still other moods that can be distinguished and described.

4. Is it true that "commitment is more important than skill" and that "knowing how" may implement antisocial motives and purposes? Give evidence to support your answer. You may wish to consult the article "The Terrifying Impact of the Fuchs Case," by Rebecca West, in the *New York Times Magazine* for March 4, 1951, p. 10. See also some of the reports and books that have dealt with the Nuremberg and other war trials.

5. Review the following books and discuss the contrasting positions set forth: George A. Lundberg, *Can Science Save Us?* (New York: Longmans, Green, 1947); Anthony Standen, *Science Is a Sacred Cow* (New York: Dutton, 1950) (Dutton Everyman Paperback, 1958); Magnus Pyke, *The Science Myth* (New York: Macmillan, 1962).

The first book, written by a man working in the social studies, posits that science is the hope for the future. The author thinks that the methods of investigation (the procedures, the logic) of science are applicable to *any* subject matter. The second book, written by a chemist, criticizes many of his fellow scientists for being so immodest in their worship of science and for making extreme claims in behalf of science. In the third book a scientist attempts to explode what he calls the "myth" that science necessarily contributes to the welfare and the happiness of man.

6. After reading this and the previous chapter and other works, write a short essay entitled "My Philosophy of Science."

7. Evaluate the following quotations:
   (1) "Even the most 'unprejudiced' science is imbedded in philosophy—sometimes in a philosophy that is not very sound or consistent."
   (2) "If science could tell with certainty all that it is capable of telling, it would still leave our most pressing questions unanswered."
   (3) "The tools of science are observation and experiment; the tools of philosophy are discussion and contemplation."
   (4) "In Western culture science . . . is the discovery of useful facts. . . . This factualness of science makes it blind to the difference between the trivial and the significant, the odious and the exquisite, the good and the bad."

(5) "If a scientific age is to be a good civilization, it is essential that increase in knowledge be accompanied by increase in wisdom or in a sense of human values."

SUGGESTED READINGS

BRIDGMAN, PERCY W. *The Way Things Are.* Cambridge: Harvard U. Press, 1959.
Since we cannot separate the observer from the "thing itself," the author stresses an "operational" approach and discusses its implications for physics, biology, and psychology. Our knowledge comes from two sources: observation and introspection.

BROWN, HARCOURT (ed.). *Science and the Creative Spirit: Essays on the Humanistic Aspects of Science.* Toronto: U. of Toronto Press, 1958.
Essays edited for the American Council of Learned Societies. The subtitle describes the book very well.

BURTT, EDWIN ARTHUR. *The Metaphysical Foundations of Modern Physical Science.* Garden City: Doubleday, 1960. (Anchor Book.)
A discussion of the scientific and philosophical development of thought from Copernicus to Newton and the implications of this development for later thinking.

FRANK, PHILIPP. *Philosophy of Science; The Link between Science and Philosophy.* Englewood Cliffs: Prentice-Hall, 1957.
A philosophy of science written from the point of view of operationalism and the unity of science movement. For the more mature student. See also the author's Modern Science and Its Philosophy.

GILLESPIE, CHARLES C. *The Edge of Objectivity; An Essay in the History of Scientific Ideas.* Princeton: Princeton U. Press, 1960.
The author traces the growth of scientific objectivity from Galileo to Einstein and shows how the sciences have become independent of theology, ethics, and politics, which set norms.

HARRISON, GEORGE RUSSELL. *What Man May Be: The Human Side of Science.* New York: Morrow, 1956.
A readable account of what science does mean and may mean in the life of man.

HESSE, MARY B. *Science and the Human Imagination.* London: SCM, 1954.
Science has room for the creative imagination and for recognition of the transcendental, as it describes the world by analogies that reflect the cultural outlook.

HULL, LEWIS W. H. *History and Philosophy of Science; An Introduction.* New York: Longmans, Green, 1959.
Considers scientific ideas from early Greek to modern times in relation to history and philosophy.

KEMENY, JOHN G. *A Philosopher Looks at Science.* Princeton: Van Nostrand, 1959.
A philosopher and mathematician deals with a wide range of subjects, including language, scientific method and explanations, life, mind, values.

MARGENAU, HENRY. *Open Vistas; Philosophical Perspectives of Modern Science.* New Haven: Yale U. Press, 1961.
A stimulating discussion of modern science in relation to human affairs, aesthetics, ethics, and metaphysics.

PIEL, GERARD. *Science in the Cause of Man.* New York: Knopf, 1961.
The author deals in a popular way with many topics, including "Science and Secrecy," "Science in America," and the like.

WERKMEISTER, WILLIAM H. *A Philosophy of Science.* New York: Harper, 1940.
A very good general text on the philosophy of science and the philosophical implications of modern science.

WHITEHEAD, ALFRED NORTH. *The Interpretation of Science.* Ed. by A. H. Johnson. Indianapolis: Bobbs-Merrill, 1961. (Liberal Arts Press.)
Selected essays that make clear the author's philosophy of science and his view of the place of science in contemporary civilization.

————. *Science and the Modern World.* New York: Macmillan, 1925. (Also a Mentor Book, New American Library of World Literature, 1948.)
A study of the relation between science and culture in the Western world during the last three centuries.

PART TWO

MAN AND HIS PLACE
IN THE WORLD

᠅ SEVEN ᠅

THE PHYSICAL SCIENCES AND PHILOSOPHICAL PROBLEMS

Every great scientific achievement and important change in scientific theory affects philosophical and religious beliefs. Consider for a moment how our views of the nature of man and the world have changed as a result of the work of men like Copernicus, Galileo, Newton, Darwin, Freud, Einstein, and Max Planck. Without doubt, other men's achievements will cause equally profound changes in the future.

In this chapter we shall consider the outlook of the physical sciences. Then we shall turn to the biological sciences and the other sciences related to man. We cannot discuss these in detail, but we can indicate some important scientific ideas, some of the philosophical questions that arise, and some of the implications of these newer views of the universe and man.

THE EARTH AND THE CELESTIAL BODIES

The term *universe* refers to the totality of things, to everything that exists. The term thus includes the earth, the sun, the stars, and their contents. The term *world* may also be used in this sense, although commonly we restrict it to the earth and its inhabitants.

Some early Greek thinkers held that the earth was round, and ever afterward this view was held by a small group of educated men. However, even as recently as a few hundred years ago, most people thought of the earth as flat and stationary. Overhead in the canopy of the sky were the sun, the moon, and the stars, with heaven beyond. Underneath the earth were hell and purgatory.

The views of Ptolemy, formulated about 140 A.D., dominated the thinking of many intellectuals during the medieval period. Ptolemy taught that the earth was a fixed sphere at the center of things—this, of course, is the geocentric (earth-centered) view of the universe. A new astronomy in the sixteenth century—the Copernican—led to what is known as the heliocentric (sun-centered) view. The earth was seen to be one among a number of planets that revolve about our sun, which is one of many suns. Somewhat later men discovered more planets and learned that the earth is one of nine planets revolving around our sun.

Our sun is an ordinary star—a "star in the foreground," which looks large because of its comparative proximity to us. According to modern scientific theory, all the planets and lesser bodies of our solar system, whose movements in space are governed by the gravitational pull of the sun, had their origin in the sun. Some may wish to read elsewhere about the nebular and the planetesimal hypotheses, and the modifications of the latter called the "tidal," "encounter," and "double-sun" hypotheses.[1]

Planets seem to us the most important part of our solar system, since it is only on certain types of planets that human life as we know it can exist. Whether or not there are other stars that, like our sun, are surrounded by planets we do not know, because planets are relatively small and only reflect light. If they do exist, we cannot see them through even our most powerful telescopes.

As we look up into the heavens on a clear night, we can see numerous stars—the stellar system. These stars are suns, some of which are many times the size of our sun. Something like 5000 stars can be seen at various times by the unaided human eye. Hundreds of millions can be viewed through powerful telescopes. The stars, of which our sun is one, are grouped in a spiral form, called a *galaxy*. The stars in our galaxy all move through space at the same rate and in the same direction, but they are said to be rotating about a center. The chemical constitution of the sun and the stars is fairly accurately known through spectroscopic analysis of light.

Our vast galaxy is apparently surrounded by even vaster spaces. Astronomers are now talking about "exterior galaxies," "extragalactic nebulae," "island universes," and even "super galaxies." Light travels at a speed of 186,000 miles per second, and today men are talking of millions of light years. Such conceptions simply lie beyond the imagination.

THE NATURE OF MATTER

Equally fascinating are the matter and energy studies that investigate the world's most minute parts. We might ask: Why is there a problem here? Why not just accept physical objects as physical objects and let it go at that? Why should a tree or a stone or a human hand be analyzed into anything

---

[1] For an elaboration of the newer views consult one of the many recent texts that deal with astronomy and the nature of the physical universe.

different from a tree or a stone or a human hand? There are several reasons, as we shall see.

First, particular things, like land forms, oceans, stones, trees, and human bodies, do change—at least they undergo alterations in their outward form. The desk on which I am writing, for example, was once part of a growing tree or trees. The elements in the tree were once elements in the soil and the atmosphere. Processes like growth, decay, weathering, and erosion are always going on.

Second, physical objects undergo or are affected by inner transformations of various kinds. They may pass back and forth between solid state, liquid state, and gaseous state. With sufficient increase in temperature, even metals become liquids or gases. Under pressure objects behave differently.

Third, though we can contact or have experience of particular physical objects through our various sense organs, we cannot experience matter itself. *Matter* is an abstract term for a concept that is applied to any or all conceivable physical things. We experience the colors, shapes, sounds, and other sensations from these physical objects, but, as we have seen in Chapter 3, understanding the nature of the origins of our sensations is one of the difficult problems we face. The history of human thought includes a great variety of interpretations of matter. While a few thinkers, the materialists, have asserted that matter is the one basic existent or that there is nothing except matter, some outstanding thinkers have denied that matter was the primary existent and instead have asserted that mind or spirit or something other than matter had primary importance. Most scientists and philosophers have not held either one of these extreme positions. For the natural scientist, however, matter, or the physical world, has been the area of major concern.

During the sixth and fifth centuries B.C. certain men became curious about the nature of the world. They started a new line of thinking and investigation that, by various paths, has led to our modern conceptions of matter. To trace this development in detail would carry us too far afield and would embrace a considerable portion of the history of philosophy and of science. The qualitative atomism of Anaxagoras was changed by Leucippus and Democritus, who died about 362 B.C., to an atomism in which the atoms are all qualitatively the same and differ only in size, shape, and velocity. Democritus, one of the early materialists, posited that the universe was made up of two parts: first, the plenum (from the Latin *plenus,* meaning "full"), or matter, composed of an infinite number of self-moving, indivisible atoms; second, the vacuum (void), or empty space. The views of Democritus had a profound effect on later thinking.

Early in the nineteenth century, when chemists and physicists were turning their attention to the constitution of matter, John Dalton (1766–1844) found in the atomic theory of Democritus a possible explanation of certain chemical and physical actions and reactions. He laid down the general outlines of the atomic theory that was widely accepted during the nineteenth century. Chemists believed that the elements were definite or fixed and that the atoms of any one element were alike, indivisible, and indestructible. Dalton and others were impressed by the numerical order and relation among the atoms and by the way in which they combined to form molecules and compounds. Since then, of course, atomic theory has undergone extensive revision.

Two methods of studying the nature of matter have been used side by side: the method of chemical and physical analysis, with instruments and apparatus; and the method of mathematical or logical speculation. The investigations are too complicated to describe here, but a few of the significant steps and conclusions can be pointed out.

Significant advances in the knowledge of the nature of matter were made in the period 1895–1900. Wilhelm Roentgen discovered X rays, and Henri Becquerel discovered that uranium affected covered photographic plates. Soon after this, in 1898, Pierre and Marie Curie discovered polonium and radium. The discovery that rays were emitted at high velocities and without any apparent external cause was something of a shock; apparently the elements were not so definite and fixed as men had assumed, and the atom was not indivisible.

The careful and elaborate research of men like J. J. Thomson, Ernest Rutherford, Niels Bohr, Werner Heisenberg, W. Pauli, and others has revolutionized our views of the material universe and ushered in the nuclear age. These men contrived models to interpret the properties of atoms. When these models gave satisfactory results and yielded testable hypotheses they were used; otherwise they were revised or discarded. The atom, it now appears, consists of a small, heavy core, or *nucleus,* which contains almost the entire mass of the atom and bears a positive electric charge. This is surrounded by one or more *electrons* at relatively great distances from the nucleus and from each other. The simplest of all atoms, the hydrogen atom, consists of a single proton as nucleus and a single electron; the composition of other elements is more complicated.

During the last few decades, many able investigators have offered both mathematical and empirical evidence in support of the view that the atom is an exceedingly complicated system, a little world in itself. Each atom appears to be a tiny planetary system in which a minute nucleus contains more than 99.9 percent of the total atomic mass. The center, or nucleus, is no simple unit, however, since there is evidence that certain composite and active nuclei emit particles, variously termed neutrons, positrons, positive mesotrons, negative mesotrons, and the like. The mesotrons are short-lived and join other particles after they are formed. Electrons, which we might call negatively charged planets, circle around the center, or the nuclear sun.

The number and arrangement of the electrons determine the chemical properties of the atom.

The quantum theory was set forth in its early form by Max Planck in 1900, and later developed by Albert Einstein and others. According to this theory, not only matter and electricity but all forms of radiant energy are atomic, in the sense that they are made up of separate items or discrete particles. Planck called the unit of energy the *energy quantum*. When a subatomic particle such as a vibrating electron or proton emits light, the light goes out as a definite quantity of energy. The quantity or amount of energy is not always the same, and it is greater for short waves than for long ones.

An example may be taken from the study of light. From the time of Newton to the nineteenth century, men accepted the corpuscular theory of light. This meant that light was held to travel in the form of tiny, rapidly moving, material particles. During the early nineteenth century this theory was discarded in favor of the undulatory, or wave, theory of light. Light appeared to travel through space in waves much as ripples cover the surface of a pond; scientists therefore assumed that there must be a medium and postulated an invisible ether. The ether theory, widely held in the nineteenth century, has dropped out of contemporary scientific thought. The evidence now seems to indicate that light has an atomic character and travels in bundles, packets, or a stream of particles, somewhat like bullets coming rapidly from a machine gun. For some purposes the wave theory serves more satisfactorily; for other purposes, the quantum theory. These two theories of light illustrate what has been called the "complementarity principle." This principle recognizes the need on occasion for dual types of descriptions and explanations of human experience, as well as the possibility that this need may be grounded in the nature of things and not merely in the limitations of man's knowledge.[2]

Something quite new, and even astonishing from the point of view of the objective science of a few decades ago, is the principle of uncertainty or indeterminacy as set forth by Werner Heisenberg and others. Some people believe that the foundations of science are undergoing radical change. According to Heisenberg, the physicist is forced to choose whether to determine the location of an electron or to ascertain its speed with precision, since he cannot do both. Position and velocity seem to be related in such a manner that no two particles can have the same potential energy, kinetic energy, and direction of spin. At least one of the conditions must be different. This would mean that in subatomic investigations the experimenter cannot, as he

---

[2] This principle, introduced by Niels Bohr, has been emphasized by J. Robert Oppenheimer in *Science and the Common Understanding* (New York: Simon and Schuster, 1954) and in other writings. Henry Margenau in *Open Vistas* (New Haven: Yale U. Press, 1961), p. 162, gives some of these contrasts or pairs of theories as follows: the kinetic theory of gases and the dynamics of molecular motions; the biological theory of life and the physicochemical description of life; introspective analysis of consciousness and its behavioristic description.

did in classical experiments, hold certain factors constant while varying others. If this were the case, it would have profound implications for the notion of cause and effect. Electrons jump from one orbit to another. Physicists are unable to predict where these electrons will go or how long they will take to reach their new position. Where they go depends on the energy of the quantum.[3] The very introduction of the measuring instruments seems to change what is under observation. Is it merely that something is lacking in the conditions of the observer and in our measuring instruments? If so, better conditions and instruments would alter the situation. Many people believe, however, that it is more than that—that it is in the nature of certain subatomic particles themselves that not all factors may be determined simultaneously, and that there is a genuine uncertainty, or chance, element in nature.

Just what this uncertainty means cannot be stated with any degree of assurance. The principle of indeterminacy has been widely accepted among scientists and has influenced thinking in philosophy. The whole issue is packed with speculation and controversy.

SPACE-TIME AND RELATIVITY

From early days, views of space and time have changed as the horizons of human knowledge have been extended. With the growth of reflective thinking, men have come to use the terms *space* and *time* each with two different meanings. A distinction has been made between perceptual space and perceptual time, on the one hand, and conceptual space and conceptual time, on the other hand. Perceptual space is the space in which we live and move— for example, the distance between objects and the areas through which these objects move. Perceptual time is the time which we experience day by day— the time at which we get up in the morning, eat our meals, meet our friends, continue at work, and retire at night. These experiences are parts of direct awareness or sense perception. We walk a certain distance, and we wait a specific time.

Conceptual space and time are the idealized space and time of geometry and other forms of mathematics. Conceptual space and time are the space and time about which we think when we ask about their nature, and when we ask whether or not there is some whole of which all the particular spaces and times are a part. They are the space and time to which the philosopher refers when he asks whether they are limited or unlimited, subjective or objective.

---

[3] Because of an increasing number of variables some problems in connection with the nature of atomic structure are staggering in their complexity. The "exclusion principle" or "Pauli principle" was introduced to exclude some possibilities, on a common-sense basis, so that men could concentrate attention on the fewer remaining possibilities. The study of the atom and the uncertainty and exclusion principles have called for new types and systems of mathematics.

Let us look, first, at the traditional view of space and time. Apart from a few philosophers like Immanuel Kant, who argued that space and time were not in the outer world but were ways in which the mind of man perceives and organizes the world, most men until very recently have thought that space and time were real, separate entities, though entities of a very special kind. Space was distinguished by the property of extension, and all the elements of space were of the same nature. Space extended in all directions indefinitely unless stopped by something different from space. Time was characterized by duration. Each instant or division of time was similar to every other bit of time, and time would go on forever unless stopped by something different outside it. Different events were distinguished and separated by two kinds of relations or intervals. One kind of relation had to do with their location or position in space; the other relation had to do with time, or their location in the continuous flow of duration. Time and space were fixed and definite, and they were experienced in essentially the same way by all normal people. While motion takes place in space and in time, it does not materially affect them.

Until early in the twentieth century, the traditional views of space and time were not seriously questioned.

RELATIVITY

A new "Copernican Revolution" in human thinking has been taking place in recent years. In 1887 Albert A. Michelson and Edward W. Morley obtained experimental results that did not fit into the nineteenth-century ideas of the physical universe. In succeeding years the difficulties increased. In 1905 Einstein suggested a new approach. With the publication of further papers ten years later and with the verification in 1919 of some of his predictions by English astronomers, Einstein's theory of relativity came to be almost universally accepted. Soon men were talking about space-time, the curvature of space, relative motion systems, and frames of reference.

What is meant, in simple terms, by the notion of relativity? Let us start by considering some common human experiences. We all know that the distance from particular cities or points on the surface of the earth varies with, or is relative to, the position of the observer. To ask the distance "to New York" is meaningless unless we have some particular point of reference in mind, and can ask the distance "to New York from. . . ."

Have you ever stood on the bridge of a wide river, looking over the railing at the water below, and then had the sudden impression that the river was standing still and the bridge moving? If one loses sight of the banks of the river, it is possible to get a sensation similar to that which one ordinarily has when looking over the rear of a moving boat. Leaning over the rear rail of a boat, one may suddenly get the notion that he is at rest and the water is moving. If you lie on your back on the grass, looking at the clouds as they go by, you may get the feeling that the clouds are still and you are moving.

Most of us have had the peculiar experience of sitting in a railway train at a station and receiving the impression that our train was moving, only to find in a minute or two that it was the train on the next track that was in motion. Until we could see the station or some other "fixed" object, we could not be certain. Again, if a train beside ours or other objects about us move as we move, we may get the impression that we are not moving but are at rest. Somewhat similar impressions may be had at an airport.

The literature on relativity contains various illustrations from moving ships. Imagine a ship with a flat topdeck steaming along a bay fairly near the shore. A man standing on the deck at a point exactly halfway between the bow and the stern of the ship rolls two balls along the deck, one toward the bow and the other toward the stern. He starts them at exactly the same time and with the same force. Another man, standing on the cliff, watches this operation from the shore. Do the balls travel the same distance? Do they travel at the same speed? Do they arrive at the bow and at the stern at the same time? Will the answers be the same for both men? Now stop and think this problem through before reading further.

For the man in the middle of the deck, the two balls will appear to arrive at about the same time, traveling the same distance at the same speed. For the man on the cliff, however, one ball will appear to move much faster and farther than the other ball, even though they both arrive at the same time. He will insist that the ball that rolled toward the bow moved at the original speed on the deck plus the speed of the ship, and that its distance was half the length of the deck plus the distance the boat moved while the ball was in motion. He will insist that the ball that moved toward the stern traveled a length equal to half the length of the deck minus the distance the boat moved while the ball was in motion, and that its speed was the original speed on the deck minus the speed of the boat. Which man is right? Obviously, they are both right. Their answers differ because one man has viewed the performance from the point of reference of the ship while the other man took the cliff as his point of reference.

Motion and the point of view of the observer are much more important than was formerly recognized. There is no one true movement or frame of reference when we are thinking about the events of the world.

SPACE-TIME

Why is the concept "space-time" coming into use? Recent investigations have shown that space and time are crucially interrelated. Leaders in this field have come to think that neither space nor time is fundamentally separate and distinct. Both are cross sections of what might be called *space-time*. Time is sometimes said to be a fourth dimension of space.

Let us look for a moment at this problem of dimensions. If we wish to locate a particular point on a plane figure, a sheet of paper, a blackboard, or even the surface of the ground, only two dimensions of space are necessary. If we wish to locate a point within space, not on a recognized surface, as in a room, we need three dimensions of space. If, however, we wish to locate an event like an explosion in midair on a moving airplane, we need three dimensions of space and one dimension of time, or three dimensions of *where* and one of *when*.

These facts seem sufficiently commonplace until we are told that these four dimensions are interchangeable, so that what is a period of time for one person may be distance in space for another. For example, if a person remains at one spot relative to the earth for a length of time, say five hours, and some-one could observe him from Mars, the observer would state that the person on earth moved through a certain distance in space, since the earth is moving rapidly. Each observer, we are told, "slices up" space-time into space and time in a manner that is dependent on his motion system or his point of view.

Expressions of time order, such as *before, after,* and *simultaneously,* are relative. Mass, length, and duration are dependent on the speed at which the observer is moving. We are also told that as velocity increases, such mechanisms as clocks tend to slow down and the human body ages more slowly.

The arrangement of stars and planets, as we may see them on a clear night, does not exist in that order except from our present view. We see one star as it existed four or five years ago, another as it existed a few thousand years ago, others as they existed a million years ago. A star could go out of existence and we could continue to "see" it for many years.

In the light of recent studies on the nature of space and of time and their relationship, it is difficult to think of one of them alone or to insist that *our* vantage point is the only one or the "correct" one. However, while space and time seem to be interrelated and interdependent, there are important differences between them which cannot be ignored. Whereas space exhibits three dimensions—length, breadth, and height—and we can come and go in space, time exhibits one dimension—from the past to the future—and there appears to be no return.

The following quotation indicates that other points of view are possible:

Doctor Abbott pictures intelligent beings whose whole experience is confined to a plane, or other space of two dimensions, who have no faculties by which they can become conscious of anything outside that space and no means of moving off the surface on which they live. He then asks the reader, who has consciousness of the third dimension, to imagine a sphere descending upon the plane of Flatland and passing through it. How will the inhabitants regard this phenomenon? They will not see the approaching sphere and will have no conception of its solidity. They will only be conscious of the circle in which it cuts their plane. This circle, at first a point, will gradually increase in diameter, driving the inhabitants of Flatland outwards from its circumference, and this will go on until half the sphere has passed through the plane, when the circle will gradually contract to a point and then vanish, leaving the Flatlanders in undisturbed possession of their country. . . . Their experience will be that of a circular obstacle gradually expanding or growing, and then contracting, and they will attribute to *growth in time* what the external observer in three dimensions assigns to motion in the third dimension. Transfer this analogy to a movement of the fourth dimension through three-dimensional space. Assume the past and future of the universe to be all depicted in four-dimensional space and visible to any being who has consciousness of the fourth dimension. If there is motion of our three-dimensional space relative to the fourth dimension, all the changes we experience and assign to the flow of time will be due simply to this movement, the whole of the future as well as the past always existing in the fourth dimension.[4]

SOME IMPLICATIONS AND CONCLUDING QUESTIONS

The brief summary statements that have been made regarding the universe, matter, space, time, and relativity serve as a reminder of some of the main points in the scientific view of the universe. Since the sciences furnish philosophy with a large part of the factual, descriptive, and theoretical knowledge on the basis of which philosophy formulates its interpretations of life and the world, the philosophy of any age is always inseparably connected with the science of that age. Any basic changes in scientific outlook are likely to produce reactions in philosophy.

On the basis of our general knowledge of scientific methods and outlook, what are some of the philosophical questions that present themselves? Of the many questions that may arise, there are six especially worth noting.

1. *Is the universe orderly or capricious, and, if orderly, what is the nature of the order?* While there may be *some* spontaneity and a degree of uncertainty even in the physical realm dealt with by the natural sciences, there does not seem to be any area that is genuinely capricious and chaotic. In fact, scientists are more and more impressed with the orderliness of the universe. From the formation and fall of the tiny snowflakes to the orbits of the planets and the solar systems, there is regularity.

If the world is orderly rather than capricious and chaotic, what is the nature of its orderliness? For example, is the world mechanistic, or is there purpose operating throughout the process?

4 William Garnett, in Edwin Abbott's *Flatland: a Romance of Many Dimensions, by A. Square* (Boston: Little, Brown, 1926), pp. xi–xii. (Reprinted, 6th ed.; New York: Dover, 1952.)

The older conceptions of a mechanical world of "dead" matter, the "Newtonian world machine," and the "indivisible atom" (the "building blocks" of the universe) seem to be breaking down. A revolution under way in the physical sciences appears to indicate that nature is not to be compared with a machine and that the concepts of possibility and of becoming are not vain human illusions. These changes have profound implications for a philosophy of inorganic nature, as well as for our views of life, man, mind, values, and the like. This question is discussed in later chapters.

2. *What is the nature of matter? What are physical things?* Earlier scientists and philosophers made clear-cut distinctions between the primary qualities of matter, like extension, solidity, figure, and motion, which were supposed to be permanent fundamental properties of matter, and the secondary qualities, like color, sound, odor, and taste, which were often thought to be more subjective or to result from the way in which the primary qualities affect knowing organisms. Primary qualities were thought to be objective and to exist in things themselves, while secondary qualities were supposed to be subjective and to exist only in minds that experience them. Matter as now viewed by scientists appears to be something quite different from the physical objects that "contain" the qualities experienced by us in our daily affairs. There seems to be little similarity between the two ways of looking at things; yet the scientific account is needed to explain some events in our everyday lives. In the newer scientific account of matter, both the primary and the secondary qualities seem to disappear, leaving us with centers of energy or force. This does not mean that matter and its qualities are not both permanent and real. They may be approaches or aspects of our world from different points of view.

One assertion regarding the nature of matter appears to be beyond serious doubt: the studies of the nature of matter lack finality. We are told that matter is energy. When we ask, "What is energy?" we are told that it is electronic in nature. When we ask, "What is electronic energy?" we are likely to be told that it is process or potentiality for doing things or that the question itself is unanswerable. There may be some truth in the whimsical remark of a physicist that "energy is a thing that is defined so that it can be understood and conserved." We shall need to follow carefully the investigations that are still under way. It is possible that matter cannot be studied successfully by itself; it may be inseparably connected with a series of processes and events yet to be considered.

3. *Are space and time limited or unlimited, and what is their nature?* Whether space and time are limited or unlimited, finite or infinite, is a problem that has puzzled men at many different periods in history. Some scientists and philosophers have thought of time as proceeding without beginning or end, and of space as extending in all directions without limit. We can move bodies,

but space and time seem to remain fixed. We can imagine that an object, like a building, does not exist, but we cannot seem to think away the space that such an object occupies. If we think of space as unlimited, then we can go in imagination to the most distant star and beyond to space that stretches out without limit. This is hard for many people to believe or conceptualize.

Yet if we think of space and time as limited or finite, we also run into difficulties. If there is an edge to space, what is beyond? If we could go to this edge and hurl a javelin outward, as the early Greeks suggested, it would either go on, in which case there is more space, or be thrown back, in which case there is an object or obstacle that also must occupy space. To think of an edge to space, or of nonspace, is difficult. If we think of time as limited, we may find ourselves saying, "There was a time when time was not."

The theories of space-time and relativity offer a new approach that seems to eliminate the older paradox. In this view, space may be finite though unbounded, for, in addition to the curvature of space in the neighborhood of matter that is said to produce a gravitational attraction, there is a curvature of space that is inherent in its nature. Let us use an example that is inexact since it takes our thoughts from the nature of space to a physical object, yet may help us to understand the point. The surface of the earth is limited, yet it is unbounded, since it curves back on itself.[5] There is no edge or end to the earth's surface. We are told that, apart from irregularities or a "puckering" near matter, the curvature of space is uniform, so that space is spherical.

4. *Is the universe "running down" or is it a continuous creative process?* This question is frequently raised in discussions regarding the nature of the universe. The principle of the "conservation of energy," included in the first law of thermodynamics, holds that energy cannot be destroyed or created— that there is a constant amount of it. The second law of thermodynamics, however, indicates that all self-acting processes in nature are tending toward a common temperature and energy level, which means that this energy is not destroyed but is unavailable for man's use. If energy tends to pass from available forms to unavailable forms, then, it is claimed, the universe is tending toward equilibrium, or is "running down."

The apparent "loss of energy" seems to be true for man's machines and for the processes that he manipulates. It may be true for some processes and systems and not for others. That it is true for the universe as a whole is doubtful. If the universe is infinite and has neither beginning nor end, there must be an infinite and creative source of energy. If, on the other hand, the universe is finite and had a beginning, there must be some source of energy that causes creative processes to overcome or outweight the destructive processes. The universe itself may be a continuous creative process.[6]

5 See Lincoln Barnett, *The Universe and Dr. Einstein* (New York: New American Library of World Literature, 1952), p. 104. (Mentor ed.)

6 See Stephen Toulmin, *et al.*, *Metaphysical Beliefs* (London: SCM, 1957), pp. 28 ff.

5. What is man's place in the universe? Are there habitable worlds other than ours? The facts and theories of the physical sciences lead us into a world that is quantitative, mathematical, and formal. These scientists are not concerned with pain and pleasure, good and evil, life and personality. This point of view is expressed by the statement, "Astronomically speaking, man is insignificant." A different view is expressed in one man's reply: "Astronomically speaking, man is the astronomer." If the great size and age of the world appear to reduce human life to insignificance, we need to remember that it is our minds which interpret, and perhaps discover meaning in, the process.

The question of whether life exists in any other part of this vast universe is being asked more frequently now that we are reaching out toward other planets in our solar system. Is the earth the one spot in all this vast space where life as we know it exists? Many scientists think that life may exist in other parts of this immense universe. The answers to questions such as this may be found in the years ahead as we press our investigation to other planets in our solar system and to outer space. Even on these "nearby" planets the atmospheric conditions are thought to be different from those that exist on the earth.

While it is possible that no other parts of the universe offer conditions favorable to the development of life as we know it, it is also possible, as some have suggested, that the universe contains a multitude of inhabited planets, some with beings much further advanced than we.[7] Even if planets surround other suns, we cannot see these planets because of the great distance and because they are lost in the bright light of their suns, as we said earlier.

6. What is the place of the knower, or the subject, in statements like, "I know that . . ."? Do we know the world as it is, or do we contribute something to the world we know—that is, do we alter what is to be known by the mere fact of our observations? The notion of the "standpoint of the observer" is coming to be investigated more fully than it was during the late nineteenth century. This may be part of the effect of the breakup of the older mechanistic world view, which seemed to leave little or no place for man. Much more depends on the "knower" or the point of view of the observer than was formerly thought. The scientist cannot leave himself out of the picture without running the danger of developing a blind spot or some dogmatism.[8]

Some philosophers will protest at this point and say that the "observer" need not be a person or a mind but may be a recording instrument, such as a photographic plate. The photographic plate, however, must be analyzed, interpreted, and explained. By itself it does not know; it is an instrument.

---

7 See Harlow Shapley, *Of Stars and Men* (Boston: Beacon, 1958). (Also in paperback, New York: Washington Square Press, 1958.)

8 See Michael Polanyi, *Personal Knowledge: Towards a Post-Critical Philosophy* (Chicago: U. of Chicago Press, 1958).

Our minds interpret the world. Do they also play some part in creating our world?

Developments in the physical sciences make it appear that matter, motion, space, time, and relativity are all bound up together and cannot be considered as separate entities. While we have yet to consider the evidence from the sciences which deal with life, including man, the emphasis on the point of view of the observer probably means that the concepts mentioned above are also bound up with evolution, life, mind, and values.

QUESTIONS AND PROJECTS

1. Review Questions

(1) In a philosophy book why are we considering developments in the various sciences?

(2) State briefly the main changes that have occurred since ancient times in man's view of the physical world.

(3) What is meant by the *world*, the *universe*, the *solar system*, the *stellar system?*

(4) Why do we often speak of "the problem of matter"?

(5) State briefly the changes that have taken place in the view of the nature of matter during the last one hundred and fifty years.

(6) State and give examples to show the difference between perceptual and conceptual space and time.

(7) Give the traditional views of space and time; then indicate why the concepts of "relativity" and "space-time" are coming to be used. Be ready to give examples that clarify the meaning of these terms.

(8) State in your own words the general conclusions that can be drawn from recent studies in the physical sciences. Be ready to discuss such questions as these: Is the universe orderly? What conclusions can be drawn regarding the nature of matter? Why is it difficult to think of space or time as either limited or unlimited? Is the universe running down or is it a creative process? What is man's place in the universe? What is the place of the observer, knower, or subject?

2. This chapter pointed out that significant changes in the sciences tend to influence philosophical thinking. What are the most recent trends in the physical sciences, and in what ways may these changes affect philosophy? For a report on interviews with some scientists see Lawrence Galton, "Science Stands at Awesome Thresholds," *New York Times Magazine,* December 2, 1962, pp. 38–39, 90, 92, 94.

3. Early in the seventeenth century Father Inchofer, outraged at the suggestion that the earth moves, is reported to have said, "The opinion of the earth's motion is of all heresies the most abominable, the most pernicious, the most scandalous: the immovability of the earth is thrice sacred; the argument against the immortality of the soul, the existence of God, and the incarnation should be tolerated sooner than an argument to prove that the earth moves." What would impel Father Inchofer to make such a statement?

4. What is your reaction to the statement of some scientists to the effect that science deals with a world of symbols rather than with the familiar substantial world of everyday experience? For example, are there two different tables or two interpretations of one table? See Sir Arthur S. Eddington, *The Nature of the Physical World* (New York: Macmillan, 1937), pp. ix–xvii; Bertrand Russell, *The Problems of Philosophy* (London: Oxford U. Press, 1912), Ch. I. (Also Galaxy paperback.)

5. Consult a standard history of Greek philosophy and become acquainted with Zeno's famous paradoxes of "Achilles and the Tortoise" and "The Flying Arrow." Zeno, a Greek philosopher of the fifth century B.C., found it necessary to deny the reality of motion. What did he assume, and how could one refute his position?

6. Compare the philosophies of time set forth by Henri Bergson and Alfred North Whitehead. Bergson's views will be found in his *Creative Evolution* (New York: Holt, 1911); and *Time and Free Will* (New York: Macmillan, 1913). For a brief account, see Joseph A. Leighton, *The Field of Philosophy* (4th ed.; New York: Appleton-Century-Crofts, 1930), Ch. XXIV, "Temporalism." For Whitehead's approach see William W. Hammerschmidt's *Whitehead's Philosophy of Time* (New York: King's Crown, 1947).

7. Is there a difference between the Occidental, or Western, and the Oriental, or Eastern, view of time? In *The Meeting of East and West* (New York: Macmillan, 1946), p. 343, F. S. C. Northrop suggests that there is such a difference. What is said to be the difference, and can you give further evidence to support or refute the claim?

SUGGESTED READINGS

ABRO, A. D'. *The Evolution of Scientific Thought from Newton to Einstein.* 2nd ed. rev. and enl.; New York: Dover, 1950.
   For the more advanced student in science and philosophy: Part III discusses "The General Theory of Relativity," and Part IV, "The Methodology of Science."

BARNETT, LINCOLN K. *The Universe and Dr. Einstein.* New York: New American Library of World Literature, 1952. (Mentor ed., Foreword by Albert Einstein.)
   A clear and interesting exposition for the layman of the theory of relativity. One of the better attempts at popularizing recent scientific trends and suggesting some implications of these views.

CHERONIS, NICHOLAS D., PARSONS, JAMES B., AND RONNEBERG, CONRAD E. *The Study of the Physical World.* 3rd ed.; Boston: Houghton Mifflin, 1958.
   See chapters that contain discussions of the recent theories of matter and its structure, the earth, planets, and stars.

EDDINGTON, SIR ARTHUR S. *The Nature of the Physical World.* New York: Macmillan, 1937. (Reprinted, Ann Arbor: U. of Michigan Press, Ann Arbor Books, 1961.)

The author discusses the new outlooks in the physical sciences, including relativity theory, the quantum theory, and notions about the nature of science. He also discusses the philosophical implications of these newer trends.

FRANK, PHILIPP. *Philosophy of Science: The Link between Science and Philosophy.* Englewood Cliffs: Prentice-Hall, 1957.
A philosophy of science written from the point of view of operationalism and the unity of science movement. For the more mature student. See also the author's Relativity: A Richer Truth.

GAMOW, GEORGE. *The Atom and Its Nucleus.* Englewood Cliffs: Prentice-Hall, 1961. (Spectrum Book.)
A paperback in which the author explains, with the use of many charts and pictures, the recent developments in nuclear science.

————. *One, Two, Three . . . Infinity: Facts and Speculations of Science.* New York: Viking, 1953.
Written to acquaint the reader with the newer views of space and time, the fourth dimension, numbers, the atomic theory, and the like.

JONES, G. O., ROTBLATT, J., AND WHITROW, G. T. *Atoms and the Universe.* New York: Scribner's, 1957.
A discussion of the structure of matter as indicated by recent astrophysical and nuclear research methods.

LYTTLETON, R. A. *Man's View of the Universe.* Boston: Little, Brown, 1961.
Chapters are included that deal with the earth, planetary and solar systems, galaxies, and the like.

MUNITZ, MILTON KARL. *Space, Time, and Creation: Philosophical Aspects of Scientific Cosmology.* Glencoe: Free Press, 1957.
A discussion of recent trends and methods in science and their bearing on representative cosmological schemes.

REICHENBACH, HANS. *Atom and Cosmos.* New York: Braziller, 1957.
Written for the nonspecialist by a man familiar with the fields of natural science and philosophy.

Scientific American. *New Astronomy.* New York: Simon and Schuster, 1956.
A nontechnical presentation of some recent discoveries regarding the solar system, stars, galaxies, and so on.

SHAMOS, MORRIS H., AND MURPHY, GEORGE M. (eds.). *Recent Advances in Science, Physics and Applied Mathematics.* New York: New York U. Press, 1956.
The recent findings and trends in atomic structure and electronuclear devices appraised by Bethe, Condon, Rabi, and others.

WEIZSACKER, C. J. VON. *The World View of Physics.* Chicago: U. of Chicago Press, 1952.
Deals with the physical world view and some philosophical implications. See the author's The History of Nature *and* Rise of Modern Physics.

EIGHT

LIFE AND ITS DEVELOPMENT

In recent decades man's attention has been directed to advances in the physical sciences, especially to the new power from nuclear fission and fusion that has been placed in man's hands for good or for evil. These achievements have been more spectacular, but no more important, than advances in the life sciences, which have great implications for our understanding of man. New knowledge in the life sciences gives rise to philosophical problems of primary importance. We turn now to questions concerning the origin, nature, and development of life and to the implications of recent scientific research and thinking in these areas.

THE ORIGIN AND NATURE OF LIVING FORMS

As man looks around him he is impressed by the amazing variety of living things on and in the earth, in the waters, and in the air. And then the microscope discloses a world of life invisible to the naked eye. Living forms seem to occupy almost every conceivable place in nature. How do organisms differ from the inorganic processes that we have been considering? Where did life come from, and what are some of its characteristics?

THE ORIGIN OF LIFE

Since primitive times, men have observed that living things tend to reproduce their kind. Does all life come from some one source or are the different kinds of life completely separate and distinct in origin? At least six answers have been suggested at one time or another.

1. All matter is alive, and there is no need to make any clear-cut distinction between organic and inorganic matter. The theory that all nature is alive or animated, a view held by a number of early Greek thinkers, was known as *hylozoism*. But from the days of ancient Greece to the present, most men have thought that there is a rigid separation between the organic

and the inorganic. Recently the discovery of viruses, bacteriophage, and filter passers, and the knowledge that living and nonliving matter are composed of the same elements, tends to make this separation seem less rigid.

2. The theory of spontaneous generation appears in the philosophical poem *De Rerum Natura,* written by the Roman poet Lucretius in the first century before Christ. It was held by many people until about 1860, when Louis Pasteur proved fairly conclusively that it was false. Men had noticed that animal forms, such as worms, insects, mice, and frogs, seem at times to come out of the earth, and had assumed that the earth, under proper conditions of warmth and moisture, could generate living forms. Decaying meat and water exposed to the air swarmed with living things. Pasteur, by comparing sterilized and unsterilized liquids, proved that these microorganisms are propagated by their kind, and that they are carried in the dust-laden air.

3. The view that life came to earth from some other planet was set forth by Helmholtz, Lord Kelvin, and Svante Arrhenius. While it is conceivable that life might arise from ultramicroscopic living forms driven by light radiation, from cosmic dust, or through organisms hidden in the crevices of meteorites, this theory is not only highly improbable but really provides no answer. It merely transfers the problem of the origin of life to another planet or star.

4. The theory of direct creation by a special act of God has taken several different forms. One, a literal interpretation of the first chapters of Genesis, confines the entire creative process to six days of twenty-four hours each. According to this view, all living species were created at one time and place. A second group of interpretations attempts to mediate between the Biblical and modern scientific accounts. The geological-day theory, the vision-day theory, and the restitution theory are examples of such interpretations.[1] To many people these views fail to do justice to either the Biblical or the scientific accounts of creative processes.

5. Living creatures emerged or developed gradually from nonliving material. From what we know today, life seems always to arise from other life. Yet as the story is pressed back, the distinction between animals and plants and between living and nonliving forms tends to disappear. Now and then some biochemist announces that he has succeeded in creating life artificially by combining carbon and other inorganic substances. Actually, no one has yet produced living forms in this manner. What could have happened or what did happen in the past is difficult to say, except that life, through some

---

[1] The geological-day theory interprets the "days" in the Genesis account as long geological periods. The vision-day theory assumes that the writer had visions, on six consecutive days, of these things being created; they were not actually created in six days. The restitution theory assumes that evolution took place, then a catastrophe destroyed everything, and God restored it as related in the book of Genesis. Read the first two chapters of Genesis. Many scholars believe there are two accounts of creation, one given in Genesis 1:1–2:4a, the other in Genesis 2:4b ff.

kind of creative process, appeared on earth. If living matter should be created from the nonliving, it would not seriously affect our general outlook on life. The chief effect of the idea would be to increase our appreciation of what has been called "nonliving" matter.

6. Philosophers and scientists today, with few exceptions, believe that the present living forms on the earth, including man, originated and developed through some process of evolution—that is, through a slow, gradual, and progressive change. This does not rule out the idea of creation by God, if God is interpreted as the creative agency or the creative synthesis, although the idea of a special act of creation at one time or place would be rejected.

THE NATURE OF LIVING FORMS

While it is usual to make a fairly clear distinction between the organic and the inorganic, the two are very closely related. Many characteristics of the inorganic world, such as physical and chemical actions and reactions, are present also in the organic realm. The chemical elements in living matter, including those in man, are the same as those in such things as water, air, earth, and the stars. Apparently no material that is present in organic matter is absent from inorganic matter.

Certain internal and external conditions do appear to be necessary, however, for life. For example, in man there must be a certain chemical balance, or equilibrium, in the blood, spinal fluid, and glandular secretions. Certain physical equilibria of temperature and pressure must be maintained, and supplies of oxygen, hydrogen, carbon, and nitrogen must be present in breathable, eatable, and drinkable forms. These are only a few of the conditions necessary to maintain human life.

Among the characteristics of living things are organization, movement, metabolism, growth, reproduction, irritability, adaptability, and dynamic equilibrium.[2] *Organization* is reflected in characteristic form and appearance. The structural and functional unit, the cell, exhibits the characteristics of life. Living things are also characterized by special kinds of *movement*. They can swim, wiggle, run, or fly. In plants, of course, movement is much more restricted. *Metabolism* consists of the processes of building up (anabolism) and breaking down (catabolism), two processes that go on simultaneously throughout life. In early life the building-up processes are dominant; in later life, the breaking-down processes. While life continues, there is a constant assimilation and transformation of matter and energy. *Growth* toward

[2] For the characteristics of living things see Claude A. Villee, *et al., General Zoology* (Philadelphia: Saunders, 1958), pp. 14 ff. For a discussion of "Living Versus Nonliving Systems" see George W. Hunter and F. R. Hunter, *College Zoology* (Philadelphia: Saunders, 1949), pp. 56 ff. Fig. 32, p. 58 of the latter book shows that where the same characteristics can be applied to both living and nonliving things there are other differences. One characteristic alone does not suffice to distinguish between a living and a nonliving system.

maturity is a characteristic of all living creatures. The young must increase in size and be prepared for the more complex functions of later life. There are definite limits to the size that any given species of animal ordinarily attains. *Reproduction* is essential if the species is to survive. Apart from some simple forms of reproduction, like cell division or budding, every animal begins life as a fertilized germ cell and develops through the embryonic and infant stages to maturity. This ability of a living thing "to form copies of itself," but copies with innovations or variations, is one of the fundamental characteristics of organisms. *Irritability* is the power to respond to stimuli, both internal and external. This sensitivity is the basis of adjustment. In higher organisms it functions through an elaborate nervous system. *Adaptability* is closely related to irritability and leads to changes that produce harmony or satisfactory adjustment to environmental situations. Living forms that are adaptable are more likely to survive changes in external conditions. *Dynamic equilibrium* is the ability to maintain a balance in the flow of matter and energy within the organism's system. It includes the power of the organism to use its own energy to meet disturbances successfully, and some living forms can restore lost parts or have the functions taken over by uninjured parts.

We see that life, within broad limits, tends to press out in all directions and endeavors to increase its range and powers. It is usually self-moving, capable of initiating an action. It is selective and inventive and is able to meet new situations and emergencies. It is self-adjusting, self-maintaining, self-preserving, and self-perpetuating. There is an interdependent relationship between the parts and the whole. Under normal conditions the parts of an organism grow and develop as one integrated whole. When we reach the very complex and highly integrated members of the animal kingdom, other characteristics and powers appear, such as heightened sensations, a higher form of memory, selective choice, consciousness, and intelligence. These new qualities are dealt with later in our study.

ORGANIC EVOLUTION

Evolution in the biological sense, or organic evolution, is a process of growth or development of all forms of life. It means that "the present is the child of the past and the parent of the future." The theory of organic evolution posits that the plants and animals we see about us today are the descendants of ancestors which were, on the whole, somewhat simpler. These ancestors were the offspring of still simpler ancestors, reaching back for millions of years to exceedingly low forms of life or to life's beginnings. The numerous species of animals and plants have developed by natural descent, with modification, from previously existing types. In general, the theory is that life proceeds "from the simple to the more complex" or "from the lower to higher forms."[3] *Evolution* is the name for this process of change; *evolutionism,* or the theory of evolution, is the interpretation of how the process proceeds.

Does the concept of evolution apply in all realms and areas of the universe, or only in the realm of animate things? Sir Julian Huxley speaks for many scientists when he says:

"Evolution in the most general terms is a natural process of irreversible change, which generates novelty, variety, and increase of organization: and all reality can be regarded in one aspect as evolution. Biological evolution is only one sector or phase of this total process. There is also the inorganic sector and the psycho-social or human sector. The phases succeed each other in time, the later being based on and evolving out of the earlier. The inorganic phase is pre-biological, the human is post-biological."[4] Again he says that "This is one of the first public occasions on which it has been frankly faced that all aspects of reality are subject to evolution, from atoms and stars to fish and flowers, from fish and flowers to human societies and values— indeed, that all reality is a single process of evolution. And ours is the first period in which we have acquired sufficient knowledge to begin to see the outline of this vast process as a whole."[5]

While some use the term *cosmic evolution,* there is disagreement as to whether or not there is universal evolution connecting all the various forms or types of changes. Certainly many of the concepts used in one area, like heredity and the struggle for existence in the area of organic evolution, are quite inappropriate when we are talking about other types of evolution. Unless it is understood that we are speaking from some one frame of refer- ence, we should always put some distinguishing adjective, such as *stellar, geological, atomic, organic, cultural,* before the term *evolution.*

In this and the following sections of this chapter, we shall consider organic or biological evolution. There are, it is estimated, well over a million species of animals. Did each species originate separately, or did it begin in some simple organism from which the present varieties of species have evolved? Practi- cally without exception, scientists and philosophers today accept the latter view, that of organic evolution, since the evidence appears so conclusive. Differences of opinion do exist, however, especially regarding details.

MISINTERPRETATIONS OF EVOLUTION

To understand clearly what evolution is, one must rid oneself of some prevalent misconceptions. First, the theory of evolution does not mean or

---

[3] The term *higher* here means increased structural complexity and range of functions, or powers.
[4] "The Emergence of Darwinism," in *Evolution After Darwin,* Sol Tax and Charles Callender (eds.) (3 vols.; Chicago: U. of Chicago Press, 1960), I, *The Evolution of Life,* p. 18. Copyright 1960 by The University of Chicago.
[5] *Ibid.,* III, *Issues in Evolution,* p. 249.

imply that all living forms are tending toward man, or that any present species is changing into any other species. It does not mean that man "came from" the monkey or is a "made-over monkey." Man has had a long ancestry, extending back through earlier species of man. Though the ape and man likely have common ancestors, the ape is not man's ancestor. The other mammals which exist today have also had a long ancestry. Most students of evolution illustrate the relationships among living creatures by a tree with many long branches. Once a branch has been separated from the trunk, or

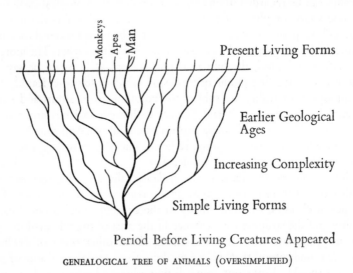

GENEALOGICAL TREE OF ANIMALS (OVERSIMPLIFIED)

main branch, it does not return; it has gone off in a new and separate direction. Existing species are represented by the tips of the branches only. Many of the branches have probably reached "dead ends," so to speak. A few others have died and disappeared in the past. There is no possibility of any present species of animal giving rise to animals which are in a different evolutionary line. To locate connections and relationships, it is necessary to delve into the distant past.

Second, the *theory of evolution* is not synonymous with *Darwinism*. Darwinism is one explanation of how one species may have arisen from another. A few years ago, when an outstanding scientist said that he did not accept Darwinism, he was quoted, incorrectly, as stating that he did not believe in evolution. One may reject Darwin's explanation of how one species arose from another, as many do, and still accept the theory of evolution.

Third, the theory of evolution is not the explanation of the nature or origin of life itself. It is the theoretical interpretation of a process, or the descriptive interpretation of how one species was derived from another. Such interpretations may be mechanistic, vitalistic, or teleological; they may be nontheistic or theistic. Just as a knowledge of the development of the individual does not imply any single attitude toward life, so an acceptance of the theory of evolution does not in itself force upon us any single philosophy of life or any one interpretation of the universe.

Fourth, the theory of evolution is not necessarily a denial of religion and of belief in God. If you do not find it difficult to believe in God when you know that the individual has come to adulthood as the result of a slow process of growth, why should the knowledge that mankind has been the result of a process of development cause so much concern? We shall return to this topic later in the chapter.

HISTORY AND THEORIES OF EVOLUTION

The doctrine of evolution originated with the ancient Greeks, but their views were largely speculative. Anaximander (c. 611–546 B.C.) thought that living creatures were brought into being on the seashore by the heat of the sun, and that man was descended from other kinds of animals. Empedocles (c. 490–430 B.C.) said that from the evolving earth came plants and animals. He had the bizarre notion that organs or members of all kinds developed separately and were brought together later, at which time only the fittest members survived. Anaxagoras (c. 500–428 B.C.) thought that the seeds of life had their source outside the earth and developed in the moisture under the influence of the sun's heat and the guidance of a directing mind. Aristotle (384–322 B.C.) studied about five-hundred species of animals and classified them. He recognized development and relationships within species only. He rejected Empedocles' idea of the survival of the fittest. Charles Darwin later paid his respects to Aristotle when he said: "Linnaeus and Cuvier have been my two gods, though in very different ways, but they were mere schoolboys to old Aristotle."

The idea of development within nature and of gradations of living creatures from lower to higher forms is found in the writings of various philosophers. It was not until 1859, however, when Charles Darwin published his *Origin of Species*, that the theory of organic evolution began to gain widespread acceptance. During the previous hundred years the ground had been prepared by a considerable group of careful investigators. For example, Linnaeus, a Swedish naturalist of the eighteenth century, had discovered that plant and animal forms could not be rigidly separated when he made a classification of species. Buffon and Cuvier in France had carried on studies in comparative anatomy. Lyell, in geology, had set forth the principle of uniformitarianism, pointing out the universal and uniform operation of causative factors in the history of the world. He said that the present must be explained by the past unless there is evidence to the contrary. Erasmus

Darwin in England and Lamarck in France had set forth a theory of evolution known as Lamarckianism, or the theory of the inheritance of acquired characteristics.

LAMARCK: THE INHERITANCE OF ACQUIRED CHARACTERISTICS

Lamarck (1744–1829) was the first man to set forth a theory of organic evolution to account for the transformation of species. He concluded that certain characteristics acquired by an organism during its lifetime are inherited by its offspring and that in this way permanent changes are brought about. Muscles and organs that are used tend to strengthen and develop; those that are not used tend to atrophy or become weak. For example, animals like the cat, which springs at its prey, develop strong hind legs; animals that run from other beasts become swift of foot; the giraffe, which reaches up to get the tender leaves of trees, develops a long neck. If we assume that slight changes brought about by use and disuse during the life of the individual are passed on to each succeeding generation and that the effect is cumulative, we have an explanation of how evolution has taken place. This interpretation emphasizes the role of the environment in modifying the organism, although Lamarck also recognized the influence of effort and desire on the part of the individual.

The theory that acquired traits or capacities can be passed on to one's offspring is simple to understand, and it has appealed to many as reasonable, but there is little evidence for such physical or biological inheritance. Most biologists now reject the Lamarckian interpretation.

DARWIN: THE THEORY OF NATURAL SELECTION

Charles Darwin (1809–1882) and Alfred Russel Wallace (1823–1913), working independently, arrived at similar conclusions, which we are now to consider. Because of Darwin's long and painstaking accumulation of evidence, together with his publication of *Origin of Species* in 1859 and *Descent of Man* in 1871, these views are usually termed *Darwinism*.

To understand Darwin's theory of natural selection, four ideas need to be recognized and kept in mind.

1. *Heredity*. Like tends to produce like. This clear fact of human experience and observation seems to operate throughout the realm of animate things.

2. *Variations*. While an animal tends to produce offspring like itself, no two animals are exactly alike. There are always slight individual variations in structure or function. These variations, according to Darwin, may occur because of organic causes or through mere chance.

3. *A Struggle for Existence*. Because there is not enough food or space for all living creatures, there is fierce competition for life, or a struggle for existence.

4. *The Survival of the Fittest.* Those offspring with the most favorable variations—that is, those best adapted to the conditions under which they must live—are the ones that survive. The rest go down in the struggle and do not propagate their kind. Those selected and preserved by nature will bring forth offspring, again with chance variations or modifications. Eventually these changes will give rise to new species.

The entire process described above is known as *natural selection*. In contrast to Lamarck who said that the adaptations made by the individual organism in its effort to survive were passed on to offspring, or inherited, Darwin posited that organisms with the most favorable chance variations survived; hence the only organisms which remained to have offspring were those with the special ability to adapt themselves to their environment. Because of variations in these offspring, certain of them possessed further special ability to adapt themselves—that is, to survive in the struggle for existence. After this process of variation and selection had gone on for a period of many generations, the organisms which survived would differ markedly from those which first struggled to adapt, and a new species would have arisen. In other words, nature, in the struggle for existence, selects the organisms most capable of adaptation to the environment. Such, then, is Darwin's famous interpretation of organic evolution—the *origin of species by natural selection*.

GERMINAL CONTINUITY AND THE MUTATION THEORY

Since Darwin's time various modifications in the theories of evolution have been proposed. We can take space to explain only two that are of the utmost importance, those connected with the names of Weismann and De Vries.[6]

August Weismann (1834–1914) set forth the theory of germinal continuity. According to this theory, the germ cells, which are not affected by changes or variations in the body cells, are passed on from generation to generation. The parent is the carrier, or the trustee, of the germ plasm that goes to produce the offspring. The germ cells are subject only to their own variations or mutations and are unaffected by what happens in the life of the parent. This explains why each generation tends to produce offspring like itself. The germ plasm is increased by a process of cell division.

In 1900 Hugo De Vries, a Dutch botanist, published a treatise, *The Mutation Theory*, which gained widespread attention and acceptance as an interpretation of the evolutionary process. A mutation is a sudden change or variation which breeds true—that is, the offspring inherit the variation. The notion that evolution might proceed by abrupt and comparatively permanent

---

[6] The reader should also become familiar with Mendel's law of inheritance and Morgan's elaboration of the gene theory. Any good biology textbook will have a discussion of the work of these men.

germinal changes, instead of by slight variations, was a new idea. The evidence set forth by De Vries has been confirmed and supported by additional evidence, so that the theory has gained wide support.

The views of Weismann, De Vries, and others may be incorporated into the Darwinian theory and the result spoken of as Neo-Darwinism. After mutations occur as permanent changes in the germ cells, why is it that some survive and others do not? The answer given by the biologist is "natural selection." Some students of evolution, impressed with the new discoveries and many changes in interpretation since Darwin's day, prefer to speak of the "modern selectionist theory" or the "synthetic theory" of evolution.[7]

THE EVIDENCE FOR ORGANIC EVOLUTION

The evidence for organic evolution, which has been accumulating for more than a hundred years, cannot be outlined in our limited space. All we can do is list the fields from which the evidence has come and give a few examples.

COMPARATIVE ANATOMY

In this field a study is made of the structural correspondence that exists among the great divisions of animals. A comparison is made of the bones, muscles, bodily organs, and tissues. Such comparison shows that the same basic limb bones and muscles have adapted themselves to meet a variety of uses as different animals have turned to running, climbing, jumping, burrowing, flying, or swimming. For instance, there is a resemblance between the arm of man, the forelimb of the dog, sheep, or horse, the wing of the bird, the flipper of the seal or whale, and the foreleg of the lizard.

VESTIGIAL REMAINS

Some of the animal organs, such as the heart, are essential to life and are called vital organs. Others, like the spleen, may be removed without causing death. A few organs and glands are useless or degenerate, and are called *vestigial*. They are organs which are developed and functional in some lower animal forms, but which have lost their functions or use in higher forms. Examples are the wings of the female gypsy moth, which are never used, degenerate eyes in various cave animals, and the well-known vermiform appendix in man. Such organs, whether now functionless or serving new functions, are interpreted as clear evidence of an evolutionary development.

EMBRYOLOGY

Embryology is the study of organisms in the early stage of development

[7] T. A. Goudge, *The Ascent of Life: A Philosophical Study of the Theory of Evolution* (Toronto: U. of Toronto Press, 1961), pp. 87–96.

from the fertilized ovum. Each organism, in its individual life history, tends to recapitulate (repeat) the various main stages through which its kind has passed. In the embryos of the whalebone whale, for example, there are rudiments of hind legs and dentition that disappear before the adult stage is reached. The early ancestors of the whale lived on land. All higher animals in their embryonic development pass through a fish-like stage with gill arches and gill clefts. In the embryos of animals with four-chambered hearts, the heart is first two-chambered, and then three-chambered, as in amphibians. The embryos of the different species of animals tend to be similar in the early stages. The lower animals stop developing at certain points; the embryos of the higher animals go on through additional stages.

TESTS OF THE BLOOD AND FLUIDS OF ANIMALS

Comparative studies of the chemical constituents of the fluids and tissues of animals, particularly the blood, show relationships among the various species. The *precipitation tests* for the blood are the most interesting and convincing. Samples of blood from the closely related higher animals are biochemically more nearly alike than samples taken from animals that are more distantly related from an evolutionary point of view. "Because of the specificity of the antigen-antibody reaction these cross reactions are a measure of the degree of similarity of the serum proteins in the different species. They tend to confirm, therefore, the relationships of man to the Primates and particularly to the anthropoid apes."[8]

FOSSIL FORMS

The science of paleontology deals with the life of past geological periods insofar as it may be studied through fossils, remains that have been preserved in the earth's crust. Remains of extinct animals that once roamed the earth and of earlier forms of animals that continue to live today have been found. The age of the fossil may be known approximately by the stratum or layer of the earth's crust in which it is embedded. The best-known and most complete set of fossils among the vertebrates is that of the horse. His development can be shown from a small animal about eighteen inches in height, through various modifications, to the majestic animal of today.[9]

GEOGRAPHICAL DISTRIBUTION

The study of the location and distribution of the plants and animals in the various parts of the world takes account not only of the distribution throughout the various counties, states or provinces, and countries, but also of their

[8] David J. Merrell, *Evolution and Genetics* (New York: Holt, Rinehart and Winston, 1962), p. 111.
[9] William K. Gregory, *Evolution Emerging* (New York: Macmillan, 1951), II, Ch. XXI.

distribution in relation to climate, altitude, mountains, valleys, bodies of water, the food supply, and the presence of enemies. For example, oceanic islands, far from continents, which have originated through the elevation of the land from the oceans, exhibit flora and fauna that contrast with those of continental islands which have been cut off from the mainland at some time in the past. Both areas show differences from the continental mainlands. Australia is a good example. It was separated from the Asiatic continent at an early time (Cretaceous period). At the time the marsupials—animals that have a pouch for carrying the young—were probably the highest animals. Australia contains more relics of these earlier mammals and fewer of the higher mammals than any other large island or continent. There is a break in the development which coincides with the geological evidence. Apparently these facts can be explained only on the basis of evolution.

DOMESTICATION AND EXPERIMENTATION

Most people are aware of the fact that dogs are domesticated wolves (or related animals). A great variety of changes in size, form, and appearance have been produced in recent years by selective breeding. New conditions of climate and food supply, as well as of training, have probably played some part. The work of Mendel with the sweet pea and of Luther Burbank with flowers, fruits, and vegetables is fairly well known. Man is sometimes able to do in a short time with science what the slower processes of unmanipulated nature might do over a long period of time, and what he does illuminates those processes.

CLASSIFICATION

The only type of classification that has proved satisfactory and useful to students of living forms is that which groups them according to their fundamental structure. Animals are classified into a dozen or more groups, or *phyla,* with many subdivisions. Animals are thus arranged in an ascending order of complexity, from unicellular organisms to man. There are no sharp distinctions between species, and it is evident that all living organisms are related, however remotely.

The evidence from the various fields of research dovetails or fits into a single pattern, forming one united theoretical whole. This is often said to be the strongest argument for evolution.

ATTEMPTS TO DISCREDIT THE THEORY OF EVOLUTION

In spite of the fact that the evidence for evolution appears to be so conclusive, a small group of people are unconvinced. The *Origin of Species* led to a controversy that has not ended completely. While a few scientists at first voiced opposition or doubt, most of the opposition came from a branch of religious conservatives, later known as fundamentalists. The latter group defended a literal interpretation of the account of creation contained in Genesis. Early Roman Catholic opposition was modified in later pronouncements, especially by the Papal Encyclical of 1951. Among the Protestants, with no central authority, the reactions were more diverse. In the United States the controversy between the religious liberals who accepted evolution and the fundamentalists who stood against it continued for some decades in denominational conventions and state legislatures. For example, during the 1920's, thirty-seven anti-evolution bills, resolutions, or riders were introduced in various states. Three states passed laws against the teaching of evolution in tax-supported schools and two states passed resolutions against such teaching.

Those who attacked the theory of evolution took one or both of two approaches. First, they rushed to the defense of the traditional statements of church doctrines and reaffirmed "the faith once and for all delivered to the saints." They attacked evolution as a godless theory. Second, they sought to discredit the theory by the use of quotations from scientists who had opposed the theory or who had expressed doubt about one or another of the interpretations of the origin of species. In some cases they ridiculed the evidence as fantastic or absurd.[10]

Some opponents of a general theory of evolution accept what they call "threshold" evolution, but reject "total" evolution. Supporters of this position may accept the large mass of evidence that shows structural and functional relationships between animal forms, but they insist that "similarity does not necessarily mean genetic kinship." There is evolution, according to this view, only within the "kinds" originally created by God and as indicated in Genesis. There are gaps, it is said, between the "kinds," such as plants yielding seeds, trees bearing fruit, birds, creeping things and beasts, and man made in the image of God. There is no "fixity of species"—there is development within the "kinds" or groups—but these groups are not genetically related. On the basis of "threshold" evolution there are gaps that exist and cannot be filled. On the basis of "total" evolution each "kind" is genetically related to earlier and more primitive groups without any limit.[11]

The controversy over the question of evolution came to its peak during the decade 1920 to 1930, and especially during the Scopes trial in Dayton,

[10] See Stewart G. Cole, *The History of Fundamentalism* (New York: Harper, 1931), Ch. XII; *Anti-Evolution Laws* (New York: American Civil Liberties Union, January, 1927); Maynard Shipley, "The Forward March of the Anti-Evolutionists," *Current History*, 29 (January, 1929); Russell L. Mixter (ed.), *Evolution and Christian Thought Today* (Grand Rapids: Eerdmans, 1959).

[11] See Edward John Carnell, *An Introduction to Christian Apologetics* (Grand Rapids: Eerdmans, 1956), pp. 236–242.

Tennessee, in 1925.[12] Since then the debate has subsided or ended in most parts of the Western world. For those who accept an historical rather than a literal interpretation of the Bible, the concept of evolution presents no difficulties.

SOME PHILOSOPHICAL IMPLICATIONS OF EVOLUTION

During the last hundred years or more, a revolution in human thinking has led to far-reaching changes in all fields of knowledge, so that we are living in a new intellectual climate. The concept of evolution has played a prominent part in the creation of the modern outlook. The intellectual revolution it has caused can be compared only with the changes brought about by the group of astronomers and physicists of which Copernicus and Newton were members or with the changes necessitated by the theories of relativity and matter that have been propounded in recent decades. For many, the concept of evolution is the most far-reaching of all, since it involves so directly man's status and place in the universe. It involves not only science and philosophy, but man's religious outlook and his educational methods. It has become the basis of research in fields as widely separated as history and medicine. Let us consider a few questions that are frequently raised and in so doing point out some implications of the idea of evolution.

1. *Does the theory of evolution explain life?* There seems to be little doubt about the fact of evolution, but considerable doubt concerning its interpretation. Does evolutionary theory explain everything, or does it leave much unexplained? Does it explain the will to live? Philosophically, natural selection or any other of these scientific explanations leaves much unexplained. They do not explain the origin or the nature of life and of mind. A biologist, pointing out that natural selection is "not the primary factor in evolution," says:

> The chief shortcoming of the process of natural selection as a causative agent lies in the fact that the mere act of sifting out the fit by exterminating forms which have varied unfavorably cannot of itself initiate *new* variations. It guides but does not create, since it can operate only after variations have appeared. Whatever it is that causes the variation to appear is plainly the primary factor in evolution.[13]

---

[12] See Ginger Ray, *Six Days or Forever? Tennessee vs. John Thomas Scopes* (Boston: Beacon, 1958). This famous trial in 1925 gained national and even international attention. John Thomas Scopes was found guilty in court of having taught evolution in the local high school. William Jennings Bryan volunteered his services as chief counsel for the prosecution, and Clarence Darrow as chief counsel for the defense. The play *Inherit the Wind* (1955) by Jerome Lawrence is a dramatization of the Scopes trial. For some of the larger issues see Gail Kennedy (ed.), *Evolution and Religion: The Conflict Between Science and Theology in Modern America* (Boston: Heath, 1957).

[13] Michael F. Guyer, *Animal Biology* (4th ed.; New York: Harper, 1948), pp. 655–656.

The terms *competition,* the *struggle for existence,* and the *survival of the fittest,* used in the discussion of evolution, also need to be carefully criticized and evaluated. Both competition and cooperation are present in nature, so that competition and struggle by no means tell the whole story. The survival of the fittest may mean only that those survive who are able to survive in some particular environment, and this may depend on various chance factors. There are many degrees and types of adaptation, as well as of fitness. In some environments only low forms of life can survive.

2. *How does the concept of evolution affect our views of man?* Does evolution degrade man, since it relates him to the animal kingdom, or does it enhance his nature, since man seems to be the crowning achievement of a long process of evolution? Since man is related to all other living creatures and is a part of the order of nature, we are forced to consider the whole question of the nature of man and his status in the order of things. At first, some men thought that the newer views were degrading to man, and there are expressions of this attitude in literature. Philosophers and many religious leaders, however, point out that, no matter how man came to be, no matter what his genesis, he is no less than what he is—a self-conscious being with unique characteristics. The nature and character of a thing is determined not so much by its beginning as by its end. Man's aspirations give him his place and his importance. Man has a great variety of characteristics not shared by any other living creature, as we shall see in the next chapter. He also has great adaptive powers and the capacity to exert some control over his own development.

3. *What has been the effect of the idea of evolution on our views of mind and knowledge?* In earlier interpretations, mind was something quite apart from nature. The "mind" attempted to contact and to know "ultimate reality." The "spectator view" of knowledge was taken for granted. The problem was to bridge the gap between mind and the world. Now the mind is more likely to be looked on as a growing instrument or function, developing in the process of evolution. The mind is thus not just an observer outside the process. If the world and life are in process of development, then it would appear that knowledge and truth—and of course minds of which they are products—may also be growing and changing. More stress is being placed on experimentation and research, tentative attitudes, and degrees of probability. As we shall see, however, there are those who hold to the existence of an unchanging reality beyond the "passing show" or the phenomenal world.

Some students of evolution speak of a shift from physical and biological to psychological and cultural evolution. "The shift from somatic genetic evolution to psychosocial or cultural evolution is a change as great as that from the inorganic evolution of the universe to the evolution of life."[14] Man's mind and mental capacity along with his ability to use spoken and

14 *Evolution After Darwin,* III, *Issues in Evolution,* p. 246.

written language have made possible a great accumulation of knowledge. Such knowledge can be stored so that it is available to future generations or to peoples distant in time and space. "Man alone among living things knows that he has evolved. Man alone is able to decide what direction or directions he desires his own future evolution to follow, and can set about acquiring the knowledge he needs to achieve the desired results."[15]

4. *How have our views of morals and values been affected by the idea of evolution?* At one time values were thought to be as fixed and specific as the species of animals; but with the coming of the theory of evolution and emphasis on historical research, it was recognized that there is a history of morality and an evolution of morals to be discovered and described. Instead of an authoritative and fixed system, morality came more and more to be regarded as a dynamic, progressive discovery of the means and conditions necessary for a well-rounded life for the individual in a society.

Morality is based on life itself. It grows out of life and its needs, and it matures along with the growing knowledge and culture of men. As morality becomes reflective, there is a far-reaching and impressive uniformity among the codes of men. And though morality may shift its base and emphasis, it neither declines nor loses its importance.

Man's capacity to judge his own conduct and to guide his actions in the light of ideals or standards has gradually increased, if we take the long view over some thousands of years. Whether there has been progress or retrogression in recent decades is more difficult to decide. At present man has within his grasp the power to destroy himself and all forms of life on earth. Unless he can quickly learn to control some of his primitive impulses, emotions, and misleading ways of thinking, the future is uncertain. One encouraging thing is that man's development is still going on; he knows that he is in danger, and he has the ability to take steps to meet the danger.

5. *What is the effect of modern views of evolution on theories of the universe?* When we turn to modern views of the universe, we find that the theory of evolution, especially in its larger aspects, has forced man to give up the older notion of a fixed and stationary world. The main concepts henceforth are more likely to be "change," "process," "development," "relativity," and "progress." There is a tendency to think of "reality" not so much as a substance, but as a process. Philosophers such as William James, Henri Bergson, and Alfred North Whitehead found in the idea of evolution the organizing principle for a philosophy in which novelty, creativity, and purpose are central. Numerous philosophies of emergent, or creative, evolution have arisen. When we consider the various types of philosophy, we shall see that they all recognize the concept of evolution, though they interpret it in different ways.

15 Goudge, *Ascent of Life*, p. 148.

Modern views of the universe tend to be more definitely "this-worldly" and naturalistic in their approach. They posit one world of reality, and the older dualisms tend to disappear. Ultimates, absolutes, and finalities either drop out of the picture or retreat to the background. This trend is a result not only of the theory of evolution but also of the entire scientific development in recent centuries. While some scientists see the course of evolution as unsteady and erratic, Sir Julian Huxley, in speaking about the over-all process, characterizes it as "A one-way process in time; unitary; continuous; irreversible; self-transforming; and generating variety and novelty during its transformations."[16]

6. *To what extent have man's views of religion and God been affected by the new intellectual climate of opinion?* The theory of evolution had far-reaching implications for religion. Three possibilities presented themselves to the religious leaders of the modern world: (1) They might attempt to retain the older, prescientific views of religion and God and to deny the theory of evolution and endeavor to discredit it. A small and belligerent group took this stand; they attempted to discredit the evidence. (2) They might set forth interpretations of religion that preserve religious loyalties without engaging in scientific controversies. In the main this is an attempt to keep the two fields apart. Religion may then be said to be concerned with value judgments, not with factual judgments, or religion may become a matter of personal piety. (3) They might accept the theory of evolution, and make whatever intellectual adjustments seem necessary. This was the course eventually taken by most religious leaders. For many people, religion too is an evolutionary product in the sense that it changes along with the growing experience and knowledge of man. Religion thus comes to be grounded more on the authority of human experience and reason. These in turn are dependent on the nature of man and the nature of the universe. These philosophers would say that God is present throughout the entire process and men are religious because they live in the kind of universe that calls forth in them the religious response. Thus God did not create the first man and then stop. The world is still in the making, and every day is a creative day.

QUESTIONS AND PROJECTS

1. Review Questions

(1) State some of the views of the origin of life that have been held at various times. Evaluate these views and indicate which appeals most to you and why.

---

[16] *Evolution in Action* (New York: New American Library of World Literature, 1957), p. 12. (Mentor ed.)

(2) What are the characteristics of living things that distinguish them from non-living things?

(3) What are the problems connected with the application of the concept of evolution to areas other than that of living things?

(4) Explain *evolution, evolutionism, Lamarckianism, Darwinism,* and *Neo-Darwinism* and indicate, where possible, the person who first set forth the theory.

(5) State a few of the fairly prevalent misinterpretations of evolution.

(6) Give the main areas of study from which the evidence for biological evolution comes. What is said to be "the strongest argument for evolution"?

(7) Discuss the reasons for opposition to the theory of evolution by some groups, and indicate the different forms the opposition took.

(8) Discuss the statement: "From a philosophical point of view, natural selection leaves much unexplained."

(9) Describe and explain the influence of the theory of evolution on our views of the nature of life, man, mind, knowledge, morals and values, the universe, and religion and concepts of God.

2. How would you answer the question asked by one student after he had read the scientific views we have been considering in this and the preceding chapter: "Do we have to accept this?"

3. How do you explain "orthogenesis," or the fact that variations and hence evolution proceed in "straight lines" or definite directions? In answering this question, give your reaction to the following statement: "I find it difficult to believe that the extravagant glories of birds, fish, flowers and other living forms were produced solely by natural selection; I find it incredible that human consciousness was such a product. How can man's brain, the instrument which created all the riches of civilization, which served Socrates, Shakespeare, Rembrandt and Einstein, have been brought into being by a struggle for wild game in the Pleistocene wilderness?"[17]

4. Discuss the relation between the theory of evolution and the account of creation in the first two chapters of Genesis. Read those two chapters and list the events as they are related verse by verse. Is there any evidence for two accounts, as many Biblical scholars claim? Note carefully Genesis 1:1–2:4a and Genesis 2:4b–3. Why are different words for God used in these two sections? Is the order of creation the same in the two accounts?

5. What is the effect of laws against the teaching of scientific or philosophical theories? The following law was passed March 21, 1925: "Be it enacted by the General Assembly of the State of Tennessee that it shall be unlawful for any teacher in any of the universities, normals, or other public schools in the State, which are supported in whole or in part by the public school funds of the State, to teach the theory that denies the divine creation of man as taught in the Bible, and to teach instead that man has descended from a lower order of animals."

6. Discuss the influence of the theory of evolution on educational theory and practice.

---

17 Jacquetta Hawkes, "Nine Tantalizing Mysteries of Nature," *New York Times Magazine* (July 7, 1957): 33.

7. Is it possible to know life from without, or objectively through the sciences, or is life, as some people claim, something that we can know only from within, or through the experience of living?

8. Give your reaction to the objection some people raise when the word *progress* is connected with the word *evolution*. Some say that we think evolution demonstrates progress only because we view it from the point of view of man.

9. A central principle in the philosophy of Albert Schweitzer is "reverence for life," by which he means all life. He says, "A man is ethical only when life, as such, is sacred to him." Should we feel under obligation to promote the will to live and destroy life in any form only when or where it is absolutely necessary to preserve "higher" forms of life?

10. What would be your reaction if life were successfully synthesized in a laboratory? Compare your reaction with that of an earlier generation to evolutionary theory.

SUGGESTED READINGS

BECK, WILLIAM S. *Modern Science and the Nature of Life.* New York: Harcourt, Brace, 1957.
A readable study of the life sciences dealing with a variety of questions from the origin of life to the nature of mind.

BERGSON, HENRI. *Creative Evolution.* Trans. by Arthur Mitchell. New York: Modern Library, 1944. (Postscript by Everett Skillings.)
An influential book by the French biologist and philosopher. Somewhat difficult for beginners but rewarding.

Evolution After Darwin. Ed. by Sol Tax and Charles Callender. 3 vols.; Chicago: U. of Chicago Press, 1960. (Vol. I, *The Evolution of Life,* ed. Sol Tax; Vol. II, *The Evolution of Man,* ed. Sol Tax; Vol. III, *Issues in Evolution,* ed. Sol Tax and Charles Callender.)
Papers and panel discussions of the University of Chicago's Darwin Centennial Celebration in 1959. About fifty scientists share their knowledge with each other and with the public.

GOUDGE, T. A. *The Ascent of Life: A Philosophical Study of the Theory of Evolution.* Toronto: U. of Toronto Press, 1961.
A philosopher discusses present-day evolutionary theory including recent changes in interpretation and their philosophical implications. Highly recommended.

GREENE, JOHN C. *Darwin and the Modern World View.* Baton Rouge: Louisiana State U. Press, 1961.
A professor of history gives a popular account of the impact of Darwin's conclusions on the religious and intellectual thought of the last hundred years.

GREGORY, WILLIAM K. *Evolution Emerging.* 2 vols.; New York: Macmillan, 1951.
An outstanding work in the field of evolution that summarizes the available evidence and

discloses the changing forms of life from primeval forms to man. Vol. I contains the textual presentation; Vol. II consists of illustrations.

HUNTSMAN, A. G. *Life and the Universe.* Toronto: U. of Toronto Press, 1959.
A biologist grapples with the following questions: What is life? Is there life everywhere? He attempts to integrate our science and our living.

HUXLEY, JULIAN. *Evolution in Action.* New York: New American Library of World Literature, 1957. (Mentor ed.)
An outstanding student of evolution marshals evidence for it and states his views.

MANDELBAUM, MAURICE. "Scientific Background of Evolutionary Theory in Biology," in *Roots of Scientific Thought,* ed. Philip P. Wiener and Aaron Noland. New York: *Journal of the History of Ideas* and Basic Books, 1957, pp. 517–536.
The aim of this paper is to show the background for the formulation and adoption of the theory of biological evolution.

PERSONS, STOW (ed.). *Evolutionary Thought in America.* New York: Braziller, 1956.
A series of eleven lectures delivered before the undergraduate conference of the program in American Civilization at Princeton University, 1945–46. Evolutionary concepts are discussed from scientific, philosophical, and religious points of view.

SIMPSON, GEORGE GAYLORD. *The Meaning of Evolution.* New Haven: Yale U. Press, 1949.
A general work in the meaning of evolution and its implications for our views of human life, ethics, and human destiny. Evolution has no built-in "goal," but man can control his own evolution and supply a purpose, according to the author.

SINNOTT, EDMUND W. *Matter, Mind, and Man: The Biology of Human Nature.* New York: Harper, 1957.
A biologist and a graduate-school dean at Yale University turns philosopher and sets forth his views of life, man, and our human prospects.

TEILHARD DE CHARDIN, PIERRE. *The Phenomenon of Man.* New York: Harper, 1959. (Introduction by Julian Huxley.)
A Jesuit paleontologist views evolution as "an ascent toward consciousness" in an attempt to reconcile his Christian faith and his scientific views of evolution.

NINE

THE NATURE OF MAN
AND THE SELF

"Know thyself," said Socrates. Too frequently, perhaps, we have gone to the white rat or the guinea pig in our attempts to study behavior, forgetting that, as Pope phrased it, "the proper study of mankind is man." Studies of life on the subhuman levels have brought us valuable information, but they fail to recognize man's unique or distinctive qualities. Man is a part of nature and partakes of nature's ways; yet he also appears to transcend or rise above nature and to exercise considerable control over it. According to John Ruskin, every man must ask and attempt to answer three questions: "Whence did I come? What am I? Whither am I going?"

THREE INTERPRETATIONS OF MAN

There are three rather distinct interpretations of the nature of man: the classical, or rationalistic, view, inherited largely from Greece and Rome; the Judaeo-Christian view, which comes largely from Palestinian sources; and the naturalistic, or biological, view, which is largely the product of the natural sciences as they have developed during recent centuries. There are various subdivisions, modifications, and transformations of these views. They are often combined, as, for example, in the medieval synthesis of the Judaeo-Christian and the classical traditions. The thinking of the man of today may contain elements from all three attitudes. Some individuals and groups, however, subscribe fairly closely to one or another of these interpretations.

THE CLASSICAL, RATIONALISTIC VIEW OF MAN

According to this view, inherited in the main from Greece and Rome and revived in a slightly different form during the Renaissance, what most distinguishes man is the fact that he is a rational being. For Plato, reason is the highest part of the soul and the function of reason is to guide conduct. It is independent and immortal in its essential nature. Only reason is able to penetrate to the very nature of things. For Aristotle, also, reason is the highest faculty of the soul. It is man's prize possession, which sets him apart from subhuman nature. The Stoics believed in a cosmic reason, or *logos,* which pervades all things. The ideal person is the wise man, who suppresses his emotions and governs his world by controlling himself. Reason must check the testimony of the senses, since the "assent of reason" is central in human knowledge.

According to this classical interpretation, man is to be understood primarily from the viewpoint of the nature and uniqueness of his rational powers. Mind is the unifying and organizing principle and, as such, is distinguished from the body. Reason is the pride and glory of man. For Socrates, Plato, and their followers, the intelligent man is the virtuous man. To know the right is to do it. Vice is the result of ignorance. The goal of human effort and the meaning of progress are the harmonious development of all of man's functions and capabilities through the supremacy and the perfection of reason in man and society.

While the classical view of man is optimistic, especially in its confidence in human reason and its view that the intelligent man is virtuous, there is an undertone of melancholy in Graeco-Roman civilization. Many Greek thinkers were impressed by the brevity and mortality of man. Nor did they believe that large numbers of men could be among the wise. History had little meaning, since it was viewed as a series of cycles or endless recurrences. A few men, such a Democritus, Epicurus, and Lucretius, interpreted man as wholly a part of nature, but they did not deny the importance of reason; they merely interpreted it in more naturalistic and mechanical terms.

THE JUDAEO-CHRISTIAN VIEW OF MAN

According to the Judaeo-Christian interpretation, man is to be understood primarily from the standpoint of his divine origin. His uniqueness is not chiefly in his reason or in his relation to nature. Man is a being created by God and made in God's image. Man stands at the point where nature and spirit meet. The fact that man is a finite creature, bound to the earth, explains his weakness and his sinfulness. The fact that man is in part a spiritual being who transcends nature explains his uniqueness, worth, and almost unlimited possibilities.

This view of man is religious and theological in its general emphasis. It places man in a meaningful and purposeful universe. Man is an expression of the intelligence and moral purpose present in the universe. Man transcends the natural conditions of life; he does not become himself until he is devoted to the highest that he knows, to God.

Man is a sinner capable of resisting the call to free obedience and fellowship with God. All too frequently man gives way to sensuality, injustice, and egoism, or pride. Sensuality is giving way to one's desires and passions.

Injustice is gaining some privilege or security at the expense of others. Pride, man's attempt to usurp the place of God, is seen in human desire for glory and power. Man's pride may be the pride of his knowledge or power or even of his virtue. Man falls into these errors when he fails to make God the center of his life.

The view that man is a creature of great value or worth is central in the Judaeo-Christian tradition. People are ends in themselves, never to be used merely as means. The right act is that which produces the good, and the good is that which has value for persons. The distinction between right and wrong is a factual one, not a mere matter of opinion, tradition, or custom. The conviction that people have great intrinsic worth is what makes a society possible; it is at the roots of our democratic faith, and it is a basic conviction underlying Western civilization.

Man is a creature of almost unlimited possibilities for good or for evil. In his weakness he may fall to the level of the animals and live as one of them, but in his strength he may rise to great heights. Man has both moral freedom and responsibility.

Christians stress love, selflessness, or social-mindedness as the supreme virtue. They believe that in the life of Jesus of Nazareth men have an expression of the creative good will necessary for personal and social reconstruction. In Judaism, justice and righteousness are stressed; religion and group consciousness are more closely associated than they are in Christianity. For many people in both groups, religion is a historical movement in which men seek to discover the intrinsic values of life. The chief end of man, in the Judaeo-Christian view, is devotion to God.

SCIENTIFIC INTERPRETATIONS OF MAN

The modern scientific interpretations of man are many and varied, depending on the science to which we turn. Certain facts are generally accepted in all these sciences, however. Man is a part of the physical order of nature, and he is subject to physical and chemical laws, as are other organisms. Like other objects, man has size, weight, shape, and color. He occupies space and time; and the laws of nature, such as the law of gravitation, apply to him as to other physical objects. Certain specific conditions must be met for life to go on. Man absorbs foreign substances into his body, where they are changed into compounds necessary for his life processes. Chemical changes take place during breathing and digestion, and as a result of glandular action. When man's body is analyzed, the same chemical elements are found in him as in air, water, earth, and stars. Thus, for some of the sciences, man is viewed with regard to his physical and chemical aspects.

From another point of view, man is said to be one of the animals. He is one of more than a million species of animals that live on the surface of the earth.

As in the plants and in other animals, the unit of man's body is the cell. He has many characteristics in common with other animals and is said to be part of the age-long process of evolution.

The men and women now living on the earth are sufficiently alike to warrant their classification as a single species, *Homo sapiens*. Modern peoples are often divided into three racial groups: the white, or Caucasoid; the yellow, or Mongoloid; and the black, or Negroid.[1] There is widespread agreement among students of racial groups that all the existing races of men had a common origin at some distant time in the past, and that the different races have developed from a common source as the result of mutations and varying geographical factors. All living races are so much alike that they can and do intermarry and produce fertile offspring. There is no justification for the claim that any one race is inherently superior or inferior to another. There are superior and inferior individuals among all the racial groups.

Let us consider the physical characteristics that set man apart from other higher animals. (1) His *erect posture*. Man's upright posture frees the arms and hands for exploration and manipulation. Whereas most other animals can only scratch, smell, taste, or bite, man may handle objects. The sense of sight achieves greater prominence and use, and the sense of smell tends to recede. (2) His *free fingers and prehensile thumb,* and the *rotation capacity of the arm.* The free flexible fingers and prehensile thumb enable man to oppose the thumb to the other four fingers in grasping objects. The well-developed collarbone, which permits the rotation of the arm, gives greater freedom and flexibility to the arm than that present in the forelimbs of many animals. For example, the forelimb of the dog is stiff and limited in range compared with the arm of man. Because of this flexibility, man is a manipulator, a toolmaker, and an inventor. (3) His *larger brain and head and more highly organized and intricate nervous system.* Not only is man's average skull capacity about three times the average skull capacity of the largest anthropoid ape, but in man the greatest development is in the cerebrum, the "seat" of the "higher mental processes." This permits more varied and subtle behavior.

There are also certain social and cultural characteristics that are developed to a greater degree, so that they set man apart from the other higher animals. These include: (1) *Articulate speech, oral and written language, or the use of symbols.* The spoken and the written word are the principal vehicles of culture. They keep the past alive and continuously feed memory and imagination. Language, in its various forms, is the instrument of both personal and social communication and is basic to human society. According to some social psychologists, the invention of writing enabled man to pass from barbarism to civilization. (2) *Inventions and great cultural advances.* These in-

[1] See Ralph L. Beals and Harry Hoijer, *An Introduction to Anthropology* (2nd ed.; New York: Macmillan, 1959), pp. 167–197.

clude the discovery and use of such things as fire, metals, tools, and machines, and social organizations of numerous types, all of which enable man to lead a fuller life. (3) *The growth of cooperation in larger and larger units.* Cooperation among individuals and groups is essential for the development of the institutions of agriculture, industry, education, science, government, and religion. In this development specialization and integration, or organization, have gone hand in hand. Human progress appears to depend on the ability of men to cooperate in larger and larger groups. Social cooperation is one condition for a good life in an interdependent society.

The strictly scientific view of man does not consider the realm of science to extend beyond the objective "facts" as disclosed by the various sciences. Man differs from the other animals in his "advanced anatomical and physiological complexity" and his more elaborate behavioral patterns. The scientific outlook may lead to the assertion that man and all his activities are determined by the laws of physics and chemistry. From the time of the early Greeks until the present, some men have asserted that the organic or "higher" forms of life, including man, are merely more complex processes which may be explained by the same laws that govern matter and motion. Vitalism asserts that living organisms owe their characteristics to some special life principle or creative synthesis. An alternative theory is that of emergences or levels, which holds that new qualities or forms appear that cannot be explained by the previous level.

AN EVALUATION OF THE THREE INTERPRETATIONS OF MAN

Modern culture is a synthesis of ideas, ideals, and ways of living that have come from the early Greek culture, the Jewish and Christian beliefs, and the scientific progress of recent centuries. The sciences study man as a physical object, as a complicated animal, as a stimulus-response mechanism, and as a social problem. These sciences have furnished us with a mass of facts or descriptive material regarding man's life and relationships. They give us valuable and expert information about segments of man's life. For example, knowledge of our metabolism, our allergic sensitivity, the Mendelian laws of inheritance, defense mechanisms, and our intelligence quotients is important. There is a great quantity of technical knowledge we could not gain by other methods. We need more, rather than fewer, such facts to live well.

The scientific view of man is one which can be accepted as far as it goes, and no limitations or barriers to the study of its proper subject matter should be placed in its way. Where it is deficient it is usually not because it is false but because it is incomplete. Neither a physicochemical nor a biological view of man is sufficient by itself. There is the danger that we may "reduce" the rich qualities of human personality to the functioning of the biological organism, and then attempt to interpret the organism totally according to physical and chemical action and reaction. The sciences, with their emphasis on objectivity, are likely to neglect what is distinctively human about man. The knowledge furnished us by the sciences, as has been pointed out, is related to our everyday experiences somewhat as a road map is related to the country through which one travels. "Just as the road maps have to leave out colors and smells of the countryside, and pleasures and discomforts of the tourists, so the scientific diagrams of human nature and behavior leave out most of its color and smell, and all of its individuality."[2] In attempting to be objective, impersonal, and quantitative, the sciences emphasize certain aspects of man and his life and ignore others. This procedure is unobjectionable if the investigator does not forget what he has done.

To limit the investigation of human experience to one or even a few of its segments is unphilosophical, since philosophy seeks completeness and a comprehensive answer to questions. Freud's interpretation of man according to "libido" or sex striving, Spengler's interpretation of man as a "beast of prey," or Marx's interpretation of man according to economic processes—these are not totally false but extremely lopsided views.

The Greek view of man as a rational being is sound insofar as it goes, yet it too is not complete. Reason gives man dignity and is the logical basis of his demand for freedom. To stress the power of creative intelligence or human mental faculties not only describes accurately a distinctive characteristic of man but is also sound social policy, since men tend to do those things or to cultivate those qualities which the group they respect expects of them. Though men are not merely rational beings, and though no man is completely and consistently rational, man is potentially a rational being. He should follow the Greeks in respecting reason and cultivating it in human society.

The Christian emphasis on man as a creature whose life has meaning in a meaningful universe, on the worth and dignity of each person, and on love and social-mindedness in human relations is sound and very necessary in our society today. This is not to deny, of course, that many earlier theological conceptions of man need to be revised or discarded. But the Christian view is crucial, since it refuses to reduce personality to uncontrolled "natural" impulses or to conceive of it as perfect. As we noted before, man lives at the point where "nature" and "spirit" meet. He has great possibilities for both evil and good. In the Judaeo-Christian view, the good and the Will of God are united; morality and religion touch all phases of life.

Under the influence of the biological sciences, modern man is likely to explain the tension in his life as a conflict between his animal characteristics and his higher aspirations, which accompany the development of his higher powers. Man is a child of nature, in continuous interaction with his environ-

[2] Robert Lowry Calhoun, *What Is Man?* (New York: Association Press, 1939), pp. 2–3.

ment, an animal living a precarious existence on a small planet. But he is also a self-conscious person, a spirit which stands outside nature. He is nature's rebel, who refuses to accept conditions as he finds them.

Man is a creature of necessity determined by the forces of nature and by his biological impulses, but he transcends those natural processes and manipulates them. In referring to these elements in the nature of man, Reinhold Niebuhr says:

> To the essential nature of man belong, on the one hand, all his natural endowments and determinations, his physical and social impulses, his sexual and racial differentiations, in short, his character as a creature embedded in the natural order. On the other hand, his essential nature also includes the freedom of his spirit, his transcendence over natural process, and finally his self-transcendence.[3]

Man may live his life totally on a biological level, where he seeks to satisfy his appetites and desires, or he may live it on a distinctly human or personal level. Unless he consciously seeks to live on the higher level and maintains deep-rooted ideals of personal honor and responsibility, he is likely to revert to the animal level.

> It is within our power to will and to attain complete selfhood; as it is also our privilege, if we so desire, to suppress the unifying and orienting impulses that reside in the forebrain and to sink back to the biological level. In this case we become animals, veneered with conventional conduct-reactions that enable us to keep our place in respectable society, but animals none the less. We then find the satisfactions of life in sensation. We engage in the scrabble for wealth and social position and power for the "kick" we get out of it and for the further pleasures their possession brings; we cease to be concerned with ideals and moralities, with the problems of personal growth and social progress.[4]

We see then that there are many interpretations of the nature of man and that they are not necessarily mutually exclusive. Each of the three main interpretations has contributed important insights. They may be combined in a synthesis that avoids the extremes of any one of them. Man can live on quite different levels; he can vegetate or he can live as a responsible person with broad interests and aspirations and great growth possibilities. Let us now examine the distinctive qualities of man as a person.

MAN AS A PERSON

We need to note the testimony from fields of knowledge other than the physical and biological sciences and the social studies. Human history past

3 *The Nature and Destiny of Man* (New York: Scribner's, 1941), I, *Human Nature*, p. 270.
4 Albert Edward Bailey, *Art and Character* (Nashville: Abingdon-Cokesbury, 1938), p. 67.

and present, philosophy, religion, and the humanities disclose important aspects of man's nature. They enable men to know more about human existence and to gain an insight into the meaning of their own lives. Much insight can also be gained through intimate association and fellowship. Those who work and play with people day after day can come to know much about life and human nature. Feeling, striving, believing, and aspiring may be irrelevant to a strictly scientific approach, but they are central in our lives.

There are other factors in connection with "man as a person" that need to be considered:

1. *Self-consciousness.* While animals are conscious, only man is *self-conscious.* This quality is the basis of personal and social responsibility. It makes possible imagination and an understanding of the whole range of meaning; imagination makes foresight and creativity possible. The philosopher Fichte is said to have given a party when his young son first used the pronoun *I,* because the use of this pronoun meant the dawn of selfhood and its wide range of powers.

2. *Reflective thinking, abstract thought, or the power of generalization.* While animals can form percepts, apparently man alone can form concepts that permit him to deal with the abstract and the ideal. Reflective thinking enables man to carry on the trial-and-error process mentally, and to distinguish between the true and the false. It enables him to retain memories of the past, to extend himself into the future, and to live in a world of new meanings. Later chapters consider man's intellectual powers in greater detail.

3. *Ethical discrimination and the power of choice.* Man has considerable power of choice. In the light of "what is," he can say "what ought to be." His conscience, his sense of "ought," his eternal restlessness, are the hope of mankind. Moral progress usually comes through the insights of "conscience-haunted" and creative individuals.

4. *Aesthetic appreciation.* Man not only can appreciate beauty but can create it. In art, the human spirit exhibits the range and depth of its appreciation and insight.

5. *Worship and faith in a higher power.* Man is a being who worships, prays, repents, and asks forgiveness. There is a dimension here that seems to be intrinsic to human existence. Even though some men become agnostic or atheistic, they tend to replace a personal God with an impersonal one—the state, the race, or some process in nature.

6. *Creativity.* This creativity finds expression in art, science, philosophy, and religion. It includes the quest for truth, beauty, and goodness, and it has expressed itself in many different ways in the civilizations and cultures of the past.

THE SELF: AFFIRMATIONS AND DENIALS

Granted the various qualities or characteristics of man as a person listed above, can we proceed further and affirm the existence of a self or subject that has a reality apart from these particular functions? What am I? Who are you? We may try to avoid or even to deny the significance of such questions, but they keep returning and forcing themselves upon us. Continuously we are saying, "I think," "I feel," "I did," "I must," and the like. Just what do we mean by "I," "me," "you"?

AFFIRMATIONS OF THE SELF

One psychologist with a long career of teaching, counseling, and study says:

> Below the level of the problem situation about which the individual is complaining—behind the trouble with studies, or wife, or employer, or with his own controllable or bizarre behavior, or with his frightening feelings, lies one central search. It seems to me that at bottom each person is asking: "Who am I, *really*? How can I get in touch with this real self, underlying all my surface behavior? How can I become myself?"[5]

In "The Riddle of Man," Emil Brunner says that this question of the self is not just one problem among many.

> Other problems may seem to us to be greater or more important, but they are still *our* problems. It is *we* who probe into the remote recesses of the world's existence; it is for *us* that the phenomena of the universe become questions. All our problems are focused in this one question: Who is this being who questions —the one behind all questions? Who is this who perceives the infinity of the world? Who is this who is tortured by all life's problems—whether in human existence or outside it? Who is this being who sees himself as a mere speck in the universe, and yet, even while so doing, measures the infinite horizon with his mind? We are here confronted by the problem of the *subject,* separated by a great gulf from all problems of the objective world. What is this to which things are objects, which they are "set over against"?[6]

The great issues of philosophy, psychology, religion, and daily living involve this question of the existence and nature of the self. It can be argued that we are objects among other objects located at particular points in time and space and with a dated existence. "A man hath no pre-eminence above the beasts, for all is vanity." However, man seems to rise above all the

---

[5] Carl R. Rogers, *Becoming a Person* (Oberlin: Oberlin Printing, 1954), pp. 16–17.
[6] From *Man In Revolt,* pp. 17–18, by Emil Brunner. Copyright, 1947, by W. L. Jenkins, The Westminster Press. Used by permission.

objects of his experience, the particular data of consciousness, and even space and time. We shall continue our discussion of affirmations in the section on "The Nature of the Self" after we have considered some of the denials.

DENIALS OF THE EXISTENCE OF A SELF

In the Orient in the sixth century B.C. the founder of Buddhism, Siddhartha Gautama, called the Buddha or the "Enlightened One," said that all things are impermanent. The doctrine of "no-self" came to be stressed in the Hinayana form of Buddhism. The doctrine is open to various interpretations and difficult to present briefly to those who do not have a background of knowledge in Buddhist philosophy. We shall merely note in passing that some Buddhist thinkers in the past and present deny the existence of a permanent self and hold a position somewhat similar to the position of David Hume considered below.

Since the seventeenth century in the West, when men turned their attention toward man's inner life, there have been a considerable number of explicit denials of the existence of a self. In contrast with Leibniz and others, who regarded the self as active and "self-propelled," John Locke (1632–1704) thought of the mind as a passive blank tablet, with action initiated from the outside through the senses. David Hume (1711–1776) carried the denials much further. He was unable to discover any permanent self. Introspection appeared to disclose only fleeting sensations that come and go, or what has sometimes been called the "empirical self." The sole content of the mind is impressions and ideas. There are some philosophers, Hume says, who think that we are continuously conscious of a self and that our immediate awareness of personal identity suffices as proof or demonstration of the existence of such a self. "For my part," he states, "When I enter most intimately into what I call *myself*. . . I never can catch *myself* at any time without a perception, and never can observe any thing but the perception".[7] These perceptions, of course, are always fleeting or temporary. When Hume says that he denies the existence of a self, he is saying that "this bundle of experiences," which he refers to as "I" or "myself," denies the existence of nonmaterial substance and a permanent self. We shall return to Hume's views in the next chapter.

Others have followed Hume's lead in denying the self, at least in any sense in which the term has been used by many philosophers in the past. For example, the author of a fairly widely used textbook in psychology speaks of "man a machine" and asserts that "a concept of self is not essential in an analysis of behavior. . . ." We are also told that "since mental or psychic

[7] *The Treatise of Human Nature*, Book I, Part IV, Section 6. See *Hume Selections*, ed. C. W. Hendel, Jr. (New York: Scribner's, 1954), p. 84.

events are asserted to lack the dimensions of physical science, we have an additional reason for rejecting them."[8]

There is a tendency to insist that what is physical, external, and measurable is more fundamental than what is not. The hypothesis of the "empty organism" or "hollow man," along with the belief that the higher animals, including man, are essentially similar in fundamental nature, has led to the view that man's nature can be known by means of studies of lower species of animals. If man is merely an animal, then investigations of simpler animals, such as the white rat or the guinea pig, will reveal man's nature.

Writing in a British journal, F. H. Heinemann says, "Man without mind. This seems to be the newest discovery of our century, made independently in this country, in America, and in Russia."[9] He is here referring to such views in England as Gilbert Ryle's attack on the self or mind as "the ghost in the machine," to metaphysical behaviorism in the United States, and to dialectical materialism in Russia. In these and other approaches, says Heinemann, "no private thoughts or feelings are allowed." The inner private sphere of the individual stands in danger of being "absorbed by the sea of stereotyped external behavior."

In a similar vein, some psychologists say that they do not wish to retain concepts and terms like *self, mind,* and *self-consciousness,* because they do not want to "drag in spooks." In their desire to be strictly objective and empirical, some psychologists and philosophers omit all reference to a self. They talk about actions, reactions, and "behavioral biographies," but not about a self. Methods devised for the study of inorganic nature, animals, and machines have been applied, often fruitfully, to the study of man. These studies disclose, however, what these different areas have in common but not what is peculiar to man. Scientific methods and postulates have clearly demonstrated their usefulness in the realm of objective phenomena. As the behavioral sciences succeed in their aim to become more like the natural sciences, they eliminate problems of meaning, value, and the knower, or self.

CRITICAL COMMENTS

Are the current denials of the self and mind, as anything more than verbal shorthand to refer to physical and psychological processes, due in part to the desire of some scientists to extend the objective methods of science to include all reality? If this desire can be fulfilled, all questions can be answered neatly and the world and man reduced to a series of logical, easily manipulated constructs. Is this denial of a self due in part to an interpretation of man as merely a product of his environment? We agree that we do not want to deal with "spooks," but there are elements of human experience that we should

[8] B. F. Skinner, *Science and Human Behavior* (New York: Macmillan, 1953), pp. 30–31, 45, 285.
[9] "Man Without Mind?" *The Hibbert Journal,* 49 (October, 1950): 54.

not ignore just because of a method that works only for certain kinds of elements. That which cannot be explained in the language of the behavioristic school of psychology may still be the most significant part of man's life. There can be no objection to these scientific methods if they are acknowledged and understood for what they are, and if their results are not treated, consciously or subconsciously, as complete and final explanations. But when the results are put forth as total explanations, whole aspects of man's life are subsumed under essentially inappropriate headings.

A psychologist gives his reaction to the contemporary denials of the significance of the self. Gordon W. Allport says:

> Up to now the "behavioral sciences," including psychology, have not provided us with a picture of man capable of creating or living in a democracy. These sciences in large part have imitated the billiard ball model of physics, now of course outmoded. They have delivered into our hands a psychology of an "empty organism," pushed by drives and molded by environmental circumstance. What is small and partial, what is external and mechanical, what is early, what is peripheral and opportunistic—have received the chief attention of psychological system builders. But the theory of democracy requires also that man possess a measure of rationality, a portion of freedom, a generic conscience, propriate ideals, and unique value. . . . Man talks, laughs, feels bored, develops a culture, prays, has a foreknowledge of death, studies theology, and strives for the improvement of his own personality. The infinitude of resulting patterns is plainly not found in creatures of instinct. For this reason we should exercise great caution when we extrapolate the assumptions, methods, and concepts of natural and biological science to our subject matter. In particular we should refuse to carry over the indifference of other sciences to the problem of individuality.[10]

THE NATURE OF THE SELF

Since the time of the early Greeks there has been a tendency on the part of philosophers to think of the "self" and "mind" as synonymous, and "to equate the self as subject with mind; and the self as object either with body or the body-mind unity."[11] Mind may be identified here with "form," or the principle of organization. This identification of self and mind is open to question. The human self seems to consist of three elements. There is the thinking, reasoning, or knowing side, called the cognitive; there is the feeling or emotional element, usually termed the affective; and there is the desiring, striving, willing, or active side, called the conative. These traditional distinctions appear to be based on fundamental aspects of or differences in human experience.

[10] *Becoming: Basic Considerations for a Psychology of Personality* (New Haven: Yale U. Press, 1955), pp. 100, 22.
[11] Reinhold Niebuhr, *The Self and the Dramas of History* (New York: Scribner's, 1955), pp. 6 ff.

THE SELF AS THE CENTER OF PERSONAL IDENTITY

The term *self,* or *selfhood,* refers to the subject or to that which persists through the changing experiences of a person's existence. The self is the perceiving, conceiving, thinking, feeling, willing, and deciding entity. If the self is a substance—and many modern philosophers and psychologists reject this view—then it is a substance of a special or unique kind. A substance, it is well to remember, does not have to be material; it may be either material or nonmaterial. If we claim that the self is not a substance, then we think of it as the center of personal identity.

There is evidence of an inner element of some sort, call it what you will—self, ego, agent, mind, knower, soul, spirit, or person. Notions such as "immediate experience" and "content of consciousness" imply an agent of some kind that has the experience. There is something that supplies unity. We say "I" or "me" in connection with experiences that happened ten years ago, five years ago, yesterday, and now. I am a unity, a subject of experience, who cannot be reduced to one part of me or to any of the particular, changing elements of my experience. If the terms *mind* and *self* are not to be identified as the same thing, then the self, or person, is that which has those experiences that we call mental.

The reality most *immediately* known to a man is his own self or ego; it is more directly and intimately known than the external world. The objective world that can be experienced, measured, and manipulated is always viewed from the vantage point of a self or knower. As one psychologist has pointed out: "We cannot profitably deny our subjective life, any more than we can deny the objective description of that life."[12] The self includes that quality of uniqueness and duration through change that enables a person to say "I" or "me." Self-consciousness is the awareness by the self of itself. Man is not only conscious of himself as an "I," he is also conscious of the fact that it is he who is conscious.

THE SELF AS INTEGRATOR OF EXPERIENCES

All experience implies the existence of a self or subject independent of and not completely submerged in the processes and events surrounding it. Through its integrating or synthesizing power, the self transcends the process in which it is involved. People experience the world as "a world of objects open to observation." They experience themselves as "an inner awareness of being alive." The person who denies selfhood as something apart from objective and observable behavior will insist that his ideas are true. But doesn't this denial of self really establish its reality? If there are such things as truth and falsity, then thinking is not merely a succession of sensations which follow one another apart from a center of personal identity that gives them

12 Carl Rogers, "Some Issues Concerning the Control of Human Behavior," *Science,* 124 (November 30, 1956): 1064.

unity. Truth and falsity, recognition, and knowledge presuppose a self or a thinker. How can one compare things apart from a comparer who stands outside the things compared? The continuity of thought that enables a man to carry on a lengthy argument or to write a book implies a continuing self or knowing subject.

A psychologist says that "the self is the organizing function within the individual. It is prior to, not the object of, our sciences; it is presupposed in the fact that one can be a scientist."[13] J. B. Pratt has said that we must accept "the reality of the self" or go on to an extreme form of naturalism and the "suicide of thought."[14] The self that knows and decides is inaccessible through the objective methods of the sciences. Karl Heim, in pointing out that we can see reality only from this central viewpoint of the self, says: "The odd thing about the ego, which takes the world of nature as the object of its perception and volition, is that although it is nearest and most familiar to us, and although each of us is immediately aware of it, yet it is downright impossible for us to describe it objectively, as we can describe a crystal or a flower or a house."[15]

THE PRIVACY OF THE SELF

There is a private character as well as a degree of permanence and transcendence about the self that is not characteristic of the body. We have a direct acquaintance with a self, and this knowledge, like other knowledge by acquaintance, is private and by its very nature (or meaning) cannot be completely described in objective terms. In relation to the objective world I speak of *my* body, *my* environment, *my* experiences. I cannot exchange the "here" or the "there" in which I find myself with anyone else. I can give an eye, a kidney, or some of my blood to another person. I cannot substitute the content of another's consciousness for my own, though I can, of course, vary or enlarge my own experiences through contact with the other person. I can never actually enter into the world of another, though by various forms of communication I can come to a large measure of understanding, sympathy, and even empathy. While there are many varying factors about me, there is a constant factor of which I cannot rid myself. Even as I think of the dissolution known as death, it is in a very unique sense *my* death that is coming.

Furthermore, the privacy of the self means no self can know, in the sense of having direct experience of, another self. The presence of the self can neither be verified objectively, as can that of objects in space and time, nor be found among the objects of consciousness. One discovers no "self" among his sense perceptions, since the self is not an object with sensory qualities. The private nature of the self makes it an entity that gives rise to difficult philosophical

---

[13] Rollo May, *Man's Search for Himself* (New York: Norton, 1953), p. 91.
[14] *Personal Realism* (New York: Macmillan, 1937), p. 296.
[15] *Christian Faith and Natural Science* (New York: Harper, 1957), p. 36. (Torchlight Edition.)

problems. Some scientists claim that they can deal with what is internal and subjective only as it manifests itself objectively in behavior and that anything beyond this must be ignored. Behavior does reveal many things, but it does not exhaust the inner and private nature of the self.

THE SELF AS TRANSCENDING TIME

The relation of the self to the time process is one of the deepest problems of human life. Man is a very limited being with a dated existence; yet he is raised above the time sequence in the sense that the self is perceived and experienced in the ever-present "now" or in what has been called the "specious present," the subjective point between the past and the future. Man has the ability to deal with the past, which may be kept alive through memory. Man also has foresight—the ability to project, predict with varying degrees of probability, plan for, and to some extent shape the future. My self, however, is inexorably bound to *my* present, though in memory I can move into the past, and in imagination I can roam into the future. I am inseparably attached to my present, which is different in quality from the series of points in the sequence; it thus becomes the *time center,* so that the past and the future are viewed from the standpoint of my *now.*

THE SELF AS UNIQUE

The self has, up to the present, defied adequate description and definition. It is apparently the case that the difficulty lies not in our intelligence, tools, and so forth, but in the nature of the very concept of "self." Terms like *life, self,* and *God* are difficult to define because noncircular definitions seem to distort their nature, and nondistorting definitions, expressed in terms similar to those we are attempting to define, merely give rise themselves to the same sorts of questions and difficulties. While we cannot define *self* to our satisfaction, it is nevertheless an important factor and concept. Some would say that the self is *the* important factor in human life. We cannot eliminate awareness, self-consciousness, and mind from our interpretations of human affairs without denying much that is central in human experience. To eliminate the self is to eliminate knowledge and to deny science. At this point the critic may say that to deny a self in the sense implied here, and to insist that it is only a "bundle of experiences" or merely an empirical self, does not deny truth and falsity, knowledge, science, and the like. In reply to the critic who would say that we are "reading in" what is not there, we would insist that he is "reading out" and that he is attributing to a bundle of separate experiences faculties or powers that he has no right to ascribe to it. Logic is the self inspecting its own methods. Mathematics is the self examining relationships apart from things. Psychology is the self describing sensations or behavior, and the like. Human history is in part an account of self-conscious, intelligent human beings—observing, thinking, and carrying out a multitude of purposes. The self is different from the material it analyzes and describes.

If two things are the same or their definitions synonymous, one may be substituted in statements for the other without loss or change of meaning. When we compare *behavior* with the *self,* this substitution cannot be made. Whether we think of self as a substance, a principle of organization, or as the unifying factor in personality, there appears to be a fundamental difference between observable behavior and the inner self. For example, bodies are in space; they can be measured. Selves and thoughts do not occupy space; they cannot be measured. Bodies fall, since they are affected by gravity; hopefully knowledge does nothing comparable to falling. To sum up, the very nature (or meaning) of *self* defies analysis (or definition) in behavioristic terms.

THE MEANING OF HUMAN EXISTENCE

Undoubtedly large numbers of people find little meaning in life and merely plod along in some dull routine. Some, seeing the evils of our time, may declare that there is no meaning in or rational justification for life. Life, for them, is "full of sound and fury, signifying nothing." Some others use one or more of the various escapes to avoid facing any of the serious questions of life. While it may be impossible to *prove* (by some logical deduction) that life is meaningful and significant, the numerous questions men ask and their search for some meaning in life indicate that they believe life has some meaning which they perchance only dimly grasp if at all.

There are two levels at which people find meaning. First, there are those who find meaning in some immediate task that needs to be done or in seeking to achieve some rather definite goals. They are working for a better world: for peace, freedom, child welfare, or any one of scores of things that need attention. In this sense to ask for the meaning of life is to ask, not for some remote meaning, but for those thoughts and actions that contribute to a rich, full, and purposeful existence. If man is to acquire a sense of meaning in life, he cannot be merely self-centered. Human experience indicates that the men and women who attach themselves to worthy tasks to which they can give themselves with loyalty and enthusiasm do find meaning in life. Devotion to something beyond oneself—to an ideal, to a person, to God— gives one a sense of mission. The meaning of life may be to grow, to extend the areas of our awareness, and to cooperate with others to help what is ideal become actual in human affairs.

There is a second question, however, that men ask. Specific acts in life can have meaning as steps toward goals, but the larger question is whether *all* of life, considered as a totality, is meaningful. This is an important philosophical question, which mature men in all ages have asked. The meaning we attribute to human life will depend, in the final analysis, on the place we assign to man in the universe as a whole, or on our world view. One of the most searching and revealing questions one can ask of any philosophy is, "What is its interpretation of the role of man"?

There is in man, it appears, a creative urge that is part of or related to the other creative forces of the universe. At times this urge expresses itself as interest, wonder, striving for fulfillment, or some form of the will to live; it manifests itself in thinking and in conscious activities. It expresses itself on a highly developed plane in the creations and achievements of science, art, philosophy, and religion. If man can acquire a feeling for his distinctive, strategic, and directive role in the general scheme of things, he may gain a new sense of meaning and direction that will give poise and significance to his life. To do this, man needs to keep clearly before him the fact of the uniqueness of the human self or the person. Interpretations of life that make man merely a physicochemical object, a physiological mechanism, or an unself-conscious animal are at best merely partial truths. It is true that man has a physical and chemical nature, that he is propelled by electronic and cellular forces, and that he can live on the animal level. But there is an "I" or a self-conscious aspect that may transcend or rise above the given order of uncon-templative nature. Any purportedly comprehensive interpretation of man that neglects or ignores his ideas and ideals, his self-consciousness, his power of abstract thought, his powers of ethical discrimination and aesthetic appreci-ation, and his need for worship and companionship is incomplete and inade-quate. As a person, man is to some extent free from the limitations that hold for the inorganic and the merely organic but unselfconscious levels of ex-istence. Man is a being who can bring his appetites and habits under the control of a consciously established purpose.

Our interpretation of man is not at an end. The succeeding chapters in this book deal with man and the mind, freedom, world views, values, religion, and similar issues.

QUESTIONS AND PROJECTS

1. Review Questions

(1) Give the characteristics or distinguishing features of each one of the three "interpretations of man." Do you agree that each has contributed important insights?

(2) From a strictly scientific point of view, what are some things we can say about the nature of man? Discuss in your own words the adequacy of the interpretations of man's nature given us by the various sciences.

(3) What is meant by "man as a person"? Explain the characteristics of man as a person listed in this chapter, and indicate whether you would add others, or omit some of those listed, or both.

(4) What is meant by the statement that the question of the meaning of the self or person is not just one problem among others but in many ways *the* basic issue in man's life?

(5) Describe some of the attempts to deny the self as something distinctive in man. Are these denials based mainly on methodological or on other considerations? Discuss.

(6) What is the reason for questioning the fairly prevalent practice of thinking of "self" and "mind" as synonymous?

(7) What is the evidence for saying that the self is not completely submerged in the nonpersonal processes of nature?

(8) Explain and give evidence for accepting or rejecting such concepts as the following in thinking about the self: "that which is the center of personal identity," "the integrator of experiences," "that which is private," "that which transcends time," "that which is unique."

(9) State your own convictions about the meaning of human experience, and critically evaluate the statements made in the chapter on this topic.

2. To a considerable extent man has learned how to control nature and eliminate natural selection. Are there dangers in this trend if man is unable to replace natural selection with intelligent selection?

3. In discussing the nature of human beings J. A. V. Butler, in *Science and Human Life* (New York: Basic Books, 1957), p. 152, protests against certain "grotesque simplifications." He says, "Because they contain mechanical contrivances, living things were regarded as machines; because they were made of chemical substances, life was a chemical phenomenon; because the nervous tissue conducts electrical currents, the brain is likened to a telephone exchange." Do you agree that man's dynamic and creative inner world cannot be so easily subsumed under scientific headings? Discuss.

4. In his book *Reality* (New York: Macmillan, 1926), p. 36, B. H. Streeter says that what a person really knows of the "inner quality of life" depends primarily on the following three things: "first, the depth and the range of his own personal experience; secondly, how far he has the imaginative sympathy to penetrate into the inner experience of others; thirdly, the extent to which he has reflected on the material so presented." Give reasons for agreeing or disagreeing with Streeter.

5. A man's skull is opened, under local anesthetic, so that he remains conscious. The ridges of the whitish-grey matter (the cortex) of the brain are exposed to view. The movements or changes that take place in the brain are shown in magnifying mirrors, so that the man is able to watch these brain changes while he perceives and thinks. Who or what is doing the watching?

6. Comment on the following statements:
   (1) "Life can be understood only by living."
   (2) "The scientist, the thinker, is being forgotten. . . . Even in science the machine

is being worshipped, while the inventor—the scientist who thought it out—is set aside."

(3) "We must deal with man as he is with a view to what he may become."

(4) "Personality is still a growing factor in the Universe. . . . Its history is marked by thousands of years, whereas that of organic nature is marked by millions."

(5) "There is no wealth but life . . . no consummation of life except in the perpetual growth and renewal of the person."

7. Review one of the following: Hannah Arendt, *The Human Condition* (New York: Doubleday, 1960) (Anchor Book); John M. Dorsey and Walter H. Seegers, *Living Consciously: The Science of Self* (Detroit: Wayne State U. Press, 1959); Harry Emerson Fosdick, *On Being a Real Person* (New York: Harper, 1943); J. W. Krutch, *The Measure of Man* (Indianapolis: Bobbs-Merrill, 1953); Rollo May, *Man's Search for Himself* (New York: Norton, 1953); Emmanuel Mounier, *The Character of Man* (New York: Harper, 1956); Leslie Paul, *The Meaning of Human Existence* (Philadelphia: Lippincott, 1950); Pierre Teilhard de Chardin, *The Phenomenon of Man* (New York: Harper, 1959); Franz E. Winkler, *Man: The Bridge Between Two Worlds* (New York: Harper, 1960).

8. Write an essay entitled "My Interpretation of the Nature and Role of Man." While you may wish to use some ideas suggested by the discussion in this chapter, do not limit yourself to them. Is the present age, with its emphasis on things and objectivity, in part responsible for the sense of meaninglessness and anxiety that many people are reported to experience?

SUGGESTED READINGS

Brown, Harrison. *The Challenge of Man's Future: Inquiry Into the Condition of Man.* New York: Viking, 1954. (Compass Book, 1956.)
The author examines man's past and present and attempts "on the basis of the clues derived . . . to examine his future" and decide how he may solve his present problems.

Buber, Martin. *The Writings of Martin Buber.* Ed. by Will Herberg. New York: Meridian, 1956.
An informative introduction followed by selections from the main writings of Martin Buber.

Butler, J. A. V. *Science and Human Life.* New York: Basic Books, 1957.
The author discusses the human implications of contemporary science and shows how scientific progress has increased man's control over himself and his environment.

Campbell, C. A. *On Selfhood and Godhood.* New York: Macmillan, 1957. (The Gifford Lectures, 1953–54 and 1954–55, revised and expanded.)
A carefully reasoned statement starting with an examination of the author's first principles. Part One, "On Selfhood," states the case for a "substantial view" of the self.

Cassirer, Ernst. *Essay on Man: An Introduction to a Philosophy of Human Culture.* New York: Doubleday, 1953. (Anchor Book.)

The life of man is viewed as a struggle between tradition and innovation. The author analyzes various symbolic forms, such as language, art, history, religion, and science, and the relation of man to culture. Man can influence the forms of social life and hasten his own liberation.

DONIGER, SIMON (ed.). *The Nature of Man in Theological and Psychological Perspective.* New York: Harper, 1962.
Part One, Views of Man's Nature; Part Two, Good and Evil in Man; and Part Three, Man's Problems and Potentialities.

HEIM, KARL. *Christian Faith and Natural Science.* New York: Harper, 1957. (Torchbook ed.)
For the self and personal existence, see Part II, pp. 35–150. An active subject must be presupposed if a natural science is possible.

KAHLER, ERICH. *Man the Measure.* New York: Pantheon, 1943.
The author deals with the history of man from primitive times to the present to gain some insight for the future. See especially "The Kingdom of Man," pp. 603–640.

LOOMIS, EARL A. J. *The Self in Pilgrimage.* New York: Harper, 1960.
A short and popular presentation that draws on the Judaeo-Christian outlook and deals with the self in history, in community, and the like.

MACMURRAY, JOHN. *The Form of the Personal.* 2 vols.; New York: Harper, 1953, 1961. (The Gifford Lectures, 1953; Vol. I, *The Self as Agent;* Vol. II, *Persons in Relation.*)
The author is critical of our philosophical tradition that sees the self as contemplative and "pure subject for whom the world is object," rather than as agent acting as a whole. The self is a person in relation to other persons. Meaningful knowledge is for the sake of action.

MUMFORD, LEWIS. *The Conduct of Life.* New York: Harcourt, Brace, 1951. (Harvest ed., 1960.)
This book, the final volume of a series, is a study of man's place in Western civilization. The author is concerned with the renewal of life and man's destiny on this planet. See also the author's The Transformations of Man.

NIEBUHR, REINHOLD. *The Nature and Destiny of Man.* 2 vols.; New York: Scribner's, 1941, 1943. (Vol. I, *Human Nature;* Vol. II, *Human Destiny.*)
A diagnosis of the ills of our culture by a theologian, and a defense of the Christian view of man and of history. Not easy reading for beginners, but a comprehensive and influential work. See also The Self and the Dramas of History.

ROGERS, CARL R. *Becoming a Person.* Oberlin: Oberlin Printing, 1954.
Two lectures by a psychological counselor on problems of personal growth and what it means to be a person.

ULICH, ROBERT. *The Human Career: A Philosophy of Self-Transcendence.* New York: Harper, 1955.
A professor of education discusses the nature of man and sets forth his own philosophical, religious, and educational beliefs.

TEN

WHAT IS THE MIND?

An interpretation and understanding of the relation between the human mind and the human body is one of the most important issues philosophy has to consider—and one of the most complex and baffling. "Among the problems with which philosophy and the various sciences have to deal, the mind-body problem is still the most intriguing . . . . Recent advances in philosophical thinking and in experimental research have made the problem even more challenging than it was, say thirty years ago."[1]

From ancient times men have tended to make a fairly clear distinction between events, substances, processes, or relations that they have called *material*, or *physical*, and those that they have called *mental*, or *psychical*. The former realm comprises the entire range of inorganic and organic matter, including animal and human bodies. The things so classified are located in space and time and are public in that they are capable of being perceived by any observer. The latter realm comprises thinking, images, sensations, desires, and the like. These events or processes are distinctively private in that they cannot be experienced by an observer, though he can be informed of them and gain sympathetic understanding.

Before proceeding further let us clarify a number of terms that are widely used and frequently confused: *soul, self, mind, consciousness,* and *self-consciousness*. Different writers often use the terms with different meanings, and this makes clarification more difficult. Plato used the term *psyche*, which is often interpreted as *soul*, to distinguish an immaterial entity, or substance, from man's animal nature. The soul came to be conceived of as immortal and separable from the body at death. Aristotle also used the term *soul*, but in a somewhat different sense, as we shall see later. The term has been prominent in some theological systems, and some people have used the terms *soul* and *self* as if they were synonymous. Philosophers now tend to avoid the term *soul* and to use other terms such as *self, mind, knower, ego,* or *agent*. Since the

1 Wolfgang Köhler, "The Mind-Body Problem," in *Dimensions of Mind: A Symposium,* Sidney Hook (ed.) (New York: Collier Books, 1961), p. 15. (New York University Institute of Philosophy.)

time of the early Greeks many thinkers have used the terms *self* and *mind* as synonymous or have equated the "self as subject" with mind, and the "self as object" with the body or body-mind unity. This use can be questioned, however, as the human self consists, to use the traditional terms, of the *cognitive* element, or the thinking, reasoning, knowing side; the *affective* element, or the feeling, emotional side; and the *conative* element, or the desiring, striving, and willing side. From this point of view, mind is to be identified with the cognitive aspect of the self and of man's life.

Mind and *consciousness* are not synonymous, although, here again, they are sometimes thought of in that way. We may or may not be conscious of our mental processes. When we arrive at a solution to some problem, we have gone through a *mental process,* but not necessarily one of which we are conscious. When we introspect these processes—that is, examine or ponder them or simply become aware of their existence—we are conscious of them. This distinction allows us to speak, for example, of animals having *mental processes* whether they are conscious or not. Consciousness is an awareness of a relation between the perceiving individual, the subject or knower, and some object of attention. When we are aware of the fact that it is we who are conscious, we speak of *self-consciousness.* We do not seem to be able to explain these immediate conscious and self-conscious experiences satisfactorily without some notion like the self. We must, it appears, hold to a personal unity or identity which persists through the various experiences of life and which makes those separate experiences "mine."

To a considerable extent, the question of what the mind is will be under consideration throughout the book, especially as we consider The Types of Philosophy in Part Three. In this chapter, however, we have the subject of the nature of the mind directly before us, and we shall give some of the possible solutions to the problem and attempt to clarify some of the issues involved.

DIFFICULTY IN STUDYING THE MIND

For several reasons there has been confusion and delay in studying the mind. First, the study of mind, of man, and of social relations in general has received much less attention in the past—and certainly much less financial support—than the study of the world around man. In our own age we have been concerned mainly with the exploitation of physical nature and the construction of machines. We have studied things and animals more than people and social relationships. When man has been studied, it has usually been those aspects of his life that belong as well to the world of things and of animals. The social studies are comparatively recent, dating from the late nineteenth and early twentieth centuries. Scientific method was applied first to mathematics and astronomy, then to physics and chemistry, later to physiology and biology, and only recently to sociology and psychology.

Second, psychology has produced conflicting schools of thought. Psychology is the special science to which we would normally look for the descriptive material on the basis of which to formulate interpretations of mind; but there is no single psychology, only psychologies. There is no agreement about what method should be used or, indeed, what subject matter should be studied. In studying mind, a number of methods may be used. The study of objective behavior, the genetic approach, involving development of the child or of the race, the study of animal behavior, abnormal behavior, physiological mechanisms and processes, introspection, "extrasensory perception"—each of these is used by one group or another.

The various psychologies emphasize different aspects of man's mind or behavior. The early development of psychoanalysis (by Sigmund Freud, Alfred Adler, C. G. Jung, and others) took place within the medical profession. According to Freud, the life energy of a person, or the structure of the personality, is divided into three parts: the *id,* the deep subconscious realm of instinct, impulse, and passion; the *ego,* the element of individuality which is capable of deliberation and which at times exercises some control over the impulses of the id; and the *superego,* an internalization of the demands of society that we call *conscience.* Subservient to three masters—the id, the superego, and a harsh external world of nature—the ego is forced to recognize its weakness, and it easily develops a sense of guilt and anxiety. Psychoanalysis has stressed conflicts and fixations within and between these personality areas, and various mechanisms for coping with these problems— for example, escape, defense, and the like. Behaviorism (developed by John B. Watson, K. S. Lashley, Clark L. Hull, and E. C. Tolman) evolved in the field of animal psychology and later was applied to the study of human behavior. The behaviorists directed attention toward the body in action and to "conditioned" behavior. Gestalt psychology (developed by Max Wertheimer, Kurt Koffka, and Wolfgang Köhler), a reaction against the analytical and atomistic methods of the older psychologies, stresses the view that the whole is more than the sum of its parts; wholes often have qualities not present in their parts. The Gestaltists, whose researches have been mainly in the area of the psychology of perception, feel that the notion of organization or pattern is fundamental to an understanding of the observations in that realm, and have extended their views to include certain aspects of personality. For these psychologists, behavior is said to be determined, not by discrete and isolated stimulus-response events, but by an integrated personality perceiving a total situation. There are other schools of psychology that are less prominent today, and there are a few psychologists who do not wish to be identified with any of the schools.

A third problem in studying the mind is that it is hard to be objective in this field, and there is the danger that in achieving objectivity we may be leaving out the very thing we are trying to study. Science tends to ignore the unique and the nonrepeatable and to deal with an order of nature from which many of man's distinctly human characteristics have been excluded. When we try to isolate "mind," often it is gone and we are left with something else. In this respect, the mind may be like the electron, which is disturbed when it is observed; the physicist, as we noted earlier, cannot discover both its location and its velocity.

There is, then, a real problem as to whether or not the mind can be studied as an objectively viewed entity. Can the same mind be subject and object at one and the same time? Can one mind be subject and another mind object? If there is an area of human existence that is private and not publicly observable, and if science is knowledge that is objectively verifiable, then science faces real problems as it attempts to study the mind and self. The interpreter of the world is trying to interpret himself or other selves, his mind or other minds, and he finds it difficult. He cannot always be sure of what he has studied, how he should interpret the results, the accuracy and relevancy of his observations and results, or what bearing these results may have on a theory of mind.

Finally, there is no agreement as to when or how mind originated in the long process of evolution. The answer will depend largely on our definition of *mind* and on our world view, or interpretation of the universe. If we define *mind* as "adaptive behavior," the account may well begin with the amoeba or some early form of life. There is a gradual increase in delicacy and complexity of reactions as we deal with more complex organisms. But there is no complete evolutionary or classifiable break, though today there is a wide gap between man and the species nearest him. If *mind* were interpreted as "abstract thought," then an account of mind would have to be confined to man.

THEORIES OF THE MIND

Numerous theories of mind have been developed through the years. The various theories can be classified under the following simple system used by G. Watts Cunningham and others: (1) mind as a nonmaterial substance, (2) mind as organic or personal unity, (3) mind as an association of experience, and (4) mind as a form of behavior.

MIND AS SUBSTANCE

This interpretation of the mind is that it is a nonmaterial entity which is indivisible and immortal. The term *substance* generally is used in philosophy to refer to some underlying reality, that in which qualities reside. Let us take two examples: Wax is a substance that has specific qualities: it is dull yellow (unless bleached or purified), plastic (when warm), adhesive, impressible, and so on. What is left when you remove the qualities? The answer is substance, or that which has the qualities. Again, take mind, which has such qualities as the ability to perceive, think, remember, and imagine. What is left when you remove these qualities? The answer again is substance, but this time it is said to be an immaterial substance. The source and chief representative of this view of mind in ancient times was Plato. His major interest was man, especially the mind of man. Plato divides the nature of man into three parts. There is, first, the rational part, the locus of which is in the brain. Man's rational element is a divine essence, or substance, not to be confused with the body in which it is imprisoned. There is, second, the feeling or sensory part of man, with its locus in the breast. There is, third, the desiring elements, or the appetites, whose locus is in the abdomen. The desiring element in man has no principle of order of its own. It needs to be brought under the control of reason. Mind and body are closely and intimately related but, according to Plato, there is a clear-cut distinction between them. The indivisible soul originated in the supersensible world of eternal Forms or Ideas, beyond this fleeting world of sense experience. The soul is marred considerably by contact with matter; it will eventually leave the body and return to its eternal abode.

Plato's interpretation of soul, mind, or reason strongly influenced the thinking of Plotinus and Augustine and, through them, the Christian Church. A view derived from Plato was widely held during the Middle Ages. In this form, or as restated by Descartes, it permeates much modern thinking.

Descartes, one of the great philosophers of the seventeenth century, supported the theory of mind as substance. In serious doubt as to the validity of the knowledge of his day and the validity of all possible knowledge, he decided to question everything and begin anew, to adopt a program of systematic doubt, and to see what he could find that was impossible to doubt. The first clear-cut conviction with which he emerged was that of the existence of the self. His famous saying is *"cogito ergo sum"*: "I think; therefore I am." Descartes found the existence of at least one mind—his own—to be beyond doubt. He went on from this to affirm the existence of other minds, of God, and of an external world of matter. The external world impressed itself upon him through his sense organs, and he could not believe that he was being deceived.

For Descartes there are two substances, mind and matter. He makes a clear distinction between them. Mind is immaterial; it is conscious, and it is characterized by thinking. Since it is substance, it cannot be destroyed except by God, who is the only nondependent substance. Matter is characterized by extension. Man's body is a part of the world of matter and is subject to its laws.

Descartes' explanation of the mind as a separate substance was the beginning of a long development in modern philosophical and scientific thinking, sometimes referred to as the "bifurcation of nature." The Cartesian dualism of mind and body (or matter) enabled men to interpret the external world in mechanical and quantitative terms and to put all other aspects of existence in the realm of mind. Separation of mind and matter is a theory held by some in all periods of history.

MIND AS ORGANIC OR PERSONAL UNITY

While Aristotle, Plato's famous pupil, subscribed to many features of the theory of mind as substance, he moved in the direction of the view we are now to consider. For Plato, ideas are eternal forms whose real existence is in another realm; the ideas we have in this world are merely copies, of varying degrees of accuracy, of these eternal Ideas. For Aristotle, forms exist *in* things or *in* the world. They are the shaping, organizing, dynamic principles that give order and direction to matter. From this point of view, soul (*psyche*) is the life principle, the sum of the processes of life, the active principle of organization of these processes. Mind or reason is the highest capacity or function of the human *psyche*. In this attempt to integrate mind and body, Aristotle moves away from Plato's position and closer to the view of the mind as process and function. Whereas for Plato the world of Ideas or eternal forms is beyond the world of sense experience, for Aristotle the forms are *in* things as the active principle of organization.

In the late eighteenth century Immanuel Kant criticized the traditional view of the mind as substance, a view which assumes that the individual can make his "self" and his "mind" direct objects of knowledge. According to Kant, all we know for certain is our experiences. The mind that does the knowing is always the subject and never the object of knowledge. For Kant there is unity wherever there is knowledge, and knowledge entails a knower. Where there is memory, there must be something to do the remembering. The organization of experiences in various ways is made possible by a principle of organization. Kant speaks of the "synthetic unity of apperception" and the "transcendental unity of apperception." There is an organic or personal unity that transcends or surpasses or is responsible for the continuity among the separate experiences. This unity we call the *self*. The self is sometimes spoken of as the locus of the forms of knowing. Sometimes, too, the self and the mind are treated as if they were identical.

For Kant, the mind is active; it forms into a system of knowledge all the materials presented by the various senses. Time and space are forms of the mind that are thrust upon nature. Mind is not a separate mental substance; it is the organization and unity of man's personal experiences.

MIND AS AN ASSOCIATION OF EXPERIENCES

Hume, in the eighteenth century, was a severe critic of the traditional view of the mind as a separate substance. Even before Kant's time, Hume attacked the dualism of Plato and Descartes. Hume did not maintain, however, as did Kant, that there was a personal unity or self. Hume carried empiricism to its logical conclusion and attacked both the idea of substance and the rationalism of his time. All knowledge comes through experience, he held, and the sole content of the human mind is impressions and ideas. Impressions are our simple and elemental experiences; they are lively and vivid. Ideas are only copies of impressions. When we introspect, we find only these fleeting experiences and ideas, which are constantly changing. There is no evidence of any substance or of any permanent self.

In his well-known section entitled "Of Personal Identity" in *The Treatise of Human Nature,* Hume says:

> There are some philosophers who imagine we are every moment intimately conscious of what we call our SELF; that we feel its existence and its continuance in existence; and are certain, beyond the evidence of a demonstration, both of its perfect identity and simplicity. . . . For my part, when I enter most intimately into what I call *myself,* I always stumble on some particular perception or other, of heat or cold, light or shade, love or hatred, pain or pleasure. I never can catch *myself* at any time without a perception, and never can observe anything but the perception. When my perceptions are removed for any time, as by sound sleep, so long am I insensible of *myself,* and may truly be said not to exist.[2]

What, then, is the mind? For Hume the mind and the faculties and properties of the mental life are nothing but an association of ideas and experiences. *Mind* is a term for the sum total of the experiences, ideas, and desires that occupy one's attention and life. It is a bundle of experiences, or a collection of sensations.

How then do we acquire the impression of unity? According to Hume, our sensations are tied together by the laws of association, which are three: the law of resemblance, the law of proximity in time and space, and the law of causation. These are based on observation, experience, habit, and custom.

Hume's general attitude is one of skepticism; he is a thoroughgoing empiricist. He hesitates to accept anything beyond the common day-by-day experiences. The critic of Hume will point out that, in the passage quoted above, he continuously uses such terms as "I" and "myself," which imply some fairly constant personal center of unity. While the self finds it difficult to be both subject and object at the same time, the critic will insist that we affirm the existence of a continuing self in the very act of denial. The sup-

[2] From *Hume Selections,* ed. Charles W. Hendel, Jr. (New York: Scribner's, 1927), pp. 83, 84.

porters of Hume point out, however, that in statements like "I deny the self" the subject and the predicate have different meanings. Hume is saying that "this bundle of experiences" (which he calls "I" or "me") denies the existence of nonmaterial substance or a constant center of personal identity. Thus he denies the more traditional concepts of a self.

MIND AS A FORM OF BEHAVIOR

For some philosophers and psychologists, mind is simply one form of behavior. For them, certain kinds of behavior lead us to postulate the existence of a mind; why not, they ask, simply study the behavior and rid ourselves of abstract and unobservable extra entities like "mind"? A few deny that terms like *mind* and *consciousness* have any real content and value; they prefer to speak of neuromuscular activity. This group is represented by the more extreme behaviorists, whom we consider in the next section. Others, like the instrumentalists, merely reject all dualisms and stress intelligent behavior. John Dewey is the chief representative of the instrumentalists. Since we consider his position in a later chapter, we shall state his views only briefly at this point.

For Dewey, *mind* ceases to be a noun and becomes an adjective descriptive of certain kinds of behavior. "There is no separate 'mind' gifted in and of itself with a faculty of thought; such a conception of thought ends in postulating a mystery of a power outside of nature and yet able to intervene within it."[3] Mind and thought become functional aspects of the interaction of natural events. Mind is simply intelligent behavior. Depending on our point of view or frame of reference, mind may be considered an aspect of nature, of an object, or of an organism. Man and nature are part of a continuum. Man is not part body and part mind. Dewey rejects all dualisms and the spectator view of mind. Nature in man is simply nature grown intelligent.

In *The Concept of Mind*[4] Gilbert Ryle also attacks the mentalism in a mind-body dualism and insists that mind is not something separate and distinct from body and matter. Mind is the way a person behaves. Mind is not another world either parallel to or beyond the ordinary world. Ryle attempts to get rid of what he calls the traditional "dogma of the ghost in the machine," and to rectify the "category mistake" or the "philosopher's myth." This mistake and myth are found when men put the facts of mental life in a category or class to which these facts do not properly belong. Ryle uses the example of a foreign visitor on a university campus. Suppose that the visitor, after being shown the college halls, library, dormitories, playing fields, administration offices, and the activities associated with them, asks to see the university. The university, he will be told, is just the organization of

---

[3] John Dewey, *The Quest for Certainty* (New York: Putnam's, 1929), p. 227.

[4] New York: Barnes & Noble, 1950. See also a discussion of this book by a number of writers in *The Journal of Philosophy*, XLVIII (April 26, 1951): 257–301.

the buildings and activities he has seen. To consider the university some counterpart to or entity beyond what he has seen would be a mistake. In the same way, to talk about "mind" or "consciousness" as some counterpart to human behavior or as some world behind or beyond the activities is a mistake. The meaningful referent of the concept "mind" is a description of how people behave.

THE MIND-BODY RELATIONSHIP

The mind-body problem is one of the persistent problems with which men have struggled for centuries. From the time of Descartes in the seventeenth century it has been an issue of the first importance. This importance is due in part to the growing influence of science, with its desire to describe the world in quantitative and mathematical terms. It is also explained in part by the trend of thought, started by Descartes, that has made a clear-cut distinction between mind and matter. If mind and body are different in nature, what can be the relationship between them? If we posit interaction, then there must be some point at which mind and body meet; there must be some quality that both have in common. If there is a common quality, then is there really a dualism?

Interpretations of and solutions to the mind-body problem are many and varied. These solutions range all the way, as we have seen, from a rather complete denial of mind and a thoroughgoing materialism, to the assertion that mind is the only fundamental reality and that what we have called *matter* is an illusion or, at most, a by-product of mind or consciousness. Most explanations, however, have avoided these extremes. There is a widespread belief that mind and body are essentially different. "The nature of the mind and its relation to the brain is perhaps the oldest, most intractable and certainly the most interesting and important of all the problems that man has put to himself on his own nature."[5]

In this section the main answers to the mind-body problem found in the literature of the past and the present are presented. No attempt is made either to give all the shades of opinion or to mention all the men who have supported the various theories.

In the diagrams, the white circles represent the mental, or mind; the solid black circles indicate the physical, or body; X represents the unknown; and the lines show the causal connections.[6]

INTERACTIONISM

Let us begin with what might be called the common-sense view, which has been widely accepted; since the time of Descartes it has been prominent

[5] J. R. Smythies, "Brain and Mind," *The Twentieth Century*, 159 (1956): 462.
[6] A number of books use diagrams similar to these. It is uncertain to whom credit should go.

in philosophical discussions. In considering the view of "mind as substance," we have seen that Descartes made a clear-cut separation between mind and matter. Mind is an immaterial or spiritual substance that thinks; matter is a substance whose chief characteristic is extension. This presentation of Descartes is a classic expression of the common-sense view. One does not have to accept Descartes' philosophy or his formulation of the position to accept interactionism.

According to interactionism, in addition to a physical causal sequence and a psychical causal sequence, the mind may cause bodily changes, and bodily changes may produce mental effects. The following diagram illustrates these connections.

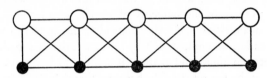

Many people have been impressed by what they believe to be a causal relationship or interaction between mental and bodily processes. Our physical condition affects our disposition; bodily changes register themselves in our mental outlook. Diseases of the brain affect our mental life and thinking. A blow on the head or chloroform fumes may cause us to lose consciousness. The mental effects of drugs, alcohol, and coffee are almost universally recognized. If one's digestion or bodily secretions are disturbed, he may become depressed. We usually cannot think clearly and concentrate unless our bodily processes are functioning rather smoothly. Furthermore, as the brain and the nervous system develop more fully, the powers of the mind also increase.

Mental experiences affect bodily processes, too. An idea strikes us, and we become animated and proceed to strenuous activity. Worry may cause ill health. Fear leads to quickened heart action and other bodily reactions. Anger or even ordinary mental effort may produce a rise in blood pressure. The conviction has been growing, especially among medical men, that mental states may lead to organic as well as functional disease, and that resistance to disease is affected by mental outlook. Teeth are said to decay more quickly when one is under emotional strain. Hypnotism has been used to produce anesthesia, to cure alcoholism, and to control other processes and actions. A blister was raised on a hypnotized patient when the experimenter told him he was being burned, though the metal that touched his skin was cold, not hot.[7]

In spite of the array of evidence and its widespread support, the theory of

7 See Aldous Huxley, *Ends and Means* (New York: Harper, 1937), p. 299.

interactionism has been severely criticized. Men have asked how two substances or entities so different in nature could possibly interact. A causal
relation between a change in the brain or nervous system and a muscular
movement can be understood. A causal relation between an idea and a
physical motion is difficult to comprehend. The two areas seem independent
and self-sufficient.

PARALLELISM

The attempt to meet the objections to interactionism led to parallelism.
According to this interpretation of the mind-body question, there is no
interaction or causal connection between the two areas. Mental processes
and physical processes are equally real, but they are not causally related;
they merely accompany each other in time.

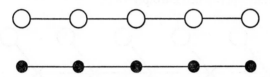

The law of causation holds good in the mental realm, since one mental
event may cause another mental event. The law of causation also holds good
in the physical realm. The illustration has been used of "two railway trains
running side-by-side on a double track." Although the trains are parallel and
appear to be moving together, they are operating on different systems and
are not causally connected.

The classic example of this point of view is the position of the philosopher
Leibniz (1646–1716). For him there is a preestablished harmony in God's
mind and creativity. Two clocks may run together and keep perfect time
because they have been made with such skill that they will always operate
in harmony. Leibniz believed that the universe had been made with such skill
that mind and matter always operate in harmony. The course of the universe
was determined by the way its elements were endowed.

Parallelism has never had the widespread support given to interactionism
and some other theories. It seems to cut the universe in two and to deny
rather than explain the problem. Sudden experiences or interruptions are
exceedingly difficult to explain on the basis of parallelism. How is it, when
the doorbell rings, that we get the idea that someone is at the door? When
we are in the midst of a train of thought, we are annoyed if unwelcome interruptions occur. Furthermore, this interpretation appears to make mind useless in the evolution and the physical struggles of men. Most of us have
believed that reflective thinking saves time and energy and that thinking
makes a real difference in the world of affairs. Thus some men have been

forced, in seeking an explanation of an apparent relationship, to adopt the doctrine of the identity of mind and body.

THE DOUBLE-ASPECT, OR IDENTITY, THEORY

According to the double-aspect theory, neither mind nor body is a completely separate and independent entity. Both mind and matter are expressions of some underlying reality that appears as "mind" when we experience it from the inside, or subjectively, and as "body," or matter, when we view it from the outside, or objectively. Mind and body are thus in a sense identical; they are two different aspects of the same thing (an unknown, X). As people, we know our inner life intimately, or at first hand; we speak of it as mental. The rest of the world we know only at second hand, or through its impression upon our sense organs; we speak of this part of our world as physical. Mind is this one reality approached introspectively.

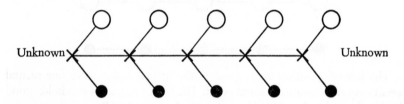

Both Spinoza and Kant regarded the mind and body as two aspects of one reality. For Spinoza, a pantheist, the one reality was God. For Kant, reality was the unknown "thing-in-itself." The two series, the physical and the psychical, thus seem to be causally connected. Members of the movement known as New Realism hold a position which is sometimes called neutral realism or neutral monism—that is, that neither consciousness nor physical things are ultimate; both may be analyzed into neutral entities.

Supporters of this view claim that it meets the objections directed against the two preceding theories. There is one integrated, spatiotemporal world, without any breaks in continuity, and so this theory preserves the law of the conservation of energy that the theory of interactionism is thought to endanger. Nor is there the mystery of how two separate, parallel series of events can operate side by side.

Those who criticize the double-aspect view argue that mental processes and physical processes are too different from each other to be explained in this way. Mind is not in space, and, to some extent, it seems to shape future events, not merely to parallel present physical events. Physical processes are extended in space and appear to be mechanically directed. The approach uses an unknown, X, to explain a difficult problem. It leaves the seeming dualism unsolved.

EPIPHENOMENALISM AND THE DENIAL OF MIND

A view of mind that has had some popularity among men of science is known as epiphenomenalism. According to this interpretation, consciousness, or mind, is an attendant or secondary phenomenon accompanying some bodily processes. Mental processes causally influence neither the physical processes nor even other mental phenomena. Matter is primary, the one real substance. The stream of consciousness is a phenomenon accompanying certain neurological changes. What we have called *mind* is a glow or shadow that appears under some conditions. Certain processes taking place in the brain and nervous system produce the sensations, feelings, emotion, imagery, thought, or other types of consciousness.

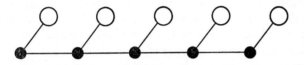

The term *epiphenomenalism* was first used and the philosophy first defended by Thomas Huxley. The position has been held by various materialistic schools of thought. One way to meet a problem is to deny its existence or to get rid of one of the offending aspects or parties. In contemporary psychology some schools tend to deny the existence of mind. In a chapter entitled "The Demise of Mind," one writer says:

> Within a strict scientific universe of discourse . . . there is no such thing as mind —at least, not with a capital "m." In everyday conversation the word is useful enough, in spite of its gaudy ambiguity of meaning; but in scientific language, except as a short-cut expression, it has no defensible place. Its career would almost be enough to rule it out.[8]

Epiphenomenalism asserts that what we call mental events are always the results of physical events, but are never the cause of other mental events or the cause of any physical events. This appears to be an extreme and arbitrary assertion that will stand or fall with the materialistic and mechanistic assumptions on which it is based. Materialism and mechanism are considered in a later chapter.

PSYCHICAL MONISM AND THE DENIAL OF MATTER

We have seen that epiphenomenalism and the various materialistic types of explanation get rid of mind as a fundamental entity. In a similar way,

---

[8] From Carroll C. Pratt, *The Logic of Modern Psychology* (New York: Macmillan, 1939), p. 26. By permission of The Macmillan Company, publishers. See also B. F. Skinner, *Science and Human Behavior* (New York: Macmillan, 1953), p. 285.

various forms of mentalism, or spiritualism, would reduce matter to a position of secondary importance and assert that mind is primary. Psychical monism is the view that the causal series is confined to the mental and that what we call *matter* is a shadow cast by thought. Matter is essentially an appearance. The body is an externalization or phenomenon of mind.

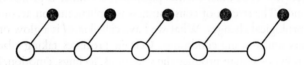

All idealists insist on the permanent significance and reality of mind.[9] They do not all claim that the body or the physical is mere appearance—that is, not all idealists are psychical monists—but psychical monism in some form is supported by idealists such as Lotze, Fechner, Eduard von Hartmann, W. K. Clifford, Friedrich Paulsen, and C. A. Strong.

Psychical monism is likely to be rejected by all but the mystics and a certain group of idealists. If mind is everything, then mind has all the qualities included in the term *matter*—for example, mind then would have extension. On the other hand, if matter is all that exists, then we shall have to endow matter with a new set of qualities not ordinarily attached to our concept of it —for example, matter then would be conscious. One tries to get rid of the problem by denying the conflict. These more extreme solutions—the denial of mind and the denial of matter—tend to give *mind* and *matter* the same meaning, and they fail to explain apparent distinctions.

MIND ACCORDING TO EMERGENT EVOLUTION

An interpretation of mind based on emergent evolution is fairly popular. The position is said to leave behind the former solutions of the mind-body problem. There is no dualism, no interaction, no extreme denial. Matter is real and mind is real. Mind is a distinct level of reality, and is as real as any other level. Mind, however, has new qualities or characteristics of its own that cannot be adequately interpreted with reference to the standards or criteria of previous levels. In *Emergent Evolution* C. Lloyd Morgan uses the pyramid to give diagrammatic expression to this view. The ladder also has been suggested. (See the diagrams on page 251.)

Supporters of this view of emergence, or the theory of levels, believe its functional approach solves many of the problems that have baffled students in the past. One of the false ideas inherited from the nineteenth century is that the real things of the world are elements. The twentieth century is discovering that reality consists of wholes. We must interpret mind as organi-

9 For definition of *idealism* see the Glossary and p. 226.

zation and activity. Just as the physicist uses the term *physical* to denote the processes described in his science and the biologist uses the term *vital* to refer to living things, we may use the term *mental* to denote the qualities and activities we discover and experience on the personal level.

Philosophically, the mind is explained by the notion of creative synthesis. Protons and electrons are organized into atoms, atoms into molecules, and these into living cells from which finally emerge consciousness and intelligent action. At each level a creative synthesis takes place, resulting in a series of new qualities. With the arrival of man there emerge a new reality and marvelous new powers, including memory, imagination, thought, and reasoning, so that the world becomes different. All these levels are equally real. Matter is real, mind is real, and moral distinctions are real. Science, art, philosophy, religion, and moral distinctions have been realized through mind. The self is the being who does or who experiences these things. The self is the living individual with his needs and interests and his capacities for feeling, thinking, and creative imagination. The self is not the mind. The self is the living being who carries on these mental processes.

CONCLUDING COMMENTS

Obviously there are many psychological methods of study and explanations of mind. The various psychological interpretations use methods, terms, and symbols that differ greatly. They almost use different languages when they set forth their explanations.

Even though a few people assert that the subject matter of psychology is so complex and elusive as to make impossible any strictly scientific treatment, some progress is being made. There are some converging lines of evidence and some quite generally accepted conclusions. For example, most psychologists recognize that the traditional structural approach is inadequate, that function and human activity are especially important, that the traditional notion of man as a purely "rational animal" needs to be modified to the extent that we recognize the importance of impulse, emotion, habit, and custom in the explanation of behavior. The extreme sensationalism of Hume and the interpretation of mind as neuromuscular activity are likewise inadequate. However, each psychological school is organized around some main emphasis and therefore tends to impose its order or system on that aspect of the complex individual that attracts its attention.

Each of the psychological interpretations has given us some valuable knowledge about mind and its powers and functions. Behaviorism has made a significant contribution in its concept of conditioning. Psychoanalysis has given us valuable information about mental conflicts and repressions. Gestalt psychology has called our attention to the qualities of wholes and to the dangers involved in dealing with parts separately. But as total explanations, these interpretations are inadequate. A combination of methods and a receptive attitude toward knowledge gained by any method and from any of these sources might be considered reasonable. Just as the psychologists differ about methods of study and interpretations of the mind, so philosophers differ about the theory of the mind and the mind-body relationship that they think offers the most adequate explanation.

To compare and contrast all the different interpretations of mind is not possible in the space available. We would like to point out, however, that the question of the truth or falsity of the various interpretations of mind is not a purely academic issue. The acceptance or rejection of particular views has widespread implications for the interpretation of other questions and for the lives we live. For example, let us consider very briefly two influential views of mind set forth by Plato and Freud. Plato's concept of the mind has been influential throughout the course of Western civilization. Freud's views have been influential during the last half century. The two views have some points in common as well as sharply contrasting points. Both men divide the psychic life of the individual into three parts, but the division and emphasis are different. For Plato, the function of reason is to be the master of life and to rule the passions. For Freud, the *id,* which represents man's passionate nature, is largely beyond the control of reason. The ego, which represents man's conscious and reflective life, is weak, easily frightened, and cowed by the passions and the pressures and dangers of the external world. Plato may give us a picture of man that is too optimistic, and that stresses too strongly the power of the intellectual elements in man's life. On the other hand, Freud has probably underestimated these elements. Freud's long study of neurotic people has given him, in the opinion of many, a somewhat distorted view of man. Since ideas have consequences for our lives and society, it is important for us to discover whether Plato's or Freud's views of mind are the correct ones. If we think that Freud has the true view we may expect less of man in the way of self-discipline and self-control than if we accept Plato's interpretation.

One of the crucial issues facing this and future ages is whether man is going to neglect and weaken his latent powers of reflection and control and permit his impulses and passions to have free sway, or whether his more or less blind and unconscious animal appetites are to be brought under control by the strengthening and recognition of his conscious and rational powers and insights. On the answer to questions such as these the future of man and civilization may well rest.

Is it possible that mind is something like life itself? We have to recognize and take account of life, even though we cannot describe and define it adequately. Life, in contrast with the inorganic, is not something that can be put under a microscope, enlarged, and directly observed. When we attempt to dissect and to analyze the higher functions of life, they seem to disappear. Mind is of a similar nature. Thinking, feeling, appreciation, and a sense of values are central in individuality, or personality. They are the very things that give sense and meaning to the human venture and to the universe itself; yet they are not things that can be counted, measured, touched, and seen.

In the evolutionary development of the human race, it was a tremendous step forward when living creatures gained the ability to see distant objects. A similar advance was made when organisms were able to hear and interpret sounds. These new powers saved time, energy, and life. When memory, imagination, and self-consciousness developed, even greater steps forward were taken. Men could "see" and "hear" what was not present. They could review the past and plan for the future. When they had acquired these powers and could make intelligent choices, it could be said that mind was actually present. Whether we use the term *mutation* or *creative synthesis* or *creative act,* the new powers that are present are of the utmost importance. The actual steps by which they arrived and the symbolism used for their interpretation, while important to know, are not so crucial for the philosopher as a realization of the significance of mind and creative intelligence. From the creative processes of cosmic evolution, to the widespread will to live expressed through a great multitude of ascending forms of life, to the wide range of mental powers leading to self-consciousness and to human personality may be a continuous process. Mind, intelligence, and self-conscious beings may be goals of the creative process.

QUESTIONS AND PROJECTS

1. Review Questions

(1) In the past, man has made a distinction between material and mental processes, or between the physical and the psychical. Why have these distinctions been made, and do you think the mind-body problem is still a live issue?

(2) Explain the various methods of studying and interpreting mind as set forth by the different schools of psychology. Is any one method sufficient, or do you think it advantageous to use many different approaches to study the mind? Discuss.

(3) Give at least three reasons for the delay and confusion in the study of mind.

(4) What problems do we encounter when we attempt to be strictly objective in our experiments with and studies of the mind or mental phenomena?

(5) State the four general theories of the nature of the mind.

(6) Distinguish between "mind as substance" and "mind as personal unity or principle of organization." How do the views of Plato, Aristotle, and Descartes relate to this distinction?

(7) State the interpretations of mind given by Hume and by the behaviorists. How adequate are these interpretations?

(8) Explain the important theories of the mind-body relationship. Be ready to present the case for and against any one of these interpretations and to indicate which side of the argument seems most convincing.

(9) Are all the interpretations of the mind-body problem mutually exclusive, or would it be possible to hold, say, the theory of interactionism and that of emergent evolution at the same time?

(10) State and explain carefully the general conclusions that can be drawn regarding mind as a result of the discussion here. Do not feel limited by the conclusions drawn at the end of the chapter, and, if you disagree with some of these, clarify the reasons for your position.

2. Which solution of the mind-body problem seems most reasonable? Be ready to state clearly and to defend that position.

3. The statement has been made that the nature and power of the mind are found not in physiological and psychological measurements but in the great literature, art, religion, and outstanding achievements of man. Do you agree?

4. In *How Our Minds Work* (New York: Philosophical Library, 1947), pp. 67 ff., C. E. M. Joad gives an example of a geometrician who, after thinking about the properties of a triangle, reaches a conclusion that he states in a formula. He carries it in his head for a time and later writes a book in which he includes the formula. It is understood by A, who translates it into French, and it is read and understood by B. The formula is included in a lecture and understood by C. Here, then, are four people who understand the same things by the formula and know its meaning; yet the sensory stimuli are different in each case. The stimuli include an idea, English letters, French letters, and sound in the form of speech. How do you explain this "synthesizing power of mind"?

5. Does reality seem to you to be monistic (one), dualistic (two), or pluralistic (many) in its fundamental nature? If it is monistic, we shall need to reduce everything to one substance (mind, matter, or a "neutral" substance). If it is dualistic, then mind and matter are the two substances. If it is pluralistic, mind and matter may still be two of the many realities. Today the concept "substance" is not popular, and many people prefer to use the term *energy* for the physical world and *process* for the mental world. The term *behavior* may be used for all processes in the world. For a statement of the case in favor of the monistic school and the dualistic reply, you may wish to consult J. R. Smythies, "Brain and Mind," *The Twentieth Century*, 159(1956):462–473.

6. Review one of the books in the "Suggested Readings" list at the end of this chapter, especially one of those by Bickel, Chennakesavan, Joad, Laslett (ed.), Rhine, Ryle, and Sinnott.

7. Comment on the following statements:
   (1) "I think; therefore I am."
   (2) "Mental events are only brain events; thinking is subvocal speech."
   (3) "One never really knows other minds."

(4) "Men are tormented by the opinions they have of things, rather than by the things themselves."

(5) "Knowledge has altered the world. We must rely on knowledge to accommodate ourselves to new surroundings."

(6) "When a person depends for his happiness upon the interests and activities of his own mind, he has become to a considerable extent independent of his material surroundings."

SUGGESTED READINGS

BICKEL, LOTHER. *The Unity of Body and Mind.* Ed. and trans. by Walter Bernard. New York: Philosophical Library, 1959.
A small book that deals with the philosophical and psychological problems of body-mind relationships and man's position in nature.

BLANSHARD, BRAND. "The Nature of Mind," in *American Philosophers at Work,* ed. Sidney Hook. New York: Criterion, 1956.
A defense of "mind" as a set of processes distinguished "through their control by an immanent end."

BROAD, C. D. *Religion, Philosophy, and Psychical Research.* New York: Harcourt, Brace, 1953.
In Part I, an outstanding philosopher examines psychical research for the light it can throw on man's powers and prospects.

CHENNAKESAVAN, SARASVATI. *The Concept of Mind in Indian Philosophy.* New York: Asia Publishing, 1960.
A study of mind in the Advaita Vedanta system of Hinduism and a comparison with Western concepts of mind.

FARBER, SEYMOUR M., AND WILSON, ROGER H. L. *Control of the Mind, Man, and Civilization.* New York: McGraw-Hill, 1961. (University of California, San Francisco Medical Center.)
A symposium in which the papers deal with mind in relation to problems of integration, drugs, society, technology, and restriction and freedom.

HOOK, SIDNEY (ed.). *Dimensions of Mind: A Symposium.* New York: Collier Books, 1961. (New York University Institute of Philosophy.)
The papers represent many points of view on "the mind-body problem," "the brain and the machine," and "concept-formation."

JOAD, C. E. M. *How Our Minds Work.* New York: Philosophical Library, 1946.
A brief, clear discussion of mind and body and the relationship between the two.

LASLETT, PETER (ed.). *The Physical Basis of Mind.* New York: Macmillan, 1950.
A little book in which seven scientists and three philosophers explain for the listening public (over the B.B.C.) their conceptions of the physical basis of mind. Clear and readable.

RHINE, J. B. *New World of the Mind.* New York: Sloane, 1953.

An account of past research, current experiments, and future possibilities in the area of extrasensory perception. See also the author's New Frontiers of the Mind *and* The Reach of the Mind.

RHINE, LOUISA E. *Hidden Channels of the Mind.* New York: Sloane, 1961.

A study of extrasensory perception and the conditions under which clairvoyance, precognition, and the like appear.

RYLE, GILBERT. *The Concept of Mind.* New York: Barnes & Noble, 1950.

A vigorous attack on the mentalism in mind-body dualism. Mind is a way of behaving, not an entity to be treated as a special instrument.

SCHRODINGER, ERWIN. *Mind and Matter.* Cambridge: Cambridge U. Press, 1958.

Six lectures on such questions as consciousness, understanding, the principle of objectivation, oneness of mind, science and religion, and sensual qualities.

SHERRINGTON, SIR CHARLES SCOTT. *Man on His Nature.* New York: Macmillan, 1941.

An outstanding physiologist sums up the results of his study of the relation of brain and mind.

SINNOTT, EDMUND W. *Matter, Mind, and Man: The Biology of Human Nature.* New York: Harper, 1957.

A biologist sees evidence of a principle of organization that brings order out of chaos, spirit out of matter. An organism is a mind-and-body unity.

WERKMEISTER, W. H. *A Philosophy of Science.* New York: Harper, 1940.

See Chapter XI, "Mind and Personality," pp. 366–424 for a clear discussion of the interrelation of mind and body and of the psychological and philosophical interpretations of personality.

❧ ELEVEN ❧

HOW FREE IS MAN?

Is man free in the sense that he has some power to choose between alternatives and to initiate action? Or is his every act predetermined? Probably no other issue in philosophy is more alive today or has more far-reaching consequences. If all events in the world, including a man's thoughts and actions, are rigidly determined by forces beyond his control, then a man can neither act differently from the way he does nor really guide the course of events even in his own life. If he could not have acted differently, should he be held responsible for his conduct?

Upon the solution to this question of man's freedom depend the answers to a great many other questions, including those as to the nature of the person, man's power of self-discipline, the status of morals, and social policy and programs. Our aim in this chapter is to clarify the issue of free will versus determinism and, if possible, to find an answer. The term *will* in modern thought refers to a person's ability to choose to perform acts of all sorts—thinking as well as doing. Today men are less likely to talk about "freedom of the will" than to use such expressions as "freedom of choice," "the power of alternative choice," and "moral freedom." Is man a "self-conscious center of free activity"? Is he capable of initiating action in accordance with ends that he selects?

THE DILEMMA OF FREEDOM AND NECESSITY

In our intimate, personal relationships with other men and women we assume that we are free to decide many issues. Many such contacts are permeated with ideas of purpose and freedom. Spontaneity is taken for granted and is felt to be the very essence of life. We assemble to decide certain questions, and we persuade others to accept our plans.

The world of the sciences is one with quite different assumptions. In the scientific world it is assumed that everything is determined (or caused) by natural laws, and determinism and often mechanism are taken for granted. The universe as a whole and all its parts participate in and are governed by an orderly causal sequence. Effects follow causes with often predictable regularity. The causal sequence is thought to hold not only in the physical sciences but in the biological, social, and psychological sciences as well. All these sciences have made considerable progress operating on the basis of a strict determinism. (There are those who claim, however, that in the natural sciences, the traditional stronghold of determinism, the doctrine of "universal determinism" may have to be given up "in an effort to understand the world of subatomic behavior."[1]) Here, then, is a seeming paradox: in our personal relations we take freedom for granted, whereas in the sciences we assume that necessity and determinism are the rule.

We wish to set forth the contrasting positions as fairly as we can. We shall first examine some positions of thoroughgoing determinism, where the tendency is to deny all freedom. This view has also been called *"hard" determinism*, or *necessitarianism*. The second position, sometimes called *indeterminism*, claims that freedom is real in the sense that some personal choices are independent of antecedent causation. We shall use William James as an exponent of this view of freedom. Finally, we shall present a third position, which recognizes both determinism *and* freedom.

THE DENIAL OF FREEDOM

Today the denial of freedom occurs most frequently as a result or a by-product of the postulate of determinism as accepted by many scientists and philosophers. Let us consider this position first, then a classic example of monistic determinism, and then other forms of the rejection of freedom of choice, such as predestination and fatalism.

THOROUGHGOING DETERMINISM AS A SCIENTIFIC DOCTRINE

There are thinkers who would agree with the Persian poet Omar Khayyām that "With earth's first clay they did the last man knead," or with the French philosopher Baron von Holbach that "Our volitions and our desires are never in our power." The German philosopher Arthur Schopenhauer thought that the course of a man's life is "as necessarily predetermined as the course of a clock" and that "a man can surely do what he wills to do, but he cannot determine what he wills."

Determinism as a scientific doctrine is the view that the entire realm of nature, including man, participates in an unbroken chain of cause and effect. All events in the world are fully explained by preceding events. The determinist is impressed by the orderliness of the universe, the universal sway of natural laws, and the progress of the sciences in explaining events as causal

---

1 See statements by Sidney Hook in the Preface and by Percy W. Bridgman in Part II, Ch. 1, of Sidney Hook (ed.), *Determinism and Freedom in the Age of Modern Science* (New York: Collier Books, 1961). (New York University Institute of Philosophy.)

sequences. He believes that all human behavior, like the happenings in the world about man, is governed by natural law and is the result of antecedent events. Wherever nature has been studied, men have found orderly causal sequences. From the orbits of the distant stars to the fall of the snowflake, natural law reigns supreme. From such sciences as physics, chemistry, biology, psychology, and sociology we discover that man too is ruled by cause and effect. His glands, complexes, unconscious drives, conditioning, folkways, and conventions all influence his life; the whole range of hereditary and environmental pressures are ever present and are powerful determining factors.

Many believers in freedom of choice can accept the statements about scientific determinism that we have made in the preceding paragraph. Some scientists and philosophers, however, carry their determinism to the point where all freedom is denied. After saying that Western thought has emphasized the importance and dignity of the individual and individual freedom, a psychologist goes on to say:

> The use of such concepts as individual freedom, initiative, and responsibility has, therefore, been well reinforced. When we turn to what science has to offer, however, we do not find very comforting support for the traditional Western point of view. The hypothesis that man is not free is essential to the application of scientific method to the study of human behavior. The free inner man who is held responsible for the behavior of the external biological organism is only a prescientific substitute for the kinds of causes which are discovered in the course of a scientific analysis. All these alternatives lie *outside* the individual.[2]

In a somewhat similar vein, a philosopher tells us that our conscious lives, including our choices and decisions and the "entire train of deliberations leading up to them," are merely the expression of unconscious urges and desires. After relating cases of people who have gone astray, he says of children who have turned out all right that it is "through no virtue of their own. . . . The machine turned them out with a minimum of damage. . . . We do not blame people for the color of their eyes, but we have not attained the same attitude toward their socially significant activities."[3] If a person's desires, as well as the acts resulting from them, are rigidly determined, then he is not responsible for his actions; he is merely the plaything of forces beyond his control.

A Classic Example of Thoroughgoing Determinism   A classic example from among the great masters is the determinism of Benedict Spinoza (1632–1677). Spinoza's philosophy is a modification of Descartes' position. For Spinoza,

---

[2] B. F. Skinner, *Science and Human Behavior* (New York: Macmillan, 1953), pp. 447–448. Used by permission of The Macmillan Company.

[3] John Hospers, "Meaning and Free Will," *Philosophy and Phenomenological Research*, 10 (March, 1950): 326–327.

God, or Nature, is the only self-existent substance. Mind and matter, or thought and extension, are attributes, or qualities, of this one substance. Nature extended is matter; Nature thinking is mind. Intellect and will are modes (modifications) of thought. The one substance—God, or the Universe —is not personal, and it does not have a purpose, since personality and purpose are limiting concepts. Spinoza has been called an atheist and an agnostic monist, as well as a pantheist and a "God-intoxicated man." The point that concerns us here is that his position is clearly a monistic determinism. There is one infinite cosmic order, a fact which excludes chance and spontaneity from nature. Reality is completely rational, and there is unity, order, and necessity everywhere.

How is it, then, that men frequently consider themselves to be free agents who may do this or that by choice? According to Spinoza, men think that they are free merely because they are conscious of many of their acts and, at the same time, they are ignorant of the causes of these actions. Men therefore go on to assume that *they* caused these acts—that is, men postulate themselves as causes of acts in the absence of other demonstrable causes. All events in the mental and moral life of man, as well as those in the physical realm, can be explained as the result of direct cause and effect. Terms like *should* and *ought,* and other expressions of praise, blame, and obligation, have no real place in the world. In the entire realm of nature, things must be simply what they are.

> Nothing happens in nature which can be attributed to any vice of nature, for she is always the same and everywhere one. Her virtue is the same, and her power of acting; that is to say, her laws and rules, according to which all things are and are changed from form to form, are everywhere and always the same; so that there must also be one and the same method of understanding the nature of all things whatsoever, that is to say, by the universal laws and rules of nature.[4]

Continuing, Spinoza tells us that he is going to consider "human actions and appetites" just as if he were considering "lines, planes, or bodies."

> Thus the madman, the chatterer, the boy, and others of the same kind all believe that they speak by a free command of the mind, whilst, in truth, they have no power to restrain the impulse which they have to speak, so that experience itself, no less than reason, clearly teaches that men believe themselves to be free simply because they are conscious of their own actions, knowing nothing of the causes by which they are determined: it teaches, too, that the decrees of the mind are nothing but the appetites themselves, which differ, therefore, according to the different temper of the body. . . . All this plainly shows that the decree of the mind, the appetite, and determination of the body are coincident

[4] From "Ethics," Part III, of *Spinoza Selections,* ed. John Wild (New York: Scribner's, 1930), pp. 205–206.

in nature, or rather that they are one and the same thing, which, when it is considered under the attribute of thought and manifested by that, is called a decree, and when it is considered under the attribute of extension and is deduced from the laws of motion and rest, is called a determination.[5]

The will, according to Spinoza, as we saw above, is a mode, or modification, of thought. Thus there can be no separation in man between thought and will. No volition can exist unless it is determined by another cause, this by another, and so on. An action is free only insofar as the cause of the action is "wholly contained in the nature and past history of the agent." Thus only the Universe, or the collective whole, can be said to be completely free.

Spinoza rejects the view, held by many determinists, that men considers various possible alternatives and then select one because of certain attractive features it possesses for them. Spinoza contends that the presence or absence of consciousness is not a decisive factor. The decision and the action are determined by man's impulses, whether or not he is aware of them at the time.

PREDESTINATION

Predestination in its most thoroughgoing form is the doctrine that God has decreed every event that is to take place, or at least that each man's destiny is fixed by divine decree. If God is omnipotent and omniscient—that is, all-powerful and all-knowing—then things must be determined by Him. This means that events in nature and human conduct, including man's will, are determined by the sovereign will of God. The view is thus theological and supernatural in its outlook and emphasis. The doctrine ranges from an extreme form, in which every event and each man's destiny are fixed, to interpretations that call for some initiative or choice on the part of the individual. Some contemporary theologians use the term *predestination* to mean that "God is seeking us even before we are aware of Him," or that "man's decision is a response to the initiative of God."

The doctrine of predestination is found in Judaic, Christian, and Islamic religious thought. Though Judaism and Christianity have placed emphasis mainly on man's responsibility to God, there is a development of the notion of predestination from passages in the writings of Paul through Augustine to John Calvin. Augustine elaborates the doctrine and gives it a prominent place in his thinking. In Calvinism the doctrine of predestination achieves its most complete expression in Christian thought. In extreme Calvinism, salvation is not dependent on anything that man can do. In traditional Islamic theology, whatever happens is the will of Allah.

In its extreme form the doctrine of predestination has always provoked

5 *Ibid.*, pp. 212–213.

protest and opposition. It seems to make God responsible for evil as well as for good, since, if God decrees what is to happen, then God rather than man is responsible for events. Modern conceptions of God do not assign responsibility for evil to Him.

FATALISM

Fatalism is the belief that some (perhaps all) events are irrevocably fixed, so that human effort cannot alter them. It is the doctrine that the happenings in the world of nature and the events in men's lives are predetermined at the beginning of time, so that no human will has a part in shaping the course of things. A man's lot is determined independently of his choices and actions; the future is always beyond his control. Fatalism holds to the notion of the inevitable appearance of an event at a specific time. Fatalism logically may set forth a definite theory of causation, but it is in fact more likely to consider the question of causes an inscrutable mystery.

> A FATALIST—if there is any such—thinks he cannot do anything about the future. He thinks it is not up to him what is going to happen next year, tomorrow, or the very next moment. He thinks that even his own behavior is not in the least within his power, any more than the motions of the heavenly bodies, the events of remote history, or the political developments in China. It would, accordingly, be pointless for him to deliberate about what he is going to do, for a man deliberates only about such things as he believes are within his power to do and to forego, or to affect by his doings and foregoings.[6]

In Greek and Roman thought the concept of Fate is prominent. It is a determining power sometimes identified with the will of Zeus (Greek), or Jupiter (the Roman god identical with Zeus), or often thought of as superior to the gods, as well as to mortal men. Fate is omnipresent in the Greek plays, especially the tragedies. The Stoics identified Fate with the course of Nature and with Providence. The Romans were influenced by the Greek beliefs regarding Fate, and they reproduced much of the spirit of Greek mythology. In place of Fate the Romans sometimes used the similar concept of Fortune.

The view that as individuals or in groups we are incapable of changing the course of events seems to have its origin or basis in the fact of human helplessness in the presence of certain inescapable evils, especially death. Fatalism is in part an emotional reaction growing out of the fact that man lives in a universe which it far exceeds his power to understand and control. Fatalism is most prevalent in areas where hopeless misery exists without any effort to relieve it and in areas without advanced means of scientific and social control.

---

[6] Richard Taylor, "Fatalism," *The Philosophical Review*, 71 (January, 1962): 56.

In time of war, fatalism often has a noticeable revival. It is likely to be prevalent among soldiers under fire. The first reaction to danger may be panic or fear or worry, but soon the attitude of fatalism may emerge as an adjustment or defense or escape reaction. The individual may say to himself, "If there is a bullet with my name on it, I'll get it anyway. If there isn't, I'll come through unscratched, so why worry?" From then on he may settle down and take events as they come. That he does not make decisions for himself—the soldier is trained to follow orders—is an additional factor in the genesis of a fatalistic attitude.

A fatalistic outlook may appeal to certain irresponsible people. If the individual cannot influence the course of events, he is not responsible for what happens. Furthermore, he does not have to exert himself strenuously; he takes what comes along, and emotionally accepts it or not; in either case, the blame is not his. Fatalism is a convenient alibi for those who are inclined to shift responsibility and blame outside forces for the course of events.

Fatalism, as a theoretical position that someone may insist on holding, is not subject to refutation. What it does, however, is to blur all sorts of important and useful distinctions. It classifies all events as the same—even those as apparently different as a man in prison who cannot go to the movies and the man who decided not to go to the movies. In modern Western civilization, with its concepts of democracy, progress, and human control, fatalism has never been a prominent attitude.

FREEDOM AS INDETERMINISM

Many people are repelled by a doctrine of thoroughgoing determinism. They want and consider the world to be "open" rather than "closed." They desire the novelty, spontaneity, and genuine creativity that they think a mechanistic or a rigid determinism precludes. We shall consider William James as the outstanding representative of this position.

WILLIAM JAMES AND INDETERMINISM

William James (1842–1910) was an able exponent of the theory of freedom of the will, or "indeterminism," as he called it. James thought that the "monistic superstition" leads men to deny freedom. Once this superstition is cast aside, the way is open for a belief in freedom, novelty, pluralism, and a world in the making. The question of free will cannot be resolved on either strictly psychological or purely theoretical grounds.[7] The doctrine of free will is essentially a moral postulate about the universe. Our sense or feeling of freedom and the existence of effort on the part of human beings point to the fact that some things are decided by human choice.

[7] William James, *The Principles of Psychology* (New York: Holt, 1896), II, pp. 572 ff.

Determinism, according to James, is the view that past factors decree what the future shall be. Consequently, the future has no ambiguous or indeterminate possibilities hidden within it. James says that indeterminism, on the other hand, is the view that the parts of the universe have a considerable amount of "loose play"—that is, not all things are causally connected and there is a genuine pluralism in the nature of things. There are genuine possibilities existing in the future. The possibilities exceed the actualities in many situations. James says that "our first act of freedom, if we are free, ought in all inward propriety to be to affirm that we are free."[8] Though freedom is a postulate—that is, an unproved rule or basic assumption from which to reason—so also are causality and uniformity. James is not afraid of the term *chance*. If we accept the real existence of chance, novelty, and spontaneity, the world is just as consistent as is the world of the strict determinist. For example, before the action we often cannot predict which of two possible ways a man will walk to his home. The indeterminists do not assert that *any imaginable* action is possible for *any* person; they claim merely that among two or more mutually exclusive choices, more than one is possible, though only one becomes actual—that is, occurs. Freedom is limited to the field of voluntary action and conscious selection.

In his essay "The Dilemma of Determinism," which the student is urged to read, James shows how judgments of regret and tragedies such as murders present a real dilemma for the determinist. If the murder has been fully determined by the rest of the universe, a judgment of regret seems inappropriate or foolish.

> Calling a thing bad means, if it means anything at all, that the thing ought not to be, that something else ought to be in its stead. Determinism, in denying that anything else can be in its stead, virtually defines the universe as a place in which what ought to be is impossible—in other words, as an organism whose constitution is afflicted with an incurable taint, an irremediable flaw.[9]

If one is a determinist the inappropriate regret for the murder leads to a larger regret and hence to a pessimism.

> When murders and treacheries cease to be sins, regrets are theoretic absurdities and errors. The theoretic and the active life thus play a kind of seesaw with each other on the ground of evil. The rise of either sends the other down. Murder and treachery cannot be good without regret being bad: regret cannot be good without treachery and murder being bad. Both, however, are supposed to have been foredoomed; so something must be fatally unreasonable, absurd, and wrong in the world.[10]

[8] William James, *The Will to Believe and Other Essays in Popular Philosophy* (New York: Longmans, Green, 1912), p. 146.

[9] *Ibid.*, pp. 161–162.

[10] *Ibid.*, pp. 163–164.

The only escape for the determinist, according to James, is in the direction of a subjectivism which assumes that a certain amount of evil is good, since it may further some higher good. Such an optimism is gained only at the price of suppressing our judgments of blame and regret. Insofar as the determinist attempts to think things through, without denying evident facts of experience, he is directed toward a pessimism or toward a subjectivism which may lead to the pathetic hope that everything really is good. This type of optimism results in an ethical indifference that is likely to bring trouble in its wake.

> The only consistent way of representing a pluralism and a world whose parts may affect one another through their conduct being either good or bad is the indeterministic way. What interest, zest, or excitement can there be in achieving the right way, unless we are enabled to feel that the wrong way is also a possible and a natural way—nay, more, a menacing and an imminent way? and what sense can there be in condemning ourselves for taking the wrong way, unless we need have done nothing of the sort, unless the right way was open to us as well? I cannot understand the willingness to act, no matter how we feel, without the belief that acts are really good or bad. I cannot understand the belief that an act is bad, without regret at its happening. I cannot understand regret without the admission of real, genuine possibilities in the world.[11]

THE CASE FOR FREEDOM AND DETERMINISM

In dealing with the problem of freedom versus necessity, many people have been led to make extreme claims and draw unreasonable conclusions from the evidence. Some, impressed by the evidence for determinism, have claimed that freedom in the sense of personal initiative and choice is an illusion. They have agreed with the player in *As You Like It* that "All the world's a stage, And all the men and women merely players." Others have been impressed by the evidence for freedom of choice and have declared that the doctrine of determinism is false.

The position to which we are now turning is that both those who deny all freedom and power of alternative choice and those who deny determinism are taking false and extreme positions. The supporters of this third position say that it is not an "either-or" issue; we need not accept freedom alone or determinism alone. This is what is sometimes referred to as a "both-and" problem. Determinism in the sense of general causation and freedom in the sense of choice between alternatives may be shown to be not only compatible but necessarily complementary.

How is it possible to accept both determinism and freedom? Let us look at determinism a little more closely, and then see why it is also possible to

[11] *Ibid.,* p. 175.

accept a degree of freedom. Determinism is a necessary scientific assumption. The scientist, to pursue his work, must follow the directive: "Behave as though every event has a cause." The idea of a dependable order of nature is the guiding principle of scientific thinking; on the basis of this assumption the sciences have made outstanding progress. Even the actions of human beings, it is claimed, arise out of a given set of conditions and have little meaning apart from those conditions. Case studies of the behavior of delinquents, as well as the life histories of other people, indicate that conduct is determined by specific causative factors. Determinism is said to be a presupposition of all intelligent explanations.

While acknowledging that determinism in some form is a necessary scientific assumption, we need to point out that there are many different kinds of determinisms or causal relationships. In the physical realm there are causual sequences of the collision type, where there is direct contact: for example, when one billiard ball strikes another and *causes* it to move. There are also gravitational, electromagnetic, and chemical causative factors. In the organic realm, vital processes are directed toward (cause) the maintenance of the organism as a whole. In the realm of human behavior, there are geographical, biological, psychological, social, and cultural determinants. The same phenomena may be explained differently by these various factors.

While determinism has been a scientific postulate, present trends in the sciences appear to be against the acceptance of any completely mechanistic or physical determinism. To what extent the principle of uncertainty or indeterminancy, as set forth by Heisenberg, has played a part cannot be stated with any degree of assurance, but this and other recent developments in science have undoubtedly had some influence. The scientists quoted below all recognize determinism and causality, but they insist that modern science does not banish freedom from the universe and certainly not from human affairs. Speaking about "opinion in physics with regard to the question of determinism as it is presented by quantum mechanics," Percy W. Bridgman says that "seldom in the history of physics . . . has there been such a radical difference of fundamental outlook between the acknowledged leaders."[12] He says also that we have gone too far in attempting to separate "the object of knowledge," the things out there in the external world, from the "instrument of knowledge" or the entire knowing process, since there can be no sharp dividing line between them.[13] Henry Margenau, another outstanding physicist, says much the same thing. He tells us that the change from the old style, or Newtonian, physics to recent quantum theory has cast new light on the problem of freedom. Whereas the older mechanistic views that embrace Newton's laws permit no freedom, the recent outlook "rescues man's

12 In Hook, *Determinism and Freedom*, p. 57.
13 *Ibid.*, pp. 74–75.

destiny from the fateful web of physical determinism" and injects uncertainties into the picture. "These uncertainties *may* harbor freedom."[14]

Arthur H. Compton says that it is "no longer justifiable to use physical law as evidence against human freedom."[15] In his *History of Science,* Sir William Dampier, discussing Whitehead's concept of organism, says:

> The doctrine of deterministic mechanism only applies to very abstract entities, the product of logical analysis. The concrete enduring entities of the world are complete organisms, so that the structure of the whole influences the character of the parts. An atom may behave differently when it forms part of a man; its conditions are determined by the nature of the man as an organism. Mental states enter into the structure of the total organism, and thus modify the plans of the subordinate parts right down to the electrons.[16]

Speaking about the relation of the behavioral sciences to the problem we are considering, one scholar working in this area says:

> We can choose to use our growing knowledge to enslave people in ways never dreamed of before, depersonalizing them . . . [or] we can choose to use the behavioral sciences in ways which will free, not control; which will bring about constructive variability, not conformity; which will facilitate each person in his self-directed process of becoming; which will aid individuals, groups, and even the concept of science to become self-transcending in freshly adaptive ways of meeting life and its problems.[17]

The position we propose is one that links determinism and freedom and stresses the causal effectiveness of man's participation in events. Man is not only a creature of his environment; he is also at times a critic and a creator of his environment. We do not defend indeterminism which holds that some decisions may be independent of any antecedent causative factors. (Indeterminism is the extreme position on the side of freedom.) On the other hand, we are rejecting the opposite extreme of "hard" or thoroughgoing determinism, which rejects freedom and, as a logical concomitant, moral responsibility. Our position may be called universal causality with the self as a causal agent, or self-determinism, or "soft" determinism.

Not only many scientists, but a considerable number of philosophers accept this general approach. In discussing the "introspectively observable fact of reflective choice," a philosopher, Brand Blanshard, says:

14 *The Key Reporter,* XXV (Autumn, 1959): 3. See also Henry Margenau, *Open Vistas,* Ch. VII.

15 *The Freedom of Man* (New Haven: Yale U. Press, 1935), p. 29. See also Arthur H. Compton, "Science and Man's Freedom," *The Atlantic Monthly,* 200 (October, 1957): 61–74.

16 *A History of Science and Its Relations with Philosophy and Religion* (4th ed. rev. and enl.; New York: Cambridge U. Press, 1949), p. 485.

17 Carl R. Rogers, in Carl R. Rogers and B. F. Skinner, "Some Issues Concerning the Control of Human Behavior: A Symposium," *Science,* 124 (November 30, 1956): 1064.

Now, what can be meant by saying that such choice, though not determined mechanically, is still determined? Are you suggesting, it will be asked, that in the realm of reflection and choice there operates a different kind of causality from any we know in the realm of bodies? My answer is: Yes, just that. To put it more particularly, I am suggesting (1) that even within the psychical realm there are different causal levels, (2) that a causality of higher level may supervene on one of lower level, and (3) that when causality of the highest level is at work, we have precisely what the indeterminists, without knowing it, want.[18]

We hold that man as a self-conscious being has the ability for personal initiative and response, that he is a center of creativity, and that within limits he is able to reshape himself, to influence the behavior of his fellows, and to redirect the processes of the outer world. What is the evidence for a degree of freedom of choice?

1. *The immediate consciousness of freedom.* Practically all men have a direct and distinct consciousness of freedom. They believe they are able to choose between alternative courses of action. After they have acted, they usually feel that they could have chosen otherwise than they did. This is an experiential fact that must be recognized. If we actually have some freedom, then it is easy to understand how this consciousness of freedom arises. If we are not free in any sense, then it is difficult to understand how this consciousness of freedom comes about. Arthur H. Compton says that "the person has a kind of firsthand knowledge of his own situation that is not gained from any physical observation. . . . There is nothing known to physics that is inconsistent with a person exercising freedom."[19]

To claim that we think we are free merely because we are ignorant of the causes of our action is not adequate refutation of this point. In many situations we know just why we are acting, but still we feel free. If the organism or the self is a center of activity, it may choose that stimulus to which it desires to respond from among a number of stimuli. The increase of self-consciousness, knowledge, and intelligence—that is, of stimuli—does not make us less free. On the contrary, we have more alternatives before us, and we have a greater sense of personal choice.

To claim that we are not free because we always act on the basis of the strongest motive is likewise an inadequate refutation of the argument for freedom. This apparent refutation is circular in that whatever motive wins is called the strongest; and it is called the strongest merely because it wins.[20] We may also say that it wins and is the strongest because it is chosen by the

---

18 In Hook, *Determinism and Freedom*, p. 26.

19 "Science and Man's Freedom," *The Atlantic Monthly*, 200 (October, 1957): 73.

20 See William H. Werkmeister, *A Philosophy of Science* (New York: Harper & Brothers, 1940), pp. 432–433.

self. We admit at once that choice or selection does involve determination by motives; free choices are not undetermined, but they are within our control. This point is elaborated further when we discuss the part played by reflection.

2. *The sense of personal responsibility.* The sense of personal responsibility that expresses itself most clearly in our feeling of obligation, or the sense of "ought," is quite meaningless if the power of choice is denied. After some actions we say, "I could not have done otherwise"; but after some other actions we say, "I ought to have done the other thing" or "I ought to have chosen differently." Sometimes we have a keen feeling of blame or even of guilt and remorse.

In some situations where we feel we have made the wrong choice, self-interest tends to lead us to shift the blame by rationalizing and projecting. Yet in spite of these somewhat selfish pressures, we often acknowledge ourselves as the causual agent and accept the responsibility and sometimes the penalty.

We experience a sense of obligation and we need to explain it, since its existence cannot be denied. If freedom is a reality and the person has some power of alternative choice, the sense of "ought" is meaningful and important.

3. *Moral judgments on human conduct and character.* We not only hold ourselves personally responsible for our own choices but hold others responsible for their actions. Praise and blame, approval and disapproval, rewards and punishments, and the norms and standards we set up in society assume human freedom. They assume that the chain of causal sequences is not fixed solely by outside determinants and that new ones can sometimes be added at will.

All judgments of conduct and character assume that men are free moral agents. Children are held responsible only in proportion to their age, experience, and degree of maturity. Why should we speak of an "age of accountability" if all actions of both children and adults are equally determined or if the adult has no more power of selection than the child? In the courts of the land we do not hold people responsible or guilty unless we believe that they could have done otherwise or that they are free moral agents. In some cases much of the court's effort is directed toward discovering the degree of guilt.

In a discussion of "Free Will and the Laws of Nature," Werkmeister says:

It is generally conceded that our ethical notions are meaningful and significant only if they pertain to free agents. In a world in which there is no freedom, *loyalty*, for example, is a meaningless word; for what sense is there in saying that a person is loyal—or truthful or honest or just—if factors and forces beyond his control determine his every word and deed, and if he cannot help doing what he does? Do we call a particle of dust loyal because gravitation and adhesion keep it securely in its place? . . . One need only ask these questions in order to see the absurdity of the very idea of moral significance in a world in which no freedom exists. Even truth and falsity lose their meaning in such a world.[21]

4. *The fact of deliberation.* Reflective thinking is another fact of human experience which indicates that man is not a mere plaything of external forces. Sometimes a man stops to deliberate before he acts. As a result of this deliberation he may select a course of action that he would not have selected without deliberation. In reflective thinking a man can place before himself a number of possible lines of action. He may consider the consequences of first this and then that line and weigh all the possibilities carefully. Reflective thinking has been called "trial and error by ideas." A man may carry out or follow through a number of lines of action in imagination and then select one of them as his actual course. In this way ideas, ideals, and goals may determine his conduct. Conduct may be guided by the anticipation of future consequences, as well as by the pressure of past or present events.

Why should a man stop and deliberate if the choice is not influenced by the deliberation? Why do we say so frequently to ourselves and to others, "Why don't you stop and think?" When hit by the racket, a tennis ball does not stop to deliberate. It goes at once, and it goes in a direction that is determined by mechanical forces. Sometimes when a man is stimulated he does not act at once and upon impulse; he stops to think. He may consider many lines of action before he chooses any one of them. His action may be influenced by what he considers to be his interests. He may decide on a course of action that runs counter to the one that appeals strongly to his emotions. He may even resolve to modify some well-established habit.

Thought and deliberation are meaningless if there is not sufficient freedom to enable a man really to choose among two or more alternatives. The difference between mere impulse and prejudice, on the one hand, and reason and knowledge, on the other hand, consists of the capacity of the latter to modify the effects of unconscious and semiconscious organic and social pressures.

FREEDOM AS AN ACHIEVEMENT

We should not forget that it is man—a thinking, self-conscious being—who has formulated the laws of nature. When we speak of the "reign of law" we need to remember that natural laws are the formulations by man of his experiences with the uniformities in nature.

21 *Ibid.,* p. 436.

We are accustomed to speak of heredity and environment as determining man's affairs, and certainly no serious student of human life can doubt the relevance of these factors. However, it should be pointed out that we do not know exactly which the hereditary and which the environmental determinants are in rats and guinea pigs, and evaluating the roles of these determinants is even more difficult in the case of man. Furthermore, when we become aware that some hereditary or environmental factor is influencing us, it ceases to be the same determinant. We may accept it and yield to its influence, we may modify it, or we may develop a negative attitude and reject or counteract it. In any case, our consciousness of it must have some effect. If a man accepts his humanity and self-consciousness, he has considerable freedom. When we are talking about subhuman species, the terms *heredity* and *environment* seem sufficient. When we are talking about mature human beings, we need to consider three factors—heredity, environment, and "personal response."

We seem to live in a world in which there is personal causation as well as mechanical causation. The two are not necessarily antagonistic; they may interact and function harmoniously. The results of scientific investigations depend on the continuous interplay of purpose and mechanism.

Supporters of the notion of freedom in its philosophical sense do not deny the evidence presented by the various sciences in support of causal relationships, nor do they claim that man is completely free—that is, not subject to causal determinants. They claim merely that the self at times is a causal agent, as well as an entity acted upon by causes, and that man has considerable power to choose among alternatives. If the things we have said about man and his powers and capabilities are correct, then people are real causes. In other words, everything is caused, and I (or the self) cause some things. If the self is a determining agent, then a degree of freedom and some kind of determinism may be combined. Self-conscious beings, at least at times, are capable of initiating events which lead to goals that are self-chosen. Human freedom is neither freedom from causes nor freedom from laws; it is the ability to act on the basis of self-chosen ends, which are themselves influenced by experiences, thoughts, motives, desires, and needs. Freedom is the power to direct mechanisms so that they contribute to fulfillment of our purposes. Without reliable cause-and-effect relationships, our human purposes would be frustrated at every turn.

No man is entirely free in this sense, yet all normal human beings have some freedom of choice. A large part of the activity of many people is determined by the immediate, pressing needs for food, clothing, and shelter. These people have little opportunity for choice or even for reflection on the goals of life. In addition, habits and social pressures hold many to stereotyped lines of action. For most of us, the times when we consciously choose and guide the course of our lives are few and fleeting. Freedom, we are suggesting, depends on growth or achievement. We gain freedom as our self-consciousness and intelligence expand and as our knowledge grows. The fundamental question is not "Is Man free?" but "How free is Man?"

Self-consciousness, as we have seen, is one of the distinctive human traits. Whereas animals are conscious, only man is self-conscious. Consciousness is awareness of the environment; self-consciousness includes the additional awareness of the contents and activity of one's own mind or self. Self-consciousness makes reflective thinking and the sense of right and wrong possible. It enables a person to consider himself as a subject and as an object of action. It is a prerequisite of freedom of choice.

Man increases his freedom with the growth of his intelligence and knowledge. If a man is faced with a difficulty and knows of only one thing that can be done, he does not have much freedom of choice. If he knows of many things that can be done, he has the possibility of greater freedom. With additional information about life and the world and with an increase in the power of reflective thinking come additional choices.

In addition to self-consciousness, intelligence, and knowledge, there are other conditions that are important for the realization of our freedom. These include physical and mental health and energy, a fertile imagination, a wide range of interests, and a society sufficiently advanced so that the elemental burdens of existence are not pressing. A man may live merely in the present, tangible, physical world of sense perception, but he need not be confined or limited to this world. He may live also in an emerging world of ideas, ideals, and values. Man seeks something higher and better; he is, by his very nature, this sort of being.

QUESTIONS AND PROJECTS

1. *Review Questions*

(1) Explain as clearly as you can the "dilemma of freedom and necessity," or the problem that centers around freedom of choice. Why is this question important?

(2) What is meant by thoroughgoing or "hard" determinism and what are its implications? Name some people who have held this position.

(3) Distinguish among *predestination, fatalism,* and *scientific determinism.*

(4) State the evidence or the case for indeterminism as William James sees it.

(5) What are the more extreme positions on the question of freedom versus determinism? What is meant by the view that this question is not an "either-or" issue?

(6) What are some important things to remember about scientific determinism if we are not to interpret it too narrowly?

(7) What is the evidence for the position that there is some freedom of choice? State this evidence as fully and clearly as possible and in your own words.

(8) Explain what is meant by speaking of freedom as an "achievement." What part do heredity, environment, self-consciousness, and knowledge play in a consideration of the problem of freedom?

(9) State the position regarding freedom and determinism set forth in this chapter; then critically evaluate it.

(10) What are the broad implications for man's life of the denial of freedom of choice, and the implications of the acceptance of the position that there is some freedom?

2. Do you agree that there are many "levels" of nature and kinds of existence? Distinguish among a stone, a dog, and a man, insofar as self-determination and freedom are concerned. Is it true that man is not only a creature of his environment but at times also a critic of his environment and one who can make things happen?

3. The frog, it is said, is so easily adapted to its surroundings and so unaware of slight changes that if it is put in a dish of water and the water is slowly heated, it will stay there until it is killed by the boiling water, although it could have jumped out at any of the early stages in the heating process. Some people behave much like frogs; others grow and are alert to new conditions, and therefore are able to control those conditions rather than being controlled by them. Describe these two attitudes, and give examples.

4. Was Socrates free or causally determined or both when he held to an ideal even though it meant death? When unjustly sentenced to death, Socrates had ample opportunity to escape, and his friends urged him to do so. Reflecting on the entire situation, he decided to stay in prison and drink the poisonous hemlock, because he considered it more just and honorable to obey the laws of the city than to break them.

5. In *The Revolt Against Reason* (London: Eyre & Spottiswoode, 1950), p. 87, Arnold Lunn raises a question about mechanism and natural law. From the point of view of a thoroughgoing mechanistic materialism, all events in nature and all the acts of man, including his thought processes, are determined by preceding physical events or causes. Every thought in the mind is the result of changes that take place in the brain or nervous system. Since natural law determines brain changes, natural law will likewise determine the way in which thoughts succeed one another in the mind. Yet the thought of "7 times 9" in a boy's mind is sometimes followed by the thought of "65." In this case we insist that something has gone wrong. We say that the brain that produces "7 times 9 are 65" is not working as well as the brain that produces "7 times 9 are 63." Even though we associate thinking with brain processes, the connection is generally disregarded when we consider the nature of thought. Thought may be true or false, correct or incorrect. When we say this, however, we move into another type of law—law that "ought to be kept, but may be broken." Do you agree with Arnold Lunn that a rigid mechanism and a rigid determinism cannot explain incorrect multiplication, to say nothing of human conduct, philosophy, and religion?

6. Describe as many different types of determinism as you can find in the philosophic literature. The book *Determinism and Freedom* (edited by Sidney Hook) listed in the Readings will give you a start. See especially Part I, Essay 1 and Part III, Essays 2 and 3.

7. Evaluate the following statements and indicate your areas of agreement and disagreement with them:

(1) "If everything is determined, let's relax; we do not need to exert ourselves."

(2) "A philosophy that denies all freedom to man cannot be lived."

(3) "From early times man has refused to accept as it is the world in which he lives."

(4) "Since man does not ultimately shape his own character, it follows that he is not morally responsible."

(5) "The impulse to frame for himself ideas or values and to strive for their realization is one of man's peculiar endowments."

(6) "The most permanent thing in creation is the demand of the human soul for freedom, the thirst after fullness of life and opportunity. These demands are written into nature itself."

SUGGESTED READINGS

ALLPORT, GORDON W. *Becoming: Basic Considerations for a Psychology of Personality.* New Haven: Yale U. Press, 1955.
A psychologist stresses the need for a "psychology of becoming" that is willing to look within man and to recognize his relative freedom.

BERTOCCI, PETER A. *Free Will, Responsibility and Grace.* Nashville: Abingdon, 1957.
Four lectures on human freedom written from a Christian perspective.

DOBZHANSKY, THEODOSIUS G. *The Biological Basis of Human Freedom.* New York: Columbia U. Press, 1957.
Five lectures dealing with some philosophical implications of modern biology. The ability of man to choose between alternatives is presented as a characteristic product of human evolution.

EDWARDS, JONATHAN. *Freedom of the Will.* Ed. by Paul Ramsey. New Haven: Yale U. Press, 1957.
Edwards, an outstanding Puritan Protestant of the eighteenth century, states his case for Calvinism in a book originally published in 1754. The editor's introduction is valuable.

FARRER, AUSTIN MARSDEN. *The Freedom of the Will.* London: Black, 1958. (The Gifford Lectures, 1957.)
A discussion of freedom of choice in the form of a "running debate between the doctrines of freedom and of necessity." Freedom is seen as "reasonable conduct."

HARTMANN, NICOLAI. *Ethics.* Trans. by Stanton Coit. 3 vols.; New York: Macmillan, 1932. (Vol. III, *Moral Freedom.*)
Morality is possible only in a world that is determined by the law of cause and effect. Man is self-determined and is responsible and free in the sense that he does have some power of alternative choice.

Hook, Sidney (ed.). *Determinism and Freedom in the Age of Modern Science.* New York: Collier Books, 1961. (New York University Institute of Philosophy.)
Philosophers and scientists discuss determinism and freedom in their respective fields and in law and ethics. Papers and discussion representing many points of view.

James, William. "The Dilemma of Determinism," in *The Will to Believe and Other Essays in Popular Philosophy.* New York: Longmans, Green, 1912.
A psychologist and one of the founders of American pragmatism states the case for indeterminism, or for freedom of choice, in its more extreme form.

Jung, C. G. *The Undiscovered Self.* Trans. by R. F. C. Hull. Boston: Little, Brown, 1958.
The author discusses the psychic forces that divide the world and makes a plea for individual integrity and freedom.

Macmurray, John. "Freedom in the Personal Nexus," in *Freedom: Its Meaning,* ed. Ruth Nanda Anshen. New York: Harcourt, Brace, 1940.
The dilemma of free will versus determinism is artificial. The important question is: Under what conditions have we most freedom of will?

Morris, Herbert (ed.). *Freedom and Responsibility: Readings in Philosophy and Law.* Stanford: Stanford U. Press, 1961.
A wide range of selections on topics such as responsibility, the will, intention and motive, negligence, causation, free will, and punishment.

Munn, Allen M. *Free-Will and Determinism.* Toronto: U. of Toronto Press, 1960.
A physicist discusses classical and contemporary physics as well as everyday living in their bearing on the problem of freedom. A functional approach that includes technical as well as more general presentations.

Weiss, Paul. *Man's Freedom.* New Haven: Yale U. Press, 1950.
The author attempts to show how man can become more human and free. For the more mature student.

Werkmeister, William H. *A Philosophy of Science.* New York: Harper, 1940.
See Chapter XII, "Free Will and the Laws of Nature," pp. 425–465 for an excellent discussion of the problem of freedom of choice in relation to the laws of nature.

PART THREE

THE TYPES OF PHILOSOPHY

TWELVE

MATERIALISM AND NATURALISM

In discussing the various types of philosophy we shall have occasion to introduce a considerable number of new terms and we shall need to clarify their meaning. Some of the types of philosophy we are to consider take us into the field traditionally known as *metaphysics*. Supporters of some of the other types of philosophy described here say they are not interested in metaphysical questions because of the mystical connotations involved. The term *metaphysics* is derived from the Greek *meta* meaning "beyond," and *physikon*, meaning "nature," from which we get our word *physics,* the science concerned with natural laws and processes and the physical world of nature. Metaphysics has traditionally been concerned with first principles and the ultimate nature of things or with a reality beyond that of immediate experience.

Philosophies vary so widely and yet overlap and agree on so many points that no one classification is ever completely satisfactory. In the three chapters which follow this one we consider in turn idealism, realism, and pragmatism, which, until recent decades, were the main schools of philosophical thought. We shall then consider two reactions against traditional philosophy—logical empiricism and existentialism.

In this chapter we shall discuss, in order, mechanistic materialism, dialectical materialism, and humanistic or empirical naturalism. Mechanistic materialism and dialectical materialism, as well as being materialisms, are also forms of realism, yet they differ from many forms of realism that we will present. Some humanistic naturalists are also pragmatists. The philosophies presented in this chapter are thoroughgoing naturalisms, but they do not exhaust this field, as we shall see. *Naturalism* and *materialism* are related terms, but they are not synonymous. All materialistic systems of philosophy are also naturalistic, but some naturalistic systems are not materialistic.

Naturalism is a theory that accepts "nature" as the sum total of reality. The term *nature* has been used in philosophy with a wide variety of meanings, ranging all the way from the physical world as observable by men to the total system of spatiotemporal phenomena. It is the world disclosed to us by the natural sciences. The term *naturalism* stands in contrast with the term *supernaturalism,* which implies a dualistic world view with some power or Being above or beyond nature. Materialism is a narrow or more limited form of naturalism, which in general asserts that there is nothing in the world except matter, or that "nature" and the "physical world" are one and the same. The term *materialism* may be defined in various ways: as the theory that extended, self-existent atoms of matter in motion are the constituent elements of the universe, and that mind and consciousness—including all psychical processes—are mere modes of such matter and are reducible to the physical elements; and as the doctrine that the universe can be fully interpreted by the physical sciences. These two definitions have identical implications. These definitions, however, tend to represent the more traditional forms of materialism. In recent times the doctrine has been expressed as "energism," which reduces everything to some form of energy, or as a form of "positivism," which emphasizes the exact sciences and disclaims concern about such things as the "ultimate" nature of reality.

> Modern Materialism holds that the universe is an unlimited material entity; that the universe, including all matter and energy (motion or force), has always existed, and will always exist; that the world is a hard, tangible, material, objective reality that man can know. It holds that matter existed before mind; that the material world is primary and that thoughts about this world are secondary.[1]

Materialists, like members of other schools of philosophy, do not agree on all points or make all the claims made in the quotation above. In the contemporary world, materialism is likely to take one of two main forms: mechanism or mechanistic materialism, with emphasis on the natural sciences, and dialectical materialism, the official philosophy of the Soviet Union, China, and other communist groups around the world. We shall now consider these two forms of materialism.

MECHANISTIC MATERIALISM

Is the world a mechanism to be interpreted solely according to the principles of the physical sciences? Can the structure, function, and behavior of living creatures be interpreted exclusively by physics, chemistry, and related sciences? We know that the same physical elements that are found in rocks and stars are found in organisms. Does this mean that the same mechanical laws operate universally?

[1] Charles S. Seely, *Modern Materialism: A Philosophy of Action* (New York: Philosophical Library, 1960), p. 7.

Materialism, in the narrow sense, is the theory that all things may be explained in accordance with the laws that govern matter and motion. Materialism holds that all events and conditions are necessary consequences of previous events and conditions. The organic or "higher" forms in nature are merely more complex than the inorganic or lower forms; the higher forms contain no new materials or forces, and the principles of the physical sciences are sufficient to explain all that occurs and exists. All of nature's processes, whether inorganic or organic, are determined and would be predictable were all the facts about previous conditions available.

From the early Greeks we have inherited two quite different interpretations of the world. The line of thought most representative of the Greek outlook is that embodied in the works of Pythagoras, Plato, and Aristotle. According to this view, the regularity and orderliness of the world are due to the presence of mind or purpose. But other Greek philosophers believed that the universe could be interpreted merely as matter in motion. The quantitative atomism of Democritus was probably the first systematic presentation of mechanism. Psychic activity is merely the motion of fine, highly mobile atoms. Epicurus and the Roman poet Lucretius popularized similar views for a short time before mechanism went into almost total eclipse during the medieval period.

From the fifteenth to the twentieth century, materialism gained considerable support in Western thought with the development of the mathematical sciences and of objective, experimental methods in the natural sciences. The world, some thought, consisted solely of physical quantities that could be measured mathematically. Descartes (1596–1650) applied mechanical concepts to the physical universe only—that is, unlike the materialists, he accepted the existence of nonphysical entities. Thomas Hobbes (1588–1679) went further and attempted to raise the science of his day to a philosophy by presenting a thoroughgoing mechanistic materialism. He explained conscious life as sensations that are movements in the brain and nervous system. By the twentieth century, various physiologists, biologists, and psychologists were employing physical and mechanistic explanations in their interpretations of all living creatures, including man. All movements, from those of the distant stars to the thoughts of man (thoughts being regarded by these men as movements), could be explained, it was asserted, without appeal to any nonphysical principles.

According to mechanistic materialism, mind and its activities are forms of behavior. Psychology, then, becomes a study of behavior, and mind and consciousness are interpreted as muscular, neural, or glandular behavior. These processes may then be explained by physics and chemistry. Values and ideals become merely subjective labels for physical situations and relations.

Materialism takes numerous forms, from the materialistic atomism of earlier times to the "metaphysical behaviorism" and "physical realism" of more recent times. Some adherents of materialism recognize a plurality of systems or orders of nature that have evolved from a physical basis, but all seek to employ one basic principle that does not look beyond the purely objective methods and terminology of the natural sciences.

For the mechanistic materialist, all changes in the world, from those involving the atom to those involving man, are strictly determined. There is a complete and closed causal series. This causal series is to be explained by the principles of the natural sciences alone, and not with resort to such notions as "purpose." Mechanistic materialism is the doctrine that the world is governed by natural laws that may be stated in mathematical terms when the necessary data are available. It is the type of metaphysics that enlarges the concept "machine" and stresses the mechanical nature of all processes, organic as well as inorganic. The mechanistic materialist claims that all phenomena are subject to the same kinds of explanation that we use in the physical sciences—that is, the concepts of mechanism, determinism, and natural law have universal application. The only world which men know or can know is the one that reaches them through the physical sense organs.

The foundations of materialism were laid by the mathematical and physical sciences; then these principles of explanation were later employed by the biological, psychological, and social sciences.

THE APPEAL OF MECHANISTIC MATERIALISM

First, mechanistic materialism has considerable appeal because of its simplicity. In accepting this approach one seems to get rid of many difficult problems that have perplexed men through the centuries. What is real in man is his body, and the tests for truth or reality are touch, sight, sound—the tools of experimental verification.

Second, mechanistic materialism is attractive because most men are occupied for a large part of the time with physical things, and a philosophy that calls these things and only these things "real" appeals to some people. The problem of obtaining food, clothing, and shelter is a constant one. The materialist is impressed with the stability and permanence of these physical things and their necessity for life. It is easy to go on from here to believe that the material things are the only real things in life—the only genuine determinants—and that what are called "nonmaterial things" depend on these physical things. If people claim that there are "things" that are not physical, these claims are said to be the result of imagination or wishful thinking.

Third, mechanism as a theory and a method has produced great results in the natural sciences. Why, then, it is asked, should mechanism not be the key to the explanation of all other things in life? Many do not feel that they have explained things adequately until they have interpreted them mechanistically. In this sense intelligibility, for many, appears to be synonymous with a mechanistic and a materialistic explanation.

Finally, mechanistic materialism, in its thoroughgoing forms, seems to relieve man of personal or moral responsibility. Moral standards and appeal to ideals have meaning only if man is to some degree a free agent. For some men this lack of responsibility is comforting, because it causes problems of ethics and morality to drop out of the picture or to become purely subjective and relative.

IMPLICATIONS OF MECHANISTIC MATERIALISM

Some thinkers have argued that if the sciences are able to explain all things by simple mechanical causation, then there is little justification for believing in God or in a cosmic purpose. The same laws operate in man as in the lower animals and the stars, and "consciousness" and "thinking" are the result of changes in the brain or the nervous system. "The universe is governed by the physical laws of matter, even to the most refined and complex processes of the human mind." "Living is merely a physiological process with only a physiological meaning."

Mechanistic materialism, as we have seen, would interpret mind and consciousness as physiological behavior of a neural, glandular, or muscular type. All human activity obeys physical laws. The action of stimulus and response in the nervous system is automatic and mechanistic. Consciousness must be discarded or interpreted as epiphenomenal (a phenomenon accompanying some bodily processes, such as a glow or emanation from the brain), and thinking is "subvocal speech"—it is talking under one's breath or silent talking—or brain movements. We are conditioned to react (or behave) to certain words as we would react to the objects for which they stand. When this happens we are said to know the meaning of the symbols or words. The law of cause and effect operates universally, and the human organism offers no exceptions.

In talking about the new image of the world that has grown up during the last three hundred years, W. T. Stace says, "The world, according to the new picture, is purposeless, senseless, meaningless. Nature is nothing but matter in motion. The motions of matter are governed, not by any purpose, but by blind forces and laws.[2]

A complete mechanism implies complete and universal determinism and rules out any real freedom of choice. One must merely accept the physical facts as they occur and as they are described by the natural sciences, except where we use material forces to alter the physical facts. These are the implications of a thoroughgoing mechanistic materialism.

[2] "Man Against Darkness," *The Atlantic Monthly*, 182 (September, 1948): 54.

CRITICAL COMMENTS

While mechanistic materialism has appealed to some people because it is a simple interpretation of the universe in line with science, the attacks on the doctrine have been many and varied. Recent developments in the natural sciences have weakened, if they have not completely shattered, the foundations of the older mechanism and materialism. Nature does not seem to be as completely determined and as mechanistic as some earlier scientists thought. Studies of the nature of matter lack finality, and men are giving more attention to such varied concepts as organism, novelty, potentiality, possibility, becoming, and the point of view of the observer. These concepts, as we have seen in the preceding chapters, seem to imply a greater degree of spontaneity and freedom than do mechanism and materialism.

Mechanistic materialism seems to be forced to do one of two things: either to deny many things that are fundamental realities to large numbers of people, or to endow "matter" with the power to become a self-conscious person interested in the promotion of truth, beauty, goodness, and love. The universe has produced men who are the discoverers of mechanisms and the builders of machines; this fact should not be overlooked. Nature has produced men with loves and hates, with hopes and aspirations, with consciousness and reason. Men strive to attain ideals. They engage in creative activity, and they look into the past and the future. Man, the observer, the discoverer, must not be forgotten.

In an age in which men are inventing even more complicated machines and elaborate computers, and in which men are writing articles on "reading machines," "teaching machines," and "thinking machines," it may be easy for some people to accept mechanistic materialism. After acknowledging "that the behavior of men can in principle be duplicated by machines," Paul Weiss says:

> What cannot be loved by one who can love, and what cannot love what can be loved, are less than human, no matter how much they look like and behave like men. Machines fail on both counts. They are not on a footing with me. They are, in short, not human, and thus cannot be said to have selves or minds, rights or responsibilities. The conclusion is not surprising, for we all know that a machine is an artifact whose parts are united so as to enable them to act together, whereas a man is a unity in which the whole governs the behavior of the parts. Only such a unity has a self, with feelings, mind, will, and the rest.[3]

A considerable number of philosophers—humanists, idealists, pragmatists, and others yet to be considered—claim that mechanism does not tell the whole story. Most people acknowledge that there are systems in the world

[3] "Love in a Machine Age," in *Dimensions of Mind: A Symposium*, Sidney Hook (ed.) (New York: Collier Books, 1961), pp. 179–180. (New York University Institute of Philosophy.)

that are best interpreted mechanistically, and few would question the value of using mechanistic interpretations in any field where they aid our understanding or control. But many do doubt the ability of mechanistic principles to supply a satisfactory basis for the explanation of *all* the facts of human existence. These critics claim that materialism is an example of the "reductive fallacy" that occurs when some complex situation or whole is described as "nothing but" some simple element or part. For example, when the materialist asserts that mind is merely a form of matter, the critic claims that he is guilty of a crude reductionism. The reductionist reduces all phenomena to one type and thereby denies or at least blurs useful distinctions.

DIALECTICAL MATERIALISM

Dialectical materialism grew out of the intense social struggle that arose as a result of the Industrial Revolution. It is connected with the names of Karl Marx (1818–1883) and Friedrich Engels (1820–1895). It has become the official philosophy of the Soviet Union and Communist China, and the doctrines of Marx and Engels have been interpreted and expanded by Lenin, Stalin, Khrushchev, Mao Tse Tung, and others.[4] We are dealing here, however, with dialectical materialism as a metaphysical position and not with the views and practices of the present regimes in Russia, China, and elsewhere.[5] In a later section of the book we will consider the social and revolutionary program that the followers of Marx claim to accept.

Dialectical materialism is not identical with mechanistic materialism, which we have just considered. Dialectical materialism, while it holds science in high esteem and claims that the sense perceptions of science provide our only real knowledge, is an approach from the point of view of politics and history rather than from that of the natural sciences. Emphasis is placed on a view of historical development in which matter in the form of the economic organization of society is regarded as basic. Thus the terms *historical materialism* and *economic determinism* are both used.

BACKGROUND FOR THE DIALECTIC

To understand dialectical materialism, we need to go back to Georg Hegel (1770–1831), Marx's teacher. Hegel was an idealist who held that the universe is an unfolding process of thought out of which develop the processes of

---

[4] For a discussion of the differences among Marxism, Leninism, and Stalinism, as well as the contemporary Soviet trends, see Herbert Marcuse, *Soviet Marxism: A Critical Analysis* (New York: Columbia U. Press, 1958).

[5] We are aware of the fact that scholars differ in their interpretation of Marx. Some prefer to stress the early writings, up to 1844, which are more subjective and humanistic, rather than the later writings, which emphasize the materialistic interpretation of history. For most Marxists and communists the later and "mature system" is the more important. See Robert C. Tucker, *Philosophy and Myth in Karl Marx* (London: Cambridge U. Press, 1961).

nature, human history, and the organizations and institutions of society. Matter, for Hegel, was less real than mind, since thought or mind is the essence of the universe. Marx rejected the idealism of Hegel. He inverted Hegel's philosophy and said that matter, not mind and ideas, is fundamental. Matter, especially as it is revealed in the economic organization of society and the modes of production, determines the social and political institutions of society. These in turn influence ethical, religious, and philosophical notions.

Though Marx and Engels rejected Hegel's idealism, they did accept his philosophical methodology almost completely. The world, according to Hegel, is in a continual process of development. All such processes of change are dialectical—that is, these changes proceed through an affirmation, or thesis, to some denial, or antithesis, to an integration, or synthesis. All development, both of things and of ideas, is brought about through the overcoming of contradictions. For example, the idea of "being" leads logically to the idea of "nonbeing." Nonbeing and being, when united, logically entail the concept "becoming." In society, to give another illustration, a trend in the direction of extreme individualism tends to generate a countermovement toward its opposite, collectivism. Out of these extremes may come a society which recognizes the value of both individual freedom and collective action.

Marx and Engels accepted the dialectic. They said that while the early Greeks discovered it, Hegel was the first to explain it fully. His mistake, according to Marx and Engels, was to give it a mystic form; when stripped of its idealistic form and turned around, the proposition that historical development is dialectical is a profound truth. The dialectical process, Marx and Engels contended, is a pattern that exists in nature. It is an empirical fact knowledge of which is derived from a study of the order of nature and supported by further knowledge of the causal interconnections brought to light by historians and scientists. Marx and Engels did not think of the dialectical process as mechanistic or completely determined. They emphasized a pluralism of factors and causal interaction, in which the production of the goods necessary for life is the predominant factor. Change and development take place continually. When a synthesis has been reached, it tends in time to generate its own contradictions (or antithesis), and so the process proceeds. There is a continuous emergence of new qualities that grow out of the interpenetration and unity of opposites.

HISTORICAL MATERIALISM

Dialectical materialism, like the earlier materialism, rejects the primacy of mind and all dualisms (such as the view that mind and body, man and nature, are different substances) as well as all forms of supernaturalism. Material forces are the societal determinants and determine evolutionary development, as well as all other phenomena—inorganic, organic, and human. Dialectical materialism is a physical realism that is sometimes spoken of as "historical materialism" or "economic determinism." In dialectical materialism, the decisive factor in historical change and human society is the production and reproduction of life. The first need is to live and therefore to attend to life's necessities. Thus the mode of production at any particular stage in history is of prime importance.

Marx and Engels had read widely in the fields of the physical, biological, and social sciences. The sciences, these philosophers claimed, disclose a world in constant change. Stability and rigidity can no longer be accepted as descriptive terms or desirable goals, since the physical universe has a history and exhibits changes through time, just as the organic world and human society do. Darwin's theory of natural selection eliminates the need for teleological concepts in the natural sciences. There was a time when no man existed, and there was an earlier time when there was no life. Quite clearly, Marx and Engels assert, everything has had a natural development with origins in the inorganic, or matter.

While Marx vigorously opposed idealism as the exclusive interpretation of reality, he did not question the existence of conscious mind. He was not a "moral materialist" stressing eating, drinking, and the acquisition of things. He wanted to free man from "wage slavery" and, to do this, he thought that changes in the material base of society were necessary.

According to dialectical materialism, man can influence his own life and history to some degree. Life has its origins in the inorganic, and man is a part of nature; therefore, man and animals differ in degree rather than in kind. Man is able to make other parts of nature serve his ends. He alone can alter the conditions of his life and, in a sense, help make his own history. The springs of action, however, reside neither in ideas, nor in men's desires, nor in their brains, but primarily in the processes of production and the class relations of society.

A PHILOSOPHY OF SOCIAL CHANGE

In dialectical materialism, action is primary and thought is secondary. There is no such thing, it is claimed, as knowledge that is mere contemplation of the world of nature; knowledge is inseparably bound up with action. In the past, Marx tells us, philosophers have explained the world in many different ways. The present task is to change the world, and that is the task and historic mission of the communists. In this task the communists do not hesitate to take direct action and use violence to obtain their objectives. In fact, most communists believe that violence is necessary to eradicate the evils in society.

Society, like all things, is always in process of change. It cannot be static, since matter itself is dynamic. Change, or the process of development, however, is not a simple, straight, or linear growth process. Small, indiscernible changes take place, apparently not altering the nature of what is changing, until finally there comes a point beyond which a thing cannot change without becoming different. Then there is an abrupt change—for example, if water is heated slowly, it gets hotter and hotter until suddenly, at a specific point, it turns to steam—and a change of state occurs. There is "a development which passes from insignificant and imperceptible quantitative changes to open, fundamental changes, to qualitative changes; a development in which the qualitative changes occur not gradually, but rapidly and abruptly, taking the form of a leap from one state to another."6 Similarly, in the economic relations of a society and in the conflict of interests between the classes, revolutionary situations arise. Interpreted in this way, dialectical materialism provides a basis for the "class struggle" and for revolutionary action.7

CRITICAL COMMENTS

While some people would classify dialectical materialism as closer to mechanistic materialism than to the humanistic naturalism which we shall consider next, others have called the communistic philosophy a *realistic humanism*. Insofar as dialectical materialism is a materialism, it is subject to the same criticisms as materialism. Insofar as it is humanistic, it is subject to the same criticisms as humanistic or empirical naturalism, to be considered later in this chapter. Let us here consider those points in dialectical materialism that are distinctive and also open to criticism.

First, the Marxian interpretation of the dialectic is open to serious question. Other historians have discovered no dialectical "necessity" in history. In addition, this concept offers no objective standard by which to judge events. Any historical event can be asserted to be the thesis, antithesis, or the synthesis in a process of change, depending on one's point of view or perspective. And while the theory of the dialectic assumes that each new stage in the process is "higher" than preceding stages, there certainly seem to be processes of disintegration and decline to be reckoned with in history. There appears to be no one-way process operating throughout the course of human history. In other words, one may, with Marx, choose to describe history solely with reference to a dialectical process of thesis, antithesis, and synthesis, but such a description ignors important distinctions and reduces all historical events to those of a single kind. Such *reductionism* is at best unenlightening and at worst stultifying and misleading as to what is really occurring.

6 Joseph Stalin, *Dialectical and Historical Materialism* (New York: International Publishers, 1940), p. 8.
7 For the communist interpretation of history and the stages of revolutionary change, see pp. 487–488.

Second, while economic factors are exceedingly important, an economic or materialistic interpretation of life and society is one-sided and false. The course of history is not so fixed and inevitable as the Marxists seem to believe. Marx apparently assumes that the blind forces of economic change are the determining factors in human history. But the productive forces in society are as much a result of human intelligence as the thoughts of man are a result of the productive forces. Dialectical materialism fails to explain why peoples living under similar systems of production have developed quite different types of cultures, and why men who share the same economic and cultural conditions often embrace quite different systems of thought. The social and ethical attitudes of people are more important than Marx was willing to acknowledge.

Third, many people will oppose the use of dialectical materialism as a philosophical justification for direct action, violence, and revolution. This philosophy places too great an emphasis on force, in the expectation that a revolution or some drastic change in the structure of society will solve most of humanity's problems. If a program is really good for the majority, leaders ought to be, and generally have been, able to persuade the people of that fact. History shows that important changes in society can be brought about through peaceful means.

HUMANISTIC NATURALISM

The term *naturalism,* as used philosophically, is best contrasted with the terms *supernaturalism,* or *other-worldliness.* Naturalism takes nature to be the whole of reality, but, as we have seen, *nature* is interpreted in many different ways. The dictionaries of philosophy give many different uses of the term *nature* in philosophical discussions.[8] When the term is used to designate a point of view, it needs a qualifying adjective to make the meaning clear. For example, there are the logical or structural or realistic naturalists, who look to mathematics and physics for their orientation. There are the poetic naturalists like George Santayana. There are the humanistic naturalists who stress the social studies, the welfare of man, and the universal applicability of the empirical, experimental methods of the natural sciences. In this section we shall deal with humanistic naturalism.

HUMANISTIC NATURALISM DEFINED

Humanistic naturalism is a philosophy that emphasizes man or human interests and affairs. It has also been called humanism, the new humanism, evolutionary naturalism, empirical naturalism, and scientific humanism. The

[8] See *Dictionary of Philosophy and Psychology,* ed. James Mark Baldwin (rev. ed.; New York: Macmillan, 1901–1905); *The Dictionary of Philosophy,* ed. Dagobert D. Runes (New York: Philosophical Library, 1942).

differences among these positions are largely a matter of emphasis. Humanism has been defined as follows: "Scientific humanism is the doctrine that men, through the use of intelligence, directing the institutions of democratic government, can create for themselves, without aid from 'supernatural powers,' a rational civilization in which each person enjoys security and finds cultural outlets for whatever normal human capacities and creative energies he possesses."9 Another definition is, "Humanism is a faith in people, in all humanity, and in science as a means of attaining truth. It is also a quest for the ethical and spiritual values of life through philosophy, science, the arts and literature."10

Humanistic naturalism is to be distinguished from two other philosophical positions: mechanistic materialism and Renaissance humanism. First, it is not to be confused with mechanistic materialism, which is based on a rigid determinism and tends to make everything subservient to the laws of the physical sciences. In contrast, humanistic naturalism emphasizes the social studies and seeks to do justice to the organic and to human interests and aspirations. It acknowledges that which is unique in man, and its defenders claim that it is as sensitive as idealism to man's interests and welfare.

Second, humanistic naturalism is to be clearly distinguished from the humanism of the Renaissance, though it has been called "Renaissance humanism modernized and brought up to date." The humanists of the Renaissance admired the Greeks—especially their reasonable and balanced lives—and they studied the classics. The Renaissance movement was to a great extent a literary one, which developed a new confidence in man and in human reason. There was a turning to classical, as opposed to ecclesiastical, studies. A modern movement, known as *literary humanism* and led by Irving Babbitt, Paul Elmer More, and Norman Foerster, advocates a classical type of liberal education and opposes the vocational education presently in vogue. This movement, resembling Renaissance humanism, should not be confused with humanistic naturalism.

Humanistic naturalism has much in common with the "Religion of Humanity" of Auguste Comte in the nineteenth century, with the pragmatism of William James, and with the instrumentalism of John Dewey. While a few of the humanistic naturalists are realists, many of them are pragmatists.

THE METHOD

The humanistic naturalists have profound respect for modern science: they accept its assumptions, postulates, and discoveries. They are especially

9 Oliver L. Reiser and Blodwen Davies, *Planetary Democracy* (New York: Creative Age, 1944), p. 212.

10 From "A Note to Authors," which gives the editorial policy of *The Humanist* (Yellow Springs: American Humanist Association, 1962), inside front cover.

interested in biology, psychology, medicine, and the social studies, since the attention of these disciplines is centered on man and his welfare. Science is viewed not as a transcript of reality but as a human construct to secure control over the world. Humanistic naturalists recognize that the "laws" of nature are formulated as such by men.

Since the final appeal in determining truth or falsity is to empirical facts or to man's verifiable experience, all distinctions between "sacred" and "secular" disappear. The humanistic naturalists claim, however, that while the term *sacred* disappears, they retain many of the rich values of human experience formerly associated with the term *sacred*. Humanistic naturalism is, therefore, a philosophy based on the empirical scientific method and interested in hypotheses and experimentation for the purpose of control.

In a book entitled *Naturalism and the Human Spirit*[11] members of a group who call themselves empirical naturalists emphasize the universal applicability of the methods of experimental inquiry. These methods, they claim, are self-correcting and indefinitely progressive; the knowledge derived in this way does not need to be checked or tested by some "higher" or nonexperimental principles. This emphasis on the universal applicability of scientific method rules out the validity of the intuitions of the mystics, a priori principles, the "primacy of spirit," and all systems of thought that accept or imply a bifurcation of nature.

Until the late nineteenth century, man and his various experiences were usually interpreted independently of the rest of nature, but the theory of biological evolution and the universal application of scientific methods led to the consideration of man and all his powers and activities as part of nature. Basic to experimental naturalism is the view that nature is the whole of reality—that is, that the natural world is all there is. Naturalism is

> opposed to all dualisms between Nature and another realm of being—to the Greek opposition between Nature and Art, to the medieval contrast of the Natural and the Supernatural, to the empiricist antithesis of Nature and Experience, to the idealist distinction between Natural and Transcendental, to the fundamental dualism pervading modern thought between Nature and Man. For present-day naturalists "Nature" serves rather as the all-inclusive category, corresponding to the role played by "Being" in Greek thought or by "Reality" for the idealists.[12]

Whatever man encounters in any area of experience is regarded as "natural."

Humanistic naturalists stress the principle of continuity. There are no sharp distinctions among intellectual, biological, and physical processes. There is, the humanistic naturalists assert, continuity from the less complex

11 Edited by Yervant H. Krikorian (New York: Columbia U. Press, 1944).
12 *Ibid.*, p. 357.

to the more complex. Intellectual processes "grow out of" organic or biological processes, and organic processes arise from physical processes without being identical with them. This is a methodological postulate—a directive for investigation—and is in no sense an attempt to "reduce" one to the other.

In *The Humanist Frame* a group of contemporary humanists distinguish among three transitional evolutionary stages. The first was from the inorganic to the biological, the second from the biological to the psychosocial, and now the third stage is emerging: "the passage from the psychosocial to the consciously purposive phase of evolution."[13]

The humanists contend that the richness of human experience and the great variety of natural phenomena can neither be "explained away" nor "reduced" to something else. This opposition to reductionism distinguishes this form of naturalism from the older materialism. The world is what it is—appears to be—in all its qualitative and quantitative variety. The new naturalism can accept the reality of physical and intellectual (mental) processes. It finds some processes mechanical and others teleological or purposive, and accepts the existence of all these processes as empirical facts.

THE HUMANIST WORLD VIEW

Humanistic naturalists regard the universe as "self-existing and not created." They have abandoned all conceptions of a supernatural Being and all forms of cosmic "support." Life is dependent on a physicochemical order, and it is likely that "life is a local and episodic phenomenon in the cosmos at large."[14] The quest for an understanding of the "ultimate" origin, nature, and goal of the universe as a whole is felt to be futile.

That the universe is indifferent to the human venture has been forcefully stated by Max C. Otto:

> It is thus a constructive social suggestion that we endeavor to give up, as the basis of our desire to win a satisfactory life, the quest for the companionship with a being behind or within the fleeting aspect of nature; that we assume the universe to be indifferent toward the human venture that means everything to us; that we acknowledge ourselves to be adrift in infinite space on our little earth, the sole custodians of our ideals.[15]

Thus humanists support an "unreservedly naturalistic" view of the universe and of life.

In the new naturalism the categories of "matter" and "motion" have

---

13 Julian Huxley (ed.) (New York: Harper, 1961), p. 7.
14 Edwin A. Burtt, *Types of Religious Philosophy* (rev. ed.; New York: Harper, 1951), p. 341.
15 *Things and Ideals* (New York: Holt, 1924), p. 289.

been replaced by the categories of "events," "qualities," and "relations." To experience change or process is to be aware of differences of the kind called "qualitative." The naturalists insist that they are not committed to any one interpretation of the nature of anything; they subscribe to neither the theory of levels nor the principle of reduction. Observation merely indicates that some objects and events differ sharply from one another and some differ less sharply. An explanation is acceptable to the extent to which it is supported by evidence. Scientific method is not limited to any field; it may deal with the processes of history, with values, with the fine arts, and with human purposes and goals.

MAN AND HUMAN SOCIETY

The "Humanist Manifesto"[16] states that humanists hold an "organic view of life," reject the "traditional dualism of mind and body," and believe that "man is a part of nature and that he has emerged as the result of a continuous process." Man with all his faculties is a part of one all-embracing natural order. He is the highest product of the creative forces of the universe, with "nothing above or beyond him" but his own aspirations.

The fact that man is a part of nature does not mean that there is nothing distinctive about him. Nature must be so interpreted as to allow man's place. The humanistic naturalists stress the worth of every human being. They claim, indeed, that they are gaining a new sense of human values. The values of life, they hold, are the products of human relationships. A realization of this fact can bring new confidence. Men are now able to look to the future with a new spirit of progress, adventure, and courageous conquest. Our task as men is to appropriate the instruments science has given us and to cooperate with the scientists in building a more satisfactory life on earth. We need to naturalize the spiritual values of life and to humanize the mechanical world of things. The humanists have a strong faith in the possibility of improving human life and in the essential unity of mankind.

The humanistic naturalists stand for human freedom—freedom of choice and the civil liberties. Most of them oppose an acquisitive society and favor a socialized and cooperative social and economic order. "The goal of humanism is a free and universal society in which people voluntarily and intelligently cooperate for the common good. Humanists demand a shared life in a shared world."[17]

16 The American Humanist Association, incorporated in 1941, actually dates from 1928, when its journal, *The Humanist,* was first published. In 1933 a group of thirty-four persons issued a "Humanist Manifesto" summing up their convictions in fifteen brief propositions. See *The Christian Century,* 50 (July 7, 1933): 743–745. Since 1933 a number of similar statements have been published, one of which is "A Statement on World Policy Drafted for the Oslo Meeting of the International Humanist and Ethical Union," *The Humanist,* 22 (January-February, 1962): 12–14.

17 "Humanist Manifesto," part of point 14.

HUMANISM AND RELIGION

Many humanists retain the word *religion* and redefine it; but some humanists prefer to substitute "the humanist way of life."[18] In either case, the
orthodox or traditional conceptions of religion are abandoned. The humanist's religion is a social product; it is loyalty to the values of life and the cooperative human quest for a better life.[19] The religious or the spiritual is not
something alien to man or imposed from without; it is a quality of man's
life that is grounded in his own human activity. The spiritual in man is man
at his best, fighting loyally and courageously for the values of life, cooperat-
ing for human welfare, projecting ideals and struggling to attain them, and
making room for sympathy and love. "Any activity," says John Dewey,
"that is pursued in behalf of an ideal and against obstacles and in spite of
threats of personal loss because of conviction of its general and enduring value
is religious in quality."[20] The essence of religion is seen as the integration of
the human personality around loyalty to some high ideal. It is "a religion
without God," but the humanists claim that it meets the needs that religion
has always met in that it unites men in devotion to human interests and
values. The humanists hope to integrate scientific, social, and religious
thought into one unified philosophy that aspires to the best possible life
for man.

CRITICAL COMMENTS

Many people commend the humanistic naturalist for his emphasis on
man and man's distinctively human traits, for his emphasis on scientific
method, and for his willingness to face facts with courage and a Promethean
will. People also admire the humanist's faith in creative intelligence and his
notion that the world is still in the making.

What will be more difficult for many to accept is the humanist's exclusive
faith in the methods of the objective sciences and in man's ability to attain a
satisfactory life in a universe that is indifferent to man's interests and aspirations. If nature has produced man, as the naturalists say, then it would seem
that man gives some indication of the nature of nature and that man probably
gives as good an indication of the nature of the universe as do rocks and stars.

The modern naturalists want to guard against the charge of anthropomorphism—attributing human qualities to the nonhuman realm. They wish
to avoid the danger of projection or of "reading into nature" our human

---

[18] The "Humanist Manifesto" of 1933 uses the term frequently. Corliss Lamont, in "The
Meaning of Humanism," *The Humanist*, 2 (Summer, 1942): 41–45, deplores the use of the term.
See discussions in succeeding issues of *The Humanist*.

[19] See Sir Julian Huxley, "The New Religion of Humanism," *The Humanist*, 22 (January-
February, 1962): 3–6.

[20] *A Common Faith* (New Haven: Yale U. Press, 1934), p. 27.

hopes and aspirations. Isn't there an equal danger that we may go to the opposite extreme and, in our desire to be strictly objective and empirical, "read out of nature" some qualities and aspects that may be present? If "wishful thinking" is a bad thing, as it is, isn't it equally undesirable to assume that the truth is contrary to what we desire?

The question as to whether the universe is friendly in the sense that there is purpose and concern for man at the center of things, merely neutral, or unfriendly to man is fundamental. Is it true, as one writer suggests, that "a cold and suspicious attitude toward the cosmos is hard to combine with a trustful and affectionate attitude toward human beings"?[21] While the humanists say that they do not make a separation between man and the process that has produced him, their critics say they do make such a separation when they see the power beyond man as "indifferent to the human venture," to repeat Otto's phrase. The creative processes of the universe have produced self-conscious beings with a degree of intelligence and a drive to search for truth, beauty, and goodness. Is it reasonable to believe that a process devoid of purpose and intelligence could produce a being like man? If man is interpreted as a part of nature and nature is simply a blind force operating without concern for the goals of man's life, is life, as some of the critics assert, likely to be seen as only a struggle for existence? Are self-interest and power eventually likely to emerge as guides for action? Does humanism leave man's ideals and standards without any secure foundation?

Many of the convictions of the humanists are acceptable to theists, especially to those who hold the position known as theistic naturalism. Theism, however, is an interpretation of the universe that affirms a cosmic support for man's ideals and values. It insists that there is meaning and moral purpose both in the universe and in man's life.

QUESTIONS AND PROJECTS

1. Review Questions

(1) Explain what is meant by *metaphysics*.

(2) Why is no one classification of the various types of philosophy wholly satisfactory?

(3) Explain the terms *naturalism*, *materialism*, *mechanistic materialism*, *dialectical materialism*, and *humanistic naturalism*.

(4) What are some of the things that mechanistic materialists affirm and deny? Why does this position appeal to some people?

[21] Walter M. Horton, *Theism and the Modern Mood* (New York: Harper, 1930), p. 82.

(5) What are the implications of mechanistic materialism for one's general philosophy of life?

(6) Critically evaluate mechanistic materialism.

(7) Explain how dialectical materialism differs from other types of materialism. How can it be used to justify revolutionary tactics?

(8) Critically evaluate dialectical materialism.

(9) What are the distinctive emphases of humanistic naturalism? How do humanistic naturalists differ from some other types of humanists?

(10) What do the humanistic naturalists say about methods of gaining knowledge, man, society, the universe, and religion?

(11) Critically evaluate humanistic naturalism.

(12) Indicate clearly the points of agreement and disagreement of the three types of naturalism discussed in this chapter. Be ready to compare these positions.

2. Critically evaluate the following statements, indicating where you agree and disagree with them:

(1) "If there is no God, then anything goes."

(2) "The mechanistic conception of life is a structural approach in the main, whereas the teleological view places emphasis mainly on function. These are complementary rather than antagonistic approaches."

(3) "In materialism the emphasis was upon order, law, immutability. In the new way of thinking which is developing, the emphasis is upon spontaneity, creativeness, initiative."

3. Is it true that there are "two atheisms," the atheism of the creed and the atheism of the deed? Max Otto, in *The Human Enterprise* (New York: Appleton-Century-Crofts, 1940), p. 291, makes such a distinction and quotes Alexander Meiklejohn's statement: "To be a materialist is to think of men, to deal with them, in external terms, as if they were 'things.'"

4. Report on dialectical materialism and its ethical implications. See "Dialectic Morality," by Donald A. Lowrie, in *Religion in Life*, 25(Spring, 1956):271–279; Herbert Marcuse, *Soviet Marxism* (New York: Columbia U. Press, 1958).

5. The humanistic naturalists are meliorists (*meliorism* means "betterment") in their attitude toward society and nature. To what extent does their philosophical position allow them to be optimistic or pessimistic? Is one position likely to overcome the other in the long run?

6. Review one of the following books: J. A. C. F. Auer and Julian Hartt, *Humanism Versus Theism* (Yellow Springs: Antioch Press, 1951); Thomas J. Blakeley, *Soviet Scholasticism* (New York: Humanities Press, 1963); Robert Daniels, *The Nature of Communism* (New York: Random House, 1962); Lloyd Morain and Mary Morain, *Humanism as the Next Step* (Boston: Beacon, 1954); Oliver L. Reiser, *The Promise of Scientific Humanism* (New York: Hafner, 1940); Adam B. Ulam, *The Unfinished Revolution* (New York: Random House, 1960); Gustav Wetter, *Dialectical Materialism* (New York: Praeger, 1959).

SUGGESTED READINGS

MECHANISTIC MATERIALISM

COHEN, CHAPMAN. *Materialism Restated.* 3rd ed.; London: Pioneer, 1943.
A defense of the tenet in materialism that all phenonema may be reduced to causative processes of an objective nature.

ELLIOT, HUGH. *Modern Science and Materialism.* New York: Longmans, Green, 1919.
An exposition of a more extreme form of materialism that reduces all existence to those processes investigated by physics and chemistry.

LANGE, F. A. *History of Materialism.* New York: Humanities Press, 1950.
A reprint in one volume of a three-volume work, published in 1925, dealing with materialism and its evaluation.

SEELY, CHARLES S. *Modern Materialism: A Philosophy of Action.* New York: Philosophical Library, 1960.
A small book that makes rather large claims regarding the principles, theory, objectives, and immediate aims of materialism.

SELLARS, ROY W., et al. (eds.). *Philosophy for the Future: The Quest of Modern Materialism.* New York: Macmillan, 1949.
The philosophy of materialism from the point of view of various philosophers and scientists.

DIALECTICAL MATERIALISM

CORNFORTH, MAURICE. *Historical Materialism.* New York: International Publishers, 1954.
An exposition of Marxist philosophy that deals with conceptions of history and science and speculates as to how the transition from socialism to communism will take place.

MARCUSE, HERBERT. *Soviet Marxism: A Critical Analysis.* New York: Columbia U. Press, 1958.
The author traces the development of Marxism through Leninism and Stalinism to post-Stalinism.

MARX, KARL, AND ENGELS, FRIEDRICH. *Basic Writings on Politics and Philosophy.* Ed. by Lewis S. Feuer. Garden City: Doubleday, 1959. (Anchor Book.)
A large collection in paperback that includes the Manifesto and many writings that have not been so widely circulated.

SELSAM, HOWARD. *Philosophy in Revolution.* New York: International Publishers, 1957.
The relation of Marx to the great thinkers from Plato to the present is discussed, showing how philosophy is related to the class struggle.

STALIN, JOSEPH. *Dialectical and Historical Materialism.* New York: International Publishers, 1940.
A forty-page presentation of dialectical materialism in the "Little Lenin Library," Vol. 25.

TUCKER, ROBERT C. *Philosophy and Myth in Karl Marx*. London: Cambridge U. Press, 1961.
  On the basis of recently published manuscripts, the author distinguishes between the earlier and later Marx and indicates the direction in which reinterpretation should move.

HUMANISTIC NATURALISM

HADAS, MOSES. *Humanism: The Greek Ideal and Its Survival*. New York: Harper, 1960.
  This work emphasizes Greek culture with its stress on the individual and man as the measure of all things.

HAWTON, HECTOR (ed.). *Reason in Action*. London: Watts, 1956.
  Five humanist writers show how humanism is related to history, man, and society.

The Humanist. Yellow Springs: American Humanist Association.
  A bimonthly journal "devoted to the realization of human values on earth in the faith that man has the goodwill and intelligence to build a decent world."

HUXLEY, JULIAN (ed.). *The Humanist Frame*. New York: Harper, 1961.
  The editor and twenty-five others present humanism in its many phases. Man is said to be entering "the consciously purposive phase of evolution."

————. *Religion Without Revelation*. New York: Harper, 1957.
  A biologist emphasizes "evolutionary humanism" and sees religion as a way of life without the necessity of revelation or a personal God.

KRIKORIAN, YERVANT H. (ed.). *Naturalism and the Human Spirit*. New York: Columbia U. Press, 1944.
  A symposium by a group of empirical naturalists.

LAMONT, CORLISS. *The Philosophy of Humanism*. 4th ed.; New York: Philosophical Library, 1962.
  A systematic presentation of humanism as philosophy by an ardent humanist.

REISER, OLIVER L. *The Integration of Human Knowledge*. Boston: Sargent, 1958.
  The author discusses the social implications of unified science and the "knowledge explosion" of recent years. He advocates a scientific humanism that provides "an individual and a world philosophy."

✳ THIRTEEN ✳

IDEALISM AND
ITS IMPLICATIONS

The term *idealist* as used philosophically has a meaning quite different from its meanings in ordinary language. Popularly the word may mean (1) one who accepts and lives by lofty moral, aesthetic, and religious standards or (2) one who is able to visualize, and who advocates, some plan or program that does not yet exist. Every social reformer is an idealist in the second sense because he is supporting something that has not yet come into existence. Those who work for permanent peace or for the elimination of poverty may be called idealists in this sense. The term may be used either as a compliment or as a term of derision. The person who stands for goals that other people generally believe to be quite unattainable or who ignores the facts and practical conditions of a situation is quite likely to be called a "mere idealist."

The philosophical meaning of the term *idealism* is determined more by the ordinary meaning of the word *idea* than *ideal*. W. E. Hocking, an idealist, says that the term "idea-ism would be more to the point."[1] Idealism, in brief, asserts that reality consists of ideas, thoughts, minds, or selves rather than of material objects and forces. Even a brief sketch of the history of idealism in its many forms would involve recounting a considerable amount of the history of philosophy from Plato to the present. Idealism has held the allegiance of many prominent thinkers, in both the Occident and the Orient, for more than two thousand years. During the latter half of the nineteenth century, idealism was the dominant Western philosophy. Since the beginning of this century, however, idealism has had to share the philosophical field with other movements. In this chapter we shall give a brief general statement of idealism, distinguish among three main types, and set forth a few of the implications of the philosophy. The reader is urged to consult the works of the idealists themselves for a more complete presentation.

[1] *Types of Philosophy* (3rd ed.; New York: Scribner's, 1959), p. 152.

WHAT IDEALISM IS

Idealism emphasizes mind as in some sense "prior to" matter. Whereas materialism says that matter is real and mind is an accompanying phenomenon, idealism contends that mind is real and matter is in a sense a by-product. Idealism thus implies a denial that the world is basically a great machine to be interpreted as matter, mechanism, or energy alone.

Idealism is a world view or a metaphysics which holds that the basic reality consists of or is closely related to mind, ideas, thoughts, or selves. The world has a meaning apart from its surface appearance. The world is understood and interpreted by a study of the laws of thought and of consciousness, and not exclusively by the methods of the objective sciences.

Since the universe has a meaning and purpose of which the development of people is an aspect, the idealist believes that there is a kind of inner harmony between the rest of the world and man. What is "highest in spirit" is also "deepest in nature." Man is "at home" in the universe and is not an alien or a mere creature of chance, since the universe is in some sense a logical and a spiritual system that is reflected in man's search for the true, the good, and the beautiful. The self is not an isolated or unreal entity; it is a genuine part of the world process. This process at its high levels manifests itself as creativity, mind, selves, or persons. Man, as a part of the cosmos, expresses its structure in his own life.

Nature, or the objective world, is real in the sense that it exists and demands our attention and adjustment to it. Nature, however, is not sufficient in and of itself, since the objective world depends to a certain degree upon mind. Idealists believe that the later and higher manifestations of nature are more significant in disclosing the characteristics of the process than are its earlier and lower ones. Idealists are willing to let the physical scientists tell us what matter is, provided they do not attempt to reduce everything in the world to that category. The idealists are willing to let the biological scientists describe life and its processes, provided they do not attempt to reduce all other "levels" to the biological or the physiological.

Idealists stress the organic unity of the world process. Whole and parts cannot be separated except by a dangerous abstraction that centers attention on single aspects of things to the exclusion of other, equally important aspects. According to some idealists, there is an inner unity, an unfolding series of levels from matter through vegetable forms through animals to man, mind, and spirit. Thus a central principle of idealism is organic wholeness. Idealists, tend to emphasize the coherence or consistency theory of the test of truth— a judgment is believed to be true if it is in agreement with other judgments that are accepted as true.[2]

---

[2] See pp. 58–60 for a discussion of the coherence theory.

TYPES OF IDEALISM

The history of idealism is complicated, since the term is broad enough to include a number of different though related theories. There are some students of philosophy who use the term in a broad sense to include all the philosophies that maintain that spiritual (nonmaterial) forces determine the processes of the universe. Idealistic philosophies thus oppose naturalistic philosophies that view these forces as emerging at some late stage in the development of the universe. In a narrower sense, the term *idealism* is used for those philosophies which view the universe as, in some crucial sense, dependent on mind.

In our discussion in this chapter we shall be referring mainly to the idealistic tradition as reflected in the thinking of some of its outstanding representatives in Western civilization. We need to keep in mind, however, that there are significant idealistic systems and movements in Asia, especially in India, within the Hindu tradition. While there are differences in outlook and emphasis between Western and Eastern idealism, P. T. Raju tells us that "the idealistic systems of the West and of India seem to be complementary to each other," and that "the orthodox Indian thought and Buddhist philosophy became idealistic when they reached their highest developments."[3] Space does not permit an elaboration of these Oriental systems of idealism, but the reader is encouraged to consult the books listed that deal with this topic.

There are many classifications of the types of idealism, yet no one classification seems to be entirely satisfactory, and there is much overlapping. We may classify the different types of idealism by the names of their representatives—Plato, Descartes, Leibniz, Berkeley, Kant, Hegel, Lotze, and Royce, to mention only a few. Each of these men contributed something distinctive. Some students, after the fashion of an early psychology that divided mind into intellect, feeling, and will, have spoken of rationalistic, affective (or romantic), and voluntaristic types of idealism. Representatives of these types would be Hegel (rationalistic), Schelling (affective), and Schopenhauer (voluntaristic). In this chapter we shall briefly consider subjective idealism, objective idealism, and personalism; this classification is useful, relatively simple, and clear.

SUBJECTIVE IDEALISM

This type of idealism is sometimes called *mentalism,* sometimes *phenomenalism.* It is the least defensible and least prevalent, and the one most frequently attacked by opponents of idealism. The subjective idealist holds that minds, or spirits, and their perceptions, or ideas, are all that exist. The "objects" of

---

3 *Idealistic Thought of India* (London: Allen and Unwin, 1953), pp. 7, 13. Others, including S. N. Dasgupta and S. Radhakrishnan, have spoken of the dominant philosophies in India as idealistic.

experience are not material things; they are merely perceptions. Things such as buildings and trees exist, but they exist only in a mind that perceives them. The subjective idealist does not deny the existence, in some sense, of what we call the "real" world; the question at issue is not its existence but *how* it is to be interpreted. It does not exist independent of a knower. The sense in which the external world is said to "exist" by the subjective idealist is very special—that is, the word *exist* is used very differently from the way it is used ordinarily. For the subjective idealist all that exists (in the more ordinary sense) are minds and their ideas.

Subjective idealism is probably best represented by George Berkeley (1685–1753), an Irish philosopher who preferred the term *immaterialism* to describe his philosophy. Berkeley accepted the psychology of John Locke (1632–1704), who said that our knowledge deals only with ideas. Locke accepted the existence of spiritual substance, ideas, and material substance. He distinguished between the primary qualities of matter (form, extension, solidity, figure, motion, number, and so on) and secondary qualities (colors, sounds, tastes, odors, and the like). The secondary qualities, according to Locke, are not in the material substance; they are in the mind or they are the way in which the primary qualities affect the mind or knower, and they vary from person to person. Berkeley went further than Locke and attempted to show that the primary qualities, as well as the secondary qualities, do not exist apart from minds. Berkeley, therefore, called both primary and secondary qualities "ideas" and concluded that what we refer to as a material object is simply a collection of ideas. Berkeley insisted that the arguments used by Locke to prove the subjectivity of secondary qualities also demonstrate the subjectivity of the primary qualities.

For Berkeley, nothing but minds and their ideas exist. To say that an idea exists means, according to him, that it is being perceived by some mind. For ideas, *Esse est percipi:* "To be is to be perceived." Minds themselves, however, are not similarly dependent for their existence on being perceived. Minds are *perceivers*. To give Berkeley's full view, we must say: To be is to be perceived (ideas) or to be a perceiver (mind). All that is real is a conscious mind or some perception or idea held by such a mind. How, Berkeley asks, could we speak of anything that was other than an idea or a mind?

When we assert that we can imagine objects existing when they are not seen, and that we do believe in the independent existence of an external world, Berkeley tells us that the order and consistency of the world of nature are real and are due to active mind, the mind of God. God, the supreme mind, is the author and the governing spirit of nature, and God's will is the Law of Nature. God determines the succession and the order of our ideas. This explains why we cannot determine merely by willing it what we shall see when we open our eyes.

The subjectivist holds that there can *be* no object, as well as no perception of it, without a knower; that the subject (mind or knower) in some way creates its object (what we call matter, or things that are known); and that all that is real is a conscious mind or a perception by such a mind. To say that a things exists is to say that it is perceived. What anything would or could be apart from its being known, no one can think or say. What we see or think is mind-dependent, and the world is a mental world.[4]

Immanuel Kant (1724–1804) is a *phenomenalist* who stands about midway between the subjective and the objective idealists. Since the world as described by Kant is in some sense a mind-made world, we will make the transition from subjective to objective idealism through his philosophy. For Kant there are three realms. There is the inner realm of subjective states, which is purely personal and not the realm of knowledge. There is the outer world of ultimate reality, the noumenon, which by its very nature is unknown and unknowable. Man's contact with this realm is achieved through the sense of duty or the moral law. There is also the world of nature, or the phenomenal world, which is the realm of human knowledge.

According to Kant, the mind has certain innate ways of working (as opposed to Locke's notion of the mind as a *tabula rasa*). Form and order are thrust on nature by the mind. Sensory experience merely furnishes mind its content. The mind is active; it forms into a system of knowledge the raw material brought in by the senses. Just as the potter takes the formless clay and fashions it into one form or another, so the mind forms or organizes the material of the senses. Thus our thoughts regarding the world are determined in large part by the structure of the mind. The understanding prescribes its laws to nature.[5]

OBJECTIVE IDEALISM

Many idealists, from Plato through Hegel to contemporary philosophers, reject both extreme subjectivism, or mentalism, and the view that the external world is in any real sense man-made. They regard the organization and form of the world, and hence knowledge, as determined by the nature of the world itself. The mind discovers what there is in the order of the world. They are idealists in that they interpret the universe as an intelligible realm, whose systematic structure expresses rational order and value. When they say that the ultimate nature of the universe is mental, they mean that the universe is one all-embracing order, that its basic nature is mind, and that it is an organic whole.

Although the term *idealism* has been used only in recent times to designate

4 For an understanding of Berkeley's position and the force of his arguments, read *The Principles of Human Knowledge*, ed. Colin M. Turbayne (New York: Liberal Arts Press, 1957).
5 See Kant's *Critique of Pure Reason*.

a school of philosophical thought, the beginnings of idealistic speculation in Western culture are often attributed to Plato (c. 427–347 B.C.). Plato called the fundamental realities *Ideas,* but for him, unlike for Berkeley, this did not mean that they are dependent for their existence on a mind, human or divine.6 Plato believed that behind the empirical world of change, the phenomenal world that we see and feel, there is an ideal world of eternal essences, forms, or "Ideas." He believed in the objective reality of our ideals and values. For Plato the world is divided into two realms. There is, first, the world of sense perception, the world of sights, sounds, and individual things. This concrete, temporal, perishable world is not the real world; it is the world of appearances only. Second, there is the supersensible world of concepts, Ideas, universals, or eternal essences. The concept "man" has more reality than any individual person has. We recognize individual things through our knowledge of these concepts or eternal patterns. This second realm contains the patterns, forms, or types that serve as standards for the things we perceive with our senses. Ideas are the original, transcendent patterns, and perceptions and individual things are mere copies or shadows of these Ideas. While reality is immaterial, Plato would not say that there is nothing real except mind and its experiences. The unchanging Ideas, or essences, which are real, are known to man through his reason. The soul of man is an immaterial essence imprisoned for a time in the body. The changing world of matter, apprehended by the senses, yields only opinion, not genuine knowledge.

Modern objective idealists typically maintain that all parts of the world are included in one all-embracing order, and they attribute this unity to the ideas and purposes of an Absolute Mind. Hegel (1770–1831) propounded one of the best-known systems of absolute or monistic idealism. His system is sometimes called evolutionary, logical idealism. Thought is the essence of the universe, and nature is the whole of mind objectified. The universe is an unfolding process of thought. Nature is the Absolute Reason expressing itself in outward form. Consequently, the laws of thought are also the laws of reality. History is the way the Absolute appears in nature and human experience. Since the world is One and since it is purposive and intelligent, it must be of the nature of thought. The world expresses itself in our thinking; our thinking does not determine the nature of the world. When we think of the total world order as embracing the inorganic, the organic, and the spiritual levels of existence in one all-inclusive order, we speak of the Absolute, or the Absolute Spirit, or God.

Instead of the fixed or static reality and the separate and complete self of traditional philosophy, Hegel sets forth a dynamic conception of a self and

6 For this reason, Plato is sometimes included with the realists. For an explanation of *realism* see the Glossary and Chapter 14.

its environment so interrelated that a clear-cut distinction cannot be drawn between the two. The self is experiencing reality at all times. The "universal" is present in all the particular experiences of the dynamic process. In such a philosophy, distinctions and differences belong to the phenomenal world and are relative to the observer; they do not affect the unity of the one purposive intelligence.

The objective idealists do not deny the existence of an external or objective reality. In fact, they believe that their position is the only one that does justice to the objective side of experience, since they find in nature the same principles of order, reason, and purpose that men find within themselves. There is purposive intelligence at the heart of nature. This is discovered, they believe, and not "read into" the world. Nature existed before me, the individual self, and will exist after me; nature also existed before the present community of selves. The existence of meaning in the world, however, implies something akin to mind or thought at the core of reality. Such a significant order of reality is given man to comprehend and to participate in. This belief in meaning and intelligence in the structure of the world is a basic intuition underlying idealism.[7]

Panpsychism is a form of idealism standing somewhere between objective idealism and personalism. Panpsychism (from the Greek *pan,* meaning "all," and *psyche,* meaning "soul") is the doctrine that reality is psychic in character —that *everything* has mind. Mind is universal throughout nature, and the whole world is "alive."[8]

PERSONALISM, OR PERSONAL IDEALISM

Personalism emerged as a protest against both mechanistic materialism and monistic idealism. For the personalist the basic reality is neither abstract thought nor a particular thought process, but a person, a self, or a thinker. Reality is of the nature of conscious personality. The self is an irreducible living unit, which can be divided only by a false abstraction. The personalists believe that recent developments in modern science, including the formulation of the theory of relativity and the growing recognition of the importance of the "standpoint of the observer," have added support to their position. Reality is a system of personal selves; hence it is pluralistic. Personalists emphasize the reality and the worth of individual people, moral values, and human freedom.

Nature, for the personalists, is an objective order; however, it does not

---

[7] Since the time of Hegel there have been many systems of objective idealism. Omitting the contemporary thinkers, we can name such outstanding idealists as Josiah Royce, Mary K. Calkins, and J. E. Creighton in the United States, and T. H. Green, Edward Caird, and F. H. Bradley in England—to mention only a few.

[8] For types of panpsychism see G. W. Leibniz (1646–1716) and Friedrich Paulsen (1846–1908) in Germany, and James Ward (1893–1925) in England.

exist in and of itself. People transcend or rise above nature when they interpret it. Science transcends its material through its theories, and the world of meaning and of values surpasses the world of nature as final explanation. Rudolf Hermann Lotze (1817–1881), Borden P. Bowne (1847–1910), and contemporary personalists have emphasized this point of view. Lotze attempted to reconcile the mechanical view of nature set forth by the sciences with the idealistic interpretation of a spiritual unity. For Bowne, self-conscious mind realizes itself through the order of nature as its vehicle of expression yet transcends it.

Nature was created by God, who is the Supreme Self in a society of persons. The Supreme Spirit has expressed Himself in the material world of atoms and in conscious selves which emerge at particular stages in the world process. There is a society of persons, or selves, related to the Supreme Personality. Ethical and spiritual values are reinforced by and gain their meaning from the Personal Creative Spirit, to whom all men are related. Personalism is theistic; it furnishes both religion and ethics with metaphysical foundations. God may be thought of as finite, as a struggling hero, working for lofty moral and religious ends. The goodness of God is retained, even though there is some limitation placed on his power. The proper goal of life is a perfect society of selves who have achieved perfect personalities through struggle.

As a group, the personal idealists have shown more interest in ethics and less interest in logic than have the absolute idealists. The personal idealists hold that the process of life is more important than any verbal forms of expression or fixed meanings, and they stress the realization of the capacities and powers of the person through freedom and self-control. Since personality has greater value than anything else, society must be so organized as to give each person fullness of life and of opportunity.

IDEALIST ARGUMENTS

The arguments used in defense of the various types of idealism fall into four major categories.[9]

1. *An argument from the analysis of matter and related concepts.* Some idealists have maintained that it makes little difference where a person begins his inquiry; if he presses far enough in his thinking, he will come to the point of view of idealism. Take, for example, the study of matter. The world of nature that men see and feel is evidently a world of appearances whose real nature is different from what it seems to be. In their attempt to explain the

9 For a more detailed discussion of the arguments for idealism, see G. Watts Cunningham, *The Idealistic Argument in Recent British and American Philosophy* (New York: Appleton-Century-Crofts, 1933). See also A. C. Ewing, *The Idealist Tradition from Berkeley to Blanshard* (Glencoe: Free Press, 1957).

various transformations that take place in matter, men have pushed their analysis from molecules to atoms, and from atoms to protons and electrons. But what are atoms, protons, and electrons? Are they anything other than mental constructs arrived at through a process of reasoning or logical analysis? Evidently the fundamental character of matter is not that of its outward appearance, and when we try to determine just what this fundamental character is, we get back to energy of some kind. If we try to stop at this point in our interpretation, the idealist will point out that psychical energy is that which is most real to us. Even though we start with so-called physical things, when we push our investigation far enough, we are forced into what appears to be a mental world. In any event, we are led to the conclusion that there are mental forces within or behind the world of nature.

2. *An argument from the nature of knowledge.* This argument varies in its emphasis, depending on whether one leans toward subjective or objective idealism. When men say that a thing exists, what do they mean? According to these idealists, they can mean only that it is perceived by them or by someone else. Men know and can know only that which is in consciousness, in some mind. To ask what objects are in themselves or apart from knowing minds is a meaningless question. Men cannot get outside their own experiences. Consequently, knowing the world-out-there implies that the world is in some sense mental or related to the mental. Men may hold to the "objective reference of thought" and insist that ideas refer to something beyond themselves. If minds have been produced by nature, are actually parts of nature, and interpret nature's ways, the same principles of rational order operate in nature as in mind. If the two realms were of entirely different orders, how could events be known and predicted as the result of thinking about the world?[10]

3. *An argument from the structure and order of the universe.* The world appears to be an orderly, intelligible structure, which exhibits direction from lower to higher forms of life and intelligence. Consider the long period through which the earth was "prepared" for the growth of life, the fairly continuous improvement in organic structure, and the increasing control exercised by the mind over the body and the environment. This long evolutionary development, culminating in the mind of man, suggests that there is purpose in the universe. The evolutionary process has produced men with knowledge and the power of reflective thought. Such concepts as "natural selection" and "emergence" are descriptive, not explanatory. This development is unintelligible unless the course of evolution is directed. The mind that knows, appreciates, and values is not a stranger appearing suddenly and accidentally in the universe.

The fact that two men can read and understand the same book in the same

10 For the discussion of the problems of knowledge, reread Chapters 2 through 4.

way is an indication that their minds are of the same fundamental kind and work the same way. They are governed by the same laws of logic and intelligibility. The fact that man is progressively coming to understand and interpret the structure of nature is an indication that there is an intelligible structure or a mind in nature. Order, intelligibility, meaning, and law seem to be at the basis of both mind and nature.

4. *An argument from man's moral character.* The idealist is likely to claim that his interpretation of the world is the only one that recognizes and satisfies the moral, aesthetic, and religious demands of humanity. The purely naturalistic view of man and the universe is inadequate, since it would render false or unsupportable man's deepest moral convictions. Man's ideals and aspirations have emerged along with man. They are man's half-conscious realization of his own inherent possibilities. The presence of moral values and a sense of moral obligation ("I ought") in the human realm requires a purposive interpretation of the world. Man's sense of moral obligation has been a directive force in human history; men have lived strenuously and died courageously to uphold their ideals. Since moral experience is always associated with minds and purposes, the facts of man's moral life point to the existence of mind and purpose in the universe. There are other and more elaborate forms of the moral argument with which the student may wish to become acquainted.[11]

IMPLICATIONS OF IDEALISM

MAN LIVES IN A FRIENDLY UNIVERSE

For the idealist there is a purposeful universe, the real nature of which is spiritual. While he accepts the interpretations of the modern empirical sciences, he points out that they are limited by the nature of the methods used and the fields investigated. The sciences tend to eliminate all mental aspects of the world and to construct a world that is "closed to mind." The laws of the universe, according to the idealist, are in harmony with the demands of man's intellectual and moral nature.

Though man is a part of the world process and in that sense "natural," he is a spiritual being in the sense that there is in him something not reducible to bare "matter." Doctrines of total depravity, as well as all interpretations of human nature as evil, are out of place in the idealist's system. Equally inadequate are all interpretations of man that would make him a mere animal or place him in the control of purely physiological or mechanical processes. Man has only begun to realize his possibilities. Moreover, it is through man and his aspirations that we find the best clue to the nature of God.

For the idealists, God is not apart from the world, but is the indwelling

11 See Kant's *Critique of Practical Reason.* See also William R. Sorley, *Moral Values and the Idea of God* (New York: Macmillan, 1918).

life principle. Though God may transcend the world process, He is also immanent in it. He is found in the processes of nature, in history, in the social order, and preeminently in the human heart. Consequently, the older distinction between the natural and the supernatural tends to break down. In monistic idealism, God is the immanent logic and purpose or the creative spirit of the cosmic process. The absolute idealist thinks of God as infinite and as the ground of all existence. The personalist, who is a pluralist, may think of God as finite. He will be a struggling hero, the Supreme Self or Person in a society of persons. In any case God's administration is no longer external, and men do not have to look to some outside agent or event for divine revelation; it is to be found in all of life.

IDEALISM AND MAN'S SOCIAL RELATIONSHIPS

What are the social implications of idealism? Does it lead to an acceptance of conditions as they are or to a spirit of reform and progress? The answer depends much on the type of idealism being considered. Idealists in general tend to have considerable respect for culture and tradition. They think of the values of life as grounded in a realm beyond the individual and the social groups. In absolute idealism the universe precedes and is superior to the particular, so that men may come to believe, with Hegel, that the absolute is expressed in history and through the institutions of society. In such cases, there is less tendency to recognize individual rights and values as opposed to those of society and the state.[12]

While Plato's philosophy has inspired many reform movements, his idealism with its view of Ideas or universals as transcendent essences led, through Plotinus and Augustine, to a conceptual separation of this world and the next; this view dominated the whole of medieval society and tended to fix all human relationships. This outlook supported the idea of a static society.

In contrast with Platonic and Hegelian types of idealism, many modern idealists, from Descartes and Leibniz to the contemporary personalists, have emphasized the person or the consciousness of the individual. Men are viewed as free moral agents capable of discovering values. Idealism thus gives an objective basis for moral values and obligations, as opposed to relativistic views, which stress customs and opinion. Self-realization, or the development of selfhood, is the supreme value to which all other values are subordinate.

EVALUATION OF IDEALISM

The fact that idealism has survived for many centuries and has been supported by many outstanding thinkers, both in the Orient and in the Occident,

---

12 Thus the philosophies of Hegel and Fichte played a part in the development of the concept of the state in Hitler's Germany.

would seem to indicate that it has filled some need. The strength of idealism is that it emphasizes the significance of the person and the mental or spiritual side of life. Idealism justifies philosophically the notion that the individual self has meaning and dignity; man has abiding worth and is superior to institutions and "things."

While accepting the modern scientific account of the world, idealism makes room for religion. Moral and religious values are present in the world of nature. Idealism is thus in harmony with many of the intuitions and aspirations of men. Idealism, its supporters claim, gives intellectual support to the spiritual intuitions of the race. The appeal of idealism is in part to the moral aspirations of men and not only on logical or epistemological grounds.

In their struggles toward a better life, many men feel that there is a power beyond them upon which they may depend for aid. Idealism gives them the assurance that mind and values are structurally part of the universe. Thus men may have a sense of confidence and come to feel "at home" in the universe.

The critics of idealism, on the other hand, say that it is vague and abstract in its terminology, that it is merely of traditional interest, and that it lacks a genuinely scientific outlook. Pragmatists such as John Dewey claim that idealism tends to substitute an antiquated attitude of other-worldliness for vigorous participation in the struggle for a new society here and now. To regard institutions as expressions of a universal reason may lead men to think more about order and stability and less about change and progress.

Realists and philosophical analysts are likely to charge that idealism goes beyond all empirical evidence and that its "proofs" resort to metaphor and flights of the imagination based on the hopes and wishes of men. The assumptions the idealist makes are those which the tough-minded person finds it difficult to accept. If the universe is an expression of mind or reason, the critic asks, why is it that experience reveals so much that is irrational and apparently purposeless, if not actually malevolent?

Other opponents charge that the idealists confuse the "accidental" with the "essential" features of objects. When idealists claim that existence is dependent on some mind, the realist is likely to insist that "being perceived" is an accidental feature of an object, whereas existence is an essential feature. The fact that we can never refer to an object without holding some idea of it does not mean that the object does not exist apart from the presence of an idea or a mind or even that it is in any way changed by the act of perception. There is the danger in idealism of equating mere thought with being or of confusing the environment with the mind that thinks about the environment.

Idealism comes in for criticism from some theologians who say that an intellectualistic view of God or an Absolute can be no substitute for a contrite heart and an act of decision. Idealism, they say, has a too optimistic view of man and the world. It does not deal satisfactorily with the problem of evil. For most people evil is a stubborn reality and the problems of evil are how to identify it, how to reduce its power, and how to eliminate it. For idealism there is the additional and insoluble problem of how there can be any evil or imperfection in the world. Monistic idealism, at least, appears to permit a too easy tolerance of evil and to justify the status quo, since whatever *is* is defined as good or as a part of the World Spirit.

QUESTIONS AND PROJECTS

1. Review Questions

(1) Give the derivation of the term *idealism* and distinguish the philosophical meaning from the common or popular uses of the term.

(2) What are the common assumptions and convictions underlying the various schools or types of idealism?

(3) Explain as clearly as you can the distinctive points of subjective idealism, objective idealism, and personal idealism.

(4) List a few Western idealists, and indicate where idealism has flourished. Can you give any reasons for its relative decline in the West in recent decades?

(5) State in your own words the major arguments for idealism. Which of these arguments are strongest, and why?

(6) What are the implications of idealism for our views of the universe, God, man, and social relationships?

(7) Evaluate idealism, indicating what you consider to be its strengths and its weaknesses.

2. Do you think there is any justification for the criticism that idealists identify spirit too readily with reason, and reason too easily with God?

3. Comment on the following statement by R. F. A. Hoernle: "There is a deep-seated need in the human mind, the roots of which strike far beneath all other needs and interests. This is the need to feel at home in the universe."[13]

4. Give your reaction to the idealism of George Berkeley. The following limerick, attributed to Ronald Knox, was written about Berkeley's immaterialism:

> There was a young man who said, "God
> Must think it exceedingly odd
> If he finds that this tree
> Continues to be
> When there's no one about in the Quad."

[13] From Edwin A. Burtt, *Religion in an Age of Science* (New York: Stokes, 1929), p. 102.

REPLY
Dear Sir:
Your astonishment's odd
I am always about in the Quad.
And that's why the tree
Will continue to be,
Since observed by
Yours faithfully,
God

5. Is Christian Science within the general framework of, or closely related to, idealistic philosophy? If so, to which of the types is it most closely related? Mrs. Mary Baker Eddy, the founder of Christian Science, said: "I gained the scientific certainty that all causation was Mind, and every effect a mental phenomenon."[14] "God is good. Good is Mind." "God, Spirit, being all, nothing is matter."[15]

6. Theosophy has been called "the body of truths which forms the basis of all religions." Look up some facts regarding theosophy and its beliefs. Does it have any relationship to idealistic thought?

7. Discuss the educational implications of idealism, and compare or contrast them with the implications of pragmatism. See J. Donald Butler, *Four Philosophies and Their Practice in Education and Religion* (New York: Harper, 1951), Chs. VIII, XIX; Van Cleve Morris, *Philosophy and the American School* (Boston: Houghton Mifflin, 1961), Chs. 3, 6, 9.

8. Review one of the following books: Edgar S. Brightman, *Nature and Values* (New York: Abingdon, 1945); A. C. Ewing, *Idealism: A Critical Survey* (New York: Humanities Press, 1950); Ralph T. Flewelling, *The Person* (Los Angeles: Ritchie, 1952); S. Radhakrishnan, *An Idealist View of Life* (London: Allen and Unwin, 1951); William Allison Shimer, *Conscious Clay* (New York: Scribner's, 1948).

SUGGESTED READINGS

BERKELEY, GEORGE. *A Treatise Concerning the Principles of Human Knowledge*. Ed. by Colin M. Turbayne. New York: Liberal Arts Press, 1957.
Berkeley's classic is made available in a paperback edition, along with a helpful introduction.

BERTOCCI, PETER A., AND MILLARD, RICHARD M. *Personality and the Good*. New York: McKay, 1963.
An exposition and critique of psychological and ethical theories of the good life with a view to developing an ideal of personality and some "universal ethical principles." The system developed is consistent with personalistic idealism but does not presuppose it.

[14] *Retrospection and Introspection* (Boston: Published by the Trustees under the Will of Mary Baker G. Eddy, 1892), p. 24.

[15] *Science and Health with Key to the Scriptures* (Boston: Published by the Trustees under the Will of Mary Baker G. Eddy, 1906), p. 113.

BLANSHARD, BRAND. *The Nature of Thought.* 2 vols.; New York: Macmillan, 1940.
An outstanding idealist makes a careful examination of human thought and knowledge. The first volume is concerned with sense perception and ideas, the second volume with creative thinking and the nature and tests of truth.

BRIGHTMAN, EDGAR SHEFFIELD. *Person and Reality: An Introduction to Metaphysics.* Ed. by Peter Anthony Bertocci with Jannette Elthina Newhall and Robert Sheffield Brightman. New York: Ronald, 1958.
An introduction to metaphysical problems from the point of view of a personalistic idealist. The author assumes some knowledge of philosophy on the part of the reader. See also the author's shorter work, Nature and Values.

BUTLER, J. DONALD. *Four Philosophies and Their Practice in Education and Religion.* New York: Harper, 1953.
See Part II, pp. 121–272 for a discussion of idealism, and pp. 525–528 for a fairly inclusive bibliography.

EWING, A. C. *Idealism: A Critical Survey.* 3rd ed.; New York: Humanities Press, 1961.
A critical discussion of the idealism that dominated philosophy during the nineteenth century. Its central conceptions are elaborated and evaluated.

———— (ed.). *The Idealist Tradition: From Berkeley to Blanshard.* Glencoe: Free Press, and Indian Hills: Falcon's Wing, 1957.
Selections from both adherents to and critics of idealism.

FLEWELLING, RALPH TYLER. *The Person; or The Significance of Man.* Los Angeles: Anderson & Ritchie, 1952. (Ward Ritchie Press.)
An outstanding personalist gives a comprehensive exposition of personalism and discusses its implications for the contemporary world.

HARRIS, ERROL E. *Nature, Mind, and Modern Science.* New York: Macmillan, 1954.
The author, an idealist, is especially critical of logical empiricism and of any philosophy which would reject the immanence of mind in nature.

HOCKING, WILLIAM E. *Types of Philosophy.* 3rd ed.; New York: Scribner's, 1958.
Part V discusses idealism—its types and applications.

LUCE, A. A. (ed.). *Berkeley's Immaterialism.* New York: Nelson, 1945.
A commentary on Berkeley's approach to the principles of human knowledge.

RADHAKRISHNAN, S. *An Idealist View of Life.* London: Allen and Unwin, 1951.
One of the intellectual leaders of India discusses man's religious experience, his nature, and his destiny.

RAJU, P. T. *Idealistic Thought of India.* London: Allen and Unwin, 1953.
An Indian philosopher discusses Vedantic idealism and Buddhistic idealism. He contends that metaphysical idealism is still the dominant philosophy in India and that the idealistic systems of the West and India are complementary.

SCHILPP, PAUL ARTHUR (ed.). *The Philosophy of Sarvepalli Radhakrishnan.* New York: Tudor, 1952. (From the Library of Living Philosophers.)
Descriptive and critical essays that deal with many aspects of the philosophy of an outstanding Hindu idealist.

WARNOCK, G. J. *Berkeley.* London: Penguin, 1953. (Also Boston: Houghton Mifflin, 1962.)
A nontechnical presentation of the views of George Berkeley as found in his various writings.

Other key works are the following: René Descartes, *Discourse on Method;* G. W. F. Hegel, *The Philosophy of History* and *Lectures on the Philosophy of Religion;* Immanuel Kant, *Critique of Pure Reason;* G. W. Leibniz, *Discourse on Metaphysics;* Plato, *The Dialogues* (especially *Phaedo*) and *The Republic,* Books VI–VII; Josiah Royce, *The Spirit of Modern Philosophy;* Arthur Schopenhauer, *The World as Will and Idea.*

FOURTEEN

REALISM AND
ITS IMPLICATIONS

In the chapter called "The Nature of Knowledge" we introduced a common-sense type of realism (naïve realism) in which a clear distinction was made between thoughts and things, knower and objects known, what is subjective and what is objective. These distinctions were at first thought to be fixed and self-evident. Upon examination difficulties were found with this common-sense or naïve type of realism. Modern philosophical realists, however, set forth and defend a position which they think will stand up under critical analysis and which they believe is less vulnerable to attack than the position of any of their critics.

Realism, with its assumption of an external world existing quite independent of the human mind, has been widely accepted throughout history. In some form or other it has had almost universal acceptance among Western thinkers; in fact, realism was not seriously questioned until the seventeenth century. Most men think of themselves as existing in the midst of a world of objects that are independent of them. The mind and the external world interact, but this interaction does not affect the basic nature of the world. The world existed before mind was aware of it and will exist after mind ceases to be aware of it.

Let us be clear about the meanings of the terms *real, reality,* and *realism.* The *real* is the actual, or the existing; the term refers to things or events that exist in their own right, as opposed to that which is imaginary, or fictitious. *Real* refers to what is. *Reality* is the state or quality of being real or actually existent, in contrast with what is mere appearance. In a popular sense, *realism* may mean devotion to fact, to what is the case, as opposed to what is wished, hoped, or desired. In philosophy, however, the word *realism* is used in a more technical sense.

WHAT REALISM IS

Realism, in its strictly philosophical sense, is the position that the objects of our senses are real in their own right; they exist independent of their being known to, perceived by, or related to mind. For the realist, the universe is so inexorably "out there" that the only thing we can do is to come to the best terms possible with it. The realist attempts to do this, not to interpret the world according to his special hopes or unverified beliefs. However, for many realists there are mental events or mental entities, as well as physical ones, that are recognized as real quite apart from any ideas we may have regarding them.[1]

A contemporary British realist, John Macmurray, says:

> We cannot get away from the primary fact that there is a distinction between things and ideas. For ordinary common sense an idea is the idea of something, a thought in our minds which *represents* the things that it is the idea of. In that case the thing is the reality while the idea is merely "how the thing appears to us." Our thought must, therefore, adapt itself to things if it is to be proper thought, that is to say, if our idea is to be true. If the idea does not correspond with the thing of which it is the idea, then the idea is false and useless. The thing will not accommodate itself to our idea of it. We have to change our ideas and keep on changing them till we get them right. Now, such a common-sense way of thinking is essentially realist, and it is realist because it makes the "thing" and not the "idea" the measure of validity, the center of significance. It makes the thing real and the idea the true or false appearance of the thing.[2]

In discussing the psychological genesis of positions other than realism, Macmurray says that, since the philosopher is so concerned with ideas, he tends to emphasize the world of ideas or thought. Since thought tends to be important *to him,* he naturally, though mistakenly, comes to think that ideas have a reality not found in things. If a man regards the life of the mind, or reflective thinking, as something higher or nobler than practical activity or than his interest in things, he may falsely come to assume that the idea is more important than the thing of which it is the idea. If he confines himself to thought, then thought seems to be the only significant thing. According to Macmurray, the realistic view is the common-sense view and the only one that will stand up amidst the practical activities of life.

Another realist, Alfred North Whitehead, sets forth his reasons for believing that the things we experience are to be distinguished clearly from our knowledge of them.[3] In defending the objectivist position of realism, which, he says, is adapted to the requirements of science as well as to the concrete

---

1 For example, E. G. Spaulding in *The New Rationalism* (New York: Holt, 1918) uses the phrase *physical entities* for entities that are correlated with a specific part of space and time, and *mental entities* for those with a specific time alone. He calls the latter *subsistents*. In the realm of subsistents we have universals and ideals. Such values as justice, goodness, truth, and beauty, though never completely attained, are nevertheless realities.

2 *The Philosophy of Communism* (London: Faber & Faber, 1933), pp. 21–22.

3 *Science and the Modern World* (New York: Macmillan, 1935), pp. 125 ff.

experiences of mankind, Whitehead makes three affirmations. First, we are *"within* a world of colors, sounds, and other sense-objects." The world is not within us, nor does it depend on our sense perception. Second, historical knowledge discloses long ages in the past when no living beings existed on earth and when important changes or happenings were taking place. Third, one's activity seems to transcend the self and to find and to seek ends in the known world. Things pave the way for our awareness. A "common world of thought" seems to imply and require a "common world of sense."

Many philosophers past and present, notably the idealists and the pragmatists, have claimed that an object known or experienced is different from the object before it entered such relationships. Since we can never know an object except as it is known or experienced by us, the object's being known or experienced forms an integral part of the object known. Thus knowledge and experience tend to modify or to constitute the object to some extent. The realist holds that such reasoning is fallacious, because it draws a false conclusion from certain accepted propositions. We cannot, of course, know a thing until we have some experience of it. It is also true that we cannot know what qualities a thing possesses when it is unknown. The only valid conclusion is that all known things are known, which is a truism, or that awareness is an element in knowledge. From this we cannot draw the conclusion either that things have no qualities when they are not known or that the experience of knowing changes them in any way or constitutes their existence. Realism insists that the widely accepted common-sense position is sound, that is, that the realm of nature, or physical objects, exists independently of us and that our experience does not change the nature of the object experienced.

An idealist's view of realism is presented below. In essential agreement with the statements of Macmurray and Whitehead, William Ernest Hocking says:

> Realism as a general temper of mind is a disposition to keep ourselves and our preferences out of our judgment of things, letting the objects speak for themselves. If we can say of idealism that it has a tendency to read the mind into nature, realism is in this respect its precise opposite. In the interest of allowing every object its full distinctive flavor, realism is inclined to de-personalize or de-mentalize the world, to see things starkly and factually in a spirit which it conceives to be at once more objective and more scientific than that of idealism.[4]

Realism is a term that covers many different trends or types of philosophies that have certain basic tenets in common. At least three tendencies are evident in modern realism. There is, first, a tendency toward materialism in some of

---

[4] *Types of Philosophy* (rev. ed.; New York: Scribner's, 1939), p. 383. (See also the 3rd ed., 1959, with the collaboration of Richard Boyle O'Reilly Hocking, p. 225.)

its modern forms. For example, mechanistic materialism is a realism as well as a materialism. Second, there is a tendency toward idealism. The basis of existence may be thought of as mind or spirit that is an organic whole. In his *Personal Realism*[5] James B. Pratt sets forth such a form of realism, which may be hard to distinguish from some types of objective idealism. Third, there are many realists who claim either that reality is neither physical nor mental but some underlying neutral substance (neutral monism) or that reality is pluralistic and consists of many types of entities, of which mind and matter may be only two. In this chapter the pluralistic type of realism receives greatest attention, since it appears to be the dominant trend today.

THE HISTORY OF REALISM

What is sometimes called Platonic or conceptual realism is nearer to modern idealism than to modern realism. Assuming that the real is the permanent or the unchanging, Plato said that the Idea, or the universal, was more real than the individual thing. For example, the concept "man" has greater reality than an individual man, John Doe.

During the Middle Ages there was a controversy between the Platonic, or classical, realists and the nominalists. The realists claimed that class terms, or more precisely the universals for which they stood, were the only realities. Classical realism is the belief that universals for which class terms stand have an existence quite independent of the particular things that appear to the senses. The nominalists insist that class terms or universals are names only, and that reality is found in percepts or individual things. Class terms are mere names or symbols and represent nothing having any existence of its own apart from the particular things that make up the class.

This controversy was very important to scholars during the Middle Ages. If realism were correct, there could be a Universal Church with authoritative dogma. All men could sin in Adam, and the doctrine of redemption and the work of Christ could apply to all humanity. If nominalism were correct, only particular churches were real; furthermore, the sin of Adam and the work of redemption would not apply to all men, and men might be free to substitute their private judgments for the decrees of the Church. The Medieval Church supported realism, since nominalism tended to undermine its authority.

Aristotle was more a realist, in the modern sense, than was his teacher, Plato. Aristotle was an observer interested in the details of individual things. He felt that reality exists in concrete things or in the process of their development. The real world is the world we sense, and form (the idea or principle of organization) and matter are inseparable. From the twelfth century on,

---

[5] New York: Macmillan, 1937.

the influence of Aristotle tended to replace that of Plato. Thomas Aquinas (c. 1225–1274) brought Aristotelian metaphysics and Christian theology into harmony and gave Medieval Scholasticism its most complete expression. His great synthesis was made within the realistic tradition. For Aquinas, as for Aristotle, the universe is composed of matter and form. Matter is united or organized by forms that have been fixed by the Creator. There are real substances with real qualities. There is a "substantial form" which makes a body what it is, and there are also qualities which may change and which are called "accidents." God created the world, but he should not be identified with the world. God is an original substance, and nature is a separate and created substance or group of substances. Created things, however, are real and possess genuine powers. The philosophy of Thomas Aquinas is called *theistic realism*.

Space does not permit a detailed account of the various groups or schools of realism that have existed during the last two hundred years. Thought from Descartes to Kant during the seventeenth and eighteenth centuries centered attention on the knower and was mainly idealistic in outlook. The position of John Locke, however, is called *representative realism*. For Locke our ideas merely represent the primary qualities of the external world, which themselves are real. In the United States, during the early decades of the twentieth century, two realistic movements that showed considerable vigor were the new realism, or neo-realism, and critical realism. The new realism was an attack on idealism, and critical realism was a criticism of both idealism and the new realism. The discussion tended to center around highly involved and technical problems of epistemology and metaphysics. Some prominent realists not associated with these groups were also active during the first half of the present century.

The rise of realism at the beginning of the twentieth century was in considerable part a reaction against various movements of the nineteenth century that tended to magnify human powers and man's part in knowledge and reality. Only a few of these trends can be listed here: the increase in human control over nature resulting from scientific advances, the great advance in human knowledge that led to a new confidence in the power of man to control his own life and affairs, the political emancipation of the individual, the concern for the inner life that made religion and theology man-centered, and the development of philosophical idealism and positivism, with their attention to man rather than to the world and nature. As a reaction to these trends, realism has tended to transfer attention from the mind that interprets nature to the world that is interpreted.

The first decade of the twentieth century was a time of intellectual ferment. In the United States, William James was challenging the monism and intellectualism of the dominant types of idealism. In England, in 1903, G. E. Moore published his noted essay "Refutation of Idealism." Similar protests arose in Germany. By 1910 six men, all teachers of philosophy in the United States, discovered that they were in considerable philosophical agreement and formed a group that published, in 1912, a cooperative book entitled *The New Realism*.[6] This movement is known as new realism, or neorealism.

The new realists reject subjectivism, monism, absolutism (belief in an Absolute or that which is without limitation), all mystical philosophies, and the view that nonmental things are either created or modified in any way by the knowing mind. The new realists claim that they are returning to the common-sense doctrine of a real, objective world which men know directly by sense perception. The outer world is actually present and is directly experienced; it is not hidden or obscured by images and sense data. The world is pluralistic, relations in it are external and objective, and analysis does not destroy the real qualities of the world. "The knowledge of an object does not change the object known."

The common objects of sense perception, the objects of scientific analysis, and relational and nonrelational qualities appear to be unaffected by our experience or consciousness of them. Our experience and awareness are *selective*, not *constitutive*: that is, we choose to give attention to some things rather than others; we do not create or alter them merely by experiencing them. For example, that "there is a chair in this room" is not affected by our experiencing or not experiencing the chair.

The new realists point out that, apart from these basic convictions, there is neither a single correct or adequate philosophy of life nor any one inevitable or necessary answer to questions regarding such things as mind, freedom, purpose, and the good. However, certain men have set forth fairly complete philosophies derived from the new realism.[7]

During the decade 1910–1920, seven men set forth a philosophy with a slightly different outlook. In 1920 they published a volume entitled *Essays in Critical Realism*.[8] While agreeing with the new realists that the existence of objects is independent of knowledge, they criticize the new realists for making the relationship between object and observer so immediate or direct. The new realism, as we have seen, was an attack on idealism; critical realism was a criticism of both idealism and the new realism.

The critical realists do not think that the awareness or perception of

6 Edwin B. Holt, *et al., The New Realism* (New York: Macmillan, 1912). The group consisted of Edwin B. Holt, Walter T. Marvin, William Pepperell Montague, Ralph Barton Perry, Walter P. Pitkin, and Edward G. Spaulding.

7 For example, Spaulding, *The New Rationalism;* Samuel Alexander, *Space, Time, and Deity* (New York: Macmillan, 1920).

8 Durant Drake, *et al., Essays in Critical Realism* (New York: Macmillan, 1920). (Reprint, New York: Peter Smith, 1941.) This group included Durant Drake, A. O. Lovejoy, James B. Pratt, A. K. Rogers, George Santayana, Roy W. Sellars, and C. A. Strong.

objects is as direct and immediate as the new realists claimed. The outer object is not actually present in consciousness. Only the sense data (mental images, or sensa) are present in human consciousness. The sense data reflect the nature of the external object, as well as the nature of the perceiving mind. Except by inference we cannot go beyond or get behind the sense data to the object from which they are derived. We have, then: (1) the perceiving mind, the knower, or the conscious organism; (2) the object, with its primary qualities; (3) the sense data, which connect the perceiving mind and the object. The critical realist thinks that the sense data give us fairly direct contact with objects. Sensa reveal in large part what objects are, and thus they indicate to us the nature of the external world. Furthermore, the critical realist believes that this approach enables us to understand and explain illusions, hallucinations, and errors of various kinds, since the sense data may be distorted.

In addition to the men most directly associated with new realism and critical realism, there are a number of equally important contemporary realists outside these groups.[9]

THE PLATFORM OF SOME REALISTS

During the late nineteen-forties a group of philosophers, mainly in the United States, organized the Association for Realistic Philosophy and later published a platform for "critical clarification and defense."[10] In the preface to a volume of essays by certain members of the group, the editor, John Wild, says:

We inhabit a universe marked by real structures which exist independently of human knowledge and desire. These structures can be known as they really are, at least in part, by the human mind, not only the more restricted patterns revealed by the special sciences, but also more fundamental ontological patterns which require philosophical description and analysis. Finally, norms are not exclusively man-made. There are norms actually founded on nature which are accessible to human cognition. . . .[11]

The platform of the Association for Realistic Philosophy attempts to clarify and defend the following theses:

I. METAPHYSICS
1. *Being cannot be reduced to either material being or to immaterial being.*

[9] In Great Britain this group includes George E. Moore, Samuel Alexander, Lloyd Morgan, Bertrand Russell, John Laird, and C. D. Broad. In the United States it includes Frederick J. E. Woodbridge, John E. Boodin, Morris R. Cohen, Evander B. McGilvary, Jacob Loewenberg, Douglas C. Macintosh, and Alfred North Whitehead.

[10] John Wild (ed.), *The Return to Reason: Essays in Realistic Philosophy* (Chicago: Regnery, 1953), pp. 357–363. (Henry Regnery Company, publisher and holder of copyright.)

[11] *Ibid.*, p. v.

2. *Empirical evidence shows that both modes of being exist in the cosmos.*

3. *This cosmos consists of real, substantial entities existing in themselves and ordered to one another by real, extramental relations.*

. . . .

II. EPISTEMOLOGY

These real entities and relations together with human artifacts can be known by the human mind as they are in themselves and can be aesthetically enjoyed.

. . . .

III. PRACTICAL PHILOSOPHY

Such knowledge, especially that treating of human nature, can provide us with immutable and trustworthy principles for the guidance of individual and social action.

. . . .

IV. HISTORY

Important truths are contained in the classical tradition of Platonic and Aristotelian philosophy.[12]

. . . .

REALISTS AND THE QUEST FOR TRUTH

Realists vary in the extent to which they lean toward empiricism or rationalism. Probably most realists would agree that we need some balance between the sources of knowledge, or a sort of federation of these sources. The realists distinguish clearly between the objects of thought and the act of thought itself. Realists on the whole stress the correspondence theory for the verification of statements: Truth is the faithful adherence of our judgments to the facts of experience or to the world as it is; it is "fidelity to objective reality." (See pp. 57–58.)

The realist likes to think that he does not shrink from hard facts. He forces his desires and interests to the background and accepts the differences among and the uniqueness of things as real and important features of the world. He is suspicious of sweeping generalizations that tend to subsume all things under one system.

Most realists respect science and are likely to stress the close relationship between science and philosophy. Yet many of them are critical of an old science which either implied a dualism or denied the realm of values. For example, Alfred North Whitehead, who set forth a "philosophy of organism," has criticized the traditional scientific outlook that separates matter and life, body and mind, nature and spirit, substance and its qualities. Such an approach empties nature of sense qualities and tends to lead to the denial of the values of ethics, aesthetics, and religion. Newton's methodology led to success in the physical sciences, but it left nature without meaning or value; some men came to believe that values and ideals are illusory and have no

12 *Ibid.*, pp. 357, 358, 360, 361, 362.

objective basis. This attitude is the result of abstracting and emphasizing certain aspects of reality and ignoring other aspects. Whitehead calls this process of abstraction the "fallacy of misplaced concreteness." It is found wherever men take one aspect of a thing and treat it as the whole. In this way arbitrary lines are drawn between what the investigator is willing to regard as important and what he proposes to consider unreal.

THE THEORY OF EXTERNAL RELATIONS

The realists quite generally deny the idealist contention that all relations are internal. For the realists many relations are external. To grasp the distinction clearly, let us contrast the two positions. A relation is said to be *internal* when it exists within and forms a part of the things related. If two things are internally related, the relationship affects their natures so that they would not be what they are if they were not related as they are. They must also be part of some larger whole, which includes them both. A man, for example, is never isolated. He is related to other men and to a larger whole, such as the family, and also to humanity, an even more inclusive whole. He is also related to the physical world and to the moral and spiritual world order. There is evidence, it is asserted, that it is these relationships that make a man what he is. Good and evil may seem to be unrelated opposites, but they are related in an inclusive moral order. The nature of each is determined partly by the existence and the nature of the other. All particular things, whether electrons and atoms or living organisms, are partly defined by, as well as depend on, their relations to other things. The supreme system that includes all relationships is what the monistic idealist means by the Absolute.

The realist says that relations are *external,* by which he means that objects are the same and preserve their independence regardless of how they are related to other objects. An object may change its relationship to other bodies without itself being changed or without its changing these other things. This is true also of the relation between a knower and an object. "Knowing makes no difference to, and neither constitutes nor alters, that which is known." The object is the same whether known or unknown, and it would be the same even if there were no existing people who could know it.

For many realists, the relations themselves, as well as the related objects, are objective as well as external. If box A is larger than box B, the relationship *larger than* is real and objective. If an orange is sweeter than a lemon, not only is the orange real and the lemon real, but the relation *sweeter than* is also real. Such a point of view, it is asserted, is more likely to lead toward a pluralistic view of the world. Matter, mind, relations, number systems, logical principles, ethical ideals, and the like may all be real. Those things which do not occupy space and time may be called *subsistents,* to distinguish them from the *existents,* which do occupy space and time.

THE THEORY OF EMERGENCE, OR THE THEORY OF LEVELS

The realists, though not the sole exponents of the theory of emergence, have given it its greatest emphasis. Three British philosophers—G. H. Lewis, C. Lloyd Morgan, and Samuel Alexander—have done much to popularize the use of the terms *emergence, emergent evolution,* and *theory of levels.*

The term *emergence* means that in the universe new qualities or new forms appear that cannot be explained by those forms and qualities that previously existed. The higher levels bring real additions, which are not mere duplications or regroupings of previously existing elements. Out of one level grows something "new," which emerges into something else that is novel, and so on. *Repetitive evolution,* in contrast with emergent evolution, holds that nothing really new appears, that each level is merely a more complex arrangement of the same elements that existed previously. From the point of view of emergence, we cannot reduce personality and mind to biological processes or reduce life to physical and chemical processes without loss or damage to the unity and special qualities of the entity with which we began.

According to the theory of emergent evolution, there are new combinations being formed that give more than an additive result. A synthesis takes place, and new qualities, powers, or activities appear. For example, protons and electrons are organized into atoms, and atoms unite to form molecules. When water, a liquid, emerges from two gases, hydrogen and oxygen, we get a whole range of new qualities in the water that the separate parts did not have. The most searching study of these separate gases would not have revealed the liquid and its qualities. With living matter we get another group of new qualities, such as growth, reproduction, and sensitivity. With the emergence of mind, important new qualities and capacities appear, and these lead to reflective thinking and awareness of values. The new qualities that appear cannot be interpreted adequately in the light of the previous parts and, until the emergence takes place, we cannot predict just what will happen. There are apparently countless levels of existence, from electrons and protons, to atoms, to chemical elements, to molecules, to crystals, to plants and animals, to mind, and to reflective thinking.

In his *Emergent Evolution* C. Lloyd Morgan has set forth a philosophy of emergence that has had wide influence on philosophy. He rejects mechanism because it fails to recognize the creative element operative through all nature and regards life as merely an elaborate "regrouping of physicochemical elements." He also rejects vitalism (belief in a life principle that directs development), because he finds creativity and the emergence of new qualities in matter as well as in life. An emergent is what results from a qualitative change of direction. A pyramid or ladder may be used to illustrate Morgan's point.

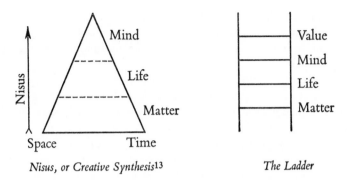

Nisus, or Creative Synthesis[13]   *The Ladder*

At each stage or level there is a new kind of relatedness. There is, however, "no mind without life; and no life without some physical basis." There are matter systems, there are life-matter systems, and there are systems involving mind at various stages of development. "Life stands to matter in the same kind of relation as mind stands to life."[14]

In the child as he develops from birth to maturity we recognize the development of new powers and capacities that were not evident at an earlier period. Similarly, in nature there is an orderly advance and development of the new. This unexplained emergence of the new produces no disorder in nature; the new is no less orderly than the old. There is in fact an "orderly constructiveness" in nature. Nature is still in the making.

> Emergent evolution works upwards from matter, through life, to consciousness which attains in man its highest reflective or supra-reflective level. It accepts the "more" at each ascending stage as that which is given, and accepts it to the full. The most subtle appreciation of the artist or the poet, the highest aspiration of the saint, are no less accepted than the blossom of the water lily, the crystalline fabric of a snowflake, or the minute structure of the atom.

> Emergent evolution urges that the "more" of any given stage, even the highest, involves the "less" of the stages which were precedent to it and continue to coexist with it. It does *not* interpret the higher in terms of the lower only; for that would imply denial of the emergence of those new modes of natural relatedness which characterize the higher and make it what it is. Nor does it interpret the lower in terms of the higher.[15]

What makes emergents emerge? There is a *nisus*, or pull, that provides evidence of a purpose operative in nature. The emergent view rejects the

13 Adapted from p. 11 of C. Lloyd Morgan's *Emergent Evolution* (New York: Holt, 1923).
14 *Ibid.*, p. 29.
15 *Ibid.*, pp. 297–298.

notion of an "alien influx into nature." Morgan does accept, however, a vast cosmic tendency and the creative and directive power of God, but this power is immanent, or indwelling, in every one of the multitudinous entities which make up the whole.

How adequate is the concept of emergence? Is it a successful way of avoiding dualism, if such avoidance is desirable? Is it open to the charge of being essentially a materialism, as some critics have suggested, since mind has emerged from life and life has emerged from a matrix of events or processes that once were admittedly inorganic? There are other possibilities, of course, including the view that mind and life have developed in a world process that has always contained life and mental processes in some form.

IMPLICATIONS OF REALISM

Whereas the pragmatists, as we shall see, emphasize "the world *of our experience,*" the realists emphasize "*the world* of our experience." The world is what it is, no matter what men think about it. Whereas the idealists emphasize mind as the primary reality, the realists tend to view mind as only one of many things that go to make up the world. The realist is suspicious of any tendency to substitute our wishes or desires for the "facts," or to make our conscious selves the center of importance in the universe. This emphasis on an external world independent of but disclosed just as it is to the mind is congenial to the natural sciences. Attention is directed not to the mind that understands but to the reality that is understood. Realism thus reflects the objectivism that underlies and supports modern science. Realism is less likely than idealism to concern itself with problems of the whole. Realism depends on reason rather than on our sentiments and wishes; it is prepared to find that the world is quite different from what men might wish it to be.

Since realism stands in rather sharp contrast with idealism and is said to "de-mentalize" the world, a statement regarding the realist's attitude toward mind is in order. In arguing that realism does not defame mind or rob it of its riches and value, one realist says, "Realism strips mind of its pretensions but not of its value or greatness. On the contrary, in leaving to other things their rights mind comes into its own . . . if it dethrones the mind, it recognizes mind as chief in the world it knows."[16]

We have spoken earlier about realism as a "disposition to keep ourselves . . . out of our judgment of things, letting the objects speak for themselves." Is there a relation between philosophical realism and what realism means in ordinary language? Does this attitude carry over into everyday affairs and affect our outlook in education, art, literature, and religion? Many people think there is a definite relationship, while others have suggested caution in

[16] Samuel Alexander, "The Basis of Realism," in *Realism and the Background of Phenomenology*, Roderick M. Chisholm (ed.) (Glencoe: Free Press, 1960), p. 186.

making such applications. The instrumentalism of Dewey has had a marked influence on the progressive education movement, as we shall see. Is it possible that philosophical realism might influence an individual to stress content-centered rather than pupil-centered education? In literature has the outlook of philosophical realism led men to stress fidelity to real life as opposed to the sentimental, extravagant, romantic, and idealistic glorification of human nature and the world? Has there been a similar influence on art forms? Realism in art avoids an imaginative treatment and limits itself to a portrayal of the object as actually observed. The realist aims at correspondence with nature; he attempts to represent his subject matter in its concrete and particular details.

While some realists deny religion any validity, there has been a revival of religious realism during the last half century. Philosophical realism has influenced thinking in the field of religion. Within Roman Catholicism a religious realism, or a realistic theism, is found in the form of neo-Thomism, or neo-Scholasticism. Neo-Thomism, a restatement of the religious philosophy of Thomas Aquinas, repudiates all relativistic philosophies as well as idealistic metaphysics. A considerable group of Protestant religious leaders have also formulated their theological beliefs within the general outlook of realistic philosophy. These beliefs have ranged from a theistic naturalism, which stresses religious values that are continuous with the natural world, to various types of supernaturalism.[17] In general we can say that the influence of realism has been in the direction of a recognition of the presence of evil in life. Realism is thus a repudiation of extreme optimism, sometimes found where the influence of idealism is prominent. This recognition does not lead to the denial of the good or of God. Real deliverance from evil is possible, since salvation may be obtained if the right adjustment to the religious Object (or God) is made.

EVALUATION OF REALISM

Realism is a broad philosophical movement that ranges from materialism at one extreme to a position very close to objective idealism at the other. Consequently it is a position not easily defended or criticized briefly. To deal with all the various types of realism is impossible. Critical evaluation of the epistemological bases of the various positions would involve many technical questions and is beyond the scope of Part Three, which acquaints the readers with the alternative types of philosophy. The presentation of each one of the types of philosophy raises questions, of course, about the soundness of other positions. The general statements about realism we make here must be

17 From the many books in this field we list one that is outstanding: D. C. Macintosh (ed.), *Religious Realism* (New York: Macmillan, 1931). In this book fifteen philosophers and theologians of the 1930's relate philosophical realism to religion.

made with caution and the realization that our statements may not apply to all realists and that most realists will not accept all these criticisms as valid.

Realism is the view that the objects of our senses are real or exist in their own right quite independent of their being known to, perceived by, or related to mind. Being known or becoming an object of experience does not affect the nature of the object or alter it in any way. Objects exist and we may be aware of them and later not be aware of them without their characteristics being changed. Objects thus may be related to consciousness, but they are not in any way created or altered by the mere fact of being known.

The realist thinks that his position is the only one which is supported by common sense, as well as by the assumptions underlying the work of the sciences. The "human mind," says Ralph Barton Perry, is "instinctively and habitually realistic: so that realism does not so much need to be proved as to be defended against criticism."[18] Referring to his own position as that of "provisional realism," Alfred North Whitehead says, "I do not understand how a common world of thought can be established in the absence of a common world of sense."[19]

The general metaphysical position of realism comes in for criticism from both the idealists and the pragmatists. The idealists claim that it is impossible to prove that there is an object independent of the knower. Realists, they say, have had to appeal to common sense, conviction, or "animal faith" (Santayana). William Ernest Hocking says that "a man knows as much as he judges; he judges as much as he questions, and no more. Knowing is acting." He does not believe that "a consistent system can be built on the *uncorrected* principles of analysis, external relations, and the independence of object from subject."[20]

Other idealists criticize the realist's classification of mind as one among many things in nature. They say that, in its attempt to be objective and scientific, realism tends to minimize man and the importance of human life. Man as a late product of the evolutionary process lives in a world most adequately interpreted by the various physical sciences; yet this explanation of man fails to present us with the whole man.

The pragmatists, too, are critical of the realist's claim that the objects of nature are independent of experience. The world is not independent of the knowing process; no line can be drawn between the two. Since this is the case, all we may claim is that "the world is *our experience*." We turn next to the pragmatists for a brief elaboration of these and related views.

[18] *Philosophy of the Recent Past* (New York: Scribner's, 1926), p. 201.
[19] *Science and the Modern World*, p. 131.
[20] *Types of Philosophy* (3rd ed.; New York: Scribner's, 1959), pp. 246, 252–253.

QUESTIONS AND PROJECTS

1. Review Questions

(1) Define the terms *real, reality,* and *realism* as they are used in philosophy.

(2) Indicate the chief characteristics of or points of emphasis in philosophical realism.

(3) According to Macmurray, why have some thinkers failed to see the validity of realism? Do you think his explanation is an acceptable one, and why? What kind of an explanation is it?

(4) Why is modern realism difficult to present comprehensively?

(5) Discuss the history of realism, indicating a few of the different forms it has taken in different periods of Western thought.

(6) Why did realism show new vitality early in the twentieth century? Where do the new realists and the critical realists of this era agree and differ?

(7) Give the main points in the platform of the Association for Realistic Philosophy.

(8) What are the areas of agreement among most modern realists?

(9) Discuss the theory of emergence, or the theory of levels, as set forth by C. Lloyd Morgan. Give your evaluation of this metaphysics.

(10) State some of the implications of realism for political thought, literature and other arts, and religion. Why are the realists critical of idealism as it affects these areas in addition to being critical of it as a general philosophical position?

(11) Evaluate realism, indicating its major strong points and weaknesses.

2. The new realists claim that they are returning to the common-sense doctrine of a real, objective world that is neither created nor modified by the knowing mind. The critics of realism claim, however, that perceptual errors refute this type of realism. Do you think the critical realists, by emphasizing the sense data and thus making the relationship between the knower and the object known less direct, have strengthened the case for realism? Give reasons for your answer.

3. Some idealists claim that consciousness of an object and the presence of the object occur together, and that therefore they are in some sense interdependent. Do you agree with the realist that this is a tautology mistaken for an axiom? The idealist rests his case on the mere copresence of consciousness and object, whereas the real issue is one of dependence or independence of existence, according to the realist.

4. Some idealists assert that the realists usually attack the weaker or weakest types of idealism and then assume that they have disposed of idealism as a whole. Are the realists' criticisms as valid against objective idealism as they are against subjective idealism? Are there points of agreement between realists and objective idealists? If so, what are they?

5. The problem of realism versus nominalism, or of universals and particulars, was especially important in the Middle Ages. A third and mediating position, known as moderate realism, was set forth by Thomas Aquinas. State the three positions as clearly as you can, and indicate why men thought the question of the relationship between universals and particulars important. You may refer here to one or more of the many standard texts in the history of philosophy, or to the encyclopedias.

6. The statement is sometimes made that George Berkeley, whose position was discussed briefly in Chapters 3 and 13, denied the existence of the real world of nature. Discuss this statement indicating: (a) in what sense it is true or false, and (b) some of the possible meanings of the term *real* as used by philosophers.

7. Review one of the following books: James K. Feibleman, *The Revival of Realism* (Chapel Hill: U. of North Carolina Press, 1947); E. B. McGilvary, *Toward a Perspective Realism* (La Salle: Open Court, 1955); Kurt F. Reinhardt, *A Realistic Philosophy* (New York: Ungar, 1962); Walter Silz, *Realism and Reality* (Chapel Hill: U. of North Carolina Press, 1956); Alfred North Whitehead, *Nature and Life* (Chicago: U. of Chicago Press, 1934); Maurice de Wulf, *An Introduction to Scholastic Philosophy*, trans. P. Coffee (New York: Dover, 1956).

SUGGESTED READINGS

Aristotle: Selections. Ed. by W. D. Ross. New York: Scribner's, 1927.
   Selections from the main works of Aristotle and an introduction by the editor.

BUTLER, J. DONALD. *Four Philosophies and Their Practice in Education and Religion.* New York: Harper, 1951.
   For a general discussion of realism, see Part III, pp. 275–392. For an extended bibliography, see pp. 528–532.

CHISHOLM, RODERICK M. (ed.). *Realism and the Background of Phenomenology.* Glencoe: Free Press, 1960.
   This work includes translations from Brentano, Meinong, and Husserl and selections from the writings of realists in England and the United States.

JOHNSON, A. H. *Whitehead's Theory of Reality.* Boston: Beacon, 1952.
   The author introduces the general reader to the heart of Whitehead's philosophy: "that permanence is as inescapable as change"; that value is a part of the universe; that God is in creative interaction with individuals.

McGILVARY, EVANDER B. *Toward a Perspective Realism.* Ed. by A. G. Ramsperger. La Salle: Open Court, 1956.
   Selections, some from previous publications, that expound the realism of McGilvary, who maintains that the world has the characteristics, physical and nonphysical, which appear in experience.

MACINTOSH, D. C. (ed.). *Religious Realism.* New York: Macmillan, 1931.
   Fifteen essays dealing with various aspects of religious realism. See especially essay XII, pp. 413–428, "Religious Realism in the Twentieth Century," by Helmut Richard Niebuhr.

MARITAIN, JACQUES. *An Introduction to Philosophy.* Trans. by E. I. Watkin. London: Sheed and Ward, 1932.

The author presents scholastic philosophy (*Aristotle enriched by St. Thomas Aquinas*), which he calls "the Christian philosophy." A clear and readable account of a type of realism accepted by many Roman Catholic scholars.

PRATT, JAMES B. *Personal Realism.* New York: Macmillan, 1937.

A clear presentation of the problems of philosophy from the point of view of a realist. Recommended for mature students.

SPAULDING, EDWARD G. *The New Rationalism.* New York: Holt, 1918.

Spaulding is one of the new realists who constructs a comprehensive philosophy.

WEISS, PAUL. *Modes of Being.* Carbondale: Southern Illinois U. Press, 1958.

A systematic philosophy that attempts to integrate the main divisions of knowledge around the basic realities: *Actuality, Ideality, Existence, and God.* Difficult for beginners.

WHITEHEAD, ALFRED NORTH. *Process and Reality: An Essay in Cosmology.* New York: Macmillan, 1930.

This work is difficult but takes one to the center of Whitehead's speculative metaphysics. See also Whitehead's Science and the Modern World; Nature and Life; Modes of Thought; *and* Adventures of Ideas.

WILD, JOHN (ed.). *The Return to Reason: Essays in Realistic Philosophy.* Chicago: Regnery, 1953.

Fourteen essays on realistic philosophy that attempt to restate various traditional realistic doctrines.

ᕱᕱ FIFTEEN ᕱᕱ

PRAGMATISM AND ITS IMPLICATIONS

Pragmatism is a philosophical movement that has come to prominence during the last hundred years, but has been called "a new name for an old way of thinking." It is a philosophy that strongly reflects some of the characteristics of American life. Pragmatism is connected with such names as Charles Peirce (1839–1914), William James (1842–1910), and John Dewey (1859–1952). Pragmatism has also been called instrumentalism and experimentalism. While it has had its main development in America, similar theories have been set forth in England by Arthur Balfour and F. C. S. Schiller, and in Germany by Hans Vaihinger.

WHAT PRAGMATISM IS

Pragmatism is an attitude, a method, and a philosophy that uses the practical consequences of ideas and beliefs as a standard for determining their value and truth. William James defined pragmatism as "the attitude of looking away from first things, principles, 'categories,' supposed necessities; and of looking towards last things, fruits, consequences, facts."[1]

Pragmatism places greater emphasis on method and attitude than on a systematic philosophical doctrine. It is the method of experimental inquiry extended into all realms of human experience. Pragmatism uses the modern scientific method as the basis of a philosophy. Its affinity is with the sciences, especially the biological and social sciences, and it aims to utilize the scientific spirit and scientific knowledge to deal with all human problems, including those of ethics and religion.

The pragmatists are critical of the older systems of philosophy, such as the various forms of materialism, idealism, and realism. They say that philosophy in the past has made the mistake of looking for ultimates, absolutes, eternal essences, substances, fixed principles, and metaphysical "block systems."

1 William James, *Pragmatism* (New York: Longmans, Green, 1907), pp. 54–55.

The pragmatists emphasize empirical science and the changing world and its problems, and nature as the all-inclusive reality beyond which we cannot go. For John Dewey, *experience* is central. Experience is the result of the interaction of the organism and its environment.

While pragmatism as systematic philosophy is comparatively recent, similar attitudes and ideas can be found in the works of a number of earlier thinkers. The word *pragmatism* was used by Kant to describe rules and standards based on experience as distinct from those he thought were above or beyond experience. He appealed to our moral nature, especially man's sense of duty, and to the will to establish the truth of certain beliefs, such as those in freedom, God, and immortality. His principle of the "primacy of practical reason" anticipated pragmatism to some extent. We shall limit our discussion of pragmatism to the views of Peirce, James, and Dewey.

CHARLES S. PEIRCE (1839–1914)

Charles S. Peirce, sometimes called the founder of pragmatism, was influenced by Kant; Peirce considered the way in which problems, including those of metaphysics, can be solved if one gives careful attention to the practical consequences of adherence to various ideas. Pragmatism is sometimes said to have originated in 1878, when Peirce published the article "How to Make Our Ideas Clear."

The philosophical writings of Peirce consist of essays and manuscripts, many of which are fragmentary or incomplete. While he never wrote a book in philosophy or organized his thoughts into systematic or final form, his literary activity covered many years. With the publication of his papers in recent decades, interest in Peirce's philosophy is increasing, and he is coming to be recognized more and more as an intellectual genius of outstanding originality. He was the rare combination of natural scientist with a "laboratory habit of mind," careful student of philosophy, and a man with strong moral convictions. He is sometimes referred to as a philosopher's philosopher rather than a public or popular philosopher, like James.

Peirce was primarily a logician concerned with the more technical problems of logic and epistemology, and the methods of the laboratory sciences. His interest in logic included attention to deductive systems, methodology in the empirical sciences, and the philosophy behind the various methods and techniques. His logic included a theory of signs and symbols, a field in which he did pioneer work. He viewed logic as a means of communication and a cooperative or public venture. Such an approach invites critical examination and seeks aid from others in its continuous quest for the clarification of ideas. Peirce wished to establish philosophy on a scientific basis and to treat theories as working hypotheses. He called his approach *pragmaticism*.

One of Peirce's main contributions to philosophy is his theory of meaning. In fact, he set forth one of the first modern theories of meaning by proposing a technique for the clarification of ideas. The meaning of many ideas, Peirce said, is best discovered by putting them to an experimental test and observing the results, since ideas are plans of action. His standard of meaningfulness, sometimes called the *pragmatic maxim,* is to ask about any proposition, "Suppose this proposition were true, what conceivable bearing might it have on the conduct of our lives?" The answer to this question will disclose the meaning of the proposition.[2]

Peirce's empiricism is intellectualistic rather than voluntaristic; that is, emphasis is on the intellect and understanding rather than on will and activity. The irritation of doubt leads to the struggle to attain belief. The end of this inquiry, which aims to dispel doubt, is knowledge. Thus he does not stress sensation or volition as much as do later forms of popular pragmatism. Peirce is critical of positivism and mechanistic determinism, on the one hand, and intuitionism and a priori principles, on the other hand. While he shares some of the positivists' views, he does not share with them the view that empiricism requires a denial of the possibility of metaphysics. In the field of metaphysics as well as in all other areas of discourse, we must avoid the belief that we have attained finality. Peirce supports "fallibilism"; even the most intelligent men are apt to be mistaken. Progressive inquiry leads to constant modification. There is chance (tychism) in nature and at times a spontaneous departure from that which men take to be law. Chance, as well as habit, plays a real part in the occurrence of events in the world. Fallibilism and an open future replace skepticism and absolutism, and pragmatism replaces fixed systems of belief in philosophy and in science. While Peirce gave his major attention to logic and methodology, his writings make clear that he left a place for an evolutionary idealism that stresses the need for a principle of love opposed to any narrow individualism in the affairs of men.

WILLIAM JAMES (1842–1910)

A complete discussion of the men who influenced William James would take us back to Lange, Mach, Pearson, and Renouvier, as well as to Peirce, and so we will have to content ourselves with a mere mention of these names.

The rapid development of pragmatism was due largely to the fertile soil it found in America and to the brilliant exposition made by William James. In his book *Pragmatism,* James contrasts the tender-minded rationalist, who usually has an idealistic and optimistic outlook, with the tough-minded empiricist, the lover of facts, who is often a materialist and a pessimist.

---

2 Note that Peirce set forth a pragmatic theory of meaning and not a new theory of truth, which was to be developed by James.

To both of these James says: "I offer the oddly-named thing pragmatism as a philosophy that can satisfy both kinds of demands. It can remain religious like the rationalisms, but at the same time, like the empiricisms, it can preserve the richest intimacy with facts."[3]

RADICAL EMPIRICISM

James defines the term *radical empiricism* in the following way: "I say 'empiricism' because it is contented to regard its most assured conclusions concerning matters of fact as hypotheses liable to modification in the course of future experience. . . ."[4] Again he says, "To be radical, an empiricism must neither admit into its constructions any element that is not directly experienced, nor exclude from them any element that is directly experienced."[5] James includes relations among the latter (directly experienced) elements.

Pragmatism, as we have seen, is the practice of looking toward results and facts instead of toward first principles and categories. It accepts the experiences and facts of everyday life as fundamental. Reality is just what it is experienced as being—flux or change. Since experience is fragmentary, pragmatists find things partly joined and partly disjoined, and accept them as they are. Consequently, they insist that reality is pluralistic rather than monistic or dualistic. There is *the given*, the data of the senses, which is brought in as stimulus from the region beyond us. Added to this is the *interpretative element*, which the conscious being supplies. The creative whole of experience, which includes both the given and the interpretative element, is the one reality we know. Knowledge is thus based directly on sense perception, or experience, which constitutes the continuous, flowing stream of consciousness.

TRUTH AS THAT WHICH "WORKS"

William James and other pragmatists make a distinct break with the traditional conception of truth. In the past, truth had meant some fixed or static relation, but James asks of a statement said to be meaningful, or capable of being judged true or false, "What concrete difference will it make in life?" "A difference that makes no difference *is* no difference," but only a matter of words. An idea becomes true or is made true by events. An idea is true if it works or if it has satisfactory consequences. Truth is relative; it also grows. The true is "the expedient in the way of our thinking," just as the right is "the expedient in the way of our behaving." Ideas, doctrines, and theories

---

[3] James, *Pragmatism*, p. 33.
[4] William James, *The Will to Believe and Other Essays* (New York: Longmans, Green, 1896), p. vii.
[5] William James, *Essays in Radical Empiricism* (New York: Longmans, Green, 1922), p. 42.

become instruments to help us meet life situations; doctrines are not answers to riddles. A theory is man-made to suit some human purpose, and the only satisfactory criterion of the truth of a theory is that it leads to beneficial results. *Workability, satisfactions, consequences,* and *results* are the key words in the pragmatic conception of truth.

FREEDOM AND MELIORISM

Morality, like truth, is not fixed but grows out of present life situations. The source and authority for beliefs and conduct are to be found in human experience. The good is that which makes for a more satisfactory life; the evil is that which tends to destroy life. James was a strong defender of moral freedom and indeterminism; he believed that determinism is an intellectualistic falsification of experience. He supported the doctrine of meliorism, which holds that the world is neither completely evil nor completely good but is capable of being improved. Human effort to improve the world is worthwhile and fruitful, and the trend of biological and social evolution is toward such improvement.

THE WILL TO BELIEVE

James devoted considerable attention to religion. The doctrines of pluralism and meliorism as well as the doctrine of the will to believe all contributed to his views of religion and of God. He acknowledged later that "the will to believe" might have been called "the right to believe."

Let us consider first James' doctrine of the will to believe. We have pointed out that radical empiricism ceases to look beyond experience for supposed necessities and metaphysical entities and stresses the present stream of consciousness. Consciousness displays interest, desire, and attention; it is volitional as well as sensory, and the will rather than the intellect is determinative. The will determines how and what we shall experience; thus thinking is empirically secondary to willing. What is selected and emphasized is thereby made vital and real; thus the world we experience is largely of our own making.

As with our sensory perceptions, so with our ideas. Those ideas that interest us and engage our attention tend to exclude others and to dominate the scene; and these ideas tend to find expression in our actions. In life, men have to make numerous decisions. How are they to make these decisions and formulate their beliefs? In some situations the evidence is reasonably certain and clear, and in these circumstances men need to act in accordance with the evidence. In other situations, where a choice between the proposed lines of action either is not forced or is trivial, they can postpone their decisions or even refrain from choosing at all. There are still other situations, however, in which men face some crucial issue where they must choose and act, since failure to decide is actually to commit themselves to one of the alternatives. If such issues are *living, forced,* and *momentous,* men need to act even though they do not have all the evidence on the basis of which they would like to make their decisions. James' doctrine of the will to believe applies to this third type of situation, where some decision is demanded by the very structure of the situation. For example, shall I marry this girl (or man) or shall I wait until I know for certain how the marriage will turn out? Here one cannot know for certain that the marriage will be harmonious and successful. All the facts are not known and one cannot wait until all the evidence is in, yet the issue is living, forced, and momentous. To fail to act is in itself a decision—not to marry this person at this time. When the will to believe leads to decision and action, it leads to discovery and conviction, or to truth and value simply through the fact that the will exists. Life's values are empirical and are found and tested in the process of living.

According to James, in many of life's experiences, man has contact with a "More." Man feels around himself that which is sympathetic and gives him "support." He is ever falling back upon his reliance on it in worship and in prayer. This sense of the "More" brings comfort, happiness, and peace; furthermore, it has been an almost universal experience among men. In the religious sense, God is the name of this ideal tendency or encompassing support in human experience.

James, as we have seen, was impressed by the novelty, freedom, individuality, and diversity inherent in our world. Consequently, he insists that God is finite. Since there are real possibilities for evil as well as for good in our world, no good, all-powerful God could have created the world as we know it. God is, however, moral and friendly, and man can cooperate with God in struggling to create a better world.

THE INSTRUMENTALISM OF JOHN DEWEY (1859-1952)

The continued growth and strength of pragmatism is to be attributed to John Dewey's prolific writings and his application of the principles of the movement to all phases of life and thought. Dewey achieved prominence in logic, epistemology, ethics, aesthetics, and political, economic, and educational philosophies. For Dewey and his many followers the term *instrumentalism* is preferred to the term *pragmatism,* but both terms are used.

Dewey was a keen and a constant critic of the classical or traditional types of philosophies, with their search for ultimate reality and their attempt to find the immutable. Such philosophies, Dewey claimed, have attempted to minimize or transcend human experience. In *The Quest for Certainty* Dewey tells us that men have used two methods to escape dangers and gain security. One has been to appease or conciliate the powers around them by ceremonial rites, sacrifices, supplication, and so on. The second has been to invent tools to control the forces of nature to man's advantage. This is the way of science, industry, and the arts, and it is the way Dewey approves. The aim of philosophy is the better organization of human life and activity here and now. Interest thus shifts from traditional metaphysical problems to the methods, attitudes, and techniques for scientific and social progress. The method is that of experimental inquiry as guided by empirical research in the area of values.

EXPERIENCE AND THE CHANGING WORLD

Experience is one of the key words in instrumentalism. Dewey's philosophy is *of* and *for* daily experience. Experience is the whole human drama, and it includes the total process of interaction of the living organism with its social and physical environment. Dewey refuses to attempt to transcend human experience or to believe that anyone else has ever done so. In the past, philosophers have attempted to discover some "theoretical super-experience" on the basis of which they might build a secure and meaningful life. Dewey insists that "experience is not a veil that shuts man off from nature"; it is the only means men have of penetrating further into the secrets of nature.

This present world of men and women, of fields and factories, of plants and animals, of bustling cities and struggling nations, is the world of our experience. We should try to understand it and then attempt to construct a society in which men can grow in freedom and intelligence.

Dewey takes evolution, relativity, and the time process very seriously. The world is in the making; it is constantly moving forward. This view of the world stands in marked contrast with the view of a fixed and permanent reality that dominated Greek and medieval thinking and has characterized many areas of modern science. Max C. Otto, in "John Dewey, Philosopher of a New Age," makes much of the fact that Dewey was born in 1859, the year Darwin's *Origin of Species* was published.

> Plato and Aristotle gave philosophic expression to the Athenian stage of culture; Thomas Aquinas brought into a workable scheme the traditions of Aristotle and Paul which were at war in medieval Europe; Francis Bacon, standing at the threshold of the seventeenth century, drew a comprehensive projection of the scientific civilization which was just beginning; Immanuel Kant, two centuries later, fashioned a world-view that provided honorable room for the physical science and the ethical aspiration of his day. In the same measure John Dewey has created a philosophy for the present age of evolution and evolution's precocious child, relativity.[6]

According to Dewey, men live in an unfinished world. Dewey's attitude

[6] In *The Social Frontier*, May-June, 1937.

can best be understood by an examination of three aspects of what we call his *instrumentalism*. First, the notion of temporalism means that there is real movement and progress in time. Men can no longer hold a spectator view of reality. Our knowledge does not merely mirror or reflect the world; it reshapes and changes it. Second, the notion of futurism bids us look mainly to the future and not to the past. The future, which is growing out of the past, will not be a repetition of it but will be in some sense novel. Third, meliorism is the view that the world can be made better by our efforts, a view also held by William James.

THE INSTRUMENTAL THEORY OF IDEAS

Basic to Dewey's philosophy is the instrumental theory of ideas and doctrines. Thinking is biological; it is concerned with the adjustment between an organism and its environment. All thinking and all concepts, doctrines, logics, and philosophies are part of the "protective equipment of the race in its struggle for existence."

Reflective thinking occurs when there is a problem or when our habits are blocked in particular crises. Intelligence is an instrument for gaining some goal or goals sought by the individual or by society. There is no separate "mind stuff" gifted with a faculty for thinking. Mind is expressed in results. Knowing and acting are continuous. Knowing occurs within nature, and sensory and rational factors cease to be competitors and are united as parts of a unified process. Ideas are plans of action to be undertaken. Scientific theories, like other tools and instruments, are made by man in pursuit of particular interests and goals. The aim of thinking is to remake experienced reality through the use of experimental techniques.

Dewey makes little use of such terms as *mind* and *consciousness*. Mind is merely the system of meanings that arise in the process of human adjustment, and consciousness is the awareness of these meanings.

MAN, NATURE, AND FREEDOM

According to Dewey's instrumentalism, man and nature are always interdependent. Man is not part body and part mind; he is naturalized within nature, and nature is so interpreted as to take account of him. Nature in man is nature grown intelligent. Nature is said to be neither rational nor irrational; it is intelligible and understandable. Nature is not something merely to be accepted and enjoyed by men; it is something to be modified and experimentally controlled.

Dewey and the modern instrumentalists have been staunch defenders of both freedom and democracy. Dewey was a defender of moral freedom, or freedom of choice, of intellectual freedom, and of the political and civil liberties, including freedom of speech, of press, and of assembly. He advocated an extension of the democratic principles in the political and social realms to all races and classes.

VALUES: ETHICAL AND RELIGIOUS

Dewey and many of his supporters reject all supernaturalism and ground both ethical and religious values solely in the natural relations of man. The values of life are capable of verification by the methods through which other facts are established.

> There exist concretely and experimentally goods—the values of art in all its forms, of knowledge, of effort and of rest after striving, of education and fellowship, of friendship and love, of growth in mind and body. These goods are there and yet they are relatively embryonic. Many persons are shut out from generous participation in them; there are forces at work that threaten and sap existent goods as well as prevent their expansion. A clear and intense conception of a union of ideal ends with actual conditions is capable of arousing steady emotion.[7]

Dewey was critical of the traditional institutional church, with its stress on fixed ritual and authoritarian dogma. He uses the adjective *religious* to describe those values through which one's personality is integrated and enriched. Any activity pursued in behalf of an ideal, because of an abiding conviction of its genuine value, is religious in quality. The term *God* may be used if it refers to the unity of all ideal ends in their tendency to arouse us to desire and action.

A NOTE ON OPERATIONALISM

A movement closely related to pragmatism and instrumentalism is *operationalism,* or *operationism.* It has many beliefs in common with the philosophy of Peirce, James, and Dewey, and it is an outgrowth of the empirical movement of recent decades. The movement began when a mathematical physicist, P. W. Bridgman, described a new theory of method.[8] His theory of knowledge has affinities with the unity of science movement and with logical empiricism, to be discussed in Chapter 16.

Central to operationalism is the conviction that "all concepts should be defined in terms of empirically performable operations."[9] Emphasis is on clarity of ideas, precision of meaning, activity, and the identification of truth with workability, as opposed to correspondence or coherence as verification criteria. The important thing about a theory is said to be "what it actually

[7] John Dewey, *A Common Faith* (New Haven: Yale U. Press, 1934), p. 51.

[8] See *The Logic of Modern Physics* (New York: Macmillan, 1927).

[9] A. Cornelius Benjamin, *Operationism* (Springfield: Charles C Thomas, 1955), p. 3.

does" and not what someone says it does or hopes it will do. Thinking and doing are closely related. Interest shifts from what a thing *is* to what it *does*. Learning and doing are inseparable, so that when a question of truth arises one should test the proposition by some set of "operations" and observe the results. Broadly stated, operationalism is the philosophical justification for the methods of science. Operationalism has been defined as "an attitude which views thought and action inseparable; which defines 'truth' in terms of the predictive content of assertions, and ethics in terms of action-directed goals."[10]

Since we shall not comment specifically on operationalism in our evaluation at the end of this chapter, it is important to note that some outstanding scientists and philosophers of science would insist that even science cannot proceed on a purely operational basis. There are theoretical constructs and useful terms that are difficult if not impossible to define operationally.

IMPLICATIONS OF PRAGMATISM

The attitudes, methods, and views associated with pragmatism and instrumentalism have implications for and applications in all areas of human thought and action. Let us consider the implications for logic, psychology, education, social philosophy, and religion.

LOGIC

Traditional, or Aristotelian, logic held sway until comparatively recently. It follows certain fixed principles or formulas, which include the "laws of thought" and the syllogism (two premises and a conclusion), the unit of deductive reasoning. The rules that are formulated enable one to determine when the conclusion follows necessarily from the premises.

The new logic of pragmatism and instrumentalism attacks the syllogism and the assumptions underlying traditional logic. The syllogistic logic, it holds, is academic, and, because it fails to conform to the facts of experience, attains certainty at the cost of novelty—it sacrifices experience, or reality. If the conclusion of the syllogism follows from the premises, it is not new information; and if it is new information it does not follow from the premises.[11] We gain new knowledge by a variety of scientific methods, including the historical method to acquire knowledge of past events, the operational and experimental methods to acquire knowledge of present conditions, and

---

10 Anatol Rapoport, *Operational Philosophy* (New York: Harper, 1953), p. 230. For a discussion of "The Present State of Operationalism" by P. W. Bridgman and others see Philipp G. Frank (ed.), *The Validation of Scientific Theories* (Boston: Beacon, 1956), Ch. II. (Reprint, New York: Collier Books, 1962.)

11 The term *new* in this sentence is somewhat ambiguous. The pragmatists are right in saying that the conclusion is logically implied by the premises. They appear to be wrong in overlooking the fact that we are frequently not aware of all the implications of a set of premises until we deduce them.

the methods of statistics and probability to aid in the prediction of future events. Since our experience is limited and relative to our particular positions in a changing world, our beliefs cannot be more than tentative. The quest for complete certainty is not consistent with a novelty-producing nature, which is always in the making. A belief is a truth-claim that we confirm or disconfirm as we test it in relation to the purpose before us. Whether the belief does or does not serve our purposes can be ascertained only through our experience and the use of "experimental thinking."

PSYCHOLOGY

Pragmatism has been among the attackers of the earlier "atomistic psychology" and the defenders of a more unified and activistic approach to mental processes. According to the earlier atomistic psychology, our perceptions consist of a number of distinct and separate sensations. For example, when we see a stone, we may get the isolated sensations of brownness, hardness, and smoothness. When these sensations occur together, we impose upon them a unity and call the complex a stone.

To the pragmatist, consciousness is a continuous flow, and experience a continuous whole. Mental activity, instead of joining together that which is chaotic and separate, tends to break up and separate that which is actually a continuous whole. The mind is active; according to the purpose it has in view, it rejects, selects, or makes additions. Thus what is believed to be real is prescribed in part by the interests, the purposes, and the temperament of the knower.

Mind is real in that it is an aspect of behavior, but its reality does not imply the existence of a transcendental reason or cosmic mind. Mind is a function the child acquires as he learns the meanings of things and activities in his environment. He learns to think as he connects what he does with the consequences that follow from his actions.

EDUCATION

The emphases on experience and experimental inquiry and the notion that knowing and acting are continuous have had direct and important implications for the field of education. One result was the Progressive Education movement, which flourished in this country in the 1930's and early 1940's, and is still influential. While not the originator of the movement, John Dewey was largely responsible for the philosophy of education underlying it. In Progressive Education, emphasis was on the student, in the belief that we learn as we live meaningfully, not on "subject matter" isolated from its living use.

We learn as we act, and we act on the basis of our interests; thus projects and activity are stressed in the learning process. Our desires do not need to be suppressed; they need to be organized and directed along useful lines. Education is the continuous reconstruction of experience; it is not the transmission of a body of beliefs but a process of growth. Education is the process of sharing experiences in associated living. The student needs to discover how to deal successfully with new and changing situations.

The instrumentalist is opposed to an education which by passive rote memorization would impose standardized subject matter on students. He is opposed to a uniform program of activities that tends to regiment or to warp the development and expression of true individuality. He wishes to give individual attention and consideration to each pupil and to encourage an active community life within the school. Initiative and independent thinking need to be encouraged and cultivated.

Education is a social process. Since knowing and doing are interdependent, people learn what they live, especially if the activities of life are self-chosen. People acquire greater freedom as they learn, especially if there is a strong desire to learn, and as they become responsible and responsive persons in a well-integrated society. The intellectual, the practical, the cultural, and the vocational are organically related. Education includes not only formal schooling but the total experience of the person with his total social and physical environment.

Though few educators today subscribe fully to the philosophy of Progressive Education as it was developed by Dewey's followers, the movement has left its mark on educational practice.

SOCIAL PHILOSOPHY

The emphasis on evolution and change, on the close relation between knowing and doing, and on the instrumental nature of all ideas and theories has focused attention on the social scene. Questions of social philosophy occupy a central position in the thinking of most contemporary instrumentalists.

Dewey and his followers have been identified with many of the liberal movements of our time. According to Dewey, the individual and the social milieu cannot be kept apart except by a false abstraction. Similarly, morality includes everything that affects human values. Ends and means are related and must be thought of as a unit. Hence the liberalism that is stressed is not the older individualistic liberalism, which fails to recognize the new conditions created by our corporate civilization. The instrumentalists' liberalism directs its energies to fundamental social change and recognizes the need for cooperative social control and organized planning in the interest of human welfare.

We have already mentioned Dewey's emphasis on freedom and democracy. Experimentation and creative intelligence require a democratic state, and any artificial barriers, whether political, economic, or racial, are condemned.

Governments, however, need to expand as the effects of private actions increase. Pragmatists accept social intelligence and negotiation and reject violence as the proper method of social change. They see the future as an open road along which we may move as human needs dictate.

RELIGION

Pragmatism is exceedingly distrustful of generalizations about ultimates; it takes its stand on empirical science and the world of experience. In refusing to define in final terms what is real, pragmatism attempts to leave behind both the older idealism and the older naturalism. It does not wish to make its world out of physical forces alone or to locate the roots of values and hence of religion and morals in another world or in an area that empirical science is unable to enter.

Religious doctrines, according to the pragmatist, arise neither from revelation, as orthodox Christianity claims, nor in the mind of some Absolute or Knower, nor as an attempt to describe the real external world. They originate in the desires of men to find suitable instruments with which to bring about certain desirable results. There are no absolutely true doctrines, since all ideas are tools subject to improvement. Doctrines are based on experience, and they will change as experience changes.

Pragmatism has influenced religion in two ways. First, it has been used by some people to defend already established ideas and emotions. William James' doctrine of the "will to believe" and his conception of truth readily lend themselves to this use. Certain doctrines, like the doctrine of the belief in the existence of God, are comforting and strengthening; their usefulness establishes their validity. Men have a right to accept certain beliefs as hypotheses and to test them in the process of living; if they lead to favorable consequences, they are valid. In this way pragmatism was used to justify some traditional and orthodox beliefs.

Second, pragmatism in its modern dress, or the instrumentalism of John Dewey and his followers, is humanistic and definitely naturalistic in its implications. This is borne out by John Dewey's *A Common Faith* and by the fact that pragmatists have been the main supporters of the new humanism, or humanistic naturalism. Instrumentalists not only oppose any trace of supernaturalism but object, on the grounds that they are useless, to discussions of traditional metaphysical and cosmological problems. Nonscientific theories about reality are irrelevant and meaningless; therefore discussions of theistic and teleological problems are no longer necessary. Emphasis is placed on nature as experienced; beyond this we cannot go, for *nature* is defined as all that has been, is, or ever can be. Nature is interpreted as pluralistic rather than dualistic or monistic. It has material, life-giving, and mental qualities.

According to Dewey, the world men know is the world they experience. There is no consciousness as a separate entity, and no objective world as something separate from man. Man is within the natural process. By his developing intelligence, however, he can view, interpret, and evaluate those aspects of the process which come within his experience. Intelligence is not just the abstract reasoning of individuals; it is a social process. Through his growing intellectual powers, man can share in the control of nature. Religion thus becomes the cooperative human quest for the good life.

EVALUATION OF PRAGMATISM

Pragmatism has grown out of certain aspects of contemporary living. It is an expression of the mood of modern technological society, with its emphasis on getting things done and on satisfactory consequences. Pragmatism is to be commended especially for its attempt to bring philosophy "down to earth" and to deal with the living issues of the day. According to Dewey, the aim of philosophy should be the improvement of human life and its environment, or the organization of life and its activities to meet human needs. We need, he says, a philosophy that makes life better here and now; the world is in the making, and our efforts will in part shape the future. If we accept the melioristic attitude and believe that life can be made better, we are likely to have a better world than we would have without such a conviction. We need to face the facts of experience and to discover and live by those principles that stand the test of time and of daily living.

According to pragmatism, our knowledge does not merely mirror or reflect the world; thinking is a creative process that reshapes the world. Ideas and doctrines are instrumental and serve the process of adjustment between the organism and its environment. Beliefs are developed and tested by experimental methods and experience. These pragmatic affirmations contain much that is illuminating.

Pragmatism has generated a liberal habit of mind and a beneficial enthusiasm for social progress. Most pragmatists have been keen supporters of democracy, human freedom, and other forward-looking movements in modern society.

However, pragmatism has had various criticisms directed against it. First, it is asserted that pragmatism has an inadequate metaphysics. Pragmatists are likely to claim that mere speculations regarding the ultimate nature of reality are a waste of time. Consequently, they turn to scientific methods of inquiry in their search for knowledge, since they believe that nature's ways can be discovered. But critics seeking for a "reality behind appearances" are not satisfied. They say that pragmatism distrusts traditional metaphysics because pragmatism does not rest on a stable foundation. If the pragmatists say that ultimate reality cannot be known, that in itself is a statement regarding the nature of reality. If the pragmatists stress experience and assert that "reality is as it is experienced" and that nature is to some extent "man-made," they move in the direction of the subjective forms of idealism. However, if they stress the objective, independent world, they move in the direction of realism. Their denial of metaphysics is in fact a confused metaphysics and a fear of facing metaphysical issues openly.

Second, it is claimed that pragmatism has an inadequate view of the mind. Mind is undoubtedly a biologically related aid to survival, as the pragmatists claim. Mind is much more, however, than an instrument for satisfying the practical needs of food, clothing, and shelter. Man is a problem-solver, it is true, but man also functions in the realm of aesthetic contemplation and of ideas and ideals. He asks about the "how" and the "why" of things. He lives to some extent in the past and in the future, as well as in the present. Dewey and other pragmatists have devoted attention to aesthetics and to man's ideals and future prospects. Some of the critics, however, think that the instrumentalist view of mind as merely a description of certain kinds of behavior is unsatisfactory.

Third, the critics attack the pragmatic view that truth is man-made and that it has no independent existence such as that claimed by realists and others. While "true propositions work in the long run," to turn the proposition around, and claim that "all propositions that work are true," does not logically follow. Some true beliefs cannot be verified; others are not useful. As truth is ordinarily understood, we do not create it by living right; we live right by grasping and following the truth. According to the critics, there is truth to be contemplated, beauty to be appreciated, and an order in nature to be discovered.

Fourth, there appears to be a serious inconsistency between the claim that philosophy is an outgrowth of social conditions and the demand for objectivity in research. If mind is an instrument to fulfill desires, how is it possible to demand impartiality in inquiry? If "men who live differently think differently," how can we have any reliable scientific knowledge?

Finally, critics ask whether or not pragmatism can be used to justify any social attitude that an individual or a group wishes to call progress. If the good is that which can be lived, is everything belonging to the evolutionary process good? Possibly pragmatism places too much emphasis on activity—the goals men do seek—and not enough on the goals men should seek.

QUESTIONS AND PROJECTS

1. Review Questions

(1) What are the distinguishing features or emphases of pragmatism?

(2) Write a brief essay on the origin and history of pragmatism.

(3) Indicate the part played by Charles S. Peirce in the development of pragmatism.

(4) Give an exposition of the philosophy of William James, indicating his views of empiricism, truth, meliorism, and the will to believe.

(5) How does the pragmatic view of truth differ from traditional interpretations?

(6) Discuss the instrumentalism of John Dewey, indicating the distinctive points of emphasis in his philosophy.

(7) What are the implications of accepting pragmatism, or instrumentalism, for logic, psychology, education, social philosophy, and religion?

(8) What do you consider to be the strengths and weaknesses of pragmatism as a general philosophy of life?

2. Are you able to accept William James' doctrine of the will to believe? What are its values and its dangers? Are there safeguards you would like to add?

3. Give an account of the life of John Dewey, emphasizing his intellectual development and the factors that influenced his thinking. See Paul Arthur Schilpp (ed.), *The Philosophy of John Dewey* (2nd ed.; New York: Tudor, 1951), pp. 3–45 (Vol. I of The Library of Living Philosophers); Irwin Edman, "America's Philosopher Attains an Alert 90," *New York Times Magazine*, October 16, 1949, pp. 17 ff.

4. Wherein does pragmatism agree with and differ from: (1) idealism, (2) realism?

5. Review Chapter 10 and list the positions on the mind-body problem that would be acceptable and unacceptable to pragmatists. Give reasons for your grouping.

6. Do you think there is any justification for the charge sometimes made that pragmatism could be used to support many widely differing systems of metaphysics or social philosophy? At one time American pragmatists had to challenge Mussolini's statement that he was following the principles of pragmatism! Is it conceivable that several hypotheses about the same thing might "work" equally well?

7. Are there beliefs that cannot be verified on pragmatic grounds? Consider beliefs about the meaning of life, the worth of man, democracy, and immortality in the light of the above question.

8. American education has come under severe criticism in recent years from a wide variety of critics. In a letter printed in *Life*, March 15, 1959, p. 114, President Eisenhower wrote:

> Educators, parents and students alike must be continuously stirred up by the defects in our educational system. They must be induced to abandon the educational path that, rather blindly, they have been following as a result of John Dewey's teachings.

John Dewey himself was a keen critic of American education, which he believed did not take sufficient account of the scientific revolution of the twentieth century and was not sufficiently creative. He proposed that the logic or thought pattern used in science be adopted as the standard in thinking about social issues, and he stressed creative intelligence. To what extent is he responsible for some of the excesses of his followers? Are the weaknesses of education due to the influence of Dewey or to the failure to apply his principles with understanding? You may wish to consult Sidney Hook, *John Dewey, His Philosophy of Education and Its Critics* (New York: Tamiment Institute, 1959).

9. Write a short essay on the contributions of George H. Mead to pragmatism. The following books may be consulted: George H. Mead, *The Philosophy of the Act* (Chicago: U. of Chicago Press, 1959); Maurice Natanson, *The Social Dynamics of George H. Mead* (Washington, D.C.: Public Affairs Press, 1956).

10. Review one of the following books: from the Suggested Readings, the books by Childs, Dewey, Feldman, James, and Otto; or, Bernard P. Brennan, *The Ethics of William James* (New York: Bookman, 1961); Gail Kennedy (ed.), *Pragmatism and American Culture* (New York: Heath, 1950); Morton Levitt, *Freud and Dewey on the Nature of Man* (New York: Philosophical Library, 1960); Ralph Barton Perry, *In the Spirit of William James* (New Haven: Yale U. Press, 1938).

SUGGESTED READINGS

BENJAMIN, A. CORNELIUS. *Operationism*. Springfield: Charles C Thomas, 1955.
   A study of operationism and its relation to empiricism and pragmatism, with special reference to the work of P. W. Bridgman.

BUTLER, J. DONALD. *Four Philosophies and Their Practice in Education and Religion.* New York: Harper, 1951.
   For a general discussion of pragmatism, see Part Four, pp. 395–482. For an extended bibliography, see pp. 532–534.

CHILDS, JOHN L. *American Pragmatism and Education.* New York: Holt, 1956.
   The author deals with the development of pragmatism and its relation to the new education.

DEWEY, JOHN. *His Contribution to the American Tradition.* Ed. by Irwin Edman. Indianapolis: Bobbs-Merrill, 1955.
   An introduction by the editor, followed by selections from some of the major works of Dewey. Readability has been a factor in the selection.

――――. *The Quest for Certainty.* New York: Putnam's, 1929. (Capricorn paperback.)
   A discussion of the relation between thought and action. Dewey's epistemology, showing that philosophy must turn to the experimental methods of science, is presented.

――――. *Reconstruction in Philosophy.* enl. ed.; Boston: Beacon, 1948. (Beacon paperback.)

In this book Dewey points out what he considers to be the defects of traditional philosophy and the new emphasis that is needed.

FELDMAN, WILLIAM T. *The Philosophy of John Dewey: A Critical Analysis.* Baltimore: Johns Hopkins Press, 1934.
A criticism of Dewey's instrumentalism, showing what the author believes to be contradictions in Dewey's philosophy and some of the reasons behind them.

GEIGER, GEORGE R. *John Dewey in Perspective.* New York: Oxford U. Press, 1958.
A readable account of Dewey's philosophy and an attempt to answer some of the misconceptions about his point of view.

HOOK, SIDNEY. *John Dewey: Philosopher of Science and Freedom; A Symposium.* New York: Dial, 1950.
A book of essays, on a wide range of topics, that attempt to bring out Dewey's main contributions and to evaluate his influence on our age.

JAMES, WILLIAM. *Pragmatism.* New York: Longmans, Green, 1907. (Also Meridian paperback.)
The beginner should start with these "popular essays" before reading The Meaning of Truth; A Pluralistic Universe; *and* The Will to Believe *by the same author.*

KONVITZ, MILTON R., AND KENNEDY, GAIL (eds.). *The American Pragmatists: Selected Writings.* New York: Meridian, 1960.
This paperback includes selections from Emerson, James, Peirce, Holmes, Dewey, Mead, Bridgman, Lewis, Kallen, and Hook.

MOORE, EDWARD CARTER. *American Pragmatism: Peirce, James, and Dewey.* New York: Columbia U. Press, 1961.
A discussion of the three leading figures in American pragmatism, with emphasis on Peirce's view of reality, James' conception of truth, and Dewey's explanation of the good.

OTTO, M. C. *The Human Enterprise.* New York: Appleton-Century-Crofts, 1940.
A readable account of how a pragmatist and humanist applies his philosophy to daily life.

PEIRCE, CHARLES S. *Collected Papers of Charles Sanders Peirce.* Ed. by Charles Hartshorne, Paul Weiss, and Arthur W. Burks. 8 vols.; Cambridge: Harvard U. Press, 1931, 1958. (Vols. 1–6, ed. C. Hartshorne and P. Weiss; Vols. 7–8, ed. A. W. Burks.)
These papers throw light on the origin of pragmatism and the development of modern logic and science, and contribute to the discussion of metaphysical problems. Fourteen of the essays from Vols. 1–6 are printed in paperback: Charles S. Peirce, Essays in the Philosophy of Science, *ed. Vincent Tomas (New York: Liberal Arts Press, 1957).*

———. *Values in a Universe of Chance.* Ed. by Philip P. Wiener. Stanford: Stanford U. Press, 1958.
Selections, divided into five groups, that attempt to bring out the various facets of Peirce's philosophy for the lay reader.

RAPOPORT, ANATOL. *Operational Philosophy.* New York: Harper, 1953.
A study of the relation between knowledge and action.

SCHILPP, PAUL ARTHUR (ed.). *The Philosophy of John Dewey*. 2nd ed.; New York: Tudor, 1951. (Vol. I of the Library of Living Philosophers.)

This volume includes a biography of John Dewey, critical essays by various students of Dewey's philosophy, a rejoinder by Dewey, and a bibliography of Dewey's writings.

VAN WESEP, H. B. *Seven Sages: The Story of American Philosophy*. New York: Longmans, Green, 1960.

This is a nontechnical introduction to the thoughts of Franklin, Emerson, James, Dewey, Santayana, Peirce, and Whitehead. The author finds considerable agreement running through the writings of these men.

WIENER, PHILIP P. *Evolution and the Founders of Pragmatism*. Cambridge: Harvard U. Press, 1949. (Foreword by John Dewey.)

The story of six men at Harvard, including William James, who worked out the pragmatic approach to philosophy.

✾ SIXTEEN ✾

LOGICAL EMPIRICISM
AND RELATED MOVEMENTS

During the last half century a number of reactions or revolts against the methods and dominant trends of Western philosophy have become prominent. In this chapter we shall briefly consider some of these new movements— logical empiricism, analytic philosophy, linguistic analysis, and some other movements that express a similiar spirit and outlook. In the next chapter we shall consider existentialism and related movements. These philosophical views are not easy to summarize or present in general terms and in a brief space, partly because the positions in some instances are highly technical and partly because the groups have been undergoing changes and realignments, so that clear-cut distinctions are difficult to make.

THE TRADITIONAL OUTLOOK

Before we consider some of these newer positions, we shall summarize the outlook to which they are a reaction. In the past two thousand years, Western philosophy, reinforced by Christianity, has attempted to furnish men with a world view, a life view, and a scale of values by which to live. One philosopher sums up this traditional outlook as follows:

The traditional Philosophy of Western Europe holds that, transcending the familiar world of things known to us by our senses and explored by science, there is another order of reality which contains values. Of these, Goodness, Beauty and Truth are pre-eminent, and constitute the grounds of ethics, aesthetics and logic respectively. In other words, it is because the universe is—or contains—a moral order that some things are right and some are wrong; because it contains an aesthetic order that some things are beautiful and some ugly, and because there is such a thing as truth that some judgments are true and some false. Many philosophers would add that the universe also includes deity and that deity is the source of the values, Goodness, Truth and Beauty, being, as religion puts it, the modes of God's revelation of Himself to man.

Metaphysics—the study of the reality which transcends and underlies the familiar world—is, therefore, in part, the study of the values and of God.[1]

THE EMPIRICISM OF LOCKE AND HUME

Alongside what is sometimes called the "Great Tradition" there developed, especially in England during the last few centuries, an empirical movement that has gained considerable strength. Including such thinkers as John Locke and David Hume, this movement was critical of metaphysics and merely speculative thinking and held that knowledge comes through our senses. John Locke (1632–1714) held that at birth the mind is like a blank tablet or photographic plate on which are registered impressions from the outside. Knowledge is sensorially derived. Through reflection aided by memory, sensations are organized into the various disciplines or bodies of knowledge. Locke denied the existence of inborn, or innate, ideas and said that universals (or Platonic Ideas) are not transcendental but rather are "the inventions and creatures of the understanding, made by it for its own use." David Hume (1711–1776) carried the empirical tradition even further. Simple ideas, he said, are copies of simple sensations, and complex ideas are formed from the combination of simple ideas or from complex impressions. The general effect of Hume's position was to deny the validity of the notion that there are abstract and general ideas. Hume attacked the traditional concepts of substance and causality and carried the skeptical implications of his position over into the fields of ethics and religion. This empiricism received further support in the nineteenth and twentieth centuries from the rise and influence of the sciences.

RECENT SUPPORT FOR EMPIRICISM

Four groups, separate at least in origin, carried on and supported the empirical tradition. They were the French positivists of the nineteenth century, the logical positivists of the Vienna Circle, the English schools of philosophical analysis, and the various schools of behavioristic psychology. These groups supported or reinforced each other though they have not actually combined. We shall consider them separately before we comment on their type of thinking as a whole.

FRENCH POSITIVISM

The tendency to base knowledge on sense perceptions and the investigations of objective science and to discard metaphysical world views led to a position known in France as positivism. Positivism would limit knowledge to statements of observable facts and their interrelations. The French phi-

---

[1] C. E. M. Joad, *A Critique of Logical Positivism* (Chicago: U. of Chicago Press, 1950), p. 27.

losopher Auguste Comte (1798–1857), a pioneer in the field of sociology and advocate of a "religion of humanity," was the founder and leading exponent of positivism. He divided the history of man into three periods, each of which is characterized by a certain way of thinking. The first period is the theological, in which imagination has free play and events are explained by the control and intervention of spirits and gods, with the world defined in animistic or supernatural terms. The second period is the metaphysical, in which events are explained by such abstractions as causes, inner principles, and substances. These abstractions replace supernatural agencies. The third, or "positive," is the final and highest period. This is the period of scientific description, which does not attempt to go beyond observable and measurable facts. Man gives up his earlier efforts to discover the causes, the destiny, and the ultimate nature of things. What, if anything, is "beyond" this world of experience is of no concern, and we should confine our attention to this world. Positivism is the final stage of human thought, and the task of science at this stage is to make the present world safe for humanity.

According to this school of thought, knowledge is valuable only because it helps people modify conditions in the material world and society. For this purpose men need to know only phenomena and the laws under which things operate. Comte replaces supernatural religion and metaphysical unity with humanity and social progress. The negative attitude of positivism toward any reality beyond the experienced order has influenced various modern schools of thought, including pragmatism, instrumentalism, scientific naturalism, and behaviorism.

LOGICAL POSITIVISM AND THE VIENNA CIRCLE

Largely because of Ernst Mach and Moritz Schlick, who succeeded Mach in 1922 as professor of the philosophy of the inductive sciences at the University of Vienna, a group of positivists made its influence felt not only in Austria and Germany but also eventually throughout the West. The members of this group, especially active during the nineteen-twenties and -thirties, were scientists, mathematicians, or men who had done their main professional work in symbolic logic and scientific methodology. Whereas the earlier positivism was founded on nineteenth-century science, the new developments were based on more recent logical and scientific concepts. The movement has been variously designated "logical positivism," the "Vienna Circle,"[2] "logical empiricism," "scientific empiricism," and the "Unity of Science Movement."

---

[2] For the work of the Vienna Circle and the recent activity of some of its members, see Jørgen Jørgensen, *The Development of Logical Empiricism* (Chicago: U. of Chicago Press, 1951); see also Victor Kraft, *The Vienna Circle: The Origin of Neo-Positivism,* trans. Arthur Pap (New York: Philosophical Library, 1953).

One member of this school of thought says:

> The forerunners of logical empiricism are, in the opinion of the members of
> the movement themselves, all those philosophers and scientists who show a
> clear antimetaphysical or antispeculative, realistic or materialistic, critical or
> skeptical, tendency—as well as everyone who has contributed essentially to
> the development of their most important methodological instrument: symbolic
> logic.[3]

The members of the Vienna Circle were especially interested in working out a secure intellectual foundation for all science. They felt that the sciences, though not now highly unified, belong logically to one coherent system. The problem was to find an inclusive terminological and conceptual system common to all the sciences and not limited to one or only a few of them. This led to a study of the language of particular sciences and an analysis of language in general in the hope of finding a universal language of science. The members of this philosophical group believe the proper task of philosophy to be the analysis of language, especially the language of science.

The approach represents a definite shift from the methods and tactics of traditional philosophy. Instead of attacking the arguments per se of the traditional philosophers, the members of this school have turned to a criticism of language in an attempt to show that the older issues are meaningless as presented. Logical positivists tend to claim that their method or approach is independent of a metaphysics. Their critics, however, challenge this claim.

SCHOOLS OF PHILOSOPHICAL ANALYSIS

Early in the twentieth century certain philosophers, including G. E. Moore, C. D. Broad, Susan Stebbing, Bertrand Russell, and Ludwig Wittgenstein, became interested in linguistic study and the logical analysis of terms, concepts, and propositions. The new emphasis was in part a reaction to the rationalistic monism of certain idealists, mainly F. H. Bradley who held a position somewhat similar to that of Hegel considered in the chapter on idealism.

Some of the late nineteenth-century rationalists who were absolute idealists had viewed the world as a single, indivisible whole in which the only self-contained entity was reality itself—the Absolute or God. One reaction to such a rigid monism was an extreme pluralism—which described the world as consisting of an indefinitely large number of separate elements—to which the term *logical atomism* was applied. Partly because of the desire to avoid the metaphysical implications of the concept "atomism," and partly because of revised analytic methods, the philosophical analysts later replaced *logical atomism* with *logical empiricism*. There were differences among the

3 Jørgensen, *Logical Empiricism*, p. 6.

logical analysts regarding metaphysical questions. In the main, however, the later analysts either avoid making metaphysical statements or reject explicitly all metaphysical questions as useless or meaningless[4] and assert that analysis is the only legitimate activity of philosophers.

The fact that Russell and Wittgenstein had come to philosophy by way of symbolic logic and mathematics was also partly responsible for the rise of philosophical analysis. The philosophical analysts and the members of the Vienna Circle also influenced each other. Could the disagreement among philosophers, they asked, be rooted in the ambiguities of ordinary language rather than in the complicated nature of the world? A belief that this might be so led some philosophers to be concerned with the language in which ideas are expressed and with an analysis of the structure of that language.

Looking back over the history of philosophy, the linguistic analysts thought they saw evidence that analysis of language had in fact always been stressed, though superficially it would appear that nonlinguistic points were at issue. They called attention to Plato's analysis of concepts like "justice," to Socrates' effort to clarify the meaning of terms like *courage, goodness,* and *piety,* and to Hume's rigorous examination of statements about causality. Analysis was not a new device but a well-established philosophical method stressed especially by the empiricists. What was new, the linguistic analysts said, was the extra rigor and precision, the increased subtlety and exactness of the symbolic methods, and the explicit claim that what is being done is linguistic analysis. Sometimes the aim is to make every statement correspond, insofar as is possible, to the data or experience to which it refers. At other times the aim is to clarify just what is at issue—a linguistic point, an empirical matter—and eliminate confusion. For example, a philosopher may be stipulating a definition when he appears to be giving a new insight about the world.

Contemporary analysts generally are empiricists, and some of them allow as meaningful only statements that are capable of empirical verification or statements as to how we use terms. Statements that are not based on experiences or that cannot be verified are regarded as nonsensical or as having some noncognitive function. All the genuine data of experience, they say, are the province of some special science. Philosophy properly deals with language— in other words, once the philosopher has decided that a statement is meaningful and makes some claim about the world and not merely about the way we use words, it is up to the scientist to verify the statement. What is new is that attention is directed toward analysis and criticism, with synthesis and the synoptic outlook pushed into the background; metaphysics and speculative philosophy are repudiated. Critical philosophy, in the form of logic, semantics, philosophy of language, philosophy of science, and epistemology, has become prominent in some colleges and universities.

4 The term *nonsense* is sometimes used in its original sense of "without meaning."

BEHAVIORISM AS A PHILOSOPHY

We have spoken of the attempt to unify the sciences under a single methodological and conceptual system. How is this unification possible in the light of such differing subject matter as that of mathematics and the physical sciences, on the one hand, and the social studies and human psychology, on the other? The attempt to unify the sciences was supported by behaviorism, a psychological method developed to study animal psychology and later applied to the study of human behavior. Behaviorism as a methodology has yielded fruitful results in psychology, but some behaviorists go much further and make behaviorism a philosophy. As a philosophy, behaviorism dismisses all questions concerning an inner life, mind, conscious states, and consciousness as meaningless. The behaviorists abandon efforts to study "mind" as anything other than certain kinds of behavior. "Thinking" is said to be talking under one's breath, movements of the vocal organs, or various neurological activities and events. Such states as fear and anger are exclusively defined by patterns of heartbeat, muscular contraction, and the like. "Stimulus," "response," "conditioning" (learning a response to a stimulus), and "determinism" are key concepts in such an approach.

Behaviorism as a philosophy supports and is supported by logical positivism. Behaviorists recognize only that which is observable. The methods of the experimental sciences are said to be adequate for testing and solving all problems in human psychology. All questions are translated into or reduced to questions that can be answered operationally. Language is cognitively meaningful only when it makes physically testable claims. Therefore, statements about man are meaningful only when they are or may be translated into statements about man's behavior.

THE PHILOSOPHY OF LANGUAGE

During the last half century there has been a growing interest in the problems of language and communication and the function of signs and symbols. This interest has led to the development of semantics, or the study of the meaning and the function of words and the relations between words and things, schools of linguistic or philosophical analysis, and symbolic logic. It has also led to a renewed attention to details of grammar and syntax. Most people take language pretty much for granted, like the air we breathe. At present, however, many specialists, including philosophers who use a "logical-analytic method," see the study of meaning and the principles and rules of language as the central problem of philosophy. The philosophers of the ancient world and the Middle Ages were concerned mainly with a reality that transcended that of the temporal world. Their search was for "being." The philosophers from the Renaissance to the nineteenth century looked inward; they were interested mainly in the self, ideas in the mind, and the problem of knowledge. While these earlier interests have not disappeared from philosophy, some philosophers restrict their attention to linguistic analysis and the details and theory of discourse. Words, definitions, propositions, hypotheses, axioms, principles of verification, and the like have come increasingly to be regarded as worthy of philosophical investigation. This field is complex and highly technical. We shall limit our discussion to a few of the issues raised.

Naming is an early step in acquiring knowledge. Ordinarily we are said not to know what a thing is unless we can name it, classify it, and locate it in some meaningful context. If we wish to say something about a thing we need a name (or symbol) for it, so that we can distinguish it from other things. The *name* is the symbol that stands for the thing named, which is called the *referent*. By this device we take a word or symbol (spoken or written) and use it to refer to something (object, quality, relation) or to connect other words that stand for things, and so on. Different names *could* have been chosen, but once a particular one is selected in a given language, there must be an element of permanency about its use if confusion is to be avoided. Words are combined into sentences, which also have meaning, and we have a language as an instrument of discourse.

The ability to use language is one of man's distinctive traits. Animals are restricted to natural cries, which are few in number and which seem to express feelings of pleasure or pain. Such sounds or expressions may accompany the presence of food, mates, or danger. With the development of consciousness, intelligence, and a social group, and with the invention and use of verbal symbols, man acquired a potentiality for freedom and knowledge that no other animal possesses.

A spoken language with an appeal to the ear has a great advantage over pictorial signs and gestures with an appeal to the eye or sight. Sound has advantages over sight in that the voice leaves the hands free, and sound radiates in many directions and can be heard even in the dark. The speaker does not need to be seen. All groups of men the world over have a spoken language. However, a spoken language has no independent objective permanence and may soon be lost from memory, and with it will be lost whatever knowledge the group may have acquired.

The development of a written language is one of the important steps in the growth of a civilization. Without a written language there would be little progress. When speech is broken into its fundamental elements, and symbols are used for these as in the alphabet, a written language comes into existence and we get a relatively permanent medium of expression and communication. A written language may be a storehouse of past knowledge, and it has the power to transcend some of the more obvious limitations of time and space and to resist the changes that take place in oral transmission. New methods of recording, of course, may give speech (spoken language) a greater degree of permanency in the future than it has had in the past.

The development of language has made possible the rapid growth of human knowledge and its extension into innumerable special fields. We cannot think without symbols. Along with great gains have also come new problems. Language has many functions. Language has a *cognitive* function: it expresses propositions that we can test for accuracy and accept or reject. This is the knowledge sought in the various sciences, as well as in philosophy. Language, however, has many other functions. Much of our language is *emotive* in one of two ways: it may be *expressive* of our feelings and moods or *evocative* and call forth an emotional response from others. Language may be *imperative*: it may command or direct in an attempt to control the actions of others. It may be *ceremonial,* as in many of our greetings and some of our conversation and ritual. Different disciplines may have their own terminology, so that we may have the language of science, of literary and aesthetic pursuits, of poetry, love, morals, and piety. Is it possible to confuse these different kinds and functions of languages and to assume that a statement is cognitive when it is emotive or imperative? May an expression of a wish be accepted on occasion as verified knowledge?

Men need to distinguish clearly between statements that point out or describe actual things in the world of nature and the way these things are related and statements that have no referent in the external world. That is, we may use language to talk about objects or to talk about language or words. When we talk about objects like pencils, desks, animals, and the like, we are said to be using an "object-language," but when we talk about this object-language itself we are using a "metalanguage." We could even take a further step and talk about the language in which we talk about the object-language, but let's not complicate this problem any more than necessary! That I said something may be true; what I said may be false. A statement may be true in one language and be false or meaningless in the other language.

Language is more intimately connected with human experience than is often recognized. Some think of language merely as a fairly accurate recording of the items of experience that seem important to the individual and to the society. People think of language as reflecting or portraying the world much as it is. However, language itself not only reflects our experiences and the environmental conditions under which it has developed, but it also has a powerful influence on these experiences. Language imposes certain perceptual viewpoints and in this way has an influence on our thoughts and actions. Language and thought may also at times take wings, so to speak, and create their own world.

Language may influence experience and thinking in innumerable and subtle ways because of our projection of the way it structures the world onto the world itself. Language may help mold the thoughts of those who use it, since there is an interaction between the culture and the linguistic forms that are in use. Speaking about language in its relation to culture, Harry Hoijer says: "Far from being simply a technique of communication, it is itself a way of directing the perceptions of its speakers and it provides for them habitual modes of analyzing experience into significant categories."[5] Concealed in the structure of different languages are a wide range of unconscious assumptions about life and the world of nature. After asserting that there are "as many different worlds upon the earth as there are languages," Clyde Kluckhohn says: "The lack of true equivalences between any two languages is merely the outward expression of inward differences between two peoples in premises, in basic categories, in the training of fundamental sensitivities, and in general view of the world."[6] These linguistic forms, like other cultural elements, usually have a long history and carry traditional meanings whose origins are obscure. While there are often difficulties in translating accurately from one European language into another, the difficulties mount as one compares the languages of groups more widely separated in historical backgrounds and cultures. For example, the English language and European languages in general tend to center attention on objects and their characteristics. These languages are traditionally regarded as subject-predicate languages. The language of the Navaho Indians in America, on the other hand, is verb-centered, so that the main attention is paid to actions and events rather than to objects. Navaho language is more specific in some areas and less so than English in other areas. The world appears somewhat different to people using different symbols, vocabularies, and languages.

Is it possible that some of the baffling problems man faces are the result of confusions in our linguistic forms and usages, and that clarification of the language might solve or at least eliminate these problems? This is the claim of the positivists. We shall now return to the questions that are raised by the linguistic analysts.

LOGICAL EMPIRICISM AND QUESTIONS OF KNOWLEDGE

Certain questions particularly concern the logical empiricist: What judgments may one make? How much may one infer from one's sense data, or the data of experience? What is meant by *meaning* and *verification*? How may one proceed through analysis to clarify language? What are the implications of the answers to these questions?

According to Immanuel Kant, who has had a powerful influence on mod-

[5] *Language in Cultures* (Chicago: U. of Chicago Press, 1954), p. 94.
[6] *Mirror for Man* (New York: Whittlesey, 1949), pp. 160, 166–167.

ern thought, there are *analytic propositions*—propositions in which the predicate is "contained in" the subject. For example: white swans are white; all bachelors are male. The predicate merely states something that is contained in the ordinary meaning of the subject; the predicate is a defining characteristic of the subject. In contrast with analytic statements, there are synthetic propositions, which cannot be verified by analyzing the statement. For example: this watch is gold; there is a chair in my office. Synthetic judgments bring two ideas together in a new relationship; propositions that tell us something about the world (and not about how we use words) and must be verified empirically are called *synthetic propositions*. While Kant believed that most synthetic propositions could be verified sensorially, he held that there are some synthetic propositions that are a priori—that is, known to be true prior to experience and not dependent on experience for verification. An example of a *synthetic a priori* proposition, according to Kant, would be: every event has a cause. Synthetic a priori propositions are necessarily true, yet they give information about the world.

According to A. J. Ayer, who combines British philosophical analysis and logical positivism, there are no synthetic a priori judgments. There are only two kinds of statements that convey knowledge and that may be judged true or false. There are, first, analytic statements or propositions, whose truth depends solely on the definitions of the terms or symbols involved. Especially good examples are found in the fields of mathematics and logic; for instance, two plus two equals four. Kant said that this kind of statement was synthetic a priori, since it seemed to be necessarily true and to give information about the world. The logical positivists insisted that the statements of mathematics were *necessarily* true only insofar as they were analytic and depended on the meaning of mathematical terms. When, however, these statements had empirical referents, they were no longer necessarily true, but depended on observation for their verification. The positivists thus believed they had destroyed the notion of the synthetic a priori. Second, there are affirmations or denials of questions of fact, synthetic statements, which may be verified empirically. All synthetic propositions—statements of fact about the world—are grounded in sense perception or are relevant to some actual or possible experience. According to this analysis, a statement is meaningful if, and only if, it is either analytic or empirically verifiable. That is, Ayer established what is referred to as the verificationist meaning criterion: nonanalytic statements are meaningful only if they are empirically verifiable.

In his *Language, Truth and Logic* Ayer makes a distinction between the "strong" and the "weak" sense of verification. He says:

It will be seen that I distinguish between a "strong" and a "weak" sense of the term "verifiable," and that I explain this distinction by saying that "a proposition is said to be verifiable in the strong sense of the term, if and only if its truth could be conclusively established in experience," but that "it is verifiable, in the weak sense, if it is possible for experience to render it probable."[7]

The weak sense of the principle leaves room for the extremely indirect method of testing some explanatory hypotheses in science. The logical empiricist would say that these hypotheses start from and eventually return to the area of empirical data and observations.

In speaking of the function of philosophy, Ayer says that the philosopher "must not attempt to formulate speculative truths, or to look for first principles, or to make *a priori* judgments about the validity of our empirical beliefs. He must, in fact, confine himself to works of clarification and analysis. . . ." He also says that "the propositions of philosophy are not factual, but linguistic in character—that is, they do not describe the behavior of physical, or even mental objects; they express definitions, or the formal consequences of definitions. Accordingly, we may say that philosophy is a department of logic."[8]

Since the task of adding to our knowledge necessarily falls to one or another of the various sciences, just what is the task of philosophy according to this approach? Logical empiricists are likely to reply that philosophy's task is the logical analysis of language, especially the language of science. Attention is given to symbolic logic and the theory of signs or symbols. Writing on logical empiricism, Herbert Feigl says that philosophy can lead us in the direction of "maturer ways of thinking, thinking which possesses the virtues characteristic of science: clarity and consistency, testability and adequacy, precision and objectivity."[9] As distinguished from the earlier types of empiricism and positivism (such as Hume's and Ayer's), Feigl says that logical empiricism emphasizes "the systematic pursuit of the problem of meaning by means of a logical analysis of language."[10]

If philosophy is primarily a study of language, how shall one proceed in making such a study? Some philosophical analysts, the ordinary linguists, think that attention should be given to ordinary language, or the forms of common speech. The language of everyday discourse is the medium for the expression and communication of men's thoughts, and it must meet the most severe test—that of continuous use. Ordinary language can be subjected to a rigorous, extended program of analysis. Other philosophers, however, con-

[7] A. J. Ayer, *Language, Truth and Logic* (2nd rev. ed.; 1946), p. 9. Published by Dover Publications, New York 14.

[8] *Ibid.*, pp. 51, 57.

[9] "Logical Empiricism," in *Twentieth Century Philosophy*, Dagobert D. Runes (ed.) (New York: Philosophical Library, 1943), p. 376.

[10] *Ibid.*, p. 377. For the history of the movement see pp. 405 ff.

tend that ordinary language is too ambiguous and there should be constructed an ideal language, one of more exact and precise signs and symbols than those in ordinary use.[11] This is a highly involved issue, which we shall not attempt to elaborate upon here. Those of our readers who have some familiarity with modern mathematical and symbolic logic will appreciate the nature and scope of the problem.

In his *Elements of Analytic Philosophy*[12] Arthur Pap distinguishes four major schools or groups in analytic philosophy. There are, first, the followers of G. E. Moore, who emphasize the language in common use. There are, second, the followers of Carnap, who advocate "the construction of ideal, formalized languages in which the basic concepts common to all the sciences ... admit of exact definitions." There are, third, the followers of Ludwig Wittgenstein, for whom philosophy does not aim at intellectual discovery but is "a method of revealing the linguistic confusions that give rise to philosophical 'problems.' " Wittgensteinians believe that most of the perennial problems of philosophy are not genuine problems at all. Finally, there are those independent philosophers—not included in any of the above three groups—who are interested in the "clarification of the foundations of the sciences" and of "knowledge in general." They are, however, engaged in rigorous, detailed analysis of terms and concepts.

Logical empiricists who limit knowledge to statements of *observable* fact make rather sweeping denials. They will not accept anything as meaningful that cannot be verified by empirical observation. The metaphysical thesis that there is "knowledge of a reality transcending the world of science and common sense" is brushed aside as nonsense: what could it possibly mean? Much of traditional philosophy is repudiated, and concepts like "being," "reality," "God," and the "purpose of human existence" are disregarded or said to be meaningless. Similarly, normative ethics drops out of the picture. Ayer says:

> [I]n saying that a certain type of action is right or wrong, I am not making any factual statement, not even a statement about my own state of mind. I am merely expressing certain moral sentiments. And the man who is ostensibly contradicting me is merely expressing his moral sentiments. So that there is plainly no sense in asking which of us is in the right. For neither of us is asserting a genuine proposition. . . .
>
> We can now see why it is impossible to find a criterion for determining the validity of ethical judgments . . . because they have no objective validity

11 There is a tendency for analytical philosophers in America to stress an ideal language, and for philosophers in England to stress ordinary language. See A. J. Ayer, *et al.*, *Revolution in Philosophy* (New York: St. Martin's, 1956), p. 101.
12 New York: Macmillan, 1949, pp. ix–x.

whatsoever. If a sentence makes no statement at all, there is obviously no sense in asking whether what it says is true or false. . . . They are pure expression of feeling. . . . unverifiable for the same reason as a cry of pain or a word of command is unverifiable—because they do not express genuine propositions.13

Metaphysical, theological, and ethical propositions are excluded from the realm of the meaningful, since they are emotive only, untestable, and give no knowledge. Only empirically testable propositions—those of the sciences —are meaningful and contain knowledge.

While no one doubts that the various sciences have achieved much and that we can look forward to even greater advances in the future, many will question attempts to limit knowledge to scientific statements. The members of the groups we have been considering in this chapter do not say that all the statements of science are true or even meaningful, but many of them do say that for a statement to be true it must be empirically verifiable. The more extreme positivists seem to combine a thoroughgoing skepticism with respect to the beliefs of religion and speculative philosophy with an almost dogmatic acceptance of the findings of the sciences. There are limitations to the methods used by the sciences, and it follows that there are meaningful propositions that are not verifiable by these methods.

A central question is: How much may one infer from what is believed to be directly experienced? Nearly all people admit that we do make inferences both in science and in philosophy. But how much may we infer, or, to put it another way, what kinds of inferences are justified? Philosophers of very different backgrounds and intellectual outlooks have claimed that their philosophies have started from what is directly known, and yet they have concluded with very different kinds of systems. Rationalists like Descartes have been willing to cast aside everything that can be doubted and to start from what is clearly and distinctly perceived. Empiricists like Locke and Berkeley likewise built their philosophies on the basis of what they took to be given in experience. May one who starts from that which is given directly in experience move on to infer the existence of other entities or realities thought to be implied or required by these experiences? How far may one go in this direction? May one infer the existence of such things as substances, a self, universals, and God? Many philosophers have thought that some such inferences were necessary; others have attacked such inferences and have insisted that one should stop with that which is immediately given in sense perception or at least with that which is open to some experimental or empirical check. If the latter view is accepted, a wide range of topics and problems that men in the past have considered to be important is meaningless.

13 *Language, Truth and Logic*, pp. 107, 108-9.

EVALUATION OF LOGICAL EMPIRICISM

Philosophical analysis and logical positivism are not identical, as we have seen, though some people speak of them as though they were. There are, moreover, differences among analysts and among positivists. Philosophical analysis is a broad movement embracing many different points of view. Some of the comments and criticisms below will apply to some forms and not to others. We are using the term *logical empiricism* in a broad sense to cover all these closely related movements. All are empirical and antimetaphysical in tendency, though even in these aspects they differ among themselves in points of emphasis.

Careful analysis is central in philosophical method and thinking. Logical empiricism as a whole has rendered a real service in stimulating philosophers to examine more carefully their assumptions, the evidence for their beliefs, and the form in which these convictions are expressed. The method of analysis has worked well in logic, mathematics, and related fields. Some people working in the field of philosophical analysis, however, have pointed out that the general results have been disappointing. For example, the attempt to reduce the notion of "a person" to sense data or even to behavior has not produced satisfactory results.[14] One philosophical analyst says:

> I believe that it could not easily be denied that in philosophy an unusually high proportion of what has been written, and indeed is written, could not unjustly be described as nonsense, and it is no service to anyone to pretend otherwise. At the same time, it happens to be true that the restrictive iconoclasm of Logical Positivism is quite alien to the spirit of philosophy today. In particular, its exclusive respect for science, mathematics, formal logic, and very plain facts is now generally admitted to be unwarranted. If any one thing is characteristic of contemporary philosophy, it would be precisely the realization that language has *many* uses, ethical, aesthetic, literary, and indeed metaphysical uses among them.[15]

A too-exclusive attention to language may lead one to lose sight of what language is supposed to represent. Philosophers in the past have insisted on their right and the need to discuss questions of science, art, morality, religion, politics, and education, as well as symbols and language. To say that philosophy may talk only about language is to transform one method of clarification into the very essence of philosophy; it is an example of reductive analysis and "losing the object."

14 See J. O. Urmson, *Philosophical Analysis* (London: Oxford U. Press, 1956), especially Ch. 10, "The Impossibility of Reductive Analysis."

15 G. J. Warnock, "Analysis and Imagination," in *The Revolution in Philosophy*, A. J. Ayer, *et al.* (eds.) (New York: St. Martin's, 1956), p. 125. By permission of Macmillan & Co. Ltd. and St. Martin's Press, Inc., New York.

After paying tribute to the clarity and vigor of much of the work of the analytic philosophers, one critic says:

> I cannot help but feel that there is something seriously wrong with a philosophy, in the mid-twentieth century, that takes no notice of war, revolution, nationalism, nuclear energy, the exploration of space, or anything else distinctive of the life of our time save the magnificent sweep of the intellect in the achievements of pure science and mathematics.[16]

In discussing the "breakdown of modern philosophy," John Wild points out that a too-exclusive attention to the tools one is using may cut one off from the problem requiring solution.

> Vision offers us an accurate analogy. It may be that I cannot see except by the use of spectacles. But to take off one pair of spectacles and to study them by another pair will not enable me to gain a panoramic view. It merely gives me another object to be fitted into such a view. To know something about the spectacles—their size, weight, refraction, etc.—will not enable me to understand vision as such, which also involves other factors. And even to know what vision is in general will not enable me to see real objects. A blind man may have such knowledge. Analytical philosophy, which surrenders objective insight to focus on the logical and linguistic tools of knowledge, is like a man who becomes so interested in the crack and spots of dust upon his glasses that he loses all interest in what he may actually see through them.[17]

Critics of logical empiricism contend that its meaning criterion and its principle of verification are too exclusive and arbitrary. The principle of verification itself is neither logico-mathematical nor empirical and by this accepted definition of meaning is itself undermined. These critics are not willing to admit that formal logic and scientific method, while of great value, exhaust the activity and reach of human reason. If no metaphysical statements are permitted, the assumptions and statements on which logical positivism rests—that there is nothing real beyond sensory experience—are meaningless also. Positivism, at least in its more extreme form, rests on materialistic or at least naturalistic assumptions. Is it true that what we know consists exclusively of propositions that are empirically verifiable or deduced from such propositions? Various metaphysical assumptions are hidden behind statements of this kind. One critic of logical empiricism says:

> Again, Ayer is troubled about the nature of verifiability. Interpreted in its "strong" sense, the verifiability principle rules out, he thinks, all but "basic"

---

[16] Abraham Kaplan, *The New World of Philosophy* (New York: Random House, Inc., 1961), p. 90. (Copyright by Abraham Kaplan.)
[17] *The Challenge of Existentialism* (Bloomington: Indiana U. Press, 1955), p. 10.

propositions . . . yet in its "weak" sense it is not sufficiently positivist, since experiences are certainly "relevant," in the wide sense of that term, to some metaphysical propositions. This, indeed, is the dilemma in which the logical positivists, like Hume before them, constantly found themselves—throw metaphysics into the fire, and science goes with it, preserve science from the flames and metaphysics comes creeping back.18

Logical empiricism, insofar as it insists that every descriptive or factual term must be in the language of science and propositions must be verifiable by sensory observation, is asserting a metaphysical doctrine. This is in fact a clear-cut materialism, which was fairly prevalent in scientific circles during the nineteenth century. Insofar as logical empiricism is materialistic the position is open to the criticisms directed against materialism.

The linguistic analysts have made it clear that philosophers have sometimes confused the various functions and meanings of language and have failed on occasion to distinguish clearly among them; such confusion has clouded philosophical issues themselves. Today it appears that there is emerging among the analysts a more liberal attitude, which includes a recognition of not just one or two but of many modes of meaning as legitimate. This hopefully presages a return to legitimacy of such issues as those of ethics, aesthetics, and metaphysics.

QUESTIONS AND PROJECTS

1. Review Questions

(1) State the traditional philosophical outlook now being attacked.

(2) Describe empiricism, indicating some of its main points and naming a few of its leaders.

(3) What four groups during the last hundred and fifty years have embraced empiricism? Indicate briefly how each group supported the empirical, linguistic, or positivistic trends.

(4) What are the different functions of language, and how may a confusion of these different functions lead to errors in thinking?

(5) Discuss the relations among language, culture, and our views of life and nature.

(6) Distinguish between analytic and synthetic propositions. Discuss the "synthetic a priori" controversy.

(7) Explain what is meant by the "principle of verification." What is the difference between the "strong" and the "weak" application of the principle?

(8) State the position of A. J. Ayer, and point out what this position implies about the function of philosophy.

18 John Passmore, *A Hundred Years of Philosophy* (New York: Macmillan, 1957), p. 392. Used with the permission of The Macmillan Company.

(9) What schools or groups are to be distinguished in the field of linguistic analysis?

(10) What are the general implications of the position that limits knowledge to propositions about sense perception and observable "facts"?

(11) Evaluate linguistic analysis and logical empiricism, indicating what you believe to be the strengths and weaknesses of these and related movements.

2. The statements below say or imply that logical empiricists and positivists sacrifice certain questions and problems to a method. Indicate the extent to which you agree or disagree with the quotations.

(1) In *The Self As Agent* (New York: Harper, 1953), p. 28, John Macmurray says: "Philosophy, like any branch of serious reflective inquiry, is created and defined by its problems; and its problems are not accidental, but necessary; grounded in the nature of experience. If I find that my method of attempting to answer them is unsuccessful, if it fails even to discover a meaning in them, then I must conclude that there is something wrong with the method, and seek a better one. To discard the problems in order to retain the method; to seek for problems which the method *could* solve, would be neither serious nor reasonable."

(2) In Carl Michalson (ed.), *Christianity and the Existentialists* (New York: Scribner's, 1956), pp. 81–82, J. V. Langmead Casserley says: "Positivist philosophers in particular behave rather like an investigation and censorship committee determined upon the suppression of inconvenient questions by calling in question and libelling the philosophical integrity of those who insist on asking them. But to censor and suppress human questioning must in the long run erode and destroy human intellectualism."

(3) In *A Critique of Logical Positivism* (Chicago: U. of Chicago Press, 1950), p. 148, C. E. M. Joad asks: "Can a man really continue to feel indignant at cruelty, if he is convinced that the statement, 'cruelty is wrong' is meaningless?" Again he says: "If Logical Positivism is correct," you can say, "one atom bomb can destroy 50,000 people" (statement of fact), but not, "it is a bad thing to destroy 50,000 people" (statement of evaluation), or rather, you can say it, but the "word 'bad' adds nothing to the factual content of the statement."

3. Many metaphysical and theological assertions are such that, if they are held with real conviction, they make a difference in human decisions and actions. What, in your opinion, will be the effects on ethics, politics, religion, and theology of the spread of the more extreme empirical views?

4. Write a short essay on one of the following topics: (1) The Relation between Philosophy and Language, (2) My Philosophy of Language. The following books will offer suggestions: Max Black, *Models and Metaphors: Studies in Language and Philosophy* (Ithaca: Cornell U. Press, 1962); J. Samuel Bois, *Explorations in Awareness* (New York: Harper, 1957); S. J. Hayakawa (ed.), *Language, Meaning, and Maturity* (New York: Harper, 1954); H. J. Paton, *The Modern Predicament* (New York: Macmillan, 1955), Ch. II, "The Linguistic Veto"; Paul W. Taylor, *Normative Discourse* (Englewood Cliffs: Prentice-Hall, 1961).

5. Without limiting your remarks to the points presented in this chapter, draw up a brief for a debate on logical empiricism. Consult the Suggested Readings. The books by Ayer will give the case for and the book by Joad the case against this philosophical position. For a shorter presentation, see A. J. Ayer and F. C. Copleston, "Logical Positivism—A Debate," in *A Modern Introduction to Philosophy*, Paul Edwards and Arthur Pap (eds.) (Glencoe: Free Press, 1957), pp. 586–618.

6. Review one of the books by the following authors as found in the Suggested Readings below: Beckwith, Blanshard, Gellner, Pears, Taylor, and Urmson.

SUGGESTED READINGS

AYER, A. J. *Language, Truth and Logic*. 2nd rev. ed.; London: Gollancz, 1946.
A defense of logical positivism by one of its outstanding protagonists. The book by Joad suggested below is a detailed and critical examination of Ayer's book. See also A. J. Ayer's The Problem of Knowledge and Logical Positivism.

BECKWITH, BURNHAM P. *Religion, Philosophy, and Science: An Introduction to Logical Positivism*. New York: Philosophical Library, 1957.
An attempt to answer questions about religion, philosophy, and science in clear positivistic terms that any intelligent layman can understand.

BLACK, MAX. *Problems of Analysis*. Ithaca: Cornell U. Press, 1954.
A rather technical discussion of various problems connected with language and logic. See also Language and Philosophy by the same author.

BLANSHARD, BRAND. *Reason and Analysis*. La Salle: Open Court, 1962.
This volume of the Paul Carus Lectures discusses the rise of analytic philosophy, states its main contentions, and subjects it to keen criticism.

GELLNER, ERNEST. *Words and Things: A Critical Account of Linguistic Philosophy and a Study in Ideology*. London: Gollancz, 1959. (Introduction by Bertrand Russell.)
A vigorous attack on the linguistic analysts of the Oxford School who, the author thinks, are limiting the field of philosophy too drastically.

HENLE, PAUL (ed.). *Language, Thought and Culture*. Ann Arbor: U. of Michigan Press, 1958.
A collection of essays in which specialists seek to clarify the various approaches to language and to show its importance in a living culture.

JOAD, CYRIL E. M. *A Critique of Logical Positivism*. Chicago: U. of Chicago Press, 1950.
A critical examination of logical positivism as represented by Ayer's Language, Truth and Logic.

JØRGENSEN, JØRGEN. *The Development of Logical Empiricism*. Chicago: U. of Chicago Press, 1951. (International Encyclopedia of Unified Science, Vol. II, No. 9.)
A monograph on the Vienna Circle, logical positivism, and the expansion of logical empiricism.

KRAFT, VICTOR. *The Vienna Circle: The Origin of Neo-Positivism*. Trans. by Arthur Pap. New York: Philosophical Library, 1953.
Part I deals with the history of the Vienna Circle and Part II with its work and influence.

PAP, ARTHUR. *Semantics and Necessary Truth: An Inquiry into the Foundations of Analytic Philosophy.* New Haven: Yale U. Press, 1958.
A comprehensive text that attempts to "clarify the nature of analytic philosophy and the basic concepts of modern semantics." Part One is historical; Part Two deals with contemporary analytic philosophy.

PEARS, D. F. (ed.). *The Nature of Metaphysics.* London: Macmillan, 1957.
A brief book of essays on metaphysics and its relation to science, history, and ethics. Written from the approach of conceptual analysis as represented by the Oxford School.

PEI, MARIO. *Voices of Man: The Meaning and Function of Language.* New York: Harper & Row, 1962.
A small book that is concerned with the history and nature of language and the study of linguistics.

REICHENBACH, HANS. *The Rise of Scientific Philosophy.* Berkeley: U. of California Press, 1957.
The author attempts to show that philosophy has proceeded from speculation to science, and he hopes the new methods of logical analysis will lead us from error to truth.

TAYLOR, PAUL W. *Normative Discourse.* Englewood Cliffs: Prentice-Hall, 1961.
A discussion of the logic of evaluating and prescribing: Part One, Evaluating; Part Two, Prescribing; and Part Three, Normative Language.

URMSON, J. O. *Philosophical Analysis: Its Development Between the Two World Wars.* London: Oxford U. Press, 1956.
A brief book that discusses the progression from logical atomism and logical positivism to contemporary philosophy. The weaknesses and strengths of analysis are considered.

EXISTENTIALISM AND RELATED MOVEMENTS

We shall now consider existentialism, another movement that represents a revolt against the methods and outlooks of traditional Western philosophy. Within existentialism there are divergent interests and points of view. Existentialists include philosophers, theologians, writers, and artists, Protestants, Roman Catholics, and Jews, theists and atheists. They agree on a few central doctrines, or at least they are grouped together in opposing certain tendencies in the modern world. Though existentialism has not had a great influence on professional philosophers in the English-speaking world, it has had considerable influence on thinkers in continental Europe and Latin America; and through Sören Kierkegaard and others it has had a marked influence on contemporary theology.

Existentialism is an attitude and outlook that emphasizes human existence— that is, the distinctive qualities of individual persons—rather than man in the abstract or nature and the world in general. We shall describe the movement briefly and then consider some of the men who have contributed to its theological, philosophical, literary, and artistic expressions.

CHARACTERISTICS OF EXISTENTIALISM

A MOVEMENT OF PROTEST

Existentialism is a revolt against some features of traditional philosophy and modern society. It is in part a protest against the rationalism of the Greek, or classical, tradition in philosophy, especially the speculative world views of men like Plato and Hegel. In such "systems" the individual self or the thinker is lost in a supersensible world, in abstract universals, or in a universal ego. Existentialism is a protest in the name of individuality against the concepts of "reason" and "nature" that were so strongly emphasized during the eighteenth-century "Enlightenment." It has some points in common with German Romanticism, with its emphasis on the emotional, intuitive, and subjective rather than on the logical, intellectual, and objective. "The refusal to belong to any school of thought, the repudiation of the adequacy of any body of beliefs whatever, and especially of systems, and a marked dissatisfaction with traditional philosophy as superficial, academic, and remote from life—that is the heart of existentialism."[1]

Existentialism is also a revolt against the impersonal nature of the modern industrial or technological age, against scientism and positivism, and against the mass movements of our time. Industrial society tends, as the existentialists see it, to subordinate the individual to the machine: man is in danger of becoming a tool or an object. Positivism and scientism recognize only the external nature of man and interpret him as part of physical processes. Existentialism is also a protest against totalitarian movements, whether fascist, communist, or whatever, which tend to crush or submerge the individual in the collective or the mass. While existentialism, in its reaction to the main stream of traditional philosophy, certainly has tendencies in common with logical empiricism, it is clear that its outlook and mood are distinctly different, especially its attitude toward the modern spirit and the technological age.

A DIAGNOSIS OF MAN'S PREDICAMENT

Existentialism is a philosophy concerned with describing and diagnosing the human predicament. In this respect, it is a reemphasis of some older ways of thinking. Some of its supporters claim that it is not just ancient and modern, but actually timeless. "Existentialism as a universal element in all thinking is the attempt of man to describe his existence and its conflicts, the origin of these conflicts, and the anticipation of overcoming them. . . . Wherever man's predicament is described either theologically or philosophically, either poetically or artistically, there we have existentialist elements."[2]

Insofar as existentialism emphasizes the human situation and man's prospects in the world, it is found in Judaism, among the early Christians, and in the attempts at self-analysis and self-understanding of philosophers like Socrates. In this sense it is indeed ancient as well as modern. As a modern movement, existentialism gained prominence only in the twentieth century. During the nineteenth century, however, certain "lonely prophets"— Kierkegaard, Nietzsche, Dostoevsky, and others—were voicing their protests and registering their concern about the condition of man. During the last half century, the expression of concern over man's sense of estrangement

---

[1] *Existentialism from Dostoevsky to Sartre,* edited, with an introduction, prefaces, and new translations by Walter Kaufmann, p. 12. A Meridian Book, published by The World Publishing Company, Cleveland and New York. Copyright © 1956 by The World Publishing Company. By permission of the publisher.

[2] Paul Tillich, "Existentialist Aspects of Modern Art," in *Christianity and the Existentialists,* Carl Michalson (ed.) (New York: Scribner's, 1956), pp. 129, 130.

and meaninglessness has grown into a strong chorus. Man, it is asserted, does not feel at home in the world in which he must make his home.

A BELIEF IN THE PRIMACY OF EXISTENCE

Existentialism emphasizes the uniqueness and primacy of existence—the inner, immediate experience of self-awareness. The fundamental drive or urge is to exist and to be recognized as an individual. If man is so recognized, he may gain a sense of meaning and significance in life. The most meaningful point of reference for any person is his own immediate consciousness, which cannot be contained in systems or abstractions. Abstract thinking tends to be impersonal and to lead away from the concrete human being and the human situation. Reality or being is existence that is found in the "I" rather than the "it." Thus the center of thought and meaning is the existing *individual* thinker.

In his play *Caligula* Albert Camus has one of the characters say: "To lose one's life is a little thing and I shall have the courage to do so if it is necessary; but to see the meaning of this life dissipated, to see our reason for existing disappear, that is what is unbearable. One cannot live without meaning."

Existentialists make a clear-cut distinction between *existence* and *essence*. Let us consider the term *existence* first. It means the state of being actual, or occurring within space and time, or it refers to "something given here and now." It is used in the sense in which selves or human individuals are recognized to exist, or to live. For the existentialists, however, the verb *to exist* has a richer and more positive content than the verb *to live*. People sometimes say of one who lives a drab and meaningless life, "He does not live, he merely exists." The existentialists would turn the sentence around and say, "He does not exist, he merely lives." Existence for them means a full, vital, self-conscious, responsible, and growing life.

The term *essence,* in contrast with *existence,* is that which distinguishes a thing from other types of objects. It is that which makes a thing what it is, or that which all things called by the same name have in common. The essence is common to the many individuals, and we may speak meaningfully of an essence even though no instances of the thing actually exist at any given time. "We distinguish between *what* a thing is and *that* it is. What a thing is we call its essence, that it is, its existence. The thing I hold in my hand is by essence a pencil. And this pencil, as I believe on the evidence of my senses, exists."[3] Once a person has grasped the idea or concept of the essence of a thing he can think of it quite apart from its existence. For Plato and many classical thinkers, the concept of, say, "man" had more reality than the percept, or the individual human being John Doe (or any group of human

3 Helmut Kuhn, *Encounter with Nothingness* (Chicago: Regnery, 1949), p. 1.

beings); they thought that the participation in the idea, or form, or essence, "man-ness" is that which makes a person, any person, what he is.

Perhaps one can most easily characterise existentialism as a violent reaction against that view of man and his world which is enshrined in Plato's *Republic*. For Plato, "existence" is a paltry, second-rate manner of being; existent entities are real only in so far as they manifest a "form" or "essence." To see the world as it *really is,* according to Platonists, is to see it as an intelligible system of essences.[4]

Existentialists reject this Platonic view and assert that there is something which cannot be conceptualized: this is the personal act of existing. Personal existence has to be experienced or "lived through" to be actually known; it cannot be described adequately by propositions alone. Thus they insist on the primacy of the state of existence rather than the primacy of the supra-temporal and supraempirical essence. Jean-Paul Sartre and some others would say that the expression, "Existence precedes essence," is the very heart of the movement, but other existentialists would not be willing to put it quite this way.

AN EMPHASIS ON MAN'S SUBJECTIVE EXPERIENCE

Existentialism places a new emphasis on man's inner life and experience and thus on his immediate, subjective awareness. There is no knowledge, the existentialists say, apart from a knowing subject. Man's inner life, with its moods, anxieties, and decisions, becomes the center of attention. Existentialism opposes all forms of objectivity and impersonality insofar as they pertain to the life of man. Objectivity, as expressed in modern science and Western industrial society and by their philosophical and psychological representatives, has tended to make the person of secondary importance to things. Life in general and man in particular have often been interpreted objectively and impersonally, so that life in fact becomes hollow and meaningless. Existentialism, in contrast, stresses the importance of man's inner life and is not afraid of introspection. It raises anew the problems surrounding that which is unique—man's individuality and personality. It represents man's rebellion against all attempts to ignore or suppress the uniqueness of his subjective experience.

Truth, existentialists say, is revealed in the subjective experience of living. We experience the truth within us. The truth about the nature of man and human destiny is not something to be grasped and stated adequately in abstract concepts or in propositions. A purely rational approach is likely to deal with universal principles that absorb the person into some all-embracing

4 John Passmore, *A Hundred Years of Philosophy* (New York: Macmillan, 1957), p. 460. Used with the permission of The Macmillan Company.

unity or system. Since the existentialists stress the intimate, concrete aspects of man's experience, or that which is unique and personal, they are likely to turn to literary and other artistic forms of expression, through which man's feelings and moods may be more vividly portrayed.

A RECOGNITION OF FREEDOM AND RESPONSIBILITY

The emphasis on personal existence and subjectivity has led in turn to a new emphasis on man's freedom and personal responsibility. The various determinisms, whether hereditary and biological or environmental, do not tell the whole story. In existentialism interest is directed not so much to mankind in general, or to man's institutions and achievements, or to the impersonal world of nature, but to the individual person and his choices and decisions. Existentialism is an assertion of the significance of personal existence and decisions even in the face of interpretations of the world that appear to eliminate meaning and significance.

Freedom is not something to be proved or argued about; it is a reality to be experienced. Man has considerable freedom within his reach if he will but grasp it. Freedom is working out the demands of one's inner nature and expressing one's genuine or authentic self; it is facing choices, making decisions, and accepting responsibility for them.

AN EMPHASIS ON HUMAN WEAKNESS AND INSECURITY

While stressing the importance of man, existentialists also realistically face the facts of human weakness, insecurity, and limitations. They have been concerned with man's sense of anxiety, despair, dread, guilt, and loneliness, and with human finitude and death. Anxiety, the existentialists assert, arises as man comes to have a sense of the meaninglessness of his life. Anguish and melancholy lead to existential despair, and this "crisis" prepares man for the "leap" into authentic existence. This may come through "faith" and dependence on God, according to the theologians, or through "resolve" and an act of will, according to some others. Existentialism is thus an assertion of the significance of the self in the face of frustration and the impersonality of modern civilization.

SOME EXISTENTIALIST THINKERS

Apart from a few characteristic affirmations and a few common denials, there are widespread differences among the views of the people who have been influential in the development of existentialism. The statement has been made that there are as many existentialisms as there are existentialists. While no one classification is entirely satisfactory, we shall group the men we consider here under three headings: existentialists as theologians, existentialists as philosophers, and existentialists in literary and artistic movements.

EXISTENTIALISTS AS THEOLOGIANS

Sören Kierkegaard (1813–1855) Kierkegaard is usually considered the founder of modern existentialism. The writings of this Danish thinker furnished the stimulus for later members of the movement. Kierkegaard is a difficult man to interpret. He is not a systematic thinker, and he glories in paradoxes. His writings are repetitious, and he devotes much space to his own moods, anxieties, and "existential introspection." He was subject to melancholy and doubt and a sense of sin and guilt induced, in part, by his father's sense of guilt. We cannot here give the details of Kierkegaard's personal life, his deformity, his home life, the Lutheran orthodoxy under which he was reared, and his broken engagement, even though these undoubtedly were responsible to a great extent for his thinking.

For Kierkegaard the central issue in life is what it means to be a Christian, or to become a whole man. He is concerned not with "being" in general, but with human existence. He wants men to come to an understanding of the central factors of existence, their own immortal souls, their destiny, and the reality of God, the absolute sovereign. There are, Kierkegaard believes, two great enemies of Christianity. One is the Hegelian philosophy so prevalent in his day. Abstract speculation, he believes, whether in the Cartesian or the Hegelian form, depersonalizes man and leads to the impoverishment of life. Kierkegaard feels that this type of thinking tends to emphasize thought and minimize or disregard the thinker. He is especially scornful of all attempts to make Christianity "reasonable" or to come to its defense with intellectual arguments. He opposes those Protestants who interpret the Divine as immanent in the world of experience or God as expressing Himself through nature, human history, and the lives of men. Philosophy and religion, he feels, deal with totally different areas and do different things. Reason deals with what occurs in time alone, whereas Christianity is concerned with eternity.

The second enemy of Christianity is the conventional churchgoer, who imagines that he lives in a Christian community and thinks he is a Christian because he performs some "good works" and is a "good citizen." The unreflective or nominal church member may be a good functionary, but he has a depersonalized religion, and he may not know what it really means to *become* a Christian. Kierkegaard is highly critical of much in the Christianity or "Churchianity" of his day, especially the "unorthodox" Christians, with their evolutionary optimism, belief in human progress, confidence in reason, and faith in the goodness of man. He opposes the activism and the social Christianity which seem to imply that one can redeem men by making changes in the social order.

According to Kierkegaard, there is an "unbridgeable gulf" between God and the world, the Creator and the creature, Supernature and nature. God stands above all social and ethical standards. How is man to overcome this gap or bridge this seemingly rigid dualism? To be suspended in doubt is to experience existential anguish. "Every man who has not tasted the bitterness of despair has missed the significance of life, however beautiful and joyous his life might be."5 When man is in anguish he must abandon reason and embrace faith. In the agonized "leap of faith," man embraces the absurd and the paradoxical. "Christianity takes a prodigious giant-stride . . . a stride into the absurd—there Christianity begins . . . how extraordinarily stupid it is to defend Christianity. . . ."6 To Kierkegaard, faith is everything.7 There must be either wholehearted obedience to God or open rebellion. Man is either for or against Christ, for or against Truth; Christianity is absolutely true or absolutely false. Kierkegaard says, "What our age lacks, however, is not reflection but passion." Factual knowledge simply cannot overcome a defect of motive and will. To be a philosopher is rightly to understand oneself as a creature of God, the absolute sovereign.

In a number of works Kierkegaard describes three "stages on life's road." The first is the aesthetic stage, which is the life of the natural man, who lives in sensuous enjoyment. This is the life of immediacy, in which the senses and emotions dominate the scene, and moral and religious demands are brushed aside. This stage by itself is the "path of perdition." The second is the ethical stage, where man arrives at the level of the "universal human." Only on this level can man retain aesthetic beauty, and only the ethical life can tie the individual to the rational and social order. At this point he begins to have some awareness of his vocation as a human being. At the third and highest stage, the religious, the religious man discovers the meaning of existence and sees himself as an individual who stands alone before God. Not only does man's relation to God go beyond the ethical stage, but at times man may rise above ethics and do what appears to be "immoral." This is "the teleological suspension of the ethical," in response to what is believed to be the will of God.

One student of existentialism says:

> Kierkegaard rejects belief in the eternal verities, as well as Plato's trust in reason as a kind of second sight. Ethics is for him not a matter of seeing the good but of making a decision. The crucial difference between an informed and unin-

5 Sören Kierkegaard, *Either-Or*, trans. David F. Swenson and Lillian Marvin Swenson (Princeton: Princeton U. Press, 1946), II, p. 175.

6 Sören Kierkegaard, *The Sickness Unto Death*, trans. Walter Lowrie (New York: Doubleday, 1954), pp. 217, 218. (Anchor Book.)

7 Sören Kierkegaard, *Fear and Trembling*, trans. Walter Lowrie (New York: Doubleday, 1954), pp. 41, 42. (Anchor Book.)

formed, a reasoned and un-reasoned, a responsible and irresponsible decision, escapes Kierkegaard. Yet he is unquestionably right that reason cannot absolve us from the need for decisions, and he sees that Greeks and Christians and modern philosophy have tried to ignore this all-important fact.[8]

Among the Protestants, Kierkegaard has been a source of inspiration for men like Karl Barth and Emil Brunner, proponents of the "crisis theology," and neoorthodox groups in Europe and America. The French Roman Catholic philosopher and "lay theologian" Gabriel Marcel is included among the existentialists, though he dislikes labels. He stresses many of the same convictions, but he was not directly influenced by Kierkegaard. The outstanding Jewish thinker Martin Buber, who also rejects the existentialist label, is nevertheless frequently included in the movement. While some thinkers do not want to be classified as existentialists because they are opposed to systems and dislike being typed, there are important trends and emphases in their thinking that make it reasonable to group them with the existentialists.

EXISTENTIAL PHILOSOPHERS

Friedrich Nietzsche (1844–1900)   Whether Nietzsche is an existentialist or not is a question about which men may differ, but in any event he has exerted a strong influence on the movement. "In the story of existentialism, Nietzsche occupies a central place: Jaspers, Heidegger, and Sartre are unthinkable without him. . . . Existentialism without Nietzsche would be almost like Thomism without Aristotle; but to call Nietzsche an existentialist is a little like calling Aristotle a Thomist."[9]

Nietzsche and Kierkegaard agree and disagree on many points. Both men lived unhappy and lonely lives, and their experiences undoubtedly colored their views of man and the world. Both opposed the rationalistic thought of the nineteenth century and concerned themselves passionately with the human predicament. They saw in each man an existential being whose life cannot be described in the conventional ways. They found much that was wrong with human nature, and they opposed what they considered the shallowness of middle-class morality. On the other hand, the points of sharp contrast stand out clearly. Whereas Kierkegaard's main problem was how to become a Christian, Nietzsche attacked Christianity and said, "God is dead." Nietzsche opposed Christianity as the enemy of reason, and his problem was how to live as an atheist. His emphasis was on life, instinct, and power, which, he felt, were being perverted by a culture that catered to misfits. He recognized the "Will to Power" as the basic human motive. He wanted to make way for the "higher man," who would embody the higher values

---

[8] Kaufmann, *Existentialism from Dostoevsky to Sartre*, p. 17.
[9] *Ibid.*, pp. 21, 22.

of the Lords of the Earth (supermen he foresaw), not the virtues of mediocrity that he thought were exhibited in Christianity, democracy, and socialism.

We need, Nietzsche says, a "transvaluation of all values." Man does not *discover* his values; he *creates* them and projects them on the world. The mind constructs its world by giving a meaningless mass of phenomena its shape and order. There is no real and permanent world but only many private "human perspectives." The will to dominate is a fundamental principle in nature, and it will produce a race of supermen. The superman who is "beyond good and evil" is to be the creator of the new values for man. Christianity, Nietzsche felt, was responsible for the agony of Western civilization, because it had transferred the highest values of mankind from this world to the next.

Nietzsche's main contribution was to confront men with the implications of existence in a world in which there were no secure values and goals. This nihilistic outlook has been reflected in much literature and art that express the sense of hopelessness and meaninglessness of today's world. Yet Nietzsche's works have some religious overtones, as evidenced in the desire to escape human finiteness and frustration and in the yearning for a new wholeness. He is one of many who see the dangers in a technical and industrial age that has discarded the guidance of human values and wisdom. Yet his own views introduce other dangers equally great.

A Note on Husserl and Heidegger   Space does not permit us to consider all the existential philosophers and to trace the development of their ideas. However, before making the transition from Nietzsche to Karl Jaspers and Gabriel Marcel, we shall discuss briefly Edmund Husserl (1859–1938) and Martin Heidegger (1889–   ). A group of philosophers, known as the phenomenologists, under the leadership of Husserl, held that we must be concerned with phenomena or what we perceive and also with the general patterns of consciousness and experience. The phenomenologists start with the human subject and his consciousness and endeavor to get back to a "pure consciousness" after man's everyday experiences and images have been stripped away. When this has been done there remains, they say, certain essential features or an "intuition of essences" indicating that something exists quite apart from and prior to experience. Members of this group claim that philosophy is the science of essences and that this phenomenological method is basic and prior to all other methods of investigating the nature of human experience. Such intuition delves more deeply into the world of existence than does scientific method or syllogistic reasoning.

Martin Heidegger, a student of Husserl, used the method of phenomenology to study the predicament of human existence.[10] His central questions have to do with man's life (human being), with his existence in

---

10 Heidegger has exerted considerable influence on existentialism, though he refuses to acknowledge any connection with the movement. He uses a difficult terminology and is often obscure.

the world of nature (concrete being), and with ultimate reality (Being as such).

The main question for Heidegger is "What does it mean to say 'I am'?" Man is a creature brought into the world without his consent. He needs to acknowledge his finiteness. He came out of the abyss, and before him lies the abyss of death. Confronted with nothingness, he is anxious, but this anxiety enables him to become aware of his existence. As man studies himself, questions of temporality, fear and dread, conscience and guilt, nothingness and death, and the like come to the fore.

Heidegger is especially critical of the men of our time who live superficially and who emphasize things, quantity, and personal power. Modern man is rootless and empty because he has lost his sense of relationship to Being in its fullness. Concrete being must be transcended so that man is open to the totality of Being as such. Only through the discovery of the dynamic nature of existence can man be saved from the chaos and frustration that threaten him. A man may (and most men do) live an unauthentic existence as a member of a collective absorbed only in the things and details of everyday affairs. But man may, if he so chooses, live an authentic human existence; he fixes his gaze on the truth as he is able to discover it, lives his life in the light of death, and views his life in a new perspective. This is heroic existence, regardless of man's final destiny. In this case a man possesses things but is not possessed by them.

Karl Jaspers (1883–   )[11] Jaspers is interested in the good life and in the self that makes decisions. For him philosophy is a guide to reasonable living; it can never be a finished system. It is a perpetual quest in which living, feeling, deciding, acting, and risking cannot be ignored. Thus Jaspers parts company with the trends in Anglo-American philosophy that stress rigorous analysis, logic, and objective science as the ways to understanding and truth. Man is always more than what he thinks he knows. In striving for meaning or orientation in the world, we can go to one extreme by stressing only the objective sciences, and arrive at positivism. We can take the opposite approach by emphasizing subject or spirit and accept some form of idealism. Jaspers thinks that matter, life, self, and mind are qualitatively different from each other and that they cannot be reduced to any common term or terms. In addition to the way of objective science and the way of metaphysics, there is the approach through an examination of personal existence. Here there are at least three areas to consider: man's immediate consciousness or selfhood, man's communication with his fellows in social life, and the various historical structures of community life—morals, law, the family,

[11] The large volume in The Library of Living Philosophers, *The Philosophy of Karl Jaspers,* edited by Paul Arthur Schilpp (New York: Tudor, 1957), gives Jaspers' autobiography, a bibliography of his writings, a glossary of terms used, and twenty-four descriptive and critical essays.

the state, and the like. While Jaspers quotes Nietzsche frequently, he is really closer to Kierkegaard. He refuses, however, to go along with either Nietzsche's anti-Christianity or Kierkegaard's "leap of faith" into Christianity.

In man, Jaspers says, we find a historically conditioned empirical self. It is conditioned by the physical and physiological background and cultural environment. This is the self studied by sciences like psychology; but there is a gap between the findings of objective psychology and the intimate human experience of love and hate, joy and tragedy, aspiration and anxiety. There is also a transcendent or authentic self, which the sciences cannot discover. As persons we have a temporal existence, yet we are not merely temporal. We live in time, yet touch existential eternity. This authentic self gives life its meaning. There are many "limiting situations," such as the restraining conditions of the environment, suffering, and death. We can be guided in part, however, by love, faith, and insight. This breaking through of the authentic self into the historical and empirical process makes choice and freedom possible. We exist in the midst of causal necessity, which is a valid postulate for science, but Being itself is not exhausted by being-subject-to-law.

Subjectivity and objectivity are both genuine aspects of reality. Subjectivity is not a passing phase or a by-product of objectivity. There is in man the breath of the transcendent, and he must strive, in spite of all difficulties, to maintain his deeper insights and his freedom. Man in nature is more than nature. Yet only through life in society and through communication can individual existence be developed and fulfilled. We cannot say just what the nature of the world is or understand Being with any completeness. But with the aid of intelligence we can keep up the quest for understanding and endure the struggle patiently.

Gabriel Marcel (1889–) Marcel is a French philosopher who has been strongly influenced by the intuitionism of Henri Bergson and the idealism of Josiah Royce. However, Marcel's existentialism grew out of his personal experience and thinking and developed independently. He tells us that he read Kierkegaard and other existentialist writers after his thinking had taken fairly definite form. While Marcel is a man of deep religious convictions, with liberal leanings, his approach is philosophical in outlook and emphasis. His life-long interests include philosophy, music, and playwriting. His plays deal with such themes as loneliness, disappointment in love, and misunderstanding.

The proper theme of philosophy, according to Marcel, is the human predicament. He is concerned with the answers to two big questions: "Who am I?" and "What is Being?" While showing his distrust of metaphysical *systems* which seem to imply that thinking has arrived at some stopping place, he does not avoid metaphysical questions. His ideas are often presented in informal and unsystematic ways—in his diaries, journals, and plays. His two-volume work *The Mystery of Being* is his most systematic statement. Marcel sees philosophy as a search moved by "an unusual sense of inner urgent need," and a "deep sense of inner disquiet." "Nothing is less patentable than philosophy." Philosophy does not attempt to view things in a purely detached objective manner, since the philosopher must be in continuous living contact with the reality in the midst of which he lives.

Marcel is opposed to all systems of thought that deprive man of his wholeness and that interpret him monolithically. He says, "The dynamic element in my philosophy, taken as a whole, can be seen as an obstinate and untiring battle against the spirit of abstraction."[12] Thus Marcel opposes a rationalism that elevates reason above life and experience, and an empiricism that goes to the opposite extreme and interprets man too exclusively as a creature of sense perceptions. He also opposes philosophies such as positivism and idealism, which identify being with only one of its modes. Marcel speaks of our world as "a broken world" that has lost its real unity and is at war with itself. He is critical of many things that go along with a mass society and tend to depersonalize man and discredit privacy, brotherhood, and creativity. "The more techniques advance, the more reflection is thrust into the background."

Two distinctions made by Marcel need to be kept in mind if we are to understand the trend of his thinking. The first distinction is that between "first reflection" and "second reflection." The first type arises from our experiences of seeing and having. It is the reflection of the "man in the street," as well as of technical and scientific man. It separates subject and object and views things from the outside, as objects of scientific study. It is the spectator view of the world. The other type of reflection transcends science, technology, and objective knowledge. It is the effort of human thought to reach beyond itself into the realm of Being. This is philosophical reflection, which has become more completely aware, so that it is able to bear witness to the presence of Being. Man is capable of nonsensuous intuition or understanding. Knowledge can be gained through philosophical reflection, including metaphysics, as well as through the objective methods of the many special sciences.

A second distinction is that between "having" and "being." Having implies a relationship between me and some object outside or independent of me. It may indicate mere possession or refer to some other internal or external relationship, as when we say, "I have a body." Being, on the other hand, involves that which I *am* and not just that which I *have*. It reaches into the depths of my nature and involves participation and some degree of tran-

---

12 Gabriel Marcel, *Man Against Mass Society*, trans. G. S. Fraser (New York: Regnery, 1952), p. 1.

scendence of the merely physical level of existence. A living person, however, cannot abolish all "having" from his life, and this would not be desirable in any event. Danger arises when man unduly emphasizes the "having" area of his experience. To make the change of emphasis from "having" to "being," one needs to avoid the fixed attitude that exclusively attends either to the self or to the object.

Central concepts in Marcel's philosophy are those of participation, transcendence, and being. The reflective man seeks to overcome the broken world and rise from the insignificant to the level of the significant. He needs to start from the realization that he is in a concrete situation "tied to a body," immersed in matter and in the historical process. My body, he says, is not external to me; I am not independent of it; yet I am more than a mere body. Through this body I function in the world and am in continuous sensuous (feeling) contact with the universe around me. Marcel uses the term *incarnation* to symbolize man's relation to the world. I am incarnate or embodied in my body, and the world of nature is thus expressed in me. Man is a part of objective nature, but he is more than a "thing"; he is aware and can evaluate his life and its activities.

Marcel wishes to avoid many of the traditional dualisms, including those held by Plato and Descartes. The traditional distinction between subject and object is too sharp. Reality is both transubjective and transobjective. Man the participant stands in contrast with man the spectator. The latter remains largely passive and is not "open to the situation." The participant allows himself to be drawn into that which he encounters, so that the oppositions are overcome. Both feeling and contemplation are modes of participation. At one extreme we are in contact and interaction with the objective world of things; at the other extreme objectivity has been transcended and we participate through prayer, meditation, or contemplation as we encounter an authentic and transcendent reality. Communion involves interpenetration without negation of one's own existence. Participation and transcendence at different levels involve the world of being, an encounter and exchange with the being of others, and the richness of the Absolute Thou or God. There is a reciprocal relation that involves the striving self and the totality to which it is related. A finite and concrete self may be in contact with a living, personal God. To refuse God is to refuse to be.

Marcel speaks of the "mystery" of being where the term *mystery* is used in contrast with the term *problem*. *Problem* is used where the person is uninvolved personally and looks at the world objectively. *Mystery* is used where there is "depth, involvement, and relationship" between the subject, or self, and that which has no stopping point or final answer. Mystery embraces all things in the world, but the world is here viewed from a comprehensive, "metaproblematic" approach. Metaphysics combines immediacy of experience, reflection, and the quest for mystery. It does not hesitate to be concerned with such problems as love, death, wickedness, and fidelity, which have no neat conclusions. Man is not able to conceptualize Being or God in any adequate fashion. Furthermore, if a man experiences the presence of God, there is no need for formal proofs or conceptualizing.

True freedom, according to Marcel, is achieved when the self is conscious of the many rich possibilities of insight and development that are open to it. Man is truly free only when he opens himself to hope, fidelity, and love and when he understands that "freedom points beyond itself ... to a transcendent reality." Love and intelligence are related to freedom, and they are the most concrete as well as the most creative things in the world.

EXISTENTIALISM IN LITERATURE AND ART

The spirit of revolt, the sense of the human predicament, and the emphasis on the inner experience of the individual have been expressed in many literary and artistic forms: in the novels and plays of Kafka, Sartre, and Camus; in the poetry of Eliot and Auden; in the paintings of Cezanne, Van Gogh, Picasso, Chagall, and de Chirico.

Whereas nature can be systematized and objectified, man's life must be experienced to be understood. Thus the emphasis in existentialism on confessions and memoirs, personal diaries and journals, autobiographies, novels, and drama. Many sensitive men have turned to these literary and artistic forms to symbolize what they experience in the depths of their lives.

The Philosophy of Life of Jean-Paul Sartre (1905–　　) Sartre's philosophy of life is an example of an outlook that is fairly widespread among certain writers and artists. Sartre's philosophy is reflected in his plays and other writings, as well as in his more philosophical works. Sartre, one of the leaders of existentialism in mid-twentieth-century France, started as a free-lance writer, taught philosophy for five years, and took part in World War II and the French Resistance. While he is most widely known for his novels, plays, and essays, his main philosophical work, *Being and Nothingness,*[13] brought him some recognition as a philosopher. He borrows much from Husserl and Heidegger and somewhat less from Hegel, Nietzsche, and others. In a short and more popular work, *Existentialism Is a Humanism,* Sartre says that "existentialism, in our sense of the word, is a doctrine that does render human life possible; a doctrine, also, which affirms that every truth and every action imply both an environment and a human subjectivity."[14] He sets forth a "phenomenological ontology" stressing human existence as the one thing we really know. Consciousness is aware of a world beyond itself which is different from or which stands over against man, but

13 New York: Philosophical Library, 1956.
14 Quoted in Kaufmann, *Existentialism from Dostoevsky to Sartre,* p. 288.

Sartre is not primarily concerned with this area. He is convinced that there is no hidden "essence" back of the things we experience. For Sartre, though not for all the existentialists, "existence precedes essence."

Man is not ready-made at the beginning. He has to make himself and to choose the conditions under which he is to live. Thus "there is no human nature, because there is no God to have a conception of it. Man simply is. Not that he is simply what he conceives himself to be, but he is what he wills, and as he conceives himself after already existing—as he wills to be after that leap towards existence."[15] Sartre is not willing to allow that man has any external support. Man must rely on his own resources; there is no meaning or purpose apart from that which he in his freedom creates. Human existence is the result of chance or accident, and there is no use trying to get around this fact, Sartre holds, by positing a God or a supreme intelligence. Sartre follows Nietzsche in denying the existence of God and in elaborating on the implications of this view.

For Sartre, there are no values external to man. Values are created by man and have no objective or permanent basis. Man has freedom to create himself and his values as he wills and acts. In this sense "everything is permissible" and man is really "beyond good and evil." Man's situation may seem meaningless, absurd, and tragic, but he can still live by the rules of integrity, nobility, and valor, and he can create a human community. Since man's destiny is within himself, his hope is in choosing and acting so that he may live. Sartre is willing to be called a realist but not a materialist, since this would imply an abandonment of man in favor of the nature outside of man.

At some points Sartre dwells on the tragic nature of life. Man in his aloneness experiences dread and anguish, and he fears the nothingness and death that are before him. Life is dominated by hate and strife. The "other" is either the stranger who does not care or the enemy who wishes to possess or dominate. Some people attempt to get rid of this human burden by shifting responsibility to the determining factors of heredity and environment, to the will of a superior power, or to the mass or collective in which a sense of personal responsibility is lost. These ways of escape are doomed to failure. While man experiences himself as fragmentary and discordant, he is of necessity free and therefore responsible for his life and decisions. This freedom, Sartre thinks, gives man dignity and saves him from being a mere object.

In speaking about the "paradox of freedom" Sartre says: "Human-reality everywhere encounters resistance and obstacles which it has not created, but these resistances and obstacles have meaning only in and through the free choice which human-reality is." Again, he says:

The essential consequence of our earlier remarks is that man being condemned

15 *Ibid.,* pp. 290–291.

to be free carries the weight of the whole world on his shoulders; he is responsible for the world and for himself as a way of being. . . . Furthermore this absolute responsibility is not resignation; it is simply the logical requirement of the consequences of our freedom. . . . Thus there are no accidents in a life; a community event which suddenly bursts forth and involves me in it does not come from the outside. If I am mobilized in a war, this war is my war; it is in my image and I deserve it. I deserve it first because I could always get out of it by suicide or by desertion; these ultimate possibilities are those which must always be present for us when there is a question of envisaging a situation. For lack of getting out of it, I have chosen it.[16]

The goal of human striving is a more ideal self—a heightened consciousness and existence that may come to free and responsible men. Yet Sartre acknowledges that this is an endless quest. While freedom appears genuine for a time, in the last analysis freedom is deceptive and the quest for it is futile; but even in failure man can retain his integrity.

For Sartre the individual stands as a tragic and lonely specimen of humanity. Man must look to himself, since there is no God and no purpose or meaning in the universe. Love is nonexistent or at best has no enduring basis, and freedom is illusory. Life is dominated by strife, and man experiences dread and anguish. Marcel, on the other hand, believes that nihilistic thinking tends to validate its own assumption by reducing the person to a mere thing. He thinks that man cannot become and remain free unless he is linked to that which transcends him. Hope and fidelity can lead a man to have sustaining contact and communion with others and with a living, personal God. To reject these contacts, Marcel says, is to refuse to be.

EVALUATION OF EXISTENTIALISM

Even from the few "existentialists" we have considered, it is evident that *existentialism* is a term used to describe widely differing viewpoints, moods, and attitudes. Yet there are some common emphases, and all existentialists are concerned with the human predicament. They deal in one way or another with the feelings of estrangement and alienation, and the separation of man from his deeper self, from his fellows, and from nature and the world, a separation many people experience in modern life. Existentialists call attention to the questions: What is man? What is the meaning of existence? What is man's ultimate destiny? How can man achieve "wholeness" in our world? They want men to think about what is involved in being a person.

The existentialists all protest against the traditional emphases in philosophy. They feel that most philosophers, in dealing with speculative questions and the formulation of systems, have overlooked the vital problems of human

---

16 *Being and Nothingness*, pp. 489, 553, 554.

existence. Consequently, philosophical thought has been divorced from practical affairs. The existentialists are equally dissatisfied with the linguistic analysis and the logical positivism of more recent years. They feel that these movements, in their effort to avoid what they regard as pseudoproblems, have themselves become enmeshed in pseudoproblems of their own making.

We can commend the existentialists for bringing certain contemporary problems of human experience and existence forcefully to our attention and for being sensitive to the discrepancy between thought and action. The intellectuals of our time all too frequently have been satisfied to watch and describe what they should have shaped and guided. The existentialists are justified in asking the intellectuals to take a stand when life and death issues are in the balance. We must recognize the need for decision and action, as well as for contemplation and analysis.

As we have pointed out, existentialism is a movement of protest and rebellion. It is a reaction against the philosophical solutions proposed by Hegel, Marx and Engels, and modern scientists. The existentialists feel that these proposed solutions are ineffective in meeting the problems of modern man. We have also noted that the positivistic and linguistic emphases and the masses of descriptive knowledge of the sciences often leave men's lives empty. Man's feeling of estrangement has increased during the last hundred years. The Industrial Revolution, the technology that has produced great cities, the collectivist trends and mass movements, the fragmentation and specialization of knowledge and life, all have tended toward the depersonalization of man. "Because the very existence of man on this earth is menaced, because the annihilation of man, his dehumanization and the destruction of his humanity and of all moral values is a real danger, therefore the meaning of human existence becomes our problem."[17]

In rejecting a false and extreme objectivity that tends to deny the distinctive qualities of the human, existentialism seems to have gone to the opposite extreme and rejected all objectivity. Thus existentialists have minimized the importance of science, nature, the external world, reason, and the many valid insights of other kinds of philosophy. If reason alone cannot solve the central problems of existence, is there any assurance that passion alone can do so? As a reaction to those who ignore the subject, existentialists tend to ignore the object. Furthermore, their critics claim that the existentialists are giving an inadequate description of even the human experience that is their prime concern. In addition to studying experience itself, men need to ask *what* it is that we experience, and hence to study the outside world.

The critics also ask how, if human reason is devalued or discredited and there are no objective standards of truth and goodness to which men may

17 F. H. Heinemann, *Existentialism and the Modern Predicament* (London: Adam & Charles Black, 1953), p. 178.

appeal, we can settle disputes except by force? Is it, some ask, mere coincidence that existentialism took root and flourished in Germany after its defeat in World War I, and then in France after its collapse in World War II? Isn't existentialism, it is asked, a retreat from reason into the fascinating world of metaphor where objective standards do not apply? In this sense it is unrelated to the historical mainstream of recent technical philosophy. This may be one reason why it has gained more support from artists, writers, and theologians than from philosophers and scientists.

Is existentialism in part the product of a particular historical epoch and of conditions that have led a disillusioned intellectual elite to center its attention on the meaningless and absurd elements in modern life? Existentialism may be the result of the swing of the pendulum away from the extremely optimistic rationalism that was the product of a different set of conditions a half century or more ago. To emphasize any one mood or set of feelings as the clue to the understanding of life and the world in their entirety is dangerous. To stress anxiety and dread, which, unlike fear, are not directed toward specific objects, is likely to lead to a sense of absurdity and nothingness. Nevertheless, existentialism has called our attention to serious frustrations and disorders in modern life and to the fact that not only modern civilization but also human existence itself is in a precarious condition.

QUESTIONS AND PROJECTS

1. Review Questions

(1) What is existentialism?

(2) Who are some of the leading existentialists?

(3) How do you explain the fact that existentialism has taken so many different forms among such diverse groups?

(4) What are the things against which nearly all of the existentialists have been protesting?

(5) Discuss the meaning of "the human predicament," "the primacy of existence," "the leap of faith," and "the truth we experience."

(6) Explain and give examples that clarify the distinction between *existence* and *essence* as used in existentialism.

(7) What is distinctive about the existentialist view of man? Indicate some major differences among existentialists concerning the nature of man.

(8) Outline the beliefs of the following men by indicating their central positive convictions and what they rejected or opposed: (a) Kierkegaard, (b) Nietzsche, (c) Jaspers, (d) Marcel, and (e) Sartre.

(9) Evaluate existentialism, and indicate what you consider its strong and its weak points.

2. Which existentialist thinker is the most sound in your judgment? Why?

3. Evaluate Kierkegaard's philosophy in the light of the following questions: What are the roles of reason, emotion, and authority in life? Should one exercise his critical faculties regarding the nature and direction of faith and decision? Are Kierkegaard's dualisms valid or distorting? Are his views on religion adequate?

4. In what respects are the following people existentialists? (a) Nicholas Berdyaev, (b) Martin Buber, (c) Fyodor Dostoevsky, (d) José Ortega y Gasset, and (e) Miguel de Unamuno.

5. Compare existentialism with logical empiricism as revolts against traditional philosophy.

6. How has existentialism been expressed in art? See Paul Tillich, "Existentialist Aspects of Modern Art," in *Christianity and the Existentialists,* Carl Michalson (ed.) (New York: Scribner's, 1956).

7. In 1958 Albert Camus, a French author, received the Nobel Prize for his literàry achievements. His main philosophical work is *The Myth of Sisyphus* (New York: Knopf, 1955). Report on Camus' philosophy of life.

8. What is the relation between Christianity and existentialism? Judaism and existentialism? Some writers see a close relationship; others have said that, while there is "no Christian existentialism," some Christians are also existentialists. The following books may help you: Arthur C. Cochrane, *The Existentialists and God* (Philadelphia: Westminster, 1956); George W. Davis, *Existentialism and Theology* (New York: Philosophical Library, 1957); John A. Gates, *The Life and Thought of Kierkegaard, for Everyman* (Philadelphia: Westminster, 1960); Will Herberg (ed.), *Four Existentialist Theologians* (Garden City: Doubleday, 1960) (Anchor Book); John MacQuarrie, *An Existentialist Theology* (London: SCM, 1955); Carl Michalson (ed.), *Christianity and the Existentialists* (New York: Scribner's, 1956); D. E. Roberts, *Existentialism and Religious Beliefs* (New York: Oxford U. Press, 1957); Roger L. Shinn, *The Existentialist Posture* (New York: Association Press, 1959) (Reflection Book); J. M. Spier, *Christianity and Existentialism* (Philadelphia: Presbyterian & Reformed Publishing, 1953).

9. Review one of the following books: K. Guru Dutt, *Existentialism and Indian Thought* (New York: Philosophical Library, 1960); Norman N. Greene, *Jean-Paul Sartre: the Existentialist Ethic* (Ann Arbor: U. of Michigan Press, 1960); Marjorie Grene, *Dreadful Freedom: A Critique of Existentialism* (Chicago: U. of Chicago Press, 1948); Karl Jaspers, *Man in the Modern World* (New York: Doubleday, 1960) (Anchor Book); George F. Kneller, *Existentialism and Education* (New York: Philosophical Library, 1958); Gabriel Marcel, *Man Against Mass Society* (Chicago: Regnery, 1952) (Gateway ed., 1962); Frederick Patka (ed.), *Existentialist Thinkers and Thought* (New York: Philosophical Library, 1962); Calvin O. Schrag, *Existence and Freedom*(Evanston: Northwestern U. Press, 1961).

SUGGESTED READINGS

BARRETT, WILLIAM. *Irrational Man: A Study in Existentialist Philosophy.* New York: Doubleday, 1958. (Anchor Book, 1962.)
 An account of existentialism written for the layman. The author gives reasons for the development of the movement and sets forth the ideas of a few of its leaders.

BLACKHAM, H. J. *Six Existentialist Thinkers.* London: Routledge & Kegan Paul, 1952. (Also Harper Torchbook ed.)
 An exposition of the views of Kierkegaard, Nietzsche, Jaspers, Marcel, Heidegger, and Sartre.

COLLINS, JAMES D. *The Existentialists: A Critical Study.* Chicago: Regnery, 1952.
 An introduction to existentialist thought and a critical evaluation from the point of view of philosophical realism and theism.

GRIMSLEY, RONALD. *Existentialist Thought.* Cardiff: U. of Wales Press, 1955.
 An exposition of the philosophy of a number of existentialists: Kierkegaard, Heidegger, Sartre, Jaspers, and Marcel. Includes a brief introduction and a postscript.

HEIDEGGER, MARTIN. *Existence and Being.* Chicago: Regnery, 1949. (Introduction by Werner Brock.)
 A long introduction and review of Heidegger's Being and Time, followed by four essays from Heidegger.

HEINEMANN, F. H. *Existentialism and the Modern Predicament.* New York: Harper, 1958. (Torchbook ed.)
 A readable account of existentialism, its various divisions and its leaders, and some critical evaluation.

JASPERS, KARL. *The Philosophy of Karl Jaspers.* Ed. by Paul A. Schilpp. New York: Tudor, 1957. (The Library of Living Philosophers.)
 A large volume that includes Jaspers' autobiography, a bibliography of his writings, a glossary of terms, and twenty-four descriptive and critical essays.

KAUFMANN, WALTER (ed.). *Existentialism from Dostoevsky to Sartre.* New York: Meridian, 1956.
 An introduction by the editor, followed by selections from the writings of nine men who have given some support to existentialist thinking.

KIERKEGAARD, SÖREN. *Fear and Trembling* and *The Sickness Unto Death.* Trans. by Walter Lowrie. New York: Doubleday, 1954. (Anchor Book.)
 These are two of Kierkegaard's best-known books. See also his Concluding Unscientific Postscript *and* Either/Or.

MARCEL, GABRIEL. *The Mystery of Being.* Trans. by G. S. Fraser. London: Harvill, 1950. (Vol. I, Reflection and Mystery; Vol. II, Faith and Reality.)
 These are difficult for beginners. Other works by Marcel include Metaphysical Journal, The Philosophy of Existentialism, *and a more popular work,* Man Against Mass Society.

MAY, ROLLO (ed.). *Existential Psychology*. New York: Random House, 1961.
A small paperbound volume in which the editor and Gordon Allport, Herman Feifel, Abraham Maslow, and Carl Rogers discuss the outlook of existential psychology.

MICHALSON, CARL (ed.). *Christianity and the Existentialists*. New York: Scribner's, 1956.
This work includes studies of Kierkegaard, Unamuno, Berdyaev, Marcel, and Heidegger.

OLSON, ROBERT G. *An Introduction to Existentialism*. New York: Dover, 1962.
This is a "topical analysis of major existentialist themes," including The Human Condition, Freedom, Authenticity, and the like.

REINHARDT, KURT F. *The Existentialist Revolt: The Main Themes and Phases of Existentialism*. 2nd ed.; New York: Ungar, 1960.
A critical evaluation of the philosophy of Kierkegaard, Nietzsche, Heidegger, Jaspers, Sartre, and Marcel.

SARTRE, JEAN-PAUL. *Being and Nothingness: An Essay on Phenomenological Ontology*. Trans. by Hazel E. Barnes. New York: Philosophical Library, 1956.
A long book which, though not easy reading, gives Sartre's philosophical outlook. His smaller book, Existentialism is a Humanism, is printed in Kaufmann's book listed above.

THÉVENAZ, PIERRE. *What is Phenomenology?* Ed. by James M. Edie. Trans. by James M. Edie, Charles Courtney, and Paul Brockelman. Chicago: Quadrangle, 1962. (Preface by John Wild.)
A small book that makes available the essays of a French-Swiss phenomenologist who presents phenomenology as a movement that merits attention.

TILLICH, PAUL. "Existential Philosophy," *Journal of the History of Ideas*, 5 (January, 1944):44–70.
An excellent presentation of the history, methodology, leaders, and central beliefs of the existentialists, and an evaluation of the movement.

WILD, JOHN. *The Challenge of Existentialism*. Bloomington: Indiana U. Press, 1955.
Lectures that discuss existentialism and evaluate it in the light of the author's realism.

EIGHTEEN

AGREEMENTS AND DISAGREEMENTS

We have examined briefly seven types of Occidental philosophy: materialism, humanistic naturalism, idealism, realism, pragmatism (or instrumentalism), logical empiricism, and existentialism. (Within these types there are, as we have seen, subdivisions.) In this chapter we shall consider some of the basic points of agreement and disagreement among these positions.

Men conduct their lives, consciously or not, in line with their conceptions of life and the world, and their scheme of values. Men cannot live without a philosophy of some kind. Human thought and interest are likely to move, broadly speaking, either toward specialization and a knowledge of the particular or toward generalization and integration. Today, in a practical age, specialization in all branches of inquiry is in vogue. While specialization, the division of labor, and departmentalization have brought great gains without which our type of civilization would be impossible, they also have led men to develop "blind spots" and to see life as compartmentalized or fragmented. However, it is not mere generalization that is desirable, but generalization based on the evidence of wide areas of human experience. Both specialization and generalization have dangers. The philosopher, in formulating a life view or a world view, needs to appeal, insofar as possible, to all the areas of human experience.

WHY MEN DISAGREE

A man's interpretation of his observations and experiences and his generalizations from them depend on his perspective. We interpret things in accordance with what we think is most significant or meaningful. And in addition to the perspectives of particular individuals and special groups of men, there are general presuppositions characteristic of a society or a civilization. Every civilization rests on a number of presuppositions about man, human nature, the nature of the world, and the things that are most worth-while.[1] These convictions are largely unconscious or subconscious, at least for most people. They are considered part of the nature of things and there-fore are seldom made explicit for critical discussion and examination. These assumptions and convictions, accepted as facts, determine the ways in which we view things. They determine the standards and institutions of a society. They are like windows through which we view the world: we do not see them, but we see other things through them. For example, the presupposi-tions about man and the world show a marked contrast as we move from the medieval age, to the outlook of the eighteenth century, to the contemporary world. During the medieval age, it was assumed that institutions were static because God had ordained them to be that way. Life in this world was thought to be a period of preparation for a future life, and faith was elevated above reason. By the eighteenth century large numbers of men were thinking of "natural law" as an explanatory notion, and "nature" and "reason" were two widely accepted concepts. In the contemporary world, largely because of the influence of the growth of science and technology, the outlook is more secular and naturalistic, especially when compared with the medieval age, and men tend to think of growth and change in this world. Thus there are certain beliefs which, for a particular age, seem to be not mere beliefs but statements of fact or necessary categories.

When we turn to the more explicit beliefs of the philosophers we find that these, too, rest on certain basic assumptions and value judgments which influence the direction of attention and points of emphasis. Systems, or schools, of philosophy are easier to understand once we recognize clearly the influence and the power of these different frames of reference or centers of attention. For example, the materialist who is interested in material things and the physical sciences is impressed with the stark reality to which we must adjust. He interprets all existence according to his basic assumption that everything is matter. He is impressed with the measurable processes of nature. He is likely to stress the senses as the only pathway to a knowledge of reality. Other men live in this same world of physical nature, yet do not draw the same conclusions from their experiences. The humanistic naturalist emphasizes the social studies and psychology. His main interest is in man and the "good life" here and now. He, too, is likely to insist that scientific method is the one and only path to valid knowledge. Yet his outlook or emphasis is quite different from that of the materialist. The idealist is impressed with the self, the human mind, and the rational order of things. He admits that a brain injury may lead to loss of consciousness and the powers of thought. However, he believes that the appearance of selves with consciousness of meaning, value, truth, goodness, and beauty is a fact of much greater sig-

[1] See Thomas E. Hulme, *Speculations*, ed. H. Read (London: Routledge & Kegan Paul, 1936).

nificance. This latter fact, the idealist thinks, needs to be taken into account in any adequate interpretation of the universe. The realist, in contrast with the idealist, stresses *the world* that we experience and insists that this world exists independent of being known by, perceived by, or related to mind. The universe is "out there" and we need to accept it and come to terms with it. He wants us to "face facts" and put reason and objectivity in control. We need, he says, to guard against letting our wishes and desires determine our thoughts and conduct. The pragmatist, or instrumentalist, stresses not the world out there but human experience beyond which, he believes, we cannot penetrate. Pragmatism is a philosophy that uses the practical consequences of beliefs as a criterion for determining their value and truth. With pragmatism interest shifts from traditional metaphysics to the problems of everyday affairs, since the pragmatist is particularly interested in thinking as a creative process that changes the world, as well as in social progress, freedom, and democracy. The logical empiricist emphasizes analysis and criticism, and thus he pursues more rigorously the precision and exactness of new logical and empirical methods. Interest shifts from synthesis and the synoptic outlook to the problems of meaning and verification. Critical philosophy in the form of logic, semantics, the philosophy of science, and epistemology becomes central and many questions raised by traditional philosophy are said to be meaningless or nonsensical. The existentialist is concerned with man's inner life and the human predicament. He fears that the traditional systems of philosophy and the newer methods of analysis both tend to forget or lose the individual thinker. He stresses the primacy and uniqueness of individual existence. For many theists, moral and religious values give meaning to existence, and God is the significant fact.

The supporters of each school are likely to appeal to reason and to accept, with certain limitations, the same set of facts about life and the world. Their line of reasoning and their interpretation of the facts, however, are not usually decisive factors in their philosophies. The main differences are due to divergencies in what they believe to be significant.

In Chapter 1 we related a story of the person who showed an aerial picture of the Parthenon together with one taken on the ground to his friends and found that they did not recognize the pictures as of the same building. Much the same sort of thing occurs in philosophy. Philosophers, theologians, scientists, and others disagree, first, because they view things from different points of view. Their personal experiences, cultural backgrounds, and training may vary widely. This is especially true of men living at different times and in different places. A second reason men disagree is that they live in a growing, changing universe. People change, society changes, and nature changes. Some people are responsive or sensitive to change; others cling to creeds and systems that were formulated some time ago and that were declarèd to be authoritative and final. A third reason philosophers disagree is that they deal with an area of human experience in which the evidence is not complete, and the missing links supplied will vary with the biases of the investigators. The evidence we do have may be interpreted in various ways by different people, and some undoubtedly misinterpret it.

If the above statements are true, then it is clear that different approaches are possible and that no one point of view is, as far as we know, the only reasonable or illuminating one. It is also clear that we should attempt to gain as comprehensive a view as possible. Yet, while Spinoza may call on the philosopher to view things from the standpoint of eternity and to include all possible perspectives, this is not really feasible; we necessarily look at things from a more limited point of view.

POINTS OF DISAGREEMENT

While there are large areas of agreement among the main schools of philosophy, there are also some fundamental differences.

First, philosophers are not in agreement about *the main task of philosophy*. There are those who claim that the special function of philosophy is analysis and criticism. This analysis may be a logical one, concerned with the rules and methods of clear thinking, the logical structure of sentences, and precision of meaning and language. Others say that the task of philosophy is to examine the assumptions, the postulates, the principles, and the terms and concepts of scientific and nonscientific discourse. Certainly criticism and analysis are a part of the task of philosophy. Many philosophers, however, claim that the primary concern of philosophy should be synthesis, integration, and the development of a synoptic view of life and the world. Philosophy's mission is to give a view of the whole, a life and a world view, and to integrate the knowledge of the sciences with that of other disciplines to achieve some kind of consistent whole. Philosophy, according to this view, attempts to bring the results of human inquiry—religious, historical, and scientific—into some synoptic view so as to provide knowledge and insight for man's life.

Second, philosophers disagree as to *whether or not a world view or a metaphysics is possible*. Logical empiricism, positivism, and some related movements, with their emphasis on sense perception and objective scientific knowledge, are skeptical about the possibility of metaphysical knowledge and the meaningfulness of metaphysical questions. Pragmatism, or instrumentalism, with its insistence that philosophy is "*of* and *for* daily experience," shifts interest from metaphysical problems to the methods and techniques for meeting man's biological and social needs. The idealists and realists, classical and modern, have been concerned with the great metaphysical questions. Many of them, including the idealists, have believed that problems of value and religion are closely related to man's conception of the fundamental nature of the universe. Many of these philosophers have believed that in man there is that which transcends the empirical and phenomenal order of nature.

Third, philosophers disagree as to *the number, nature, and status of "substances."* Philosophies are monistic, dualistic, or pluralistic, and this distinction cuts across the various systems of philosophy. Some idealists and some materialists are pluralists, as are the pragmatists. Whereas the monists are more likely to be rationalists, the pluralists are likely to be empiricists and to emphasize the varied nature of reality. Dualism, a rather widely held popular view, has not been so widely held among philosophers, though some outstanding thinkers—like Plato and Descartes—have strong dualistic strains in their thinking.

Fourth, philosophers disagree as to *whether or not the world (or nature) is purposeful.* A few philosophers and a considerable number of artists and literary men have pictured the world as purposeless and meaningless. The world, it is said, is ruled by blind forces that are indifferent to man's aspirations, if not actually hostile to them. Nature is matter in motion, operating according to blind forces and laws, and not on the basis of "final causes" or purposes that are related to a cosmic mind or to God. Some philosophers—certain existentialists, for example—say, however, that even though the universe considered as a whole is meaningless, man can create meaning and purpose in his own life.

Many philosophers, including the idealists and a considerable number of realists, as well as various scientists cannot view the world and life as purposeless and meaningless. Teleology is the view that the universe is governed by purpose. A sense of direction and purpose is common in human experience and cannot lightly be brushed aside. This in itself does not prove a larger purpose, but supporters of this view cannot understand how purpose can arise in a universe devoid of all purpose. Life in general bears evidence of direction and a sustaining purpose; it is by nature goal-seeking. The parts and functions of organisms usually contribute to the welfare of the whole and appear to realize ends. Human purposes and the quest for values, they say, indicate the need for a teleological rather than a nonteleological interpretation of nature.

POINTS OF AGREEMENT

There are significant points of agreement as well as disagreement among different systems of philosophy. The large measure of unity on some points would appear to indicate that these common presuppositions or convictions are considered by many philosophers to be reasonably well established.

First, practically all philosophers agree that there is some *order in life and the universe,* and that part of their task is to discover the nature of this order. While philosophers cannot agree among themselves as to the specific characteristics of the process in the midst of which they live, they all see that part of the business of philosophy is to understand the process as fully as possible. Is the world a rational order expressive of some cosmic mind and purpose? Is the world process mechanistic, vitalistic, or teleological? Is meaning to be found in personal relationships and growth—growth as people, growth in knowledge and understanding, growth in sympathy and appreciation, or growth that extends the areas of our awareness? Is meaning to be found in God and in man's relation to God?

As we have seen from previous discussions, some movements in contemporary philosophy reject speculative questions about the nature of the universe. The analysts are concerned mainly with the meaning of such questions and answers. There are many others, however, who believe that such questions are important and cannot be permanently avoided.

Second, philosophers stress *intelligence and the importance of the search for knowledge.* Each philosophical school claims to make a reasonable or logical appeal to men. Accuracy and clarity are almost universally recognized as desirable, but when large and complex issues are facing men these are often not easily attainable. Nevertheless, there is agreement that thinking is better than not thinking, that to be rational is better than to be irrational. While some men are in fact unreasonable, the value of rationality is denied by almost no one.

While philosophers respect logic, what they accept as *logical* is often influenced by certain presuppositions or assumptions. Even the "logical conclusions" of a school of philosophy may be greatly influenced by its general outlook. They may be based on only a segment of human experience or distorted by "blind spots." For this reason, a philosophy that consciously attempts to furnish a broad area of experience and reality from which to draw premises, and that attempts to make its presuppositions clear, becomes very necessary.

Third, philosophers appear to agree that *experience*—the total conscious events that make up a person's life—*must be the foundation or the starting point of philosophical inquiry.* Of course, experience needs to be analyzed and organized if its nature and meaning are to be made clear. Some philosophies, like pragmatism, or the instrumentalism of John Dewey, give experience a central position, and others do not, but this is merely a matter of emphasis; no philosophical school would deny the importance of experience in some sense.

Fourth, philosophers seem to be in substantial agreement that *there is an external reality of some kind,* or that something exists outside the experience of the person. All modern philosophical schools are to some extent realistic in outlook. While there are sharp differences of opinion as to just what is beyond us and how it is to be known, the knower, or the self, is distinguished from a "not-self," or object.

Fifth, there is considerable agreement among philosophers about *the importance of investigating notions like the "good," the "true," and the "beautiful,"* even though these concepts are interpreted in different ways. Values are generally recognized as warranting philosophical thought. Wherever men are living we find them implicitly or explicitly making value judgments. Some experiences are welcomed or sought as good, true, or beautiful; other experiences are shunned as evil, false, or ugly. The main controversy in this field has to do with the nature of values and their place in the universe. Are values objective, subjective, or both? Questions of value are raised in the next chapter.

Sixth, all philosophies accept *the findings of modern science and the validity of the scientific method and outlook.* There does not seem to be any controversy concerning modern views of matter, space-time, evolution, and the like. Differences of opinion do arise over the adequacy, finality, and proper scope of scientific interpretations. Some would say that scientific method is the only method of discovering knowledge; others will insist that this method must be supplemented if we are to achieve a full conception of the nature of things.

Seventh, men can have a *religious interpretation of life* and the universe on the basis of any one of the three main philosophical approaches (idealism, realism, and pragmatism). Idealism traditionally has been friendly to religion, and there are pragmatists like William James and realists like the "religious realists" who have emphasized the positive religious implications of their approach. A person can also be nonreligious within the general philosophical framework of any one of these schools, and certain groups, such as the materialists, repudiate religion.

Religious philosophies that are idealistic tend to retain the emotional tone— one of warmth—of traditional religion. The world is conceived of as friendly, and the outlook is usually theistic. Religious philosophies that are pragmatic tend to be more definitely naturalistic, humanistic, empirical, and melioristic.[2] Religious philosophies that are realistic take many different forms, from Neo-Thomism to some of the process philosophies. Many realists affirm the existence and reality of evil as well as of good; for them the religious problem is to adjust to a world that makes definite demands upon us.

In speaking of the universally accepted values on the basis of which a genuine world community can be built, a Chinese scholar says:

We only need to discuss briefly three fundamental ones. Take, first of all, the

2 See John Dewey, *A Common Faith* (New Haven: Yale U. Press, 1934).

ideal of unity. It is common to practically all great systems. We find in Christianity, Islam, and Judaism the One God and the One Kingdom. We find in Buddhism the gospel of universal salvation. We find in Hinduism *Brahma*, the One and No Other, of which the multiplicities of the phenomenal world are merely parts. We find in Confucianism the ideal of one world-family. This ideal of unity is so universal among mankind that if we are really true believers in any gospel, we cannot help a feeling of universal brotherhood.

Or take another fundamental human ideal, the sanctity of the individual. The individual has been suppressed in some places at all times, and for some time in all places. But as an ideal it is universal.[3]

In speaking of the third universal ideal, the "Golden Rule," Chan says: "Like the ideal of unity, it is found in practically all great systems."[4] Confucius said, "Do not do to others what you do not want them to do to you." Jesus of Nazareth said, "Whatever you wish that men would do to you, do so to them; for this is the law and the prophets."

IS SYNTHESIS POSSIBLE?

These types of philosophy present the major alternatives. The student of philosophy will need to decide whether he will fully accept one type of philosophy or attempt some combination or synthesis. A genuine synthesis that brings together the insights of the various philosophies into an integrated whole appears difficult, if not impossible, since there are issues on which these philosophies have taken contrasting, contrary, or even contradictory stands. The method of eclecticism, which attempts to select the best from several types of philosophy, has never been very successful either. Eclecticism is not generally respected, because unity must not be gained at the expense of consistency.

There is a tendency for the realist, the idealist, and the pragmatist each to think that the other points of view are false or inadequate. The realist finds it difficult to see how one can call something knowledge if the process of knowing changes or makes a difference to the thing known. To the idealist it is inconceivable that knowledge is possible if the supposed object of knowledge is wholly independent of the knower. There must be, he believes, some mutual involvement of mind and object. A mere collection of things or of facts has no meaning—there is no real knowledge unless and until the mind sees in the facts a law or an idea that the facts express or portray. The pragmatist, or instrumentalist, refuses to transcend human experience or to

---

3 W. T. Chan, "The Unity of East and West," in *Radhakrishnan: Comparative Studies in Philosophy,* W. R. Inge, *et. al.* (eds.) (New York: Harper, 1951), pp. 113-114. By permission of George Allen & Unwin, Ltd.
    4 *Ibid.,* p. 115.

look for some theoretical superexperience. The world is in the making or in the process of change. He accepts experience and tries to make the most of it, since the only thing man can know or talk about intelligently is human experience.

The different philosophies bring out and develop aspects of experience and phases of the truth that might otherwise be neglected or overlooked. For example, each of the three main tests of truth—correspondence, coherence, and utility—seems to be important for certain areas of human experience. Probably each of these tests is used by all of us at various times.

In *Beyond Realism and Idealism*[5] Wilbur Marshall Urban maintains that realism and idealism will be found to be complementary—that there is an irrefutable element in each position. The ordinary man is both realist and idealist. He feels that the world contains an objective or physical realm of nature as well as minds and other things that belong to an ideal realm. Not only does man often live by and for love, honor, justice, and God, but at times he is willing to suffer and die for them.

According to Urban, the "problem of knowledge" arose as a result of the "physiology of knowledge" of Locke, Berkeley, Hume, and others. The terms *idealism* and *realism* appear comparatively late in the history of philosophy. Each of these terms has assumed many meanings and has been attached to quite different movements of thought. The term *idealism* has embraced such diverse doctrines as mentalism, transcendental idealism, and objective idealism, which might be viewed as a form of spiritual realism. The term *realism* has been used for naïve realism and for various types of critical and logical realisms, some of which differ little from some of the idealisms. Realism has been in considerable part a protest against the forms of idealism that admitted "no reality other than the world of thought." Most modern idealists, however, agree with the realist's criticism of this extreme form of mentalism.

Both realism and idealism, according to Urban, are "necessary life forms of the human reason." Each contains an element of truth, or a postulate, that is irresistible. In the case of realism, this is the "postulate of antecedent reality." All realism affirms the conviction that reality is prior to knowledge of it. This realistic postulate is found in Plato's idealism, in medieval philosophy, and in continental rationalism. The notion of the primacy of the physical object in knowledge is a later and, many would say, dangerous assumption. Genuine knowledge, according to the realist, presupposes the "mind-independent" character of the object of knowledge. The purpose and meaning of knowledge is to portray accurately something beyond it or apart from it.

In the case of idealism, "mind-dependence," in the sense of relevance to

5 London: Allen & Unwin, 1949.

mind, is a requirement of an adequate theory of knowledge (or epistemology). Unless the content of knowledge has some meaning for mind, how is knowledge possible? We cannot describe or interpret anything that is out of all relation to mind. This is something quite different from claiming that the object known is created, determined, or constituted by the mind that apprehends it. Idealism insists, according to Urban, upon the "postulate of relevance to mind."

Both of these basic postulates can be held together—and, in fact, must be held together, according to Urban. "Without either minimum the significance of knowledge is lost." Each of these philosophies arises from a logically unsupported judgment of value, and the differences arise from these underivable first principles (axioms). Denial of the postulate underlying either philosophy refutes itself and makes the opposite principle meaningless also. A pansubjectivism or mentalism that puts everything in the mind is untenable. On the other hand, a panobjectivism (only physical objects exist) leaves no room for knowledge, truth or falsity, right or wrong, and is equally absurd.

Various other writers have indicated their belief that the disagreements between idealism and realism may be overcome. C. I. Lewis says, "It may be that between a sufficiently critical idealism and a sufficiently critical realism, there are no issues except false issues which arise from the insidious fallacies of the copy theory of knowledge."[6] Norman Kemp Smith is convinced that "idealism and realism, properly understood, are compatible." He speaks of "the development of an idealistic philosophy on realistic lines."[7] Urban says that Kemp Smith's statement is in line with what he has in mind. Writing about idealism and realism, Samuel Alexander says that "no sane philosophy has ever been exclusively the one or the other."[8]

SOME COMPREHENSIVE VISION NEEDED

In an earlier chapter we pointed out that beliefs do in fact make a difference in life. Our beliefs express themselves in action. Consequently, they affect the tone or quality of our personal lives and they influence the society in which we live. Most thinking men are concerned with questions about the nature of man, the nature of the world, and the values by which men live. For many people, however, it is difficult in an age of increasing specialization to look beyond some segment of life and achieve a comprehensive view. Yet it is in just such an age that we need the larger view to give us balance and enable us to see our specialty in its proper perspective. "It is one of the great misfortunes of our era that, as men and women everywhere become increas-

6 *Mind and the World-Order* (New York: Scribner's, 1929), p. 194.

7 Quoted by Wilbur Marshall Urban, *Beyond Realism and Idealism* (London: Allen & Unwin, 1949), p. 217.

8 *Space, Time and Deity* (New York: Macmillan, 1920), I, p. 8.

ingly interdependent, their training and occupations become increasingly concerned with special subjects and special interests."9

The principles of objectivity and neutrality stressed in a scientific age have their rightful place, and they have served us well. There are times when we have to disregard the human factor, to suspend judgment, and to wait until the evidence is in before we announce the results of a project. But these are not principles on the basis of which we can live our entire lives. If we attempt to do so, we become mere observers and spectators, rather than participants in and directors of life.

Many people believe that we need a sense of direction and that we must make commitments and "stand up and be counted" on many important questions. Sir Walter Moberly has said that "thought divorced from responsible action is sterile." Albert Einstein said, "Concern for man and his fate must always form the chief interest of all technical endeavors." J. H. Oldham tells us, "There are some things in life . . . that we cannot know by research or reflection, but only by committing ourselves." Our commitments must be "experimental commitments," to be restated and remolded as new evidence becomes available.

If philosophy should abandon the task of attempting to see life as a whole and become simply another specialty, then others will respond to the demand and take over the traditional task of the philosopher. Philosophy will not decline, but it may be carried on by scientists, theologians, historians, and writers, some of whose treatises must even now be labeled philosophical. One philosopher states this issue clearly:

> Every man has a philosophy, in short; and if it is not provided—formulated, criticized, improved—by those identified as philosophers in the prevailing division of labor, others will inevitably perform that function. At various periods of history various groups have performed it—priests, poets, scientists, statesmen, and occasionally even professors of philosophy. In our time, journalists, psychiatrists, literary critics, and nuclear physicists seem to be carrying the burden. . . . In the arts and sciences, in law, medicine, politics, or religion, questions continually arise which, because they are so speculative, so broad in scope, or so inextricably involved with values, are habitually dismissed as being too philosophical in character to be considered there. I have no quarrel with those who hold that such questions belong in philosophy; but what is to be done if philosophers also refuse to consider them? I am saying only that the division of labor in society must not be allowed to go so far as to leave no place at all for those great questions which cannot be divided, and for which every man presupposes some answer or other in going about his business or just in living his life.10

9 John Nef, *A Search for Civilization* (Chicago: Regnery, 1962), p. VII.
10 Abraham Kaplan, *The New World of Philosophy* (New York: Random House, Inc., 1961), pp. 4, 5–6. (Copyright by Abraham Kaplan.)

QUESTIONS AND PROJECTS

1. Review Questions

(1) Discuss the advantages and disadvantages of specialization and generalization.

(2) Explain what is meant by the perspectives or presuppositions of groups of men or particular civilizations. Give specific examples.

(3) Show how the presuppositions held by different men may help explain the various types or schools of philosophy.

(4) Apart from the different premises underlying the philosophical schools, give other reasons, including psychological and cultural ones, that help explain why men differ in their philosophies.

(5) Explain why you agree or disagree with the statement that our reasoning is often not the decisive factor in our conclusions.

(6) Indicate some of the specific issues on which philosophers have differed most sharply.

(7) What are some fairly specific points of agreement running through most of the different systems of philosophy? Indicate why these areas of agreement must not be pressed too far.

(8) What are the problems that confront the person who attempts some combination or synthesis of the various philosophies? Critically evaluate the points stressed by Urban in *Beyond Realism and Idealism*.

(9) Do you agree or disagree with the statements by Moberly, Einstein, and Oldham regarding the need for responsible commitments? Is it possible that these can be experimental commitments? Discuss.

(10) Discuss the quotation from Abraham Kaplan at the end of this chapter. Do you agree or disagree with the statement that there is need for some comprehensive vision of things and that if philosophers do not assist in meeting this need the task will be done by others?

2. To what extent is philosophy an individual matter, and to what extent is it a cooperative venture? Are individuals or groups more likely to develop "blind spots" and biases?

3. Can two philosophers who disagree each contribute something of real value? May their views actually supplement each other? Can you suggest conditions under which or examples when this may be the case? When may it not be true?

4. What beliefs seem most important to you? Can you defend them? Do these beliefs appear consistent, and do they lean to one type of philosophy? If so, to which one?

5. In *The Fundamental Questions of Philosophy* A. C. Ewing says that our mental processes have been subjected to a threefold classification, represented by the distinction between the affective (feeling), the cognitive (knowing), and the conative (striving or willing) aspects of our nature. While these tend to function together, one may be dominant at a particular time or in a particular person. Explain how these varied personal dispositions may be a source of differences among philosophers.

6. Does man have a "metaphysical sense"? A philosopher uses this expression in

referring to the claims made on man's life and thought by "that which transcends the phenomenal and empirical order of nature's events."[11] A biologist who refers to himself as a humanist, writing on "The Evolutionary Vision," says, "All dominant thought organizations are concerned with the ultimate, as well as with the immediate, problems of existence or, I should rather say, with the most ultimate problems that the thought of the time is capable of formulating or even envisaging. They are all concerned with giving some interpretation of man, of the world which he is to live in, and of his place and role in that world—in other words, some comprehensive picture of human destiny and significance."[12]

7. In Part Three we considered materialism, humanistic naturalism, idealism, realism, pragmatism, logical empiricism, and existentialism. Make a chart listing these main types of philosophy at the top of a long sheet of paper. In the left margin, leaving an inch or more space, list such things as metaphysics, epistemology, view of man, view of freedom of choice, and so on. Fill in the positions of these schools on the various issues. You may wish to draw vertical and horizontal lines before you make your comments. If carefully thought out and checked for accuracy, the chart will highlight the agreements and disagreements among the systems of philosophy.

8. In this chapter, a Chinese scholar, W. T. Chan, pointed out three fundamental values "common to practically all great systems" on the basis of which a world order can be built. Discuss these values. Do you think they are basic? Can you add others to the list?

9. Discuss the following statements:

(1) "A metaphysical system is but a probable hypothesis."

(2) "The choice is not between some kind of metaphysic and no metaphysic; it is always between a good metaphysic and a bad metaphysic."

(3) "Reality means that to which we must pay respectful heed if we are to gain our ends."

10. Review one of the books by Adams, Emmett, Hartshorne, or Pepper from the Suggested Reading list, or one of the following: Elijah Jordan, *Metaphysics: An Unfinished Essay* (Bloomington: Principia, 1956); Charles Morris, *Paths of Life* (New York: Braziller, 1956); Edward Thomas Ramsdell, *The Christian Perspective* (New York: Abingdon-Cokesbury, 1950); Wilmon H. Sheldon, *America's Progressive Philosophy* (New Haven: Yale U. Press, 1942).

SUGGESTED READINGS

ADAMS, GEORGE P. *Man and Metaphysics.* New York: Columbia U. Press, 1948.

  A small but stimulating book that deals with man's "metaphysical sense" and with such topics as science, knowledge, and consciousness.

[11] George P. Adams, *Man and Metaphysics* (New York: Columbia U. Press, 1948), Preface and Ch. 2, "Man's Metaphysical Sense."

[12] Julian Huxley, in *Evolution After Darwin,* Sol Tax and Charles Callender (eds.) (3 vols; Chicago: U. of Chicago Press, 1960), III, *Issues in Evolution,* pp. 251–252. Copyright 1960 by The University of Chicago.

Contemporary British Philosophy; Personal Statements. Ed. by H. D. Lewis. New York: Macmillan, 1956. (Third Series.)
  A score of British philosophers express their convictions on a variety of topics. See especially A. C. Ewing, "The Necessity of Metaphysics," and H. J. Paton, "Fifty Years of Philosophy."

EMMET, DOROTHY M. *The Nature of Metaphysical Thinking.* New York: St. Martin's, 1956.
  An introduction to metaphysics in which the author conceives of metaphysics as "in some sense an analogical way of thinking."

HARTSHORNE, CHARLES. *Reality as Social Process: Studies in Metaphysics and Religion.* Glencoe: Free Press, 1953.
  Fourteen essays written over a period of more than a decade. See Chapter 4, "A Synthesis of Idealism and Realism."

HOCKING, WILLIAM ERNEST. *Types of Philosophy.* 3rd ed.; New York: Scribner's, 1958.
  A discussion of seven major types of metaphysics that includes some critical evaluation.

KAPLAN, ABRAHAM. *The New World of Philosophy.* New York: Random House, 1961.
  An introduction concerning the nature of philosophy is followed by nine lectures treating various Occidental and Oriental philosophies.

LERNER, DANIEL (ed.). *Parts and Wholes.* Glencoe: Free Press, 1962. (The Hayden Colloquium on Scientific Method and Concept.)
  Eight scholars from various fields discuss the limited nature of human knowledge and the fact that empirical knowledge is concerned with parts and not with wholes.

LEVI, ALBERT WILLIAM. *Philosophy and the Modern World.* Bloomington: Indiana U. Press, 1959.
  A stimulating and informative interpretation of twentieth-century intellectual history; Part One deals with the problem and Part Two with sixteen of the leaders, from Bergson to Wittgenstein and Whitehead.

NORTHROP, F. S. C. *The Meeting of East and West.* New York: Macmillan, 1946.
  The author attempts to state the ideological assumptions of the Western and Eastern cultures, and then to formulate a solution that he thinks will help solve the cultural conflicts of our time. Stimulating and provocative, but difficult.

PEPPER, STEPHEN COBURN. *World Hypotheses; A Study in Evidence.* Berkeley: U. of California Press, 1942.
  A survey of metaphysics and an analysis of issues on which men agree and disagree.

SHELDON, WILMON HENRY. *God and Polarity: A Synthesis of Philosophies.* New Haven: Yale U. Press, 1954.
  A large volume in which the author contends that the pairing principle (polarity) pervades reality. See especially Chapter 3, "The Rival Types of Philosophy." See also the author's earlier work, Process and Polarity.

URBAN, WILBUR MARSHALL. *Beyond Realism and Idealism.* London: Allen and Unwin, 1949.
  The author maintains that there is an irrefutable element in both idealism and realism, and that these philosophies are complementary. Difficult reading for beginners.

PART FOUR

THE REALM OF VALUES

NINETEEN

THE NATURE OF VALUES

Life forces us to make choices, to rate things as better or worse, and to formulate some scale or standard of values. We praise and blame, call actions right or wrong, and declare the scene before us beautiful or ugly. Each individual man has some sense of values, and no society has been found that is devoid of some value system. If we do not make our own choices, time, our friends, or other external forces will decide for us, which is in a sense our decision too. Therefore, the question is not so much whether or not we are going to have standards, convictions, loyalties, and ideals around which our lives are organized, as whether these are to be consistent or inconsistent, life-promoting or life-destroying. To ignore the role of values is to have a very distorted or one-sided view of man and his world. "Decency and thuggery, love and hate, beauty and ugliness, justice and tyranny—such are the matters about which most men are far more concerned than they are about fact and falsehood."[1]

Since the time of the early Greeks, men have written about the theoretical side of the problem of values. In recent decades the study has taken on a new interest and importance. The word *axiology,* derived from the Greek *axios,* meaning "worthy," is coming to be used for the study of the general theory of value, including the origin, the nature, the classification, and the place of values in the world. *Ethics,* the study of values in human conduct, and *aesthetics,* the study of values in art, are special fields within axiology.

WHAT IS A VALUE?

A crucial philosophical distinction is that between a factual judgment and a value judgment. Judgments about such things as the distance between New York and San Francisco, the make or type of some particular automobile, or the age of a friend are factual. Factual judgments are descriptive

1 Harold A. Larrabee, *Reliable Knowledge* (Boston: Houghton Mifflin, 1945), p. 601.

statements of empirical qualities or relations. Judgments about such things as whether or not a particular picture is beautiful, one ought to visit a sick relative, or your friend's behavior is right are evaluative. Value judgments appraise the worth of objects, acts, feelings, and so on. In his outstanding work, *General Theory of Value*,[2] Ralph Barton Perry quotes three sets of statements that refer to the same object, "England." The first is a dictionary statement giving the location, the number of square miles, the population, and other information. The second is from Shakespeare's *Richard II* and includes such lines as, "This royal throne of kings, this scepter'd isle" and "This blessed plot, this earth, this realm, this England." The third is from Lissauer's "Song of Hate," which appeared in Germany during World War I, and includes such lines as, "We have but one single hate" and "We have all but one foe—England." Clearly the last two selections are in a different class from the first. They express positive and negative value judgments.

One of the main issues in the area of values today is whether value judgments express knowledge or feelings. When I say that the Mona Lisa is beautiful, that kindness is good, and that murder is wrong, am I making assertions about things that are true or false or am I merely expressing preferences, making entreaties, or issuing commands?

While we can ordinarily distinguish between judgments of fact and judgments of value, we cannot separate them completely. There is an interaction between facts and values. For example, if I am a student, the answer to the question of whether I should go out for football (or some other sport) or spend more of my time on my studies will depend in part on the facts regarding my health, intellectual ability, and standing in course work. If I am weighing the merits of two men (or women) as prospective life partners in marriage, I should seek out and consider many facts, and make certain that intelligence, as well as immediate feelings, plays an important part in my decision. The observable characteristics of things enter into our appraisals of value. If facts or conditions change, our evaluations often change too. That is, value judgments are generally fact-dependent.

There is little agreement among philosophers, however, as to how the term *value* is to be defined. In general, we can say that value judgments are judgments of appraisal.

Value judgments may be thought of merely as expressions of one's feelings and desires—that is, as subjective. For example, a value has been called an emotion or "sentiment of approval or disapproval," the satisfaction of a human want or desire. Others think of a value as the quality of objects or situations that have worth—that is, as an objective quality of things, such as

---

2 New York: Longmans, Green, 1926, pp. 1–2. See also Perry's *Realms of Value, A Critique of Human Civilization* (Cambridge: Harvard U. Press, 1954), for a recent discussion of value judgments.

"that quality of things that evokes an appreciative response." Still others interpret value as some combination of the above, as we shall see.

Does a thing have to be desired to have value? Let us compare two statements. Edgar S. Brightman says that "in the most elementary sense, value means whatever is actually liked, prized, esteemed, desired, approved, or enjoyed by anyone at any time. It is the actual experience of enjoying a desired object or activity. Hence, value is an existing realization of desire."[3] Dorothy Lee says, "By human values, by *a* value or a system of values, I mean the basis upon which an individual will choose one course rather than another, judged as better or worse, right or wrong."[4] The first quotation emphasizes the desire and approval, the second quotation emphasizes the things or the situation about which the judgment is made. While something with value is something desirable and is usually desired by men, its value is not the fact that it happens to be desired by someone. I may even desire to kill, set fire to homes, to steal—things that are not in themselves desirable. Being desired is thus only part of the meaning of *valuable*. Not all things that are desired are valuable, and some things that are not desired by many people today are undoubtedly valuable.

Some scholars claim that *value* is indefinable and that good, beauty, and obligation are direct and immediate experiences. " 'Good' is a simple notion, just as 'yellow' is a simple notion," says G. E. Moore.[5] Good, he tells us, cannot be defined in the sense of being analyzed as something else such as, desire, pleasure, self-fulfillment, following nature, or obedience to the law or to God. The attempt to do this is what Moore calls the "naturalistic fallacy." While we cannot analyze and define *good,* we can tell what things are good, just as we can tell what things are yellow. We should not, he says, confuse goodness with good things. "Good is good and that is the end of the matter." Value qualities are distinctive and unanalyzable. Whether something is good or bad in itself is known to us by intuition. We ought always to pursue that action that will produce the most good or at least more good than evil.

Can we agree with Moore that without the direct experience there can be no adequate understanding of values? Yet the numerous attempts to define and analyze *value* are an indication that many scholars believe that such effort can aid in the clarification of our thinking about values.

DO WE DISCOVER VALUE OR CREATE IT?

The basic issue in value theory has to do with the nature of values and their place in the scheme of things. What is the relationship of values to the mind

---

[3] *Person and Reality* (New York: Ronald, 1958), p. 283.

[4] Abraham H. Maslow (ed.), *New Knowledge in Human Values* (New York: Harper & Row, Publishers, Incorporated, 1959), p. 165.

[5] *Principia Ethica* (New York: Macmillan, 1903), p. 7.

that does the evaluating? Are values only in the mind, in the sense that they pertain only to the imagination, the thinking, the interests, and the desires of the person? Or are they outside the mind, in the sense that they belong to things, just as temperature, size, and shape do? Or does the truth lie between the two extreme positions, so that values are both subjective and objective?

VALUES AS SUBJECTIVE

Those who believe that values are subjective think that value statements express sentiments or emotions of liking or disliking, and nothing more. Eating, drinking, playing, listening to music, observing a gorgeous sunset—all are valuable in that they evoke pleasurable feelings, or furnish us with experiences that we enjoy.

George Santayana tells us that "there is no value apart from some appreciation of it." Emotions as well as consciousness are necessary for the existence as well as the apprehension of good in any form. "Values spring from the immediate and inexplicable reaction of vital impulse, and from the irrational part of our nature."[6] Dewitt H. Parker says that

> values belong wholly to the inner world, to the world of mind. The satisfaction of desire is the real value; the thing that serves is only an instrument. . . . A value is always an experience, never a thing or object. Things may be *valuable,* but they are not values. We project value into the external world, attributing it to the things that serve desire.[7]

In a later volume, published posthumously, Parker defines value as "either a joy-giving activity or passivity or else as the assuagement of desire." The satisfaction of desire may take any one of a number of forms: "(1) satisfactions in relatively spontaneous activities or passivities; (2) satisfactions arising from meeting the objectives of conscious desires; (3) satisfactions arising from the meeting of personal-social standards set for these satisfactions."[8] These are not separate satisfactions, as they are closely related and the common factor is the allaying of desire.

Those who present arguments for the subjective interpretation of values are likely to stress the fact that values—judgments as to goodness and beauty—have varied from individual to individual, from group to group, and from one age to another. If values were wholly objective, would judgments vary? Values are in some sense subjective in that they depend upon a relationship between an observer and that which is being evaluated.

6 *The Sense of Beauty* (New York: Scribner's, 1899), pp. 18–19. See also Willard Arnett, *Santayana and the Sense of Beauty* (Bloomington: Indiana U. Press, 1955).

7 *Human Values* (New York: Harper & Brothers, 1931), pp. 20–21.

8 *The Philosophy of Value* (Ann Arbor: U. of Michigan Press, 1957), pp. 14, 20. (Preface by William K. Frankena.)

VALUES AS OBJECTIVE

Those who consider values objective believe that they are strictly out there in our world to be discovered. The value fact—some quality, or some assemblage of qualities—calls forth our judgment. Something independent of the observer appeals to man's "moral sense" or "aesthetic faculty." A man takes an interest in those things and experiences that appear to him to possess value; it is not his interest that creates the value.

We must make a clear distinction—according to objectivism, or value realism—between the act of judging on the one hand, and the thing or situation about which the judgment is made, on the other. C. E. M. Joad gives the following analogy:[9] People differ in their judgments about temperature, yet we do not say that temperature is subjective. In this case we can check their judgments with a thermometer, and declare them correct or incorrect. In ethics and aesthetics there are no thermometers, but there are criteria on the basis of which correct judgments are made. If I judge a landscape to be beautiful, it is not my judging that is beautiful but the colors and shapes before me. There is a quality present that is independent of my judgment. Values seem to reside in objects just as truly as do color, smell, temperature, size, and shape.

Such widely varying systems as the philosophies of Plato and Aristotle, medieval realism, Neo-Thomism, and various types of modern realism and idealism agree that values are in some sense objective. For Plato the world of concepts, universals, and values is the real and permanent world. There is a hierarchy of values—leading up to the Good or the supreme value—that determines the organization of the world. For Aristotle the relation of a thing to its end or value is an essential part of its nature. The objectivity of value is central also in medieval thought. Roman Catholic philosophy, as a whole, holds that truth, goodness, and beauty exist in their own right.[10]

Various modern realists have formulated positions on the status of values. For E. G. Spaulding, values are "subsistents" (entities not in space or time, but held to be real) rather than "existents" (entities in space and time). As subsistents they are independent of human desire and preference; they are in our world to be discovered. Such values as truth, goodness, and beauty are not subject to the misfortunes of this slowly evolving natural process of discovery.[11] Another realist, John Laird, speaks of values as "tertiary qualities." They are different from the primary and the secondary qualities of our experience. Tertiary qualities are recognized in our immediate experience,

---

[9] *Philosophy for Our Times* (New York: Nelson, 1942), p. 193.

[10] For the Catholic philosophers, God is the ultimate ground and source of values. The ontological status of values is prior to their psychological apprehension. Sense experience is only partial and contradictory. The right use of reason will lead us to a perception and appreciation of the eternal values.

[11] *The New Rationalism* (New York: Holt, 1918), p. 498.

and they are real and permanent, even though they cannot be defined in the same ways as primary and secondary qualities. After pointing out that beauty resides in things, such as the sky, sea, sunset, and flowers, Laird says: "Nature, indeed, is infinitely beautiful, and she seems to wear her beauty as she wears color or sound. Why, then, should her beauty belong to us rather than to her?"[12]

In *An Analysis of Knowledge and Valuation*[13] C. I. Lewis contends that our judgments of value—our judgments of good and evil, right and wrong, better and worse—are a kind of genuine empirical knowledge that is comparable to empirical knowledge in other fields. These judgments of value, he believes, are subject to the same criteria of validity that we apply to other judgments. Valuations represent one type of "empirical cognition" and are true or false depending on the evidence that can be obtained for or against them. They are neither a priori knowledge nor merely subjective states. The fact that value judgments are related to certain conditions and that we verify them empirically does not mean that they are subjective. Value qualities, like other qualities such as hardness and color, are qualities that we can experience. "Knowledge, action, and evaluation are essentially connected. The primary and pervasive significance of knowledge lies in its guidance of action: knowing is for the sake of doing. And action, obviously, is rooted in evaluation."[14]

The supporters of the view that values are objective will point out that beauty and goodness are valued by all, and that, among cultured people, there is a large measure of agreement as to aesthetic value judgments. The objectivist may point out that, after a few years of debate, a Universal Declaration of Human Rights was approved by the General Assembly of the United Nations. Furthermore, the objectivist will claim that these agreements concerning fundamental values reflect the physical, psychological, and social conditions and needs of men everywhere. If values were subjective, they would reflect one's own desires, interests, or wishes exclusively. Yet whether the values to be sought are social, moral, or aesthetic, our choices are definitely limited. Individuals and groups that depart too radically from the accepted norms tend to eliminate themselves from the acceptable. Experience and training in the realm of values tend to make men's judgments more and more uniform.

Furthermore, the media through or the conditions under which we make value judgments have been rather restricted in scope. There is considerable agreement the world over that for beauty the important media are nature, music, painting, sculpture, poetry, and architecture. In the realm of morals

---

12 *A Study in Realism* (New York: Macmillan, 1921), p. 129.
13 La Salle: Open Court, 1946.
14 *Ibid.*, p. 3.

there is also considerable agreement as to what constitutes a situation that merits valuation. The exceptions are less numerous than the broad areas of agreement.

VALUE AS A RELATION BETWEEN VARIABLES

The subjectivist will have to admit that value judgments are made about objective entities, and the objectivist will have to admit that these judgments are in some sense mind-dependent. The theory we are now considering asserts that both subjective and objective factors are necessary for the existence of values. Valuation is a special kind of relation which discloses to people who are sensitive and receptive the fact that something is good or beautiful.

Two contemporary students of aesthetics and values make this third position clear. C. J. Ducasse says:

> The question whether beauty is objective or subjective is thus not answerable by saying simply "yes" to one and "no" to the other of the alleged alternatives. The only correct answer is that *beauty is that property of an object which consists in capacity of the object to cause pleasure in a subject who contemplates it.* Beauty, that is to say, is a character of some objects, but a *relational* character of them— the character, namely, that consists in their having to certain minds (subjects) the relation just described. The question whether beauty is objective or subjective is thus exactly parallel logically with the question whether poisonousness is objective or subjective. . . . Experiencing pleasure, like dying, is not a capacity but an *event,* which some things are capable of causing in some human beings. On the other hand, beauty, like poisonousness, is not an event or a quality, but a *capacity*—the capacity some things have of causing pleasure in *some* contemplative beholders of them.[15]

In *Aesthetic Quality* Stephen C. Pepper sets forth a position he calls "contextualism." He points out that in beauty "conditions both of an impersonal and of a personal nature must be fulfilled."[16] There are three elements that must be considered. There is, first, a system of impersonal qualities or strands, the given event, of which there is a relational element known by analysis and a qualitative aspect known by intuition. The art object—a statue, let us say—must be seen under certain favorable conditions. There is, second, a "system of personal strands," an organism with interests, moods, and cultural background. Certain conditions again must be met, such as a receptive mood and an adequate experience. When a system of personal relations contacts a system of impersonal relations, an act of perception takes

---

[15] *Art, the Critics, and You* (New York: Oskar Piest, 1944), pp. 90–91.
[16] New York: Scribner's, 1938, p. 227. See also Pepper's *The Basis of Criticism in the Arts* (Cambridge: Harvard U. Press, 1945), Ch. III; and his *The Sources of Value* (Berkeley and Los Angeles: U. of California Press, 1958).

place. Third, the perception is enriched and deepened by our interests and experiences. Symbolism, imagination, and ideas are at work, and an aesthetic experience is the result. Beauty is the "enhanced quality of texture." Positive aesthetic value is called beauty; negative aesthetic value is called ugliness. Value is the cooperative result of an interaction between personal and impersonal elements.

THE SELECTION AND RANKING OF VALUES

How are we to select and rank the values by which we are to live? There is widespread agreement about the existence of certain groups of values: religious, moral, aesthetic, intellectual, scientific, economic, and the like. There is not nearly the same measure of agreement concerning their number, nature, relationship to each other, rank in a scale, and the principles to be used in selecting them.

In an attempt to deal with values from a genetic and biological point of view, Dewitt H. Parker says there are in man "dominant systems of interests" which "contain values qualitatively alike" and which belong together. To quote Parker:

> They have their own laws of functioning, their unique and characteristic standards and norms, and they are commonly embodied in institutions. Thus about the religious interest is built the church; about the scientific interest, science and education; about ambition and the closely allied interest in self-preservation, the state and industry; about the aesthetic interest and the interest in workmanship, the arts; about love, friendship, the family, and the community.[17]

A survey of human affairs led Parker to list the following as major interests and values:

> self-preservation or health; comfort, the interest in a maximum of sensuous pleasure; ambition, the interest in securing a place of consideration and power in the social order; workmanship, the interest in the efficient making and using of things; love in its various forms, as sex love, parental love, friendship, generic love, community love, and ideal love; knowledge; play; art; religion. . . . Characteristic of these is their ability to create norms, and a certain resulting absoluteness. Upon them is based the "ought," the imperative.[18]

From the time of the ancient Greeks to the present, many philosophers have stressed three values as superior to all others: *goodness, beauty,* and *truth.* These values are said to be self-sufficient. While there have been attempts to

---

[17] *Human Values,* p. 45.
[18] *Ibid.,* p. 46.

reduce one to another or to make one supreme, these attempts have not been widely accepted. To goodness, beauty, and truth some would add happiness.[19] Others would subsume these values under the heading of religious value.

PRINCIPLES OF SELECTION

We shall make no attempt to set forth a rigid classification of values as higher or lower. There are, however, certain principles that are quite generally accepted in philosophical discussions.

1. *Intrinsic values are to be preferred to those that are extrinsic.* Something is intrinsically valuable (good in itself) when it is valued for its own sake and not for its capacity to yield something else. Something is extrinsically valuable (good for something) when it is a means to the attainment of other things. Most of the things we see and use in our everyday activities, from books and typewriters to buildings and institutions, have extrinsic value.

Intrinsic and extrinsic values are not necessarily mutually exclusive. The same things may be valued for themselves and for what they may bring, or a thing may be valued now intrinsically and later extrinsically. For example, knowledge may be valued as a good in itself and also as a means to other things that have value, such as economic success or power. A great work of art may be valued for itself, or it may be viewed as an instrument for making profit or achieving distinction. Those things that are sought as good in themselves are the *ends* we seek in life. The other things are the *means* we use to attain these ends.

2. *Values that are productive and relatively permanent are to be preferred to those that are less productive and less permanent.* Some values, like the economic, tend to be used up in the activities of life, whereas values like friendship tend to increase as they are used. To share the values of the mind and spirit with other people does not lessen their value for us. Physical and economic values, while necessary for life, are not permanently satisfying as ends in themselves. The long record of human experience shows that the social, intellectual, aesthetic, and religious values tend to give more permanent satisfaction than do the material values. The productive and permanent values tend also to be the intrinsic values.

3. *We ought to select our values on the basis of self-chosen ends or ideals.* The values we seek ought to be *our* values, and these values ought to be consistent with each other and with the demands life makes on us. "That man is free," said T. H. Green, "who is conscious of being the author of the law he obeys." Self-discipline based on a well-thought-out scale of values is the mark of a mature man.

4. *Of two values, the greater ought to be selected.* Conversely, when we are

[19] See Joad, *Philosophy for Our Times,* p. 128.

forced by some life situation unavoidably to choose between two evils, the lesser evil ought to be chosen. We must always act so that there is some gain or advance in the total values of life. In his *Moral Laws* Edgar S. Brightman says:

> We like health and we like overindulgence in foods and drinks which undermine health; we like educational success, social success, and economic success, yet the attainment of all three at the same time by the same person is sometimes impossible. My interests as a member of a political party or of a church or of the economic order may conflict with my interests as an autonomous moral person; yet I value the party and the church, as well as autonomy. The Axiological Law steps into this conflict with the rule of reason and asks the person to make a rational selection of values. Since we cannot have everything that we like because our likes are mutually exclusive and even destructive, we need to decide what values we shall pursue.[20]

SCIENCE AND HUMAN VALUES

The issue of the relation between science and values has led to much discussion in recent years. Is the scientist, as scientist, to deal with values? There are both affirmations and denials to be found in the literature on this subject. The fact that scientific method is an exceedingly valuable method of investigation is not controversial and neither is the fact that scientific research has given us valuable knowledge and useful instruments with which to control nature and improve man's life. In Chapter 6 we dealt briefly with the value and achievements of science. In addition to great advances in applications, science helps satisfy our intellectual curiosity about many areas. It gives us great new powers of prediction and control. We do need to acknowledge, however, that there are great dangers in the unwise or evil use of the new knowledge and new instruments.

Scientists, especially anthropologists, sociologists, and psychologists, have gone to all the inhabited areas of the earth and have studied the value systems of numerous tribes and racial and national groups. They can tell us how these people live, about their behavior in work and play, about the choices they make and the values these choices imply. They can compare one group with another. In this descriptive sense some scientists do deal with values. In fact, without knowing the value system or the standards of a group, it is difficult to understand its culture. The standards may be largely unconscious, so that they have to be inferred from the actual choices and behavior.

The editor of a book in which anthropologists tell about their investigations and express their convictions says:

[20] Nashville: Abingdon-Cokesbury, 1933, p. 127.

While nobody questions that values are an appropriate subject for the moralist and the philosopher, the study of their manifestation among different peoples is also a proper subject of inquiry for sociologists and anthropologists. It is, in fact, quite impossible to understand the behavior of a people without knowing their own value assumptions. But the scientific study of values must remain a study of them; it is not concerned with evaluating these values—which is the philosophers' or moralists' task.[21]

The scientist can tell us what is or was actually valued by different groups, primitive and modern. He does not, as scientist, deal with the question of what *ought* to be valued. He is neither dealing with judgments of value as better or worse nor attempting to set up a scale or standard of values. In this latter sense, there is fairly general agreement that value judgments cannot be established by objective scientific methods. Once an ethical premise is given or accepted, the scientist may aid us by indicating what means are feasible to attain the valued ends.

On the basis of descriptive studies, some scientists have come to accept ethical relativism and to claim that there are no fixed standards to which people may appeal. Yet on the basis of the equally great and changing variety of opinions and beliefs as to what is true and false, these same men do not usually claim that there are no objective standards of truth to which we may appeal. We must accept the evidence of the great diversity of values at the descriptive level; this has never been an issue among philosophers. The real issue has to do only with the conclusions to be drawn. One student of both philosophy and anthropology states this issue clearly:

> None of the parties to the disputes in Athens doubted that different people valued different things. The relativity of values at the descriptive level has never been a problem for philosophy. But the Sophists deduced from it that values are essentially relative. Socrates and Aristotle concluded from the same data that lots of people do not know what is really good.[22]

Some values are relative in the sense that they relate to questions of age, sex, intelligence, culture, technology, and other conditions. In this sense values vary depending on circumstances. There are, however, a large number of things that all men of intelligence and good will value—health, knowledge and wisdom, pleasure and happiness, courage, kindness, honesty, love, friendship, gratitude, beauty, and the like. These values have a basis in man's nature and the nature of the world in which he lives. They are necessary for

---

21 Walter Goldschmidt (ed.), *Exploring the Ways of Mankind* (New York: Holt, Rinehart and Winston, 1960), p. 418.

22 Ethel M. Albert, "Social-Science Facts and Philosophical Values," *The Antioch Review*, 17 (Winter, 1957–58): 407.

the continuation of life and the development of man, and are accepted by people the world around.

In an age of unparalleled scientific development, people claim that much mental disease and crime are due to the fact that life for many has become intolerably dull and empty of meaning. This in turn is in part due to a loss of a sense of direction in men who have no sustaining values, and to the manipulation of emotions and thoughts through the new techniques of control in the hands of special-interest groups. In *New Knowledge in Human Values* a psychologist speaking for the contributors, most of whom are scientists, says:

> This volume springs from the belief, first, that the ultimate disease of our time is valuelessness; second, that this state is more crucially dangerous than ever before in history; and finally, that something can be done about it by man's own rational efforts.[23]

Part of the problem we face in modern society stems from the fact that we have depended too exclusively on factual judgments, and forgotten that such knowledge is instrumental only and may be used for either good or evil ends. This knowledge increases our power to realize our intentions, but it does not give us standards by which to select these intentions or enable us to discriminate among competing value systems. Carl R. Rogers notes that during World War II German rocket scientists were perfecting guided missiles. They worked faithfully for Hitler, and their goal was to destroy Russia, Britain, and the United States. Later, following their capture, they worked with equal zeal for totally different objectives. Rogers goes on to say that "if behavioral scientists are concerned solely with advancing their science, it seems most probable that they will serve the purpose of whatever individual or group has the power."[24] He says further:

> My point then is that any endeavor in science, pure or applied, is carried on in the pursuit of a purpose or value that is subjectively chosen by persons. It is important that this choice be made explicit, since the particular value which is being sought can never be tested or evaluated, confirmed or denied, by the scientific endeavor which gives it birth. The initial purpose or value always and necessarily lies outside the scope of the scientific effort which it sets in motion.[25]

23 Maslow, *New Knowledge*, p. vii.
24 "Some Issues Concerning the Control of Human Behavior," *Science*, 124 (November 30, 1956): 1061. (A Symposium by Carl R. Rogers and B. F. Skinner.)
25 *Ibid.*, p. 1062.

VALUES AND HUMAN SOCIETY

Many keen observers and writers have been calling our attention to the loss of a sense of values and to the resulting deterioration of large segments of contemporary society. They tell us that we have been living under the illusion that more automobiles, labor-saving devices, and the like will bring happiness and usher in a better life. Without a strong sense of values and of direction, however, the human spirit tends to weaken or deteriorate. Technical devices can liberate man from drudgery and open up new possibilities for cultural development; they can also have a dehumanizing effect and be potentially dangerous if there is no self-discipline and dedication to enduring values.

In *The Abuse of Learning*[26] Frederic Lilge has studied the reasons for the failure of an educated Germany to prevent the excesses under the Nazi regime. He points out that, in Germany throughout the nineteenth century, with the rapid development of specialization and of science and technology, value studies were pushed aside or also became technical and the concern of specialists only. The result was a nation of highly trained specialists interested in the facts in their respective fields but unconcerned about the larger problems of the community and the world. Confusion of values and moral paralysis made possible the triumph of Nazism.

Ortega y Gasset, in *The Revolt of the Masses*,[27] attempts to diagnose the crisis of modern Europe and the reasons for the rise of the totalitarian mass movements. He notes that from the sixth to the nineteenth century the population of Europe was never more than 180 million; by the time of World War I the population had risen to 460 million. While these new hundreds of millions of people were arriving on the scene, education was becoming highly vocational, at least for the masses. They were taught "the technique for modern life"—a knowledge of our tools and machines—but no feeling for their great historical or cultural heritage. They were left without a moral code and without standards. When these are lacking there is no real culture, and we get the mass-man, the modern barbarian. Ortega y Gasset classifies as barbaric a large proportion of the "intelligentsia."

The steady increase in the crime rate, especially among juvenile offenders, is disturbing.[28] In "Man Without Values" Erich Kahler points out such

---

26 New York: Macmillan, 1948.

27 New York: Norton, 1932.

28 For example, in 1961 the crime rate was ten percent above the average for the previous three years (1958 through 1960). Whereas the national population increased seven percent during a five-year period, the increase in crime was thirty-four percent. That is, the rate of growth of crime was out-stripping the population growth by nearly five to one. See Uniform Crime Reports of the Federal Bureau of Investigation as reported in *The World Almanac and Book of Facts for 1963* (New York: World-Telegram and The Sun, 1963), p. 310.

symptoms as our "lack of a definite style of life" and the "change in our atti-tude toward crime and moral offense."

> The most frightening aspect of our present world is not the horrors in them-selves, the atrocities, the technological exterminations, but the one fact at the very root of it all: the fading away of any human criterion, the disruption of the contents and substrata of human responsibility. There is a fatal correlation, a vicious circle in which we seem to be caught: Without a human community there is no human responsibility of the individual, and without such respon-sibility, without true morality in this purely human sense, no human community can maintain itself.[29]

An experienced teacher who has observed widely and written much about trends and conditions in contemporary society says:

> My own experience as a teacher in getting student reactions to situations that involved the acceptance or the moral reprobation of senseless criminal violence, makes me believe that perhaps as much as a third of our student population of college grade may, for all practical purposes, be considered moral imbeciles, or at least moral illiterates. So poorly have the moral values that still remain partly operative been transmitted to these students that they are potential, if not active, delinquents. Though they have been screened by intelligence tests and per-sonality tests before entering college, they have not yet acquired the moral values and purposes that would enable them to function as full-grown human beings. Masked by more adult habits that they share with the rest of the com-munity, their values remain infantile, if not brutally criminal.[30]

Whether the above statement is reasonably accurate or extreme in its appraisal of the moral values of college students, the reader will have to decide for himself. There are within each one of us great potentialities for good and for evil. If some trends and conditions are discouraging, we need to remember that things do not have to be this way. A basic question we need to face is whether in the value systems we promote we are encouraging and strengthening the selfish and animal impulses that are present in us all, or reinforcing and cultivating the more altruistic and creative aspects of our nature. On the answers to questions such as these the future of our civilization may well depend. Can we agree with the following statement by a student of human nature?

> [I]t looks as if *there were* a single ultimate value for mankind, a far goal toward which all men strive. This is called variously by different authors self-actualiza-tion, self-realization, integration, psychological health, individuation, autonomy,

29 *The Tower and the Abyss* (New York: Braziller, 1957), p. 224.
30 Lewis Mumford, *The Conduct of Life* (New York: Harcourt, Brace & World, Inc., 1951), p. 154.

creativity, productivity, but they all agree that this amounts to realizing the potentialities of the person, that is to say, becoming fully human, everything that the person *can* become. . . .

[T]he human being has within him a pressure (among other pressures) toward unity of personality, toward spontaneous expressiveness, toward full individuality and identity, toward seeing the truth rather than being blind, toward being creative, toward being good, and a lot else. That is, the human being is so constructed that he presses toward fuller and fuller being and this means pressing toward what most people would call good values, toward serenity, kindness, courage, knowledge, honesty, love, unselfishness, and goodness.[31]

These are values, along with others, that the world religions and the great philosophers have been stressing through the years. The great task before man today is to discover anew the genuine values of life and to share them with his fellow men. Man must learn to unify and harmonize the world of facts with the world of values. Facts and means may serve the values and ends of human existence.

QUESTIONS AND PROJECTS

1. Review Questions

(1) State why the problems of value are important issues in any society.

(2) Discuss the problem of defining the term *value*.

(3) What distinguishes factual judgments from value judgments?

(4) What are possible answers to the question, "Do we discover value or create it?"

(5) State the case *for* or *against* each of the three general approaches to the nature of value. Which position do you favor? Why?

(6) In this chapter lists of values were given. List what you consider to be the main values and see whether you can arrange them in some order of importance. Indicate those that you think are intrinsic, those that are usually extrinsic, and those that may be either intrinsic or extrinsic.

(7) Give the "principles of selection" that you think ought to govern men in the realm of values.

(8) Write a statement on "Science and Human Values," indicating the nature of the relationship between science and values. Give reasons for accepting or rejecting the view that the scientific study of values necessarily remains at the descriptive level and that the scientist, as scientist, is not concerned with what ought to be valued.

(9) Do the explanations given by Lilge and Ortega y Gasset for the confusion of values in modern society sound reasonable to you? Discuss.

(10) Do you consider the quotation from Lewis Mumford (p. 346) reasonably

[31] Maslow, *New Knowledge*, pp. 123, 126.

accurate or extreme in its appraisal of the morals of college students? On what evidence do you base your answer?

(11) Discuss the statement made in the quotation at the end of this chapter that there is a "single ultimate value for mankind." If there is such a value or goal, how would you describe it?

2. It has been said that men are willing to die on the battlefield for values for which they are frequently unwilling to live and work in peacetime. Is this true? Why or why not?

3. Many people talk about and claim certain rights. We hear about the rights of women, of labor, of capital, of underdeveloped nations, and so on. What is the relationship between rights and values? For a brief discussion, see Harold H. Titus, *Ethics for Today* (3rd. ed.; New York: American Book, 1957), pp. 210–224.

4. Can science by itself show us the direction in which we should move, or is the world revealed by science a "valueless" world? See George A. Lundberg, *Can Science Save Us?* (New York: Longmans, Green, 1947); C. E. M. Joad, *Philosophy for Our Times* (New York: Nelson, 1942). The former seems to say that science can deal with values; the latter says that "science leaves out value," something we very much need. See also Abraham H. Maslow (ed.), *New Knowledge in Human Values,* and other books in the Suggested Readings.

5. Some years ago the Art Museum Commission of St. Louis purchased an Egyptian bronze cat. The cat, about fifteen inches in height, cost $14,400. The money was paid from a fund that had been raised by taxation for the operating cost of the museum and for acquisitions. A storm of protest, including demonstrations and parades, immediately broke out, since the city's relief funds were exhausted and there was considerable unemployment and hunger in the city. The action of the Commission was defended and attacked by various groups. Here was a real conflict between values. For a brief discussion of this case, see Harold A. Larrabee, *Reliable Knowledge* (Boston: Houghton Mifflin, 1945), pp. 613–616. Give your reaction to this controversy. Point out similar conflicts of values that have occurred in other areas of public life.

6. Comment on the following statements:
(1) "We cannot study what cannot be measured. . . . The greatest affront to the spirit of the age is to indulge in value judgments."
(2) "Lives are made by what they omit, but most of all by what they include."
(3) "Tell me what you like, and I'll tell you what you are."

7. How would you explain the following statement from a philosophy of life written by a veteran soon after World War Two? What does it indicate about his educational experience, attitude toward life, and standard of values?

I regret very much having to graduate. I shake with fear at the thought of being thrown on my own and having to make my own living. I have no confidence in my ability to earn the material things in life which are very important to me. Often I think about re-enlisting in the Navy as there I do not have any responsibility. Time takes care of advancement and retirement and I can be excused from moral responsibility.

8. Write a paper (1000–2000 words) entitled "My Philosophy of Values," in which you contrast what most people in our society put first (an empirical question) with what you think are the most important values in life (a normative question).

SUGGESTED READINGS

ALBERT, ETHEL M., AND KLUCKHOHN, CLYDE. *A Selected Bibliography on Values, Ethics, and Esthetics in the Behavioral Sciences and Philosophy, 1920–1958.* Glencoe: Free Press, 1959.
    A valuable bibliography of about two thousand research articles and books dealing with the question of values.

HALL, EVERETT WESLEY. *Modern Science and Human Values: A Study in the History of Ideas.* New York: Van Nostrand, 1956.
    Part I is a discussion of the development of a value-free science, Part II of the development of conflicting points of view in the field of values. Fact and value are not to be confused, since they are different. See also the author's What Is Value?

JACOB, PHILIP E. *Changing Values in College.* New York: Harper, 1957.
    A study of the extent to which American colleges are influencing standards of conduct. The evidence indicates that, with exceptions, the influences are slight.

KEETON, MORRIS. *Values Men Live By: An Invitation to Religious Inquiry.* New York: Abingdon, 1960.
    A discussion of the values emphasized in the religions of the world and "the idea of the divine as the proper object of our primary loyalty."

LEPLEY, RAY (ed.). *The Language of Value.* New York: Columbia U. Press, 1957.
    A book of essays each of which considers some aspect of the language of value. Part I, Essays; Part II, Comments and Responses. See also Value: A Cooperative Inquiry, *edited by Lepley; and Lepley's* Verifiability of Value.

LEWIS, CLARENCE IRVING. *An Analysis of Knowledge and Valuation.* La Salle: Open Court, 1946.
    A comprehensive defense of the naturalistic theory which holds that judgments of value are forms of empirical knowledge and thus are subject to the same standards of inquiry and verifiability. Difficult for beginners.

MASLOW, ABRAHAM H. (ed.). *New Knowledge in Human Values.* New York: Harper, 1959.
    Part I includes fifteen addresses or papers presented to a conference sponsored by the Research Society for Creative Altruism; Part II includes comments and replies.

MORRIS, CHARLES. *Varieties of Human Value.* Chicago: U. of Chicago Press, 1956.
    The author reports on his research into man's preferences for various forms of the good life

and his efforts to find a cross-cultural scale for measuring values. See also The Open Self.

MUMFORD, LEWIS. *The Conduct of Life.* New York: Harcourt, Brace, 1951.
   A study of contemporary Western civilization, with emphasis on the problems of man's nature, values, and the possibilities for a renewal of life.

MYRDAL, GUNNAR. *Value in Social Theory: A Selection of Essays on Methodology.* Ed. by Paul Streeten. New York: Harper, 1958.
   See the Introduction by Paul Streeten, and Parts One and Three for a discussion of "the relation between values and analysis of facts in social theory." Part Two is a study of the Negro problem in relation to the problem of values.

NORRIS, LOUIS WILLIAM. *Polarity: A Philosophy of Tensions Among Values.* Chicago: Regnery, 1956.
   A discussion of a method of dealing with the opposing elements of experience: subjectivity and objectivity, freedom and determination, sacred and secular values, and the like.

PARKER, DEWITT H. *The Philosophy of Value.* Ann Arbor: U. of Michigan Press, 1957. (Preface by William K. Frankena.)
   After a brief summary of the author's Human Values, *theoretical questions are discussed and illustrated with concrete examples.*

PEPPER, STEPHEN C. *The Sources of Value.* Berkeley and Los Angeles: U. of California Press, 1958.
   A study of how men derive and experience values, and an attempt to set forth an adequate theory to explain them.

PERRY, RALPH BARTON. *Realms of Value: A Critique of Human Civilization.* Cambridge: Harvard U. Press, 1954.
   A sequel to the author's earlier General Theory of Value. *After defining value, the author applies his general theory to the pursuits and institutions that make up civilization.*

SCHROECK, HELMET, AND WIGGINS, JAMES W. (eds.). *Scientism and Values.* Princeton: Van Nostrand, 1960.
   A collection of essays in which the authors critically evaluate the work of the scientist, mainly the social scientist, in relation to questions of fact and value.

WIEMAN, HENRY N. *The Source of Human Good.* Chicago: U. of Chicago Press, 1946.
   Part I discusses the general nature of value, and Part II specific kinds of value.

TWENTY

ETHICS AND THE
MORAL LIFE

Within morality and ethics there are a number of areas of interest and study. First, there is the wide range of human conduct that embraces motives and other inner springs of action as well as the overt acts themselves. Here we consider the conduct of individuals, or personal morality; the conduct of groups, or social morality; and the cultural patterns of national and racial groups. The study here is in part descriptive of what occurs and in part an attempt to distinguish what *is* from what *ought* to be. Second, there are the various ethical theories or moral philosophies set forth to explain *why* people act as they do, and what the principles are by which men live or ought to live. From the time of the early Greeks men have formulated principles of explanation and have set forth ethical theories. Third, there is the area of critical ethics or *metaethics*. Here interest is centered on the analysis and meaning of the terms and language used in ethical discourse and the kind of reasoning used to justify ethical statements. This area has received considerable emphasis in recent years, but it involves some highly technical and controversial issues. In this chapter we shall give our attention mainly to the first two areas, to what is termed *normative ethics,* or the problem of finding principles by which to live. Normative ethics seeks to establish a norm or standard for action so that men may choose their own actions with greater understanding and be able to evaluate critically the practices and institutions of society.

Men are continually judging their own conduct and that of their fellow men. Some acts are approved and are called right or good. Other acts are condemned and are called wrong or evil. Moral judgments have to do with the actions of human beings, and in particular with their voluntary actions, insofar as questions of right and wrong are involved. We do not usually hold people responsible for actions over which they have no control. Normative ethics is the study of the principles underlying the morally relevant forms of human conduct.

The terms *morals* and *ethics* are closely related in original meaning. The first term comes from the Latin *moralis* and the second from the Greek term *ethos*. Both terms meant "the custom or way of life." These terms are sometimes used as if they were synonymous. Today, however, there is a tendency to use the terms *morals* and *morality* to refer to the conduct itself, and *ethics* and *ethical* to refer to the study of moral conduct or the system or code that is followed. We speak of "a moral act" and "an ethical system or code."

The terms *right* and *good* are frequently used in ethics and need to be understood. The word *right* comes from the Latin *rectus,* meaning "straight" or "in line." In popular usage it implies conformity to some standard. The term *good* applies to that which has desirable qualities, satisfies some need, or has value for human beings. Some intuitionists and deontologists (*de,* meaning "from," and *ontology,* meaning "that which exists" or "being") contend that, in the field of ethics, right and wrong are fundamentally irreducible to anything else and are immediately recognized. Such theories are opposed to axiological, teleological, or value-based ethics that make goodness the central ethical concept. Teleological theories support the view that an act to be right must make some contribution to the goodness of man or the world. The position we are taking in this chapter is that *right* refers to conduct that brings about the greatest possible good in the situation. From this point of view, right is based on the good and the good is that which has value for people. This position has strong support in moral philosophy and in the common-sense reactions of men in their everyday activities.

SOME FACTS OF THE MORAL LIFE

First, life is such that everyone has continually to make decisions. Some of our decisions are trivial; others are so important that they affect our entire lives. Generally, too, our decisions and actions affect others as well as ourselves. In addition, we make claims on other people, and they make claims on us. Some of the well-recognized claims we speak of as "rights" and "duties."

Second, to have any orderly social life, we must have agreements, understandings, principles, and rules of conduct. There is no human society that does not have well-established codes or rules of procedure. We cannot choose whether or not we shall have them; we can only decide whether or not they are to be reasonable and well adapted to the needs of life under existing conditions. Some of these agreements are unconscious and embedded in the customs and traditions of the group and the habits of the individual; they are simply taken for granted. Others are semiconscious or wholly conscious and may be subjects for discussion. For example, when two people agree to take a trip together they will agree on certain central questions like when they will leave and how they will travel. That one of them will not bring his inlaws or his dog or change the schedule without the consent of the other is an unconscious or implicit agreement. In marriage, in calling a physician when someone is sick, and in making a deposit at a bank, while there may be some formal agreements, most of the rules of procedure are taken for granted and not articulated until some special circumstance arises to bring them to light. As the conditions and needs of life undergo change, these agreements and codes may be modified and changed.

Third, there is a development or evolution of morals, just as there is of social life and institutions in general. Throughout the history of human society, moral standards have varied from the primitive customs followed unreflectively by early man to the carefully reasoned theories of life of modern man. Moral practices and standards depend on the stage of social development, the general level of intelligence, and the knowledge available at the time. Even today we find men living at all stages of moral development; there are primitive codes existing alongside more advanced ethical standards. Morality grows out of life itself and is an attempt to discover and live the good life—which is the healthy, the happy, the socially useful, and the rich or fully developed life.

Fourth, morality is coextensive with life itself; it is not some separate area or sphere of life. A moral problem is not just a moral problem; it is also a personal, social, economic, political, or international problem.

TWO UNSATISFACTORY APPROACHES

The moral confusion of our time has been increased by two quite different approaches to the problems of morality. The first is the age-old tendency of men to hold blindly to some belief or line of conduct and to appeal to some authority for its support. The second and more recent tendency is that of men to claim that morality is relative and that there are no fixed moral standards which all men need to follow. The ethical relativists regard morality as a matter of personal or group opinion, preference, or custom.

THE APPEAL TO AUTHORITY

Reliance on authority has been widespread in human history. The authoritarian was almost entirely in control in the past, and even today most people behave as though right conduct means conduct in obedience to some established authority. For some people it is a matter of habit and inertia; they are glad to let others do the thinking or deciding for them, since they do not want to assume the responsibility. Others want the assurance of certainty that comes when they invest some established authority with final wisdom and infallibility.

The authorities that have been followed are many and varied. They include custom and tradition, a moral code, a creedal statement, a church or other institution, a sacred literature or some portion of it, "natural" law, the commands of the state or of some "divinely ordained" rulers, and the word of some individual.

In the chapter "The Sources of Knowledge," we noted that much of our knowledge is gained through the testimony of others, or from authority, and that authority which is open to free and honest examination is a legitimate source of knowledge under certain circumstances. We also noted, however, that authority accepted on blind faith and without regard for the extent to which it may harmonize with experience and reason is a dangerous thing. Today we live under rapidly changing conditions, and we face problems upon which the ancient authorities were silent. They do not tell us whether or not it is right to join a trade union, develop intercontinental ballistic missiles, and so on and on. Authoritarian ethics are likely to delay progress in a changing society. They are also likely to be destructive of a sound moral perspective, since acts are condemned because they violate the code rather than because they are injurious to human welfare. The questionable, the unimportant, and the universally recognized acts of wrongdoing are put on the same moral level. Furthermore, whatever tends to discredit the authority tends to discredit all its pronouncements, leaving one with no system at all.

Many people in our society accept custom as the basis of right and wrong. While many customs are beneficial insofar as they represent a sort of collective wisdom, custom is not a good gauge of morality. To accept custom and tradition as the standard is to submerge the individual's morality in that of society. In the past, progress has come mainly through some individual's challenging the customary actions of the group. While custom and moral demands will ordinarily coincide, we need to remember that there are good customs and bad customs. Our recognition of this fact shows that we are at least implicitly appealing to some standard beyond mere custom.

Divine law in one of its forms is not as certain a standard as it may appear to be at first. Even if we decide that it is right to do the "will of God," there is no hard and fast set of rules that can be identified as "God's will." The codes and commands attributed to God are most diverse, and they have changed with the development of the group and with changed conditions. Many modern religious leaders say that God inspires men to discover the good and to live in pursuit of it. They do not think of ethics as an authoritarian and fixed system.

The role of authority has been weakening in modern society. This is so partly because of the influences of the Renaissance, the Reformation, modern science, the democratic spirit which stresses the worth of the person and his right to think and to judge for himself, historical studies, and rapid changes in our mode of living and working. The modern attitude is not "as it was in the beginning," but "prove all things" and "hold fast only to that which can stand the test of living."

ETHICAL RELATIVISM AND SUBJECTIVISM

At the opposite extreme from authoritarianism we find a number of closely related positions of which ethical relativism and subjectivism are two examples. Some people, having rejected the older authorities, have discovered no new ones, at least none that have any objective validity. Many people have also been influenced by the facts, presented by the anthropologists, concerning the great diversity of moral practices and codes found among the peoples of the world. Man's views of what is right and wrong have varied from time to time and from place to place. What is right at one place may be wrong at another place. Morals, it is said, come from the *mores,* the folkways that have grown up and are considered the right ways.[1]

The ethical relativists claim that there are no standards accepted by all men everywhere, and that custom can make anything appear right. The ethical relativists do not merely say that what some people *think* is right in one place or at one time is *thought* to be wrong by some other people in another time or at another place; that is quite obvious. What they claim is that what *is* right at one time or place *is* wrong at another time or place (or even at the same time and place, if judgments differ) because there are no objective or universal standards. The ethical relativists find it difficult to reconcile the development and historical relativity of morals with the claim to any non-relative validity. They seem to assume that if moral judgments change they do not have any objective validity. We must realize, however, that if moral judgments are related to human needs, and if there are needs that are common to all men, there will be some standards applicable to all.

Subjectivism in ethical theory is also a protest and reaction against the older authoritarian codes and rationalistic systems. There are a number of types of subjectivism, of which three are as follows: that when I call an action "right" or a state of affairs "good" I mean that people in general approve it; that when I use such terms they mean merely that *I* give my approval; that I do not mean to *assert* anything at all, since I am simply *expressing* a feeling or an emotion.

The subjectivists in ethical theory are saying that whatever an individual or a group thinks or feels to be good *is* good—for him or it. Ethical statements, they say, refer to the feelings and emotions of men; therefore there are no permanent principles of morality and no objective standards on the basis of which we may judge an act right or wrong. The subjectivists claim that ethical terms express and arouse emotions and so stimulate action.

The objectivists in ethical theory will say that when I say an act is right

[1] They will probably quote William G. Sumner's *Folkways,* Edvard A. Westermarck's *Ethical Relativity,* and James G. Frazer's *The Golden Bough.*

I am asserting something about the quality of the act itself and not merely expressing a feeling or asserting a preference. There is a world of difference, the critics say, between the statement "X is right" and "I like or approve X." They further say that slavery, lynching, murder, and arson are wrong and that people who feel otherwise are either stupid or perverse.[2]

THE ETHICAL STANDARD

Since the time of the early Greeks and Hebrews, men have been reflecting on the principles and problems of right and wrong. Ethical thought has expressed itself in many different forms and types of explanations. We shall consider here five types that have been influential and that have persisted to the present day. We shall discuss Kant as the ablest representative of formalism, John Stuart Mill as an outstanding proponent of utilitarianism, or the pleasure theory, Herbert Spencer as a representative of nature as the standard, and Plato as one who stands for the theory of the realization of the person or self. We shall then consider the Christian ethic and the teachings of Jesus of Nazareth as found in the New Testament.

THE MORAL LAW AS THE ETHICAL STANDARD

One of the great systems of ethics was formulated by Immanuel Kant (1724–1804). To appreciate Kant fully, one needs to go directly to his ethical writings, especially his *Metaphysics of Morals* and his *Critique of Practical Reason.* Kant's moral philosophy is sometimes called *formalism,* because he was looking for moral principles that are inherently right or wrong apart from any particular circumstances. These moral principles, or laws, according to Kant, are recognized immediately or directly as true and binding.

Kant inherited the Christian reverence for divine law and the worth of the individual self. He was also profoundly influenced by the Greek and the eighteenth-century respect for reason. According to Kant, moral philosophy is properly concerned not with what is, but with what ought to be. In man there is a sense of duty, the "I ought," or the moral law, which is logically prior to experience and which springs from a man's innermost nature. The moral law results from the will governed by reason. The moral law brings man into contact with the very order of the universe itself, since the laws of nature and the laws of reason are essentially one.

Next to the moral law, or the sense of duty, Kant emphasized the good motive or the good will as central. "Nothing can possibly be conceived in the world, or even out of it, which can be called good without qualification,

---

2 For an excellent criticism of ethical relativism by Brand Blanshard see "The New Subjectivism in Ethics," *Philosophy and Phenomenological Research,* 9 (March, 1949): 504–511. See also Brand Blanshard, *Reason and Goodness* (New York: Macmillan, 1961), especially Ch. V.

except a Good Will." The one thing that is important is that a man should *will* the good. Intelligence and courage are usually good, but they may be used to promote evil. Happiness may be gained in ignoble ways. A man may contribute to charity because he wants publicity or lacks the courage to refuse requests. The good will is the dutiful will, which acts solely out of respect for the principle of duty. If a man acts from a good motive, the act is good regardless of the consequences. Kant does not say that consequences are not to be considered or that they are unimportant. He does say that the moral quality of the act is not determined by the consequences.

If the will or the motive is governed by reason and not by mere desire, it is absolute and unconditional—that is, obeying it is one's duty, admitting of no exceptions. This call to duty that comes from within is the moral law or, to use Kant's phrase, "the categorical imperative." He gives us three criteria or formulations of the moral law.

The Principle of Universality "Act in conformity with that maxim and that maxim only, which you can at the same time will to be a universal law." Actions should spring not from desires or inclinations but only from principles that can be universalized. Kant uses the example of the man who, after a series of misfortunes, contemplates suicide. When he attempts to universalize such behavior, he realizes at once that it cannot be approved. If everyone were to commit suicide, it would lead to the elimination of mankind. Kant, it will be observed, universalized the general type of conduct and not the particular act under particular circumstances. The latter interpretation might lead to extreme laxness; the former leads to a rigorism that admits few if any exceptions to moral principles.

The Principle of Humanity as an End, Never as Merely a Means "Act so as to use humanity, whether in your own person or in the person of another, always as an end, never as merely a means." This principle has received more widespread approval than any other part of Kant's moral philosophy. People, as rational beings, are ends in themselves and should never be used merely as means to other ends. We may use physical things as means, but when we use a person simply as a means, as in slavery, prostitution, or commercial exploitation, we degrade him and violate his being as a person.

The Principle of Autonomy The moral laws that a man obeys are not imposed on him from the outside. They are the "laws which he imposes upon himself." The sense of duty and the reason which man obeys come from within; they are expressions of his own higher self.

PLEASURE AS THE GUIDE IN ETHICS

The next three ethical theories we consider are teleological—that is, they judge conduct as right or wrong, not on the basis of some inherent quality, as in formalism, but in relationship to some end or goal that is considered good. The doctrine that pleasure or happiness is the greatest good in life was known until recently as *hedonism.* The term *Epicureanism,* from Epicurus, an early Greek exponent of the pleasure theory, has also been used. Since the time of Jeremy Bentham and John Stuart Mill in the nineteenth century, the term *utilitarianism* has been used.

According to John Stuart Mill (1806–1873), utilitarianism "accepts as the foundation of morals, Utility, or the Greatest Happiness Principle, holds that actions are right in proportion as they tend to promote happiness, wrong as they tend to produce the reverse of happiness." Mill's brief but brilliant treatise *Utilitarianism* should be read by all students of moral philosophy. Mill accepts the general position of Jeremy Bentham (1748–1832), who uses the phrase "the greatest happiness of the greatest number." Bentham asserts that nature has placed man under the guidance of two masters, pleasure and pain. Man is a "pleasure-seeking, pain-avoiding" creature. Bentham states his theory in quantitative terms and hopes to establish utilitarian ethics on a strictly scientific basis. In answering the criticisms directed against Bentham's position, Mill modifies the position and adds some new elements.

The most important change that Mill makes in utilitarianism is to add a qualitative standard. Human beings with refined faculties are not satisfied with the pleasures of the body; they seek the higher pleasures of the mind. Once a man has lived on a higher level, he can never really wish to sink into a lower level of existence. This is because of the human sense of dignity. "It is better to be a human being dissatisfied than a pig satisfied; better to be Socrates dissatisfied than a fool satisfied."

Mill vigorously defends utilitarianism against the charge that it encourages selfishness. He maintains that the good of all men or the greatest happiness of the greatest number must be the standard of what is right in conduct. Since we live in an unjust society, some have to sacrifice themselves for the happiness of others. Such sacrifice is not an end in itself; it is a means to the greater happiness of a larger number of people. While all people may not actually seek happiness, they ought to do so. To promote not individual pleasure but the greatest total happiness is the essence of Mill's position.

The utilitarians stress the consequences of conduct. The morality of an act depends, not on the motive from which it originates, but on its effect on society. Motives are relevant to our estimation of the characters of people, but not of actions. In some situations, however, where unforeseen conditions prevent desirable effects, we may approve the act because of its intended consequences.

NATURE AS THE GUIDE IN ETHICS

Nature or biological development has been accepted by some as the guide in ethics. This position is sometimes called the ethics of naturalism or the ethics of evolution. Though the position goes back to Democritus and the Stoics in ancient times, it received its main support in the eighteenth-century doctrines of natural law and natural rights. In the nineteenth century, the doctrine of natural selection as set forth by Charles Darwin gave further support to the appeal to nature. Nature, it was said, selects those best fitted to survive; thus man should accept nature and be guided by her laws.

Herbert Spencer[3] (1820–1903) popularized the concepts of "evolution" and "nature" and applied them to all realms of thought. The greatest good, he said, is a long life and harmonious adaptation to the environment. It is wise for man to trust in nature and avoid interference with her processes. We can trust nature, he thought, since her ways tend to eliminate evils and bring happiness and progress. Individuals must be free from all unnecessary interference by the state. The position of Spencer supported an individualistic, or *laissez-faire,* point of view. Apart from protecting men from foreign enemies and checking crime, he said, the state has few, if any, duties.

Others have pointed out that a distinctive trait of man is his ability to think and to choose, and that, if some ways of living appear better than others, man ought to exercise his power to control nature. Modern society does not seem content to let nature take its course.

THE DEVELOPMENT OF THE PERSON: SELF-REALIZATION

This theory considers as right that which tends to promote the development of all the normal capacities of man as a thinking, feeling, and acting person. Many able philosophers in both ancient and modern times have subscribed to this theory. It has been called by various names—perfectionism, eudaemonism, energism, and self-realization. We will discuss Plato as the first outstanding representative of this theory.

In his great work *The Republic* and in other writings, Plato says that there are three active principles within man. There is, first, the rational part. This is the mind, or intellect, whose proper function is to rule the body. Reason alone comprehends the true nature of things. There is, second, the feeling part of man. This consists of the sensations and the heroic virtues. There are, third, the appetites, or the desiring part of man. There is no principle of order among human passions except as the appetites are controlled by reason. Each part or function has its proper place and role in life, and when the three parts operate in harmony, each carrying out its own function, there is order and peace.

Corresponding to the nature of man, the well-ordered society is also made up of three parts: the rulers, who use their training and insight to rule the state; the officials and warriors, who execute the laws and protect the state; and the workers, artisans, and peasants, who provide the material necessities

3 *Principles of Ethics* (New York: Appleton-Century-Crofts, 1900).

of life. The well-ordered society results when each group carries out its functions in harmony with the other parts of society.

The virtues grow out of the nature of man and the organization of society. Arising from reason in man and corresponding to the rulers in the state is wisdom. Accompanying the feeling side of man and corresponding to the officials and warriors in the state is courage. Two virtues, however, are all-inclusive, since in the good society they will be found among all segments of society. They are temperance, or self-control, and justice, or righteousness. They make possible a harmony of functions within man and the harmonious adjustment between man and society. Man's life and the organization of society should thus harmonize with the moral order of the universe. The greatest good is the harmonious development and the maximum richness of life.

Aristotle, in his *Nicomachean Ethics,* wrote the first really systematic treatise on ethics. His position differs from that of Plato mainly in emphasis. Reason, well-being, and moderation are the central concepts. Just as the excellence of the sculptor lies in the skill with which he applies his art, so the excellence of man lies in the fulfillment of his function as a man. The function peculiar to man is his life of reason. He should live in the light of reason, and so by principles that are valid for all men. The highest good is *eudaemonia,* or well-being. The good life avoids the extremes of both excessive repression and excessive indulgence. The good life involves the harmonious development of the normal functions of the organism. St. Thomas Aquinas (c. 1225–1274) incorporated the views of Aristotle into the philosophy of the church; they are influential today in Neo-Thomist thought.

The theory of self-realization has emphasized the development of all the functions of the person as the greatest good. Nothing short of the harmonious development of all sides of man's nature may be accepted as a satisfactory standard. Furthermore, the emphasis is social as well as individual. Personal welfare is bound up with social welfare. Not only cooperation and sharing but often sacrifice are necessary so that the greatest good for man may be attained.

THE CHRISTIAN ETHICAL IDEAL

The Christian ethical ideal has been a powerful influence in Western civilization. Is the Christian ethic an example of formalism or of the theory of self-realization, which emphasizes the development of people? It has been identified with both these views and, on occasion, with the happiness theory. There are many Christians, however, who claim that Christianity is unique in its outlook and emphasis.

Central to all types of Christian ethics have been the teachings of Jesus as found in the New Testament; Jesus left no writings. He did not formulate an entirely new set of ethical principles. Practically every element of his teaching had been advanced by some prophet or teacher who preceded him. He did bring together certain central convictions of morality and religion in a simple and direct fashion and exemplified them in his own life as no other person has done. Inheriting a rich legacy of morality from Judaism, he gave it a new form. He took the rather exclusive nationalistic morality of his day and made it into a universal morality that embraced all men. Christians believe that he revealed the heart of the moral issue.

Central to the ethical teachings of Jesus is his emphasis on the value of the self, or person. Each man is to be treated as an end in himself. Man is of greater value than anything else. When asked a question regarding the observance of the Sabbath, the most sacred of institutions at that time, Jesus replied, "The Sabbath was made for man, not man for the Sabbath." People are ends in themselves; all other things are means.

A closely related notion is Jesus' principle of the progressive growth of personality. Men must grow or they deteriorate. "First the blade, then the ear, then the full grain in the ear." He saw even in the fallen woman and the hated tax collector the potentialities for progressive growth.

For Jesus morality was inner and positive, a matter of the "heart" or a disposition of the feeling and will. Goodness resided not, as for the Greeks, in knowledge and intelligence but in the inner springs of action. Love was the supreme virtue or character trait. When asked about the great commandments, Jesus said, "Thou shalt love the Lord thy God with all thy heart, and with all thy soul, and with all thy mind, and with all thy strength; this is the first commandment. And the second is like, namely this, Thou shalt love thy neighbor as thyself. There is none other commandment greater than these." Each man is under an obligation to promote the interests of the other people with whom he comes in contact. Love, unselfishness, selflessness, or social-mindedness received a new emphasis in human relations.

In the teachings of Jesus, ethics and religion are closely related. To live the good life is to obey God. Throughout history some Christians have thought that Christian ethics is a repository of final and absolute truth revealed by God. For an increasingly large number of Christians, however, the Christian life is a quest for the good under the inspiration of devotion to the ideals of Jesus. Men are encouraged to discover the tasks that need to be done, and then to view these tasks as a part of man's duty to God.

Christians have not always agreed about the nature of Christian ethics or its relation to the various types of moral philosophy. For example, is Christian ethics an ethics of duty, obligation, or obedience quite apart from the goodness of anything? Or does Christian ethics judge actions right or wrong according to whether they promote or hinder some end considered to be good in itself? There are two broad types of religious ethics, and these two approaches are found in Judaism, Christianity, and other religions. The first view is that ethical duties neither have nor need a justification or reason beyond the fact that they are God's will. This is an attempt to keep ethics strictly theological and to insist that it must be expressed in theological concepts. The more conservative form of this approach is a Biblical or creedal literalism in which religion is viewed as a final body of truth that has been completely revealed. All one needs to do is to discover this truth and obey its laws. Those who accept the historical approach to Biblical literature and the results of modern scholarship seek divine revelation in the events recorded in the Bible; they seek the "Word behind the words." God does not require certain things because they are right; they are right because God requires them. The business of ethics is to ascertain what God expects men to do.

According to the second type of religious ethics, men are inspired by their view of man and of God and their love of God to discover the good and to live so as to achieve it. Loyalty to Christ or to God means leading the best possible life in the situation in which men find themselves. The religious or ethical spirit is best expressed as a supreme concern for people. Men discover through experience and their growing knowledge the tasks that need to be done; then these tasks are viewed as part of their duty to God. Religion is thus a strong motivating force, which emphasizes both purity of motive and the continuous quest for a more abundant life for all men.[4]

THE BASIS OF THE MORAL LIFE

We have considered five possible answers to the question "What is the greatest good?" Though these views are quite dissimilar, they agree that there are higher and lower forms of conduct, and that we have an obligation to follow the higher if we can discover it. These theories will agree in their moral judgments in the majority of cases. The disagreements arise in a consideration of the exceptional or borderline cases. The Kantian notion of the moral law as guided by reason includes the principle of humanity as an end in itself. The utilitarian principle of the greatest happiness and the appeal to follow nature, if these are applied in enlightened ways, are likely to lead to conduct that recognizes people's needs. The theory of self-realization and the Christian ideal both stress the development of people, though in different frames of reference.

RIGHT IS PERSON-AFFIRMING

In the realm of morality, we call an action right because it has value for people or promotes the welfare of society as a whole. To be moral is to respect

4 For a discussion of the relation between morality and religion and the Judaeo-Christian ethical ideals, see Harold H. Titus, *Ethics for Today* (3rd ed.; New York: American Book, 1957), pp. 521–541. See also books by Thomas, Ramsey, and others at the end of Ch. 32 in *Ethics for Today*.

personality, in ourselves and in others. We may say then, very broadly, that right is person-affirming; wrong is person-denying. To a person who is morally mature, an act that is beneficial to people is a good act, and an act that is harmful is an evil act, regardless of whether other members of the community approve or disapprove of the action. If there is no clear-cut right course of action, as sometimes is the case, then the right choice is that which promotes the greater or greatest value or, negatively, the lesser evil.

When a mature person faces a question of right and wrong for which his past training and experience give him little or no immediate guidance, he seeks to discover all the relevant factors in the situation. Then, in the light of his evaluation of the total situation, he makes his decision. The essence of reflective morality is the ability and the willingness to weigh all the facts in a situation and to base one's choice on the results of such reflection. Reflective morality consists not only in making personal decisions but also in making clear the reasons for one's decisions.

LIVING MAKES DEMANDS ON US

Life makes demands on us and thus places us under obligation, so that we have both duties and rights. In every normal creature there is an urge, growing out of the life process itself, toward the expansion and fulfillment of its existence. Morality grows out of life and its needs; it arises from the nature of ourselves as people and from the nature of the world in which man lives. Let us consider some of the demands on man.

1. *Physical demands.* There are physical needs that must be met by appropriate decisions and actions. If a man lives one way, he survives and remains healthy. If he lives some other way, his life is difficult, or he may actually die. Man needs fresh air, sunshine, certain temperature conditions, food and drink, exercise, and sleep if his body is to function well. The way these needs are satisfied is determined in large part by the anatomical and physiological nature of man and by the environmental conditions under which he lives. Ordinarily we do not think very much about these things until something goes wrong and life is affected; then we make known our demands—for pure milk, health measures, the elimination of pests, better ventilation, and the like. We have a moral obligation neither to ruin our health nor to live so that we become diseased. We condemn the actions that bring harm to ourselves and others; we approve the actions that maintain or promote conditions beneficial to man.

2. *Psychological and social demands.* There are basic urges and desires that arise from our psychological makeup and social needs. These urges express themselves in similar ways wherever human beings are found. In these areas, too, life makes demands on us. Anger, fear, jealousy, and worry are harmful to the body, and tend to disrupt social life. Except under special conditions,

when they act as a warning or aid in coping with great evils, they are to be avoided. Love and good will tend to be beneficial to the body and promote social welfare. Certain traits, like unselfishness, friendship, honesty, courage, and self-control, are almost universally approved. Other traits and practices, like selfishness, treachery, murder, theft, and cheating, are almost universally condemned. The desirable or approved traits are called virtues; the undesirable traits are called vices. The judgment that a man who possesses the first set of traits is a good man and a man who possesses the second set is an evil man is not artificial and arbitrary. Such distinctions are based on the nature of man and the demands of society.

Man must associate with his fellows in innumerable ways. Only through cooperative effort can men gain adequate food, shelter, and protection and establish institutions such as the family, school, church, and state. Out of social interaction and cooperation develop folkways, mores, and institutional practices. Regulations express themselves outwardly in customs and laws; inwardly they register themselves in a sense of duty, in expressions of approval and disapproval. Social life makes demands upon us: to keep our agreements, to follow the customs, to obey the law. We have a moral obligation to keep our agreements unless exceptional conditions make this impossible, to follow the customs unless we are convinced they are detrimental to the general welfare, to obey the laws and to seek their improvement. These demands arise from the nature of people as they express themselves in community relations.

3. *Intellectual and spiritual demands.* Men recognize intellectual and spiritual demands, too. There is a moral obligation to be informed on significant matters and to behave as intelligently as possible. Intelligence tends to save time, energy, and at times even life itself. To be reasonable means to be consistent and moderate. The early Greeks believed that reason ought to be in control of the appetites and desires, and that only if it were could man lead a satisfactory life. This conviction, accepted by Christian thinkers though not stressed as much as love or unselfishness, is a basic belief underlying Western civilization. There is an almost universal conviction, expressed in the religious and ethical systems, that the satisfactions of the mind and spirit are more desirable and lasting than the satisfactions of the body.

While knowledge and intelligence are necessary for a mature morality, they are not sufficient. Intelligence alone is not sufficient, since clever men are sometimes vicious; knowledge may be used for destructive purposes. All the great ethical systems and moral codes that have survived over long periods of time have emphasized love and compassion as the very heart of morality. Love may lead to self-sacrifice under certain circumstances. The statement of Jesus, often called the Golden Rule—"Whatever you wish that men would do to you, do so to them"—is the very center of Christian morality. The same principle was set forth by Confucius for the Chinese, and the same general idea has been expressed in the ethical teachings of other great religions.

Human attitudes and actions must conform to the needs of man and to the basic structure and processes of the universe, or life will be a failure. If there exists in the universe a creative spirit that makes for truth, beauty, and goodness, then man must cooperatively relate himself to this purpose to realize the good life. There is, it appears, an order of things that is independent of man and unaffected by his wishes, desires, and beliefs. To oppose it is to court frustration and pain. To live in harmony with it is to find satisfaction and happiness and to fulfill man's basic nature.

MOTIVES, MEANS, AND CONSEQUENCES

Finding the right course of action is not always simple. When conflicts of interest arise, the solution may require the very greatest intelligence and goodwill, and even then we may be in doubt as to whether or not we have acted rightly. In judging conduct we have to consider motives, means, and consequences. There is no part of the process that we can disregard.

1. *Motives.* Motives, as Jesus, Kant, and others have pointed out, are basic for a determination of morality. A good motive is a prerequisite to conduct that we approve without qualification. If a good motive is present when an act, through some unforeseen factor, leads to harmful effects, we tend to disapprove less severely and to say, "Anyway, he meant well." When people ask, "What is right in this situation?" their intentions are usually good and they are trying to find the right way of carrying them out.

2. *Means.* Just as there may be many motives for desiring something, there may be many means of achieving it. We expect a man to use the best means available to carry out his purpose. We condemn the student who cheats to pass his examination. On rare occasions we may approve an act when means are used that under other conditions would be condemned. Take the classic example of the theater manager who finds his theater on fire backstage while a play is in progress. He wants to protect the audience, and immediately recalls similar occasions in the past when the audience became panicky and stampeded, resulting in injury and loss of life. He goes before the audience, therefore, gives a false reason for stopping the play, and the theater is emptied without injury or loss of life. To say that any means may be used provided it can be shown that the end is good would be to state a dangerous principle, but there are rare occasions in which the goodness of the end outweighs certain evil means that seem unavoidable. Good consequences can ordinarily be achieved only by the use of good means. Once chosen, the means become part of the general effect of an act.

3. *Consequences.* We expect the general consequences of an act that we call

right to be good. Ordinarily when people ask, "What is right?" they are thinking about the consequences of the action. Conduct is right if it proceeds from a good motive, through the use of the best available means, to consequences that are good. If these conditions are not fulfilled, men will condemn the action or they will approve only with reservations. Rarely do they approve an action when the results are evil. In the case of the surgeon operating with skill on a patient who dies in spite of all efforts to save him, we approve the action because the motive was good and because, in the light of the knowledge available at the time, it was thought that this action was the one most likely to bring good consequences.

SOME IMPLICATIONS OF THIS APPROACH

1. We have an *objective basis for morality*. When we make ethical judgments we assert something that may be either true or false, depending on the available evidence. Whether or not an act is right or wrong is a fact to be discovered. This means that distinctions between right and wrong are not mere matters of opinion, custom, or emotion. Some acts are right and others wrong, regardless of what the members of the community think about them. Whether an act has good or evil results can usually be ascertained by an appeal to human experience or to other evidence at hand.

2. This interpretation recognizes the *dynamic, functional, and experimental nature of morality*. Moral judgments grow out of life and are affected by changing conditions. While men may differ in their views of right and wrong, just as they do in their conceptions of what is true and false, they may hope to be able to resolve these differences with additional insight. This interpretation places a premium on man's growing knowledge. The more we know about our own selves, about social relations, and about the universe around us, the more likely we are to be able to make accurate ethical judgments. Knowledge and research in all fields take on new significance.

3. The view presented here *recognizes the element of truth in moral relativism, while opposing its more extreme claims*. There are, of course, personal elements in moral judgments, and these judgments are not absolute (that is, admitting of no exceptions), as we have seen. With an objective standard there is nothing to prevent an action from being objectively right for one person and wrong for another. For example, A is a strong swimmer who has taken life-saving lessons. B is unable to swim. A's duty to rescue a drowning person is great, whereas B has no such obligation, because he has no ability to effect such a rescue. Physical, biological, psychological, and social conditions influence our decisions. If the conditions of life undergo change and if there is a development in man's knowledge of himself and the world, there will be changes in his moral codes.

4. The suggested approach *can be accepted by those who hold variant philosophical positions*, since it is not dependent on a single metaphysical approach.

It may be held by realists, idealists, pragmatists, and others. It is compatible with a humanistic and naturalistic, as well as with a theistic, view of man.

QUESTIONS AND PROJECTS

1. Review Questions

(1) Explain the three areas of interest and study in the fields of morality and ethics.

(2) Clarify the use of such terms as *morals, moral judgments, ethics,* and *metaethics.*

(3) Indicate some facts of the moral life that prompt thinking men to give attention to questions of right and wrong or to moral standards.

(4) Evaluate authoritarianism in ethics. When is it advisable to accept the testimony of others, and when is it inadvisable or dangerous?

(5) What is ethical relativism? What reasons are advanced for it? Evaluate this position critically, indicating its strengths and weaknesses.

(6) What is subjectivism in the realm of morals? Critically evaluate this point of view.

(7) What are the central points in the following positions: (a) formalism, or Kant's appeal to the moral law; (b) pleasure as the guide to morality; (c) nature as the moral standard; and (d) the development of persons or self-realization as the moral standard?

(8) What are some distinctive emphases in the Christian ethical ideal?

(9) Clarify the distinctions between the two contrasting types of ethics found in religious systems. Evaluate these contrasting positions.

(10) What is the evidence for the view that morality grows out of life and its needs, and that moral judgments for mature people are not mere matters of opinion?

(11) Indicate the role in moral conduct of motives, means, and consequences.

(12) State the ethical theory set forth in the latter part of this chapter, and give some of the implications or conclusions that follow from an acceptance of this approach. In what respects do you agree or disagree with the position?

2. What are the two or three most crucial moral issues facing men today? Support your views.

3. State in your own words what you consider the basis of the distinction between right and wrong. Are you able to affirm that there is "an independent order of things" which is unaffected by human wishes and beliefs and which should play a part in our moral judgments?

4. Is moral experimentation possible? If so, in what areas? If we are to experiment, what principles should be kept in mind? See Harold H. Titus, *Ethics for Today* (3rd ed.; New York: American Book, 1957), Ch. 13, "Experimentation in the Field of Morals," and Ch. 29, "Next Steps in Moral Evolution."

5. Discuss the following quotations:

(1) "Ethics can never be a fixed code; it is only a series of suggestions."

(2) "Ethics is useless, for we do not need theories to tell us how to act."

(3) "One ought always to prefer the greater to the lesser good when either of these can be chosen but not both."

(4) "Love in itself supplies no means and end or principle of selection. Unless guided by insight it can lead to disaster."

6. "For whoever would save his life will lose it; and whoever loses his life for my sake, he will save it." (Luke 9:24) Do you agree or disagree with the writer who says that this is "the greatest discovery ever made"? Is it also true that man needs to lose himself in some cause to find satisfaction in life?

7. In a chapter "Our Double Morality," in *Strength of Men and Nations* (New York: Harper, 1959), William Ernest Hocking calls our attention to the fact that our traditional notions of morality are mainly personal. But a considerable part of our lives is lived in one or more of the numerous "groups-for-doing-things"—from boys' gangs to political parties—where the standards or rules for action are sometimes in conflict with the conventional standards. A divided or double morality, he says, is "fatal for morale" and may involve "acute moral suffering." Do you agree with Hocking? Can you give examples of conflicting standards as men move from home and church circles to their business, professional, or political activities?

8. Review one of the following: From the Suggested Readings, the books by Cahn, Garnett, Johnson, Lewis, and Schneider; also, Marquis W. Childs and Douglass Cater, *Ethics in a Business Society* (New York: New American Library of World Literature, 1954) (Mentor ed.); R. Corkey, *A Philosophy of Christian Morals for Today* (London: Allen and Unwin, 1961); George P. Grant, *Philosophy in the Mass Society* (New York: Hill & Wang, 1960); Robert T. Harris, *Social Ethics* (New York: Lippincott, 1962); D. J. B. Hawkins, *Man and Morals* (New York: Sheed & Ward, 1960); Richard LaPiere, *The Freudian Ethic* (New York: Duell, Sloane and Pearce, 1959); T. V. Smith, *The Ethics of Compromise and the Art of Containment* (New York: Starr King, 1956).

SUGGESTED READINGS

AIKEN, HENRY DAVID. *Reason and Conduct: New Bearings in Moral Philosophy.* New York: Knopf, 1962.
Essays, written over a period of years, that deal with problems of moral philosophy. The author is seeking answers to "questions of analytic ethics" as well as trends in ethical theory.

BLANSHARD, BRAND. *Reason and Goodness.* New York: Macmillan, 1961.
This book, based on the Gifford Lectures, discusses the recent conflicts in ethical theory with emphasis on the tension between reason and feeling and between Greek and Christian ways of thinking. A clear statement of some difficult issues.

CAHN, EDMOND. *The Moral Decision: Right and Wrong in the Light of American Law.* Bloomington: Indiana U. Press, 1955.
Through discussion of cases and judicial decisions, the author demonstrates the relation between morals and the law.

GARNETT, A. CAMPBELL. *The Moral Nature of Man.* New York: Ronald, 1952.

A critical analysis of ethical terms and principles that includes a discussion of intuitionism, naturalistic ethics, and ethics and religion.

HILL, THOMAS ENGLISH. *Contemporary Ethical Theories.* New York: Macmillan, 1950.
This volume surveys and classifies the moral theories of the present century in an attempt to clarify concepts of the right, good, and duty.

JOHNSON, F. ERNEST (ed.). *Patterns of Ethics in America Today.* New York: Collier Books, 1962.
Following the editor's introduction, six leaders discuss the ethics of Judaism, Roman Catholicism, Protestantism, and the Ethical Culture movement, and national ethics and ethical frontiers.

JOHNSON, OLIVER A. *Rightness and Goodness: A Study in Contemporary Ethical Theory.* The Hague: Nijhoff, 1959.
A discussion of the two major ethical traditions in the West. The author says that goodness is the fundamental concept and our first duty is to "maximize goodness."

LEWIS, CLARENCE IRVING. *The Ground and Nature of the Right.* New York: Columbia U. Press, 1955.
A carefully reasoned discussion that deals with the rational basis for value judgments as the guide to action.

RICE, PHILIP BLAIR. *On the Knowledge of Good and Evil.* New York: Random House, 1955.
A critical study of the various types of value theory in an attempt to find a solution to the problems of ethics that will be adequate for today.

ROSS, WILLIAM D. *Foundations of Ethics.* New York: Oxford U. Press, 1939.
According to the author, the "right" is not derived from the good. There are prima facie obligations, or synthetic a priori judgments, like the axioms of mathematics, that are arrived at by intuitive processes. Abstract and difficult.

SCHNEIDER, HERBERT W. *Morals for Mankind.* Columbia: U. of Missouri Press, 1960.
The author sees a morality for mankind in the making and points out some conditions necessary for building a world-wide community.

SINGER, MARCUS GEORGE. *Generalization in Ethics.* New York: Knopf, 1961.
A long subtitle, "An Essay in the Logic of Ethics, with the Rudiments of a System of Moral Philosophy," sums up the book very well. The author sets forth a "rational morality."

WARNOCK, MARY. *Ethics Since 1900.* Oxford: Oxford U. Press, 1960. (Home University Library of Modern Knowledge.)
This book gives a readable account of ethical theory in the twentieth century. One consequence of the excessive emphasis on an analysis of ethical language is that "ethics as a serious subject has been left further and further behind."

WERKMEISTER, W. H. *Theories of Ethics: A Study in Moral Obligation.* Lincoln: Johnsen, 1961.
This book is a critical evaluation of the ethical controversies, especially in the field of analysis and theoretical ethics, that have arisen during the last few decades.

TWENTY-ONE

AESTHETICS AND THE
PHILOSOPHY OF ART

In this chapter we shall consider the aesthetic experience, some of the theories that men have set forth to explain aesthetic values and the nature of art, and the place of art and the aesthetic response in modern society. While man generally concerns himself first with the bare necessities for survival, he has never considered the mere continuation of existence a sufficient goal. Man is in part a creature who thinks and decides, but he is perhaps primarily a feeling being, with a wide range of responses. His emotional reactions and feelings need to be cultivated and refined along with his thoughts if he is to become mature. The aesthetic appeal of man's environment has occupied him greatly throughout the years. He makes judgments, favorable or unfavorable, about what he hears, sees, and reads. He is interested in his general appearance, the clothes and ornaments he wears, and his environment.

Aesthetics holds insights and surprises for the inquiring mind. Beauty in some form is recognized by men everywhere, but our experience and understanding are enriched and broadened as we proceed with a study of aesthetics and the factors that underlie the aesthetic experience.

THE AESTHETIC EXPERIENCE

THE NATURE OF THE AESTHETIC EXPERIENCE

Since *aesthetic experience,* as distinct from the philosophy of art, pertains to the perceptual level of human experience, let us make clear the distinctions among a *sensation,* a *percept,* and a *concept.* As a result of a stimulus we receive a *sensation* through one of our sense organs. We may see, hear, touch, smell, or taste something. Such sensations may be unorganized or vague and convey little or nothing in the way of ideas. But when these sensory impulses are organized into units or wholes so that we recognize objects, such as stones, trees, books, or people, we speak of *percepts* or *perception.* I have a sensation of redness; I perceive an apple. When we move from particular things to general ideas, class terms, or universals, we enter the realm of concepts.

When I see a particular man, John Doe, I have a percept. When I talk about man or humanity, I am talking not about any particular person but about what is common to men in general, or the *concept* "man." In philosophy, theology, and theoretical science we generally deal with conceptual problems.

Aesthetic experience that is the result of perceptual experience is most frequently visual or auditory, but it is not limited to these areas. It may be related to our sense of touch, taste, or smell. Aesthetic experience includes any pleasurable absorption in these perceptual experiences insofar as it arises from a disinterested contemplation of phenomena, whether natural or man-made. The aesthetic "emotion" may be aroused by artistic productions, in which the artist has attempted to evoke an aesthetic response, or it may be aroused by many different kinds of objects or experiences that occur, sometimes quite unexpectedly, in everyday living.

While cultural, intellectual, associational, and sentimental factors may enter into the experience of an aesthetic object and supplement the response, the aesthetic aspects are unique and must not be identified or confused with these accompanying characteristics. Hunter Mead says:

> I personally would argue that the more of these supplementary values the artist is able to add, the more broadly significant the work will be, and the more moving will be our response to it as an inclusive human experience. But always I would insist that *unless there is this central core of strictly aesthetic value,* arising from the presentation of perceptual relations which we find it rewarding to contemplate in themselves and for their own sake, the object is not a work of art or an "aesthetic object" in *any* sense of the word. It may still give us a pleasing and even deeply moving experience—art has no monopoly on pleasurable or moving experiences—but it cannot be a truly artistic one. The aesthetic alone can give us art, although all great art embodies other values in addition. But no abundance of these subordinate value-experiences can by itself constitute art; the aesthetic is the irreducible minimum of the artistic.[1]

In discussing the aesthetic attitude and aesthetics, James L. Jarrett says:

> Aesthetics is the study of aesthetic experience, aesthetic attitude, aesthetic quality, aesthetic value and derivatively of closely related topics such as artistic creativity, artistic standards, beauty and its opposites. . . . One takes an aesthetic attitude toward a work of art or some part of nature when he deliberately *opens himself to the qualities of the experience.*[2]

In discussing the nature of the aesthetic mood or attitude, Mead[3] gives

[1] Hunter Mead, *An Introduction to Aesthetics,* p. 61. Copyright 1952 The Ronald Press Company.
[2] James L. Jarrett, *The Quest for Beauty,* pp. 2, 106. © 1957. Prentice-Hall, Inc., Englewood Cliffs, N. J.
[3] *Introduction to Aesthetics,* pp. 13 ff.

three characteristics of the aesthetic attitude. There is, first, the aspect of detachment, in which a person during the experience is released from the practical concerns of everyday living. Second, the true aesthetic attitude is disinterested and nonpossessive. "To appreciate without the itch to acquire, to love without longing to possess, to contemplate with joy and satisfaction but without thought of social advantage, economic gain, or practical exploitation: this is to achieve the disinterested attitude which is fundamental to the aesthetic mood."[4] Third, the aesthetic attitude is impersonal and thus involves "the temporary elimination of certain expressions of the personality." One is absorbed by the aesthetic object. In a sense one gets "outside himself," transcends his narrow interests and acquires a new perspective. This mood carries detachment and disinterestedness a stage further.

WHAT THE AESTHETIC EXPERIENCE CAN DO FOR US

The aesthetic experience, in addition to bringing immediate pleasure and satisfaction by revealing certain experiential elements of reality, can also fortify us in various ways to meet the practical demands of life. The aesthetic response to music, for example, may be therapeutic. It may stimulate or soothe us; it may change the rate of the heartbeat, ease digestion, or affect other bodily processes. The aesthetic experience may help renew our spirits, exciting us and giving us courage and enthusiasm for some strenuous task. The power of the aesthetic experience in its different forms to create various moods, from patience to a spirit of sacrifice, is well known.

The aesthetic experience and response may help create a social bond between diverse individuals and groups by arousing sympathy, furnishing understanding, and producing a desire for harmonious relationships. The presence of beauty, whether in nature or in art objects, tends to make our lives qualitatively richer.

Plato says that even ordinary human beings, if they are reared amid masterpieces of painting, sculpture, architecture, and so on, will be ennobled thereby. If artists are gifted to discern and disclose the nature of the beautiful and graceful, "then will our youth dwell in a land of health, amid fair sights and sounds, and receive the good in everything; and beauty . . . shall flow into the eye and ear, like a health-giving breeze."[5] The young will imbibe a taste for beauty and decency and this will affect their entire lives.

THE AESTHETIC EXPERIENCE, BEAUTY, AND THE ARTS

How are the aesthetic experience, beauty, and the arts related? There are

4 Hunter Mead, *An Introduction to Aesthetics*, p. 18. Copyright 1952 The Ronald Press Company.
5 Plato, *The Republic* (New York: Scribner's, 1928), p. 114. (The Modern Student's Library. Introduction by Charles M. Bakewell.)

wide differences of opinion as to what objects call forth the aesthetic response, and what beauty really is. Our concepts of beauty may differ not because of the nature of beauty itself, but because of varying degrees of preparation in discerning beauty. Therefore, if we cannot perceive beauty in objects that others find beautiful, it may be wise to withhold judgment until we are capable ourselves of making a competent analysis of the aesthetic experience.

Aesthetic experiences are basic and fundamental to art, and we should refuse to call anything *art* that does not have aesthetic value. Some people, however, divorce art from the aesthetic experience and link it to other interests and values that have little or no relation to the aesthetic—that is, art is used for propaganda, prestige, camouflage, and so on. Art justifies aesthetic analysis only insofar as it has genuine aesthetic value.

THE PLACE OF BEAUTY

Definitions of *beauty* are many and varied. It has been defined as "truth," "the expression of an ideal," "an assemblage of properties satisfying the aesthetic sense," "harmony in diversity," and "an intrinsic quality of things themselves." While definitions do not agree, there is no uncertainty concerning the fact of beauty. Fortunately for most of us, beauty in some form is almost continuously present. Even those who live in comparatively drab and unpleasant surroundings find frequent opportunity to experience beauty in an expression, a face, a garment, a trinket, a bit of cloud or sky, the sunset, or a landscape. While men differ widely in their capacity for appreciation of beauty, some enjoyment is apparently possible for all.

In much contemporary as well as traditional aesthetic theory, art is what is beautiful, and what is not beautiful is not art. From this point of view, all discords and irregularities are not beautiful and therefore not art. The modern trend in the interpretation of art, however, is away from this traditional identification of art exclusively with beauty. If an artist is endeavoring to give certain experiential qualities artistic form, then he must be free to express the ugly as well as the beautiful.

According to the modern interpretation, the artist must portray things as he "sees" them, and so in many instances he must express the misery and the injustices, the ugliness and brutality, which are a part of his vision of life. Some works of art are not beautiful, and some beautiful things, like landscapes, are not works of art. The possession of beauty, however, may be taken as the criterion for art that is likely to continue to appeal to man.

MEDIUM, TECHNIQUE, FORM, AND SUBJECT MATTER IN ART

In the work of art the aesthetic experience is related to at least four elements. First, there is the medium (or media). The material used varies as we pass from one art form to another—from painting to sculpture to music—

and it also varies within any one field. A statue, for example, may be made from any one of several different materials. The material (the medium) enters into the total effect, but it alone does not determine the aesthetic response.

Second, there is the technique. This includes the method of artistic execution as a particular formal arrangement as, for example, in cubism. It also includes the skill with which the artist carries out this arrangement or the ability with which he organizes or handles his material. Technique may make all the difference between an excellent and a mediocre or poor performance of a musical composition or a dance, or an excellent or poor painting. The aesthetic experience may be enriched by awareness of the skill involved. However, if the skill in execution is not quite perfect or is too prominent it may lead to a loss of that sense of the qualitative whole so essential to aesthetic appreciation.

Third, there is the form of the work of art. Form has to do with the arrangement and order of the various parts of the whole. A melody is an arrangement of tones; a dance is an arrangement of movements. Certain formal requirements need to be met if a work is to stimulate the aesthetic response. While there is no general agreement as to what formal requirements must be met, a list of these requirements usually includes unity, order, rhythm, balance, proportion (including harmony and symmetry), integrity, depth, and, for some forms of art, functionality. The parts need to be arranged in aesthetically satisfactory ways, so that there is no artistically unwarranted tension or lopsidedness, and the execution needs to reveal mastery of the art (or good technique).

Fourth, there is content or subject matter. The subject matter is what the work has to deal with, and this may cover the whole range of experience including portraits, animals, sunsets, trees and meadows, waterfalls, adventure, love and hate, and the like. Here we come to the aesthetic object that may be or depict some of the familiar things of life, or may portray emotions, impressions, and insights in symbolic form. In his work the artist may disclose features of our world that we would not observe apart from his insights.

Some art critics have said that in art the "how" is everything and the "what" is not important. This is the form-content controversy that is one of a number of philosophical issues, like the epistemological status of the art object and the "who's to judge?" problem, that we shall be unable to discuss in a single chapter.

THEORIES OF ART

The theories of art that have appeared throughout human history are many and varied, and no one theory is generally accepted. Some of the more popular interpretations are set forth briefly here. As will be seen, the theories overlap and are often different in kind. Some describe the genesis of works of art, others the nature of works of art, still others the artist, and so on. An acquaintance with them, however, will help one see the breadth and the richness of the field and may also help eliminate some false impressions about the nature of art. Critical comments are reserved until the end of this part.

ART AS IMITATION

The notion of art as imitation has been prominent since the time of the ancient Greeks, when it received support from both Plato and Aristotle. Objects of beauty were not considered to be fundamentally different from other objects known through the senses. Plato, a great lover of the arts as well as their severe critic, makes some reference to them in nearly all of his *Dialogues*. A central idea is that works of art imitate something. Painting and sculpture depict objects and people. Music imitates human moods and emotions. For Plato, however, the art object or reproduction is only an imperfect copy of the subject. Plato also gives some support to other explanations of art, as we shall see.

Aristotle, Plato's pupil, finds in imitation a natural tendency that he regards, along with the pleasure that comes from recognition of the object or scene portrayed, as the explanation of art. Painting grows out of the desire to make likenesses of people and things. The theater imitates men in action: comedy mimicks people, and tragedy is an imitation of some of the events of real life. Through imitation we seek to portray the universal, or that which is common to many particular things.

This early interpretation of art, because of its simplicity and the fact that it seems to answer many questions and solve many problems, has had a strong influence on later thinking. In one form or another, it has persisted until comparatively recent times.

ART AS PLEASURE

A popular notion is that the artist is a person who delights in beauty and spends his time in the creation of beautiful objects. Quite clearly the artist does take pleasure in his work and seeks to please others with his product. According to some people, then, the proper function of art is to give pleasure, and this is the basis on or standard by which it should be judged. If objects of art give pleasure, they are called "good art." People go to art galleries and to theaters to be entertained or pleased. The purpose and meaning of art, it is said, is to give aesthetic pleasure. Aesthetic pleasure is a very special type of pleasure related to the aesthetic experience.

Plato, while denying that pleasure is the highest good or what gives meaning to life, gave some support to this interpretation of art by combining the notion of pleasure with the notion of imitation—art is the imitation of what is pleasant.

ART AS PLAY

An explanation of the nature of art that is related to the pleasure theory and to the notion that art is an escape from life is the theory that it is related to play and grows out of the surplus energy of the individual. Men must work because they need to provide such things as food, clothing, and shelter for themselves and their dependents. Such labor involves stress, effort, deprivation, and sustained concentration for the sake of other ends. Play, in contrast, is a free and spontaneous discharge of the excess energy of the organism. It is undertaken, not because it is a means to something else, but because our abundant energy needs expression in some form. Art is of this nature; it is spiritual play and relaxation in its highest form.

The idea that art is a form of play appears to have originated with Immanuel Kant. In *The Critique of Judgment,* published in 1790, Kant refers to the contrast between art and labor, suggesting that art is more closely related to play because it is an occupation agreeable in itself. Following this suggestion, the poet Friedrich Schiller developed the theory in greater detail, showing how the energy of man is expressed by his creative imagination through the pursuit of the arts. Through art there is a harmonious blending of man's rational, imaginative, and sensuous natures.

ART AS EMPATHY

In recent decades the idea of art as empathy has been popular among some psychologists. The word *empathy* is used by a number of psychologists and students of art to refer to the "sympathetic motor attitudes" and agreeable feelings that we experience in the presence of art objects. These motor attitudes or muscular tensions will be evident to anyone who has been an interested and enthusiastic spectator at a football or baseball game. We almost literally push and hold back. Our muscles tighten and relax in response to the events on the field. After such a game, we may feel a sense of physical exhaustion. When we listen to a song, we tend to move in time to the rhythm and possibly beat with our fingers or foot, or we move the muscles of our throat. If we see an acrobat, a runner, or a skater about to fall, our muscles tense and we brace ourselves. Someone else's facial expression may evoke a similar expression from us, as when a baby smiles in response to our smile.

While we are not usually conscious of these movements and attitudes, they are nevertheless present when we perceive a picture, statue, or other work of art. According to the empathy theory, the aesthetic experience is an empathic one; people experience, to a lesser degree, what they would experience if they were participating in the situation or performing the actions that they perceive and that the work of art depicts. The theory thus emphasizes the motor aspects of certain psychological or physiological processes. Attention is given to figures and lines that suggest certain motor sets. The directions of lines are said to be important. Vertical lines convey a sense of dignity and strength. The Doric column, for example, is said to "rise." The high arches of the Gothic structure are elevating; we stretch ourselves, and our eyes follow the unbroken line upward. Diagonal lines are the lines of action or of strenuous exertion, as in the famous pictures of athletes. Horizontal lines suggest repose and relaxation; they can also be used to convey a notion of speed.

ART AS COMMUNICATION

Many scholars think that communication is indispensable—in fact, central —to art and that the urge to communicate is the most adequate explanation of the artistic impulse and the aesthetic response. Their theories range all the way from the views of certain mystics for whom art reveals the ideal, the universal, or the absolute, to those who think that art is the "language" of the emotions and who make no metaphysical claims for it.

The person who has an experience which he considers to have led to a genuine insight into the abiding and significant elements of life or of nature usually feels a compulsion to share that experience with his fellow men.

In *What Is Art?* Leo Tolstoy gives a clear-cut presentation of art as communication.

> Speech transmitting the thoughts and experiences of men serves as a means of union among them, and art serves a similar purpose. The peculiarity of this latter means of intercourse, distinguishing it from intercourse by means of words, consists in this, that whereas by words a man transmits his thoughts to another, by art he transmits his feelings.[6]

Feelings and emotions are contagious. When we see or hear an expression of emotion, it tends to evoke a similar response in us. One man laughs and others laugh with him. In a similar way excitement, suffering, fear, courage, determination, respect, and love can be communicated to others.

> *To evoke in oneself a feeling one has once experienced and having evoked it in oneself then by means of movements, lines, colours, sounds, or forms expressed in words, so to transmit that feeling that others experience the same feeling—this is the activity of art.*

[6] Trans. Aylmer Maude (London: Oxford U. Press, 1938), p. 121. Used by permission of the publishers and of the representatives of the late Aylmer Maude.

Art is a human activity consisting in this, that one man consciously by means of certain external signs, hands on to others feelings he has lived through, and that others are infected by these feelings and also experience them. . . .

We are accustomed to understand art to be only what we hear and see in theatres, concerts, and exhibitions, together with buildings, statues, poems, and novels. . . . But all this is but the smallest part of the art by which we communicate with one another in life. All human life is filled with the works of art of every kind—from cradle-song, jest, mimicry, the ornamentation of houses, dress, and utensils, to church services, buildings, monuments, and triumphal processions. It is all artistic activity. So that by art, in the limited sense of the word, we do not mean all human activity transmitting feelings but only that part which we for some reason select from it and to which we attach special importance.[7]

Artists find themselves emotionally stirred or inspired, and they wish to communicate this feeling to others by creating some object that conveys or embodies it. In speaking of art as essentially a form of language, Ducasse says that it is "the language of feeling, mood, sentiment, and emotional attitude," which is to be distinguished from "the language of assertion through which we express opinions, facts, and the like."[8]

ART AS EXPRESSION

The view of art as expression is closely related to that of art as communication. The difference between the two interpretations is one of intent. Some people feel that in art we express some deep emotion, some insight, or some intuition that we are unable to express adequately by our ordinary language and gestures. The artist's dominant interest is to express this insight. Whether or not it is communicated to others or evokes a similar feeling in them is secondary, though the artist, like other people, is likely to appreciate sympathetic understanding.

The artistic impulse selects and intensifies some things and rejects or disregards others. The artist seeks to find the forms, qualities, and materials that will best express and in turn direct the attention of his audience or public to what he seeks to emphasize. A work of art is thus an expression of the artist's inspiration, preference, or sense of values.

The artist wishes not only to express and to share his insights but to elicit a sympathetic response from his fellow men. In this way his own feelings and insights are heightened, and others come to participate in the creation of these same values. Art is social and helps not only to extend our personalities but to unite the members of the social group.

7 *Ibid.*, pp. 123–125.
8 C. J. Ducasse, *Art, the Critics, and You* (New York: Piest, 1944), pp. 52–53.

According to the Italian philosopher Benedetto Croce, art is intuition that is expressed. Art must be clearly distinguished from a purely physical event, from a utilitarian act, from a moral act, and from conceptual knowledge. Theories that attempt to explain art as philosophy or religion or history or science are taking the wrong approach. Intuitions, however, are fragmentary and imperfect so long as they are only in the stage of sensation. Expression is essential if intuitions are to become realities and to play a part in human affairs.

ART AS A QUALITY OF EXPERIENCE

In *Art as Experience* John Dewey criticizes the separation of art from the common everyday experiences of men and its relegation to the museum and the art gallery. Art, he says, is too frequently identified with some painting, statue, or symphony apart from the human experience out of which it arose. Art is compartmentalized and put into a separate realm where it is cut off from other forms of human experience, or "spiritualized" and set above the experiences of everyday life.

In earlier times art was associated with common objects: domestic utensils, the bow and the spear, personal adornment. Art brought an enhancement of the processes of life. According to Dewey, our task today is to restore continuity between the forms of experience that are works of art and the common events of life.

Art, Dewey says, is a quality that permeates an experience, and it should "idealize qualities found in common experience." There is an aesthetic aspect to all normal experiences. We should be able to see this quality in the grace of the baseball player, the delight of the housewife in carrying out her duties with care, and the satisfaction of the intelligent mechanic in a good piece of work.

Art not only reflects experience but enriches it and draws from it a new significance. The place that art occupies in the experience of a people is an indication of the sophistication of that civilization. Art is a judgment on the quality of life and a means of promoting its development.

A CRITICAL EVALUATION OF THEORIES OF ART

Most contemporary students of art find the theory of imitation quite unsatisfactory, and it is not widely held today. Imitation is secondary, not primary, in art. If it were primary, then color-photography might well be the most perfect art form. While there appears to be an imitative element in much painting, certainly many forms of art, such as music, poetry, and architecture, do not merely describe and imitate. The capacity of any art, even landscape painting, to "copy" natural phenomena is definitely limited. The natural scene is undergoing continual change, and the variety of colors, shades, and movements cannot be exactly duplicated. Furthermore, any artist depicts what *he* sees and what interests or appeals to him, and no two artists have the same experiences.

While most works of art give pleasure to many, pleasure-yielding itself is certainly not an adequate criterion of art. Some art, such as tragedy, does not give much pleasure, in the usual sense of the world. The artist who creates the work of art usually does find pleasure in his creative activity, but pleasure accompanies creative activity in many different fields, and thus does not distinguish art from these other disciplines.

The interpretation of art as play is not widely held at present. Even if it could be shown that art was related in its origin to play, that would not necessarily mean that this is a satisfactory statement of its present value. To think that a thing is explained fully by its origin and needs no further analysis or logical interpretation is an example of the genetic fallacy. Undoubtedly art can serve, for the artist and others, as a form of escape; some turn, for escape, to the theater, motion pictures, paintings, poetry, and novels. But others go fishing, take a sea voyage, or even turn to drink or suicide for the same purpose.

Psychological and physiological explanations of art, like the theory of empathy, undoubtedly throw much light on the aesthetic impulse and add to our knowledge of the means of communication and expression. Many will question the adequacy of the theory of empathy, however, as a philosophy of art. If accepted, it may need to be combined with other explanations. The artist may be a person who sees in certain total situations new possibilities or rich qualities that elude the rest of us. The artist may be more sensitive than other people to certain values and try to communicate to others his vision and insight.

The interpretations of art as communication, as expression, or as a quality of experience have much in common. In the opinion of the author, these theories are the most adequate. Each of them can be so stated that it will assume or embrace the others. The various theories agree that there is an aesthetic experience which is unique. They agree that this experience is worthwhile, that it enriches life. There is a sense of obligation to seek and maximize beauty and to share the aesthetic experience with others.

The realization that art is not the sole source of the aesthetic experience and that artists often are interested in objectives which have little to do with aesthetics has led some students of aesthetics to be critical of the philosophies of art set forth above. The following statement of the distinction between craft and art expresses the sense of dissatisfaction with the traditional philosophies of art.

C. Hillis Kaiser says that the term *craft* denotes "those activities done for an end other than the activity itself"—for example, rug-making and building

—whereas *art* denotes those activities "done for the sake of the activity itself" —for example, playing the harp. In other words, art is engaged in for its own sake and not for some end beyond the activity. Kaiser says: "If anyone asserts that it is the end of art to represent physical things or ideal realities, to communicate thoughts or feelings, to teach or instruct, to amuse, to stimulate to thought or action, to improve by arousing useful emotions, he will in every instance be asserting that art is a kind of craft." From this point of view, most of the philosophies of art "can be abolished at a stroke by showing that each presupposes art to be a form of craft." Aesthetic apprehension is an instance of knowledge by acquaintance. Genuine art is that form of expression which "makes things for the sake of the pleasure derived from the aesthetic apprehension of them."[9] Only so far as an activity stimulates or recreates aesthetic values does it enter into the realm of aesthetics.

To enlarge the range and depth of our aesthetic response is to extend the area of our awareness and to enlarge and enrich life as a whole. In these experiences, personal desires and anxieties tend to be set aside; we transcend our narrow selves and gain a new understanding of life and a new scale of values. Fortunate indeed are those people of acute sensitivity who are able to find continuous aesthetic satisfaction in the everyday experiences of life.

> It is through daily, even hourly use of this perceptual awareness and aesthetic sensitivity that life is genuinely and permanently enriched. And since for most of us frequent contact with great painting, good music, and beautiful scenery is impossible, the solution clearly lies in securing as much aesthetic experience as possible from ordinary daily living. Admittedly, these everyday experiences will seldom have the breath-catching intensity or thrilling scope of great art and magnificent scenery, but since the press of practical affairs does not often spare us the time for sustained enjoyment of powerful aesthetic emotions, the minor character of these incidental perceptual experiences has its advantages. Their frequency and ubiquitous accessibility will compensate for what they may lack in scope and intensity, and many persons of acute sensitivity find the larger part of their abundant aesthetic satisfaction in the common pattern of everyday living.[10]

ART AND CULTURE

Art, as we have seen, is an integral part of life and cannot be separated from the daily activities of men and women. What men see and feel is intimately connected with what they think and know. Art grows out of the aesthetic response. It is also an expression of the personality of the artist and a reflection of the spirit or outlook of the age in which it is produced. Except in those

---

[9] *An Essay on Method* (New Brunswick: Rutgers U. Press, 1952), pp. 41, 42, 44, 49.

[10] Hunter Mead, *An Introduction to Aesthetics*, p. 140. Copyright 1952 The Ronald Press Company.

cases where the artist attempts to imitate or copy some earlier art form, his art is to some extent an expression of the culture, while at the same time it influences and may help direct that culture. For example, medieval art is an expression of the theological aspirations and outlook of that era. During the Renaissance the growing interest in nature and the spatiotemporal world led to a change in artistic expression; artists portrayed what they experienced in their daily lives. Portrait painting and, later, still lifes and landscapes reflected this growing interest in man and nature. This changing interest led, through various routes, to the Impressionism of the nineteenth century, and its new ways of depicting nature and the world.

The impressionists exhibited a friendly interest in nature and the world in which they lived. Apart from the use of new techniques and methods, the artists of this era did not vary greatly in their aims from the traditions of art prevalent during the two preceding centuries. While desiring to paint nature as they saw it, they experimented with various new techniques, including unusual color combinations, loose brush work, and painting "on the spot" or from immediate sense impression, without great attention to detail. The late nineteenth century was a period of great optimism and complacency, especially among the upper class groups in Western societies. The world of nature was regarded as a worthy object of the artist's attention, which he might portray in various ways. During this period, however, among an increasing number of artists, there was growing dissatisfaction and uneasiness with the traditional forms of art. The impressionism of the period was "brilliant but messy." Artists were also unhappy about the decline of craftsmanship brought about by the machine processes of the Industrial Revolution. Various young artists decided to abandon the older forms and begin anew. Painters like Van Gogh and Cézanne gave up the imitation of nature as the main goal or object of painting. In architecture Frank Lloyd Wright pioneered in stressing the functional features of a building. He swept away unnecessary trimming, moulding, and cornices. Similar innovations were made in other arts.

The art of the twentieth century grew out of feelings of dissatisfaction with the old order. The revolt against a growing mechanization, depersonalization, and the demand for conformity was most pronounced in art and literature, though it was not confined to them. The revolt became strong during the second decade of the century with the outbreak of World War I and the revolutions and tragic events that followed. Gone was the old confidence in progress, in the value systems and philosophies of the nineteenth century, and in a friendly nature. Artists and writers were merely among the first to sense the many signs of change and to reject a world grown sordid and impersonal. Freud's disclosure of the superficial role of reason and the depth of the irrational in man, and the totalitarian mass movements, were among the many factors that led to further disillusionment and to attacks on reason, the goodness of man, and the old order in general.

The protest of the artist against the world as he finds it is expressed in the nonobjective and abstract art of recent decades. Much modern art is characterized by the absence of recognizable "objects" and by the distortion of form with parts arranged in unusual ways. Fantastic, wierd, and mystical symbolism is also used. In every art there is some attempt to "refashion" the world, but in modern art this tendency is more pronounced. The artist, it seems, is attempting to portray the confusion and conflicts in our society, and then to recreate the world in a manner more to his liking; either mood may be dominant in a particular work of art.

The expressionists turned to abstract and nonobjective art forms in an attempt to portray by the use of symbols the emotions aroused in the artists by objects and events. Expressionism is a technique that may be used for different objectives. The expressionists want to face the facts of poverty, suffering, the disinherited, and the ugly. Some expressionists feel so keenly about these problems that they tend to believe "that the insistence on harmony and beauty" is "only born out of a refusal to be honest."[11] In abstract art all "subject matter" is discarded and there is an attempt to express a mood or an emotion by colors and lines alone. In cubism, artists like Picasso seek simplicity and order with a rhythmical distribution of forms, such as cubes, cones, and cylinders, in which "form" comes first and "subject" second. The surrealists, impressed by the writings of Freud and others and conscious of the power of irrational impulses and passions in man, seek with dream pictures and other symbolic means to represent the chaotic impulses of the id. They cease to look outward or to exhibit interest in physical nature; instead they center attention on the exploration of the hidden depths of the self.

What is interpreted by many people as chaos and obscurity in modern art is also evident in some movements in philosophy and in the vast social changes of our time. Perhaps art is "saying" something very important— that ours is a segmented and confused era, but one which is looking for meaning and a sense of direction. When our age has achieved a greater unity of purpose, we can hope that that unity will be expressed by the artist.

QUESTIONS AND PROJECTS

1. *Review Questions*

(1) Define *aesthetics, aesthetic experience, art,* and *philosophy of art.*

[11] E. H. Gombrich, *The Story of Art* (London: Phaidon, 1949), p. 429.

(2) What specific evidence can you cite to indicate that the aesthetic experience has occupied a prominent place in life among all peoples?

(3) Give the distinctive characteristics of the aesthetic mood or attitude.

(4) What is the relation of the aesthetic experience to art objects?

(5) What are the personal and social values of the aesthetic experience—that is, what can it do for us as individuals and as a society?

(6) What are the relations among the aesthetic experience, beauty, and the arts?

(7) In the work of art the aesthetic experience is related to what four elements?

(8) What are the theories or explanations of art set forth in this chapter? Evaluate them, and indicate which you would be most likely to accept or reject on the basis of this evaluation.

(9) Indicate whether you agree or disagree with John Dewey when he says that the aesthetic is a quality that should permeate all experience, and that we tend too much to think merely of museums and art galleries when we think of the aesthetic experience and art.

(10) Discuss the distinction between a craft and an art, and indicate whether or not you agree with the statement that theories of art tend to view art as a craft.

(11) Discuss the relation between art and culture. Give examples that illustrate your points.

(12) Give some reasons for the rise of the "modern" art of the twentieth century. Why did this art break with the more traditional forms?

(13) Do you agree with the statement that art is saying something very important to and about our age? Explain your answer carefully.

2. What kinds of experiences or situations have called forth an aesthetic response in you most frequently? To what extent are these responses purely aesthetic, and to what extent are they the result of supplementary associational values?

3. What more can be done in the educational process to cultivate the aesthetic experience? Specifically, what would you do with the usual public-school classroom to make it a part of education in aesthetics?

4. Plato, Tolstoy, and others have raised the question of the relation of art to morals. Is the production and enjoyment of art subject to the principles of ethics, or are art and morality two separate and autonomous fields? You may wish to consult Jacques Maritain, *The Responsibility of the Artist* (New York: Scribner's, 1960); Harold Taylor, "Moral Values and the Experience of Art," in *Art and Intellect* (Garden City: Doubleday, 1960). In your discussion, comment on the following:

(1) "Art for art's sake."

(2) "Art, like other interests, can flourish only in a sound and whole society, and the law of soundness and wholeness in life is morality."—Ralph Barton Perry

(3) "Just as physical things cannot exist without the support of a physical environment, so moral life cannot go on without the support of a moral environment."—John Dewey

5. In *What We Live By* (New York: Simon and Schuster, 1932) Abbé Ernest Dimnet raises the question why, if art is naturally "elevating," artists often have the reputation of being lax as far as social and moral standards are concerned. Are artists less bound

by conventions—and if so, in what sense—than other members of society, or is the "artistic temperament" different from the scientific, the philosophical, or the religious temperament? Are the feelings of the artist likely to be stirred more easily than those of others?

6. Is there justification for the statement that, while art creates sentiments and emotions, these sentiments and emotions do not carry over into everyday life? Art, it is asserted, induces a contemplative attitude toward life. The artist wants to enjoy life as it is, not to change or reform it. For example, we go to the theater and see a murder enacted. We do nothing; indeed, we may applaud the performance. We are spectators, and we assume a passive attitude. Is this example typical?

7. Is there any justification for the statement that while there is so much want and suffering in the world, it is "wrong to waste so much money on expensive and useless luxuries like art"?

8. What is the relation between art objects and practical objects?

9. What are the main periods in the history of art? How are these changes or periods to be explained? (You will need to consult some good history of art.)

10. Should there be any censorship of art? Some groups vigorously oppose any type of censorship; others favor some censorship. Is censorship desirable? Is it likely to be successful? In what sense? Discuss the following statement: "Probably censorship should be limited to cases of (a) obscenity, and vulgarity which is not necessary to artistic effect or moral purpose; (b) the representation of crime and vice in such ways as to teach them to the innocent, to excite morbid curiosity, or to stimulate brutality; (c) the presentation of anything that would arouse fear, resentment, hatred, or ill-will towards foreign peoples, a lust for successful war, or a touchy and pugnacious spirit; (d) anything obviously libellous."[12]

11. Pablo Picasso, when asked to explain modern art, is said to have replied: "Do you require an explanation for the song of a bird?" Discuss this reply with some care.[13]

SUGGESTED READINGS

BEARDSLEY, MONROE C. *Aesthetics: Problems in the Philosophy of Criticism.* New York: Harcourt, Brace, 1958.
Written for the beginner who is interested in the problems of aesthetics and in the critical evaluation of artistic form and the arts.

DEWEY, JOHN. *Art as Experience.* New York: Putnam's, 1934.
The leading instrumentalist gives his view of art as a quality of experience.

[12] From Durant Drake, *The New Morality,* p. 248. By permission of The Macmillan Company, publishers, New York, 1928.
[13] Bartlett H. Hayes, Jr., *The Contemporary Arts* (The American Library Association, in cooperation with the Public Affairs Committee, 1962), p. 1.

DUCASSE, C. J. *Art, the Critics, and You.* New York: Piest, 1944.
   This stimulating book interprets art as a form of language that communicates emotion.

ELSEN, ALBERT E. *The Purposes of Art.* New York: Holt, Rinehart and Winston, 1962.
   A work that uses many illustrations in its survey of world art. Art is seen as an expression of the philosophy and beliefs of the age in which it appears.

GOMBRICH, E. H. *The Story of Art.* London: Phaidon, 1949.
   Written in nontechnical language and with many illustrations to help young people gain an appreciation of our artistic heritage.

JARRETT, JAMES L. *The Quest for Beauty.* Englewood Cliffs: Prentice-Hall, 1957.
   A general book dealing with aesthetics and art that brings in a considerable amount of illustrative material.

LANGER, SUSANNE K. (ed.). *Reflection on Art: A Source Book of Writings by Artists, Critics, and Philosophers.* New York: Oxford U. Press, 1958. (Galaxy Books, 1960.)
   Includes the contributions of twenty-six people to art criticism and aesthetics.

LEVICH, MARVIN. *Aesthetics and the Philosophy of Criticism.* New York: Random House, 1962.
   The seven parts of the book deal with different problems in aesthetics. Essays are included from writers of the past and present.

MEAD, HUNTER. *An Introduction to Aesthetics.* New York: Ronald, 1952.
   A book that emphasizes the nature and range of the aesthetic experience and distinguishes between aesthetics and the philosophy of art.

PEPPER, STEPHEN C. *The Work of Art.* Bloomington: Indiana U. Press, 1955.
   A brief book of six lectures on works of art and the problem and object of art criticism.

SEWALL, JOHN IVES. *A History of Western Art.* rev. ed.; New York: Holt, Rinehart and Winston, 1961.
   A discussion of art, period by period, from the early Greeks to the twentieth century. A large volume that concludes with a chapter by John Canaday on contemporary art.

STOLNITZ, JEROME. *Aesthetics and Philosophy of Art Criticism.* Boston: Houghton Mifflin, 1960.
   An introductory text that discusses the aesthetic attitudes, the leading concepts used in the field, some of the influential theories of art, and the function of art criticism. Illustrative photographs are included.

WARBEKE, JOHN M. *The Power of Art.* New York: Philosophical Library, 1951.
   A readable discussion of aesthetic qualities and the arts that shows the author's conviction of the power of the arts to mold the character of peoples and civilization.

WEISS, PAUL. *Nine Basic Arts.* Carbondale: Southern Illinois U. Press, 1961.
   This is a companion volume to the author's earlier book, The World of Art.

⁕❧ TWENTY-TWO ❧⁕

ORIENT AND OCCIDENT: CONTRASTING VALUE SYSTEMS

Late in the nineteenth century an English poet, Rudyard Kipling, could reasonably say, "Oh, East is East, and West is West, and never the twain shall meet." Today this older provincialism and isolationism have gone or are going. The Occident and Orient are meeting, and what is needed is an understanding of each other's values. During the last few decades there has been increasing interest throughout Western countries in Oriental or Eastern philosophy and culture,[1] and this interest is reflected in our educational institutions and media.

There is, of course, no single Oriental, or Eastern, philosophy or value system, just as there is no single Western philosophy or set of values. The Eastern systems are as diverse as the Western. There are also characteristic differences in thinking as we move from India to China to Japan. We shall necessarily limit our attention to the main positions of the dominant cultures of Asia.

Western philosophy has its source mainly in Greek, Roman, and later European thought, and within those cultures. Western philosophy and standards of value have also been profoundly influenced by the Judaeo-Christian interpretation of life and the world. Eastern or Oriental philosophy and ways of life include those systems of thought and patterns of behavior found among non-European peoples from North Africa and the Near East to China and Japan. Students of East-West relations have pointed out that until about the sixteenth century the West and the East were at pretty much the same stage culturally, and that some of the major differences have devel-

[1] See Kurt F. Leidecker, "Oriental Philosophy in America," in *American Philosophy*, Ralph B. Winn (ed.) (New York: Philosophical Library, 1955), pp. 211–220, for a discussion of this topic.

oped in recent centuries with the more rapid development by the West of science and technology.[2]

Let us point out two sources of misunderstanding between East and West. First, there is a tendency for people in the West to assume that, because many Asian nations are economically and technologically underdeveloped, they are necessarily morally and culturally less advanced than we are. A second source of misunderstanding has been the Western tendency to compare our own achievements and ideals, not with Eastern achievements and ideals, but with what we consider the idiosyncracies and shortcomings of Oriental peoples. Comparison is unfair and unreasonable unless we compare things that are similar.

Our plan in this chapter is, first, to point out some broad differences in outlook between the value systems of East and West. Second, we shall examine briefly some characteristic emphases in the dominant cultures of India, China, and Japan. We shall limit our attention to Hinduism, Buddhism, and Confucianism, and the way in which these religions, along with Shintoism, have influenced Japanese culture. Finally, we shall draw a few general conclusions.

POINTS OF CONTRAST

There are a few broad differences in outlook between East and West. First, as we pointed out in Chapter 2, the East and the West tend to view the objective or natural world of the senses from different perspectives. The West has tended in recent times to emphasize the sensorially perceived world, and so has moved ahead in science and technology. The Greek influence is seen in knowledge that is empirical, descriptive, and highly specialized. The Oriental thinker, especially as influenced by Hinduism and Buddhism, is more likely to emphasize the inner nature of the self and a reality beyond the world of the senses, which is regarded as fleeting and illusory. This outlook has value implications.

Second, and partly as a result of differences in theories of knowledge (epistemology) and views of reality (metaphysics), the Orient and Occident exhibit considerably contrasting attitudes toward human desires and their fulfillment or control. In the West there is a tendency to emphasize desires and the need to satisfy them. The effort to satisfy desires has led to a striving or a struggle to get ahead in the here and now, and to an interest in things and the comforts and pleasures of this world. It has led to competition, the

2 Vera Micheles Dean, *The Nature of the Non-Western World* (New York: New American Library of World Literature, 1957), p. 18 (Mentor ed.); Barbara Ward Jackson, *The Interplay of East and West* (London: Allen and Unwin, 1957), Lecture I; Sir S. Radhakrishnan, *East and West* (New York: Harper, 1956), Lecture I.

acquisitive society, and sometimes unrest and even war. In the East, on the other hand, there is greater emphasis on discipline, self-control, moderation, detachment, and even renunciation. The typical Oriental is less attached to the things of this world. We can understand, then, his reaction to Western motion pictures and to what is sometimes called "Madison Avenue," and why he sometimes says that Western civilization is superficial. This Eastern position is more marked in Hinduism and Buddhism than in Confucianism and Shintoism. Buddhism, however, with its claim that suffering and misery come from desire and striving and its stress on release from desire and the suffering it brings, has had a strong influence in China, Japan, and other Asian countries. In reply to charges by some people in the West that this attitude is negativistic or life-denying, the Buddhists and Hindus says, "Not so, it is merely the renunciation of lower values for those that are higher and more enduring."

Third, thinkers in the West put more emphasis than do most Eastern thinkers on the reality and the value of time. In the West we find process philosophies and concepts of creative evolution and progress that hold that good is on the rise and evil on the decline. Thus time has a role in man's salvation. For the Hindu or the Buddhist, on the other hand, the good is not in this present world of things, and it is not to be gained by manipulating nature, altering society, or seeking pleasure for ourselves. The good is found through the quest for the One within or beyond, or in attaining nirvana.

Apart from these differences regarding the value of certain kinds of knowledge, the role of desires, and the nature of the time process, there is considerable agreement about morals and values. The virtues and values are much the same in the different cultures. That is, the things approved and called good and the things disapproved and called evil differ only in minor details. Differences are to be found mainly in the ranking of values. For example, filial piety and respect for ancestors rank much higher in Confucian ethics than in most Western ethics. Love and compassion, man's freedom, and man's responsibility are emphasized in both Eastern and Western systems.

INDIA AND HINDU CULTURE

To set forth even the central points in Hindu philosophy and culture in a few pages is difficult. There are divisions and subdivisions into which we cannot go, and the experts themselves vary in their interpretation of this philosophy. The problem is further complicated by the fact that there are no exact equivalents in English for some Indian terms and concepts. We shall try to avoid the technical terms, however, and to set forth what appear to be the dominant trends among Hindu thinkers. We shall follow, in the main, the systematization of the teachings of the Upanishads[3] as set forth by Sankara, one of the greatest Indian philosophers. We shall not deal with the more technical questions of metaphysics and epistemology except where brief statements are necessary for an understanding of the system of values involved.

PHILOSOPHY AND LIFE

India's value system is much more otherworldly than that of either China or Japan. Love of life for its own sake is secondary. As Radhakrishnan says, "Early in India's history a definite direction has been given to man's mind. To be, to hold the soul in its serenity is the end of man. There is in us the principle of subjectivity which is free from the pressure of external influences."[4]

Philosophy (*darsana*) in the Hindu tradition means "seeing the truth," and applying this truth to the problems of everyday life. Thus for Indian thinkers the purpose of studying philosophy is not merely to gain knowledge for its own sake or to satisfy one's curiosity, but to discover and to live the highest kind of life or the life that will bring permanent self-realization or bliss. One must discover the basic truths for himself, not just accept them on blind faith or from the testimony of others. Unless one has convictions and lives in accordance with them, he is not really a philosopher. In Hinduism it is very difficult to separate philosophy and religion.

BRAHMAN AND THE SELF

Central in Hindu philosophy is the emphasis on the one unchanging reality that transcends space, time, causality, and all particular things. This Absolute cannot be comprehended by human thought or adequately expressed in words and concepts. According to the nondualistic view (which emphasizes the oneness of existence) only Brahman is real, and the individual souls and the universe are illusory manifestations of Brahman. For some others, the self and the physical world may be real, though they are finite and imperfect. There are also differences among philosophical thinkers as to whether the ultimate reality is nonpersonal, superpersonal, or personal. But all agree in the possibility of every soul's attaining liberation from the bondage of the physical world.

Closely allied to the concept of Brahman is the concept of the self, or soul, or *atman*. The true self of each person is identical with Brahman. From the transcendental standpoint, the self is immortal, free, and one with Brahman.

3 The Hindu scriptures are the Four Vedas, which consist of the Mantra, or Samhita, and the Brahmanas. The Upanishads are the concluding portion of the Brahmanas and they represent philosophic Hinduism. See *The Upanishads*, trans. Swami Nikhilananda (4 vols.; New York: Harper). (Vol. 1, 1949; Vol. 2, 1952; Vol. 3, 1956; Vol. 4, 1959.)

4 Radhakrishnan, *East and West*, p. 21.

The divine nature of the self is veiled, but not destroyed, by false images and ignorance. The true destiny of the self is the realization of this relationship with Brahman. From the phenomenal standpoint, there are many individual selves, enmeshed in the world of affairs and seeking deliverance from the round of births and deaths. Thus we need to distinguish between the real and the empirical self.

What are the relations among Brahman, the self, and the universe that man perceives? In describing the world view of Advaita Vedanta (one of the main nondualistic systems within Hinduism), a Hindu scholar says: "We now know the advaitic world-view in general. Brahman is the sole reality, and it appears both as the objective universe and as the individual subject. The former is an illusory manifestation of Brahman, while the latter is Brahman itself appearing under the limitations which form part of that illusory universe."[5] The objects of the empirical world, while of a certain order of reality, are appearances in that they depend for their existence on a higher reality. The individual self, however, is not illusory in this sense. The self is Brahman appearing under limiting conditions. It is not negated in the way physical objects are negated. Vedanta philosophers prefer the term *nondualism*, rather than *monism*, to express the idea of the oneness of existence. Swami Nikhilananda says that "from the philosophical standpoint, Hinduism is nondualistic, and from the religious standpoint, monotheistic."[6]

THE GOAL OF LIFE AND THE FOUR ASHRAMAS

The goal of life is to achieve release or liberation (*moksha*) from the cycle of rebirths created by ignorance. This release is the highest of human ends, far surpassing pleasure, wealth, and all the other things for which great numbers of people strive. Unless a man achieves release in this life, which is rare indeed, he is destined to repeat the round of more existences. According to Hinduism, no soul is eternally damned. The law of *karma*, the law of sowing and reaping, determines the form that will be taken in each new existence. This is the law of cause and effect in human life. A man through his conduct determines his own destiny. A life of evil may even lead to rebirth as a sub-human creature, and a life of goodness may lead to a more favored human existence or to ultimate liberation from the round of rebirths. Thus the doctrines of *karma* and rebirth are said to be grounded in the moral structure of the universe. They permit freedom and ethical advance in that they are under man's control and are not determined by cosmic or environmental forces completely beyond his influence.

The theory of *karma* and rebirth determines one's position in the caste system of India. This system has long been connected with the social aspect of

5 M. Hiriyanna, *The Essentials of Indian Philosophy* (London: Allen and Unwin, 1949), p. 158.
6 *Hinduism: Its Meaning for the Liberation of the Spirit* (New York: Harper, 1958), pp. 7–8.

Hindu ethics, and it has been under attack in recent years. Various outstanding leaders of Hinduism have called attention to the abuses of the caste system and have taken steps to bring about its reform. Today, to discriminate on the basis of caste is a punishable offense. The caste system has, however, the strong support of tradition and custom, even though it no longer has a legal status. The *Bhagavad Gita* (literally "Song of the Blessed One"—part of the devotional scripture of Hinduism) provides divine sanction for dividing human beings into four groups. There are first the men of wisdom, the brahmins, whose virtues include austerity, cleanliness, and righteousness. They are men of learning, insight, and faith. Second, there are the men of action and valor, the *kshattriyas,* whose virtues include heroism, resourcefulness, and generosity. Third, there are the men of desires and acquisitive enterprise, the *vaisyas,* who give attention to trade and agricultural pursuits. Finally, there are the *sudras,* those capable only of manual labor. Beyond these are the outcasts. Caste for a person is determined by his past actions and duties. The belief that one's present social status or class is regulated by the law of *karma* makes the system highly resistant to change. Unless one accepts the doctrine of rebirth and the law of *karma,* it appears difficult, if not impossible, to give any satisfactory ethical justification for the inequities of the caste system.

Swami Nikhilananda says that Hindu ethics differs both from modern scientific ethics and from utilitarian ethics. It "prescribes the disciplines for a spiritual life." Again he says, "Hindu ethics is mainly subjective or personal, its purpose being to eliminate such mental impurities as greed and egotism for the ultimate attainment of the highest good. . . . Objective ethics, which deals with social welfare . . . is based upon the Hindu conception of *dharma,* or duty, related to a man's position in society and his stage in life."[7]

The concept of the four *ashramas,* or stages in the life of the individual, relates the goal of liberation and perfection to the needs and tasks of daily life in society. While a person should seek spiritual fulfillment, he should not neglect his social obligations. A man's duties are set not only by his caste, but by the stage of life at which he has arrived. The stages in life's development are held before each man as an ideal, although practice may vary widely. The four stages are: (1) the life of the student, normally from age five to twenty-five; (2) at twenty-five the person is expected to marry and become a householder and assume the responsibilities of parenthood and other social obligations; (3) as his grandchildren arrive and as his skin begins to wrinkle, he retires to the forest for meditation and reflection, through which he seeks illumination; and (4) by means of austerities and rigid self-control he seeks union with Brahman. If he is successful in the fourth stage, struggle and strife cease and he gains peace and freedom through union with the all-embracing

[7] *Ibid.,* p. 57.

World Soul. The inner spirit of man is the focus of attention, and its development, illumination, and release are the highest values. Other values that are stressed include *ahimsa,* or noninjury to living things, compassion, renunciation of worldly attachments, simplicity, humility, and courage.

CHARACTERISTICS OF THE INDIAN PHILOSOPHICAL OUTLOOK

In "The Spirit of Indian Philosophy," Sir Sarvepalli Radhakrishnan,[8] after pointing out the diversity of views held by Indian thinkers, indicates seven attitudes that are characteristic of the Indian philosophical mind. These are, first, "concentration upon the spiritual." Philosophy and religion are closely related. Man is spiritual in nature and is primarily interested in his spiritual destiny and not in material welfare. Second, "belief in the intimate relationship of philosophy and life." Philosophy is not a mere intellectual exercise; it is for life and to be lived. Third, the "introspective attitude" and concern for the inner life. The inner spirit of man, the subject rather than the object, is the focus of attention and gives the best clue to the nature of the universe. Fourth, the affinity with idealism. Since reality is "ultimately one and ultimately spiritual," the tendency is toward nondualistic idealism. Fifth, the acceptance of direct perception as the only method through which reality can be known. When the mind becomes free from the impurities of attachment and aversion through the practice of yoga or spiritual disciplines, it perceives truth directly, as one perceives a fruit lying on the palm of one's own hand. Reason is useful but insufficient; it leads the seeker as far as it can and then bows out. To know reality is to experience it or to become one with it. Sixth, a "consciousness of tradition" and an acceptance of the insights of seers who have lived in the past. This has not, however, made Indian philosophy dogmatic or creedal in its nature. Seventh, an "over-all synthetic tradition." The systems of thought are seen as complementing each other. This stress on the synthetic vision has made possible an intellectual and religious tolerance toward differences within Hinduism and toward other faiths and systems of thought. Hinduism is thus not a fixed and uniform doctrinal system; it is broad, inclusive, and tolerant of different points of view.

THE BUDDHIST QUEST FOR ENLIGHTENMENT

Buddhist philosophy has much in common with Hindu philosophy, but it also departs radically from it at certain points. Siddhartha Gautama, the founder of Buddhism, was born in North India about 563 B.C. As a result of his teaching and influence, Buddhist thought flourished in India for more than a thousand years. Today it is found mainly in Ceylon, Burma, Siam, Tibet, China, Korea, and Japan. In the course of its expansion it has changed consid-

[8] S. Radhakrishnan and Charles A. Moore (eds.), *A Source Book in Indian Philosophy* (Princeton: Princeton U. Press, 1957), pp. xx–xxvi.

erably. Gautama, though reared in luxury and under sheltered conditions, became greatly concerned about the widespread misery under which men live, especially the suffering of disease, old age, and death. He left his home and family and wandered into the forest in search of the truth about the meaning of existence. We shall not follow the steps in his quest, except to mention that after trying various methods, starting with severe penance, asceticism, and the mortification of his body, he turned to a course of self-discipline marked by less severity. Finally, after a number of years, the mystic vision began to unfold. The truth, it is said, flashed into his mind and he became the "Enlightened One"—the Buddha. Contrary to the spirit of his teaching, Gautama was later idolized and deified, and temples, ceremonies, and a priesthood arose.

Buddhism makes a fundamental break with Hinduism in its rejection not only of the Vedic scriptures but also of the concepts of Brahman and *atman*—the metaphysical absolute and the changeless self. Experience, it is said, gives no clear indication of such an all-inclusive World Soul. Gautama rejected the authority ascribed to the ancient gods and urged men to rely mainly on the resources within themselves. He also rejected the caste system, since wisdom and not birth or caste is of importance. He was impressed by ceaseless change, which seems to pervade everything, and by finiteness and suffering. Gautama was not only a man of great human sympathy and goodwill; he was a thinker of great philosophic power who decided to spend his life in teaching others to gain understanding.

THE FOUR NOBLE TRUTHS

The central core of Buddhist philosophy is found in the Four Noble Truths. Let us examine them in order. There is, first, the fact of the existence of suffering. Unhappiness or pain accompanies the experiences of birth, illness, failure to satisfy desires, separation from friends and loved ones, old age, and death. The problem of suffering is the universal problem of life in a world that is finite and changing. Even the more fortunate are unable to ward off old age and death. The second noble truth discloses to men the cause of suffering. Suffering is caused by selfish desires, or *tanha,* which in its original and literal meaning is "thirst." These desires or cravings are many, and they tend to grow or increase as men attempt to satisfy them. A man wants ten thousand dollars, then he wants a hundred thousand, then a million, and his wants do not cease. This kind of desire is the real cause of unhappiness, but it is encouraging to know that it is within our control, and that something can be done about it. If men will rise above desires and ally themselves with values to which these desires are irrelevant, they may find a serenity unaffected by any of the calamities that befall them.

The third noble truth is that release is possible. Striving or desire can be destroyed or blotted out. The main obstacle is man's ignorance of the true nature of the self and of the "chain of causation." Man's ignorance leads him to crave particular things that do not bring real happiness, and these unsatisfied cravings lead to the round of births and deaths. If man can gain enlightenment, the wheel of existence may be ended and nirvana gained. The fourth noble truth is that there is a way out through the *Noble Eightfold Path*. Right knowledge about the nature of one's self is a means of removing evil and suffering.

THE NOBLE EIGHTFOLD PATH AND NIRVANA

The Noble Eightfold Path consists of the following steps: (1) Right understanding. Men need to realize that the cessation of suffering comes through the elimination of ignorance and of craving, desire, and thirst. Without understanding, men do not know the direction from which release is to come. (2) Right aspiration or purpose. Without this man is not likely to make a start or to put forth vigorous effort. (3) Right speech. The individual is to be truthful, kind, and humble, and never to gossip, slander, or boast. (4) Right conduct. Man must not harm other living creatures and must avoid killing, stealing, eating meat, intoxication, and other evils. (5) Right mode of livelihood. His mode of living and his vocation should be in harmony with the goals toward which he is aspiring. (6) Right striving or effort. Discipline is necessary in the attainment of an honorable character. (7) Right mindfulness. One's thoughts are important, and they must not be permitted to wander or dwell upon desires that need to be suppressed. (8) Right concentration. When man is able through meditation and concentration to identify himself with truth, the goal of mystic illumination is reached. At this point he is no longer subject to rebirth, and he may enter nirvana.

What is *nirvana?* Literally the term means extinction, ceasing to be, or state of nothingness. Does this mean that Buddhist thinkers have set forth a philosophy of escape? That is how it is interpreted by some in the West and a few in the East. This, however, is a superficial interpretation, which in no way explains the sense of joyous fulfillment and the appeal of Buddhism to large numbers of people. What is extinguished is the finite, changing self, with its selfish cravings whose fulfillment cannot bring real enjoyment. There is the blotting out of that with which the unenlightened person identifies himself, but not the extinction of the essential personality. The elimination of man's lower nature, of ignorance, lust, and hate, is the liberation that is nirvana. Cessation of striving is said to bring a sense of liberation or freedom, peace and contentment, joy, insight, and love or compassion for all living beings.

Li An-Che and Fa Tsun give the following "ten virtues" or traits of character that are universally accepted by Buddhists:

(1) [N]ot to kill anything living; (2) not to take what has not been given; (3) not to fornicate; (4) not to tell a lie; (5) not to abuse or revile; (6) not to talk foolishness; (7) not to slander; (8) not to be avaricious or covetous; (9) not to think upon doing harm or mischief; and (10) not to entertain heretic notions. By being virtuous one is happy. No one else is responsible for one's misery. The only source of misery is ignorance. One who is ignorant of this fact is tempted by selfish interests.[9]

The law of *karma* and the doctrine of rebirth were retained by Buddhists. The law of *karma* is a strong incentive to choose the right or the good and avoid what one believes to be evil. If a man realizes that he is his own savior as well as his own destroyer, his sense of responsibility is likely to be keen. One should give aid to others, however, whenever this is possible, physically through alms-giving and the like, and spiritually through knowledge and enlightenment. The great positive virtue is compassion for all living creatures.

DIVISIONS WITHIN BUDDHISM

While Buddhism arose in India and flourished there for more than a thousand years, it is found today mainly in the other countries of Asia. In the course of its development, Buddhism moved from primitive Buddhism and split into two main branches with various subdivisions within each of these branches. The first branch, Theravada ("Doctrine of the Elders"), or Hinayana ("Small Vehicle"), or Pali Buddhism, prevails mainly in Ceylon, Burma, Siam, and Tibet. It is a more fundamentalist, rigorous, individualistic philosophy of escape from suffering. The second branch, Mahayana ("Great Vehicle") Buddhism, is found mainly in China, Mongolia, Korea, and Japan. It is a more broad-minded philosophy with a universal outlook, and it stresses the virtues of wisdom and love. Without minimizing individual enlightenment and freedom from illusion, there is greater stress on compassion for all living beings. For example, a Bodhisattva is one who, like Buddha, having attained enlightenment, refuses to enter nirvana so as to be able to continue to serve his fellow men. Whereas Hinayana Buddhism conceives the Buddha as a man and stresses individual enlightenment, in the Mahayana branch of Buddhism the Buddha is more likely to be conceived as the transcendental eternal principle or Absolute, which may bring release to all men.

EMPHASES IN CHINESE PHILOSOPHY

Chinese civilization was old when Western civilization was in the process of formation. About the sixth century B.C., Confucius and Lao-tzu attempted to organize the wisdom of the time into a more orderly system. Both men lived in a period of unrest and confusion, and they sought to restore peace and

9 "Buddhist Tradition," in *The Year Book of Education, 1951*, ed. J. A. Lauwerys and N. Hans (London: University of London Institute of Education by Evans Brothers, 1951), p. 648.

harmony among men and between them and the order of nature. Lao-tzu taught that behind all existence is the impersonal *Tao* (Way). *Tao* is the way the universe works; it is the reality that is immanent in nature and man. We shall return to this conception. Confucius revised and systematized the earlier classics. He was an able teacher and administrator, with a practical turn of mind, more interested in helping his people live well than in considering speculative questions. The teachings of Confucius were reaffirmed by Mencius (Meng-tzu), a Chinese philosopher who lived a century later. For twenty-five centuries Chinese ethical ideals, in the form known as Confucianism, have been influential in the development of Chinese culture. Until 1905, examinations in the Confucian Classics were the basis of appointment to the Civil Service. The introduction of communism in China in the mid-twentieth century is challenging the traditional ways of thinking and doing things. What permanent effect this will have on Chinese civilization remains to be seen.

THE PLACE OF PHILOSOPHY IN CHINA

Philosophy among the Chinese has tended, on the whole, to be practical and this-worldly. The interest is in achieving a harmonious adjustment to other people, to society in general, and to the demands of nature. There is less emphasis on questions of logic, epistemology, and metaphysics than on moral problems and social philosophy. Chinese writers, furthermore, tend to set forth their convictions in the form of aphorisms, illustrations, and stories that convey general meaning but omit analytical precision, systematic reasoning, and argument. For example, in the *Confucian Analects* the paragraphs consist of only a few words or perhaps a few sentences, and there is often little logical connection between the paragraphs.

One Chinese philosopher says:

> The place which philosophy has occupied in Chinese civilization has been comparable to that of religion in other civilizations. In China, philosophy has been every educated person's concern. In the old days, if a man were educated at all, the first education he received was in philosophy. When children went to school, the *Four Books,* which consist of the *Confucian Analects,* the *Book of Mencius,* the *Great Learning,* and the *Doctrine of the Mean,* were the first ones they were taught to read. The *Four Books* were the most important texts of Neo-Confucianist philosophy.[10]

THE ORDER OF NATURE

Traditional Chinese philosophy, according to Y. P. Mei, is predominantly a system of ethical realism. Operating through man's life and the

[10] Fung Yu-lan, *A Short History of Chinese Philosophy,* ed. Derk Bodde (New York: Macmillan, 1948), p. 1. Used with the permission of the Macmillan Company.

universe is "one all-pervading principle, rational and ethical in nature."[11]
For the Chinese, says Francis C. M. Wei, "orderliness and regularity are the
fundamental characteristics of the universe."[12] The concepts of Heaven and
the *Tao,* or Way, are prominent. Heaven, for the Confucians, is the dependable order of the Universe and the ground and guardian of the moral
law. Heaven not only governs human affairs in accordance with the moral
order of things but gives mankind a disposition inclined toward harmony
and the right. *Tao,* for the Taoists, as we have seen, is the way the universe
works and the reality that is immanent in nature and man. The *Tao* of
Heaven transcends nature and man, gives meaning to the universe, and helps
men do things in the right way. When Heaven is described in personal terms,
it may be thought of as God or Providence; this outlook may lead toward an
ethical idealism. When Heaven is described in impersonal terms, it may be
regarded as the "law of nature" or as fate, which determines natural and
human events. This attitude may support a humanistic naturalism.

In Chinese philosophy the stress is on the dynamic and changing nature
of the process in the midst of which we live. This resembles some Western
"process" philosophies. From early Chinese thinking the concepts "Yang"
and "Yin" have been inherited. *Yang* is the positive force that is the initiating,
creative factor in existence; *Yin* is the more passive and receptive factor.
Through the interaction of these two forces, natural processes go on.

MAN AND PERSONAL TRAITS

Man occupies a high place in the general scheme of things; he alone can
understand the order of things and live according to a moral ideal. The normal
person ought to aspire to be a superior man. He should strive for his own
development, renounce worldly lusts, and become a courteous gentleman.
A gentleman exhibits integrity of mind in that he is honest with himself and
with others. He is sincere in speech and action and is moderate in all things.
He avoids avarice, quarrelsomeness, and covetousness, and delights in aiding
others. Such a superior man does not go to excess in any direction. He exercises moderation and strives for the "golden mean" or the "just medium,"
which enables virtue and happiness to continue and increase.

The center of Confucius' teaching is the concept of *Jen,* which has been
variously translated as human-heartedness (Derk Bodde, Fung Yu-lan),
that by which a man is to be a man (Chan), the virtue of perfect humanity
(Wei), compassion (Lin Yutang), and man-to-manness (E. R. Hughes).
Jen is that which distinguishes man from animals, and all the virtues, like
reciprocity, loyalty, trustworthiness, and courage, are expressions of it.

11 Quoted in Charles A. Moore, editor, *Essays in East-West Philosophy,* (Honolulu: University
of Hawaii Press, 1951), p. 301. (East-West Philosophers' Conference.)
12 *The Spirit of Chinese Culture* (New York: Scribner's, 1947), p. 91.

In Chinese society the eminence accorded men in the various walks of life stands in contrast with that in Western society, where the more aggressive business leaders who acquire great wealth have the greatest prestige. In China the position of honor is given to the scholar and sage; next comes the farmer, who provides the food; then the artisan, who makes the instruments for men to use; then the merchant; and finally the soldier. As a result of the recent revolutionary changes in China, the prestige accorded to the different social groups may be different in the future.

THE GOOD SOCIETY

The concepts of the community and of social propriety are central in Chinese culture. The basic institution is the family, which usually contains as a household not only the parents and unmarried children but all the sons with their wives and children and other dependent relatives. Prestige and authority rest with the oldest male or, under certain conditions, with his widow or mother. Reverence for ancestors and elders is strong in Chinese society.

Proper attitude and conduct depend on one's relation to the person with whom he is dealing. That is, different attitudes are called for depending on whether a man is dealing with his parents, his wife, an official or ruler, a child, a younger or elder brother, or a neighbor. Different men also have different duties according to their abilities and their station in life. This is the basis of the five types of personal relationships, or the concept of social propriety. Briefly, these types are: (1) The relations between ruler and subject, where benevolence and loyalty are stressed. The state is only the larger household or community and exists to secure material blessings and long life for the people. Government exists by the consent of the governed. (2) The relations between father and son. Here kindness in the father and filial piety in the son are the central virtues. (3) The relation of husband and wife. The man treats his wife with consideration. The woman respects and follows her husband. Monogamy is the rule but concubinage is accepted and regulated, especially if there are no sons to carry on the family traditions. (4) The relations of elder and younger brothers, where gentleness and deference are in order. (5) The relation of friend and friend, where there is respect and mutual consideration.

The Chinese value system, which grows out of life and the order of nature, is, on the whole, humanistic, naturalistic, and practical in emphasis. The ideal social order is one in which each individual and section of society performs its natural duties. When man acts in harmony with nature and his fellows, he lives in peace and in a well-ordered and harmonious society.

Before the introduction of Buddhism into China, Chinese thought and ethical ideals were dominated by Confucianism and, to a lesser extent, by

Taoism. Confucianism was concerned mainly with personal and social relations, whereas Taoism, at least at its higher or more sophisticated levels, cultivated a sense of oneness or unity with the order of the universe and put less emphasis on man-made conventions and rules. When Buddhism was introduced into China, many educated Chinese adopted it because of its comprehensive and systematic character. For a number of centuries many of the ablest Chinese thinkers were Buddhists or were profoundly influenced by Buddhist ideas. Later the leaders of the revival of Confucianism, often called Neo-Confucianists, elaborated their views, with the presence and challenge of Buddhism consciously before them. The Neo-Confucianists, however, continued to emphasize the *Four Books*.

THE VALUE SYSTEM OF THE JAPANESE

In Japan we find a culture and value system that have been strongly influenced by Confucianism and Chinese culture and also by Buddhism and Indian culture. Yet the Japanese have remolded these acquisitions into something distinctive and uniquely Japanese. "What she has adopted she has also adapted to her own use." The fact that these people with a common ancestry and language live on a chain of islands separated from the mainland of Asia has enabled them to develop distinctive traits in comparative isolation.

EARLY DEVELOPMENTS

The Japanese value system goes back to a primitive tribal society in which life was centered around the family, the villages, and small neighborhoods. In this situation religious values and moral standards were scarcely distinguished from each other or from the problem of keeping order and making a living. The veneration of the sun, worship of the *Kami* (the nature spirits), reverence for the spirits of ancestors, respect for and loyalty to parents, older people, and all those in positions of authority, were part of one's duties. *Shinto* is the name used to cover many activities and beliefs. At an early date it was the tribal folk religion centering around the family and local shrines, but eventually it became a patriotic state cult connected with the chieftain and court. During the early centuries of the Christian era the influences of Chinese culture, especially Confucianism, and Indian cultures by way of Buddhism were making themselves felt. The Confucian emphasis on loyalty was carried over into the evolving ethical code of the warrior class. Buddhism was introduced and changed on Japanese soil. Zen became the most influential sect of Buddhism in Japan. Zen is from the Japanese *zazen,* to sit and meditate. Zen Buddhism came to serve not only people seeking salvation and wisdom, but also soldiers; it strengthened their power of self-discipline and gave them poise and courage even in the face of death.

THE MILITARY CODE

The period from about 1100 to 1600 saw the development of the code of the samurai or warrior class, the *bushi,* whose code is known as *Bushido.* This was a time when many of the Japanese values that have persisted were codified. This code was dominant not only in the Tokugawa Period, 1600–1868, when a group of military leaders (*Shoguns*) were the real power in Japan, but right down to 1945, when the Japanese defeat in World War II gave it a major blow. The code stressed an almost Spartan life. The samurai man was taught to lead a "sober, restrained, and frugal life," to live simply, to seek only the necessities in food, clothing, and shelter, not to desire great possessions, to rise early and avoid idle talk, and not to engage in frivolities. I. O. Nitobe, in *Bushido, the Soul of Japan,* emphasizes the following as distinguishing marks of the Bushido code: loyalty, personal honor, rectitude or justice, courage or the spirit of daring, benevolence, politeness and modesty, veracity, self-control, education, suicide or redress, and "The Sword, the Soul of the Warrior." *Bushido* involves a willingness to face death when honor demands it, since life itself is of less value than one's honor. An abridgement of the code in the eighteenth century includes the following. "We have sworn to do four things: (1) We will be second to none in performance of our duty. (2) We will make ourselves useful to our Lord. (3) We will be dutiful to our parents. (4) We will attain greatness in charity."[13] This abridgement does not supersede the *Bushido* code. All the older duties are included in these general terms.

INDIVIDUAL VIRTUES AND CULTURAL VALUES

The code of the samurai does not differ greatly from that of the merchant and the peasant, or worker on the land, since the warrior code came to be accepted by all classes. Merchants and peasants, like others in society, are expected to be honest, to work hard, and to place public interest above private gain. While some character traits are generally or universally desirable in that they apply to all men, many duties depend on the status of the person, his social role, or the particular circumstances. One man is ruler, another subject. One has different obligations to one's father, older brother, younger brother, neighbor, mere acquaintance, or a stranger. Thus we have a situational ethics with a complicated mass of obligations. Rigid adherence is expected to a detailed set of social conventions. Formalized behavior tends to prevent conflicts and make possible a smoothly functioning society in which political values are primary, with loyalty as the outstanding virtue. Loyalty ranges all the way from absolute loyalty to emperor and country to filial piety as the main obligation in the family group. It includes loyalty to public officials and to one's employer.

[13] Quoted by Robert N. Bellah, in *Tokugawa Religion: The Values of Pre-Industrial Japan* (Glencoe: Free Press, 1957), p. 90.

Robert N. Bellah lists Japanese cultural values under three categories: First, there is respect for learning, study, or scholarship. Second, there are the aesthetic values. The Japanese are an artistic people and cultivate the aesthetic sense. Third, there are the values centering around the family; filial piety is central here. The family, rather than the individual person, tends to be the unit of society. However, in the dominant Japanese value system filial piety is subordinate to loyalty to the emperor and state.

Before our brief discussion of changes that are taking place in modern Japan, we shall point out some general characteristics of the Japanese value system. First, Japanese standards and values are based mainly on a respect for external authority. The authority of the emperor, the elders, or tradition is always present. There is little or no emphasis on individual freedom and initiative and the need to work out an inner personal scale of values. While most people in all countries are outer-directed rather than inner-directed, the Japanese as a people have been more willing than Westerners to make their personal desires and wills subordinate to social standards and to accept authority.

Second, Japanese standards are based on an aristocratic, hierarchical, and hereditary tradition. Another way of stating this would be to say that the vertical lines, to those above or in authority, are stronger than the horizontal lines, which run to the peer group. There are political, military, and social hierarchies. Edwin O. Reischauer says, "No major people in the world places greater emphasis on hierarchy than do the Japanese."[14] This is also seen in the respect for age and in the attitude of obedience to and reverence for government, people in positions of responsibility, and parents and elders.

Third, adherence to the code of approved behavior seems to be the result largely of a "sense of shame before society." Ruth Benedict has drawn a distinction between "shame cultures" and "guilt cultures." Guilt cultures, more characteristic of the West, rely on man's developing a conscience and on some degree of inner control. Shame cultures are found in Japan and many other Eastern societies. People living in shame cultures are held in line by fear of ridicule and rejection by others or by the group. One must avoid *faux pas,* errors, and misbehavior that would bring a loss of "face." For example, one should not joke or laugh at another's expense, "go easy" on criticism and abuse, and be careful how one refuses requests. Honor is exceedingly important. A person desires to avoid not only personal shame but also family or we-group shame and loss of respect, as well as more formal punishment. Shame or loss of self-respect can lead to suicide.

The Japanese value system and rules of conduct contain contradictory elements, as do the systems of other societies. Conformism and the desire for self-expression, the suppression of emotion at times and emotional out-

14 *The United States and Japan* (Cambridge: Harvard U. Press, 1957), p. 163.

bursts on occasion, military ruthlessness and a basic compassion and normally peaceful ways of living, are a few of these contradictory aspects.

MORAL CRISIS IN MODERN JAPAN

During the nineteenth century, unable to stem the forces that were threatening her comparative isolation and bringing her into the modern commercial and technological age, the Japanese reacted in two ways. The first reaction was to reach back into the past and strengthen the ancient faith under a strong central government, with the emperor as its head. The second reaction was to modernize technologically and attempt to beat the West at its own game. The Meiji Restoration of 1868 (which restored direct rule to the Emperor Meiji), a new Education Code, military, commercial, and industrial development, military excursions on the Asian continent, and various crises and wars resulted.

In the Education Code, which set up a new system of public education, the emphasis was on national morality of an authoritarian type. Emphasis was placed on the divine origin of Japan and its people, the divinity of the emperor, and the messianic destiny of the nation, as well as on various desirable personal and social character traits. Various means were used to strengthen the national value system. R. P. Dore, in speaking of Shinto, tells how "the emphasis was shifted from the teachings of 'sincerity' and 'purity' as the norms of personal relations to the political requirements of loyalty, patriotism, harmony, and the martial spirit."[15]

With startling suddenness, defeat and surrender came at a time (August, 1945) when the general public was not prepared for them. Defeat seemed to deny the validity of the very foundation of Japanese national life and to undermine the national morality.

The Japanese discovered that the occupation forces were anxious to help them discover better ways of living. Japanese moral standards, traditions, and expectations seemed to be thrown rather quickly into reverse. Furthermore, the occupation leaders assumed the superiority of democratic ways. They praised freedom as the basis for mature and responsible moral decisions. What was to become of the Japanese emphasis on conformity and authority? What was to be the basis for moral action after the emperor, publicly before the Diet (legislature) and the nation, disclaimed his divine origin, the racial superiority of the Japanese people, and the divine destiny of the nation? The whole value system seemed to be shattered. This is what usually happens when morality is authoritarian and when the authority is overthrown or questioned; moral standards need to be more adequately grounded to survive.

Defeat, surrender, and the occupation are only outstanding events in a

[15] *City Life in Japan: A Study of a Tokyo Ward* (Berkeley: U. of California Press, 1958), pp. 347–348.

long series of rapid changes that Japan has been undergoing for nearly a century. They include industrialization, urbanization, secularization as a result of a weakening of the traditional religions, the introduction of foreign ideas and ways of doing things, and modernization along many lines. All of these changes or trends caused and are still causing severe strains and conflicts in the national tradition, the value system, and ways of doing things.

In 1961 an observer of Japanese life reported as follows: "Sixteen years after World War II, she has recreated almost everything she lost—except a set of values." Again, "The Emperor was not simply the symbol of authority and morals but their source. When the Emperor gave up his power, he also left empty the source of national morality, and the search seems to be for something to take its place."[16]

On the negative side, there has been a weakening of family ties, increased juvenile delinquency, divorce, and sexual immorality, a high rate of suicide, and a feeling of frustration and anxiety. On the positive side, there is the attempt to set up a new and more adequate system of education and the existence of a strong will to survive and succeed.

Japan, as we have said, is in the throes of rapid social change. She may be moving away from a closed, tradition-bound, authoritarian society, which emphasized duties or obligations rather than rights, toward a more open society, which will emphasize the individual as well as the group, and in which individual rights will be respected along with duties. If this is the case, the turmoil and frustration of the present period could lead to a brighter future.

CONCLUDING CONSIDERATIONS

A philosophy that includes a scale of values underlies each society and gives it some unity and sense of direction. In fact, a civilization is in considerable part a set of ideas, ideals, and values that acts as the cohesive force to hold the various parts of society together. When these values are weakened or lost and are not replaced by others equally constructive, the society tends to break up into conflicting groups, each claiming autonomy. In an era in which revolutionary changes are occurring and old orders are being destroyed, it is well to be aware of the role of value systems.

Today East and West face many of the same dangers and problems. The traditional societies in the East are under strain as they move into the modern scientific age. The West has moved rapidly ahead in science and industry, but it is facing a moral crisis and a lack of a sense of direction. The need today is for a more adequate value system, one which considers people as ends, which makes use of all modern knowledge, and which is dedicated to

16 A. M. Rosenthal in *New York Times*, September 24, 1961, p. 24.

peace and the sharing of the values of civilization with all men and women the world around. If men behave as they do merely because of tradition, custom, law, or outside pressure, they are not in the highest sense moral. Unless men have a consciously chosen scale of values and know what they are for and what they are against, they will be adrift in a changing world.

The cultures of the West, of China, and of India are explained in part by Gerald Heard as attempts to answer "three master questions."[17] The West has become interested in the question "Where am I?" Here interest is directed primarily to external nature, and this quest has led to experimentation that has culminated in modern science. China has asked, "What am I?" or "How am I related to other men?" Here the social solution or "man-to-manness" is considered most important. India has stressed the question "Who am I?" and has turned toward the inner life, psychological exercises, and methods of detaching oneself from the passing "outer show." The answer to one question, however, is not enough; all three questions must be answered. There is no one way to truth and no one answer to all the problems of life.

Both East and West need to ask what values they have to share with others and what they may receive from others. The East, through one or more of its various cultures, may help the West to realize the importance of self-discipline, moderation, and nonattachment; that selfish desire is the cause of much suffering; that an attitude of tolerance toward other religions and points of view is desirable; that filial piety, respect for authority, and the principle of noninjury have a place in society; and that the things of the empirical world are not eternal. Among other things the West can contribute to the East are the idea of the worth of the individual person; religion as a personal commitment to one God; the ideal of freedom and democracy; scientific method and the need for experimentation; technology and a wide range of social services. There is need now for the two groups to cooperate in creating an international order based on goodwill and law.

The educated, intellectually mature people in these various cultures relate to each other fairly well. There are differences, especially in emphasis, but the things approved and the things disapproved are generally much the same from group to group. Greater differences are found in the metaphysical and religious backgrounds, but even in these areas there is much common ground. No single culture, system of thought, or group has a monopoly on an awareness of human values and on insights.

If conformity to doctrines is to be regarded as the final test, believers in different creeds will be profoundly alien to one another; if modes of life are taken into account, religious men will be like one another. The view that our creed represents the truth and those who deny it are heretics who deserve to be liquidated,

17 *The Human Venture* (New York: Harper, 1955), pp. 16 ff.

is a dangerous one. . . . There are no fundamental distinctions between the East and the West. Each one of us is both Eastern and Western. East and West are not two historical and geographical concepts. They are two possibilities which every man in every age carries within himself, two movements of the human spirit. There is tension in the nature of man between his scientific and religious impulses. This tension or tumult is not a disaster but a challenge and an opportunity.18

QUESTIONS AND PROJECTS

1. Review Questions

(1) Why is it important to study Oriental philosophy, especially value systems? What problems are involved in making such studies?

(2) What are some of the main sources of misunderstanding between East and West?

(3) Discuss briefly the agreements and differences between East and West in their attitudes toward the world of the senses, human desires, the time process, and human values in general.

(4) Discuss the following in the Hindu tradition: the aim of studying philosophy; the relations among Brahman, the self, and the universe; the goal of life and the steps to achieve it.

(5) Give the distinctive characteristics of Indian philosophy.

(6) Discuss the following in Buddhism: what it accepts and rejects in Hinduism; the four Noble Truths; the Eightfold Path; and Nirvana.

(7) What are some virtues or character traits that are stressed by Buddhists?

(8) Discuss the place of philosophy and the general value system found in traditional Chinese civilization, especially under Confucianism.

(9) Discuss the origins, native and foreign, of the Japanese value system, and trace its development and characteristics to the nineteenth century.

(10) Explain what is meant by "the moral crisis in modern Japan." What are the reasons for this crisis?

(11) What are some conclusions to be drawn from a study of the value systems of the Occident and the Orient? What are some contributions the Orient can make to the Occident, and vice versa?

2. Study the philosophy of the Moslems and the philosophical backgrounds and value systems of such faiths as Zoroastrianism. Write a statement explaining their central outlooks and systems of value.

3. Yoga and other disciplines of concentration and meditation are said to help people direct their lives and attain union with the ultimate reality. On this subject see Swami Nikhilananda, *Hinduism: Its Meaning for the Liberation of the Spirit* (New York: Harper, 1958), Chs. V–VIII; William S. Haas, *The Destiny of the Mind, East and West* (New York: Macmillan, 1956), Ch. XI, "The Yoga Technique," pp. 214–235.

18 Radhakrishnan, *East and West*, pp. 40, 120.

4. Thinkers in the Orient tend on the whole to be tolerant of opposing doctrines, and they reject the view that there is only one way to truth and salvation. Western thinkers tend to look for flaws or theoretical loopholes that will furnish grounds for criticism, and they often seem more anxious to tear down than to build up. Does the following statement by a Western philosopher seem to you fair or too severe?

> All philosophy is—should be—reasoning plus experiment. Nevertheless, the experiment of seeking pure theoretical proof has been tried in the West and has resulted in perennial bickering and a retreat today into the ivory tower of methodology and language-structure, without the slightest prospect of emerging to look at the real world. *Seen only from its own contemplative perspective,* Western philosophy has been a complete failure.19

5. Discuss the following quotations:

(1) "The backwardness of any people is merely the field of activity in which it has not specialized." "The strength of one culture is often the weakness of another." "No single culture can realize all the possible human values." Is it true that each culture tends to specialize in some area or aspect of life?

(2) "Most of the ills of the world come from men not being able to sit in a room quietly and think." May the hermit or the person who spends much time in meditation and thought be as influential and effective as the "man of action"?

6. Review one of the following books: Vinoba Bhave, *Talks on the Gita* (New York: Macmillan, 1960); Kenneth Cragg, *The Call of the Minaret* (New York: Oxford U. Press, 1956); Vera M. Dean, *The Nature of the Non-Western World* (New York: New American Library of World Literature, 1957); William S. Haas, *The Destiny of the Mind, East and West* (New York: Macmillan, 1956); Gerald Heard, *The Human Venture* (New York: Harper, 1955); Barbara Ward Jackson, *The Interplay of East and West: Elements of Contrast and Cooperation* (London: Allen and Unwin, 1957); Sokyo Ono, *Shinto: The Kami Way* (Rutland: Tuttle, 1962); D. T. Suzuki, *Zen and Japanese Culture* (New York: Pantheon, 1959).

7. Discuss the popular view that the West is materialistic and the East is spiritual. Is the impression a true one? In your reply take account of religion, art, and other elements of our culture, past and present.

8. In *The Meeting of East and West* (New York: Macmillan, 1946), Ch. II, F. S. C. Northrop discusses Mexican culture as an example of a synthesis of the values of various cultures. What, according to him, are the distinctive elements in Mexican culture?

9. Judaism and Christianity are Eastern in origin. To what extent do their value systems agree with and differ from the Eastern philosophies considered in this chapter?

19 W. H. Sheldon, "Main Contrasts Between Eastern and Western Philosophy," Charles A. Moore, editor, *Essays in East-West Philosophy* (Honolulu: University of Hawaii Press, 1951), p. 297.

SUGGESTED READINGS

BELLAH, ROBERT N. *Tokugawa Religion: The Values of Pre-Industrial Japan.* Glencoe: Free Press, 1957.
  An interesting study of the traditional values of Japanese society and the part these values have played in recent Japanese history.

BURTT, EDWIN A. *Man Seeks the Divine: A Study in the History and Comparison of Religions.* New York: Harper, 1957.
  An excellent discussion of the religions of East and West, with considerable emphasis on the underlying thought forms or philosophy.

CONZE, EDWARD. *Buddhist Thought in India: Three Phases of Buddhist Philosophy.* London: Allen and Unwin, 1962.
  This book discusses the main themes of Buddhist thought as it developed in India through three different stages.

CREEL, H. G. *Chinese Thought from Confucius to Mao Tse-Tung.* Chicago: U. of Chicago Press, 1953.
  A nontechnical history that takes into account the social and political background of the movements of Chinese thought.

DORE, R. P. *City Life in Japan: A Study of a Tokyo Ward.* Berkeley: U. of California Press, 1958.
  This book reports the results of a careful study of the levels and standards of living, outlook, religion, and moral standards of one section of Japanese society. The study shows how the old value system is changing under new conditions.

Essays in East-West Philosophy. Ed. by Charles A. Moore. Honolulu: U. of Hawaii Press, 1951.
  Papers read at the second East-West Philosophers' Conference in 1949. An attempt at world philosophical synthesis in the areas of methodology, metaphysics, ethics, and social philosophy.

FUNG YU-LAN. *History of Chinese Philosophy.* Trans. by Derk Bodde. 2 vols.; Princeton: Princeton U. Press, 1952, 1953. (Vol. I, 1952; Vol. II, 1953.)
  A systematic account of Chinese thought from early times to the modern world. Written for the Western reader. See also the author's A Short History of Chinese Philosophy.

GARD, RICHARD A. *Great Religions of Modern Man.* New York: Braziller, 1961. (*Buddhism,* ed. Richard A. Gard; *Hinduism,* ed. Louis Renon; *Islam,* ed. John Alden Williams.)
  The above volumes, along with three others (on Catholicism, Judaism, and Protestantism) give selections and deal with the traditions, values, and significance of the great religions.

History of Philosophy Eastern and Western. London: Allen and Unwin, 1952. (Sponsored by the Ministry of Education, Government of India; Sarvepalli Radhakrishnan, Chairman, Editorial Board, Vols. I and II.)
  A history of philosophy, written by many Oriental scholars, that includes all the main Eastern philosophies, as well as the development of philosophy in the West.

KEETON, MORRIS. *Values Men Live By: An Invitation to Religious Inquiry*. New York: Abingdon, 1960.
    A discussion of the values emphasized in the religions of the world and "the idea of the divine as the proper object of our primary loyalty."

MOORE, CHARLES A. (ed.). *Philosophy and Culture—East and West*. Honolulu: U. of Hawaii Press, 1962.
    This is a complete report of the third East-West Philosophers' Conference held at the University of Hawaii, Summer, 1959. The aim was "to consider the practical implication of comparative philosophy for cultural institutions as a basis for world understanding and cooperation." See also the reports of the two previous conferences, edited by Charles A. Moore.

MURTI, T. R. V. *The Central Philosophy of Buddhism: A Study of the Madhyamika System*. London: Allen and Unwin, 1955.
    A historical and critical exposition of an absolutist form of Buddhism called the Middle Path. By negating all partial knowledge, adherents hope to attain perfect wisdom and freedom. Difficult for beginners.

NIKHILANANDA, SWAMI. *Hinduism: Its Meaning for the Liberation of the Spirit*. New York: Harper, 1958.
    A readable yet comprehensive discussion of the various beliefs and practices of Hinduism. Highly recommended.

NORTHROP, F. S. C. *The Meeting of East and West*. New York: Macmillan, 1946. (Paperback, 1960.)
    The author attempts to state the ideological assumptions of the cultures of the West and the East, and then to formulate a solution that he thinks will help solve the cultural conflicts of our time. Stimulating and provocative but difficult.

Philosophy East and West: A Journal of Oriental and Comparative Thought. Ed. by Charles A. Moore. Honolulu: U. of Hawaii Press.
    Consult this journal for articles dealing with philosophical synthesis and for a comparative study of Eastern and Western philosophy.

POTTER, KARL H. *Presuppositions of India's Philosophies*. Englewood Cliffs: Prentice-Hall, 1963.
    An attempt to identify the basic assumptions and commitments that underlie Indian thought.

RADHAKRISHNAN, SARVEPALLI. *East and West: The End of Their Separation*. New York: Harper, 1956.
    A brief book of three lectures by a philosopher-statesman of India on the challenge and the opportunity confronting the leaders of East and West.

———, AND MOORE, CHARLES A. (eds.). *A Source Book in Indian Philosophy*. Princeton: Princeton U. Press, 1957.
    Selections from the major philosophical systems of India, together with some introductions and a general introduction on the "History of Indian Thought."

REISCHAUER, EDWIN. *The United States and Japan*. Cambridge: Harvard U. Press, 1957.
    The author discusses the relations between the two countries and gives valuable comparisons of the two cultures. See especially Part Two.

SUZUKI, BEATRICE LANE. *Mahayana Buddhism.* London: Marlowe, 1948. (Introduction by D. T. Suzuki; Foreword by Christmas Humphreys.)
A brief book written for the person with no knowledge of Buddhism. Includes selections from Mahayana scriptures and other writings.

SUZUKI, D. T. *Zen Buddhism.* Ed. by William Barrett. Garden City: Doubleday, 1956. (Anchor Book.)
The selections discuss the background, meaning, techniques, and philosophy of Zen Buddhism.

TWENTY-THREE

RELIGION: ITS NATURE
AND FORMS

Along with art, philosophy, and science, religion has been one of the dominant concerns of mankind. In fact, it developed earlier and has been more widespread than these other activities. A study of man and his problems would not be complete without some consideration of his religious beliefs and practices. A philosophy of religion is a doctrine of the truth about religion and its relation to life. However, religion is not easy to describe, or define, because it is a growing, dynamic thing, elemental, personal, and broad in scope.

Religion differs from both science and philosophy in emphasizing personal adjustment and commitment. Religious people think that their convictions are fundamentally true. They believe that this is a person-producing process in the midst of which we live, that the factors which have produced personality in the past are still operative, and that people may live in fellowship with the source of personality and goodness, that is, with God.

THE ORIGIN AND GROWTH OF RELIGION

What caused man to become religious? Numerous explanations have been given—fear, awe, an instinct, a faculty of some kind. Many of the answers are either false or quite inadequate, but two of the numerous interpretations of the origin of religion merit attention. Together they probably furnish us with the most adequate answer to the question.

1. Religion grew out of man's will to live or his quest for the completion and fulfillment of life. It is part of his struggle for a fuller life and a more adequate adjustment to the world. Religion is part of the ever-present quest for life that expresses itself on the lower levels in the search for food, shelter, and safety, and on the higher levels in the search for the social, intellectual, and spiritual values.

2. Religion grew out of man's awareness or recognition of a more ideal

411

world that gives meaning and significance to his life. Religion is man's response to the presence and appeal of an unseen world that evokes his awe, reverence, and confidence. Stated theologically, religion grew out of man's response to God. The search may be a double one, in which man is searching for God and God is seeking man's voluntary commitment. The awareness or recognition on man's part has been a slowly developing one.

Primitive man, in contact with a little-known and sometimes frightening world of nature, found himself in circumstances beyond his control or the control of his group. His early reaction was one of caution and awe.

> The simplest and therefore, probably, the earliest philosophy of nature is the belief in a widely and indefinitely diffused *power* or *influence* (mana). This power is believed to be operative wherever anything striking or unusual happens. It produces catastrophes, diseases, death; it is present in conception and birth; it causes plants and animals and human beings to increase and multiply; it gives prowess to the great warrior and skill to the mighty hunter; it works in the medicine man, in the good canoe, and in the deadly spear. The gods and the evil spirits wield it. It is liable to break out anywhere, especially in unusual occurrences. Mana is not evenly distributed and does not work in an orderly manner, since it is subject to the control of gods, heroes, and demons, although in its essence it is distinct from them. It is not soul or spirit but *power*.[1]

A second stage in the development of religion is *animism*. Nature comes to be regarded as filled with innumerable spirits; every part of it is alive, so to speak. Men attribute a kind of soul to all the phenomena of nature. The trees, brooks, mountains, stars, and other objects are held to be the dwellings of spirits. All things are thought of as possessing a life somewhat like man's own; it is thought that the spirits of things may be influenced by rites of various kinds.

Out of the mana reaction and animism, and continuing on in later stages, arise such conceptions and practices as taboo, magic, totemism, and fetishism. Something that is *taboo* must not be touched because it is mysterious or dangerous. *Magic* attempts to bring about certain desired ends by mysterious powers or the aid of spirits. The *totem* is an animal thought to have some relation to the group and its welfare. Totemism is the belief that there is an intimate and mysterious relationship between some object, usually a species of animal, and the group; the totem is this object. A *fetish* is an object which is supposedly endowed with power or in which a spirit resides.

Following animism is *spiritism*, at which stage the spirits become "free" and are able to move about. The spirits may be of many different kinds—the spirits of natural objects, great Nature Spirits (Sun, Moon, Stars), or the spirits of departed ancestors. The belief in many spirits or the worship of

---

[1] Joseph A. Leighton, *The Field of Philosophy* (rev. and enl. ed.; New York: D. Appleton-Century, 1930), p. 13. Used by permission.

them is called *polydaemonism*. Some writers speak of animism and spiritism as connected with the tribal stage of human culture.

When the spirits are given names and personalities, we have *polytheism*, or belief in many gods. The spirits are elevated to the status of gods and dwell above or beyond the world inhabited by men. With the change from tribal to national life, this transition from polydaemonism to polytheism is likely to take place. The gods usually come to be invested with human faculties and passions. There arise stories about the gods and their actions and stories to account for the world, for man, and for beliefs and customs. These stories, or *myths*, are known collectively as *mythology*. Myths are found among all early peoples. Mythology is not itself a religion; it is a primitive theology, or interpretation of religion.

Monotheism, or the worship of one god, may take a number of forms. One god may be elevated over the others in a heavenly hierarchy or pantheon. For example, Zeus became supreme among the Greek gods, and Jupiter among the Roman gods. This is sometimes called *monarchianism*. When the worshiper devotes his attention exclusively to one deity, though recognizing that other gods exist, the religion is called *monolatry* or *henotheism*. This stage is seen among the early Hebrews, who recognized Jehovah as their God, but Baal as the god of the Philistines.

There is an interesting development of the idea of God among the early Hebrews as reflected in the writings of the Old Testament. In earlier portions of these writings, God is represented as a "local" deity residing on Mount Sinai and walking in the garden in the cool of the day. During the wanderings of the Israelites in the desert, He is pictured as traveling in an ark, or holy chest. At a still later date He is thought of as residing at Jerusalem, or He is considered the God of Palestine. When the Israelites wandered from this land, they left the presence of their God. During the prophetic period and as a result of the Babylonian exile, the prophets assured the people that God was the God of all mankind and, moreover, that He loved righteousness and justice and hated iniquity and injustice. The idea of God becomes increasingly ethical and spiritual: God is interested in sincerity, purity, mercy, and truth.

The history of religion includes the history of the development of the religious acts or rites through which man has sought to come into harmonious contact with God. Forms of prayer have tended to progress from simple appeals for help to more elaborate prayers with the emphasis on fellowship, communion, and meditation. Institutions or organizations have developed to provide fellowship for the worshipers and to carry out a religious or social program. Scriptures, or sacred literatures, and systematized statements of belief have arisen in connection with most religious groups.

Today there are four religions that claim universality, in the sense that they have the truth and therefore a mission to all mankind. In order of historical development they are Buddhism, Judaism, Christianity, and Islam (Mohammedanism). There are also many religions that are more closely associated with racial, national or sectional groups, such as Confucianism, Taoism, Hinduism, and Shintoism. (Judaism is also sometimes included here.)

While some general stages or steps in the growth of religion may be pointed out, there is no particular line of development through which all religions have passed or must pass. Religion is a growing, dynamic force that has expressed itself in many and varied forms. The stages in religious development are related to the stages in the development of civilization and culture as a whole. The history of religion is not a record of unbroken progress; we find arrested development and, at times, decadence.

THE NATURE OF RELIGION

On the North American continent there are hundreds of different religious groups, each claiming that it has the truth. Some groups have sought independence over questions of church organization. Some, like the Roman Catholic Church, have an elaborate hierarchical organization; others, like the Baptists and Congregationalists, have a simple, democratic form of organization. Religious bodies are also separate because of questions of ceremony and ritual. Groups like the Episcopalians have a fairly set ritual, whereas the Quakers (Friends) have eliminated practically all ceremony and ritual. In addition, churches are separate because of issues of theology. Some groups accept elaborate statements like the Apostles' Creed, the Nicene and Athanasian Creeds, and the Westminster Confession; other groups say that matters of belief should be left to the individual conscience. Different religious groups accept differing interpretations of the sacred literature: should it be interpreted literally or symbolically, or should it be taken simply as a record of the developing moral and religious life and problems of the past?

Is religion primarily a set of beliefs? What part do knowledge and intelligence play? As we examine the history of religion, it is evident that the "I believe" element has been prominent. Some men have been put to death for not believing "what they ought" to believe. A few men, including Hegel the philosopher and Tylor the anthropologist, have interpreted religion as belief. Intellect and explanation are essential, they say, to any high religion. Religion must be intellectually respectable or it will lose its appeal. Yet it is a matter of fact that some people who have been able to explain the creeds and theologies have not been considered genuinely religious, and that others who have not been able to explain their convictions have been considered religious. Theology may be to religion only what botany is to plant life. Intellect, while valuable and even essential to any mature religion, is not enough. Religion is not merely believing, not just a philosophy.

Is religion largely a matter of emotion? What part does feeling play in religion? Probably the most thoroughgoing case for the interpretation of religion as feeling was set forth by Schleiermacher, a German theologian of the last century. For him, pure religion was pure feeling, a feeling of absolute dependence on God.

We know from history and from contemporary life that the emotional element has been prominent in religion; yet emotions are not enough. Emotions are in great danger of leading one astray unless they are accompanied and guided by intellect. There have been men in history whose emotions have been "worthy," but whose actions and influence have been wrong, because of such a lack.

Religion is under attack by many people in the modern world. Many of them are attacking what is in fact not the central concern of religion. In the past, men built great organizations to aid them in spreading their religious ideals and carrying out their tasks in the world. Occasionally men have forgotten about the main tasks and have become concerned primarily with the organization. Again, religious organizations have established symbols to remind men of the objects of devotion, and sometimes men have centered attention on the symbols and neglected what they symbolized. Organizations and ritual may be promoted merely because they arouse emotion.

Religion cannot be segregated from the rest of man's life. It is the reaction of a man's whole being to his object of highest loyalty. Religion at its best must be felt and thought; it must be lived; it must translate itself into action. Religion is not a segment of life, nor is it connected with any one time or place. It is not just ritual, ceremony, doctrines, or the church, even though these may all be aids in stimulating it. The great religious leaders of the race have spoken of religion as a vital, personal experience. This experience grows out of real needs—the need for courage and companionship. Micah speaks of man's chief duty "to love mercy, to do justly, and to walk humbly with thy God." For Jesus the great commandments were love of God and love of one's neighbor. Whether religion has been interpreted as man's cooperative quest for the values of life or as "the Spirit of God in the soul of man," it has been stressed as involving the whole of life.

TYPES OF RELIGIOUS PHILOSOPHY

A philosophy of religion, as we have pointed out, is an attempt to find the truth about religion in its relation to life, and to organize that knowledge into a systematic whole. A *religious philosophy* is a philosophy of life set forth from the point of view of some religion or of some religious tradition. In Chapter 22 we considered the value systems of some of the dominant religions and cultures of Asia. In this section we shall point out a few of the characteristics of Judaism and Islam before we turn to Christianity. We shall distinguish between Roman Catholic and Protestant Christianity and then note the special emphases in fundamentalism, liberalism, and neoorthodoxy within the latter group.[2]

JUDAISM

Judaism is one of the oldest of the world's major living religions. It has contributed much to Christianity and to Islam. The most cherished writings of the Jews include the Old Testament (Law, Prophets, and Writings), the Mishnah, or the traditional doctrine of the Jews as developed chiefly in rabbinical decisions, and the Gemara, or the commentaries on the Mishnah. The following four beliefs are central in Judaism: (1) *Ethical monotheism,* or the doctrine of the "One Only and Holy God." This is sometimes said to be the central teaching of Judaism and its gift to the world. "Hear, O Isreal, the Lord our God, the Lord is One." (2) *The one true God has revealed his sovereign will through the Prophets.* Here Abraham and Moses are especially important, but revelation is progressive and is continued through the scribes and rabbis. (3) *God has chosen Israel to be His servant* to bring men to a true knowledge of God. Israel has a mission to all mankind. This does not endow the Jews with special privileges, but it does give them special responsibilities. (4) *God's will for man affects all of life.* It applies to all people and to all times and places. Religious duties are especially emphasized in connection with the home, the family, and the welfare of the group. Judaism is a way of life; religion and morality are bound together. To do God's will one must "do justly, love mercy and walk humbly with God." The ideals of truth, justice, humility, faithfulness and loving-kindness are held in high regard. The Jew has special responsibilities for his family and his community. One should not only support his immediate family, but he has special responsibility for other relatives, and must contribute to the welfare of the community. Charitableness is not optional; it is an absolute precept. Jews are noted for a love of learning; education and intelligence are highly respected.

There are three divisions within modern Judaism. Orthodox Judaism is rigorous about ritual observances, the dietary laws, and the keeping of the Sabbath. It stresses the absolute authority of the revealed Law and looks for the coming of the Messiah. Conservative Judaism, while continuing rabbinical Judaism, claims the right to adapt the traditions to the conditions of the modern world. There is a less rigid formulation of the requirements than among the orthodox groups. Reform Judaism stresses the ethical teachings of the prophets and the growth of a Messianic age of justice, truth, and

---

[2] Religious philosophies could be differently classified as religious humanism or humanistic naturalism, supernaturalism, and theistic naturalism. Humanism is considered in Chapter 12. Supernaturalism includes all those religious philosophies which are dualistic or in which the natural and the supernatural stand in sharp contrast. Theistic naturalism, on the other hand, shifts emphasis from the supernatural and the other-worldly to spiritual values that are continuous with or within the natural world.

peace. Judaism is regarded as an evolving religious experience that is subject to change.

ISLAM

Islam is the newest of the world religions, and Moslem philosophy is inseparably connected with it. While Mohammed is the founder of this way of life and the term *Mohammedanism* is often used, the term *Islam,* which means "submission to God," is preferred. One who accepts this way of life is a *Moslem.* Moslem philosophy is a blend of Arabic, Jewish, and Christian elements united into a working whole by leaders such as Mohammed and by the Arabic people. Reacting against the Arabic polytheism of his day, Mohammed drew ideas from Judaism, especially from the Hebrew prophets, and from Christianity.

The doctrines underlying the religious outlook of Islam, and those accepted by orthodox Moslems, are usually stated as follows: (1) *Belief in one absolute and transcendent God.* Allah is the omnipotent ruler of the universe and His will is supreme. He has decreed the processes of nature and He judges, punishes, and rewards men. Since men stand constantly in the presence of Allah, there is no need of mediators in the form of priests, sacraments, and churches. (2) *Belief in angels.* There are good angels, who may intercede for men, and there is an evil angel. (3) *Belief in the Koran,* which is inspired and verbally infallible. According to the account, the angel Gabriel appeared and revealed to Mohammed the contents of this sacred book.[3] (4) *Belief in the Prophets of Allah, of whom Mohammed is the last and the greatest* and the one commissioned to deliver Allah's message to men. Abraham, Moses, and Jesus of Nazareth are also recognized prophets. (5) *Belief in a time of judgment* when mankind will be judged for its deeds. There is a heaven and a hell, but eventually all Moslems are to be saved.

Moslem thinking on the whole has been legalistic and authoritarian, but there have been some attempts to set forth new philosophical interpretations. Must one accept the authority of revelation, or may one bring all the doctrines to the court of reason? The issue of faith and reason has troubled thinkers in the Moslem world, as elsewhere. For some, union with a supreme being of love and mercy rather than mere submission to authority and tradition becomes central.[4]

---

[3] In addition to the Koran, the Sunna (Customs of the Prophets), the Hadith (traditions), and the Ijma (agreement) aid followers in gaining the right interpretation of doctrine, and they cover points not dealt with in the Koran. In the Koran will be found expressions of high ethical ideals and a passion for righteousness, contrasted with the use of inspiration to condone sensuality and settle minor disputes in Mohammed's harem.

[4] One outstanding Moslem leader, al-Ghazzali (1058–1111), occupies a position in Moslem philosophy somewhat like that of Thomas Aquinas in Roman Catholicism, especially as regards the roles of reason, faith, and revelation.

In the Moslem view of man, all sincere Moslems are equal before Allah, and therefore they should not seek special privileges. Equality, brotherhood, compassion, and justice are to be expressed, especially toward all Moslems, and toward all men insofar as this is possible. Happiness comes by following the way of righteousness and seeking to do Allah's will. Moslem morality has been closely related to religion and has been a mixture of the primitive and the modern. Truthfulness, hospitality, alms-giving, abstinence from gambling and the use of alcohol as a beverage, and the like have been stressed. At the same time slavery and polygamy are permitted. The problem of reconciling the view that man is responsible for his life with the doctrine of predestination set forth in sections of the Koran is a dilemma that has been perplexing to many Moslems.

Moslems made real contributions to philosophical thinking during the early centuries of the Middle Ages. They translated and discussed various works of Aristotle and Plato and helped introduce these works to the West. On the whole, however, there has been a tendency to concentrate on individual events rather than on philosophical principles. The influence of the Koran, tradition, and the "consensus of the community" has made for a conservative outlook, so that changes are resisted or come slowly.

CHRISTIANITY: ROMAN CATHOLICISM

Roman Catholics, like orthodox Christians of other groups, accept certain historical formulations of the faith, such as the Apostles' Creed and the Nicene Creed (an expansion of the Apostles' Creed), as well as certain later formulations or pronouncements by official persons or bodies. The *Summa Theologica,* the long doctrinal and philosophical work of Thomas Aquinas, supplies the most systematic explanation of the fundamental beliefs of the Roman Catholic Church. According to Aquinas and present-day Thomists, human reason is competent up to a point, and reason and natural law support the faith of the Church. Reason is competent to prove the existence of God and the immortality of the soul. Theology, however, deals with questions that are above reason and that can be answered only through revelation. The doctrines of the trinity and the incarnation are of this type. They are mysteries of faith that no human mind can completely comprehend.

The Apostles' Creed is the summary of belief most widely used by Catholics and many Protestant groups as well. It reads as follows:

> I believe in God, the Father Almighty, Creator of heaven and earth; and in Jesus Christ, His only Son, our Lord; who was conceived by the Holy Ghost, born of the Virgin Mary, suffered under Pontius Pilate, was crucified, died, and was buried. He descended into hell; the third day He rose again from the dead; He ascended into heaven, sitteth at the right hand of God, the Father

Almighty; from thence He shall come to judge the living and the dead. I believe in the Holy Ghost, the Holy Catholic Church, the communion of saints, the forgiveness of sins, the resurrection of the body, and life everlasting. Amen.[5]

Roman Catholicism holds the conviction that it is the true religion whose dogma is infallible, and therefore the Church is an authoritative body. Accepting this thesis, the Church insists on obedience from its officials and the laity. Authority is traced from Christ, who is God, to the Apostles, who were given power to appoint their successors. Thus, it is asserted, there is an unbroken line to the Bishop of Rome, the Pope, who is infallible when he speaks *ex cathedra,* or as the representative of Christ on earth, in defining a doctrine concerning belief or morals. The Church regards these statements as expansions or interpretations of doctrine, not additions. The doctrine of the Church is unchanging. The Church claims that it is *one* in doctrine, authority, and worship; *holy,* observing God's will and therefore deserving obedience; *catholic,* or universal; and *apostolic* in its ancestry.

Through the Fall, man is prone to sin, or corruption. This is evidenced by the fact that he frequently chooses evil over good. The Church, through its seven sacraments, provides "grace," by which a person is able to overcome his inclination to evil. The Mass is the central act of worship.

The Roman Catholic Church holds that God created the world and Christ established the Church. In such a theologically interpreted world it is natural and reasonable for a divinely appointed Church to exercise authority in such broad areas as education, marriage, and the interpretation of the Scriptures, and in more specific ways, such as censorship of reading matter.

PROTESTANTISM

While the term *Protestant* is sometimes taken to mean "one who protests," the original meaning was "one who makes a solemn declaration or affirmation to profess a conviction." Protestants believe that they retain the insights of the great Jewish prophets and of Jesus, as well as the inner living spirit of Catholicism. While agreeing at many points with Roman Catholicism, they claim that their views are closer to New Testament Christianity.

In general, Protestants, in contrast with Roman Catholics, have at least four rather distinctive convictions: (1) The *sense of immediacy* in the relation between God and man. Man can approach God directly and commune with him. Because of this, Protestants have simplified ritualistic and institutional forms and have rejected the attempt to set up intermediaries between God and man. Prayer is personal and direct: "The Spirit beareth witness

5 *A Catechism of Christian Doctrine* (Paterson: St. Anthony Guild Press, 1949). (Rev. ed. of Baltimore Catechism, No. 3.)

with our spirit that we are children of God." (Romans 8:16) (2) The concept of the *universal priesthood of believers*. This is the evangelical principle, as distinct from the institutional or sacramental principle. This, it is claimed is the true apostolic succession. A man's private interpretation is corrected by the fellowship in the light of religious experience and insight from the Bible, reason, and research. (3) Use of *the Bible as the "Word of God,"* or a unique record of the relation between God and man. Protestants have insisted that the Bible be printed in the language of common use and put in the hands of the people. (4) *Belief in the worth of the natural relations of men*. Protestants have believed that they could meet God in the common experiences of life and serve him in the common tasks. They have tended to emphasize freedom for the individual and to place less emphasis than Roman Catholicism on rites and dogma.

This freedom has led to denominational divisions among Protestants. We shall consider the philosophical difference among these groups, not the ritualistic and institutional differences. While any classification of these differences is somewhat arbitrary, three Protestant movements may be distinguished: fundamentalism, liberalism, and neoorthodoxy.

Fundamentalism   The Protestant Reformers of the sixteenth century, especially Martin Luther and John Calvin, set forth the general framework of what came to be known as Protestant orthodoxy. Different denominational groups or sects had their special emphases, which we cannot stop to consider.[6] During the four centuries following the Reformation, great changes were taking place in the life and thinking of the people in Western Europe and, later, in America. The rise of new social and economic classes to power and influence, the growth of democracy and the demand for liberty and tolerance, the development of modern science, the opening up of many new fields of study, including biblical criticism and comparative religion—all had their effect on the outlook of modern man. During the latter half of the nineteenth century and the early decades of the twentieth century, liberalizing tendencies became prominent in many Protestant circles. Opposition to these innovations was solidified when a series of pamphlets, *The Fundamentals,*[7] began to appear in 1909 and millions of copies were distributed over the Protestant world. Later, organizations were formed to combat "modernism," and the term *fundamentalism* came into fairly general use to designate a certain type of conservative Protestantism.

[6] See Leo Rosten (ed.), *A Guide to the Religions of America* (New York: Simon and Schuster, 1955).

[7] Published by the Testimony Publishing Co., Chicago, Ill., and widely distributed free of charge with the "compliments of two Christian laymen." For details regarding the various pamphlets see Norman F. Furness, *The Fundamentalist Controversy, 1918–1931* (New Haven: Yale U. Press, 1954), pp. 12 ff.; Gabriel Herbert, *Fundamentalism and the Church* (Philadelphia: Westminster, 1957), Ch. II.

Fundamentalism aims to preserve the fundamentals of the faith and to combat the attempt to reinterpret the Bible and theology in the light of modern knowledge. Christianity, from this point of view, is a fixed set of beliefs that have been stated by the church fathers, the Reformation leaders, and the traditional creeds.

The doctrines stressed by the fundamentalists are usually five: (1) The *infallibility or the inerrancy of the Bible*. While most accept a literal interpretation, some do realize that parts of the Bible have to be interpreted symbolically. The doctrine of the verbal inspiration of the scriptures—that the actual words of the Bible were inspired by God—arose in the early modern period in response to the Roman Catholic claim of papal infallibility on matters of faith and morals. (2) The *deity of Christ and the virgin birth* as stated in the various creeds. (3) The belief that Christ by his death on the cross achieved a "*substitutionary atonement*" for the sins of mankind. (4) The *physical or bodily resurrection of Christ*. (5) The *bodily* "*Second Coming*" of Christ to establish His kingdom in person on the earth.

The fundamentalists have opposed the so-called "Social Gospel" with its application of Christian principles to the social, political, and economic order and efforts to achieve international peace through mere man-made organizations, such as the United Nations. They await Christ's return, at which time history will end in a catastrophe.

Liberal Christianity   Liberal Christianity, or evangelical liberalism, is based on the conviction that Christianity and the knowledge about man and the world as revealed by modern research are not in conflict but are essentially in accord with each other. Liberalism is an attempt to interpret man's abiding religious experience in the light of modern knowledge, including the theory of evolution. Christianity is not, the liberal would insist, one set creed. Jesus left no fixed system or creed to which men must subscribe. Rather, he invited each person to begin a spiritual adventure in fellowship with God.

While there is no set of doctrines that can be called the tenets of liberalism, here are some points the liberals are likely to emphasize: (1) That *Christianity is a dynamic and growing religion,* which consists not in repeating what our predecessors have said but in "what the spirit of the living God reveals to us as true or good." From this point of view, the Bible is interpreted as a record of God's unique disclosure of himself to men who were responsive to His call. (2) That *revelation is progressive* and continuous. God works within the historical process and through nature and the lives of men. Authority is based not just on an inerrant scripture or church or creed, but on a combination of inner experience, the Bible as interpreted historically, the life and teachings of Jesus, and God's continuous revelation through history, nature, and men who are searching for truth. (3) That *God is personal* and One with whom men may have fellowship and communion, and that in the person and life of Jesus we have a unique expression of the nature and will of God. Jesus believed that the relationship between God and himself was different from that shared by other men, and he sought to lead men into a similar vital relationship. He imparted to men a unique quality of spiritual life. To be saved is to share his attitude, his spirit, and his moral character, and to live a sacrificial life. (4) That emphasis should be placed on the *worth and dignity of man as a child of God* and on his inherent possibilities, not merely on the fact that he is a sinner in need of redemption. The Christian is committed to a continuous struggle against all that tends to degrade men. (5) That *the struggle against evil is both personal and social.* Selfishness, pride, and idolatry express themselves in both personal and social forms. Sin and immorality cannot be completely separated; inhumanity, cruelty, racial prejudice, economic injustice, and war are real sins against the real God and must be continuously opposed. Christianity must be thought out, deeply experienced, and lived in all of life's relationships.[8]

Liberalism may express itself within the intellectual framework of idealism, realism, pragmatism, or existentialism. While many liberals prefer the term *supernaturalism,* since they think of God as above and beyond nature, others prefer the term *theistic naturalism* to describe their position.

Theistic naturalism is a religious philosophy that finds God and the values of religion in the natural world. It thus shifts emphasis from the supernatural and the other-worldly to spiritual values that are continuous with the natural world. There is no rigid separation of God and nature, though God is not nature, and He is not to be identified with nature. He is immanent or operative as one aspect of the natural world, and He is found in man, in history, and in nature. Theistic naturalism makes it possible for man to believe in an ever-present cosmic support for his ideals and values. Since God is in this close relationship with man and nature, He is discovered through religious experience and with the aid of human reason.

Neoorthodoxy   In recent decades there has developed a theological movement that is critical of both fundamentalism and religious liberalism. It is a return to orthodoxy, but an orthodoxy that has learned much from liberalism while departing sharply from it on a number of central issues. What is called *neoorthodoxy*—or, sometimes, *crisis theology*—is represented in Europe by Karl Barth, Emil Brunner, and others who have been profoundly influenced by Sören Kierkegaard (1813–1855), and in the United States by Reinhold Niebuhr, Paul Tillich, and others. The movement began in Germany; by the third and fourth decades of the twentieth century it had come to have considerable influence in England and America. Many would say that it is the dominant movement in theology today.

[8] Harry Emerson Fosdick was one of the leaders of the liberal movement in theology. His autobiography, *The Living of These Days* (New York: Harper, 1956), gives a good account of liberalism and its relation to fundamentalism and neoorthodoxy. See especially Chs. VI-X.

The neoorthodox theologians, or new supernaturalists, subscribe to the following: (1) The *Bible as the "Word of God."* This does not mean that they take the Bible literally; they agree with the liberals in accepting the principles of literary and historical criticism of the Bible. Myths like the creation stories are considered symbolic ways of stating truths that cannot be presented in their fullness with rational consistency. These theologians speak of the "Word behind the words" and insist that God is found in special events and in His relationship with men. The Bible merely reports these happenings, and the accounts are subject to the errors of human reporting and transmission. (2) *Revelation as the primary source of Christian truth.* The neoorthodox leaders are critical of the use, from Origen and Aquinas to modern liberalism, of reason, natural theology and philosophy, and mystical experience as ways to discover God. There is a renewed emphasis on a revealed theology that does not ignore the paradoxes and contradictions of existence. Faith rather than reason is emphasized. There is an almost suspicious attitude toward reason, secular philosophy, and science. Neoorthodoxy claims that God is not found in nature as such or in secular history apart from special revelation. (3) Emphasis on the *transcendence and sovereignty of God.* We cannot describe God and His ways in the conceptual forms of our world, so that any statements we make about Him must be very inadequate. We can know God only as He speaks and reveals Himself to us. Christ is God who has broken into history and revealed to men the nature and love of God. (4) Emphasis on *man's sinfulness,* which expresses itself most clearly in pride and idolatry. The term "original sin" is retained but interpreted to mean, not that man inherits guilt from Adam's sin, but that man tends rather naturally to fall into the sin of overemphasizing his own interests and importance. Sin takes the form of pride in power, in knowledge, and in moral "goodness." Sin is not so much immorality and sensuality as rebellion against obedience to God. Justification comes through faith in the forgiving grace of God. (5) *Emphasis on the tragic alternatives of life.* The Christian ethic is an "impossible possibility." Jesus taught a perfect and therefore impossible ethic, according to Barth and Niebuhr. The liberals are wrong, they say, in stressing the goodness of man and belief in progress. In society, compromise with evil appears necessary, and any advance faces the peril of corruption. A measure of justice is possible only by working out some harmony among the conflicting interests of men and also of social groups.

PRESENT TRENDS WITHIN PROTESTANTISM

There appears to be a growing movement, looking beyond the theological movements mentioned above, which may retain the valid insights of both liberalism and neoorthodoxy. In "Beyond the Usual Alternatives"[9] Paul Tillich contrasts the "theology of crisis," which has been profoundly influ-

9 *The Christian Century,* LXXV (May 7, 1958): 553–555.

enced by the political and cultural crises of the early twentieth century, with what he terms the "theology of progress," or the liberalism that had its origin in the more optimistic era before the world wars and revolutions of recent decades. Both of these movements, he believes, may be temporary phases in the theological development of our time, though both make some lasting contribution. The "theology of crisis," which has replaced the older liberalism in many circles, stands "for the lasting crisis in man's relationship to God," for the distinction between the infinite and the finite, and for the divine judgment upon all human activity, cultural and religious. From the "theology of progress," which failed to understand the depth of man's predicament, Tillich says we can learn that "the progressive activity of man which is going on in every moment of his historical existence . . . can lead to creation as well as destruction." Religion, Tillich, believes, is "not a sphere alongside others, but the dimension of depth in all spheres of human life." Future theologians, he says, need to give more attention to Biblical studies, to relate theology to secular culture and use the insights gained in psychology and philosophy, and to consider their religion in relation to the other great religions of the world. Karl Barth, who wrote about God as "wholly other" in his earlier books, has recently written a book on *The Humanity of God.* Roger Hazelton says that the " 'church-against-the-world' emphasis of twenty or thirty years back is now being radically questioned and superseded by a far more positive appreciation of the secular and the cultural, and on explicitly Christian grounds."[10]

QUESTIONS AND PROJECTS

1. Review Questions

(1) How does religion differ from (a) philosophy, (b) science, (c) art? In answering this question you will need to keep in mind the discussions in previous chapters.

(2) Discuss the origins of religion, and trace the steps in its growth from the early mana reaction to monotheism.

(3) Trace the development of the idea of God among the early Hebrews.

(4) What are some of the main issues that have produced separate religious groups?

(5) Discuss the roles of belief, emotion, organization, ritual, and symbol in religion. Give your reaction to the statement that religion is "the reaction of a man's whole being to his object of highest loyalty."

(6) What are the distinctive emphases in Judaism?

10 In Ralph C. Raughley, Jr. (ed.), *New Frontiers of Christianity* (New York: Association Press, 1962), p. 248. See also Henry P. Van Dusen, *The Vindication of Liberal Theology* (New York: Scribner's, 1963).

(7) Discuss briefly the Moslem philosophy and religious outlook.

(8) What are some of the main points of agreement and disagreement between Roman Catholics and Protestants?

(9) Indicate the distinctive beliefs or emphases of the following Protestant groups: (a) fundamentalists, (b) liberals, and (c) the neoorthodox theologians.

(10) Is there any evidence of a new theological outlook that may leave the older divisions behind? What are likely to be some of the characteristics of a new theological movement?

2. How do you explain the following facts: (a) most men have expressed some religious devotion or attachment, and (b) there are some strong antireligious movements in the modern world?

3. Discuss the relation between religion and philosophy, indicating the extent to which you think that religion needs support from philosophy and whether or not religion has anything to fear from philosophical investigation and discussion of religious questions.

4. What parts do the following play in religion: the church, the scriptures, ceremony, prayer, worship?

5. What is the relation between morality and ethics, on the one hand, and religion, on the other? Can they develop separately without loss? For a discussion and bibliography, see Harold H. Titus, *Ethics for Today* (3rd ed.; American Book, 1957), pp. 503–541.

6. How are the various world religions related? The following books will give you help in discussing this question: E. L. Allen, *Christianity Among the Religions* (Boston: Beacon, 1961); Nels F. S. Ferré, *The Sun and the Umbrella* (New York: Harper, 1953); Joseph M. Kitagawa (ed.), *Modern Trends in World Religions* (La Salle: Open Court, 1959); Stephen Neill, *Christian Faith and Other Faiths: The Christian Dialogue with Other Religions* (New York: Oxford U. Press, 1961); S. Radhakrishnan, *East and West* (New York: Harper, 1956), pp. 120–131; Paul Tillich, *Christianity and the Encounter of the World Religions* (New York: Columbia U. Press, 1963); Arnold Toynbee, *Christianity Among the Religions of the World* (New York: Scribner's, 1957); Arnold Toynbee, *An Historian's Approach to Religion* (New York: Oxford U. Press, 1956).

7. Review one of the following: Harold A. Bosley, *The Philosophical Heritage of the Christian Faith* (New York: Harper, 1944); L. Harold DeWolf, *The Religious Revolt Against Reason* (New York: Harper, 1949); W. Burnet Easton, Jr., *Basic Christian Belief* (Philadelphia: Westminster, 1957); Nels F. S. Ferré, *Faith and Reason* (New York: Harper, 1946); Edward LeRoy Long, Jr., *Science and the Christian Faith* (New York: Association Press, 1950); Robert Leet Patterson, *Irrationalism and Rationalism in Religion* (Durham: Duke U. Press, 1954); Philip Henry Phenix, *Intelligible Religion* (London: Gollancz, 1954); Harold K. Schilling, *Science and Religion* (New York: Scribner's, 1962); Harlow Shapley (ed.), *Science Ponders Religion* (New York: Appleton-Century-Crofts, 1960).

SUGGESTED READINGS

BROWN, ROBERT MCAFEE. *The Spirit of Protestantism.* New York: Oxford U. Press, 1961.
A readable account of Protestantism, which deals with basic preliminaries, affirmations, and ongoing Protestant concerns.

———, AND WEIGEL, GUSTAVE. *An American Dialogue: A Protestant Looks at Catholicism and a Catholic Looks at Protestantism.* Garden City: Doubleday, 1960. (Foreword by Will Herberg.)
The subtitle describes this book very well. It is a fair but frank discussion of the disagreements, agreements, and problems of the two faiths in a pluralistic society.

BURTT, EDWIN A. *Types of Religious Philosophy.* rev. ed.; New York: Harper, 1951.
A valuable volume that presents the major types of religious philosophies—Roman Catholicism, the main branches of Protestantism, humanism—and discusses other basic issues in religious philosophy.

DE WOLF, L. HAROLD. *Trends and Frontiers of Religious Thought.* Nashville: National Methodist Student Movement, 1955.
This book is a discussion of liberal, fundamentalist, and neoorthodox reactions to our cultural situation, elements of agreement among them, and "the road ahead."

FINKELSTEIN, LOUIS, ROSS, J. ELLIOT, AND BROWN, WILLIAM ADAMS. *The Religions of Democracy.* New York: Devin-Adair, 1941.
Three leaders of their respective faiths present Judaism, Catholicism, and Protestantism in the hope of creating understanding of each other's position.

HERTZBERG, ARTHUR (ed.). *Judaism.* New York: Braziller, 1961. (In Great Religions of Modern Man series, ed. Richard A. Gard.)
A readable presentation with chapters on teaching, doctrine, and so on.

HORDERN, WILLIAM. *A Layman's Guide to Protestant Theology.* New York: Macmillan, 1955.
A readable account of changes within Protestantism during the last half-century. Gives an understanding of fundamentalism, liberalism, and neoorthodoxy.

HOOK, SIDNEY (ed.). *Religious Experience and Truth.* New York: New York U. Press, 1961. (New York University Institute of Philosophy.)
Essays by theologians and philosophers that discuss "The Meaning and Justification of Religious Symbols," "The Nature of Religious Faith," and "Meaning and Truth in Theology."

PELIKAN, JAROSLAV. *The Riddle of Roman Catholicism.* New York: Abingdon, 1959.
Parts of this book deal with the evolution of Catholicism, the genius of Roman Catholicism, and a theological approach to Roman Catholicism.

Religion in American Life. Ed. by James Ward Smith and A. Leland Jamison. 4 vols.; Princeton: Princeton U. Press, 1961. (Vol. I, *The Shaping of American Religion;* Vol. II, *Religious Perspectives in American Culture;* Vol. III, *Religious Thought and Economic Society: The European Background,* by Jacob Viner; Vol. IV, *A Cultural Bibliography of Religion in America,* by Nelson R. Burr.)

The first two volumes contain essays on a wide range of topics, including Judaism, Catholicism, education, philosophy, theology, and the like. The titles of the other volumes speak for themselves.

SCHMITT, PAUL F. *Religious Knowledge.* Glencoe: Free Press, 1961.
The author reviews the claims to knowledge made by the world religions and then subjects these claims to analysis in the light of the "contemporary status of the theory of knowledge" and of religious experience.

SOPER, DAVID WESLEY. *Major Voices in American Theology: Six Contemporary Leaders.* Philadelphia: Westminster, 1953.
The leaders presented are Edwin Lewis, Reinhold Niebuhr, Nels F. S. Ferré, Paul Tillich, Richard Niebuhr, and Robert L. Calhoun.

TILLICH, PAUL. *The Theology of Paul Tillich.* Ed. by Charles W. Kegley and Robert W. Bretall. New York: Macmillan, 1952. (Vol. I, Library of Living Theology.)
Fourteen essays on various aspects of Tillich's theology. Also contains autobiographical reflections, a reply to interpretations and criticisms, and a bibliography.

WIEMAN, HENRY NELSON. *Man's Ultimate Commitment.* Carbondale: Southern Illinois U. Press, 1958. (Paperback, 1963).
A liberal theologian elaborates his empirical religious philosophy that emphasizes creative interchange between people.

PHILOSOPHIES OF RELIGION

MACGREGOR, GEDDES. *Introduction to Religious Philosophy.* Boston: Houghton Mifflin, 1959.

PATTERSON, ROBERT LEET. *An Introduction to the Philosophy of Religion.* New York: Holt, 1958.

THOMPSON, SAMUEL M. *A Modern Philosophy of Religion.* Chicago: Regnery, 1955.

TRUEBLOOD, DAVID ELTON. *Philosophy of Religion.* New York: Harper, 1957.

WELLS, DONALD A. *God, Man, and the Thinker.* New York: Random House, 1962.

Readings in the Philosophy of Religion and Religious Philosophy. In these books will be found selections from the religious classics, ancient and modern.

ABERNATHY, GEORGE L., AND LANGFORD, THOMAS A. (eds.). *Philosophy of Religion: A Book of Readings.* New York: Macmillan, 1962.

BRONSTEIN, DANIEL J., AND SCHULWEIS, HAROLD M. (eds.). *Approaches to the Philosophy of Religion: A Book of Readings.* Englewood Cliffs: Prentice-Hall, 1954.

MACGREGOR, GEDDES, AND ROBB, J. WESLEY. *Readings in Religious Philosophy.* Boston: Houghton Mifflin, 1962.

MOURANT, JOHN A. *Readings in the Philosophy of Religion.* New York: Thomas Y. Crowell, 1954.

TWENTY-FOUR

RELIGION:
BELIEF IN GOD

In some form, belief in God has always occupied a central position in religious faith and practice. Man feels a sense of dependence on something beyond the empirical world. William James speaks of a "More" which man feels about him and to which he responds in worship and in prayer. The sense of dependence may take many forms, depending on the stage of intellectual and cultural development of the individual or the group. In the practice of the illiterate hill man who smears a stone with butter to appease his god, of the woman who asks the forest god to heal her sick child, of the Mohammedan who kneels and prays at the sunset hour, and of the worshipers who offer their prayers in churches and cathedrals—in all these there is a similar faith and response. Beyond creedal, formal, and doctrinal differences all religions share a common sense of companionship and an assurance that there is "that which" hears and responds.

In considering belief in God, three things should be kept in mind. First, there is a difference between God and the idea of God. Men deal in symbols in every field, and symbols are bound to change as men grow in intelligence and knowledge. To say that God *is,* however, means that the idea of God is not merely an idea in the minds of men, but refers to what is objectively real or to that which exists quite independent of the awareness. Second, men were worshiping a God long before doctrines and philosophical problems concerning God arose. When man discovered other groups with different ideas of God, the question arose as to which ideas, if any, were right. With the growth of knowledge, the older conceptions came to seem inadequate. Thinking men were forced to defend the older views, modify them, or give them up. Third, no person's view of God is either final or adequate. Our knowledge is growing and incomplete. In addition man finds it difficult to express satisfactorily some of his deepest convictions. The religious man is likely to say that what he discovers is "not propositions but a Presence."

Let us clarify some of the terms used in discussions about the existence of God. In the previous chapter we traced the development among the Hebrews of the idea of God to the belief in one God, or monotheism. Belief in one God may take any one of three forms. *Theism* is the belief in a personal God who is creator of the world and immanent in its processes, and with whom we may come into intimate contact. *Deism,* popular among eighteenth-century thinkers, emphasizes the transcendence of God. God is the creator and lawgiver, who permits His creation to administer itself through natural law. This view has been called the "watchmaker view" of the universe, because God creates an instrument, the world; then He permits it to operate without His interference. *Pantheism* is the belief that God is all, and all is God. There is one single divine substance, and God is thus identical with nature, or with the universe. There are also terms that express disbelief or doubt about the existence of God. The term *atheism* means "denial of God." *Agnosticism* is the view that knowledge of God is limited or impossible; it is possible neither to affirm nor to deny God's existence.

OBSTACLES TO BELIEF IN GOD

1. The presence of evil and pain in our world has been a great obstacle to religious faith. Evil has been called "the atheistic fact." "How," some people ask, "can we hold to the existence of a good and loving God who is all-powerful and at the same time all-benevolent when there is so much evil and suffering in the world?" Nature is cruel, it is said, or at best neutral. There is much pain and suffering from sickness and disease. There is mental agony from such things as fear, worry, and mental disorders. There is suffering that results from human ignorance, selfishness, and perversity. There are the social evils—poverty, depressions, wars, and the like. Finally, there are the natural evils—cyclones, earthquakes, floods, pestilence, and so on.[1] The world seems immoral because the innocent frequently suffer for the deeds of evil men or from nature's vagaries.

We must admit that pain, suffering, and evil are not imaginary or trivial or a hidden form of good. They are real and serious. There is no neat and easy answer to the problem of evil. However, a number of things may be pointed out. Much suffering is caused directly by man and is due in part to his freedom of choice. When a person with some freedom operates in a world of natural law, the possibility of evil is always present. Education and training in self-discipline may eliminate some evils. We are making progress, for instance, in eliminating disease. The fact that we are bound up with others in human society brings some disadvantages and suffering along with many

[1] See W. Macneile Dixon, *The Human Situation* (New York: Longmans, Green, 1937), Part I. (The Gifford Lectures 1935–37.)

advantages. We are slowly discovering nature's ways, and we can guard against some of her evils, like earthquakes and floods.

G. T. W. Patrick tells us that there are grounds for believing that the presence of evil does not justify any indictment of nature or of God.[2] After calling our attention to the large demands we make on life, he says that if we think of the world as in process of growth, our difficulties begin to disappear. In the process of the realization of values, as higher levels are reached the lower levels become outdated and sometimes may even be considered evil. The virtues of one age may be the vices of the next. Evil is something to be overcome, eliminated, or transformed. A good world seems to require some human freedom, some obstacles to overcome, and dependable laws. A life requiring some resistance, rather than one of total ease, is conducive to growth and progress; but this condition permits evil as well as good.

2. Belief in God is said by some people to be "unscientific" and merely the result of "wishful thinking." They say, "Get rid of the illusion that there is any reality of this kind and face the facts." Such people may point to the increase in mechanistic interpretations of the physical universe and their application to the realm of the mind and the self, as well as to other areas of life. When the religious person protests and says that the unbeliever's views are false because belief in God is functioning in the lives of others, the critic replies that the belief lacks evidence of the type he can accept and that the belief persists not because it is true but because it is comforting.

The question of evidence or why many intelligent men continue to believe in God will be raised in a later section of the chapter after we have considered the question of the nature of God. Since the question is frequently raised, let us comment briefly at this point on the statement that some ideas that lack objective verification are accepted merely because they are comforting. We may admit at once that religion is comforting to some people, even though very disturbing to others. Religion is also sometimes used as an escape, but many other things are used as escapes—art, poetry, novels, alcohol, and even science. A belief is neither true nor false because people wish it to be so. Where wishful thinking leads a person to read in what is not there, it is a dangerous thing. Yet ignoring what does exist is equally dangerous. The arguments for or against belief in God are as strong or as weak as the world views on which they are based. If a person accepts materialism, mechanistic naturalism, or positivism in one of its many forms, or if he insists that the objective method of the natural sciences is the one and only method of knowing, he will reject belief in God, unless he puts "faith" in a separate area—which most men find difficult to do.

2 *Introduction to Philosophy* (rev. ed.; Boston: Houghton Mifflin, 1935), pp. 403–405.

WHAT IS THE NATURE OF GOD?

One occasionally hears it said that God and religion cannot be grasped by concepts or explained by propositions, and that statements about the nature of God and arguments for belief in God are useless. According to this point of view, one just accepts the existence of God on faith, or one does not accept it, and that is all there is to it. While we can agree that no definitions and statements are final or even adequate, men have always felt an urge to explain their experiences and to justify their convictions. If religious leaders fail to discuss their beliefs with members of their own group, with critics, and with unbelievers, theology tends to become divorced from the culture and thinking of the time, and soon these leaders find they are unable to talk to men meaningfully.[3] If faith and reason have no point of contact, no reasoned defense can be given for the claims of faith, and men will be likely to become atheists.

Is religious knowledge totally different from the kinds of knowledge we have been discussing? If faith has no evidential base, empirical or rational, then it may move off in any direction; there will then be no check on it and no limitations to its claims. The claims of faith, it appears, do go beyond what there is evidence for, but faith moves in a direction indicated by the evidence or reason. Once having committed ourselves to some belief or action through faith, we often find that our faith is a step to discovery and achievement. This is true in all areas of life and not only in religion.

For a considerable part of Christian history, a distinction between natural and revealed knowledge has been assumed. The Roman Catholic Council of Trent declared that scripture and the unwritten tradition were given at the dictation of the Holy Spirit. The leaders of the Protestant Reformation emphasized the notion of human nature as corrupt and said that reason could give no reliable knowledge of the divine. The revelation of which the Bible speaks, however, is not a body of facts but a personal relationship expressed in images or symbols.

Conceptions of God have been many and varied. In the last chapter we saw how the idea of God has changed with the development of human knowledge and civilization. This development is still going on. God may be "the same yesterday, today, and forever," but ideas of Him certainly do change. In addition to the ideas of God set forth by various theologians, the numerous religious sects, and some scientists, we have scores of ideas of God promulgated by various philosophers.[4] There is the God of the various schools of idealism. The monistic idealists have thought of Him as universal

---

[3] See Roger Hazelton, *On Proving God* (New York: Harper, 1952), Preface and Ch. I.

[4] See Charles Hartshorne and William L. Reese, *Philosophers Speak of God* (Chicago: U. of Chicago Press, 1953), for selections from both classical and modern works on God.

Mind or Spirit or as the Absolute; He is the perfect, all-inclusive Reality.[5] There are the views of the personal idealists who think of God as personal and finite, and there are the conceptions set forth by pragmatists such as William James and by various realists. There are numerous ideas of God centering around the notion of emergent evolution.[6] Some of these conceptions of God have been mentioned in our consideration of the various types of philosophy.

The ideas of God prevalent in Western civilization have been influenced by three main points of view. The first is the Hebrew, or Jewish, conception of God. God is the creator of the universe, the king and judge, the lawgiver, the Superperson Who orders persons and things by His personal will. He is a sovereign Who dwells apart from man. He demands righteousness and justice, and He rewards or punishes His subjects according to their thoughts and deeds. God is seen as acting in the empirical world through events in history, as well as in the supraempirical realm.

A second source of the idea of God is Christianity, as it is revealed by the New Testament writers. Jesus of Nazareth carries on the Jewish outlook to a great extent, but sets forth a view of God that is more personal and intimate. God is a personal Being with whom men may have fellowship and communion. Statements frequently used to describe Him are: "God is Father," "God is Spirit," "God is Love." God holds a man responsible for his actions. God has established a moral order in the universe: "For whatsoever a man soweth, that shall he also reap."

The third source is the Greek conception of God. Greek thinking was more speculative and metaphysical than the intimate, personal ways of thinking of the Hebrews and early Christians. For Aristotle, who profoundly influenced the Christian conception of God, God is "pure form." God is the uncreated Creator of the universe. God is the intelligent, perfect, and transcendent Being.

Jewish and Christian ideas of God came into contact and were unified with the Greek ideas of substance. The resulting synthesis is the God of Christian theology and of the creeds. During the medieval period there was a tendency to think of the nature of God (His qualities or "attributes") as in contrast with the nature of man. Consequently, men thought of God as eternal, one, omnipotent (all-powerful), omniscient (all-knowing), and omnipresent (everywhere). Today, however, religious philosophy is likely to begin with an analysis of human nature and experience. There is an increasing tendency to think of God's nature and activity as blending with the nature and activities of men rather than as remote from experience.

[5] See the views of Hegel, F. H. Bradley, B. Bosanquet, and Josiah Royce.
[6] See the views of L. Morgan, S. Alexander, E. G. Spaulding, and J. E. Boodin.

From this point of view, God's purpose is carried out in the world in part through the cooperation and activity of men.

Today men recognize in human nature and in the empirical world in general certain kinds of activities that make for health, happiness, and a longer and better life. They tend to say, "That is what we mean by the presence and nature of God." Men tend to transfer to a higher power, called God, those qualities which they feel are permanent and of real worth and on which man is dependent. God is thus identified with whatever is producing the greatest good in life or in our world. This conception of the nature of God may be illuminated by the following statements:

God is immanent. God is said to be operative within the structure of the universe, taking a vital part in its processes and in the lives of men. This view is to be distinguished from the older supernaturalism, which viewed God as operating from outside the natural order; it is to be distinguished as well from pantheism, in which God and the universe are one. According to the doctrine of immanence, God is conceived as the principle of intelligence, purpose, and causation operating within the creative processes of the world.

God is transcendent. Men also believe that there is a Being, a Spirit, or a Person who transcends the world process. Immanence and transcendence are not contradictory terms. "It is the Transcendent who is immanent, and it is the Immanent who transcends."[7] God is said to exist prior to the world and to be superior to it. Thus "nature" and the "supernatural" may be thought of as separate, and God may be conceived of as operating from above or apart from the world. Those who overemphasize transcendence see God's nature as contrasting sharply with the nature of man and the empirical world. He is thought to exist in a realm beyond the reach of experience. His deeds are arbitrary and basically incomprehensible to man's finite mind.

God works in lawful and orderly ways. As we study our world, we find an orderliness that is universal and dependable. Some principle of organization or law appears to be present. Our view of God must be in harmony with the processes that we discover in our world.

God is intelligent and His ways are purposeful. The world lends itself to intelligent analysis and comprehension. Consequently, we may assume that mind plays a prominent part in its processes. While God may be more than personal, intelligent, and a Being who acts with purpose, we cannot assume that He is less.

God is good and beneficent. Belief in God represents the conviction on the part of men that there is an "eternal goodness." Whenever men have been confronted with what appeared to be a choice between defining God as

[7] William Temple, *Nature, Man and God* (New York: Macmillan, 1934), p. 298.

good or as all-powerful, they have been willing to admit limits to His power rather than to His goodness. God is then felt to be struggling with us and for us. Furthermore, the character that man has attributed to God has always tended to represent the highest moral standards of the age.

WHY DO MEN BELIEVE IN GOD?

Belief in God is a conviction and a faith held by many. They are anxious to know if such a belief is intellectually respectable in the light of modern knowledge. We need at this point to keep clearly in mind that there is a close relation between definitions of *God,* the nature of God, and the types of proof for His existence. Definitions and conceptions of the nature of God that think of Him as absolute and eternal (all-powerful, all-knowing, and everywhere) start from certain premises and proceed inferentially. For example, because men explain events by cause and effect in their everyday lives, they assume that there is a cause of the process as a whole; because they strive for completion and a greater degree of perfection, they assume that there is that which is complete and perfect. We shall see this type of reasoning when we present the traditional "proofs" of God's existence. On the other hand, if men appeal directly to human experience and interpret God with respect to certain elements or aspects of experience, or certain "good things" that reveal, they believe, a more than surface depth to human experience, then we have a different approach. If we define *God* as "beneficent purpose," then to prove that God exists we must prove that love and purpose exist.

We shall present first certain traditional arguments for belief in God and raise questions about them, since the first two of these, at least, are not widely used or accepted today. We shall then discuss some arguments from human experience.

THE COSMOLOGICAL ARGUMENT

The cosmological argument is deductive and based on the "principle of sufficient cause"—that every event is caused. The world is an event, or effect; therefore it must have had a cause, outside itself, sufficient to account for its existence. There must be a cause of the series of causes that we experience. Thus we come to a First Cause or to a self-existent Being. The First Cause could not be material, since this would involve the qualitatively less (matter) being able to produce the qualitatively greater (mind or spirit)—an absurd notion. We are led to a self-dependent entity or Spirit or God.

In the Aristotelian-Thomistic tradition, as represented by Catholic theologians, the cosmological argument for the existence of God has been given considerable emphasis. We must, it is affirmed, differentiate between the accidental and the essential features of reality, or between the temporary objects of experience and those that are permanent. Every event or change presupposes a cause, and logically we must go back to an uncaused, self-existent cause or to a self-existent Being. God is thus immanent in the universe of which he is the constitutive principle. God is the condition of the orderly development of the universe, as well as its permanent source or ground.

> There exist in the world motion or change; beings and events newly brought into being; things which are and are capable of not being; things graded in degrees of perfection, whose perfection, which consists in being, is more or less limited, obscured, mingled with imperfection; irrational natures disposed towards an object or end, as is proved, not only by the complex system of the universe or the structure of living organisms, but even by the simple aptitude of every agent to produce its specific operation. To account for these various facts we are compelled—for under pain of absurdity we are obliged to stop at an ultimate explanation of existence—to admit a cause which moves without being moved, causes without being caused, cannot lack existence, contains in its purity the perfection of which things partake in greater or less degree, possesses an intellect which is the final ground of all natures and the first principle of all things. Such a cause we term *God;* it is pure act, deriving its existence from itself (*a se*).[8]

David Hume and others have criticized this argument for the existence of God. They ask, "What was the cause of the First Cause?" and they suggest that the series of causes may have had no beginning. If every event must have a cause, why, it is asked, do we stop with God? If there can be uncaused events, then is a concept of God really necessary? To these criticisms some supporters of the argument have replied that this argument is not just a temporal argument from effect to cause but an argument in the "order of being," in that God is said to be the "highest order of being" and, as such, He is the "uncaused cause" of whatever exists.

THE ONTOLOGICAL ARGUMENT

The ontological argument for the existence of God was first set forth and formally defended by Anselm in the Middle Ages. It has been given a number of forms by various scholastic and some later thinkers. The argument attempts to prove the existence of God from the idea of God entertained by the human mind. Anselm said that we have an idea of a perfect being, and that this is what we mean by God. God is "that than which none greater can be conceived." Now if God is merely an idea in our minds, we could easily conceive

[8] Jacques Maritain, *An Introduction to Philosophy*, trans. E. I. Watkin (London: Sheed and Ward, 1932), p. 258.

of something greater than this, namely a God who existed not merely in our minds but in reality. If God were only in thought and we could think of something greater than God, this would contradict our agreed-upon definition of God. We could add existence to the idea and think of a being who was not merely thinkable but had independent existence. Thus it is a contradiction to say that perfection (God) does not exist. Atheism is contradictory and is eliminated as a reasonable position.

This argument, too, has come under severe criticism. It represents the mental outlook of a prescientific age and does not carry great weight today. We can conceive of all sorts of things existing, like mermaids, that apparently have no existence. That is, I can define *mermaid* as having existence, but I still do not know whether or not the "defined-as-existing mermaid" actually exists. We cannot deduce the existence of a being from the idea of that being. Furthermore, to say that perfection exists does not inform us about the further nature of that which is thought to exist.

THE TELEOLOGICAL ARGUMENT

The teleological argument, or the argument from design or purpose in the world, has been given more attention than the two preceding ones. The order and the progress in the universe disclose an immanent intelligence and purpose. Take, for example, the long process of development leading to the human brain and the mind of man. The process has produced minds that begin to understand the world, and it has produced thought and understanding. How could this occur unless the course of evolution were directed?

In discussing modern forms of the teleological argument, W. R. Matthews says:

> The whole controversy between a religious and an atheistic theory of the universe might be summed up in the question, What is the environment? On the one hand, it is possible to conceive the environment as merely "nature," a complex of elements of a non-mental kind; but if we do so . . . we can find no help from it in explaining the ideals by which man finds himself challenged and inspired. On the other hand, we may conceive the environment to be not only natural but spiritual and believe that we exist not simply as animals who are environed by a neutral "nature" but as spirits who live and move in God. If we adopt this deeper conception of the environment we have an intelligible solution of our problem concerning ideals and values. Man's apprehension of his "affinity with truth, goodness, and beauty" is indeed his response to the environment; and his struggle for spiritual life is, as he has always felt it to be, an effort to escape from shadows to the truth, to apprehend behind and within the lower environment which appears and passes that higher environment which is and abides. . . . When we dwell upon one aspect of the universe alone—the physical in abstraction from the mental and spiritual—man may appear dwarfed

and insignificant in comparison with the stupendous frame of things; but when we refuse to be deceived by this abstraction and unite the two aspects, we are compelled, as I believe, to form a different estimate. Man, who knows and values and appreciates, is no alien in the universe. He is the revelation of its nature. In him the universe discloses itself in its real inner being—not as dead system but as living Spirit.[9]

The teleological argument has had many able supporters, past and present, who argue from the presence of order and design in the world to the source of that order in a purposeful God. While Kant was severe in his criticism of the cosmological and ontological arguments, he said that the teleological argument must be "mentioned with respect." He pointed out, however, that the most the argument from design does is to point to a designer who is not necessarily an omnipotent creator of the world. Other critics have felt that the Darwinian doctrine of natural selection has weakened the force of the teleological argument.

THE MORAL ARGUMENT

The moral argument for belief in God is based on man's moral nature and his sense of values. The argument has been stated from a number of points of view. We shall mention very briefly three general approaches which have been developed in philosophical literature.

One form of this argument is based on man's conscience, sense of obligation, or sense of duty. If man were merely an aspect of nature, a command to obey nature's ways or to depart from them would be meaningless. The sense of duty at times may even lead man to deny the will to live. Man's sense of duty implies a God as its source and the guarantor of the significance of the moral life.

Again, it is said that moral goodness and happiness ought to go together in a reasonable and just world. The man who is morally good should be happy, and the evil man should be unhappy. Yet there is in fact no such constant correlation. Therefore there must be a God who will eventually uphold intelligence, justice, and purity of motives, and make the good man happy.

A third form of the moral argument is based on the objectivity of values. Man and his values are part of the process of nature. Man's moral standards developed within the process of evolution, are an expression of it, and are an aid to survival and enrichment of life. In arguing that our activities of appreciation are responses to an order of intrinsic meaning and value which

9 *The Purpose of God* (New York: Scribner's, 1936), pp. 118–119, 127. For similar types of arguments by a biologist who sees design in nature, see Edmund W. Sinnott, *The Biology of the Spirit* (New York: Viking, 1955); *Matter, Mind, and Man: The Biology of Human Nature* (New York: Harper, 1957).

is not less real than the order of physical events, H. W. Wright says, "The attributes of value, the permanent correlation of diverse qualities, the capacities for reorganization and adaptation, the intrinsic and expressive harmonies are features of existence no less actual and important than its strictly physical attributes."[10] He protests against the assumption that the earlier stages of evolution proceeded within the space-time frame only and not within the organizing unity of intelligence and value as well.

Kant, who criticized the previous arguments for belief in God, said that God must exist if the moral order is to be intelligible. Many since his day have further elaborated this point of view. The argument, however, has its critics, who say that, while moral experience implies some norms and ideals, these do not need to be perfect norms or to be located outside the natural order. Furthermore, if the argument implies that only those who ground their standards in theistic beliefs lead morally acceptable lives, the evidence does not appear to support it.

THE ARGUMENT FROM PERSONAL EXPERIENCE

Belief in God is part of an age-old tradition among practically all peoples. There is a long line of testimony from the seers and the ordinary people of all nations. "The fact that a great many people, representing a great many civilizations and a great many centuries, and including large numbers of those generally accounted the best and wisest of mankind, have reported direct religious experience is one of the most significant facts about our world."[11] Most men who believe in God feel that they know Him because of some personal experience or experiences. While some men believe in God on intellectual grounds, it is hard to convince people on that basis alone. Many people are aware of a sense of "lift" or "pull" in various experiences of life. For others the religious experience may appear as a sense of dependence or companionship. When knowledge is descriptive or intellectual, men are likely to say, "I think." When knowledge is experiential or by acquaintance, they are more likely to have conviction and to say, "I know."

For some people the sense of "lift" or "pull" or companionship occurs most strongly when they are in contact with the order and beauty of nature. Poetry, especially, abounds in testimony to this effect; poems like Bliss Carman's "Vestigia" and Helen Hoyt's "Discovery" are good examples. People have felt that they saw evidence of God in "His footprint in the sod," the sunset, the stars, growing life, and autumn leaves.

For others the "more" or the plus in life's experiences may come through contact and experiences with other individuals or with groups, especially in group worship. For still others the experience of the reality of God comes

10 *The Religious Response* (New York: Harper, 1929).
11 David Elton Trueblood, *Philosophy of Religion* (New York: Harper, 1957), p. 145.

through meditation and prayer. Prayer arises from the needs of people; it has been persistent and central throughout the history of religion, though it has taken a great many forms. Through these various experiences many men have felt that they sense the presence of God and that they have come to know Him as a reality. The great quantity of devotional literature that has appeared and been widely used during the last two or three thousand years is a fact to be recognized.

This belief in God has been subject to attack by individuals and groups in ancient as well as in modern times. There will always be people who are unable to accept evidence that appears conclusive to others, and those who do not have vital religious experiences themselves or do not recognize them as such. Atheism, however, has had little staying power. It has tended to take some of the morale and drive out of life and often leads to pessimism, cynicism, and a sense of futility.

While it is possible for the critic to say that all religious experiences are imaginary or illusory, another explanation holds that men live in the kind of universe that calls forth such responses. All experience, we are told, takes place in response to stimuli. Vision is the response of sensitive protoplasm to light waves; hearing, to sound waves. The mental, moral, and religious development of man is likewise a response. From this point of view, men are religious because of their nature and the nature of the universe in which they live. Men live in a person-producing universe. If men use the term *God* for that in the universe which is producing life, health, goodwill, beauty, truth, and personality, then there seems to be little doubt about the existence of God. Most men, however, will insist on putting more content and meaning into the idea of God than these terms alone imply. They will say that they are conscious of a Presence that gives meaning and enrichment to their lives.

We need to admit that there can be no final and conclusive "proof" of God's existence that all men will accept; also that no conception of God will be final or adequate. In a recent work, John Baillie quotes with approval the statement of William Temple to the effect that "all occurrences are in some degree revelation of God," and the statement of Paul Tillich that "there is no reality, thing, or event which cannot become the bearer" of revelation.[12] Is God continuously revealing Himself to all who will respond? Among the variety of ideas and experiences that men claim are revelations, how may we decide what is genuine? Clearly we need to exercise some critical judgment, here as elsewhere, when questions of knowledge are involved. Religious knowledge does not appear to be something wholly separate and distinct from knowledge that men have in other fields. God

12 In John Baillie, *The Idea of Revelation in Recent Thought* (New York: Columbia U. Press, 1956), pp. 70, 74.

may speak to men and guide them in many ways, among these through their growing intelligence and through past and present leaders and events. Experience, reason, faith, and revelation may be closely related. Revelation and discovery may be different aspects of one dynamic process.

BELIEF IN GOD AND A FUTURE LIFE

The question of whether or not there is "a life after death" has engaged the interest and thought of men from earliest times. Belief in immortality, resurrection, or some form of future life was widespread in primitive times and is present in theistic religions today. The belief is closely related to the belief in God, although the two beliefs are not inseparable. If we accept the existence of God, it is comparatively easy to believe in some future life. If we do not believe in God or some other nonmaterial "ground of existence," the belief in an afterlife is hard to support.

Religious rites have tended to emphasize the great experiences or the "crises" of life, such as birth, marriage, and death. Normal, healthy people shrink from thoughts of death, which run counter to the passion for living. There is also the fact that, though man is a creature who seeks companionship, he must die alone. From the time of Job until the present, men have asked, "If a man die, shall he live again?"

Let us admit at once that immortality is an issue that cannot be definitely proved one way or the other. Science presents no clear data acceptable to large numbers of people, and scientists can be lined up on both sides of the question. Religious leaders past and present are almost unanimously on the affirmative side. But a few people say that the belief in survival after death is a delusion and the result of wishful thinking.[13] The difficulties arise as a result of certain scientific interpretations of the universe that describe the world as material and universally lawful. Some biological, physiological, and psychological interpretations of man leave little or no place for mind or consciousness; when the body dies, the person, it is said, simply ceases to exist.

Belief in *immortality* may mean quite different things. There is biological immortality, or the continuance of the germ plasm generation after generation. In this sense there is no question about immortality. There is social immortality, or the inheritance of influence or of some social contribution; this too is generally unquestionable. While few men become famous in history, one's influence or contribution does go on even after he is forgotten. There is also impersonal immortality, which means that the person or the self is merged with the world soul, is joined in union with an Absolute or with Brahman as in Hinduism. In Oriental religions the self may enter lower forms than man as determined by the law of sowing and reaping, or *karma*.

---

13 Among those who oppose would be the materialists, positivists, and many humanists. See Corliss Lamont, *The Illusion of Immortality* (New York: Philosophical Library, 1962).

It may, however, finally escape the wheel of rebirths and gain unity with Brahman. Doctrines of *karma,* reincarnation, and the transmigration of souls are not confined to Hinduism, though they are prominent there. The views stated above, however, are not what most people in the West mean by the terms *survival* and *immortality.* They think of a personal immortality that includes the persistence of personal identity in some sphere or plane other than the present earthly one. Do you or do I as a conscious self persist after what we call death?

Among Christians in the West there is a division of opinion over what survival after death means and how the doctrine should be stated. On the one hand there are those who talk about immortality of the "spiritual" part of man—the spirit, soul, or self is immortal, or does not die. On the other hand, there are those who find the term *immortality* unsatisfactory and use the term *resurrection.* They stress man as a unit, spirit and body, who dies totally and who may be "resurrected totally" by God. The former view is the Greek idea, found in the writings of Plato and others, of a self or an eternal essence which is imprisoned in the body but which later escapes from time and history to eternity. This view has strongly influenced Christian thinking. The latter view is said to represent the Jewish notion of immortality. This view is found in a few passages in the Hebrew Old Testament, and it was held by the Pharisees in New Testament times. It became prominent among early Christians who found in the accounts of Jesus' resurrection an assurance that God had won a victory over "the law of sin and death." Fundamentalist and neoorthodox theologians object to the term *immortality* and speak instead of the "resurrection faith."

Questions of an afterlife center around the issue of the nature of the universe and the nature of human selfhood. If one thinks that human personality is a brief episode or an epiphenomenon, then survival is out of the question. If one believes in the existence of God or accepts the view that what has produced people is still at work in the universe, he may think of death, like birth, as a transition to another existence rather than the end of life.

In addition to appealing to various religious doctrines and convictions, those who defend a belief in personal immortality are likely to point to the lawfulness of the universe, the nature of man, and the objectivity of values. Science, philosophy, and religion all assume that the universe is lawful. (Science sometimes leaves people out of this picture of the universe, because science starts with the postulate of objectivity and the elimination of the personal factor.) The universe appears to be a purposeful and intelligible order. It has produced people with knowledge, beauty, goodness, love, and a desire for truth; without people these things do not endure. Man seems to be overprovided for this life. He is not satisfied when he meets his physical needs; he has moral convictions, mental powers, and aspirations. There is that in man which is not confined to space and time. Finally, it is said that immortality is a demand of man's moral life and is necessary for the conservation of values. Man's deep-seated sense of moral responsibility implies immortality. This outlook is so deeply rooted in man's nature that even great tragedies do not blot it out completely. In the main this conviction that death is not the final victor has been the conviction of the prophets, the poets, and the seers of the race, as well as of great masses of ordinary people. Immortality is a faith and a hope held by many.

WHAT DIFFERENCE DOES IT MAKE?

Does a belief in the existence of God make any real difference in human affairs—in man's personal life or in social relationships? In the first place, a belief in God enables man to explain what otherwise is unexplained or is explained in a less satisfactory manner. From this point of view, it satisfies an intellectual demand. Man wants to know whether he lives in a world that is composed of material substances and mechanical forces alone or one in which the characteristics of personality, intelligence, moral purpose, or creative goodwill are structurally present. He wants to know whether or not he is an "infant crying in the night" with "no language but to cry." This is one of the most momentous questions man can face.

The idea of God or the sense of the divine presence in human affairs not only has been persistent and widespread in history but has gripped men and compelled them at times to follow a course of action counter to powerful natural passions and desires. It has sometimes been more compelling than fear, hunger, sex, and the will to live. Tyrants have not been able to stamp it out.

Every craving or desire has its possibility of fulfillment or realization. This is true of thirst, hunger, love, and sex. Is this feeling of dependence on God alone deceptive? Most people cannot think so. In the crises of life, few people give a negative answer. While there are problems growing out of a belief in God, there appear to be more problems involved in a denial of such belief.

People have to have something beyond themselves for which to live or there is less enthusiasm for life. If they do not worship something high—the great values of life or God—they will worship something of less value. Recent history seems to indicate that the "something less" is likely to be money, machines, the state, race or blood, or even themselves. Loyalty can give life meaning and a sense of direction or integration. Loyalty to a high ideal can help make that meaning good; to a low ideal, evil or distorted.

Lack of belief in God and in a meaningful universe is likely to express itself in a lowered enthusiasm for life. "Atheism," says William Pepperell Montague, "leads not to badness but only to an incurable sadness and loneliness."14 It tends to take morale and drive from life and to lead to pessimism and a sense of futility. If something in the cosmos is not concerned about loyalty, truth, and goodness, why should we be much concerned?

Belief in God has had a steadying effect on life and has contributed to mental health and personal stability. In this connection the famous statement by the psychiatrist C. G. Jung is appropriate: "Among all my patients in the second half of life—that is to say, over thirty-five—there has not been one whose problem in the last resort was not that of finding a religious outlook on life." Jung's patients had become mentally ill because they had lost that integration "which the living religions of every age have given to their followers."

Belief in God has implications for our personal lives, as well as for society. It gives us a point of reference by which we are able to judge our own lives and such social institutions as the state. Belief in God gives significance and worth to personal life, and it tends to check the natural tendency of man toward pride or egotism, in which he tends to set himself up as God.

A further comment about the issue of an afterlife is in order. This, too, appears to have implications for living. Oriental views of a rigidly determined "wheel of rebirth" appear to lead to a fatalistic acceptance of things as they are. Otherworldly notions may lead people to lose interest in the opportunities for improvement in this world. Medicine and public health measures, for example, are likely to flourish among people who love life and have a high respect for man's life in this world. On the other hand, an extreme secularism may lead a man to center his attention almost exclusively upon pleasures and material possessions, which do not permanently satisfy the deepest longings of man. Men who have a high respect for the significance and meaning of life will make human living as rich as possible in the present and will look toward the future with confidence and hope. What men believe does make a difference in life's decisions.

QUESTIONS AND PROJECTS

1. Review Questions

(1) What are some of the forms of expression that belief in God has taken in various places and throughout the years?

(2) Indicate some things that need to be kept clearly in mind when one considers the problem of belief in God. Do you agree that our knowledge in this, as in other fields, is never adequate or final?

(3) Why are pain and evil often obstacles to a belief in God? Does the presence of evil justify an indictment of nature or of God?

14 *Belief Unbound* (New Haven: Yale U. Press, 1930), p. 67.

(4) Discuss the assertion that belief in God is unscientific and the result of wishful thinking.

(5) What in your judgment is the relation between faith and revelation, on the one hand, and reason and experience, on the other? Discuss the different meanings of the terms *faith* and *revelation* and indicate which of the various meanings appear most adequate to you and why.

(6) What have been the main sources of influence of the idea of God prevalent in Western society? Indicate the ways in which these various sources differ in emphasis and outlook.

(7) In what ways do modern views of God tend to differ from earlier, especially medieval, conceptions?

(8) What are the historic or classic arguments for belief in God? Do some of these arguments appear to have more weight than others?

(9) Explain what is meant by the "argument from personal experience" as a basis for belief in God. Give some examples of the different forms such experience may take.

(10) Discuss the problem of a life after death, indicating the different forms the belief may take, why some people find belief in a future life difficult to accept, and why others think the belief reasonable.

(11) What differences does belief in God make in human affairs?

2. Do you agree or disagree with Montague (*Belief Unbound*, pp. 6–7) when he says that the question of the existence of God and of religious truth or falsity is one of the most momentous issues we face because it determines whether the things we care for most are at the mercy of the things we care for least? Discuss.

3. Are naturalism (of the nontheistic type) and optimism "steeds galloping in opposite directions"? What is the effect on morale of a rejection of cosmic support or belief in God? G. K. Chesterton is reported to have remarked that if we are to be truly gay, we must believe that there is some eternal gaiety in the nature of things. Another person asks, "Why be brave in a stupid cause? Why, then, be brave in a cosmic cause that is utterly without significance?" How would you answer these questions?

4. In the play *R. U. R.*, Karel Capek pictures a manufacturer making mechanical men, or robots, who do the work of the world. The robots do all sorts of things, and they are very efficient. However, they become destructive and destroy their creators and themselves. The play ends with the manufacturer trying to discover the secret of life and to make creatures that will feel pain. Is it true that pain and suffering play an essential part in life? Discuss.

5. Do you agree with the statement that the important question is not why there is suffering and trouble, but how we are going to meet it or use it when it comes? Why or why not?

6. Is it possible for men to think of God as both transcendent and immanent and be consistent in their views? Explain why you think this is or is not possible.

7. Comment on the following statements, and tell to what extent you think they can be accepted:

(1) "The man who refuses to face facts doesn't believe in God."

(2) "A little philosophy inclineth man's mind to atheism, but depth in philosophy bringeth man's mind about to religion."—Francis Bacon

(3) "Originally God made man in his image, and man has ever since returned the compliment."—Voltaire

(4) "The God of any group of people is the object of their highest loyalty, adoration, allegiance, awe, reverence, devotion."—Durant Drake

8. Review one of the following: John Baillie, *The Idea of Revelation in Recent Thought* (New York: Columbia U. Press, 1956); Nels F. S. Ferré, *Searchlights on Contemporary Theology* (New York: Harper, 1961); Erdman Harris, *God's Image and Man's Imagination* (New York: Scribner's, 1959); Daniel Thomas Jenkins, *Believing in God* (Philadelphia: Westminster, 1956); Henri de Lubac, *The Discovery of God* (New York: Kenedy, 1960); Frederic W. H. Myers, *Human Personality and Its Survival of Bodily Death,* ed. Susy Smith (New Hyde Park: University Books, 1961); H. Richard Niebuhr, *Radical Monotheism and Western Culture* (New York: Harper, 1960); Jaroslav Pelikan, *The Shape of Death; Life, Death, and Immortality in the Early Fathers* (New York: Abingdon, 1961); William G. Pollard, *Chance and Providence* (New York: Scribner's, 1958); Roger Lincoln Shinn, *Life, Death, and Destiny* (Philadelphia: Westminster, 1957); William J. Wolf, *Man's Knowledge of God* (New York: Doubleday, 1955).

SUGGESTED READINGS

BARTH, KARL. *The Humanity of God.* Richmond: Knox, 1960.
A small book in which Barth evaluates nineteenth- and twentieth-century theology and says that "genuine deity includes in itself genuine humanity."

CAMPBELL, C. A. *On Selfhood and Godhood.* New York: Macmillan, 1957. (The Gifford Lectures, 1953–54 and 1954–55, revised and expanded.)
An examination of the author's first principles. Part Two deals with Godhood and its relation to selfhood, which is discussed in Part One.

COCHRANE, ARTHUR C. *The Existentialists and God.* Philadelphia: Westminster, 1956.
God in the thought of Kierkegaard, Jaspers, Heidegger, Sartre, Tillich, Gilson, and Barth.

COLLINS, JAMES. *God in Modern Philosophy.* Chicago: Regnery, 1959.
A good discussion of the different kinds of philosophical interpretations of God during the period from Nicholas of Cues, Calvin, and Bruno, to Newman and Whitehead.

FARMER, HERBERT H. *Towards Belief in God.* New York: Macmillan, 1943.
A clear and stimulating discussion of the grounds for a belief in God. God is not merely an abstract idea; He is a living personal will.

HARRIS, ERDMAN. *God's Image and Man's Imagination.* New York: Scribner's, 1959.
The author discusses various interpretations of God. Chapters are included on the God of the theist, of the Bible, of the cults and sects, and so on.

HARTSHORNE, CHARLES, AND REESE, WILLIAM L. *Philosophers Speak of God.* Chicago: U. of Chicago Press, 1953.
Selections from over fifty writers, from Lao-tzu, Plato, and Sankara, to Whitehead, Berdyaev, and Radhakrishnan, as examples of philosophical conceptions of God.

HAZELTON, ROGER. *On Proving God: A Handbook in Christian Conversation.* New York: Harper, 1952.
An attempt is made to supply the reader with what he needs in the way of proof of the existence of God.

HOCKING, WILLIAM ERNEST. *The Meaning of Immortality in Human Experience.* rev. ed.; New York: Harper, 1957.
The meaning of immortality is discussed in the light of the scientific knowledge of the day and a world view that gives meaning to human existence.

HORTON, WALTER MARSHALL. *Christian Theology: An Ecumenical Approach.* New York: Harper, 1955.
Written for classes in theology. While recognizing the differences of interpretation among Christian groups, the author believes that the basic needs of humanity are universal.

SMITH, JOHN E. *Reason and God: Encounters of Philosophy with Religion.* New Haven: Yale U. Press, 1962.
The author attempts to speak for the Christian in philosophy. After supplying some historical background, he evaluates various contemporary movements in theology and philosophy.

STIERNOTTE, ALFRED P. *God and Space-Time: Deity in the Philosophy of Samuel Alexander.* New York: Philosophical Library, 1954. (Foreword by Henry Nelson Wieman.)
A critical examination of the realism of Alexander, with emphasis on his view of God and deity.

TEMPLE, WILLIAM. *Nature, Man and God.* New York: St. Martin's, 1953.
A comprehensive and profound presentation of some of the great themes of philosophy and theology. See especially Lectures X and XI, which deal with questions of immanence and transcendence.

PART FIVE

THE SOCIAL SCENE

TWENTY-FIVE

THE CIVIL LIBERTIES

The age-old fight for freedom continues unabated in the Americas, Europe, Asia, and Africa. Man's struggle for freedom goes back until it is obscured in the dim past. A familiarity with some of the great landmarks, documents, and events that are milestones in the battle for liberty and civil rights is useful and interesting. These are too numerous to discuss here, but they would include the Magna Carta (1215), the French Declaration of the Rights of Man and Citizen (1789), the American Bill of Rights (the first ten amendments to the Constitution, 1791), and the Universal Declaration of Human Rights (adopted by the United Nations Assembly, 1948). Recent Supreme Court decisions in the United States also play a significant part in this story.[1]

The various bills, petitions, and declarations of human rights, past and present, lead us to ask, what is a right? How may we support a claim on the part of men to certain rights like the rights to freedom, a fair trial, security, education, and so on. Rights are based on our conception of the nature of man and values—topics that we have considered in previous chapters. A right is a claim to a condition that is indispensable for growth and a well-rounded or full life. If there is a right to life, then there is a right to the conditions that make a good life possible insofar as these conditions can be made available. As human beings we have a right to demand some things if their absence will retard our development and their presence enrich us, provided it is well within the means of society to make these things available.

If rights are based on values and the nature of man, then they change in a changing society. An example of how rights emerge and are recognized is furnished by education. Two centuries ago education was not considered a right for all men. Later, when men discovered the value and the need for an education that could not be supplied by every home, this recognition led to the acceptance of education as the right of every child. In a similar way men talk about the right to freedom of speech, press, assembly, and religion. They also talk about the right to vote and be elected, to have a fair trial, to work and to receive a living wage, and to conduct a business.

[1] See books in the Suggested Readings by Irwin Edman, Osmond K. Fraenkel, Robert M. MacIver, and Andrew D. Weinberger.

In this chapter we shall be thinking mainly about the civil liberties, of which the rights to think, speak, and write are especially important to philosophers. These and related freedoms are not granted by the state or any group in society even though the state may need to exercise some control where conflicts of rights occur. If the state grants these rights, then the state can take them away, and that is what freedom-loving men in the past have not been willing to admit. These rights are human, social, natural, or God-given rights based on the nature of man and the conditions necessary for his development and the common good.

Four kinds of freedom need to be distinguished. There is, first, freedom of choice, or moral freedom. This issue was dealt with in Chapter 11. There is, second, freedom from external restraint, or physical freedom. This has been a particularly important issue where totalitarian governments are in power. Freedom from external compulsion is not the main question being discussed in this chapter, yet it is important.

> A dog, who, left to himself, might lie contentedly all day long in the shade of a tree, whines miserably if tied to the same tree for five minutes. Tom Sawyer's pals were willing to give up their most cherished possessions for a turn at white-washing his fence, but "by jingo, they would wail like fettered injuns" if told they must do the same at home. The union steward, who, on holiday, will go tramping across country from dawn to dusk and then spend the evening in the pub, would call a strike if half that amount of energy were required at "work." All are protesting the same thing: compulsion, restriction of their freedom to choose what it is they want to do.[2]

There is, third, the field of the civil liberties, or civil rights. This encompasses the broad area of political freedom, including equality before the law, trial before an impartial tribunal, and the right to vote or be elected. Central in this area are freedom of speech, thought, and conscience, freedom of the press, freedom of assembly or organization, and a share in the control of the conditions of life. This shall be our area of concentration in this chapter.

There is, fourth, social and economic freedom. Here the question arises, for example, of whether there should be control or legislative regulation of a man's business, professional, or other activities, or whether these should be free from all interference. This is the issue of individualism and governmental control discussed in the next chapter.

FREEDOM AND ORDER

There is a strong Anglo-Saxon tradition of civil liberties, based on English common law and practice and on American constitutional law and practice.

2 Allan M. Munn, *Free-Will and Determinism* (Toronto: U. of Toronto Press, 1960), p. 7.

It is a tradition of man's seeking to safeguard and maintain freedom while preserving order. Human beings desire freedom, but they also want order and security. Order is necessary for the maintenance and enlargement of the area of freedom, but these values sometimes appear to be in conflict. The problem is to maintain a balance that will protect the rights of the individual and of the community, for there is danger if government has too little or too much power.

Some of the great pages of history relate the struggles that have grown out of the democratic faith and spirit and out of the attempt to secure freedom under law and order. Men want to eliminate the artificial restrictions and barriers to their personal development and expression. They wish to curb arbitrary and irresponsible power and to broaden the area of political and economic liberty. For example, history tells us of the elimination of slavery, serfdom, and peonage from most parts of the world, the growth of representative assemblies, the broadening of political and religious freedom, the emancipation of women and minority racial groups, and the like. The fight continues and is not likely to end in our time. After centuries of struggle and debate, free societies have worked out certain principles and safeguards and have sought to guarantee some of them in formal legal enactments.

The legal safeguards set up to assure fairness in the administration of justice include rules of procedure to prevent arbitrary arrest. One is not to be arrested on mere suspicion, but only for "probable cause." When a person is arrested without a warrant, he is to be taken without unnecessary delay before a judge for arraignment. He must be permitted to secure counsel. A writ of *habeas corpus* by a judge requires the person to be presented and cause shown why he should be detained rather than set free. To keep prisoners incommunicado or prevent them from obtaining counsel is unlawful, as are the third degree, or brutal and inhumane treatment, forced confessions, and unreasonable search and seizure. These are just a few of a long list of safeguards that are intended to prevent abuses and help obtain justice.

Order, one necessary element in the possession of liberty, requires the enforcement of law by some governmental authority. The enforcement of law entails the use of power, which sometimes takes the form of physical restraint or the use of force against those who would violate the law. The men who exercise the authority and administer the laws are fallible; they occasionally show excessive zeal and go to extremes. When a crime is committed the public may become emotionally aroused and demand immediate and drastic action. Law enforcement officers are often under pressure from the underworld and special interest groups, and there is temptation in the form of bribery. Furthermore, some people tend to think that the promotion of worthy ends, such as the protection of society and the reduction of crime, justifies the use of any means, even the bypassing of procedural regulations.

For this reason law enforcement officials must always be subject to scrutiny and judicial supervision. We want effective law enforcement, but it is better that some guilty men escape than that innocent men be deprived of their freedom and wrongly punished.

There is disturbing evidence that even democratic societies are lax in the enforcement of the legal safeguards for our freedom and that certain attitudes and practices persist which in the past have been associated with totalitarian regimes. In *The Price of Liberty*, which marshals evidence of some dangerous trends, Alan Barth says:

> It is the thesis of this book that liberty is being imperiled today for the sake of order. There has taken place in recent years a significant shift in the threat to civil liberty in the United States—from a neurotic anxiety about protection of the community against Communist subversion to an almost equally neurotic anxiety about protection of the community against crime.[3]

One serious element in the danger we face is the willingness of the public to permit, or at least to ignore and fail to condemn, the use of unlawful means in the interest of reducing crime. This, however, is shortsighted. When people become indifferent to human rights for others and lose respect for law, they are well on the road toward losing their own rights and freedoms. A society that does not maintain justice for every group is likely to lose it eventually for all groups. Once we struggled to safeguard our freedom from monarchs and dictators.

> The danger of royal tyranny had been dealt with by dispensing with royalty. But the threat of popular tyranny was perhaps even greater. For it entailed dangers of two sorts: the danger that officials vested with authority to maintain order might use it to suppress liberty; and the danger that a majority of the people, impatient to accomplish this purpose, might override all opposition, silence dissent, crush diversity, and deal arbitrarily with any who might resist its will.[4]

The problem of maintaining our traditional liberties has been increased in recent decades by new kinds of tribunals—congressional committees, loyalty boards, and the like—which function quite differently from the regular court system. No impartial judge would express to newspaper reporters or in public addresses opinions about a case which had not yet been decided and in which the evidence had not been presented. Yet this has been done by the heads of the new bodies, and some men have been condemned merely because they have had some contact with people who were guilty or were merely thought

[3] New York: The Viking Press, Inc., 1961, p. ix.
[4] *Ibid.*, pp. 32–33.

guilty of some offense. These and other pronouncements by men in public life have given rise to phrases like "trial by publicity," the "smear campaign," and "guilt by association."[5] Some groups seem to want to stifle all criticism, all innovation, and all unorthodox opinion. We read about the banning of books and magazines from libraries, the censorship of textbooks, and the demands for loyalty oaths. We want loyalty, of course, but these methods are unlikely either to create it or to lead to the discovery of disloyal people.

In addition to a possible suppression of a minority by the majority, there is the danger, even in a democracy, of the manipulation and control of the majority by a powerful and strategically placed minority. The many new techniques of control of public opinion by the printed page, radio, television, and other propaganda media have created a new problem. After telling us that as a nation we have "lost one thousand daily newspapers" in a two-decade period and that there are over one hundred cities in which the one remaining paper and the one radio station are under the same ownership, Morris L. Ernst, an attorney who has handled many legal cases in the realm of communication, says:

> We face an obstacle, a serious bottleneck, in seeking to improve the market place of free thought when the main pipelines to the minds of most men are owned by a few people who have been said by our highest court to be restraining the only priceless commodity known to man—the precious freedom of ideas.[6]

FREEDOM OF SPEECH

Freedom of thought, speech, press, assembly, and religion are among the most cherished rights and liberties. We may sum up these freedoms in the expression "freedom of speech," since many of them—such as freedom of press and of assembly—are really means of expressing our thoughts or of communicating with others.

In democratic countries today there are two general positions regarding freedom of speech. The advocates of one position claim that there should be complete freedom of speech, with no limitations except the usual laws against slander, libel, and indecency in public places. Opposing are those who claim that there should be additional limitations.

[5] See Alan Barth, *The Loyalty of Free Men* (New York: Viking, 1951); *Loyalty in a Democracy* (New York: Public Affairs Committee, 1952) (Public Affairs Pamphlet No. 179); William O. Douglas, *The Right of the People* (Garden City: Doubleday, 1958), Lecture II; William O. Douglas, *Freedom of the Mind* (New York: American Library Association, and Public Affairs Committee, 1962).

[6] "The Preservation of Civil Liberties," in *The Future of Democratic Capitalism*, Thurman W. Arnold, *et al.* (Philadelphia: U. of Pennsylvania Press, 1950), p. 20. (Perpetua ed., New York: A. S. Barnes, 1961.)

COMPLETE FREEDOM OF SPEECH

The advocates of complete freedom of speech believe that opinions on matters of public concern should be freely expressed without interference. No one should be restrained for merely talking or for expressing a point of view. This appears to be the position that the First Amendment to the United States Constitution seeks to protect: "Congress shall make no law respecting an establishment of religion, or prohibiting the free exercise thereof; or abridging the freedom of speech, or of the press; or the right of the people peaceably to assemble, and to petition the government for a redress of grievances."

Thomas Jefferson in his day and the American Civil Liberties Union in ours have both supported this position. Jefferson says, "It is time enough for the rightful purposes of civil government for its officers to interfere when principles break out into overt acts against peace and good order." In discussing freedom of speech, the American Civil Liberties Union says:

> There should be no control whatever in advance over what any person may say. The right to meet on private property and to speak freely should be unquestioned. Meetings in public places may properly be regulated by permit but without any discrimination whatever on account of the political program or views expressed. The fullest freedom of speech should be encouraged by setting aside places in streets or parks for use without permits, and in the use of public buildings for public meetings of any sort.[7]

In the nineteenth century an Englishman, John Stuart Mill, stated the case for complete freedom of speech in his treatise *On Liberty:*

> If all mankind minus one were of one opinion, and only one person were of the contrary opinion, mankind would be no more justified in silencing that one person, than he, if he had the power, would be justified in silencing mankind. Were an opinion a personal possession of no value except to the owner; if to be obstructed in the enjoyment of it were simply a private injury, it would make some difference whether the injury was inflicted only on a few persons or on many. But the peculiar evil of silencing the expression of an opinion is, that it is robbing the human race; posterity as well as the existing generation; those who dissent from the opinion, still more than those who hold it. If the opinion is right, they are deprived of the opportunity of exchanging error for truth: if wrong, they lose, what is almost as great a benefit, the clearer perception and livelier impression of truth, produced by its collision with error.[8]

Speech, it is claimed, is different in kind from other behavior. Any possible

7 *Civil Liberty* (New York: American Civil Liberties Union, August, 1943), p. 2. (Pamphlet.)
8 John Stuart Mill, *Utilitarianism, Liberty and Representative Government* (New York: Dutton, 1910), p. 79. (Everyman's Library.)

harm from complete freedom of speech is more than balanced by the harm resulting from restraint.

THE LIMITATION OF FREEDOM OF SPEECH

Those who hold that limitations on freedom of speech are necessary under certain conditions may be divided into at least three groups. The differences among them are largely matters of emphasis. There are those who believe in what has been called the "public-utility test" or the "clear and present danger test." Freedom of speech is protected, it is said, as a means to the public welfare. If there is a "clear and present danger" to public welfare, which may be increased by the expression of certain sorts of opinions, society has a right to interfere and to protect itself. A good illustration of this is the Supreme Court decision in the case "Schenck versus United States," an appeal from conviction under the Espionage Act in World War I. The defendants had mailed circulars urging opposition to the draft. The Court's opinion, written by Mr. Justice Holmes, said in part:

> We admit that in many places and in ordinary times the defendants in saying all that was said in the circular would have been within their constitutional rights. But the character of every act depends upon the circumstances in which it is done. . . . *The question in every case is whether the words used are used in such circumstances and are of such a nature as to create a clear and present danger that they will bring about the substantive evils that Congress has a right to prevent.* It is a question of proximity and degree. When a nation is at war many things that might be said in time of peace are such a hindrance to its effort that their utterance will not be endured so long as men fight and that no Court could regard them as protected by any constitutional right.

A slightly different position is the "standard of rational discussion," which may be thought of as a special form of the "danger test." This test differs in that it is said to be a positive theory to promote civil liberty. The test of rational discussion would protect the presentation of all grievances, and would even permit suggestions of violent resistance to government. It would guarantee free speech for fascists or communists or members of any other group, provided there was an opportunity for rational discussion. It would not, however, shield violent activity or protect the communist or fascist meeting where any expression of opposition would be met by violent abuse or physical force.

A second doctrine of limitation is to deny freedom to individuals or groups who would eliminate freedom if they were in control. Some writers have expressed opposition to the policy of granting freedom of speech and assembly to antidemocratic groups that have vowed to eliminate freedom and democratic institutions if and when they gain power. Some people, using this criterion, would keep all fascist and communist groups or speakers off the air and deny the use of the mails to fascist and communist publications.

A third group that demands conformity to some standard of orthodoxy appears to be growing in strength. Partly because of fear, propaganda, hysteria, and our effort to achieve security, the members of this group appear ready, either consciously or unconsciously, to give up many of our traditional safeguards and freedoms. Two problems arise at once. The first is, if we are to penalize nonconformity, we must have some standard of orthodoxy. Who is to set this standard? Is it to be one or more of the vigilante groups now attempting to gain power? Is it to be the people who control our organs of communication? Is it to be some institution, like a church or a political party? Is it to be the government, the state itself? If the state determines the standard of orthodoxy, is it not then acting like a totalitarian state?

The second problem is that such standards of orthodoxy are likely to create an atmosphere in which independence and originality are stifled and men cease to think. When this occurs, stagnation and decay are near. "If we penalize critics, we will cut ourselves off from criticism. If we cut ourselves off from criticism, we are likely to make mistakes. If we wish to avoid mistakes, we must create an atmosphere which encourages criticism."[9]

FREEDOM OF EXPRESSION IN THE UNITED STATES

In the second half of the twentieth century in the United States, both gains and losses for the civil liberties have been recorded. The Supreme Court recently handed down some notable decisions on behalf of civil rights and civil liberties: the Civil Rights Act of 1957 established a Civil Rights Commission; the government took steps to revise its security program; and various individuals and groups raised voices of protest against what they considered to be ominous trends. The situation today shows in some respects an improvement over the hysteria of 1953.

However, in the late fifties and early sixties, nearly two decades after the close of World War II, various men were deploring restrictions that were depriving the country of the services of able scientists. One scientist said: "Our security program . . . has deprived us of the services of certain scientists on any basis, public or private. . . . How many able scientific minds have been permanently lost to the country? Ten percent would, I think, be a conservative estimate. . . . The loss is incalculable. . . . Thought-control inhibits the bold thinking that is the foundation of notable scientific achievement."[10] A specialist in high-energy nuclear physics says that security regulations are not only hampering scientific advance but making it difficult to

[9] Henry Steele Commager, "The Pragmatic Necessity for Freedom," in *Civil Liberties Under Attack*, Clair Wilcox (ed.) (Philadelphia: U. of Pennsylvania Press, 1951), p. 16.

[10] G. Brooks Earnest, President of Fenn College, in *The Spokesman*, November, 1957.

train young nuclear physicists in a field that may be all-important in the years ahead.[11]

Some writers and speakers have been deploring the "climate of secrecy" that is found in some branches of the federal government and the numerous cases of censorship that have come to the public's attention. Some recent opinion surveys indicate that various freedoms guaranteed by the Constitution are not so widely prized or respected as one could wish. For example, in a national survey of teen-agers' views, the Purdue University Opinion Poll found that a majority of high-school students favor "third degree" methods and think that the "police should censor books, movies, radio, and television." Forty-one percent see no reason for maintaining freedom of the press.[12] In another study, two sociologists interviewed university students and teachers in the public schools of one state. More than seven out of ten students would deny an accused person the right to confront his accuser. Among both teachers and students, about three out of four think there are circumstances in which a person ought to be subject to double jeopardy in courts of law.[13]

Space does not permit us to give the details of some of the numerous "cases" involving the denial of traditional liberties in education, art, religion, the banning of books and of speakers, and security clearance. In some parts of the country people are afraid to do what they believe to be right, even to obey the law of the land or to write or speak about what they consider true and just. This fear has been especially prevalent in areas of racial tension. Teachers have been dismissed for discussing international organization, civil liberties, race relations, and other "controversial" topics. We are living in a period of "cold war" and international tension. The government has a right to protect itself, and laws against subversive activity should be enforced. On the other hand, defamatory emotional outbursts by disturbed or timid and insecure individuals who are not adequately informed about the nature of the world struggle may make matters worse rather than better.

Justice William O. Douglas believes that the time has come for us "to become the champions of the virtues that have given the West great civilizations." These virtues include the ideas of "justice, liberty, and equality." The rights of the people, the civil liberties, "distinguish us from all totalitarian regimes." The real enemies of freedom are everywhere, and they flourish wherever injustice, discrimination, and arbitrary power exist. Justice Douglas contends that there is "no free speech in the full meaning of the term unless there is freedom to challenge the very postulates on which the existing

---

[11] *The Columbus Citizen,* Columbus, Ohio, January 16, 1958, editorial page, quoting M. Stanley Livingston at Massachusetts Institute of Technology.

[12] *Civil Liberties* (New York: American Civil Liberties Union, November, 1957).

[13] For these and other figures see *Time,* September 9, 1957. See also Samuel A. Stouffer, *Communism, Conformity, and Civil Liberties* (Garden City: Doubleday, 1955); and J. L. O'Brian, *National Security and Individual Freedom* (Cambridge: Harvard U. Press, 1955).

regime rests." Of the importance of freedom of expression and the seriousness of restraint, he writes: "We have witnessed in this country a virtual witch hunt that has had a paralyzing effect on students, teachers, scientists, and writers. The unorthodox become suspect; the nonconformist is clouded with the same suspicions as the subversive. We have forced our scientists to live guarded lives."[14] Referring to the loyalty investigations that dealt so frequently with mere indiscretions and unpopular opinions, he says: "The effects on the government services have been devastating, especially in critical areas of policy formulation. Condemnation of public servants for their beliefs or expressions has the inevitable result of substituting pallid orthodoxy for the independence of thought, ingenuity, and boldness of decision which effective public service demands."[15]

In *The Blessings of Liberty*[16] Zechariah Chafee, Jr., of the Harvard School of Law, who was a lifelong student of civil liberties, believes that the "tangible civil liberties" will be better protected in the decade ahead. By these liberties he means such things as fair trial in the courts of the land and the elimination of the "third degree" and of legal barriers against the members of minority racial groups. For other civil liberties he expresses concern. He says: "There is much more cause for apprehension, however, when I think of the future of the more subtle freedoms proclaimed by the First Amendment, those concerned with our believing, our thinking, our expression of our thoughts by voice and print, and our association with others to exchange or promote ideas." Chafee lists and discusses twelve "encroachments on the ideals of freedom of speech, press, and assembly which have taken place since 1945."[17] While we have had other periods when intolerance and repressive methods were on the increase, such as the period immediately after World War I, "the present situation differs from conditions in 1919–20 in at least four ways." While "the danger of bad acts is greater" because of the world situation, "the internal danger from unrest seems . . . very much less than it was thirty-five years ago." Furthermore, "resistance to suppression is weaker," and finally, "the most striking difference from the earlier Period of Struggle lies in the subtlety of the suppressions now employed. . . . There is ever so much more suppression today through proceedings which have no juries, no substantial supervision by judges, and vague definitions of wrongdoing."[18]

In his discussion "Forty Years with Freedom of Speech," Chafee expresses his concern over actions in the last decade "which disturb a man who loves the

14 From *The Right of the People*, p. 83, by William O. Douglas. Copyright © 1958 by William O. Douglas. Reprinted by permission of Doubleday & Co., Inc.
15 *Ibid.*, pp. 121–122.
16 Philadelphia: Lippincott, 1956.
17 *Ibid.*, pp. 19–38.
18 *Ibid.*, pp. 81, 82, 83.

kind of country in which he grew up and fears that that kind of country will soon disappear unless present trends are checked."[19] He says:

> I am disturbed by the gradual erosion of many fundamental human rights which were cherished by the Americans in 1791. . . .
>
> I am disturbed by the growing number of perjury prosecutions which look as if they were brought to put men in prison, not really for lying, but for some long-past personal activities or utterances which could not themselves be punished. . . .
>
> I am disturbed by the strong tendency to establish an American party-line. Loyalty and integrity are more and more getting tested by qualifications about what is in a man's mind which go far beyond the old-fashioned determination to support and defend the Constitution of the United States.[20]

Speaking at the Columbia University Bicentennial in 1955, Adlai E. Stevenson said, "I wonder if today mass manipulation is not a greater danger than economic exploitation; if we are not in greater danger of becoming robots than slaves."[21] Another speaker at the same celebration, Alfred Whitney Griswold, the late President of Yale University, also voiced his concern for freedom. "Though we celebrate freedom here tonight, over a large part of the earth the concrete definition of it has utterly ceased and in our part it has slowed almost to a standstill. Why so? On the other side of the iron curtain the reason is obvious. But at home? Why should the life process of freedom falter among its creators?"[22] Speaking to the Yale graduating class in 1957, President Griswold concluded his address as follows:

> Gentlemen of the graduating class: the society into which you now graduate is not as free as the one which produced the principles by which you have been educated. Bit by bit we have exchanged our freedom—voluntarily, for the most part, involuntarily to some extent—for security, for productive efficiency, for creature comforts. But far from discounting the value of those educational principles, this puts them at a premium. Again and again in all kinds of occupations individuals educated in accordance with those principles continue to prove their effectiveness in our society, even in the innermost sanctums and strongholds of organization. Civilization can lose just so much of its freedom without losing all of it. The presence of individuals educated in these principles, who cleave to them and live according to them, is sorely needed to prevent such a catastrophe, to hold the balance between freedom and organization, to insure the continuity of the creative process without which organization is futile.

---

19 *Ibid.*, p. 91.
20 *Ibid.*, pp. 92, 97.
21 Quoted by Gerald W. Johnson in *Peril and Promise* (New York: Harper, 1958), p. 21.
22 *In the University Tradition* (New Haven: Yale U. Press, 1957), p. 3.

My moral, then, is plain and my charge to you is simple: To do good you must first know good; to serve beauty you must first know beauty; to speak the truth you must first know the truth. You must know these things yourselves, be able to recognize them by yourselves, be able to describe, explain, and communicate them by yourselves, and wish to do so, when no one else is present to prompt you or bargain with you. This knowledge has been the purpose of your education. Hold true to that purpose. No price, no mess of potage, can equal its value to your country and yourselves.[23]

WHY FREEDOM OF EXPRESSION IS IMPORTANT

Freedom of speech is important, first, because it is a basic condition for the development of a well-rounded personality. If people cannot express themselves, they feel stifled and stunted. If they cannot think freely and express their thoughts, it will not be long before they cease to have thoughts worthy of expression. They become something less than well-developed human beings. They tend either to develop slave minds and slave habits or to become physically and emotionally rebellious. Personal self-consciousness, intelligence, and creativity develop best in a free atmosphere, where men can think and talk together freely.

Second, freedom of speech is the basis of democracy. We cannot have a democracy unless we grant to the minority the right to become the majority, if it is able to do so, by peaceful methods of persuasion. If we are to have an alert, intelligent electorate seeking peaceful solutions to present conflicts, free discussion, criticism, and even opposition are essential. Each man knows more about his desires and needs than does someone else who may be removed from his way of life and problems. Consequently, a man ought to have the right to discuss policies and to criticize them. When rulers are cut off from criticism, they are likely to rule in their own interests or at least to fail to see things from the point of view of the average citizen. Irresponsible power tends to be used in the interests of the group that possesses the power.

Third, repression tends to drive opinion underground, where it may become dangerous. "Repression," said Woodrow Wilson, "is the seed of revolution." If an idea is false, the best way to destroy it is to expose it. Repression may keep alive and intensify existing antagonisms. Revolutions occur when reactionaries obtain control of society and attempt to stifle all change and progress; they occur when there are grave injustices that men are unable to remedy peacefully.

Fourth, freedom of speech is a condition for the development of new ideas. Some of our most prized ideals and institutions arose only a short time ago as a protest against some previous way of life. For example, a hundred and fifty years ago the idea of free or tax-supported schools was considered

[23] *Ibid.*, pp. 160–161.

radical and dangerous. For progress we need new ideas. None of our institutions is perfect; each needs the free play of criticism so that the process of healthy growth may continue. Critics tend to break the hard crust of custom and make progress possible. If the institution suppresses the critic, it may seem to strengthen itself for a time, but it does so only at the price of the new life that it needs.

For the reasons given above, the civil liberties are among our most important rights.[24] For a considerable portion of the population, especially for minority groups, they exist only in a very limited form. The civil liberties need to be extended and strengthened. The limitations or restrictions on freedom of speech ought to be few. These few might include laws against slander, libel, indecency in public places, utterances that excite or terrify (such as shouting "Fire!" in a crowded theater), and immediate and passionate incitement to riot. Restriction beyond these should be limited to periods of crises, such as times of great danger or of war.

There should be no restrictions on the presentation of opinion on social, political, economic, scientific, or religious issues. Society or the state should proceed cautiously—if it proceeds at all—in restricting the expression of opinions. Law enforcement officers find it difficult to distinguish between "preserving the peace" and "preserving the status quo." From "maintaining law and order" they easily move to "defense of the established order." This is likely to mean no criticism, or agitation, or tampering with things as they are—that is, no progress.

The "clear and present danger" test sounds reasonable, but it is easy to see a danger in anything that is a little different. The lower courts have stretched the danger idea to what has been called "remote bad tendency."[25] If fascists and communists are to be prevented from exercising freedom of speech, where can we draw the line? Many people tend to call anyone whom they dislike by names such as these. A few years ago the advocates of social insurance were called communistic; now such measures are taken for granted by practically all parties in democratic countries. The standard of rational discussion appears to be a sane test. But when is discussion rational and sane? Some people think that only discussion in line with their views is really rational. Chief Justice Hughes gives us this word of caution:

> The greater the importance of safeguarding the community from incitements to the overthrow of our institutions by force and violence, the more imperative is the need to preserve inviolate the constitutional rights of free speech, free

[24] See Charles R. Nixon, "Vital Issues in Free Speech," *Ethics*, XLII (January, 1952): 101–121.
[25] In the Abrams Case, a prison sentence was given for distributing pamphlets that were not *shown* to have lowered morale or to have hindered war work. It was merely felt that the pamphlets might do so.

press, and free assembly, to the end that government may be responsive to the will of the people and that changes, if desired, may be obtained by peaceful means. Therein lies the security of the republic, the very foundation of constitutional government.[26]

The principles of freedom, including the civil liberties and the civil rights, have been sources of strength in those Western nations in which they are deeply grounded. To abandon them now would be to give up an important element of our strength. The right of freedom of thought and expression is not a privilege granted by the state, to be withheld or granted at will. It is a natural right, or at least a human right, based on the nature of man and on those conditions necessary for the development of human personality. To maintain that the state is supreme is to say that the state can dictate in moral, religious, and intellectual matters; it is to entertain the totalitarian point of view. A free society furnishes the conditions in which science, art, philosophy, religion, and a high civilization are most likely to flourish.

QUESTIONS AND PROJECTS

1. Review Questions

(1) What are some of the great landmarks in the age-old fight for human freedom?

(2) Distinguish among four different kinds of freedom, and indicate the two kinds of freedom to be discussed in this and the next chapter.

(3) Explain the problem of maintaining a just balance between freedom and order, and relate it to the need for legal safeguards in the administration of justice.

(4) What trends and institutions in our society are creating new threats to freedom?

(5) What support can be found for the view that opinions on questions of public concern should be expressed without interference?

(6) What are the arguments of those people who hold that some limitations of freedom of speech are necessary under certain conditions?

(7) What advantages and what disadvantages or dangers can you see (a) in the "danger test," (b) in demanding conformity to some standard of orthodoxy?

(8) What gains and what losses in the area of civil liberties are to be noted in the United States since midcentury? Give evidence for your answer.

(9) We have quoted statements from leaders in a number of fields expressing their concern over the state of civil liberties in the contemporary world. Are such statements valid? Support your answer. Do you consider the statements justified in the light of present conditions?

(10) Why is freedom of expression important?

2. What are the principal threats to civil liberties in society today?

[26] Quoted in *The Columbus Citizen*, Columbus, Ohio, January 8, 1937, editorial page.

3. Why is "academic freedom," or freedom in the field of education, so important? Do you agree with the statement by James P. Baxter III that "freedom in education ... underlies all the others, and anything that weakens it necessarily threatens them"? See James P. Baxter III, "Freedom in Education," in *Civil Liberties Under Attack*, Clair Wilcox (ed.) (Philadelphia: U. of Pennsylvania Press, 1951), pp. 129–154; Robert M. MacIver, *Academic Freedom in Our Time* (New York: Columbia U. Press, 1955).

4. What political, moral, and other issues are involved in the question of censorship? See Walter M. Daniels (ed.), *The Censorship of Books* (New York: Wilson, 1954) (The Reference Shelf, XXVI, No. 5); William Dix and Paul Bixler (eds.), *Freedom of Communication* (Chicago: American Library Association, 1954); Robert B. Downs, *The First Freedom: Liberty and Justice in the World of Books and Reading* (Chicago: American Library Association, 1960); *Freedom Through Dissent* (42nd Annual Report; American Civil Liberties Union, July 1, 1961 to June 30, 1962), pp. 1–15; Harold C. Gardiner, S.J., *Catholic Viewpoint on Censorship* (Garden City: Hanover, 1958); *The Student's Right to Read* (Champaign: National Council of Teachers of English, 1962).

5. Discuss the following statements, indicating the extent to which you agree or disagree with them, and why.

(1) "Remember it is much easier to fight to keep the freedoms you have than to fight to regain the freedoms you have lost."

(2) "This country with its institutions belongs to the people who inhabit it. Whenever they shall grow weary of the existing government, they can exercise their constitutional right of amending it, or their revolutionary right to dismember or overthrow it."

(3) "There is no right to be wrong."

(4) "The worst enemy of freedom is the man who obeys the community because he fears it."

6. Review one of the following books: From the Suggested Readings those by Barth, Chafee, Commager, Douglas, Gellhorn, Hook, Muller, or Weinberger; Eugene C. Blake, *Christian Faith: Bulwark of Freedom* (Houston: Elsevier, 1956); Edward Dumbauld, *The Bill of Rights and What It Means Today* (Norman: U. of Oklahoma Press, 1957); Paul G. Kauper, *Civil Liberties and the Constitution* (Ann Arbor: U. of Michigan Press, 1962); Milton R. Konvitz, *Fundamental Liberties of a Free People* (Ithaca: Cornell U. Press, 1957); John Lord O'Brian, *National Security and Individual Freedom* (Cambridge: Harvard U. Press, 1955); Calvin O. Schrag, *Existence and Freedom* (Evanston: Northwestern U. Press, 1962).

SUGGESTED READINGS

ADLER, MORTIMER J. *The Idea of Freedom: A Dialectical Examination of the Conceptions of Freedom.* 2 vols.; Garden City: Doubleday, 1958, 1961.
Two large volumes published for The Institute for Philosophical Research. Volume I sets

forth topics and theories discussed under the heading of "freedom," and Volume II sets forth the presuppositions and the arguments given for these different theories of freedom.

BARTH, ALAN. *The Price of Liberty.* New York: Viking, 1961.
The author discusses liberty and human rights with emphasis on the administration of justice. He fears that liberty is now being imperiled for order and security. See also The Loyalty of Free Men, *where the author discusses the loyalty program and its dangers.*

CHAFEE, ZECHARIAH, JR. *The Blessings of Liberty.* Philadelphia: Lippincott, 1956.
A comprehensive coverage of the problems of freedom of speech, press, and assembly, with emphasis on the period since 1945.

COMMAGER, HENRY STEELE, et al. *Civil Liberties under Attack.* Ed. by Clair Wilcox. Philadelphia: U. of Pennsylvania Press, 1951. (Swarthmore College, William J. Cooper Foundation.)
Six specialists discuss different aspects of the problem of freedom and civil rights. Clear and readable.

COMMISSION ON CIVIL RIGHTS. *The 50 States Report.* Washington, D.C.: U. S. Government Printing Office, 1961.
Reports submitted to the Commission on Civil Rights by the State Advisory Committees, 1961. The reports show the differences in outlook and activity among the various states.

Cornell Studies in Civil Liberty. Ed. by Robert E. Cushman. Ithaca: Cornell U. Press.
A series of books including: Security, Loyalty and Science, *Walter Gellhorn, 1950;* The House Committee on Un-American Activities, *Robert H. Carr, 1952;* The States and Subversion, *edited by Walter Gellhorn, 1952;* The Federal Loyalty-Security Program, *Eleanor Bontecou, 1953. These and other books in the series deal with special problems in the area of the civil liberties. They are well documented.*

DOUGLAS, WILLIAM O. *The Right of the People.* New York: Doubleday, 1958.
A member of the United States Supreme Court discusses the dangers to freedom and makes a vigorous defense of the principles underlying our freedoms.

EDMAN, IRWIN. *Fountainheads of Freedom: The Growth of the Democratic Idea.* New York: Reynal & Hitchcock, 1941. (In collaboration with Herbert W. Schneider.)
Two hundred pages of commentary by Edman and four hundred pages of statements and documents by the leaders of freedom, from the Hebrew prophets and the early Greeks, to George Bernard Shaw and John Dewey. An excellent list and source book for the classics in the field.

FRAENKEL, OSMOND K. *The Supreme Court and Civil Liberties.* New York: Oceana, 1960.
A discussion of decisions relating to civil liberties by the Supreme Court. Published for the American Civil Liberties Union in its fortieth anniversary year.

GELLHORN, WALTER. *American Rights: The Constitution in Action.* New York: Macmillan, 1960.
A professor of law discusses a broad range of topics—police and court procedures, freedom of speech and of movement, desegregation of the schools, and the like.

HOOK, SIDNEY. *Political Power and Personal Freedom: Critical Studies in Democracy, Communism and Civil Rights.* New York: Criterion, 1959.
    Essays that discuss "basic beliefs central to the free world in its struggle for survival." See especially Part Three, "Problems of Security and Freedom."

MACIVER, ROBERT M. (ed.). *Great Expressions of Human Rights.* New York: Harper, 1960.
    A discussion of fourteen documents that are landmarks in the history of human rights. The documents are printed in the Appendix.

MILL, JOHN STUART. *On Liberty.* Ed. by Alburey Castell. New York: Appleton-Century-Crofts, 1947.
    A classic statement of the need for society to recognize the right of the individual to think and act for himself. First published in 1859, this essay has a crucial message for the twentieth century.

MULLER, HERBERT J. *Issues of Freedom.* New York: Harper, 1960.
    A small book, in the World Perspective series, edited by Ruth Nanda Anshen. It considers freedom in relation to culture: Part One, "The Premises of Inquiry"; Part Two, "The Basic Cultural Factors."

OPPENHEIM, FELIX E. *Dimensions of Freedom: An Analysis.* New York: St. Martin's, 1961.
    This work is a study of the meanings and interrelations of such concepts as freedom, control, and power, and a behavioral analysis of their function in society.

WEINBERGER, ANDREW D. *Freedom and Protection: The Bill of Rights.* San Francisco: Chandler, 1962.
    A foreword on "Personal Liberty in Today's World," followed by Part One dealing with "The Bill of Rights in History," Part Two, "The Bill of Rights Today."

❦ TWENTY-SIX ❧

INDIVIDUALISM AND GOVERNMENTAL CONTROL

In addition to political liberty and freedom of expression, man wants many things, including health, security, knowledge, a high standard of living, and happiness. How can these things best be obtained? Can a man gain them by living independently and seeking to further his interests thereby, or must he obtain them through group action and legislation?

A basic struggle in the world in which we live is between personal demands and group regulation. It is expressed in many ways and by various slogans: individualism versus governmental control, free competition versus a planned economy, free enterprise versus governmental regulation, private property versus public ownership. We shall confine our discussion to questions relating to individualism and governmental control in general and not attempt to discuss all the different ideologies to which they relate.

THE RISE OF INDIVIDUALISM

Since the fourteenth century Western society has changed from one dominated by the church and a moral and religious ideal to one dominated by commerce and industry and interested primarily in production and profits. It would be interesting to trace the full development of the doctrine of sovereignty and the rise of the modern independent state, as well as the early growth of the commercial class. We shall need to confine our attention, however, to the period since the beginning of the Industrial Revolution.

When the Industrial Revolution began in England in the eighteenth century, there were in existence numerous antiquated laws and regulations which prevented the free movement of labor and merchandise. Some of these restrictions had originated under an agrarian feudalism, and they were defended by the landed interests. The merchant and manufacturing classes demanded freedom for the acquisition of markets and raw materials, the hiring and firing of labor, and the movement of labor from one area to another.

Because law was the voice of government, government was taken to be the great enemy of freedom. The new cry from business came to be: "Let us alone"; "Hands off"; "*Laissez faire.*" This slogan, in one or another of its many forms, has been heard from the eighteenth century to the present: "Men must be free to pursue their self-interest"; "There must be free enterprise"; "The economic man must have freedom from interference"; "There should be a minimum of governmental control."

In other areas of life the same kind of separation was taking place. Artists, demanding freedom of art from moral and religious ends, were proclaiming "art for art's sake." Education in the nineteenth and twentieth centuries was also becoming secularized, specialized, and independent. Objective and disinterested inquiry, bound by no social obligation or purpose, became the order of the day.

This tendency toward the independence and separation of functions in society was reinforced by an economic theory that developed in the eighteenth and nineteenth centuries in connection with the rise of the new industrial system. This theory took slightly different forms, known variously as individualism, *laissez-faire* individualism, and economic liberalism. The founders of this social philosophy were a group of writers in France in the eighteenth century known as the physiocrats, and a group of writers in Great Britain, among whom were Adam Smith (1723–1790), Thomas Robert Malthus (1766–1834), and David Ricardo (1772–1823). The physiocrats argued that social, political, and economic phenomena are governed by natural laws that are the same as or similar to those Newton disclosed as operative in nature. There is a "natural harmony of interest"; therefore any attempt to control or to regulate society is not only useless but harmful. The British writers took a similar stand. Adam Smith shared the faith of the physiocrats in a simple system of natural order and liberty, in enlightened self-interest, in free competition, and in reduced functions of government. In this system men might attain the maximum satisfaction of their desires with a minimum of sacrifice. Malthus thought that remedial legislation did no permanent good, since population tends to press on the food supply, and, therefore, misery and poverty tend to continue. Ricardo pointed out that wages tend to seek the level of the minimum of subsistence. If wages were increased, then the population would increase and force wages down to the subsistence level again. As a result of such thinking, economics came to be called "the dismal science."

The theory of individualism was an outgrowth of the doctrine of natural law and of natural rights held so strongly in the eighteenth century. Natural laws, it was argued, would regulate prices, wages, and hours in the most equitable way. Consequently, there must be no interference with the laws of competition and supply and demand.

During the nineteenth century the theory of individualism gained some support from the English utilitarians (Jeremy Bentham and John Stuart Mill). It received support also from the theory of evolution, with its emphasis on natural selection—the struggle for existence and the survival of the fittest. Herbert Spencer, at the end of the nineteenth century, held that man should let nature take its course and should not interfere in most areas. He regarded education, the postal service, and the making of roads as outside the proper jurisdiction of government. Apart from protecting the nation from foreign aggression and preventing crime, the state has few functions. The strongest members of the society will succeed and will propagate their kind, and the race will be strengthened.

In its personal application, the philosophy of individualism is the doctrine of self-interest. The individual, it is said, should be free to pursue his own interests as long as he keeps the peace and does not interfere with the rights of others. He should be free to make as much money as he can and to spend it as he sees fit. There is a need for men who are industrious, resourceful, thrifty, and self-reliant, and who have initiative and a spirit of adventure.

In *The Spirit of Enterprise* Edgar M. Queeny says that "individualists owe nothing to any man, they expect nothing from any man; they acquire the habit of always considering themselves as standing alone, and they are apt to imagine that their whole destiny is in their own hands." After vigorously attacking practically all governmental functions and planning, he goes on to say that "to realize the four freedoms, we need only one freedom—Freedom."[1]

In its economic application, individualism is the doctrine of the "economic man." He is the person who consults his own interests and who is guided in his business activities by the profit motive. Such a man is free to produce, to buy and sell, or to refrain from such activities, under conditions set by himself. He regards his property as something that can bring him profit.

In its political application, individualism is the doctrine of noninterference, the view that the government should confine itself to the suppression of fraud and violence, to the protection of property, and to the enforcement of contracts. If some restrictions are necessary, as most individualists realize they are, they should be kept to a minimum. The governmental policy is one of *laissez-faire*—let people act economically as they please.

The philosophy of individualism finds ethical justification in the assumption that the policies stated above will bring the best results in the long run. If a man seeks his own interest through free competition, the result will be

[1] New York: Scribner's, 1943, pp. 17–18, 242.

both material and social progress. Any form of governmental ownership or control will tend toward the creation of indolence and laziness, lack of technical progress and creativity, inefficiency, bureaucracy, and possibly totalitarianism.

THE GROWTH OF GOVERNMENTAL CONTROL

Whereas the individualism, or what is sometimes called the classical liberalism, that was prevalent during the nineteenth century stressed the freedom and the rights of the individual left to his own initiative in society, the contemporary liberals, the supporters of the social-service view of the state, stress social as well as individual rights and represent a tendency away from *laissez-faire* individualism. A century ago a man could find relative independence and security by shouldering his ax and gun and pressing out into the wilderness. This is not so today. Let us see what has happened during the last century and why a considerable degree of governmental control is present in our society.

First, there is the pressure from scientific and technical advances. Man's life has probably changed more in the last century or two than in the previous five thousand years. A worker in ancient Egypt would have known how to use the simple tools used by our forefathers in the eighteenth century. Those same forefathers would be completely mystified by our elaborate machines. Even a hundred and fifty years ago on this continent each village was practically self-sufficient. Men had ready access to certain raw materials, they owned their simple tools, they controlled the conditions of their labor, and they owned the finished product, which they used or sold to someone they knew. Under these conditions, few regulations were needed.

With the coming of the Industrial Revolution, all this was changed. The new machines were expensive, and their purchase and operation required large amounts of capital. The new factories had to be situated near water power or coal supplies. The handworkers could not compete with the new machines, and the workers lost control of the tools of production and so of the means of gaining a living. At first the Industrial Revolution affected chiefly the textile industry, but during the latter part of the nineteenth century there took place what is sometimes called the Second Industrial Revolution, which affected especially the basic industries of iron and steel. The evolving industrial system became more highly specialized and more impersonal. There was a separation of ownership from management and of both from labor. New business and financial classes came into power. Great vertical and horizontal mergers took place. Competition tended to beget combination. Along with the development of large-scale industry and mass production went such legal or technical devices as the limited liability of shareholders in corporations, the trust or the trusteeship, the holding company, the interlocking directorate, and other devices for amassing great economic power. Yet the law continued to apply the concept "individual" to these organizations.

Second, as large business organizations came to have a dominant position in society, the business leaders discovered that they could control or modify the effects of free competition. The early supporters of *laissez-faire* individualism did not foresee the possibility of manipulation or concerted action on the part of business executives. Control from within enabled industrial leaders to manipulate supply and demand, prices, and wages. The earlier economy was characterized by small, individually owned business units, relatively free competition, flexible or fluctuating prices, and approximate equality in bargaining power. The modern economy is characterized by huge business units, agreements and understandings, inflexible or fixed prices, and inequality in bargaining power. Business has not remained individualistic. Free market adjustments have been largely eliminated by various collective devices.

As the workers came to realize that economic freedom without economic power was putting them at a disadvantage, they formed labor unions for the purpose of collective bargaining. Consumers, much later, saw the need to protect themselves, and consumers' organizations were formed. In the largest part of our economy, collective action is the rule, though men continue to talk about individual initiative, free competition, and free enterprise.

Third, from the beginning of the Industrial Revolution until the present, business and manufacturing interests have actively sought governmental favors and support. The holders of economic power have engaged in politics for the purpose of securing economic benefits for themselves. Among these benefits we find the following: (1) *Grants of land and mineral resources.* A public domain of about 2,186,862 square miles has been reduced by grants or by sale at nominal prices to about 300,000 square miles, most of which is arid soil, forests, or mountain land. (2) *Subsidies.* Cash subsidies, tariff rebates, and cash loans frequently have been made in connection with the development of railroads, waterways, and shipping. (3) *Tariffs.* Manufacturing groups have sought and obtained high protective tariffs, which have enabled them to secure millions in extra profits through higher prices to consumers. (4) *Franchises.* Through franchises some companies have acquired the sole right to operate tramways and subways and to sell gas or electricity. (5) *Diplomatic aid abroad.* The consular officers are in part agents for the promotion of business enterprise.

Fourth, conditions that grew out of the Industrial Revolution led the public to demand new forms of governmental protection. Within a short time the factory sytem produced evils so serious that protective legislation was necessary. Factory laws passed in the nineteenth century were concerned with such things as safety, sanitary conditions, and hours of work. Today laws deal with numerous things, such as conditions of labor, grading and inspection of products, safeguarding of food supplies and drugs, regulation of corporations, and conservation of natural resources. Unable to secure results without it, individuals have asked for legislative protection against infected milk, impure water, polluted streams, and obnoxious fumes. Legislation and control are part of the price we pay for more knowledge, technical and scientific advances, wealth, and a growing population, and few people would be willing to give up these controls.

Fifth, during the last century a score or more of our most important social and economic functions have been taken from the realm of private ownership and control and are now being operated as public services. The government now owns and operates, in whole or in part, such services or functions as: the post office; the construction, lighting, and repairing of streets, roads, and bridges; schools and colleges; museums; parks; art galleries; libraries; auditoriums; health centers and hospitals; waterworks; gasworks; tramways; wharves and harbors; coinage; weights and measures; waterpower sites; and irrigation projects. Services that tended to be monopolistic and that were essential to the welfare of nearly everyone are now almost completely operated by some governmental agency as a public service. Certain functions are too important from the point of view of social welfare to be left in private hands.

These facts seem to indicate that we are no longer an individualistic or *laissez-faire* society. This is further pointed up by the fact that practically all economic activities and services not included in the above list are now carefully regulated, inspected, or controlled. The amount of air, light, and space that must be provided for workers, when and how wages are to be paid, the way packages are to be wrapped and labeled, and how wares may be advertised—all these are regulated to some degree. More and more people are demanding an intelligent control of resources for the common welfare.

EVALUATION OF THE CONTRASTING POSITIONS

Both individual freedom and governmental control, carried to extremes, lead to serious abuses. For example, the old individualism was too frequently a cloak for greed and indifference to human welfare. It tolerated conditions that crushed many individuals and permitted the few to control the means by which the many had to live. No longer can society tolerate the unlimited exploitation of people and the principle of "every man for himself." Liberty must not mean the freedom to live in misery or to starve. Self-interest is inadequate as the main motivating force in human affairs. Where ills are socially created, they must be borne and remedied by society.

Governmental control, like individualism, can become destructive. The fascist principle of "the individual for society" is destructive, as are the communists' control over all phases of life and their reliance on force to achieve objectives. There is danger in too rigid and too complete control over social and economic life.

The individualist and the supporter of the social-service view of the state are concerned primarily with somewhat different values. The individualist wishes to protect individuality, initiative, and self-reliance. These character traits have genuine value. The person who supports a greater degree of community or governmental control wishes to achieve the values that come through sharing, cooperation, and group action. How are these differences in attitude and emphasis to be reconciled?

The test of any regulation, program, or institution is what it does to people, to men and women. The goal of enlightened action ought to be the development of the person. No regulation or institution—not even the state—ought to be considered an end in itself. When regulations, restraints, and institutions serve the interests of men, they are good; when they fail to promote human welfare, they are evil or useless. We want the control or legislation that gives us health and greater freedom; we do not want the type of control that crushes individuality. If restraints and social measures make for liberty in the larger sense and serve human needs, they are to be approved.

We need considerable external control, but we do not want or need internal control, or the standardization of our thinking and inner life. We must be free to think, to speak, to criticize, and to work for a fuller life. Society and the state have the responsibility to see to it that every individual has the opportunity to become a "whole" person.

THE FAR RIGHT AND THE FAR LEFT

The preservation of freedom has been made more difficult in recent decades by the presence of extremist groups, often called the *right* and the *left*, or the *far right* and the *far left*. However, it is not to be assumed that these two groups are at the opposite ends of the political and socioeconomic poles. While they differ as to what they accept and reject, they have much in common, as we shall see. The term *right* or *rightist* comes from European legislative assemblies, especially the French, where the conservatives, monarchists, royalists, and the like sit in the assembly to the right of the speaker, and the liberals, radicals, socialists, and communists sit to the left of the speaker. The rightists are those who are the thoroughgoing conservatives, who wish to keep things as they are. They may, of course, be reactionaries, in that they may wish society to revert to some previous state or condition. The leftists, in contrast, are those who advocate extreme or thoroughgoing changes in society, which changes may or may not be brought about by action of a revolutionary nature.

The contemporary world is in a state of crisis over the question of the direction in which it should move, if at all. To place the various groups and social philosophies in a straight line and put the fascists at the right and the communists on the left with democratic groups in the center, as is frequently done, is the result of a misconception. With such a placement a move in any direction may be labeled fascistic or communistic, and democratic societies are forced to remain static in a world that is changing rapidly. The result of such classification may be a "closed society," emphasizing fixity, rather than an "open society," in which there is free discussion, fruitful inquiry, and continuous search for better ways of doing things.

How can we explain the rise of extremist groups, the name-calling, the bitter charges and countercharges, the emotional excesses, and the muddled thinking that threaten the existence of an orderly society? We have been through a period of war, cold war, and social change. Such periods are times of irritation and frustration for many people. Frustration and fear easily lead to emotional disturbance, panic, and aggressive action. Insecure and immature people fall back on what is safe and orthodox and strike out in anger at any groups or ideas that are different or that for some reason they oppose. Many individuals have stopped doing their own thinking and tend to accept slogans and stereotypes. They automatically oppose those who do not accept such "canned" thinking. Thus they line up in hard-and-fast formations. We are told that what attracts our attention tends to influence our conduct. Too many people have centered their attention on what they hate and fear. A few decades ago it was fascism, and more recently it has been communism. Many people have tended to concentrate on these totalitarian groups in a negative way rather than on our free, democratic, Judaeo-Christian heritage in a positive way. Consequently, we stand in danger of "imitative disaster"— of copying the tactics and mental traits of the groups we oppose.

The extremist groups to the right and to the left have a number of common traits: (1) Black-and-white thinking, or the tendency toward oversimplification and the elimination of a middle ground. The extremist groups feel that they have a monopoly on virtue and truth; others are gullible or mistaken, but they never are! (2) The conspiratorial or "devil" view of events and history. Any mistake or failure is called a betrayal. (3) The use of many labels and slogans. People who do not agree are "capitalist imperialists" or "communists" ("reds" or "comsymps"). (4) A keen distrust of democratic institutions, the democratic process, and human nature. Extremists tend to support minority control, some elite group, an aristocracy, or a dictator. They want to control the books used in schools and libraries and to silence criticism of their positions and tactics.

Rightist and leftist groups, however, have various points of disagreement as well as many common traits. The far left tends to oppose capitalism, free enterprise, private property, the profit motive, middle-class democracy, imperialism, colonialism, and independent labor unions. The far right is opposed to all forms of collectivism. In the name of antifederalism, rightists demand complete withdrawal of government from the regulation of business and industry and the supervision of health, education, and welfare. The extreme right is opposed to a graduated income tax, collective bargaining, the closed shop, extension of social security measures, the supreme court, ministers who preach a social gospel, social planning, the United Nations, and international aid programs.

For years many people have been alerting us to the dangers of communism and the leftist groups. In the early years of the nineteen-sixties, President Eisenhower, President Kennedy, and a number of state governors considered it important to warn the public against the rising influence of the right wing. We have been told that "there are approximately a thousand voluntary organizations in the United States today which may be called rightist."[2] Today many self-appointed vigilantes believe that the country is in the grip of a ruthless conspiracy and that their mission is to watch scientists, teachers, religious leaders, the schools and universities, labor leaders, financiers, diplomats, and others for any signs of unorthodoxy, heresy, or new and unfamiliar ideas. Many other people wonder if the extreme rightists are unwittingly following the communist line and tactics by sowing distrust and destroying people's faith in free institutions.

If, as a result of these extremist groups of the right and the left, communities are being disrupted and men and women are afraid to think and express their thoughts, then great damage is being done to our type of civilization. The development of the arts and sciences and philosophy and religion, as well as of people, calls for an open and not a closed society.

SOCIAL PROBLEMS DEMANDING ATTENTION

Most of us agree that we want to live in a relatively free society and defend what we call "the free world." Freedom is not an unlimited thing. There are different kinds of freedom, and they impinge on one another, since every freedom is exercised at the expense of some other freedom. To take a very simple example, I must curtail my freedom to run my television set at top volume all night if I want to exercise my freedom to live in an apartment building. The more complex the society, the more complicated the task of adjusting freedoms for the attainment of our goal: the greatest amount of freedom for all people in the society.

2 Ralph D. Ellsworth and Sarah M. Harris, *The American Right Wing* (Washington, D.C.: Public Affairs Press, 1962), p. 2. (A Report to the Fund for the Republic.)

While the men and women of the free world enjoy a large measure of freedom of action, there are many who believe that this freedom will be difficult to maintain in the years ahead. This is so partly because of certain impersonal forces, such as increasing mechanization, which are threatening our freedom, and partly because of the new techniques of control available to selfish men who crave more power.

If we are to retain our freedoms, our society will need to face and solve a number of pressing problems. They are problems whose solutions will call for the cooperative effort of men from many fields. They involve important questions of social philosophy, and they are all related to questions of individualism versus governmental or other forms of social control.

1. *Eliminating war and establishing international law.* This problem has become especially acute by virtue of our having learned to split the atom before we learned to unite mankind. Unless we can revise our obsolete ways of thinking and acting and achieve international control of atomic weapons and a greater degree of world order, we are likely to lose our liberties and see greatly increased control over life—if, indeed, human life itself is not destroyed. Freedom and the garrison state are not likely to exist side by side for any great length of time. This is our most urgent problem and one with which we shall be occupied in the decades ahead. It is made more threatening by the problem of overpopulation.

2. *Solving or easing the problem of overpopulation.* One impersonal force that threatens human freedom is the rapid increase in population the world over, due in considerable measure to "death control" without a large measure of "birth control." Thousands of years were required for the race to achieve the size of one billion members; this occurred in about 1830. Then in one century, or by 1930, a second billion was added. A third billion may be added by 1965. A recent United Nations' estimate is that, if present trends continue, it will take only fifteen years to add a fourth billion and about another ten years to add a fifth. In some parts of the world the population is doubling every twenty years. This problem of increasing numbers of people in relation to natural resources and living space is a central problem of mankind, even though it may not become acute in countries like the United States and Canada for some decades.

Intelligent people should not wait for famine, disease, and war to ease this problem temporarily. Birth control is possible and necessary if we are to avoid great disasters in the future. The solution of the problem runs counter to the religiously sanctioned traditions of some groups. But unless the overpopulation problem is solved, many other problems will be difficult, if not impossible, to solve.

3. *Eliminating overorganization, or the unnecessary regimentation of peoples.* Social pressure of this type, when it leads to insecurity and unrest, calls forth

more control and authority on the part of governments, military and business groups, and labor organizations. This in turn leads to greater control and more elaborate organizations. While organization is essential, too much organization can stifle freedom and the creative spirit. When an individual not only works for an organization, a government, corporation, labor union, laboratory, or the hierarchy of a church, but also surrenders his critical faculties through unquestioning obedience to it, he loses a part of his individuality and his freedom. He becomes a pawn, a robot, or an automaton.

Speaking of our supercorporations or "concentrates," Samuel Eliot Morison says: "The success of these concentrates refutes the charge of creeping socialism; but the power that they wield is terrific; their ability to affect the lives of you and me is frightening; and their lack of a guiding philosophy is appalling."[3] When great power resides in a small interrelated group of men who have great influence in or control of the large corporations, the military establishments, and the machinery of government, the situation is dangerous for democracy and a free society.

4. *Protecting people and groups from the new techniques of manipulation and control.* The excessive control of life tends to halt personal development and destroy security and mental health, with a resulting increase in neurotic symptoms. Especially under urban conditions, people tend to feel lonely and insignificant, and they easily become irresponsible seekers after amusements that arouse their emotions and make little demand on their intelligence. A few decades ago Adolf Hitler used the radio and loudspeaker to deprive millions of people of independent thought and a sense of personal responsibility. Since his time, knowledge of the techniques for manipulating people has greatly increased. In elections and political controversies, in sales campaigns, and wherever powerful groups wish to win adherents, the arts of the propagandist, with the help of the motivation analysts, are used to appeal to human weaknesses, to stir strong emotions and direct them at will, and thus to engage in wholesale mind-manipulation.

For some time it has been known that people in large groups are more suggestible and can be easily manipulated; the area of study here is known as crowd psychology. Now new techniques are being discovered and improved for the control of single or isolated individuals. Evidence gained under war conditions, in concentration camps, and from studies of animals has made clear that torture, fear, anxiety, and anger or rage may be used to bring a person to the breaking point, so that the mind "goes on strike," as it were. When this happens, new and different behavior patterns may be established with comparative ease. Under conditions of fatigue and illness, suggestibility is heightened. The new methods of manipulating individuals without their

---

3 *Freedom in Contemporary Society* (Boston: Little, Brown, 1956), p. 87. (Atlantic Monthly Press Book.)

being aware of the fact that they are being controlled are frightening to those who believe in the free person in a relatively free society. Experiments in "subliminal projection" (images that stimulate people below the threshold of perception, or learning that is not conscious) on the television or motion picture screen have been carried out. We read about such things as subliminal projectors, "whispering machines," and "sleep teaching" to influence people during their sleep. We also are told about chemical persuasion, where drugs are used to increase suggestibility, to aid in extracting confessions, and to change one's outlook and response. The danger in our world is that the modern lovers of power will use the new devices of "social engineering" for selfish purposes.[4]

5. *Mastering science and technology so that they become instruments of freedom.* Science yields power, but it may be power for good or for evil. Science yields knowledge, but this knowledge can heal or destroy. The solution of the problem of how best to use scientific knowledge lies in the realms of politics, morality, and religion. This issue is sometimes forgotten by those who believe that the solution of all our problems is just to get most of the bright young people to specialize in science.

6. *Conserving natural resources so that the resources of the earth may be shared with future generations.* We can permit fertile areas to become deserts, or we can conserve our soil, minerals, forests, gas, and oil for the use of posterity. This is a problem to which we must give more attention in the future than we have in the past, or we shall face a situation in which we shall have diminishing resources along with an increasing population.

7. *Reconciling freedom and order.* Freedom is important, but order and security are also values, and the point at which one ends and the others begin will always, in a free society, be the subject of discussion and controversy. As conditions change and needs vary, there is nothing to prevent an intelligent society from freely choosing to move in one direction at one time and to reverse this trend at a later time.

8. *Making democracy and justice effective in all areas of our life.* This is an unending task. The machinery or apparatus of government must keep abreast of the changing conditions of society, but more important are the spirit or attitude and the convictions that must be kept fresh and alive in the hearts and minds of the people.

9. *Using leisure time intelligently.* The creative use of leisure time is a problem in contemporary society, since machines are making leisure possible for an increasing number of people. While a certain degree of leisure appears to be essential for the growth of civilization, an increase in the amount of

[4] See Aldous Huxley, *Tyranny Over the Mind* (Garden City: Newsday, May 31, 1958); Aldous Huxley, *Brave New World Revisited* (New York: Harper, 1958); Vance Packard, *The Hidden Persuaders* (New York: McKay, 1957).

leisure does not necessarily mean an advance in civilization. If modern life, which makes greater leisure possible, merely increases boredom and adds nothing to our sense of beauty, our ability to live in rich fellowship with others, and our insight into the meaning of life, it may sap our nervous energy and lead to physical and moral deterioration.

While many resourceful people will be able to provide for their own recreation and leisure time, many—probably most—will depend on activities organized by groups and institutions. National, state, and city parks, public libraries, community centers, recreation grounds, and neighborhood clubs for artistic, intellectual, and recreational purposes will play a prominent role in their lives. Such services can add to human happiness and creativity.

10. *Clarifying and reinforcing the values on the basis of which a free society may endure.* The problems we have listed above are, in the last analysis, intellectual and moral problems. A free society makes strong demands on human nature, since it functions effectively only where a large number of its members respect integrity, fair dealing, and other things above money, personal power, and physical comforts. The values on the basis of which our civilization has developed are not likely to be strong or enduring unless they are reinforced by deep religious convictions, such as are found in the Judaeo-Christian tradition. Unless men believe that their values are enduring and that their life has meaning, they are not likely to make sacrifices to maintain these values when conditions become difficult.

QUESTIONS AND PROJECTS

1. Review Questions

(1) Discuss the basis and nature of the tensions between the desire for individual freedom and the need for some degree of governmental control.

(2) What are some of the historical landmarks that highlight the conflict between the desire for individual freedom and the attempts by government or other groups to control the freedom of the individual?

(3) Trace some of the important steps in the rise of individualism in recent centuries, indicating some of the movements and doctrines in the eighteenth and nineteenth centuries that reinforced the trend toward individualism.

(4) Show how the philosophy of individualism can be stated from a personal, an economic, and a political point of view.

(5) Trace the steps in the growth of social legislation during the last century or two.

(6) State the values at stake in the issue of individualism versus governmental control. Is this an "either-or" or a "both-and" issue?

(7) What ought to be the basis for evaluation of any regulation, program, or institution? Discuss.

(8) What problems for democracy and a free society have been raised by the presence of extremist groups on the right and on the left?

(9) In what ways do the extremist groups of the right and the left agree and disagree? Be specific.

(10) What are some conditions for an effectively functioning and relatively free society?

(11) List the three or four social problems that you consider most important today, indicating why you select these particular problems.

2. Make a list of events—including elections, court decisions, industrial changes, and significant declarations—that indicate a trend toward: (1) individualism, (2) greater governmental control. What over-all conclusions are to be drawn from this list?

3. Are there principles that limit or ought to limit the right of the community to interfere with the individual? State the principles you accept, and defend them.

4. Some years ago a majority of the citizens in one state developed a strong "personal liberty complex" that was directed against the compulsory vaccination law. There were then very few cases of smallpox, and the law was repealed. As the number of cases of smallpox increased, in some years doubling, more and more people began to wonder if that was the kind of freedom they really wanted. Eventually a majority decided to reenact the law. Should all the people have been forced to accept vaccination? Do people have the right to reject public health measures?

5. Statements are sometimes made to the effect that we are living in two eras: that we are living physically in a modern atomic or space age, while many of our social ideas, habits of life, and political and economic institutions belong to the nineteenth or eighteenth century or earlier. Give examples to justify these assertions.

6. Indicate why you agree or disagree with the following statement by Samuel Eliot Morison in *Freedom in Contemporary Society* (Boston: Little, Brown, 1956), p. 29:

> In my opinion, the growth of democracy in the United States has not contributed to the growth of political freedom. And the reasons, I think, are clear: (1) Political education has never caught up with political power. (2) The religious sanction to government has declined, with commensurate loss of public virtue; character and intelligence are losing the race to greed and selfishness. It is only by comparison with totalitarian governments, where the religious sanction is wholly wanting, and where free rein is given to cruelty and other abominable traits of human nature, that we are reconciled to the milder ills and supportable disadvantages of democracy.

7. Indicate which of the following activities you would leave to personal choice without governmental regulation, which you would prefer to see handled by some voluntary group or cooperative society, which by a state or local government, and which by the national, or federal, government. Give reasons for your choices.

(1) Traffic regulation; (2) the building of roads, highways, cross-country freeways, and bridges; (3) operation of a post-office system; (4) establishing standards for weights and measures; (5) operation of schools and colleges; (6) control of harbors, wharves, and lighthouses; (7) regulation of currency; (8) handling pure food and drug problems; (9) control of child labor; (10) wage legislation; (11) slum clearance; (12) establishing stock market standards; (13) handling rural electrification; (14) the installation of telephones in private homes; (15) the raising of pigs in one's own backyard: (16) determining the location of one's dwelling or home; (17) deciding the location of one's business; (18) choosing the school to which one's children are to be sent.

8. Review one of the following books: From the Suggested Readings those by Allen, Ayers, Cahn, Ellsworth and Harris, Girvetz, Greene, Morison, and Myrdal; Maurice Bruce, *The Coming of the Welfare State* (London: Batsford, 1961); E. H. Carr, *The New Society* (Boston: Beacon, 1961); Walter Gellhorn, *Individual Freedom and Governmental Restraints* (Baton Rouge: Louisiana State U. Press, 1956); Joseph S. Himes, *Social Planning in America: A Dynamic Interpretation* (Garden City: Doubleday, 1954); Richard Hofstadter, *Social Darwinism in American Thought* (Boston: Beacon, 1961); K. M. Panikkar, *In Defense of Liberalism* (New York: Asia Publishing, 1962); Rockefeller Brothers Fund, *The Power of the Democratic Idea* (Garden City: Doubleday, 1960); David Spitz, *Democracy and the Challenge of Power* (New York: Columbia U. Press, 1958); Overton H. Taylor, *The Classical Liberalism, Marxism, and the Twentieth Century* (Cambridge: Harvard U. Press, 1960).

SUGGESTED READINGS

ABERNATHY, GEORGE L. (ed.). *The Idea of Equality; An Anthology.* Richmond: Knox, 1959.
Selections from ancient and modern sources which show the variety of meanings that have been attached to equality.

ALLEN, FREDERICK LEWIS. *The Big Change: America Transforms Itself 1900–1950.* New York: Harper, 1952.
A sketch of the major changes in the character and quality of life through the "democratization of our economic system."

AYERS, C. E. *Toward A Reasonable Society: The Values of Industrial Society.* Austin: U. of Texas Press, 1961.
The author attempts a reevaluation of Western society and suggests the direction in which man needs to move if he is to harness the forces of nature for human use. He defends modern technology and scientific humanism.

BREDEMEIER, HARRY C., AND TOBY, JACKSON. *Social Problems in America: Costs and Casualties in an Acquisitive Society.* New York: Wiley, 1961.
Through illustrative readings, the authors attempt to show the genesis of social problems, not to offer statistics or to present solutions.

BURNS, EDWARD MCNALL. *Ideas in Conflict: The Political Theories of the Contemporary World.* New York: Norton, 1960.
The central political philosophies of our time are discussed in four parts: Liberal and Democratic Theories, Theories of Collectivism, Theories of Conservatism, and Theories of World Conflict and World Order.

CAHN, EDMOND. *The Predicament of Democratic Man.* New York: Macmillan, 1961.
The author discusses questions of citizenship, responsibility, and equality, and the extent to which individuals are morally involved in "the wrongs of government."

EBENSTEIN, WILLIAM. *Today's Isms: Communism, Fascism, Capitalism, Socialism.* 3rd ed.; Englewood Cliffs: Prentice-Hall, 1961.
A readable account, with attention centered on the conflict between an aggressive totalitarianism and a free way of life.

ELLSWORTH, RALPH E., AND HARRIS, SARAH M. *The American Right Wing.* Washington, D.C.: Public Affairs Press, 1962. (A Report to the Fund for the Republic.)
A pamphlet that attempts an accurate evaluation of the many right-wing groups and their programs.

GIRVETZ, HARRY K. *From Wealth to Welfare: The Evolution of Liberalism.* Stanford: Stanford U. Press, 1950.
A discussion of liberalism from the seventeenth century to the mid-twentieth century. Part One, Classical Liberalism; Part Two, Contemporary Liberalism.

GREENE, THEODORE MEYER. *Liberalism: Its Theory and Practice.* Austin: U. of Texas Press, 1957.
A discussion of the liberal attitude and creed, and the quest for a faith and a cause to meet the challenge of world-wide tension.

HARRIS, ROBERT T. *Social Ethics.* New York: Lippincott, 1962.
This work demonstrates how ethics and social philosophy are related. Parts of the book emphasize in turn liberty, fraternity, equality, and the individual in a liberal democratic society.

KIRK, RUSSELL. *The Conservative Mind from Burke to Santayana.* Chicago: Regnery, 1953.
A discussion of British and American thinkers who have respected tradition. See also Kirk's A Program for Conservatives.

LASSWELL, HAROLD D. *National Security and Individual Freedom.* New York: McGraw-Hill, 1950.
A discussion of the conflict between statism and democracy. The author considers issues such as civilian supremacy, freedom of information, civil liberties, and a free economy.

MORISON, SAMUEL ELIOT. *Freedom in Contemporary Society.* Boston: Little, Brown, 1956.
A readable discussion of political, economic, and academic freedom. These freedoms have been built up from the three concepts "government under law, government by consent, and natural rights."

MYRDAL, GUNNAR. *Beyond the Welfare State: Economic Planning and Its International Implications.* New Haven: Yale U. Press, 1960.
Economic planning is increasing among people who live in a modern organized society. There is no alternative to international disintegration except to work for a "welfare world."

NORDSKOG, JOHN ERIC. *Social Change.* New York: McGraw-Hill, 1960.
A wide selection of readings on social change, conceptions of change, and progress and trends in the various areas of society.

ROKEACH, MILTON. *The Open and Closed Mind.* New York: Basic Books, 1960.
A discussion of prejudice, dogmatic thinking, the way systems of belief are formed, and the connection between belief and personality structure.

ROUCEK, JOSEPH S. (ed.). *Contemporary Political Ideologies.* New York: Philosophical Library, 1961.
The author discusses a variety of movements including Marxism, socialism, and the new democracies. See especially his section on Cross Currents, in which he discusses the American welfare state.

TWENTY-SEVEN

THE PHILOSOPHY OF HISTORY

What is the future of Western civilization? Is it destined to follow the score or more of other civilizations that have grown, flourished, declined, and disappeared? Since the pages of history are strewn with the wrecks of past civilizations, it is appropriate for us to ask questions concerning the meaning of history and the relation between specific events and the course of history as a whole. Are there ends that are being achieved and values that are being built up? Is there progress in the direction of rationality, liberty, individuality, justice, and human welfare? Is there pattern, order, a plot, a theme, a development that we can discern? Books on the philosophy of history have been appearing, especially in recent decades, that attempt to answer these questions. Let us examine a few of the earlier and then a few of the contemporary philosophies of history. We are using the phrase *philosophy of history* for various inquiries into the nature of history and the course of historical events and the attempt to evaluate the various interpretations of history.

THE DENIAL OF MEANING IN HISTORY

Perhaps human history is a meaningless and accidental phenomenon. Those who deny that there is any meaning, pattern, or purpose in history are the *historical nihilists*. Those who assert that we do not and cannot know whether or not there is pattern or purpose in history are the *historical skeptics*. Those who claim that any pattern which seems to be present in historical development is not actually present in history but is merely a creation of human minds or imagination are the *historical subjectivists*.

In his essay "A Free Man's Worship" Bertrand Russell says that "man is the product of causes which had no prevision of the end they were achieving."[1] The human venture, he says, is the outcome of "accidental collocations of atoms." Consequently, the whole edifice of man's achievement must eventually be "buried beneath the debris of a universe in ruins." This, however, is

[1] *Mysticism and Logic and Other Essays* (New York: Longmans, Green, 1918), p. 47.

not the prevalent view of history and civilization among either philosophers or other students of human society.[2]

PHILOSOPHIES OF HISTORY BEFORE 1900

Five philosophies of history have been selected for presentation in this section. The first two represent the characteristic viewpoints of the ancient world and the medieval world. The following three represent interpretations by influential men of the eighteenth and the nineteenth centuries. These are followed by an examination of some recent or contemporary philosophies of history.

HISTORY AS CYCLICAL

A theory of history quite widely held in ancient times, especially by the Greeks and the Romans, was the theory of world cycles. This is the view that in the course of history there are periods of progress and decline. History moves in cycles like the seasons or like a wheel, but over long periods of time; there is a series of changes leading back to a starting point or original state as the process repeats itself. Many Greek thinkers believed that they were living in one of the periods of decline, a period of degeneration and decay following a glorious Golden Age. The Stoics accepted the theory of cycles, and they appear to have been responsible for passing it on to the Romans, where it is reflected in the writings of Marcus Aurelius and Seneca. Seneca believed that human life is periodically destroyed and that each new cycle begins with a Golden Age of innocence and simplicity. Arts, inventions, and, later, luxuries lead to vice and deterioration. Fate, or *Moira*—the fixed order of the universe—must be accepted with resignation.

The theory of cycles was revived in the nineteenth century by Nietzsche, and early in the twentieth century by Spengler. Spengler's view is considered later as a modern theory of cycles.

THE PROVIDENTIAL VIEW OF HISTORY

According to the providential interpretation, history is the working out of a divine purpose. The providential view was held by the early Jews and by the Christians, and it was reemphasized by Augustine and the medieval church leaders. In one form or another it is held by numerous people today.

In his *City of God* Augustine sets forth in comprehensive fashion the providential view of history as the revelation of God's purpose. He explains the drama of salvation, from the creation through the fall and the redemptive process to the end of the world and eternal reward or punishment. There are two cities existing side by side in the world. The City of God, the "Divine

2 For other illustrations of pessimistic interpretations, see John Herman Randall, *The Making of the Modern Mind* (rev. ed.; Boston: Houghton Mifflin, 1940), pp. 580 ff.

City," includes all the souls predestined to be saved—those saintly men of old, as well as the faithful of today who live close to God. The Church is the visible representation of the City of God on earth. The City of Satan, the "Earthly City," includes those who are devoted to purely worldly pursuits and who are impious and corrupt. History is the scene of conflict between the two cities, these two moralities, these two orders of life, which are diametrically opposed. On the day of reckoning, when the Lord appears, the blessed will receive their just reward and the wicked their just punishment.

Augustine thought that God was at work in human affairs and that society was moving in the direction of righteousness and peace. He could not think that God would be defeated. Many thinkers during the Middle Ages, however, thought men existed only for the purpose of attaining salvation and happiness in another world. They were not especially concerned about gradual improvement of or in this world. Instead of believing in progress, they believed that history was the story of degeneration from an original state of perfection.

The providential view of history has remained the prevalent theory of Western Christendom. In one form or another it is held by most Roman Catholics and Protestants today. However, even within this view there has been a tendency to give man a larger share of responsibility for the events of the world. God expresses Himself through occasional and unique manifestations of His presence, or He is constantly present in history and in nature.

ROUSSEAU—THE CORRUPTING INFLUENCE OF CIVILIZATION

In 1750 the Academy of Dijon, France, gave a prize for the best essay on the question of whether the development of the sciences and the arts had contributed to the improvement of morals. The prize went to Jean Jacques Rousseau (1712–1778), who attempted to show that mankind deteriorates as civilization advances. The soul of man is corrupted as the sciences and the arts become more perfect. Misery has increased as man has departed from the simpler and more primitive ways of living.

Rousseau felt that human nature is good, yet human society is evil. While he stressed the corrupting influence of civilization on the masses, he did not, as is so often claimed, advocate a return to primitive conditions. Rousseau opposed formal education. He proposed that children be protected from a corrupt society and be permitted to grow in a state of natural simplicity, so that their innate goodness might have an opportunity to develop. In the field of government, Rousseau stressed equality and democracy. However, his emphasis on the "general will" as expressed through majority rule, which appears to be democratic, in reality gives the state near absolute power.[3]

---

[3] Among Rousseau's more important works are *Emile* (1762), which gives his theory of education, *Social Contract* (1762), and *Confessions* (published posthumously).

HISTORY AS THE EXPRESSION OF REASON OR SPIRIT

By the eighteenth century, reason was beginning to replace faith as the central idea in interpretations of history. This new view is seen in Kant's *Idea of Universal History*, published in 1784, and in the work of many of Kant's successors, especially Hegel, whose *Philosophy of History* was published in 1837, six years after the author's death. Hegel's work, an elaborate metaphysics of history as seen by a monistic idealist, will serve as an example of this point of view.

Hegel's general thesis is that reality is spirit manifesting itself in nature, in human history, and in the actions of man. History is the development of spirit through successive stages. When spirit reaches the stage of rational freedom, it is fully conscious. World history belongs, not to the realm of matter, but to the realm of spirit. Whereas the essence of matter is gravity, the essence of spirit is rational freedom. Reason in history, rather than providential intervention, is emphasized.

The historical process proceeds from level to level, through the dialectic movement, from thesis to antithesis to synthesis. All change, all thinking, and all life proceed from affirmation to denial, or from claim and counterclaim to a new integration, which later develops a new opposition, and so the movement continues. Development takes place in "waltz-time," so to speak, with its beat of "one, two, three, one, two, three," instead of in a straight or smooth line. Each finite thing or event tends to generate its opposite; then the opposites tend to be absorbed into some higher unity.

According to Hegel, individuals and groups find their fulfillment in society, in the form of the state. The state is society organized to make law possible. Statutory law and morality are both self-imposed limitations which make action and freedom possible. Spirit, as the capacity to act, requires freedom under law. History thus begins and ends with the state, which is an expression of the Divine Idea on earth. Progress consists of successive transformations of the state as the World Spirit is more and more completely embodied in its activity and organization.

Human history, according to Hegel, began in Asia and has been moving westward with the sun. In the early Oriental kingdoms there was no individual freedom. Authority and obedience to the will of the ruler were enforced. The second or intermediate epoch in history is represented by Greece and Rome. In this stage there was some recognition of the rights and duties of the person. Some men were free and others were slaves. Concepts of justice, equity, and law began slowly to emerge. The third and final stage of history begins with Christianity and is seen in Western Europe. There is a tension between the inner and the outer, between the particular and the universal. The individual resists the pressure of the objective and external and often seeks escape in some subjective world of his own creation. The universal and the particular unite: religiously, in the Incarnation, where the divine and the human meet; socially and politically, in a social organization based on reason and morality—that is, in the modern state. The individual voluntarily identifies his own will with that of a supreme individual, the monarch. There is, then, no further conflict between the inner and the outer, the particular and the universal, the individual and society, for a synthesis has taken place. The synthesis that begins with the rise of Christianity is completed in Germanic culture. Hegel's nationalism, rather than the demands of reason, led him to many of the conclusions about the place of his own nation in history.

THE ECONOMIC INTERPRETATION OF HISTORY

The economic interpretation of history has had its most widespread influence during the last one hundred years. In 1848 Karl Marx and Friedrich Engels published *The Communist Manifesto*, a document that has inspired many revolutionary movements. Later Marx published his great work *Capital*, the first volume of which appeared in 1867. The philosophy of Marx and Engels is usually called dialectical materialism.[4] For Marx, economic factors are central determinants in man's historical development. History is interpreted as a record of class conflict in which the means of production, distribution, and exchange exert a determining influence on the social process. Changes in the economic structure of society cause changes in class relations, and these influence the political, social, moral, and religious customs and traditions. Let us consider briefly the stages of history according to this point of view.

Five types of productive systems can be distinguished. Four of them have appeared in succession in human society. The fifth is forecast for the immediate future or is now taking form. The first is the system of primitive communism. It is the first economic stage and is characterized by the communal ownership of property, by peaceful relations, and by a lack of technology. The second stage is the ancient or slave system of production. It is marked by the rise of private property, which comes into existence when agriculture and cattle-raising tend to displace hunting as a means of livelihood. Soon aristocratic, upper-class groups enslave other men. Conflict of interest appears as the minority groups gain control of the means of support. The third stage is characterized by military feudal groups in control of a large number of serfs. The feudal nobles appropriate the surplus products from the serfs, who eke out a bare living.

The bourgeois, or capitalist, system of production comes in with the increase of commerce and inventions and the division of labor; this is the fourth stage. The factory system creates the industrial capitalist, who owns and controls the instruments of production. The worker has only his labor power, and he is forced to offer himself for hire. Just as the hand mill creates

4 See discussion in Ch. 12, pp. 211–215.

a society with a feudal structure, the steam engine creates a society with the capitalist employer.

The history of society since the breakup of the primitive communal society is a history of class struggle. During the last hundred and fifty years industrial capitalism, with its doctrine of self-interest, has split society into two opposed groups: the bourgeois, or owning, group and the proletarian workers. Since the owning class controls the key institutions of society and will permit no thoroughgoing changes by peaceful means, the way out is "the forcible overthrow of all existing social conditions."

After the revolution, according to dialectical materialism and communist philosophy, there are two stages of society. There is, first, a transitional stage, the period of the dictatorship of the proletariat, or working class. During this interval, revolutionary social changes are made and classes are abolished through the elimination of private ownership of the means of production, distribution, and exchange. The second stage after the revolution is the fifth and final type of productive system. It is the "classless society," or pure communism. In this era, conflicts and exploitation will have ended, and all men and women will be assured of the means to achieve a good life. The state will cease to be a class instrument, and the dialectic will cease to operate in a classless society. There is supposed to be freedom, equality, peace, and abundance. Society will realize the formula "From each according to his ability, to each according to his need."

RECENT PHILOSOPHIES OF HISTORY

At the beginning of the twentieth century, Western civilization seemed to most people to be secure and dominant. There was great confidence in science, democracy, and human progress. Two wars in a generation, however, have done much to undermine that confidence. For some decades a number of students of history have been telling us that our civilization is in a period of decline. The first of six philosophies of history which we are now to consider is the outstanding representative of that point of view. The other five present a more hopeful view of the future.

SPENGLER AND THE DECLINE OF THE WEST

Oswald Spengler was an unknown teacher of mathematics in Munich, Germany, until he startled the intellectual world with his *The Decline of the West*, a two-volume work completed in 1917 and published after the close of World War I.[5] Recently there has been a renewed interest in Spengler

[5] See Oswald Spengler, *The Decline of the West* (New York: Knopf, 1945); *Today and Destiny: Vital Excerpts from The Decline of the West* (New York: Knopf, 1940) (Introduction and Commentary by Edwin F. Dakin); *The Decline of the West* (abr. ed.; New York: Knopf, 1962). For a critical evaluation of Spengler's work see the book by H. Stuart Hughes listed at the end of this chapter.

and a growing fear that he may be right. After examining many past cultures —Egyptian, Chinese, Hindu, classical Greek and Roman, and Arabic—he turns to contemporary Western culture which, he says, is now in a period of decline from its great creative heights.

Spengler uses the term *culture* to include the institutions and productions of a people in their entire historical development. The term *civilization* is reserved for the declining stage of that culture. This declining stage is a period of decay, senility, and skepticism. A culture is an organism, like a flower or an animal, that grows and decays. There is no continuous and universal world culture. History is pluralistic, or made up of many cultures; there is, therefore, no single straight line of development.

Each culture passes through four fairly distinct stages. We may think of these stages as analogous to the seasons, or to the stages in the life of a person. There is, first, spring or childhood, the time of the germination of life and early growth. In the culture this may be the time of settlement and conquest, when people live close to the soil. There is, second, summer blooming or youth. It is the prime of life and a time of ripening consciousness. In the West this was the period of the Renaissance. There is, third, autumnal fading, the time of ripest maturity, which is soon to lead to decline. It is marked by the rise of cities and commerce. Finally comes winter, or old age and death, when quality is replaced by quantity, beauty by utility, and the war lords come to inherit the earth.

In the critical stage of decline, we witness the following trends and characteristics: (1) There arise great cities in which life becomes artificial, fast, and shallow. The cities whirl with machines and are crowded with workers devoid of property and middle-class business groups devoid of what is commonly thought of as "culture." (2) There develops the dictatorship of money, which is another sign of decay. Distinction tends to pass to the men of wealth. They do not create; they merely accumulate and exchange. Money destroys first intellect and then democracy. The body prospers, but the soul decays. (3) Man becomes the slave of the machine and the industrial system. After creating "the entrepreneur, the engineer, and the factory-worker," the machine "forces the entrepreneur not less than the workman to obedience. Both become slaves, and not masters, of the machine, that now for the first time develops its devilish and occult power."[6] (4) The growth of imperialism, Caesarism (absolute government), and war are characteristic of civilization, or the declining stage of culture. Imperial dictators attempt to seize the citadels of power. (5) There is a tendency toward race suicide. Many people, especially in the cities, become sterile, or childless. The propagation of ignorance outruns the propagation of intelligence. (6) Skepticism develops, and religion, philosophy, and science tend to crystallize into fixed forms in an effort to suggest security.

[6] Spengler, *Decline of the West*, 1945, II, p. 504.

These, then, are some of the evidences of decline, according to Spengler. He considers the decline inevitable. Most students of history and philosophy, however, find it difficult to accept either his method of reasoning or his world view. The analogy between animal organisms and human culture is not sound. In addition, Spengler ignores the large degree of borrowing from one culture by another and the fact that men are now able to discover the trends of history and to do something about them. His chief contribution has been to jolt the West out of its superficial optimism.

SCHWEITZER AND THE NEED FOR AN ETHICAL WORLD VIEW

Albert Schweitzer is one of the great figures of our age. While working at his hospital in Africa he has written two volumes of his *Philosophy of Civilization*, and two more are projected. He sees civilization in an actual process of decay. The "suicide of civilization is in process," and the parts that are left are no longer safe. Human progress does not go on constantly or automatically; it depends on human effort. Until the middle of the nineteenth century, the material and moral forces of society developed side by side. In recent years, however, moral energy has declined, while the application of intelligence in the material sphere has moved ahead rapidly. Our age has come to emphasize scientific, technical, and artistic achievement. Schweitzer tells us that "material achievements . . . are not civilization, but become civilization only so far as the mental habit of civilized peoples is capable of allowing them to work towards the perfecting of the individual and the community."[7] Whether there is more or less material development is not the important criterion in judging man's development. What is essential is that reasonable men should keep control of material conditions.

Among the signs of intellectual and spiritual fatigue Schweitzer includes the decline in respect for thinking and for an ethical world view; the decline of optimistic and ethical convictions concerning the meaning of life and of the universe; our superficial and narrow specialization, with its misplaced confidence in *facts;* increasing racialism and nationalism; the growth of inhumane ideas and actions and their failure to arouse popular indignation; and the recrudescence of superstition.

The reconstruction of our age, according to Schweitzer, will come only with recovery of a theory of the universe that is both optimistic and ethical. "Civilization is founded on some sort of theory of the universe, and can be restored only through a spiritual awakening and a will for ethical good in the mass of mankind."[8] An ethical foundation is the basis for civilization. Our age, says Schweitzer, must recover its reverence for life. There is in

---

[7] Albert Schweitzer, *The Philosophy of Civilization,* trans. C. T. Campion (New York: Macmillan, 1949), Part II, *Civilization and Ethics,* p. 5.

[8] *Ibid.,* Part I, *The Decay and Restoration of Civilization,* p. 78.

man and in all organic beings a will to live. The only adequate standard for a civilization is the value it places on life.

Progress is an internal process that comes in and through personalities. "If men can be found who revolt against the spirit of thoughtlessness, and who are personalities sound enough and profound enough to let the ideals of ethical progress radiate from them as a force, there will start an activity of the spirit which will be strong enough to evoke a new mental and spiritual disposition in mankind."[9]

SOROKIN AND OUR SENSATE CULTURE

In a four-volume work entitled *Social and Cultural Dynamics*[10] P. A. Sorokin of Harvard tells us that we face a crisis that is more serious than any other in recent times. The whole of civilization is involved in it. According to Sorokin, there are three essentially different types of cultures. First, there is the Sensate, whose major principle is that "the true reality and value is sensory." The real is that which we see, hear, smell, touch, or otherwise perceive sensorially. This culture is the materialistic, empirical, utilitarian society of today, in which men seek sensual enjoyment primarily. Second, and standing in contrast to this Sensate type of culture, is the Ideational culture, which avoids the sensual and the frivolous and stresses the religious and the ascetic. Such a culture is unified around the principle of a super-sensory and superrational God. Third, and intermediary between the above types of cultures, is the Idealistic, which is partly sensory and partly super-sensory.

The crisis of our society, according to Sorokin, is nothing less than the decline of the dominant Sensate culture of our Western civilization. This culture has given man tremendous power over nature and the social and cultural world. However, it has left man devoid of self-control—the power to control his emotions and appetites.

> The Sensate culture did its best in the way of degrading man to the level of a mere reflex mechanism, a mere organ motivated by sex, a mere semi-mechan-ical, semi-physiological organism, devoid of any divine spark, of any absolute value, of anything noble and sacred. Such a debasement now becomes increas-ingly dangerous for the Sensate man himself. Hence the urgency of the shift from Sensatism to Idealionalism, from the subjugation and control of nature by man to the control of man by himself.[11]

9 Albert Schweitzer, *Out of My Life and Thought: An Autobiography*, trans. C. T. Campion (New York: Henry Holt and Company, 1933), p. 281. (See also the 1949 edition with Postscript by Everett Skillings.)

10 New York: American Book, 1937–1941, IV; P. A. Sorokin, *Social and Cultural Dynamics* (rev. and abr. ed.; Boston: Sargent, 1957).

11 P. A. Sorokin, *Fluctuation of Social Relationships, War, and Revolution* (New York: American Book, 1937), p. 539. (Vol. III of *Social and Cultural Dynamics*.)

We are passing through a "grim transition" from the Sensate to a different stage of the cultural cycle. The crisis is accompanied by an unusual number of social, economic, political, intellectual, and moral problems, including delinquency and crime, family disintegration, poverty, mental disease, suicide, charlatanism in religion, revolutions, and wars. While Sensate values lead to an abundance of material things, their creative and constructive possibilities are soon exhausted. We have reached this stage in Western society. According to Sorokin, we cannot stop the transition from taking place; we can only hasten the change and make it less violent, or we can attempt to stop it, slow it up, and make it more violent. There is no alternative.

The crisis, Sorokin says, will continue until our Sensate culture is replaced by one more adequately based. Only a change in social values and a transfer of loyalties, based on a recognition of a new sense of duty, justice, love, sacrifice, and God, will release the creative forces needed for the new society. "Let us hope that the grace of understanding may be vouchsafed us and that we may choose, before it is too late, the right road—the road that leads not to death but to the further realization of man's unique creative mission on this planet!"[12]

Lasting peace, Sorokin tells us, cannot be achieved without a pronounced increase in love, sympathy, and voluntary cooperation. There is "no peace or survival without altruism." Our present culture tends to generate the egoistic and competitive forces that lead to strife and war. There are two possibilities before us. We can "drag the conscious and superconscious to the level of the unconscious" and thus crush and deny the human personality; or we can bring these unconscious forces under the control of the conscious, and even subject these to the influence of the superconscious. Man can control himself and his institutions in the interest of high purposes. This is the paramount problem and task of humanity.

WHITEHEAD'S PHILOSOPHY OF CIVILIZATION AND HISTORY

In a number of books, especially in *Adventures of Ideas* and *Science and the Modern World,* Alfred North Whitehead sets forth a philosophy of civilization that warrants attention. Fortunately, his views, expressed in many different books and articles, have been made readily available in a single volume by A. H. Johnson, a student of Whitehead's philosophy.[13]

For Whitehead there are certain qualities or factors that are essential for any high civilization. "A man, or a society, is civilized if *truth, beauty, adventure, art, peace* are the *dominant* qualities, and if these five qualities are

12 P. A. Sorokin, *The Crisis of Our Age* (New York: Dutton, 1941), p. 326.
13 *Whitehead's Philosophy of Civilization* (Boston: Beacon, 1958).

exhibited in all phases of experience."[14] In addition to these basic elements, there are other, closely related, factors: "the recognition of the importance of each individual, freedom of thought and action, tolerance, the use of persuasion rather than force, wisdom."[15] In addition, *"ideas, great men, economic activities, technological devices, the facts of 'geography,' God*—all influence the behavior of human beings."[16] Whitehead thinks that any single or monistic interpretation of history is inadequate and misleading.

The chief influences on Western civilization are Greek, Palestinian, and Egyptian. However, though learning from the past is valuable, one must not be too closely wedded to it. Whitehead believes that there is a "strong creative process at work," and art, science, philosophy, and religion all have constructive parts to play in this process. Let us consider the part which each one of these areas plays in the development of a civilization. Through beauty, the aesthetic experience, and art, something of eternal value may be disclosed that may bring a sense of relaxation and exaltation. Science has made contributions to speculative thought and has eased the burdens of life, but it does not appear to be an essential ingredient of civilization, since there have been comparatively high civilizations where achievements in science were exceedingly small. Philosophy, Whitehead believes, is necessary for civilization because it attempts to bring facts and values into some orderly relation; and, since "the civilized mind is vitalized by a 'noble discontent,' the philosophic attitude of 'criticism'" is valuable. "Men are driven," Whitehead says, "by their thoughts as well as by the molecules in their bodies."[17] Creative ideas bear fruit slowly, but they do have great power. Religion is also a central element in civilized living, since some transcendent aim is necessary for a full and creative life. Religion is the source of moral energy and may free a person from narrow particularity. Religion directs man's attention to "what is permanent in the nature of things." Leaders like the Hebrew prophets and Jesus have been able to alter the course of history.

What are our prospects, according to Whitehead? The future is open; there is no inevitable progress or decline. There will be "either adventurous advance or a deadly lethargy of decadence." There is, however, a creative process at work, and if men can align themselves with it and rise to the occasion, the possibilities for the future are great. Our society, on the whole, has put too much emphasis on efficiency in material production and not enough upon the moral, aesthetic, and spiritual values.

14 *Ibid.*, p. 1. In *Adventures of Ideas* (New York: New American Library of World Literature, 1955), Part IV, "Civilization," Alfred North Whitehead devotes several chapters to these concepts. (Mentor ed.)
15 Johnson, *Whitehead's Philosophy*, p. 11.
16 *Ibid.*, p. 22.
17 *Adventures of Ideas*, p. 53.

TOYNBEE ON THE GROWTH AND DECLINE OF CIVILIZATION

One of the monumental studies of civilization was made by an English scholar, Arnold J. Toynbee, working under the auspices of the Royal Institute of International Affairs. *A Study of History*[18] is a twelve-volume work that deals with the growth and decline of civilization and suggests causes and patterns of historical change. Toynbee believes that we need to study society as a whole (for example, Western civilization), not just states or nations, since it is difficult to understand the parts separately. How can we understand the Industrial Revolution or the parliamentary system by studying a single nation or group of people? These movements have affected many peoples over areas much larger than any state or nation. We need to feel and comprehend life as a whole. Toynbee deals not only with the factual history of peoples but also with the aspirations and ideals expressed in their literature. After studying twenty-one civilizations, he says that Western civilization is in danger of losing its vitality and creative power. Western man, so confident at the turn of the century, has now become very anxious about his own future.

Evolution shows persistent trends, and personality is a growing factor in the universe. There are, however, two alternating forces or phases in the rhythm of the universe.[19] This can be seen in nature, as in the tides and seasons, and in all of life. These phases are variously termed "action and reaction," "Yin and Yang," "withdrawal and return." They are affected by various "challenges and responses." The challenges range from climatic factors to elements in the social environment. Ease is inimical to civilization; civilization is in considerable part the successful response by a society to a challenge. Prominent growth factors include self-determination, or development of man's inner life, and the work of the creative individuals or creative minorities. In static primitive societies, men look toward the past and the older generation. In developing civilizations, men admire and follow the creative personalities. Toynbee believes that evolution shows a trend from matter to life, from lower life to higher life, and from higher life to mind and spirit.

The causes of the breakdown of civilizations are neither cosmic forces outside human control or acts of God, nor are they racial degeneration, loss of command over the physical environment, or pressures from the outside. "The chief danger to man is man."[20] Among the important causes are militarism, "the commonest cause of the breakdown of civilization during

---

[18] Arnold J. Toynbee, *A Study of History* (12 vols.; London: Oxford U. Press, 1939, 1954, 1959, 1961).

[19] *Ibid.,* I, p. 201.

[20] *Ibid.,* IV, p. 121.

the four or five millennia,"[21] and the loss of self-determination, a loss that is spoken of as "the ultimate criterion of breakdown." Most civilizations in the past have broken down "through their own acts," before any outside or "alien human force succeeded in dealing them a potentially mortal blow."

Toynbee says that "the nature of the breakdown of civilizations can be summed up in three points." The first is the "failure of creative power in the minority." When the creative minority degenerates into a mere dominant minority that endeavors to keep by force a position it no longer merits, society begins to disintegrate. Second, there is an answering withdrawal of allegiance on the part of the majority. It ceases to admire, to imitate, or to follow the minority that has ceased to be creative. There is, third, "a consequent loss of social unity in the society as a whole."[22] A declining civilization radiates force instead of maintaining unity through creative leadership and admiration. The "idolatry of institutions" and of techniques may lead to a loss of creativity. This may lead in turn to complacency or worship of the past.

Mankind appears once more to be in a period of rapid change, and Western civilization is in the midst of grave troubles. In the past, a challenge, a crisis, or a time of troubles has had widely differing effects. Some societies have been crushed or have passed into oblivion; some, in going down, have given rise to vigorous new societies; and some have summoned latent energy to meet the challenge and, in the very act of struggle, have achieved a renaissance. The processes of change and the times of troubles tend to split a society into factions with their characteristic institutions: the dominant minority, depending on force, creates a universal state; a creative minority, emerging within the proletarian majority, creates a universal church; and other proletarian groups create "barbarian war-bands" (groups within or without the society that seek to conquer it). This is a pattern which, Toynbee says, has occurred many times in the past.

According to Toynbee, the crucial questions confronting Western man are not military, or economic, or even intellectual, but essentially moral and religious. Consequently, he devotes considerable space in his later volumes to questions of religion. If the world manages to preserve the peace and keep its population within limits, the most urgent need will be for the revival of religion. Man cannot live without freedom, and apart from religion, its spiritual citadel, freedom may be lost. Christianity and the other living religions bring mankind into touch with a living and a loving God. These religions, however, need to get rid of their parochialism and exclusiveness.

---

21 *Ibid.*, III, p. 150.
22 *Ibid.*, IV, p. 6.

Without abandoning their own convictions, adherents of all the higher religions need to subordinate their ancient rivalries and take a more united stand against a common threat to their existence—that is, against the worship of collective human power.[23]

In volume ten of *A Study of History* Toynbee raises questions about the prospects of Western civilization, the only extant civilization that does not show indisputable signs of being in disintegration. Is it rational, he asks, to expect to see only one out of twenty-one civilizations succeed in avoiding the fate of all the others? One serious cause for concern is the fact that Western society is worshiping idols. The most dangerous idolatry is worship of the state; this is one basic cause of war. This false national religion has been the cause of the decline of most civilizations in the past. Yet we may hope that a society that has eliminated slavery may succeed in abolishing the worship of the state, militarism, and war. This is one great challenge we face.

In *Civilization on Trial*, in which Toynbee speaks of, among other things, the twin dangers of war and class, he asks, "What shall we do to be saved?" He says that in politics we need to establish a "constitutional co-operative system of world government." In economics we need to find "working compromises . . . between free enterprise and socialism." In the life of the spirit we need to "put the secular superstructure back onto religious foundations."[24] While he thinks that the first two tasks demand immediate attention, he says that the third is the most basic and important one.

While our Western society is in danger of decline, Toynbee maintains, in contrast with Spengler, that the disintegration can be halted. Our Western society has a bias toward machinery, and its main interest and effort at present are directed toward putting scientific discoveries to practical use; in this the West has been very successful. But a civilization may go down while its material techniques are being refined. Civilization needs a profound moral and spiritual transformation if it is to continue to progress. Our destiny depends on our response to the challenge of our time.

Toynbee's massive work, which attempted to cover the whole range of human history, was subjected to sharp criticism by many specialists in particular areas on which he had written; most of these criticisms, however, do not deal with points emphasized above.[25] In 1961, in reply to his critics, Toynbee published a large volume, *Reconsiderations*,[26] in which he admits

---

[23] In addition to his discussion of religion in *A Study of History*, Toynbee has written two books that deal with this problem: *An Historian's Approach to Religion* (New York: Oxford U. Press, 1956) (Gifford Lectures, 1952–53); *Christianity Among the Religions of the World* (New York: Scribner's, 1957).

[24] New York: Oxford U. Press, 1948, p. 39.

[25] See M. F. Ashley Montagu (ed.), *Toynbee and History* (Boston: Sargent, 1956), for a collection of critical essays and reviews.

[26] Toynbee, *A Study of History*, XII, *Reconsiderations*.

the truth of some of the criticisms, rejects others, and points out the need for some revisions of his approach. Toynbee's history still stands, however, as one of the most discussed and important historical works of our time.

QUIGLEY ON THE DEVELOPMENT OF CIVILIZATIONS

In *The Evolution of Civilizations* Carroll Quigley attempts to develop analytical tools to aid in the understanding of history and the rise and fall of civilizations. He shows the influence of Toynbee but hopes to avoid what he considers some inadequacies of Toynbee's method and theories. (We shall omit Quigley's discussion of the various civilizations that have existed before our own Western society.) History, Quigley insists, is a continuum, and every civilization undergoes a continuous change as it comes into being, passes through various experiences over the centuries, and eventually ceases to exist. History does not lend itself easily to periodization and division. These are always arbitrary, imaginary, and to some extent subjective. Yet some classifications are more useful than others. Quigley believes that the method used in science—that is, gathering evidence, stating an hypothesis, and then testing this hypothesis—can be used in history and the social sciences, though no answer is ever final.

As civilizations rise and fall, they tend to pass through seven stages. First, every civilization "begins with a mixture of two or more cultures." There is, second, a period of gestation or preparation for the third stage, a period of expression and growth in many directions: growth in production, population, land area, and knowledge. When the rate of expansion begins to decline, a fourth stage, the "Age of Conflict," the most critical of all the stages, comes into existence, with its class conflicts, wars, and growing irrationality. A new way of renewal may be found that enables the civilization to expand again and gain new vitality. If no way of renewal can be found, a "universal empire," the fifth stage, may emerge from the conflicts and give a period of peace and relative prosperity. This soon leads to a "stage of decay," the sixth stage; and, as a result of a growing weakness, the society is taken over by "outsiders" in a "stage of invasion," the seventh stage, and that civilization ceases to exist. This last stage is also a period of mixture for a new society.

In the above development, Quigley distinguishes between instruments, often referred to as "instruments of expansion" or "social instruments," on the one hand, and institutions, on the other hand. "An instrument is a social organization that is fulfilling effectively the purpose for which it arose."[27] Such instruments of expansion are essential to any growing or healthy civilization and exhibit three characteristics: First, a society must be so organized that it has "an incentive to invent new ways of doing things." Second,

[27] Carroll Quigley, *The Evolution of Civilization: An Introduction to Historical Analysis* (New York: The Macmillan Company, 1961), p. 49.

there must be an "accumulation of surplus"; some wealth must be available beyond what is immediately consumed. Third, this surplus must be used for new inventions or for investment in some creative effort. "An institution is an instrument that has taken on activities and purposes of its own, separate and different from the purposes for which it was intended."[28] This is another way of saying that institutions tend to lose their original purpose, become ends in themselves, block development, and weaken the organization and society. An example of this in military history is the attachment to obsolete techniques, and there are instances in the churches, political and business groups, labor unions, and nearly all other institutions of society. When there is strain or the tension of development there may come reform, circumvention when the duties are given to another organization, or reaction and the triumph of vested interests.

What is the prospect for Western civilization? We cannot trace the development of the West through various early stages, and therefore the reader is especially urged to read the long chapter on "Western Civilization."[29] In brief, the West has already had three periods of expansion and has moved from stage three, expansion, to stage four, the period of conflict, three times.[30] Reform and circumvention have occurred twice. By 1930 the West had become institutionalized into monopoly capitalism and was in another major crisis. In our age, in addition to the wars, class conflicts, and market crises, there has been a great upsurge of irrationality.

> All the characteristics of an age of irrationality began to appear on all sides—increased gambling, increased smoking, the growing use of alcohol and narcotics, a growing obsession with sex and with perversions of sex, an increasing mania for speed, for nervous tension, and for noise; above all, perhaps, a growing tendency to regard violence as a solution for all problems, be they domestic, social, economic, ideological, or international.[31]

If the West does reform, which appears likely, it could enter a great new era of expansion. If it fails to do so, the threat from Russian civilization will increase.

BUILDING A HIGHER CIVILIZATION

Building and maintaining a high civilization in which man can develop his latent potentialities is our all-inclusive social purpose. It is a continuous

---

28 *Ibid.*, p. 49.

29 *Ibid.*, pp. 210–265.

30 The three periods of expansion are approximately 970–1270 (feudalism), 1420–1650 (commercial capitalism), and 1725–1929 (industrial capitalism). The three ages of conflict are 1300–1430 (Hundred Years War), 1650–1815 (Second Hundred Years War), and 1900 to the present (Boer War to the present).

31 Quigley, *Evolution of Civilization*, p. 259.

task. If we relax our efforts, even for a short period, the work of centuries may be lost. If we take our civilization for granted, our own futures may be endangered. If our ideals have become vague, it may be because we have failed to reinterpret them in the light of new conditions and to show their modern applications.

The crises through which we have passed in recent decades—depressions, threats from fascism, communism, and war—are due in large part to the fact that modern culture has lost its bond of unity, its common standards and convictions which alone give a basis for life. Life has been broken into fragments or compartments. This is caused partly by our retreat from the use of creative intelligence in social affairs, partly by a false method of knowing—a method that emphasizes only what the sense organs reveal—and considerably by the isolation of highly specialized fields and studies. As specialists we tend to see life in fragments and to lose a sense of its unity, meaning, and wholeness. Assuming that progress was inevitable, we thought that any additional "facts" would automatically accelerate the rate of progress. We see now the folly of that approach. Progress is possible but not inevitable. Awareness of facts must be supplemented by an awareness of values.

Progress should not be measured primarily by material things or scientific inventions. The conquest of nature does not necessarily mean either moral improvement or greater happiness. Progress has to do mainly with the achievement of human values; it is the development of those qualities that are distinctively human.

To believe in progress and in the possibility of progress at any specific period in history is reasonable. We live not only in an orderly universe, as we have seen, but also in one that is dynamic, and that appears to be moving in the direction of life, self-consciousness, intelligence, freedom, and the realization of values. If this is true, then meaning and moral purpose do exist in the universe, as well as in man's life.

If we are to build a higher civilization, we must use the means at hand. The intellectual framework for comprehension of man's life and culture may be provided by a study of philosophy. Philosophy must furnish a life view and a world view and contribute to man's understanding of many of his major problems. The organizations and institutions of society can be aided by the social studies. The creation of efficient means, or the implementation of our social purposes, is the work of all of the sciences. Religion can furnish the motivation and the great loyalties which enable men to feel that the tasks before them are preeminently worthwhile. Man may take the great new inventions and the marvelous powers that are now available and use them so that they will create not destitution, suffering, and war, but human welfare, happiness, and lasting peace.

QUESTIONS AND PROJECTS

1. Review Questions

(1) What is meant by "philosophy of history"?

(2) What are some leading questions and problems in the area of the philosophy of history?

(3) State the views of history that were held: (a) by the early Greeks, (b) by orthodox Christians.

(4) State the central points in the philosophies of history of Rousseau, Hegel, and Marx.

(5) Give a brief exposition of Spengler's philosophy of history including an evaluation of his method and point of view.

(6) Give the distinctive points of emphasis in the philosophies of history set forth by Schweitzer, Sorokin, and Whitehead.

(7) According to Toynbee what are the main factors in (a) the breakdown of civilizations and (b) the growth of civilizations? What are the prospects for Western civilization, and what must the West do if it is to continue to advance?

(8) What does Quigley say about the problem of institutions in any society? What institutions may be obstructing the development of Western society today?

(9) Discuss the problem of building and maintaining a high civilization. What in your opinion are the central elements in human progress?

2. Spengler and some other students of history have severely criticized the city and urban life as tending to produce materialism, skepticism, selfishness, and other undesirable traits and attitudes. Is there any justification for such an indictment? If so, what is it? If not, why have there been so many critics of the city? You may wish to consult Lewis Mumford, *The City in History* (New York: Harcourt, Brace, 1961).

3. The charge has been made that, as a result of the amazing scientific advances of the last century, science is making life trivial by leading men to think only of material things and gadgets. Is there any justification for this charge? Have we tended to place too much confidence in the ability of science alone to save our civilization from decline?

4. Do you agree with the statement that "progress is possible but not inevitable"? In what does progress, for individuals and societies, consist? Many of the books in the Suggested Readings deal with such questions. In answering, you may wish to consult a series of articles on progress that appeared in *The Personalist* during 1945. These articles deal with some fundamental issues that are still timely.

5. If men are to plan for the future or for the advancement of civilization, they need a sense of direction and some national goals. What in your opinion are the goals and values to be sought? You may wish to consult the series of articles on our national purpose, written by leaders from many professional groups, that appeared in *Life* magazine during 1960.

6. What are the encouraging and discouraging trends or conditions in twentieth-century Western civilization? Would you agree that the fact that many mature people the world around are disturbed about what is called "the crisis of our times" is in itself encouraging? Discuss.

7. In some parts of the world, a flood or a famine is accepted with resignation. In other places, men refuse to accept these blows or defeats as inevitable. What factors cause the differences in attitudes? Discuss the part a philosophy of life plays in everyday affairs.

8. Report on one of the philosophies of history as set forth by Auguste Comte, Nicholas Berdyaev, Benedetto Croce, and Giambattista B. Vico.

9. Critically review one of the following books: Philip Bagby, *Culture and History* (Berkeley: U. of California Press, 1959); John Baillie, *The Belief in Progress* (London: Oxford U. Press, 1950); Edward Hallett Carr, *What is History?* (New York: Knopf, 1962); J. V. Langmead Casserley, *The Bent World* (New York: Oxford U. Press, 1955); M. C. D'Arcy, *The Meaning and Matter of History, A Christian View* (New York: Farrar, Straus and Cudahy, 1959); Christopher H. Dawson, *The Historic Reality of Christian Culture; A Way to the Renewal of Life* (New York: Harper, 1960); Charles Frankel, *The Case for Modern Man* (New York: Harper, 1956); T. M. Greene, *Our Cultural Heritage* (Houston: Elsevier, 1956); Louis J. Halle, *Men and Nations* (Princeton: Princeton U. Press, 1962); John Nef, *A Search for Civilization* (Chicago: Regnery, 1962); Paul Weiss, *History: Written and Lived* (Carbondale: Southern Illinois U. Press, 1962).

SUGGESTED READINGS

COHEN, MORRIS R. *The Meaning of Human History.* La Salle: Open Court, 1947.
   A philosophy of history which covers such topics as metaphysics and history, the various factors that are influential in history, patterns of historical development, and the task of the historian. The author is critical of all monistic theories of historical change.

GARDINER, PATRICK (ed.). *Theories of History.* Glencoe: Free Press, 1958.
   Selections from the outstanding earlier writers on the philosophy of history are followed by contemporary contributions. The editor provides helpful introductions and comments.

HEILBRONER, ROBERT L. *The Future as History.* New York: Harper, 1960.
   The author discusses "the historic currents of our time and the direction in which they are taking America." Our society is not basically concerned with moral issues. "History is likely to go against us for some time."

HOCKING, WILLIAM ERNEST. *The Coming World Civilization.* New York: Harper, 1956.
   An outstanding philosopher discusses the character of our civilization, the possibility of a single world civilization, and the role that Christianity and other religions may play.

HUGHES, H. STUART. *Oswald Spengler: A Critical Estimate.* New York: Scribner's, 1952.
   A useful little book dealing critically with Spengler, his times, the sources of his ideas, and the influence of his work.

JOHNSON, A. H. *Whitehead's Philosophy of Civilization.* Boston: Beacon, 1958.
   Whitehead's social philosophy, including his philosophy of history, education, and religion, is here made available in condensed form.

KOCH, ADRIENNE. *Philosophy for a Time of Crisis: An Interpretation with Key Writings by Fifteen Great Modern Thinkers.* New York: Dutton, 1959.
   The author writes Parts One and Five dealing with general problems in the area of philosophies of history. The other parts include selections from philosophical writers, religious philosophers, and humanistic philosophers.

McNEILL, WILLIAM H. *The Rise of the West.* Chicago: U. of Chicago Press, 1963.
   A study of world history showing the interdependence of civilizations and how Western civilization has become the leader of a growing world civilization.

MULLER, HERBERT J. *The Uses of the Past.* New York: Oxford U. Press, 1952.(Also Mentor Book, New American Library of World Literature, 1954.)
   A series of studies of former societies, which the author hopes will throw light on the crisis of contemporary society; he contends that the whole past is summed up in the present.

QUIGLEY, CARROLL. *The Evolution of Civilizations: An Introduction to Historical Analysis.* New York: Macmillan, 1961.
   The author outlines seven stages through which civilizations tend to pass.

SCHWEITZER, ALBERT. *The Philosophy of Civilization.* Trans. by C. T. Campion. New York: Macmillan, 1949. (Part I, *The Decay and Restoration of Civilization;* Part II, *Civilization and Ethics.* Paperback, 1960.)
   The author examines what he believes to be the decay of modern civilization and suggests the causes of decline and of possible renewal. He stresses the reverence for life and the need for an optimistic and ethical life view and world view. See also Out of My Life and Thought.

SOROKIN, PITIRIM A. *The Crisis of Our Age.* New York: Dutton, 1941. (Reprinted in Everyman's Library, 1957.)
   We are living at a turning point of history. The author, a sociologist, criticizes our "sensate" civilization and says we need to rediscover "ideational" and "idealistic" values. See also his Reconstruction of Humanity and Social Philosophy of An Age of Crisis.

SPENGLER, OSWALD. *Today and Destiny: Vital Excerpts from The Decline of the West.* New York: Knopf, 1940. (Arranged with Introduction and Commentary by Edwin F. Dakin; based on translation by Charles F. Atkinson.)
   A useful work for those interested in a briefer presentation than that in Spengler's two large and discursive volumes.

SWABEY, MARIE T. *The Judgement of History.* New York: Philosophical Library, 1954.
   A philosophy of history in which common sense, scientific, and philosophical views of history are set forth, as well as the author's belief in "values beyond the flux of temporality."

TOYNBEE, ARNOLD J. *A Study of History.* 12 vols.; London: Oxford U. Press, 1939, 1954, 1959, 1961.
   These volumes deal with the growth and decline of civilizations through the ages and suggest causes and patterns of historical change. For an excellent abridgement (by D. C. Somervell) see A Study of History, in two volumes.

WALSH, W. H. *An Introduction to Philosophy of History*. London: Hutchinson's University Library, 1951.
A discussion of the logic of historical thinking is followed by an attempt to arrive at a metaphysical interpretation of history.

WARBURG, JAMES P. *The West in Crisis*. Garden City: Doubleday, 1959.
The author claims that, while the external threat exists, the great danger to the West comes from within. Here is a readable discussion of the nature of these inner weaknesses.

WHITEHEAD, ALFRED NORTH. *Adventures of Ideas*. New York: New American Library of World Literature, 1955. (Mentor ed.)
The author deals with the influence of "certain ideas in promoting the slow drift of mankind towards civilization." The four divisions of the book are: Sociological, Cosmological, Philosophical, Civilization. Stimulating for mature students.

TWENTY-EIGHT

PHILOSOPHY AND THE EDUCATIONAL VENTURE

What is the relation of philosophy to the educational venture on which we are embarked? An education that fails to consider the fundamental questions of human existence—the questions about the meaning of life and the nature of truth, goodness, beauty, and justice—with which philosophy is concerned is a very inadequate type of education. "There can be no successful democratic society," says Alfred North Whitehead, "till general education conveys a philosophic outlook."[1]

Whenever a serious problem arises in society, whether it has to do with personal, domestic, or international relations, someone is almost certain to insist that "education is the cure." No one seems to think that we should have less education or fewer educational institutions. There is almost universal agreement that education is a good thing *if* we can get the right kind. We cherish our schools and colleges as among the institutions basic to a society that is free and democratic. To close the schools or to have the books and records unread for even a few generations would lead, we all feel, to the loss of our cultural heritage and our civilization.

Mere education, however, is not enough. The important thing is the kind of education. We often hear that "education is power," but we need to remember that it may be power for life and human welfare or power for death and destruction. We can teach people to be selfish, narrow, and jingoistic, or we can give them an education which broadens their sympathies and outlook and makes them cooperative members of a world society.

CRITICISM OF CONTEMPORARY EDUCATION

Although we have more "formal" education than ever before, and although faith in the power of education has become almost a fetish, there

[1] *Adventures of Ideas* (New York: New American Library of World Literature, 1953), p. 125. (Mentor ed.)

is a widespread and growing dissatisfaction with educational methods and practices. Mark Van Doren goes so far as to say that "it is impossible to discover a man who believes that the right things were done to his mind."[2] Most people seem to feel that they were taught too much, too little, or the wrong things. Walter Lippmann has said that during recent years we have been removing from the curriculum of studies the ideas, ideals, and values which are the basis of Western civilization, and he fears that the prevailing educational system is destined, if it continues, to destroy Western civilization.[3]

In a book which grew out of a series of studies in England, Sir Walter Moberly makes a statement that applies equally well to education in America. He says:

> Our predicament then is this. Most students go through our universities without ever having been forced to exercise their minds on the issues which are really momentous. Under the guise of academic neutrality they are subtly conditioned to unthinking acquiescence in the social and political *status quo* and in a secularism on which they have never seriously reflected. Owing to the prevailing fragmentation of studies, they are not challenged to decide responsibly on a life-purpose or equipped to make such a decision wisely. They are not incited to disentangle and examine critically the assumptions and emotional attitudes underlying the particular studies they pursue, the profession for which they are preparing, the ethical judgments they are accustomed to make, and the political or religious convictions they hold. Fundamentally they are uneducated.[4]

In speaking about the "three errors which help to account for the weaknesses of contemporary education" in the Western world, Gilbert Highet says that the first is the mistaken notion that schools exist mainly to train students to be integrated with their group or "adjusted to family and community." While there is some value in a fairly uniform pattern of culture, a central aim of education should be "to train the individual mind" and to help people "to maintain personal independence." The second error is "the belief that education is a closed-end process, which stops . . . as soon as adult life begins." In reality, education is a lifelong process. The third error, he says, is the view "that learning and teaching ought to have immediate results, show a profit, lead to success." The primary function of education is rather to "benefit the entire personality" and lead to a richer life, so that men can appreciate the riches of the past and live creatively in the present and future.[5]

2 *Liberal Education* (New York: Holt, 1943), pp. 1–2.

3 "The State of Education in This Troubled World," in *Vital Speeches of the Day*, VII (January 15, 1941): 200–203. See also Lippmann's *Essays in the Public Philosophy* (Boston: Little, Brown, 1955), pp. 73 ff.

4 *The Crisis in the University* (London: Student Christian Movement Press, 1949), p. 70. Used with the permission of the Student Christian Movement Press and The Macmillan Company.

5 *Man's Unconquerable Mind* (New York: Columbia U. Press, 1954), pp. 75 ff.

Let us summarize a few of the criticisms that are being directed against contemporary education, remembering, of course, that these criticisms do not apply to *all* schools.

1. Our educational institutions, it is asserted, have no clear and consistent conception of their educational aims—that is, there is no adequate sense of direction, mission, or goals to be achieved. While a student may get many good courses in a variety of subjects, this knowledge often is not organized or integrated into any consistent whole. The knowledge is likely to be presented in separate packages. Departmentalization and specialization have gone so far that we tend to see life and the world in small, unrelated fragments and to miss a sense of unity and meaning. Since our educational institutions often fail to deal with the basic or living issues, their graduates are often unable to think clearly and coherently. We cannot assume that, by gathering more and more "facts," a person necessarily gains understanding and wisdom about his life and the world in which he lives.

2. The stress in our educational institutions is too frequently on hours, points, grades, courses, and passing examinations at set intervals. The system, it is said, has tended to place emphasis in the wrong place and to fix attention on false standards. The symbols or externals tend to usurp the place of what should be the real goals. A student tends to work for marks or for credits on the registrar's records. Often he is willing merely to "get by," and he exhibits a passive attitude. If he is able to get the credits, he feels satisfied, whether he knows very much or not. The student, it is said, "studies to pass but not to know." Often he does pass and then discovers to his sorrow that he cannot meet the demands of later life. The genuine goal of the educational process should be understanding and wisdom, not hours, grades, or credits.

3. Our schools and colleges, it is said, do not impart any common set of ideas, ideals, and convictions to their graduates.[6] Frequently it is difficult for one graduate to have a high-level conversation with another graduate because they have little common knowledge and few, if any, common interests. Practically the only thing present-day undergraduates have in common is the fact that they have successfully managed to "pass" 120 to 128 semester hours of work.

Even more serious than the lack of a common body of knowledge is the lack of common ideals and convictions. Education too frequently fails to build up any vital affirmations, convictions, and discipline. There has been a dangerous separation of science and research from human values and

---

[6] This criticism has come from many people in recent years, and some recent studies have furnished considerable evidence in support of it. See Philip E. Jacob, *Changing Values in College* (New York: Harper, 1957); Edward D. Eddy, Jr., *The College Influence on Student Character* (Washington: American Council on Education, 1959); Marjorie Carpenter (ed.), *The Larger Learning* (Dubuque: W. C. Brown, 1960).

loyalties. As a nation of specialists, we tend to apply our technical skill to our separate fields and to assume little or no responsibility for human affairs and social relationships. As a result of this attitude, our knowledge and our new techniques may be used just as readily by vicious men to destroy our civilization as by men of goodwill to advance human welfare. Too frequently, confusion, moral indifference, and cynicism have been products of the exposure of young people to the "educational process."

The failure of the schools and colleges to measure up to their highest possibilities is to be explained partly by lack of respect for scholarship and education on the part of the general public. The highly educated person may find that a graduate-school degree, the ability to speak good English, and a keen mind are handicaps among some sections of the population; he may be ridiculed as an "egghead." Anti-intellectualism is still strong in our society, although the realization that we may be falling behind some other nations in scientific and cultural achievements may help somewhat to banish a distrust of the human mind and eliminate an anti-intellectualism that could bring disaster.

LIBERAL EDUCATION THROUGH THE YEARS

Since early classical times, the liberal arts have held an important place in education because these studies were felt to provide a clear, broad, and rational perspective on the world. The name derives from the Latin term *artes liberales,* which was applied to those studies thought suitable for a freeman as opposed to those deemed adequate for a slave.

The subjects embraced by the heading of *liberal arts* have changed from time to time. In the Middle Ages, for example, the liberal arts included grammar, rhetoric, and logic or dialectic (the "Trivium"), and arithmetic, geometry, astronomy, and music (the "Quadrivium"). During the Renaissance, there was a tremendous growth of interest in classical language and thought; as a result, Greek and Latin came to play an important part in the liberal arts. Thus the colleges founded during the colonial period in America stressed the Greek and Latin classics, the art of argumentation, and—since they were founded with a view to propagating the Christian faith—the Christian classics.

Until the latter half of the nineteenth century, most college courses were prescribed, or required, so that students had little choice in the selection of the subjects to be studied. The courses usually required at that time included English, the classical languages, mathematics, moral philosophy, and the Bible or the Christian religion. All college graduates had almost identical educational backgrounds, since they had studied the same subjects in similar ways. Two conditions, however, were to lead to the introduction of a system which would permit college students to select the courses they desired to study. The first was the rapidly increasing number and importance of new courses, especially in the natural sciences and the social studies. The second was the growing emphasis on the "individual." The interests and needs of the individual, it was maintained, should come before any fixed program of studies. About 1860 President Charles W. Eliot of Harvard was advocating this "elective" system. By 1884 the only required courses at Harvard University were freshman courses, and only a few of these were prescribed. In spite of considerable opposition, the method of free election spread rapidly throughout the United States, though the amount of freedom varied considerably from institution to institution.

The rapid multiplication of courses and a marked increase in student enrollment, along with the elective system, led the critics to point out certain potential dangers. They noted that the individual tends to be neglected in such a system of mass education, and that there was a noticeable shallowness, superficiality, and confusion of ideas on the part of many of the products of the system. This was caused in considerable part by the lack of integration in the student's course of studies. We have already considered some of the criticisms that arose.

The attempt to meet the criticisms and to avoid the dangers mentioned above led to various changes in educational methods and requirements. For example, students were required to select a field or department as a "major" in which to concentrate during the last two years of their college course. Sometimes the student was required to select one or two "minor" fields for similar but less thorough concentration. In some cases "group requirements" were set up. The student might be required to select a certain number of courses or hours from three or four groups or divisions, such as the natural sciences and mathematics, the social studies, the languages, philosophy, religion, and the fine arts.

During the last few decades there has been a trend in the direction of general courses that cut across departmental lines. Many schools still emphasize such courses, but there is some evidence that the enthusiasm for general education may be declining. This is caused in part by the menacing world situation and the demand for courses calculated to aid more immediately in military defense and the conquest of space. There is a growing emphasis on intensifying educational effort by such programs and devices as supervision and guidance, honors courses, tutorial systems, seminars, comprehensive examinations, workshops, and field trips. In the future it is probable that students will take fewer courses and spend more time in the library, laboratory, and language clinic and in independent study. Most schools, however, are likely to require a "core" of subjects that are believed to be necessary for all students, regardless of their vocational or life plans.

SOME TYPES OF EDUCATIONAL THEORY

Today there are major disagreements in educational theory and practice. The sharpest conflict is between the formalists, sometimes called "essentialists," who tend to emphasize the more traditional subject matter, and the descendants of what was called in the thirties and forties "Progressive Education," the experimentalists, reconstructionists, and those who claim that learning begins with "felt needs" and problems and is concerned with satisfactory life adjustment, freedom, democracy, and cooperative living.

The formalists claim that there is a certain body of knowledge that forms the basis of human culture and that should be taught to each generation. There is thus a tendency to stress subject matter, discipline, industry, thoroughness, and logical organization.

Insofar as content itself is concerned, the formalists divide roughly into two schools—with gradations between, as might be expected. The task of education, according to one school, is to transmit to oncoming generations the cultural heritage of the past. Liberal arts education, it is said, rests on subject matter that has withstood the test of time—that is, on the Great Books, or the classics. Human problems are similar from age to age; we face much the same problems Plato, Aristotle, the prophets of Israel, Dante, and Kant faced. Studying the great masters will prepare us to understand the timeless elements in these problems. It will also give us the common background and common fund of information essential among educated people. A study of the great minds of the past, as well as of the present, is, the classicists feel, the most effective way to develop our latent human capacities.[7]

The other school of formalists stresses "basic" rather than traditional knowledge. They ask for a "hard core of fundamental learning" as the basis of the curriculum and stress such courses as English grammar and composition, history, mathematics, science, and foreign languages.[8]

In contrast with formalists, certain "modern" educators, the experimentalists and others, direct our attention to the interests and desires of the individual, problems of life adjustment, training for citizenship, or vocational

---

[7] Robert Maynard Hutchins and Mortimer Adler have been leaders in stressing the Great Books as basic in education.

[8] Note especially the writings of Arthur Bestor, Admiral Hyman Rickover, and the publications on education of the Council for Basic Education. See also *General Education in a Free Society* (Cambridge: Harvard U. Press, 1945); *The Pursuit of Excellence: Education and the Future* (Garden City: Doubleday, 1958). (The Rockefeller Brothers Fund.)

training. The raw materials of the learning process, it is claimed, are found in the situations that the person faces as he functions in society. Since people learn as they live, much of the curriculum, for some of these groups, consists of activity programs and projects of various kinds.[9]

Shall education train men mainly for citizenship in present-day society? Those who advocate this approach maintain that the critical question to be asked of any educational program is, "What does it contribute to the promotion of the culture of contemporary society?" Information regarding the past and skill in the manipulation of modern techniques are merely instruments used to help solve the pressing problems of our time. The great thinkers of the past, whether in philosophy or science, were concerned with the culture and problems of their own day. We should follow their example, not merely learn their ideas, language, and methods. Education, it is claimed, is essentially growth in the direction of good adjustment to life.

Shall we emphasize the training of young people for specific vocations? In sharpest contrast with the classicists' ideal is the view that education should be mainly a preparation for one's lifework. The rapid increase of courses in recent decades reflects this view. Further evidence of the spread of this position is the trend of technical and professional schools to devote almost their entire attention to preparation of their students for some specific profession or trade.

Some students of education are able to accept neither the more formal and traditional subject-matter approach nor the emphasis on the satisfaction of interests and desires as found in some recent movements. For example, in *Education and the Common Good* Philip H. Phenix says that neither the subject-matter approach nor the attention to interests and life adjustment gives us an adequate standard for determining the proper content of instruction. The study of traditional subject matter may not train one to meet adequately the demands imposed by modern civilization. An approach in which values are stated as interests, desires, or wants and in which beliefs in an objective good and right are discarded may reinforce human selfishness. According to Phenix the educational venture is a moral one in that it seeks to promote successful conduct based on objective standards of worth. There are real or objective values on which agreement is possible. The main goal of education in any field, whether physics or race relations, should be the promotion of loyalty to that which is excellent. Loyalty of this sort would embrace not only the intellectual virtues, but also the good as opposed to that which is immediately pleasure-producing.

9 This movement has its roots in the writings of Rousseau and Pestalozzi. Its more recent advocates in America were Horace Mann and John Dewey. For an elaboration of the philosophy of John Dewey and his relation to Progressive Education, see pp. 263–269. Van Cleve Morris in *Philosophy and the American School* (see Suggested Readings) discusses these and other groups and movements.

The most important product of education is a constructive, consistent, and compelling system of values around which personal and social life may be organized. Unless teaching and learning provide such a focus, all the particular knowledge and skills acquired are worse than useless. An "educated" person whose information and ability are directed to no personally appropriated worthy ends is a menace to himself and to society. A highly sophisticated society educated to no coherent way of life is likewise by its very learning made the more prone to disease and degeneration.[10]

While some institutions follow one or another of these movements exclusively, many institutions try to give a balanced recognition to the merits of the classical, vocational, and social educational theories, and require general education courses as well as those in more specialized fields. Some educators see their task as purely intellectual; others desire to combine the search for knowledge with the quest for the good, the beautiful, and the holy. There is much discussion and a considerable amount of experimentation in education at present. This is a sign of vitality and growth and would appear to give promise of a more effective educational program in the future. However, since educators do not agree on the dimensions of *formal* education in general, we can hardly expect agreement at all points on what liberal arts education should be.

CHARACTERISTICS OF A WELL-EDUCATED PERSON

At almost every college commencement some senior holds out his diploma to his friends and says, "Well, here's the proof—I'm educated." To some people "being educated" means getting through college and getting a degree of some kind. Needless to say, this attitude, if it represents a serious position, is quite mistaken. Mere possession of a diploma—or any other symbol, for that matter—is no proof of education.

There are certain characteristics that identify the educated man.

1. To be educated means to know at least one field with some thoroughness. Education should be in part a preparation for one's vocation. The principal danger here is not so much that students will neglect this practical element in an education as that many will wish to stop at this point.

2. To be educated means to be able to communicate with others, to be able to speak and write one's native language with a high degree of competence. Those who cannot communicate freely live in a small and isolated world. It is highly desirable that an educated person know at least one language besides his native tongue. Knowledge of a foreign language enables a person to learn about a foreign culture; this may extend the range of his

10 Philip H. Phenix, *Education and the Common Good* (New York: Harper and Row, Publishers, Incorporated, 1961), pp. 17–18.

sympathy and his tolerance, as well as broaden his understanding. Only through communication are we able to acquire the understanding of our rich cultural heritage so essential for the development of the individual.

In studies of competently trained specialists who were not succeeding very well—accountants and engineers, for example—the difficulty has been found to be their inability to communicate. They were unable to write clear and effective reports or to go before groups, such as Boards of Directors, and state their views or findings adequately. Ideas that cannot be imparted or made clear to others lose their effectiveness.

3. To be educated means to be able to live in a changing world and to entertain new ideas. In a sense every age is an age of change, but in our time changes have come with a rush. The fact that ours is a dynamic time creates new problems. History, as someone has said, is "ahead of schedule." The splitting of the atom, with the release of great new sources of energy, and other wonders of the new space age are most surely heralds of even more significant changes ahead. Our ability to entertain new ideas is, then, particularly important today.

The attitude people take toward change is one of the most revealing things about them. There are the "stand-patters," who resist change and shrink from anything that is different. They seem to believe that nothing should ever be done for the first time; yet this attitude, if universally adopted, obviously would lead to stagnation. At the opposite extreme are the "root-and-branch" people, who want to get rid of everything that is old. The revolutionists would destroy the ancient good as well as the evil. Between the stand-patters and the revolutionists are those who seek to retain the old values and the good of the past while displaying a readiness to use new discoveries and insights. They want a dynamic integration of the past and the present. They realize that the present has grown out of the past and they want the future to grow out of the present by a process of orderly and intelligent change.

4. To be educated means to be able to get along with others. Living cooperatively with other individuals and groups is one of the major problems of our age. The history of civilization is in part the story of man's learning to become involved in larger and larger relationships. The progress of the "we" concept from family to tribe, tribe to clan, clan to nation, and nation to world order is a part of this development. We need to learn to be interested in others, to be able to entertain them, and to live peacefully together. To be educated is to achieve an understanding of the statement "We are members one of another." This is the problem of all group living.

We need a new emphasis on the right to live. If a man does not become interested in the vital rights of other men and stand ready to defend them, he will soon find his own interests and rights endangered. Unless a community is prepared to use its combined efforts for the defense of a single victim of lawless violence or other injustice, there can be neither law, nor justice, nor freedom. This principle, which has been emphasized by mature moral codes the world over, applies with equal force to nations and to individuals.

5. To be well-educated means to be able to entertain oneself, to develop a rich inner life and a wide range of appreciations and inner controls. Real education takes place *within* the person, who needs to develop a wide range of interests so that he feels in good company even when alone! Some people apparently are so shallow that they are "bored to tears" if they have to spend an hour or two by themselves. They must turn on the radio or television, or gain entertainment from some other external source, so that their attention may be directed outward.

In general, we apparently have been changing as a people from inner-directed to outer- or other-directed persons.[11] Once we prized individuality and diversity; now we seem to be trying to be like everyone else. What we are losing is integrity—the integrity of the person who does his own thinking, develops and follows his own scale of values, and lives by some coherent personal philosophy of life.

If a man acts merely because of custom, the law, fear, or some other outside pressure, he is not genuinely mature. If the authority in life is external, a man tends to resist it or become docile. If the controls are inner and self-chosen, they are followed with less resistance and greater energy. Something inside the person must provide the motivation and the drive. Self-control or inner discipline is a prerequisite of high achievement in any field—sports, the sciences, or the humanities.

6. To be educated is to be sensitive to the larger spiritual order of which man is a part. Man's life is not self-contained. He is linked to a reality that reinforces him and with which he may have fellowship. Man is a creature involved in, and acted upon by, the flux of nature; yet his detached consciousness of his involvement enables him to exercise some control over this flux. Man is an animal organism, it is true; but he is able to study himself as an organism, to compare and to interpret living forms, and to inquire about the meaning of human existence. To do so he must be able in some sense to stand outside of, or to be somewhat removed from, the life and conditions that he judges and compares.

An outstanding philosopher and psychologist, William James, referred to what he termed a *More,* which surrounds man's life and which he experiences. When man enters into harmonious relations with the "More," energy flows

---

11 See David Riesman, *et al., The Lonely Crowd* (New York: Doubleday, 1953). (Anchor Book.) See also William H. Whyte, Jr., *The Organization Man* (New York: Simon and Schuster, 1956).

into his life and new zest and assurance are added. All peoples have referred to this same experience, but their interpretations or descriptive symbols have varied. For the early Greeks it was the *logos,* the Word; for the Hindus it is Brahman; and for the Hebrew-Christians it is God, or Spirit.

EDUCATION: A NEVER-ENDING VENTURE

We said earlier in this chapter that an education that fails to come to grips with the fundamental questions of human existence is very inadequate. While these basic questions can be introduced and discussed in a book or a course, they cannot be answered with any finality. We are growing people in a changing world, and the fundamental questions of philosophy and human existence will be facing us throughout our entire lives and calling for more complete answers. One is seldom satisfied with earlier answers, and the quest is lifelong.

If we are to achieve excellence in living, we need to believe in something and have a sense of direction. An individual who does not have some strong convictions is likely to be deficient in morale. A society that does not have a sense of values and thus a sense of direction and purpose will never be a great society or achieve excellence in areas of possible achievement. The development of habits of intellectual inquiry, high standards of moral integrity, a willingness to face facts, and a devotion to truth are essential as we move into an uncertain future. Ignorance and lack of a sense of personal responsiblity are forms of immorality. Life is an invitation to creativity—to individual growth and achievement, and to the creation of a society in which people have an optimum opportunity for fulfillment. These conditions are not likely to be present apart from an improvement of both public and private education and a greatly increased and continuing program of adult education.

One source of weakness in our society is a lack of respect for the mind at a time when "we are confronted on all sides by problems requiring vast amounts of intellectual power. The great immediate task, then, is the development of this power. That is one reason why our teachers are still more important than our generals."[12]

Early in this century William Rainey Harper, an outstanding president of the University of Chicago, made a short but significant speech to a group of entering freshmen. As reported by one member of the group, he said:

Young gentlemen, you have come here in hope of furthering your education. If you are to do this, it would be well for you to have some idea of what an

[12] John Cogley, "People Can Be Awakened . . . ," *Bulletin,* No. 13 (Santa Barbara: Center for the Study of Democratic Institutions of the Fund for the Republic, March, 1963), p. 7.

educated human being is. Then you will know what to aim at here, what this institution exists to assist you to become. An educated man is a man who by the time he is twenty-five years old has a clear theory, formed in the light of human experience down the ages, of what constitutes a satisfying life, a significant life, and who by the age of thirty has a moral philosophy consonant with racial experience. If a man reaches these ages without having arrived at such a theory, such a philosophy, then no matter how many facts he has learned or how many processes he has mastered, the man is an ignoramus and a fool, unhappy, probably dangerous. That is all.[13]

QUESTIONS AND PROJECTS

1. Review Questions

(1) Discuss and give your reaction to the statement by Alfred North Whitehead that general education needs to convey a philosophical outlook, and to the statement that "education is the cure" for most of our problems.

(2) Three criticisms of contemporary education were given. State them, and indicate whether you think these criticisms can be applied fairly to your own school or to schools and colleges in general. Do you agree or disagree with the opinions expressed by Lippmann, Moberly, and Highet?

(3) What have been some of the principal changes in liberal arts education from ancient times to the present?

(4) What are some of the major types of educational theory, and how do their supporters defend them?

(5) What are some of the characteristics of a well-educated person?

(6) In the light of the discussion in this chapter and your own past educational experience, what suggestions do you have for the improvement of education—at your own school and in general?

2. What is the primary function of education as a whole and of liberal arts education in particular? Should everyone have a liberal arts education? Why or why not?

3. What courses, if any, should be required of all students obtaining a liberal arts education? Should a subject be required because it is (a) a tool subject, (b) good discipline, (c) one that *may* come in handy sometime, (d) vital cultural background, or (e) necessary to know to live well in the world? Should philosophy be required or optional? Why?

4. Does a belief in a liberal arts education imply any basic convictions concerning man and human society? If so, what are these convictions?

5. How do you explain the difference between the ideal educational situation, in which students are eager to learn and students and teachers feel a sense of comradeship

---

[13] *Crisis in Education*, pp. 57–58, by B. I. Bell. Published by the McGraw-Hill Book Company, Inc., 1949.

in a common cause, and the situation, too often found, in which students exhibit a passive attitude and are content merely to "get by"?

6. How far, and in what manner, should the state or nation participate in higher education? What are the advantages of such participation, and what are the dangers? Is there any truth in the statement that education will always be biased in favor of the dominant class in any society?

7. What are the best methods or procedures for handling "controversial" issues in the classroom?

8. What is the basic difference between education and propaganda?

9. Some years ago, after visiting many college and university campuses, E. Stanley Jones, who had recently returned from India, wrote: "First, I was converted to American youth. I expected to find a blasé, fed-up, sophisticated group of young people, but instead I found the finest raw human material that this country has ever produced—frank, upstanding, prepared, but confused, and, when you can get to it, wistful and hungry. They are far finer and more open than the students of ten years ago. But one thing they do not have—they have no cause. They are all dressed up and do not know where to go. Nothing grips them supremely. And the tragedy is that they do not see it."[14] Do you think that a person visiting campuses today could reasonably make a statement to the effect that students do not have a cause and that nothing grips them supremely? What is your analysis of the situation? Give reasons for your reply.

10. Write a short paper: "My Philosophy of Education."

11. Review or critically evaluate one of the following books: Kenneth Brown, *Not Minds Alone* (New York: Harper, 1954); Christopher Dawson, *The Crisis of Western Education* (New York: Sheed and Ward, 1961); *Education in a Free Society* (Pittsburgh: U. of Pittsburgh Press, 1960) (Pitcairn-Crabbe Foundation, Lecture Series 20); C. S. Fletcher (ed.), *Education for Public Responsibility* (New York: Norton, 1961); Edmund Fuller (ed.), *The Christian Idea of Education* (New Haven: Yale U. Press, 1957); John W. Gardiner, *Excellence* (New York: Harper, 1961); Samuel B. Gould, *Knowledge Is Not Enough* (Yellow Springs: Antioch Press, 1959); Sir Walter Moberly, *The Crisis in the University* (New York: Macmillan, 1950); Nevitt Sanford (ed.), *The American College* (New York: Wiley, 1962); George P. Schmidt, *The Liberal Arts College* (New Brunswick: Rutgers U. Press, 1957); Herbert A. Thelen, *Education and the Human Quest* (New York: Harper, 1960).

SUGGESTED READINGS

AMERICAN PHILOSOPHICAL ASSOCIATION, COMMISSION ON THE FUNCTION OF PHILOSOPHY IN LIBERAL EDUCATION. *Philosophy in American Education: Its Tasks and Opportunity.* New York: Harper, 1945.

[14] "The University Christian Mission," *The Christian Century,* 56 (January 4, 1939): 10. Copyrighted by The Christian Century Foundation and used by permission.

A study of the task of philosophy in the educational process. Suggestions are made regarding the teaching of philosophy.

BESTOR, ARTHUR EUGENE. *The Restoration of Learning; A Program for Redeeming the Unfulfilled Promise of American Education.* New York: Knopf, 1955.
  The author outlines the kind of education he thinks essential to avoid the superficiality and aimlessness of much education in the past. See also the author's earlier Educational Wastelands: The Retreat from Learning in Our Public Schools.

BLANSHARD, BRAND (ed.). *Education in the Age of Science.* New York: Basic Books, 1959.
  This work is a report on seminar discussions, sponsored by the Tamiment Institute, in which more than a score of teachers and critics examine American education from various points of view.

BRAMELD, THEODORE. *Education for the Emerging Age.* New York: Harper, 1961.
  This book discusses the strength and weakness of education in dealing with cultural changes. The author stands with the reconstructionists.

BROUDY, HARRY S. *Building a Philosophy of Education.* 2nd ed.; Englewood Cliffs: Prentice-Hall, 1961.
  A discussion of current educational problems, with the author's commentary: Part I, Man, Society and the School; Part II, Values in the Educational Enterprise.

CARPENTER, MARJORIE (ed.). *The Larger Learning: Teaching Values to College Students.* Dubuque: William C. Brown, 1960.
  In this small book five people present papers that deal with the problem of how values can be taught in courses in various fields of study.

DEVANE, WILLIAM C. *The American University in the Twentieth Century.* Baton Rouge: Louisiana State U. Press, 1957.
  According to the author the university should be the intellectual conscience and leader of our time. The book deals with the growth of the American university and its relationship to society.

DEWEY, JOHN. *Experience and Education.* New York: Macmillan, 1958.
  The educational implications of Dewey's philosophy are explained. See also Dewey's Democracy and Education: An Introduction to the Philosophy of Education.

EHLERS, HENRY (ed.). *Critical Issues in Education: An Anthology.* New York: Holt, 1955.
  Selections, questions, and bibliographies on various topics, including freedom for teachers and learners, religion and public education, racial issues, and classroom methods and materials.

GRISWOLD, ALFRED WHITNEY. *In the University Tradition.* New Haven: Yale U. Press, 1957.
  A small book of addresses and articles dealing with liberal education in a free society.

HUTCHINS, ROBERT M. *The University of Utopia.* Chicago: U. of Chicago Press, 1953.
  The author is critical of a specialization that does not educate people, and he describes what he considers a more ideal education. He calls for a broad discipline in the liberal arts. See other books by Hutchins.

MATHEWSON, ROBERT HENDRY. *A Strategy for American Education.* New York: Harper, 1957.
  Deals with the meaning of education for living and stresses the need for changes in methods, attitudes, and values.

MAYER, FREDERICK. *Philosophy of Education for Our Time.* New York: Odyssey, 1958.
  Emphasis on the need for a philosophy of education to implement the total educative process. The author outlines such a philosophy. See also the author's A History of Educational Thought.

MOBERLY, SIR WALTER. *The Crisis in the University.* New York: Macmillan, 1950.
  A discussion of the failure of the universities to measure up to their possibilities. Written from a Christian and British point of view.

MORRIS, VAN CLEVE. *Philosophy and the American School.* Boston: Houghton Mifflin, 1961.
  The author discusses five different philosophies and indicates their implications for educational theory as well as for classroom practice.

PARK, JOE (ed.). *Selected Readings in the Philosophy of Education.* New York: Macmillan, 1958.
  A source book that covers a wide range of educational and philosophical thought—Pragmatism, Idealism, and Realism— as well as the Catholic, Protestant, and Jewish outlooks.

PHENIX, PHILIP H. *Education and the Common Good.* New York: Harper, 1961.
  The author distinguishes between the life of desire and the life of worth. A central task of education is the promotion of a system of values in all areas of life.

ULICH, ROBERT. *Philosophy of Education.* New York: American Book, 1961.
  A philosophy of education that emphasizes basic philosophical issues. The survival of our way of life depends on "a combination of equality and quality" that can "set the mind and spirit free." Part One stresses the "Theoretical Groundwork," and Part Two stresses "Education in Action."

WILDS, E. H., AND LOTTICH, K. V. *The Foundations of Modern Education.* 3rd ed.; New York: Holt, Rinehart and Winston, 1961.
  A text that deals with the "foundations of education theory in ancient and medieval times," as well as with modern educational theories and their evaluation.

WOODRING, PAUL. *A Fourth of a Nation.* New York: McGraw-Hill, 1957.
  This book deals with the problems of formulating a philosophy of education for the American people. It discusses current issues and makes proposals for a more adequate program.

Year Book of Education: Education and Philosophy. Ed. by George Z. F. Bereday and J. A. Lauwerys. Yonkers: World Book, 1957.
  More than forty people discuss the relationship between philosophical systems and educational practices around the world.

GLOSSARY

Philosophical terms are sometimes used with special meanings by particular writers. The following definitions and explanations attempt to give the meaning that a term has in this book. In general we include only terms used in philosophical discussions whose meanings are different from those in ordinary English usage and terms that can be defined in a short space. Reference works that will be helpful are:

Concise Encyclopedia of Western Philosophy and Philosophers. Ed. by J. O. URMSON. New York: Hawthorn.

Dictionary of Philosophy. Ed. by DAGOBERT D. RUNES. New York: Philosophical Library.

Dictionary of Philosophy and Psychology. Ed. by JAMES MARK BALDWIN. New York: Peter Smith.

Encyclopedia of Religion. Ed. by VERGILIUS FERM. New York: Philosophical Library.

Encyclopedia of Religion and Ethics. 6 vols. and Index. Ed. by JAMES HASTINGS. New York: Scribner's.

Webster's New International Dictionary. 3rd ed.; or *The Oxford English Dictionary.* 12 vols. and Supplement; or one of the other good standard dictionaries.

ACQUAINTANCE   Immediate or intimate knowledge as distinct from knowledge by description; knowledge *of* as contrasted with knowledge *about*.

AESTHETICS   That branch of philosophy concerned with art and the nature of the aesthetic object, experience, and values.

AGNOSTICISM   A profession of ignorance, especially the claim that it is impossible to demonstrate conclusively either the existence or nonexistence of God.

ANALYSIS, ANALYTICAL METHOD   The resolving of anything into its elements or constituent parts; an attempt to find and examine the simple elements that make up any whole. The term *philosophical analysis* is sometimes used to designate the method of a group of empiricists interested in linguistic study and the logical analysis of terms, concepts, and propositions.

ANIMISM   The primitive belief that nature is filled with innumerable spirits. All things are thought of as possessing a life somewhat akin to man's life.

ANTHROPOMORPHISM   The attributing of human qualities to the nonhuman realm or to nature. The term may refer to the portrayal of God as having human form or human characteristics.

ANTINOMY   Used by Kant to refer to mutually contradictory conclusions each of which may be deductively proved but which cannot both be true.

A POSTERIORI   Refers to knowledge that is stated in empirically verifiable propositions. *A posteriori* reasoning, in contrast with *a priori* reasoning, is inductive.

A PRIORI   Refers to knowledge that is self-evident or to principles recognized to be true apart from observation or experience, in contrast with *a posteriori*.

ATHEISM   Denial of the existence of God.

ATTRIBUTE   A property, characteristic, or quality of something.

AUTHORITARIANISM   The belief that knowledge is guaranteed or validated by some source; an uncritical acceptance of testimony as opposed to an independent effort to discover what is true or false.

AXIOLOGY   The study of the general theory of value or a study of those things that have value.

BEHAVIORISM   A theory of psychology which asserts that the proper subject matter of human psychology is "the behavior or activities of the human being."

BEING   That which exists; sometimes used for the infinite, God, or ultimate reality.

BUDDHISM   The religion founded by Siddhartha Gautama, born about 563 B.C. in North India. It gradually spread to Ceylon, Burma, China, Japan, etc. In India it declined or merged with Hinduism.

CAUSALITY, CAUSATION   The relation of cause and effect, or the relation between events, as when one produces or alters the other. Science is concerned with cause-and-effect sequences.

CAUSE   That which occasions an effect or leads to some change.

CIVIL LIBERTIES   Refers mainly to the freedoms of thought, speech, press, assembly, worship, and conscience.

COGNITION   The attainment of knowledge of something; the mental process by which we become aware of objects of perception or thought.

COHERENCE   A theory of the test of truth that stresses the consistency or harmony of all our judgments. A judgment is said to be true if it is consistent or coheres with other judgments that are accepted or known to be true. Quite generally accepted by idealists.

COMMUNISM   A system of economic organization in which the tools of production are held in common. The modern Marxian form is based on revolutionary tactics. There are differences among Marxism, Leninism, and Stalinism as forms of communism.

CONCEPT   A general idea, as distinct from a percept. I may have a concept of "man" or "humanity," but I have a percept when I see a particular man, John Doe. We have percepts of particular, experienced objects; we have concepts of universals, classes, and unexperienced objects.

CONDITIONING   A psychological term used for a particular type of learning process: the conditioned reflex, conditioned response, conditioned stimulus, conditioned emotion. The term was originated by Pavlov to explain learned in contrast with unlearned responses. A response originally initiated only by A (a biologically adequate stimulus) comes to be initiated by B because of B's association with A.

CONFUCIANISM   The philosophy of Confucius, mainly ethical and political, which combined various elements in Chinese culture to become the basis of Chinese custom, law, and education.

CORRESPONDENCE   A theory of the test of truth that stresses "fidelity to objective reality"; the view that truth is that which conforms to fact or agrees with the actual situation. Widely held by realists.

COSMOLOGY   The study or theories of the origin, nature, and development of the universe as an orderly system.

CRITICAL REALISM   A form of realism of the early twentieth century that was critical of both idealism and new realism. Critical realists insist that only sense data are present in consciousness, but that they indicate the nature of the external world.

DEDUCTION   An inference in which the conclusion follows logically from one or more premises. When the conclusion does so follow, the deduction is said to be valid.

DEISM   A belief that affirms the existence of a God Who has created the universe but Who remains apart and permits His creation to administer itself through natural laws—a view fairly prevalent in the seventeenth and eighteenth centuries.

DETERMINISM   The view that human choice is entirely controlled by previous conditions. The realm of nature, including man, is an unbroken chain of cause and effect.

DIALECTIC   A method of reasoning used by Hegel and others in which contradictions or opposites are synthesized. Thought proceeds from thesis to antithesis to synthesis.

DIALECTICAL MATERIALISM   A philosophy founded by Marx and Engels and supported by Lenin and Stalin. The dialectic (see above) is united with historical materialism. Communist philosophy in the twentieth century is dialectical and materialistic, and has been used to justify sudden changes and revolutionary activity.

DUALISM   The theory that reality is composed of two different substances, so that neither one can be reduced to the other. Spirit and matter, mind and body, good and evil, are often designated as the opposing realities.

ECLECTICISM   The practice of selecting or combining parts from various schools or types of philosophy. The eclectic is likely to believe that he is selecting the best from various philosophers.

EMERGENCE, EMERGENT EVOLUTION   The view that in the development of the universe and life, new forms with new qualities appear that cannot be explained by an analysis of the previous level—for example, matter, life, mind, values.

EMPATHY   Used by some psychologists and students of art to designate the motor attitudes, muscular sets, or feelings we experience in the presence of objects or people when we identify with them, reacting not so much toward them as *with* them as they act.

EMPIRICAL NATURALISM   Used by certain groups of humanists and others to emphasize the universal applicability of the methods of experimental inquiry. Nature is the whole of reality, and nature is to be studied by empirical methods.

EMPIRICISM   The view that knowledge comes from experience or through the senses, in opposition to *rationalism*. Its more extreme form may be called *sensationalism*.

ENTELECHY   A nonmaterial force, vital principle, or purpose that enables a form to come to realization. Some would use the term for the agency responsible for life and growth.

EPIPHENOMENALISM   Refers to the view that mind is a mere secondary phenomenon accompanying some bodily processes. Matter is primary, the one real substance.

EPISTEMOLOGICAL DUALISM   The view that there are two separate kinds of entities involved in the knowing process (sense data present in consciousness, and the external world).

EPISTEMOLOGICAL IDEALISM   The view that the objects of knowledge, or the qualities which we perceive by our senses, do not exist independently of a consciousness of them; may be called *subjectivism*.

EPISTEMOLOGICAL REALISM   The view that there is an independent reality apart from minds, and that we do not change it when we come to experience or to know it; sometimes called *objectivism*.

EPISTEMOLOGY   Theory of knowledge; that branch of philosophy which studies the sources, nature, and validity of knowledge.

ESSENCE   The substance or intrinsic nature which makes a thing what it is. The term has been used for the *concept* of a thing and for the immediately experienced quality. Ordinarily *essence* is considered distinct from *existence*.

ETHICAL NATURALISM   Theories that explain the meaning of ethical terms by reference to human nature or the satisfaction of human interests, or that make their appeal to observation and experience. Nonnaturalists believe that ethical judgments express nonempirical intuitions or insights.

ETHICAL RELATIVISM   The view that, of the same situation, X, it may be asserted both that "X is good" and that "X is bad" and that the two statements are not contradictory, since the meaning of *good* is relative to certain other factors, including who is making the statement.

ETHICS   The study of moral conduct. The term may also be applied to the system or the code followed.

EVOLUTION   The theory of evolution is an interpretation of how the development of living forms has taken place. *Organic evolution* is the name for the process of change; *evolutionism* is the theory of how the process proceeds.

EXISTENCE   (1) For Thomists, *existence* is the act of being as ordinarily contrasted with essence; it is the state of occurring within space and time. (2) Existentialists use *existence* in a limited sense, so that *to exist* applies to personal experience and calls for creative commitment. (3) The term is often used as the opposite of *essence*.

EXISTENTIALISM   An attitude and outlook in philosophy, theology, and the arts that stresses the human predicament or man's feeling of anxiety, and emphasizes human existence and the qualities distinctive of individuals rather than "man" in the abstract or nature and the world in general.

EXPERIMENTALISM   Suggested by some people as a substitute term for *pragmatism* or *instrumentalism*.

EXTRASENSORY PERCEPTION   Used by the "parapsychologists" for the view that the ordinary senses are not the only channels of cognition.

FAITH   An attitude of trust in the reality or truth of something that cannot be demonstrated or proved.

FASCISM   A social philosophy that rejects democracy and freedom and glorifies the state as an instrument of power; a form of totalitarianism.

FATALISM   The belief that events are irrevocably fixed so that human effort cannot alter them, though sometimes things appear otherwise. "What is to be, will be."

FINITE   Limited.

FIRST PRINCIPLES   Propositions that are basic or self-evident.

FORMALISM   Adherence to prescribed forms. In education, *formalism* has meant the tendency to emphasize subject matter and traditional methods. In ethics, *formalism* has meant the view that certain types of acts follow fixed moral principles, so that circumstances do not alter cases.

FREEDOM OF CHOICE, FREE WILL   The doctrine that man has some genuine power of alternative choice; the power of self-determination.

GENETIC   Having to do with the origin or development of a thing or an organism.

GESTALT   Literally, form, pattern, or configuration. The word is used for a school of psychology that, in reaction to the older analytical and atomistic methods, stresses the idea that the whole or the organism is not merely the sum of its parts.

GOD   A being or entity with divine powers of whom there are numerous conceptions.

HEDONISM   The doctrine that the chief good in life is pleasure. A modern type of hedonism is called *utilitarianism.*

HINDUISM   The religion and philosophy of the people called Hindus, who live mainly in India. See pages 389–393.

HUMANISM   A doctrine that emphasizes distinctively human interests and ideals. The humanism of the Renaissance was based on the Greek classics. There is a modern literary humanism that stresses a classical type of liberal education. Religious and philosophical humanism emphasizes man but abandons all concepts of the supernatural.

HYLOZOISM   The theory that all nature is alive or animated; a view held by a number of early Greek thinkers. See ANIMISM, a contrasting view, in which nature is thought to be filled with many spirits.

IDEALISM   The theory which asserts that reality consists of ideas, thought, mind, or selves rather than of matter. There are many types of idealism.

IDENTITY PRINCIPLE   The Law of Identity, or the First Law of Logic: All A is A.

IDENTITY THEORY   Another name for the double-aspect theory, which contends that mind and matter are expressions of some one underlying reality whose nature is unknown.

IDEOLOGY   Used for any systematic group of ideas concerning various political, economic, and social issues (for example, communist ideology). The term *ism* is sometimes used for these systems of thought.

IMMANENT   Indwelling, or operating within the process. A God who is immanent is in the structure of the universe, taking a vital part in its processes and in the lives of men. The term is used in contrast with *transcendent*—though God may be thought of as both immanent and transcendent.

IMMORTALITY   The doctrine that the self or soul survives the destruction of the body. The term usually means personal survival after death, an afterlife.

INDETERMINISM   The theory that personal choices in some cases are independent of antecedent events. William James, for example, held that there are genuine possibilities existing in the future, and that the universe has a considerable amount of novelty, chance, and spontaneity.

INDIVIDUALISM   A theory that stresses the free individual or the "self-directing power of personality." Individualism is opposed to regulation and governmental control.

INDUCTION   Reasoning that attempts to reach a conclusion concerning all the members or uninspected members of a class after inspection of only some of them. Inductive knowledge is empirical. The conclusion of an inductive argument, unlike that of a deductive one, is not logically necessary.

INSTRUMENTALISM   Another term for the pragmatism of John Dewey and others. Instrumentalism stresses experience and interprets thinking, ideas, and doctrines as means for the adjustment of an organism to its environment.

INTERACTIONISM   A theory of the mind-body relationship that regards mind and matter (body) as two separate substances that influence each other.

INTROSPECTION   A person's inspection of his own thoughts and feelings; a psychological method of study that is in contrast with the study of objective behavior, though the two methods may be used together.

INTUITIONISM   The view that knowledge can be gained by direct apprehension, in contrast with the processes of conscious reasoning or of immediate sense perception.

ISLAM   The religion of the Moslems, the followers of Mohammed.

JUDAISM   The religion of the Jews. It includes doctrines, rites, and ceremonies extending from Old Testament to modern times.

JUDGMENT   The act of asserting or denying something. Judgments are expressed in propositions.

KNOWLEDGE   A verifiable proposition. The problem of knowledge has to do with the sources, nature, and validity of ideas, propositions, and arguments.

LAISSEZ-FAIRE   A phrase meaning "let alone," used in economics, politics, and social philosophy; the doctrine of governmental noninterference; sometimes spoken of as *laissez-faire* individualism.

LIBERALISM   A social and political philosophy favoring freedom of the individual and the rational consent of man, as opposed to the authoritarian ideal.

LOGIC   That branch of philosophy which deals with the nature and problems of clear and accurate thinking and argument.

LOGICAL EMPIRICISM   A school of thought that would limit meaningful propositions either to those that are empirically verifiable or to those that are analyses of definitions and relations among terms. Empirically verifiable propositions are the concern of the sciences, and analysis of definitions and relations between terms is seen as the specific task of philosophy.

LOGICAL POSITIVISM   See LOGICAL EMPIRICISM and POSITIVISM.

MARXISM   The social philosophy of Karl Marx who, with Friedrich Engels, wrote the *Communist Manifesto*. *Marxism* and *Communism* are not synonymous. See COMMUNISM and DIALECTICAL MATERIALISM.

MATERIALISM   In its extreme form, the view that nothing is real except matter. Mind and consciousness are merely manifestations of such matter and are reducible to the physical elements.

MEANING   The intent, purpose, or explanation of something; that which a thing signifies or is intended to express.

MECHANISM   The theory that everything is to be explained by mechanical principles, or by the laws that govern matter and motion.

MELIORISM   The view that the world is neither entirely good nor entirely evil but can be made better through our efforts.

METALANGUAGE   The language that we use to talk about language itself, in contrast with an *object language* that we use to talk about the world.

METAPHYSICS   Literally, after or beyond physics—a critical study of the nature of reality. Metaphysics is divided into ontology and cosmology.

MIND (1) The conscious and rational element in man, or in the universe; (2) man's entire psychic experience; (3) adaptive behavior in organisms.

MONISM The theory that there is one fundamental reality, which may be mind, matter, God, or some neutral or unknown substance.

MONOTHEISM The belief that there is only one God.

MORALS The conduct and codes of conduct of individuals and groups. Moral judgments refer to the actions of human beings insofar as they are considered right or wrong. See ETHICS.

MYSTICISM The belief that an immediate consciousness of God or a unity with the Divine is attainable.

MYTHOLOGY A collection of myths or stories associated with primitive religions, or the study of such stories. Myths arise out of man's unscientific efforts to account for the world around him.

NAÏVE REALISM The common-sense view of the world that is uncritical in its acceptance of sense perception and of man's ability to know the world.

NATURALISM A theory that accepts the empirical world as the whole of reality. Naturalism is opposed to *supernaturalism* and is likely to hold that the interpretation of the world given by the natural sciences is the only satisfactory one.

NATURE Has various meanings, including (1) the essential character or distinguishing quality of a thing; (2) the system of all phenomena in space and time.

NEOSUPERNATURALISM A contemporary theology or religious philosophy that is dualistic and other-worldly in its approach. Stress is placed on a God Who is transcendent and Who comes to men in a "crisis," or Who reveals Himself through a special revelation. Sometimes called *crisis theology* or *neoorthodoxy*.

NEO-THOMISM The modern formulation of the philosophical and theological doctrines of Thomas Aquinas (1227–1274).

NEW REALISM A movement of the early twentieth century that was critical of idealism and insisted that things are neither created nor modified by the knowing mind. Experience is *selective*, not *constitutive*.

NIHILISM The doctrine that nothing exists; therefore, nothing can be known or have value. The term more often is used to refer to the social doctrine that conditions are so evil that the present social order ought to be swept aside or destroyed to make room for something better.

NOMINALISM The theory that "universals" or general terms are only names and represent no objectively real existents; all that exist are particulars.

OBJECTIVE Existing independently of the subject, the self, or the knower; pertaining to what is external rather than internal, in the sense that its existence is unaffected by one's thoughts and feelings, which are internal or subjective.

OBJECTIVISM The view that there is an independent reality apart from minds. Also called *epistemological realism*.

OBJECT LANGUAGE The language that we use to talk about the world, as opposed to the one that we use to talk about language (*metalanguage*).

OBLIGATION That which a person is bound to do, or is under a necessity to do, because of some promise, agreement, duty, or law.

ONTOLOGY That branch of metaphysics which has to do with the nature of ultimate reality or being.

OPERATIONALISM, OPERATIONISM   A movement closely related to pragmatism or instrumentalism, which defines concepts as "empirically performable operations"; to define a term is to indicate what operation it represents.

PANPSYCHISM   The doctrine that all reality is psychic in character, or that everything has mind.

PANTHEISM   Literally, "all God." God is coextensive with the universe.

PARALLELISM   A theory which asserts that mind and body are two separate substances; there is no interaction or causal connection between the two areas.

PARAPSYCHOLOGY   The name for a school of psychology that is concerned with studying "extrasensory powers." *Para* means "alongside of" or "beyond."

PARSIMONY   The principle that, other things being equal, we should always take the simpler explanation as the valid one. This principle is known as "Occam's razor."

PARTICULAR   In logic, an individual member of a class.

PERSONALISM   A type of idealism which asserts that reality is a system of personal selves. The self is said to be an irreducible living unit. Nature, though real, does not exist in and of itself.

PHENOMENALISM   The belief that we can know only phenomena and not the ultimate nature of things. We merely know objects as they appear to our senses.

PHENOMENOLOGY   A school of philosophy of which Edmund Husserl (1859–1938) was a leader. It starts with the human subject and his consciousness, the experiencing knower, and attempts to build a "theoretical science" that might serve as a root science for all the special sciences.

PLURALISM   The theory that reality consists of not one or two but many substances. Pluralism stands in contrast with both monism and dualism.

POLYTHEISM   Belief in many gods.

POSITIVISM   The belief that only empirically verifiable or analytic propositions are meaningful, and that metaphysics is impossible.

POSTULATES   Fundamental assumptions used as a basis for developing a system of proofs, but not themselves subject to proof within the system. While some logicians use *axioms* and *postulates* as synonymous, for others an axiom is a self-evident truth and a postulate is a presupposition or premise of a train of reasoning and not necessarily self-evident. In this latter sense, all axioms are postulates, but not all postulates are axioms.

PRAGMATISM   A school of philosophy founded by C. S. Peirce and William James and further developed by John Dewey. It emphasizes experience, experimental inquiry, and truth as that which has satisfactory consequences.

PREDESTINATION   The doctrine that all events in man's life have been decreed or determined from the beginning of time by the sovereign will of God.

PRIMARY QUALITIES   The qualities that are said to inhere in material substance and that do not depend on a knower. These qualities are usually thought to include form, extension, solidity, motion, and number. John Locke and others have distinguished between primary and secondary qualities.

PROBABILITY   The likelihood, possibility, or chance of an event occurring or of a statement being true. Even the strongest inductive argument is said to render its conclusion only highly probable.

PROGRESSIVE EDUCATION   A movement led by John Dewey and others that criticizes formalism in education and emphasizes the interests of the individual, freedom, and learning by doing.

PROPOSITION A sentence that is either true or false (Aristotle). Many present-day logicians call such sentences *statements* and reserve the term *proposition* for what the statement means or expresses.

PROVIDENTIAL VIEW OF HISTORY The doctrine that God directs the course of history and that He has a plan and a goal, so that good will ultimately prevail.

PSYCHICAL MONISM An interpretation of the mind-body problem held by some idealists, which claims that the causal series is confined to the mental and that what we call *matter* is a "shadow" cast by thought. Mind is primary, and matter is essentially an appearance.

RATIONALISM The view that the mind has the power to know some truths that are logically prior to experience and yet not analytic.

REALISM The doctrine that the objects of our senses exist independently of their being known or related to mind. See CRITICAL REALISM, EPISTEMOLOGICAL REALISM, NAÏVE REALISM, and NEW REALISM.

REASONING The process of drawing inferences.

REDUCTION The analysis of a whole into its parts or units, or the explanation of later stages in a developing process by the earlier and simpler stages. The "fallacy of reduction" arises when we attempt: (1) to explain the whole by the simple units; (2) to explain the later stages by the earlier stages; (3) to take something that is commonly thought to be real and reduce it to an appearance of something else.

RELATIONS, INTERNAL AND EXTERNAL Two things are internally related when the relationship affects their natures. A relation is external if the natures of the objects are unaffected by the relationship.

RELATIVISM The view that truth depends on time, place, and the thinking and point of view of the observer, and that there is no absolute truth. See ETHICAL RELATIVISM.

REVELATION Used in theology for the communication to man of the Divine Will.

RIGHT In an ethical sense, *right* means "conforming to moral standards" and is used when speaking of acts. People and situations are judged *good* or *bad*.

RIGHTS Those things to which people have a just claim.

SCHOLASTICISM Applied to the methods and doctrines of the Schoolmen, or the Christian philosophers of the medieval period. The main concern of this group was the reconciliation of the Christian doctrines with reason and the philosophy of Aristotle.

SCIENCE (1) Used collectively to denote the many sciences; (2) a method of obtaining knowledge that is objective and verifiable; (3) a body of systematic knowledge built up through experimentation and observation and having a valid theoretical base.

SCIENTIFIC METHOD The processes and steps by which the sciences obtain knowledge. The plural form, *scientific methods,* is preferred, since various methods are used by scientists.

SCIENTISM The view that science is the *only* avenue to human knowledge; the term has come to mean an idolization of science.

SECONDARY QUALITIES The sense qualities (color, sound, taste, odor) that John Locke and others claimed were determined by the mind and not by the external world. See PRIMARY QUALITIES.

SELF   The person, subject, ego, knower, or the "I"; the unity that persists through changes.

SEMANTICS   A study of the meaning of words and linguistic forms, their function as symbols, and the part they play in relation to other words and to human behavior.

SENSATE CULTURE   Used, especially by P. A. Sorokin, to characterize a culture whose major principle is that "the true reality and values are sensory." Such a culture is materialistic, empiricistic, and sensual.

SENSATIONALISM   An extreme form of empiricism which asserts that knowledge is essentially sensory and which emphasizes the feelings and senses as value determinants.

SENSE DATUM   The image or sense impression. Sense data are the immediately given contents of sense experience, such as colored patches and shapes, which, according to some epistemologists, serve as cues to the presence and nature of perceived objects.

SKEPTICISM   Skepticism may vary from the attitude of uncertainty, doubt, and the questioning of all assumptions until they are confirmed, to the claim that knowledge is impossible and therefore the quest for truth is in vain.

SOCIALISM   A political and economic theory that advocates the public ownership and management of the principal means of production, distribution, and exchange. There are various types of socialists.

SOLIPSISM   The view that I alone exist, the *reductio ad absurdum* of subjectivism.

SOUL   The conception of an immaterial entity. The soul has been identified with mind, consciousness, and personality, and has been regarded as the locus of man's mental and spiritual life. Some people have ignored the concept as of no scientific value.

SPIRITISM   The belief in many freely moving spirits—a stage following animism. The worship of spirits is called *polydaemonism*.

SPIRITUAL   The term includes such nonmaterial human values as goodness, truth, beauty, holiness, and love.

SPIRITUALISM   The belief that all that exists is spirit (a form of idealism). The term is now used almost exclusively to refer to the beliefs and practices of those who seek to communicate with "departed" spirits.

STOICISM   A school of philosophy founded by Zeno about 308 B.C. in Greece. The Stoics believed that a cosmic reason pervades the universe and that the wise man should exercise self-discipline and accept his lot.

SUBJECTIVE   That which pertains to the subject, the self, or the knower; that which exists in consciousness but not apart from consciousness. The term stands in contrast with *objective*.

SUBJECTIVISM   (1) The view that reality consists of conscious beings and their mental states; (2) the position that all we can know is the subject and his sensory and mental states; (3) the theory that value statements are about feelings, and therefore values have no independent status.

SUBSISTENTS   Entities that, though they do not occur in space or time, are held by some philosophers to be "real" in some sense. In the realm of subsistents would be universals, ideals, and numbers

SUBSTANCE That which exists in and of itself; that in which attributes, properties, and qualities reside.

SUPERNATURALISM Belief in that which is above or beyond the empirical world. In traditional thought, the supernatural implies a dualistic world view. God is transcendent, though He may also be immanent.

SYNOPTIC VIEW A general view of the whole.

TAUTOLOGY In contemporary logic, a tautology is a statement that is necessarily true because of its logical form, e.g., "Black dogs are black."

TELEOLOGY Literally, the theory of ends or purposes; the doctrine that there is design or purpose operating in the universe as a whole and that this principle is needed to supplement other types of explanations.

THEISTIC NATURALISM A religious philosophy that emphasizes God's immanence in nature. Some theistic naturalists view God as an aspect of nature, or as a process or tendency within the natural order rather than beyond it.

THEOLOGY Literally, the theory or study of God. In practice, the term is used for the system of doctrines of some particular religious group or individual thinker. Natural theology stresses reason and empirical evidence; revealed theology emphasizes revelation.

THOMISM The philosophical and theological doctrines formulated by Thomas Aquinas. See NEO-THOMISM.

TOTALITARIANISM The view that the state is supreme and its interests take precedence over those of all other groups—political, economic, scientific, or religious. Fascism is totalitarian in theory and in practice; communism is so in practice.

TRANSCENDENT That which is beyond what is given in experience. In theology the term means that God is outside of or beyond nature. *Transcendence* stands in contrast with *immanence*.

UNIVERSALS General terms or characteristics, as distinguished from the individual cases or instances of them. See NOMINALISM and the text references to Plato's realism.

UNIVERSE Used to refer to the totality of things, including the whole of space and time and their contents.

UTILITARIANISM An ethical theory which claims that utility, in the sense of the greatest happiness of the greatest number, should be the aim of acts and the criterion by which we judge them.

VALIDITY Applied to reasoning, validity is formal correctness; an inference is valid if it conforms to the laws of logic. The validity of an argument is independent of the truth or falsity of the premises.

VALUE That which has worth; that which is desirable. Whereas factual judgments are descriptive, value judgments appraise worth.

VERIFICATION Confirmation or disconfirmation of a proposition; testing or checking a statement.

VITALISM The view that living organisms owe their organization and development to a life principle or an entelechy that gives direction or purpose to the process. This is in contrast with a mechanistic explanation of life.

WORLD VIEW The sum of the beliefs that an individual or the members of a society hold about the universe and the place and destiny of man within it; a philosophical view of the universe.

INDEX